The Exceptional Child

The Exceptional Child 8e

INCLUSION IN EARLY CHILDHOOD EDUCATION

K. Eileen Allen
Glynnis E. Cowdery

CENGAGE
Learning·

Australia • Brazil • Mexico • Singapore • United Kingdom • United States

CENGAGE Learning

The Exceptional Child: Inclusion in Early Childhood Education, **Eighth Edition**

K. Eileen Allen and Glynnis E. Cowdery

Senior Product Manager: Mark Kerr

Content Developer: Kate Scheinman

Content Coordinator: Paige Leeds

Product Assistant: Coco Bator

Media Developer: Renee Schaaf

Sr. Marketing Manager: Kara Kindstrom

Content Project Manager: Samen Iqbal

Senior Art Director: Jennifer Wahi

Manufacturing Planner: Doug Bertke

Rights Acquisitions Specialist: Bobbie Broyer

Production Service: Jill Traut, MPS Limited

Photo Researcher: Saranya Sarada

Text Researcher: Christina Taylor

Copy Editor: Bill Clark

Text and Cover Designer: Lisa Delgado

Cover Image: Four Year Olds Making Handprints: © Sarah Rice/Star Ledger/ Corbis, Three preschool children working together on colorful shape puzzle: © Matt Hess/Golden Pixels LLC/ Corbis, Portrait of beautiful young girl on the playground: © Dennis Kuvaev/ Shutterstock.com, Boy with Down syndrome reading book in kindergarten: © iStockphoto/Moodboard_Images.

Compositor: MPS Limited

For product information and technology assistance, contact us at
Cengage Learning Customer & Sales Support, 1-800-354-9706

For permission to use material from this text or product, submit all requests online at **www.cengage.com/permissions**
Further permissions questions can be e-mailed to
permissionrequest@cengage.com

Library of Congress Control Number: 2013940729

ISBN-13: 978-1-285-43237-3

ISBN-10: 1-285-43237-1

Cengage Learning
200 First Stamford Place, 4th Floor
Stamford, CT 06902
USA

Cengage Learning is a leading provider of customized learning solutions with office locations around the globe, including Singapore, the United Kingdom, Australia, Mexico, Brazil, and Japan. Locate your local office at **www.cengage.com/global**

Cengage Learning products are represented in Canada by Nelson Education, Ltd.

To learn more about Cengage Learning Solutions, visit **www.cengage.com**

Purchase any of our products at your local college store or at our preferred online store **www.cengagebrain.com**

Printed in the United States of America
1 2 3 4 5 6 7 17 16 15 14 13

Brief Contents

Contents

SECTION 2
Likenesses and Differences among Children

SECTION 3
Planning for Inclusion

Preface

A Comprehensive and Accessible Guide

This eighth edition of *The Exceptional Child: Inclusion in Early Childhood Education* provides a comprehensive guide for teachers, two- and four-year college students, and for early childhood teachers and child care personnel in in-service training programs—all of whom will be working in inclusive early childhood settings. It is an equally valuable guide for parents, as well as for clinicians working with teachers to provide a viable setting for children both with and without special needs. The clinicians most commonly involved with teachers are speech and language therapists, audiologists, physical and occupational therapists, nutritionists, psychologists, social workers, behavior analysts, pediatricians, and nurses.

The combination of theory, philosophy, and best practices that comprise this text will help to ensure that inclusion in early childhood programs is carried out in the best sense of the concept:

> *That children with special needs attend school, child care, and recreational programs with their typically developing peers; that inclusion is much more than a place, a curriculum, or teaching strategy; that inclusion is about belonging, being valued, and having options; that inclusion is about accepting and valuing human diversity and providing the necessary support so that all children and their families can participate in programs of their choice.*

In this edition of *The Exceptional Child: Inclusion in Early Childhood Education*, we address many basic issues facing teachers, parents, and individuals working in an inclusive setting. These issues include how to:

▶ work effectively with a group of young children, one or more of whom may be significantly challenged in physical, cognitive, language, social, or behavioral development.

▶ apply the developmental-behavioral approach to make classroom management effective and positive.

▶ arrange the environment so that every child has developmentally appropriate learning opportunities.

▶ translate significant research findings about the relationship of early brain and language development into classroom practices.

▶ ensure that every child, with his or her own interests and capabilities, is both included with and accepted by other children.

- arrange optimal learning activities at both the individual and the group levels.
- include parents and caregivers in ways that incorporate and value their firsthand knowledge in planning for their child's learning.
- facilitate optimum speech, language, and communication development.
- facilitate pre-academics and cognitive learning, as well as overall intellectual development.
- facilitate adaptive, self-care, and independence skills.
- plan and facilitate transitions to other programs in ways that support inclusion.

Text Philosophy

Developmentally appropriate practice (DAP) is emphasized as basic to effective teaching. Research findings in reinforcement theory and early childhood special education give teachers well-tested and developmentally appropriate teaching strategies. The focus of these strategies is on the intentional teaching of skills that put a child's physical, cognitive, or social development back on track. For these strategies to be DAP-compatible, teachers must use them in the context of ongoing assessment of a child's developmental status, interests, and learning styles.

Language Usage

Both vocabulary and language in this text will be familiar to most teachers and students, despite overlapping terms. For example, terms such as *exceptional, special,* and *atypical* are used interchangeably, reflecting the mixed usage within the field. The same holds true for words commonly used, such as *normal* and *typical,* to describe the vast majority of children who are more similar than different in their development.

Words that may be unfamiliar, or that have special meaning, appear in boldface in the text and are defined in the glossary. Use of *person-first* language reflects respect for individuals with developmental disabilities.

Both the acronyms of IDEA and IDEIA are used interchangeably in this text to refer the Individuals with Disabilities Education Act Amendment of 1997, and most recently renamed as the Individuals with Disabilities Education Improvement Act of 2004, PL 108-446.

Text Organization

The nineteen chapters that comprise the eighth edition are grouped by content into four major sections.

Section 1 gives an overview of early intervention and public policy, providing the background and foundation material for the text as a whole. Chapters 1, 2, and 3 set the scene for the chapters that follow by defining inclusion. These chapters also provide an updated review of public policy related to early intervention and describe the major types of inclusive early childhood programs.

Section 2 concentrates on children and their similarities, as well as their differences. Chapters 4 and 5 offer a detailed exploration of typical and atypical development; an overview of types and causes of developmental disabilities; and an expanded look at genetic, chromosomal, and metabolic disorders.

Section 3 concentrates on planning for inclusion. The chapters focus on partnerships with parents and their participation in the inclusion process, as well as their participation in the writing of the individualized education program and/or individualized family services plan (IEP/IFSP). This section also includes information on the preparation of teachers for working in inclusive classrooms and functioning on an interdisciplinary child-study team.

Section 4, comprising most of the second half of the text, focuses on what teachers do in their classrooms on a day-to-day basis. This is the heart of the book—the "how to"—and it provides teachers with information they need in order to apply the philosophy, principles, and strategies that make inclusion work for all children.

New Features and Updates

▶ The new, larger trim size and beautiful color design with outstanding color photos makes this eighth edition even more engaging and accessible.

▶ The learning objectives correlated to the main sections in each chapter show students what they need to know to process and understand the information in the chapter. After completing the chapter, students should be able to demonstrate how they can use and apply their new knowledge and skills.

▶ The text has been thoroughly revised to reflect current National Association for the Education of Young Children (NAEYC) standards—especially those related to inclusion, developmentally appropriate practice, and early childhood education. Every chapter starts off with a list of the NAEYC standards addressed within the chapter.

▶ Digital Downloads include the text's figures as well as a complete version of the Skills Profile for students to download, often customize, and use in the classroom! Look for the Digital Download label that identifies these items.

▶ Did You Get It? quizzes allow students to measure their performance against the learning objectives in each chapter. One question for each learning objective is featured in the textbook to encourage students to go to the book's accompanying website, CengageBrain.com, take the full quiz, and check their understanding.

▶ There are twenty-one TeachSource Video Connection boxes included in this edition. The TeachSource videos feature footage from the classroom to help students relate key chapter content to real-life scenarios. Critical-thinking questions provide opportunities for in-class or online discussion and reflection.

▶ Every chapter has at least one new Connections box highlighting recent brain research or relating to English language learners and diversity.

▶ The new edition contains many recent research findings related to young children with special needs—such as information about hearing and vision problems, leukemia, autism, ADD/ADHD, and current brain research related to young children with disabilities.

- The text also contains a description of current legislative activities on behalf of young children and their families, including an update on the reauthorization of IDEA and No Child Left Behind. Current coverage of Response to Intervention (RTI) is also included.

- The text includes updated and expanded information on many topics, including universal learning design, childhood obesity and school health guidelines, the appropriate use of technology in early childhood programs, quality indicators of an inclusive classroom, family-center practices, augmentative and alternative communication systems, and English language learners.

- Comprehensive and up-to-date website listings are included at the end of each chapter.

- New "Section Wrap Ups" have been added to this edition. These Section Wrap Ups include "Special Focus" features written by parents and professionals that provide a real-life, first-person perspective on inclusion. There are application questions at the end of each Special Focus piece.

- The full-color photos in this edition illustrate key concepts within the text.

Chapter-by-Chapter Changes

The eighth edition of *The Exceptional Child* has been updated in a myriad of ways. The most significant of these revisions are:

- Chapter 1: Information on the importance of nurturing relationships to brain development in infants and children.

- Chapter 2: Expanded information on a child care center's responsibility under the ADA. Updated information on No Child Left Behind and the Vaccines for Children's program.

- Chapter 3: Information on the aspects of culturally competent early childhood programs.

- Chapter 4: Research showing the importance of everyday experiences to brain development.

- Chapter 5: Expanded information on categories of disabilities under IDEIA. Updated content for intellectual and emotional disorders.

- Chapter 6: A reference chart for signs of a hearing impairment as well as description of sign language around the world.

- Chapter 7: Expanded information on universal design for learning (UDL). A discussion of research demonstrating the connection between physical activity and brain development. Information on the Centers for Disease Control and Prevention's School Health Guidelines to Promote Healthy Eating and Physical Activity.

- Chapter 8: Updates on the autism spectrum and attention deficit disorders, based on DSM-5, as well as a discussion of advances in the area of autism research.

- Chapter 9: Additional content on family-centered practice and the importance of family involvement.

- Chapter 10: New content on the role of the family in the assessment process, including information on cultural, ethnic, and linguistic differences. Expanded information on how to write IEP Goals.

- Chapter 11: Material on preparing teachers to work with culturally diverse children.

- Chapter 12: A review of research on mirror neuron networks and their relation to learning by imitation.

- Chapter 13: A checklist that can be used by parents when looking for a program or by program staff to determine if their program is effectively including every child, as well as a checklist for age-appropriate design for outdoor play.

- Chapter 14: A description of how visual cues can be used to support self-care routines. A discussion of how snack time provides an opportunity to practice many skills in addition to self-care.

- Chapter 15: An explanation of how the Tiered Framework for Intervention provides a model for supporting the social and emotional development of all children, while also providing the systematic intervention that some children need to acquire social and emotional skills.

- Chapter 16: Additional information on augmentative and alternative communication systems. Updated information on English language learners (ELL).

- Chapter 17: Expanded information on the appropriate use of technology and interactive mediation tools in early childhood programs.

- Chapter 18: A discussion of the importance of children's executive function skills as the foundation for learning and social interaction, and the link between early school success and social-emotional development.

- Chapter 19: Updated information on transitional kindergartens and the practice of red-shirting kindergarten-aged children, as well as additional information on the role of service providers and parents during transitions.

Ancillaries for the Student

Early Childhood Education CourseMate

Cengage Learning's Early Childhood Education CourseMate brings course concepts to life with interactive learning, study, and exam-preparation tools that support the printed textbook. Access the eBook, Did You Get It? quizzes, Digital Downloads, TeachSource videos, flashcards, and more in your Education CourseMate. Go to **CengageBrain.com** to register or purchase access.

TeachSource Videos

The TeachSource videos feature footage from the classroom to help students relate key chapter content to real-life scenarios. Critical-thinking questions provide opportunities for in-class or online discussion and reflection.

Ancillaries for the Instructor

Early Childhood Education CourseMate

Cengage Learning's Early Childhood Education CourseMate brings course concepts to life with interactive learning, study, and exam-preparation tools that support the printed textbook. CourseMate includes the eBook, quizzes, Digital Downloads, Teach-Source videos, flashcards, and more—as well as EngagementTracker, a first-of-its-kind tool that monitors student engagement in the course. The accompanying instructor website, available through login.cengage.com, offers access to password-protected resources such as PowerPoint® lecture slides and the online Instructor's Manual with Test Bank. CourseMate can be bundled with the student text. Contact your Cengage sales representative for information on getting access to CourseMate.

Online Instructor's Manual with Test Bank

An online Instructor's Manual accompanies this book. It contains information to assist the instructor in designing the course, including sample syllabi, discussion questions, teaching and learning activities, field experiences, learning objectives, and additional online resources. For assessment support, the updated test bank includes true/false, multiple-choice, matching, short-answer, and essay questions for each chapter.

PowerPoint® Lecture Slides

These vibrant Microsoft® PowerPoint lecture slides for each chapter assist you with your lecture by providing concept coverage using images, figures, and tables directly from the textbook!

Cengage Learning Testing Powered by Cognero

- ▶ author, edit, and manage test bank content from multiple Cengage Learning solutions
- ▶ create multiple test versions in an instant
- ▶ deliver tests from your LMS, your classroom, or wherever you want

Acknowledgments

The authors express their great appreciation to the following lifelong friends, family, and colleagues who gave generously of their time, energy, and talent in making the eighth edition of this text the best yet.

- John, Henry, and Callie Cowdery, who, although patient, were very happy when the book was complete
- Kim Crane, friend and third-grade teacher
- Clarie Peterson, preschool teacher
- Ann Gordon, consultant, retired professor
- Leslie Kowitz, parent
- Lynn R. Marotz, R.N., Ph.D., assistant professor and associate director of the Edna A. Hill Child Development Center at the University of Kansas
- Susan R. Sandall, Ph.D., associate professor, College of Education, University of Washington at Seattle

Eileen would especially like to give equally heartfelt words of appreciation to her coauthor, Glynnis Cowdery, who enabled this text to go to press.

Finally, the authors want to acknowledge the help of the following reviewers, who provided useful input during the revision process:

- Marnie Anderson, Harrisburg Area Community College
- Rashida Banerjee, University of Northern Colorado
- Deborah Bruns, Southern Illinois University Carbondale
- Mary Cordell, Navarro College
- Christine Davis, Triton College
- Jennifer Dobbs-Oates, Purdue University West Lafayette
- Elizabeth Elliott, Florida Gulf Coast University
- Cyndra Gasperini, Pitt Community College
- Kelly Hantak, St. Charles Community College
- Dana Hilbert, Cameron University
- Sharon Hirschy, Collin County Community College
- Shari Johnson, Southwest Wisconsin Technical College
- Abigail Kelley, Baystate College

- ▶ Holly Kirk, Itawamba Community College
- ▶ Sharon Little, South Piedmont Community College
- ▶ Suzanne Mira-Knippel, Southwestern Community College
- ▶ Charlynne Murphy, Woodland College
- ▶ Esther Ntuli, Idaho State University Pocatello
- ▶ Tiffany Paine, Trinidad State Junior College
- ▶ Dorothy Phalen, Adelphi University
- ▶ Megan Purcell, Eastern Kentucky University
- ▶ Karren Streagle, Virginia Commonwealth University
- ▶ Sara Wasserman, Montclair State University
- ▶ Chun Zhang, Fordham University

The authors' experience in early childhood education and inclusion spans seven decades. Eileen is a pioneer in the field. Both Glynnis and Eileen have been teachers and facilitators of effective and developmentally appropriate programs. Glynnis is currently involved in supporting community preschools educating children with special needs. Both authors have observed and participated in the changing face of inclusion and celebrate how far the field of early childhood education and inclusion have come.

If you have questions or feedback about this text, please e-mail Glynnis Cowdery at gecowdery@gmail.com.

Eileen and Glynnis, November 2012

K. Eileen Allen started out in the late 1940s as a parent participant and subsequently as a lay teacher in a parent co-op in Seattle, Washington. At age thirty-four, the mother of three children, she took her first college course. During the next ten years she taught full-time and also completed her bachelor's degree at the University of Washington. Concurrently, she began her teaching career as an assistant teacher in the Developmental Psychology Laboratory Nursery School at the University of Washington. Through what she describes as a series of serendipitous events, she became head teacher and was soon engaged in research and the publication of significant findings in child development and child learning.

A decade later, having also completed advanced degrees, she assumed the role of director of the laboratory preschool and coordinator of teacher training and research at the Experimental Education Unit, a part of the University of Washington's Child Development and Mental Retardation Center in the medical school. There she served on a pediatric interdisciplinary team and published her first book, *Early Intervention: A Team Approach* (Allen, Holm, & Schiefelbusch, 1983).

Her next career move came in 1973, when she joined the faculty of the Department of Human Development at the University of Kansas in Lawrence. There, Eileen continued to teach, conduct research, and publish several college textbooks.

Throughout her career, Eileen has been active in national and international organizations focused on the development of young children and their families. For more than fifty years, she has been an active member of the National Association for the Education of Young Children (NAEYC), beginning in those long-ago days when it was called NANE (the National Association of Nursery Education, pronounced "nanny"). Eileen was also an original member of the NAEYC Commission on Developmentally Appropriate Practice, helping to draft the first DAP handbook. She served on the Commission on Early Childhood Teacher Education and participated in drafting the first set of published guidelines. Also, as a founding member of National Association of Early Childhood Teacher Educators (NAECTE), an affiliate of NAEYC, she became its second president. The Council for Exceptional Children (CEC) was another focus for Eileen in the 1960s; she served as a member of its governing board. During these years, she was a founding member of DEC (the Division of Early Childhood, an affiliate of CEC) and was elected as one of its early presidents.

While teaching at the University of Kansas, Eileen became active in the Society for Research in Child Development (SRCD), serving on the editorial board and as chairperson of the national interdisciplinary committee. At this time she was selected to be a congressional science fellow, and she devoted her energy to children, youth, and family issues in the 101st Congress.

In 1987, Eileen retired from the University of Kansas and returned to her home in Seattle, Washington. She continued to write and to advocate for children and families well into her eighties when her loss of vision become too limiting. Consulting as a child development specialist was also a part of her retirement activities. (Eileen considers her two years as a consultant to Microsoft's efforts to design developmentally appropriate programs for toddlers and preschoolers a highlight of her retirement.) Now in her nineties and with severely limited vision and mobility, she most recently coauthored a book with Judith R. Starbuck entitled *I Like Being Old: A Guide to Making the Most of Aging*. Eileen spends as much time as possible at her peaceful cabin on the shore of the Hood Canal, enjoying retirement with fewer external demands.

Glynnis Edwards Cowdery received a B.A. in Psychology from Hood College, Frederick, Maryland. She worked at the Kennedy Institute in Baltimore, Maryland, providing treatment and conducting research with children with severe self-injurious behavior and feeding disorders. She then received an M.A. in Early Childhood Education and Applied Behavior Analysis from the University of Kansas in Lawrence. She served as a lead teacher in the university's Inclusion Lab Preschool.

There she met coauthor Eileen Allen and worked as her teaching assistant. Upon completion of her degree, Glynnis moved to the Boston area to work for the May Institute. There she designed and directed a preschool serving children with autism and children who were typically developing. She later moved to Northern California, where she has provided in-home parent training, served as a director of an early intervention program, consulted with public schools, and designed classrooms for children with autism. She is a parent of two young adults, who played on Eileen's beach as preschoolers when Eileen and Glynnis were working on the fifth edition of this textbook. Glynnis is extremely involved in her community and with local public schools. She also serves as a city arts commissioner. She provides behavioral and inclusion support services to community preschools and local school districts.

The Exceptional Child

An Inclusive Approach to Early Education

OBJECTIVES

After reading this chapter, you should be able to:

1-1   provide a definition of *inclusion*.

1-2   describe an overview of the history of inclusion.

1-3   provide a rationale for inclusion in early childhood education.

1-4   discuss the implications for teachers and their responsibilities to ensure effective inclusion.

1-5   outline the potential benefits of inclusion.

1-6   identify concerns and challenges about inclusion for children with and without disabilities.

. . . .

naeyc

The following NAEYC Standards are addressed in this chapter:

STANDARD 1 Promoting Child Development and Learning

STANDARD 2 Building Family and Community Relationships

CONNECTIONS

- Chanda, a young child with Down syndrome, attends a local child care program while her parents are at work. A speech-language pathologist and physical therapist come to the program every week to work with her and meet with her teacher.
- After preschool, in a class with six children with disabilities and six children without disabilities, Devon, a little boy with autism, takes swimming lessons at the local community center.
- Jonathan, a second grader with severe communication delays, participates in the youth choir at his church.
- All of these children are involved in inclusive programs.

inclusion children with special needs attend preschool, child care, and recreational programs with their typically developing peers

This book is about inclusion in the lives of young children such as Chanda, Devon, and Jonathan. **Inclusion** means that children with special needs attend preschool, child care, recreational programs, and school with typically developing peers. In an inclusive program, all participants are accepted by their peers and other members of the community and are supported in an appropriate manner that ensures that their needs are met (Stainback & Stainback, 1996).

Inclusion is not merely a place, or an instructional strategy, or a curriculum; inclusion is about belonging, being valued, and having choices. Inclusion is also about accepting and valuing human diversity and providing the necessary support so that all children and their families can participate successfully in the programs of their choice. Furthermore, inclusion is about accepting all children and their families and supporting their participation in the program. This means that programs must be sensitive to and respectful of different cultural values, beliefs, and practices. Program staff need to change their practices to accommodate the cultural beliefs and practices of children and families; these accommodations will result in programs that facilitate belonging and promote optimal child development.

A major change in public educational policy came about with the Education for All Handicapped Children Act (PL 94-142) in 1975. (This law was renamed the Individuals with Disabilities Education Act [IDEA] when it was reauthorized in 1990 as PL 101-476 and amended as PL 105-17, the Individuals with Disabilities Education Act Amendment of 1997, and most recently as the Individuals with Disabilities Education Improvement Act of 2004, PL 108-446. Both the acronyms of IDEA and IDEIA are used interchangably to refer to this law.) This law entitles everyone with a disability,

The emphasis in inclusive education is on providing the support necessary so that children can participate.

© Cengage Learning

from birth to age twenty-one, to a "free and appropriate public education" (FAPE). In addition, this federal law requires every child with a disability to be educated in the **least restrictive environment.** This means that children should be educated in the environment most like the educational environment of their peers who are typically developing, where the child can be successful with appropriate supports in place. Chapter 2 includes more information on legislation and policy.

For more than three decades, parents and professionals have been working to provide free and appropriate education for all children in the least restrictive environment. The first attempt at implementing this vision was called **mainstreaming.**

The term **integration** also has been used to describe the inclusion of children with disabilities in programs for typically developing children.

Some educators argue that there are clear-cut differences between integration and mainstreaming; others use the terms interchangeably. Both terms refer to children with disabilities being placed in full-time or part-time programs designed for typically developing children. You may also encounter the terms **reverse mainstreaming** or **integrated special education.** These terms are used to describe special education classes that also include some typically developing children. In a reverse mainstreaming or integrated special education class, the majority of the children have identified special needs, the lead teacher has special education training, and only one-quarter to one-third of the children are typically developing.

The difference between mainstreaming and inclusion is philosophical. In mainstreaming, children with disabilities had to "be ready" to be integrated into the mainstream. The emphasis was placed on helping the child with disabilities meet the existing expectations of the classroom. Often the child with disabilities was regarded as a visitor in the classroom and was actually assigned (according to school records) to a special education class (Schorr, 1990). In inclusive education, children with disabilities are full-time members of the general education classroom. The emphasis in inclusive education is on providing the support necessary so that the children can participate in ongoing classroom activities. Support may include adaptation of the curriculum, materials, or instructional practices. Support may also include additional staff, consultation, or specialized training for the existing staff. Support services, such as speech therapy and physical therapy, are conducted in natural places in the school environment, including the classroom, gym, and playground.

This chapter focuses on current perspectives on inclusive education for young children. A brief overview of effective practices will be given; the specifics of what to do are reserved for the remaining units of the text. The outcomes of inclusive education, the benefits of inclusion, and some of the barriers to inclusion will also be discussed.

least restrictive environment (LRE) the most normalized environment in which the needs of a child with disabilities can be met appropriately; often, the LRE is interpreted as the environment in which typically developing children function

mainstreaming enrolling children with disabilities along with typically developing children in the same classroom

integration children with disabilities and typically developing children enrolled in the same program

reverse mainstreaming special education classes that also include some typically developing children

integrated special education including a few typically developing children in classes where the majority of children have special needs

Inclusion Defined 1-1 ☀

"Inclusion is a right, not a privilege for a select few" (*Oberti v. Board of Education in Clementon School District*, 1993). The call for inclusion continues to come from families, professional organizations, and advocacy groups. Inclusion means:

> providing all students within the mainstream appropriate educational programs that are challenging yet geared to their capabilities and needs as well as any support and assistance they and/or their teachers may need to be successful in the mainstream. But an inclusive school also goes beyond this. An inclusive school is a place where everyone belongs, is accepted, supports, and is supported by their peers and other members of the school community in the course of having their educational needs met. (Stainback & Stainback, 1996)

Inclusion is not a set of strategies or a placement issue. Inclusion is about belonging to a community—a group of friends, a school community, or a neighborhood. Ehlers (1993) describes three ways to view inclusion: through beliefs and values, through experiences, and through outcomes.

The *beliefs and values* that every family brings to inclusion reflect the unique history, cultural influences, and relationships of that family (Harry, 1998; Luera, 1993). Family choices must drive the inclusion process. The family identifies the community to which it belongs and in which the child is to be included. The concept of "goodness of fit" (Thomas & Chess, 1977) is essential when developing inclusive programs. An inclusive program must consider the uniqueness of every child and family and how it can address the child's strengths and needs as well as family priorities.

The beliefs and values that influence inclusion occur at the levels of the family, the community, and society (Peck, 1993). A family's belief system will have a direct impact on its views about inclusion.

The sociopolitical context in which children and families live and work also impacts inclusion. This includes how our society views high-quality early childhood care and education for all children. In other words, if providing high-quality child care for typically developing children is not a societal priority, providing high-quality child care for children with disabilities will not be a priority either.

The *experience* of inclusion varies from child to child and from family to family. The goal is to create a match between the program and the child and family. Inclusive classrooms are caring communities that support the ongoing development of participants (Salisbury, Palombaro, & Hollowood, 1993). Inclusion requires planning, teamwork, and support. "Our values and beliefs will help define our experience with inclusion; in turn, our experience will shape future values and beliefs" (Odom et al., 1996).

The *outcomes* observed and reported by the parents and teachers of children in inclusive educational programs are broad-based and holistic. These outcomes include some of the developmental changes observed in segregated special education programs (e.g., improved communication skills, improved motor skills). They also include important changes in social behavior and a general sense of belonging. Many parents of children in inclusive educational programs report that their child received his or her first invitation to a birthday party or to play at a friend's house after being involved in inclusive education. Some parents report that they feel more included in the community because their child is attending a "regular" school.

Billingsley et al. (1996) propose three outcomes of inclusive education. These three interrelated concepts are membership, relationships, and development.

Membership includes the child's interactions with groups: being a member of a class, being a member of a small group within a class, and being a member of non-school-related groups (e.g., children's choir at church). The defining criterion is that other members of the group are willing to make accommodations for the child with disabilities to support inclusion and membership.

The *relationships* concept looks at the different roles that children play in their interactions with peers. For example, in the majority of interactions with peers, is the child with disabilities receiving help? Does the child with disabilities have opportunities to be in the role of helping other children? Are there reciprocal or play and companionship types of interaction? Looking at relationships this way allows us to provide useful descriptions of the peers in the child's social network.

The *development* concept looks at more traditional types of early childhood special education outcomes: changes in participation in classroom routine and rituals, changes in social-communicative behavior, changes in functional skills, changes in pre-academic skills, and other goals that are included on a child's **individualized education program (IEP)** or **individualized family service plan (IFSP)** and plan for the

individualized education program (IEP) a document that is mandated for every student with a disability (ages three to twenty-one) by PL 94-142. The IEP is the blueprint for the services the child receives and must be developed every year. It describes the child's current level of functioning and includes short- and long-term goals and objectives. Parents must approve all IEPs.

individualized family service plan (IFSP) similar to an IEP. The IFSP describes services for very young children with disabilities (ages 0–3) and their families. The IFSP is mandated by PL 99-457. The IFSP is written collaboratively and describes the child's current strengths and needs. The IFSP describes what services will be provided and the major expected outcomes. Plans for the transition at age three are also included in the IFSP.

FIGURE 1-1

The Division for Early Childhood and the National Association for the Education of Young Children Joint Position Statement on Early Childhood Inclusion

Definition of Early Childhood Inclusion

Early childhood inclusion embodies the values, policies, and practices that support the right of every infant and young child and his or her family, regardless of ability, to participate in a broad range of activities and contexts as full members of families, communities, and society. The desired results of inclusive experiences for children with and without disabilities and their families include a sense of belonging and membership, positive social relationships and friendships, and development and learning to reach their full potential. The defining features of inclusion that can be used to identify high quality early childhood programs and services are access, participation, and supports.

© Cengage Learning

TeachSource Digital Download Download from CourseMate.

unique outcomes found in inclusive educational settings. This outcome framework also can be used to guide the development of goals and objectives for inclusive educational programs. (See the discussion of IFSP and IEP development in Chapter 10.)

The Division for Early Childhood and the National Association for the Education of Young Children approved a joint position statement. *Early Childhood Inclusion: A Joint Position Statement of the Division for Early Childhood* (DEC) *and the National Association for the Education of Young Children* (NAEYC) (2009) provides a shared national definition of inclusion. The document was developed through a collaborative national process that the National Professional Development Center on Inclusion (NPDCI) coordinated. This document is anticipated to have significant positive impact on the early childhood field. This shared definition of inclusion is found in Figure 1-1.

Jerlean Daniel, Deputy Executive Director of NAEYC, summarizes the need for this shared definition as follows:

Early childhood finally has a clear definition of inclusion. It is amazing that we have gone this long without a definition for an idea that gives children with and without disabilities an equal opportunity to learn together. In its place, with the best of intentions, individuals, programs, and schools have created their own working definitions based upon interpretations of federal laws, and the idiosyncrasies and politics of assorted venues where young children with disabilities are served. The DEC/NAEYC joint position statement on Early Childhood Inclusion's designation of the three primary components of inclusion, access, participation, and support offers the field a rich, substantive framework for what it means to serve all children well. (Early Childhood Community, 2009.)

naeyc

Did You Get It?

Why is the concept of "goodness of fit" considered to be essential when developing inclusive programs?

- **a.** The family identifies the community to which it belongs and in which the child is to be included.
- **b.** Goodness of fit takes into account the idea of an inclusive program considering the uniqueness of every child and family and how it can address the child's strengths and needs as well as family priorities.
- **c.** The term implies compatibility.
- **d.** Inclusion reflects the cultural influences of the family.

Take the full quiz on CourseMate.

1-2 Historical Perspective of Inclusion

1-2a ■ Early Attitudes

The number of children with disabilities in the educational mainstream has increased steadily over the past thirty years. This is in marked contrast to the way children with disabilities were viewed in the past. Caldwell (1973) gives the following description of the stages our society has gone through in its treatment of people with disabilities.

Forget and hide Until the middle of the twentieth century, families, communities, and society in general seemed to try to deny the existence of people with disabilities. As much as possible, children with disabilities were kept out of sight. For example, families often were advised immediately to institutionalize an infant with an obvious disability such as Down syndrome.

In 1950, the National Association for Retarded Children (now the ARC) was founded. Efforts were put into motion to identify children with disabilities and to bring them out of attics and back rooms. Members of President John F. Kennedy's family also were influential through their public acceptance of their own family member with mental retardation.* The Kennedys' acceptance went a long way toward breaking down the social stigma attached to a family that allowed a child with a disability (especially a child with mental retardation*) to be seen in public.

Screen and segregate About the same time (1950), special education began in public school systems. These first special education classes often provided little more than custodial care. Caldwell describes it this way:

> My first experience in lobbying was in Jefferson City, Missouri, where we were trying to get classes for the educable and trainable mentally retarded.* The children would be tested, labeled, segregated into a special facility, and virtually isolated again. These special facilities would keep them out of everybody's hair … and [avoid] the irritation of not only the parents but also the teachers. … It would also get them out of the way of other children who would supposedly be held back by them. (p. 5)

The screen-and-segregate period lasted more than twenty years, at which point the constitutional rights of people with disabilities began to be recognized.

Identify and help The identify-and-help period came about during the 1960s as a result of political and social activities. Caldwell summed up this period thus: "We have not abandoned concern with screening, with trying to find children who need help. … We now try to make the search earlier in hopes of affording early remediation or more accurately, **secondary prevention**" (p. 5; emphasis added).

secondary prevention refers to the early identification of handicapping conditions (or potentially handicapping conditions) and providing appropriate intervention services before the condition worsens or affects other areas of development

Include and support Since Caldwell's significant contribution, we have seen further change. In 1986, Madeleine Will, then assistant secretary at the Office of Special Education and Rehabilitative Services (under the U.S. Department of Education), in an annual report regarding the status of special education programs, proposed what has been called the Regular Education Initiative. She cited concerns about some unintended negative effects of special education "pull-out" programs. Her report suggested that greater efforts to educate

---

* The term is now intellectual disability.

mildly and moderately disabled students in the mainstream of regular education be pursued (Will, 1986). Further contributions to include and support were made by the passage of the Americans with Disabilities Act in 1990, and the rulings in both the *Holland* and *Oberti* court cases (*Board of Education, Sacramento School District v. Holland*, 1992; *Oberti v. Board of Education of Clementon School District*, 1993). These two court cases resulted in rulings that demonstrated clear support for inclusive educational programs. Further support comes from the National Association of State Boards of Education (1992) in the document *Winners All*, which calls for inclusive education for all students. The underlying assumption of the include-and-support period is that people with disabilities should be included as full members of society and that they should be provided appropriate supports, such as education and accessible environments, to ensure their inclusion and meaningful participation.

Did You Get It?

What created the period of "identify-and-help," as identified by Caldwell?
  a. President John F. Kennedy's family's acceptance of disabilities.
  b. Custodial care of first special education classes.
  c. Report by Madeline Will.
  d. Political and social activities.

Take the full quiz on CourseMate.

Rationale for Inclusive 1-3 ☼ Early Education

Early childhood education has gained widespread acceptance in our society during the past quarter century. The rationale for inclusive early childhood programs will be discussed in terms of ethical issues, socialization concerns, developmental considerations, and the always pressing issue of cost effectiveness.

1-3a ■ The Ethical Issue

The rights of children with disabilities to as full a life as possible is a major ethical force among advocates of inclusion. Dunn (1968) first brought the unfairness of segregated education for children with disabilities to the public consciousness. He asserted that special classes, for the most part, provided inadequate education for children with developmental delays. The integration of children with disabilities runs parallel to the multicultural approach to early education. According to Derman-Sparks (1988–1989), the common goal is to gain acceptance in our educational system for children with noticeably different cultural, intellectual, or physical characteristics. Until this is accomplished, ethical issues related to any kind of segregation in our schools remain unresolved.

1-3b ■ The Socialization Issue

Including young children with disabilities in the educational mainstream implies equal social status with children who are developing typically. Inclusion promotes awareness. Members of the community become more accustomed to children with developmental disabilities; this leads to greater acceptance. It cannot be overemphasized that young children with developmental disabilities are entitled to the same kinds of enriching early experiences as typically developing children. As Haring and McCormick (1994) point out, "separating young children with handicaps [disabilities] from normal experiences creates distance, misunderstanding, and rejection. … Moreover, separating these youngsters from the *real world* means that there must be reentry. Reentry problems can be avoided by not removing the child from normal settings" (p. 102). Young children with disabilities who play and interact only with other children with disabilities will not learn normal social skills. Play with typically developing children must be an integral part of any program designed to promote healthy development (Lieber, Schwartz, Sandall, Horn, & Ashworth Wolery, 2003; Wolery & Wilbers, 1994).

Preschool children who are typically developing need to get to know children with disabilities, especially children whose disabilities are obvious—children who are visually and hearing impaired, physically challenged, or less able cognitively. During their early years, children who are typically developing, unless otherwise influenced, seldom have trouble accepting children who are developmentally different. In fact, the disability may not even figure in a child's efforts to describe a classmate with a disability. One parent tells the following story:

> Andrea came back from preschool saying she wanted to invite Katie home for lunch the next day. I could not figure out who Katie was. Andrea tried to describe Katie's hair, then her new jacket, then her paintings. I still couldn't place her. Finally Andrea said, "Katie's the one who comes with shiny ribbons in her hair," and I knew immediately who Katie was. She was the child in the wheelchair who always had big colorful bows at the ends of her braids! Apparently, using a wheelchair was not one of Katie's outstanding characteristics for my child.

Children who are typically developing need to get to know children with disabilities.

© Cengage Learning

1-3c ■ Developmental Issues

The significance of the early years in laying the foundations for lifelong learning is well established. During these early years, children acquire a broad range of basic skills in all areas of development. Figure 1-2 lists these skills.

A quality early childhood program can assist all children in acquiring the developmental skills mentioned in Figure 1-2. The experience is of special benefit to children with disabilities or children at risk for developmental problems. Each day, they will

Young children seldom have problems accepting children who are developmentally different.

encounter a variety of challenging materials, equipment, and activities, planned and unplanned.

There will be interactions with all kinds of other children who serve as models to imitate and to play with, children who will help and who will need help. There will be teachers who understand the regularities and irregularities of development and will assist every child in taking advantage of sensitive learning periods and teachable moments.

Sensitive periods The majority of young children will acquire basic developmental skills on their own. Some of this learning seems to come about more readily at particular points in time, known as developmentally **sensitive** or **critical periods**. During these periods, the child appears to be especially responsive and able to learn

sensitive (or critical) period a time when a child is especially responsive and able to learn a particular skill

FIGURE 1-2

Basic Developmental Skills

1. They learn to move about, to get from one place to another independently, to explore and experiment.

2. They become skilled at grasping, holding on to, releasing, and manipulating evermore complex objects.

3. They become increasingly able to take care of their personal needs: toileting, dressing, eating.

4. They acquire their native language and use it in a variety of ways to get what they need (and prefer) from others in their environment.

5. They develop the ability to think, generate ideas, solve problems, make judgments, and influence others.

6. They respond with increasingly sophisticated words and gestures when others speak to them or attempt to influence them.

7. They discover ways of getting along with and interacting with others—those who are like themselves and those who are different.

© Cengage Learning

TeachSource Digital Download Download from CourseMate.

from specific kinds of stimulation. The same stimulation at other times seems to have little impact on development. It is important that all children be in an enriched and responsive learning environment during these periods. For children with developmental problems, this may be even more essential (Olswang & Bain, 1991).

A developmental disability or delay often prevents a child from reacting in ordinary ways during a sensitive period. Parents, especially if they are inexperienced, may not recognize signals from their child or they may read these signals incorrectly. In contrast, teachers in an inclusive classroom, where there is a range of developmental differences among children, tend to pick up on many subtle behavioral variations and many different forms of communication.

Critical learning periods that are not recognized and not used are common among infants and children with sensory deficits. Think of the learning experiences so readily available to children who are typically developing: hearing the difference between the doorbell and the telephone; puzzling over a bird call, a flash of lightning, or an angry face. The typically developing child turns automatically, dozens of times a day, to look at and listen to and learn from specific things at specific moments. These same cues, quite literally, *are not there* for the child with a **sensory deficit**. Without special assistance and opportunities to follow the leads of other children who are responding to what is going on, the child with a sensory impairment is isolated from everyday events.

sensory deficit a loss in one or more of the five senses: vision, hearing, touch, taste, smell

Language acquisition appears to be especially tuned to a sensitive period in development. A child with a hearing impairment may never acquire truly adequate language if the hearing loss is not treated prior to what is thought to be the critical period for language development. On the other hand, a child whose hearing problem is identified early may experience fewer problems in language development. A combination of appropriate treatment and a special education program for children with hearing impairments or an inclusive preschool (or a combination, depending on the child's age and severity of hearing loss) allows critical learning periods to be built on as they occur.

Children who are physically disabled also are denied critical learning opportunities, but for different reasons. Many cannot move around. They cannot explore their environment. They may not be able to open doors, get into cupboards, run to the window, or learn by simply getting into mischief. Contrast this with physically able children who are on the move from morning to night. They are touching, reaching, running, tumbling, climbing, getting into this and that. They try adults' patience at times, especially during critical learning periods, when they seem to be in constant motion, as in the following example:

The infant who is learning to walk is forever on the go. Once walking is mastered, a great cognitive advance seems to take place. Then comes another surge of motor development. The child learns to run, jump, and climb, practicing these skills relentlessly. On the other hand, children who do not walk until late childhood may have continuing problems. They may never get good at activities that involve sustained running, jumping, and climbing. Even more serious, they may have missed other critical aspects of early learning during the sensorimotor stage when cognitive development and motor activity are so interdependent.

Teachable moments For teachers in an inclusive setting, another concept of developmental significance is that of **teachable moments**. These are points in time when a child is highly motivated and better able to acquire a particular skill such as walking, riding a tricycle, or learning to count. All children, including those with severe disabilities, have many such teachable moments every day. They occur during daily routines and activities. It is important that teachers

teachable moments points in time, perhaps associated with critical periods, when a child is highly motivated and better able to acquire a particular skill

recognize these opportunities and make sure they lead to developmentally appropriate learning experiences. Teachers also can help parents understand the significance of teachable moments and guide them in recognizing these moments and finding ways of responding. The inclusive classroom is an especially suitable place for parents to observe teachers and try out various ways of working with their child.

The infant who is blind and getting ready to learn to walk is an illustration of a teachable moment. First, though, think about developmental sequences and the sighted infant. Walking usually is preceded by a period of just standing, then holding on to furniture, and finally cruising about. Most infants do this spontaneously; no teaching is necessary, and no special arrangements are needed.

On his or her own, the baby who cannot see may barely progress beyond the standing stage. The baby seems to sense that it might be too risky to step out. What is needed is someone who recognizes *pulling-to-stand* as a teachable moment and helps the baby build on it. Experienced parents usually recognize the sign; inexperienced parents may not. The teacher in an infant program, whether center-based or in-home, is geared to such moments and ready to provide encouragement. Once pulling to stand is mastered, the baby's hands may be moved along the tabletop to teach the fundamentals of cruising. (Usually the baby's feet follow

Connecting Developmentally Appropriate Practice to Brain Research

THE IMPORTANCE OF RELATIONSHIPS

Research has shown that secure loving family relationships contribute significantly to a child's developing brain. As cited in Dann (2011), Cairns states:

It is now clear that the brain of the developing infant is more radically shaped and structured by the quality of interactions between the infant and the environment than we had previously thought. Children whose environment is hostile or lacking in nurture end up thinking with a very different brain (Cairns, 2002, p. 46).

If children are not given adequate stimulation there may be fewer connections being made in the brain. For young children who experience disruption in attachment due to abuse or trauma, the brain is affected biochemically. When children experience trauma, this can lead to stress. Increased stress levels produce high levels of hormones, which alter the neurobiology of the brain and central nervous system. The caregiver's role is to reduce the impact of stress; if a child does not receive this support from a caregiver, the child is likely to have difficulties controlling stress levels. This will lead to the child either dissociating or shutting down to avoid being totally overwhelmed by the high level of stress.

These responses are likely to become part of the brain's response in the future, resulting in more extreme fight, flight, or freeze reactions related to stress.

Dann also states that it may be tempting to say that the damage is already done and that these children will always struggle with their learning and their relationships, but this fails to recognize the importance that future teaching and learning may have on the child's ability to cope with stress and to learn. She goes on to state that evidence is still emerging within neuroscience research. She cites Wilson (2002, 197) who contends, "the notion of the first three years as a critical period for brain development is not as yet substantiated by the research." The brain retains plasticity well beyond the early years and that "even in situations of child neglect there can often be recovery." This hope of recovery makes the need for quality programs and well-trained educators even more significant.

Your Turn

Relate the idea above to the issue of sensitive or critical periods as described in the book. Why does this information make the need for quality programs even more significant?

Sources: Dann, R. (2011). Look out! "Looked after"! Look here! Supporting "looked after" and adopted children in the primary classroom. *Education 3-13: International Journal of Primary, Elementary and Early Years Education, 39*(5), 455–465.

Cairns, K. (2002). *Attachment, trauma and resilience: Therapeutic Caring for Children.* British Association for Adoption and Fostering: London.

Wilson, H. (2002). Brain science, early intervention and "at risk" families: Implications for parents, professionals and social policy. *Social Policy and Society 1*(3), 191–202.

almost automatically as they learn to walk along, using furniture for support.) Teachers also make sure the environment is safe by keeping things off the floor so the baby does not experience frightening falls that may discourage further cruising.

As an infant becomes skilled at cruising, another teachable moment occurs: lifting one hand and one foot, as if ready to try a step with less support from the furniture. Again, the infant who cannot see will need special encouragement and a safe environment. Pieces of equipment and furniture, for example, should be left in the same place. It is frightening to reach for the support of a familiar table or chair to find it is no longer there.

The infant also needs someone to describe what he or she is doing and promote more of it: "You walked to *Delia's* chair. Can you *walk* back to the piano? "You have your *hand* on the *rocking* chair. Let's go find the *rocking* boat." Simple games such as "Find Maryanne" (from the direction of the teacher's voice) also build on teachable moments and keep the baby moving.

The more the infant who is visually impaired (or any other infant with or without a disability) moves about, the more the infant learns in every area of development. In fact, a major reason for using teachable moments is to keep the child involved in the process of learning. Hanson and Lynch (1995) put it this way:

> The child learns to be motivated and engaged in the environment and to seek interactions both with the social aspects of the environment—people—and with the nonsocial or physical aspects of the environment of toys, materials, and household items. (p. 210)

Imitation Another important rationale for inclusive early childhood settings is that young children with disabilities will observe and imitate more advanced skills modeled by typically developing children (Goldstein, 1993). The logic is sound. Imitating others is a major avenue of learning for everyone, old and young alike.

Young children learn by doing. If children with developmental problems are to learn to play appropriately, they must have children to imitate and play with. If children with behavior problems are to learn to share and take turns, they must have opportunities to imitate and interact with children who know how to share and take turns. If a young child with severe communication problems is to learn to initiate conversations, there must be peers available who are interesting and appropriate conversational partners. In a segregated classroom where there are only children with autism, it is unlikely that children will do much talking or modeling of appropriate language skills for each other—a powerful argument for inclusive education.

Throughout the day, all children have teachable moments.

© Cengage Learning

14 SECTION 1 | EARLY INTERVENTION AND PUBLIC POLICY

If children with developmental issues are to learn to play appropriately, they must have children to play with and imitate.

© Cengage Learning

1-3d ■ The Cost Issue

The cost of providing inclusive early education services is of concern to parents, program providers, administrators, and other program consumers. Although the economic aspect of early childhood special education programs is important, "it is not the only, or even preeminent perspective that one might wish to use" (Barnett & Escobar, 2000, p. 560).

The existing data on the cost of inclusive education programs suggest that these programs can be an economical alternative because they take advantage of existing program structures rather than creating parallel and often duplicate structures (Odom, Parrish, & Hikido, 2001; Salisbury & Chambers, 1994). The cost of providing appropriate educational services for young children with special needs can be reduced by capitalizing on existing programs in the community. This saving is a related benefit of inclusion but should not be the primary factor driving the agenda of inclusive education in a school district.

Another aspect of the cost issue is the large number of children, both with and without disabilities, who continue to go unserved. Simply put, there are not enough quality early childhood programs to go around. Investing public money in segregated rather than inclusive facilities should be seen as a setback—philosophically and financially—in meeting the developmental needs of *all* children.

Did You Get It?

What issue is raised by Haring and McCormick with regard to the separation of children with disabilities?
   a. Awareness will be minimized.
   b. Healthy development by playing with typically developing children is required.
   c. By separating young people from the real world means that reentry is required, and reentry problems can be avoided by not removing the child from normal settings.
   d. Children who are typically developing need to get to know children with disabilities.

Take the full quiz on CourseMate.

1-4 Supporting Inclusion: Implications for Teachers

The mere act of placing children with diverse needs together in a classroom does not ensure successful inclusion. "Inclusion depends on teachers' attitudes towards pupils with special needs, on their capacity to enhance social relations, on their view on differences in classrooms and their willingness to deal with those differences effectively" (Skipper, 2006. p. 9). Particular skills are needed to facilitate successful interactions. Many of these skills stem from knowledge of child development, as discussed in Chapter 4; the other skills are discussed in detail under various headings throughout the text. Effective inclusion requires specific planning and implementation by teachers, Figure 1-3 lists some of their responsibilities.

FIGURE 1-3

Teachers' Responsibilities for Effective Inclusion

- Individualizing programs and activities to meet each child's specific needs and abilities

- Arranging a highly engaging learning environment that encourages appropriate behavior

- Recognizing that all children belong and that although a specific behavior may be inappropriate in a particular setting, the goal is to support the child in learning a more appropriate alternative for that behavior

- Recognizing the value of play as a major avenue of learning for all children; at the same time, recognizing that play skills often have to be taught to children with disabilities, many of whom neither know how to play nor play spontaneously

- Arranging a balance of large- and small-group experiences, both vigorous and quiet, so that all children, at their own levels, can be active and interactive participants

- Structuring a learning environment in which children with diverse abilities are helped to participate together in a variety of activities related to all areas of development

- Creating a nurturing environment by providing a curriculum that emphasizes friendship, caring, and respect for diversity

- Assessing children's progress periodically and using this information to adjust curriculum and instruction

- Providing a flexible curriculum by making adjustments to the instruction and environment to address children's needs

- Supporting the development of all children by creating a learning and playing environment that includes a range of materials and activities to ensure that the lowest-functioning children can be independent and the highest-functioning children are challenged

- Collaborating with other team members (i.e., speech therapists, parents, occupational therapists, paraprofessionals) regarding progress and intervention

© Cengage Learning

TeachSource Digital Download Download from CourseMate.

The mere act of placing children with and without disabilities together in a classroom does not ensure successful inclusion and peer interaction.

© Cengage Learning

1-4a ■ Structuring Child-to-Child Interactions

The effectiveness of inclusion depends on ongoing interactions between children with diverse needs. Merely placing children with disabilities in the same settings as their typical peers will not automatically lead to social interactions and acceptance (Gutierrez, Hale, Gossens-Archuleta, & Sobrino-Sanchez, 2007; McGregor & Vogelsberg, 1998). Guralnick and his colleagues continue to conduct research on this issue (Guralnick & Neville, 1997). One of their early efforts (Devoney, Guralnick, & Rubin, 1974) indicated that children with and without disabilities played together *when the teacher structured the environment to promote such interaction.* (Chapters 13 and 15 discuss ways for teachers to accomplish this.) An interesting sidelight in the Devoney study was that children with disabilities, playing with children who are typically developing, played in a more organized and mature way than had been characteristic of their earlier play.

In another study, focused on imitation in an inclusive classroom, Garfinkle and Schwartz (1998) demonstrated that children with autism can learn to imitate their peers during small-group activities. After the imitation training, the amount of time that children with and without disabilities played together in small groups during free-choice time increased.

A wide variety of strategies can be employed to increase interactions between typical children and those with disabilities, including teaching typical peers specific initiation and interaction skills, using

▶❙❙ **TeachSource** Video Connections

© Cengage Learning 2015

Bobby: Serving a Student with Special Needs in an Inclusive Elementary Classroom

Bobby is a first grader with Down syndrome. Interviews of Bobby's classroom teacher, special education support teacher, and mother provide insight into the supports needed for Bobby to be successful in a first-grade general education classroom.

After watching the video, discuss the following:

1. What are the supports that are being provided so that Bobby is learning and thriving in his first-grade class?

2. Review the preceding list on teacher responsibilities for effective inclusion and note examples you observed in the video.

Watch on CourseMate.

cooperative learning structures for small-group instruction, and teaching students with disabilities critical social skills (Skipper, 2006). From the ever-growing library of research, it is apparent that the teacher's structuring of play activities is essential. Planning for an inclusive early childhood program must focus on activities that lead to children with diverse needs working and playing together.

1-4b ■ Planning Activities

Curriculum planning for inclusive settings also requires teachers to integrate the goals and activities on the children's IFSPs/IEPs into ongoing classroom activities. Using an **activity-based approach** to planning draws from the strong traditions of early childhood education and special education to best meet the learning needs of young children with disabilities (Pretti-Frontczak & Bricker, 2004). This approach allows teachers to use traditional early childhood activities such as dramatic play, art, nature walks, and water play to address specific goals and objectives across the developmental domains (e.g., cognitive, social, communication, motor, self-care).

Teachers structure the learning environment so that children with and without disabilities can interact and learn together.

© Cengage Learning

1-4c ■ Professional Collaboration

activity-based approach teachers use dramatic play, art, building with blocks, and other early childhood materials to provide developmentally appropriate learning experiences

interdisciplinary team refers to several different professionals working together on a common problem

In addition to classroom practices, inclusion requires the integration of professional efforts. Administrators, teachers, aides, volunteers, and members of the **interdisciplinary team** need to work together. Professional growth comes with collaboratively searching for ways to provide for children with disabilities in the inclusive setting. Part of the search includes looking for ways to develop a partnership with parents. This means listening to parents, consulting with them, and learning from them. In fact, all the participants—children, parents, teachers, classroom staff, and clinicians—can learn from each other in an integrated program. Early childhood teachers, however, receive a special bonus. In learning to meet the needs of children with disabilities, they become more skilled at meeting the needs of *all* children.

Did You Get It?

What significant children to children outcome was visible in the Devoney study?
- a. When the teacher structured the environment, the children with and without disabilities played together.
- b. When the children with disabilities played together with typically developing children, they played in a more organized and mature way than had been characteristic of their earlier play.
- c. Demonstrated that children can learn to imitate their peers during small-group activities.
- d. The amount of free time that children with and without disabilities played together in small groups during free-choice time increased.

Take the full quiz on CourseMate.

1-5a ■ Benefits for Children with Disabilities

In addition to the philosophical and legal issues discussed earlier, there are many clear benefits of educating young children with special needs in inclusive programs. In a review of the research into developmental outcomes in inclusive settings, Lamorey and Bricker (1993) noted that generally, children made significantly better gains in the areas of social competence and social play, and similar gains in the other developmental domains. The improved benefits in the social domain may be due to an emphasis on social development in programs that have implemented inclusive educational programming. There is also some evidence that the academic achievement of students with disabilities in inclusion settings is higher than that of students in segregated settings (Peters, 2004).

Children with developmental problems are likely to benefit from a quality inclusive preschool experience because these programs feature:

- more stimulating, varied, and responsive experiences than special classrooms composed of children with limited skills.

- curriculum activities that build on a child's strengths and preferences rather than a **deficit model** focused on what is *wrong* with the child.

  deficit model curriculum focuses on a child's disabilities and delays; tries to remedy what is "wrong" with the child

- opportunities to observe, interact with, and imitate children who have acquired higher-level motor, social, language, and cognitive skills.

- implicit motivation to "try a little harder," in that children who are typically developing often expect and encourage improved behaviors on the part of less skilled children.

- opportunities to learn directly from other children. It appears that a child with developmental delays can learn certain skills more easily from another child than from an adult; another child's explanations and demonstrations are often closer to the capabilities of the child with developmental delays than are the adult's explanations and demonstrations.

Research also indicates that inclusive settings are more stimulating and responsive to young children with disabilities than environments serving only children with special needs. There are greater demands for appropriate social behaviors. There are opportunities for observational learning and interactions with peers who are typical. Children with disabilities also engage in higher levels of play when they are with typically developing children (Guralnick, 1990).

1-5b ■ Benefits for Typically Developing Children

Children who are developing typically may have greater access to early childhood programs when there is full implementation of the preschool component of PL 99-457. As noted in the section on the cost issue, many typically developing children who would benefit from an early education program are not being served. As more inclusive programs become available, many more enrollments for all children will become available.

Developmental progress The progress of children who are typically developing is not adversely affected by placement in inclusive classes with children with developmental disabilities. This finding has been demonstrated at preschool and elementary ages (Buysee & Bailey, 1993; Sharpe, York, & Knight, 1994). In studies that have compared the amount of teacher attention to individual students and students' rate of engaged learning time in classrooms with and without students with disabilities, there are no differences, again suggesting no negative impact on instructional opportunities in inclusive classrooms. Carter and Kennedy (2006) reported that children who are typically developing, who were in inclusive classrooms, demonstrated greater appreciation of diversity and at the same time raised expectations of their classmates with severe disabilities.

Summarizing a number of studies, Thurman and Widerstrom (1990) suggest that children who are typically developing benefit from integrated programs "at least to the same degree and sometimes to a greater degree than would have been expected if they had attended nonintegrated preschools" (p. 39). Another conclusion to be safely drawn from the current research is that the developmental outcome for children in inclusive programs depends on the quality of teaching, rather than on integration.

peer tutoring one child instructing or assisting another

Peer tutoring A well-documented benefit of inclusion for children who are typically developing is **peer tutoring**—one child instructing another. It appears that both the child being tutored and the child doing the tutoring receive significant benefits from the experience. The common sense of this is readily apparent; most of us have discovered that, given an unpressured opportunity to teach someone else something we know (or are learning), our own skill and understanding are increased. The same is true of children. As pointed out by Spodek, Saracho, and Lee (1984), voluntary peer tutoring among young children of all developmental levels can promote:

- social interactions among children who are disabled and non- disabled.

- acceptable play behaviors.

- appropriate and enhanced use of materials.

Peer tutoring provides an exciting and challenging stretch for children to use their own creativity and ingenuity.

Developing sensitivity Rafferty, Boettcher, and Griffin (2001) surveyed 244 parents of children who attended a community-based preschool in New York. Almost all parents surveyed reported that inclusion helped typically developing children to

Children who are typically developing who grow up with opportunities to interact with children with disabilities are likely to be more tolerant in later years.

© Cengage Learning

understand differences in others. The children developed sensitivity and became increasingly aware of their own strengths and weaknesses. McGregor and Vogelsberg (1998) state that typical children who have the most contact with children with disabilities express more accepting attitudes toward those with disabilities. In addition, girls express more accepting attitudes toward children with disabilities.

1-5c ■ Benefits for Families

In general, parents' attitudes about inclusion were influenced by their experiences with inclusion (Lamorey & Bricker, 1993; Palmer, Fuller, Arora, & Nelson, 2001). Parents of children with disabilities were most often positive in their responses, although they did identify some concerns (see below). Attitudes of parents of children who are typically developing improved as experience with inclusion increased. In a study involving 125 parents of non-disabled children who attended inclusive preschool programs, Peck, Carlson, and Helmstetter (1992) found that parents perceived their children's experience as generally positive and were supporters of inclusive education. In addition, Peck and his colleagues found that parents reported that their children were more accepting of human differences and had less discomfort with people with disabilities and people who looked or behaved differently than they did.

1-5d ■ Benefits for Society

Not only does inclusion have positive effects on all children, it appears to be of long-term benefit to society. Children who are typically developing who grow up with opportunities to interact with children with disabilities are likely to be more tolerant in later years. They tend to mature into adults with greater understanding and respect for those less able in our society (Kishi & Meyer, 1994). Many teachers report that most young children, unless influenced by inappropriate adult attitudes, have a natural acceptance of individual differences. They are unlikely to make negative judgments and comparisons about children who are developmentally disabled. When they do comment or ask questions, it is because they need to learn about whatever it is that is unfamiliar about the child with a disability.

Did You Get It?

What implicit attitude displayed by typically developing children to those who are less skilled results in an increased learning benefit?
   a. Motivation to "try a little harder."
   b. More stimulated and varied experience.
   c. Curriculum activities focusing on strengths.
   d. Imitation of skills.

Take the full quiz on CourseMate.

Concerns and Challenges of Inclusion 1-6

It is inappropriate to frame the discussion of inclusion around questions such as "Does inclusion work?" or "Is inclusion right for our program?" Inclusion is the law. All early childhood programs that receive federal funds must include children with special needs. With passage of the Americans with Disabilities Act (ADA), it is also against the law for private early childhood programs to refuse to serve a child because of disability. It is important, however, to discuss the concerns that parents and professionals have about inclusion and to work together to overcome challenges that may interfere with providing quality inclusive programs for all children. (See the "Case Study" box below for further discussion of this issue.) It is also important to note that successful inclusion can look different for each child. One child might be able to learn in a neighborhood preschool without extra support or specialized services, while another might require the assistance of a shadow aide or paraprofessional for all or part of the day. The discussion that follows identifies the most common concerns about inclusion and provides brief glimpses into research findings that address those issues.

1-6a ■ Will Special Needs Be Served?

Parents and teachers have expressed concern that the special needs of children with disabilities may not be met adequately in inclusive early childhood programs. They feel that teachers may not have the time or the skills. They also are concerned that children will not receive specialized support services, such as occupational therapy, physical therapy, and speech therapy. The opposite is also of concern: If a program is meeting the special needs of children with disabilities, then what about the typically developing children? Are they going to be shortchanged?

These concerns have been addressed in a number of research studies. By and large, the data indicate that parents believe their children (with and without disabilities) benefit from integrated programs. These findings are based on well-structured programs with knowledgeable teachers. Little parental satisfaction is found with poor-quality programs, integrated or otherwise. In a review of a number of research studies, Lamorey and Bricker (1993) state that in general, the needs of the children were met in inclusive programming. Some parents were concerned about the quality of training received by teachers in inclusive programs. This indicates that there is a need for different types of training in early childhood education. Professionals need to work on adapting preservice training for teachers in early childhood, early childhood special education, and related therapy fields. Training should prepare professionals to work together to deliver quality services to children with special needs in inclusive programs (Odom & McEvoy, 1990; Washington, Schwartz, & Swinth, 1994).

Case Study ■ How much to share? ■

One of the challenges faced by parents of children with special needs is how much information to share about their child with potential early childhood programs. Some parents have faced rejection from care providers when they hear the child has special needs, often before they have even met the child. On the other hand, once parents have found a program, it is critical that the staff have the information needed to provide proper care and effective teaching. Think about how you would approach this issue as a parent. What types of questions could you ask a program to determine whether it is a good fit? What are the potential problems, if any, of not sharing enough information or sharing too much information?

Many researchers have documented that parents of typically developing children report that their children are learning important social and academic lessons from their experiences in inclusive classrooms (McGregor & Vogelsberg, 1998). A similar reaction is found among parents of children with disabilities. Guralnick (1994) reported the following:

> Particular benefits to children with special needs were noted in relation to promoting the acceptance of children with disabilities in the community, preparing the child for the real world, encouraging children with special needs to learn more, and providing opportunities to participate in a wider variety of interesting and creative activities. (p. 180)

It is important to note, however, that these same parents voiced concerns about inclusion. These concerns included the quality of specialized services available in an inclusive setting and the possible rejection of the children with disabilities by their peers. Palmer, Borthwick-Duffy, Widaman, and Best (1998) and Palmer, Fuller, Arora, and Nelson (2001) found that parents whose children display the most significant disabilities are less likely to favor inclusion. These parents who opposed inclusion wrote statements indicating that the severity of their child's disability precluded the child from benefiting from inclusion or that the general education program would not be accommodating or welcoming.

Researchers have demonstrated and assert that there does not appear to be any basis for the fear of children being slighted, as an examination of successful programs at the preschool level demonstrates (Rafferty, Piscitelli, & Boettcher, 2003; Thurman & Widerstrom, 1990). Thurman and Widerstrom (1990) also refer to their personal experiences: "Individualized programming for the children with disabilities often spilled over into better practices with the nonhandicapped children. Teachers who thought mainly in terms of group activities learned, through their work with special children, to plan for individual differences among all children more effectively" (p. 40). In general, teachers' attitudes are favorable toward inclusion once they have actually worked with children with disabilities in an inclusive setting.

1-6b ■ Concerns about Inappropriate Behaviors

Another frequently expressed concern is that normally developing children will learn immature or inappropriate behaviors from classmates with disabilities. Again, this is an unfounded fear. This is not to imply that typically developing children do not imitate other children. They do. They should. Imitation is an important avenue for learning. But typically developing children imitate each other. Rarely (and then only briefly) do they imitate the atypical behaviors of another child. The exceptions are those children who get undue attention from teachers and parents for imitating inappropriate behaviors. Data collected by a group of researchers working with autistic children and reported by Odom and McEvoy (1988) indicate that "normally developing children did not imitate the unusual and stereotypic behavior of children with autism" (p. 259).

1-6c ■ Will Children with Special Needs Be Teased?

One of the important reasons to pursue inclusion is for the potential impact it can have on the attitudes of typically developing peers in regard to their classmates

Parents of typically developing children report that their children are learning important academic and social lessons from their experiences in an inclusive classroom.

© Cengage Learning

with special needs. It is believed that children without disabilities who grow up with the opportunity to interact with children with disabilities are more likely to show greater understanding of individuals with disabilities (Daley, 2002).

Friendship and interactions do not just happen magically. Teachers must set up opportunities and model behavior for all children. Adults must answer children's questions about disabilities openly and honestly. They must model accepting behavior. This encourages children with and without disabilities to form friendships and encourages children who are non-disabled to assist their peers with disabilities.

1-6d ■ A Final Word about Inclusion

Much has been learned about inclusion over the years, and there is still much to learn. Some feel that because inclusion is the law, all children should therefore be enrolled in regular education regardless of their special needs. Other professionals feel that inclusion is one of several possibilities for students with special needs. Simpson and Sasso (1992) take this idea one step further by stating that full inclusion should be subjected to empirical verification and that data should become the basis for making decisions about which children and youth should be integrated.

As stated earlier, inclusion is about values and beliefs, but it also must be about what works best for each child. Care must be taken to ensure that when a child is placed in an inclusive setting the child is also provided with adequate support to succeed. When a child is not able to learn in an inclusive setting, it is because planning and support were not provided.

Diane Twachtman-Cullen, a speech pathologist at the Autism and Developmental Disabilities Consultation Center in Cromwell, Connecticut, lists the following as some of the "worst practices in inclusion":

- insisting on inclusion at all costs.
- settling for a mere physical presence in the classroom.
- giving priority to the inclusive education model over the individual needs of children.

- providing little or no training to staff.
- keeping the paraprofessional out of the loop.
- teaching rote information so that the student can pass mandated tests instead of teaching needed skills.
- watering down the curriculum.
- failing to teach children about the nature of disabilities and how to interact with peers who have a disability (Dybvik, 2004).

Did You Get It?

In addition to caring about the values and beliefs of each child in an inclusive setting, what is essential to provide?
- a. Adequate support to succeed.
- b. Fun.
- c. Insistence on inclusion at all costs.
- d. Physical presence.

Take the full quiz on CourseMate.

Summary

▶ Including young children with developmental disabilities in regular early childhood programs is the law.

▶ The reasons for inclusion are based on ethical, social, developmental, and philosophical arguments. No longer is it acceptable, or legal, to keep children with disabilities out of the social and educational mainstream.

▶ There are many benefits to participating in an inclusive early childhood program for children with disabilities, including opportunities to interact with and imitate children who have acquired a higher level of language, play, and social skills.

▶ Children who are typically developing are provided significant learning experiences in helping less able children acquire a variety of skills—motor, social, and intellectual.

▶ A common concern, expressed by parents and teachers, is that the special needs of children may not be adequately met in an integrated program. Another is that children who are typically developing will receive less than their share of attention if children with disabilities are properly served. Then there is the concern that children who are typically developing will learn inappropriate and bizarre behaviors from atypical children. Numerous research studies demonstrate that these anxieties are largely unfounded. In fact, the opposite is true. The advantages of inclusion for all children are numerous and well documented.

▶ While inclusion is the law, many professionals caution that it is not enough just to place a child with special needs in an inclusive setting; adequate support must be provided.

Key Terms

activity-based approach, 18
deficit model curriculum, 19
inclusion, 4
individualized education program (IEP), 6
individualized family service plan (IFSP), 6

integrated special education, 5
integration, 5
interdisciplinary team, 18
least restrictive environment (LRE), 5
mainstreaming, 5
peer tutoring, 20

reverse mainstreaming, 5
secondary prevention, 8
sensitive (critical periods), 11
sensory deficit, 12
teachable moments, 12

Student Activities

1. Arrange a panel discussion on the pros and cons of inclusion. What are your beliefs and values concerning the law of inclusion? Do you think there are situations where inclusion might not be the best option? If so, identify some examples.

2. Talk with a teacher in an infant center or early childhood center. Ask about the types and numbers of children with disabilities in the program. What accommodations have they made for these students?

3. Observe an early childhood setting. Record any episodes of a child learning through observing, imitating, or peer tutoring.

4. Set up a simulated parent conference with three other students. Two of you play the child's parents and two the child's teachers. The parents' concern is that their typically developing three-year-old may not get enough attention because a child who is blind is scheduled to be included in the program. Role-play a discussion of the situation.

5. Review the DEC/NAEYC Joint Position Statement on Inclusion. How do you think this statement can be used to encourage the development of quality inclusive programs?

6. Do some research to determine the possible services that could play a part in supporting a child with special needs in an inclusive environment. Determine whether any of these services are being provided by your local school district.

Review Questions

Part 1. Briefly respond to the following items.

1. Define inclusion.
2. What are some possible outcomes of inclusion?
3. Name and briefly describe the four stages of public perception in reference to children with disabilities.
4. What do inclusion and culturally unbiased curriculum have in common?
5. Define and give an example of a teachable moment.
6. What is peer tutoring?
7. Of what benefit to society is inclusion?

Part 2. Respond to the following items in list.

1. List five responsibilities of the teacher in an inclusive preschool.
2. List three major concerns that parents and teachers have about inclusion.
3. List five arguments in favor of inclusion for young children with developmental problems.

Helpful Websites

The Council for Exceptional Children (CEC)

http://www.cec.sped.org

CEC publishes *Exceptional Children* and *Teaching Exceptional Children*. Of particular interest to early childhood education is one of CEC's affiliate groups, the Division for Early Childhood Education. (A number of other divisions also focus to some extent on issues related to young children.)

The Division for Early Childhood (DEC)

http://www.DEC-sped.org

DEC is a division of the Council for Exceptional Children. Their website contains position statements on a variety of issues, ranging from inclusion to interventions for challenging behaviors. The site includes reproducible checklists for parents and administrators and a professional's self-assessment for child-focused interventions.

Kids Together, Inc.

http://www.kidstogether.org/index.htm

The Goal of Kids Together, Inc. is to remove barriers that exclude people with disabilities. The website includes links to resources on such topics as IEPs, inclusion, assistive technology, and building communities.

 Visit the Education CourseMate for this textbook to access the eBook, Did You Get It? quizzes, Digital Downloads, TeachSource Video Cases, flashcards, and more. Go to CengageBrain.com to log in, register, or purchase access.

Federal Legislation: Early Intervention and Prevention

OBJECTIVES

After reading this chapter, you should be able to:

2-1   discuss how the early intervention and civil rights movements set the stage for current legislation for individuals with disabilities.

2-2   explain the impact of landmark legislation for people with disabilities.

2-3   identify the components of No Child Left Behind (NCLB) 2001 (PL 107-110), including recent changes made.

2-4   highlight the landmark case law for the inclusion of all children.

2-5   provide an overview of public policy and gifted children.

2-6   describe three pieces of legislation designed to prevent developmental disabilities in children.

• • • • • • • • • • • • • • • • • •

naeyc

The following NAEYC Standards are addressed in this chapter:

STANDARD 1 Promoting Child Development and Learning

STANDARD 2 Building Family and Community Relationships

STANDARD 6 Becoming a Professional

CONNECTIONS

- Angelo is a toddler with cerebral palsy. His parents use the school's ramp each morning to bring him to class in his wheelchair. His teachers use the ramp to the play yard so that Angelo can join his friends in outdoor activities.
- Sid, a five-year-old with Down syndrome, attends kindergarten at his neighborhood school. He participates in a variety of classroom activities with other children with and without disabilities.
- Paula is a four-year-old with a severe hearing impairment. During circle time, as children play musical instruments, the teacher taps out a rhythm on a large drum. The teacher places Paula's hand on the drum so she can feel the vibration.

Federal legislation that provides special services on behalf of infants and children with developmental disabilities (or at risk for acquiring disabilities during the developmental years) has been expanding steadily. Since the 1960s, Congress has passed a number of laws that support early identification, prevention, and treatment of developmental delays.

The legislation emphasizes family support and participation, thereby recognizing that infants and young children are best served in the context of a strong and healthy family. The support for inclusion of children with disabilities in general education programs is also contained in this legislation. This support has been strengthened in the past several decades by court decisions that promote children's rights to be educated alongside their peers in community-based programs. Some of these court cases (also called **case law**) are described briefly in this chapter.

case law how courts interpret and implement laws

Early identification, intervention, and prevention of developmental disabilities are traditional principles among researchers and practitioners in early childhood education.

The laws that support these concepts and the impact of the legislation on children, families, and early childhood teachers are the focus of this chapter.

2-1 The Early Intervention Movement

Early intervention has become a popular social educational movement. Where did it begin? How did it unfold? Where are we now?

2-1a ■ Environment and Experience

The recognition of the importance of early intervention began with a reevaluation of institutionalized infants and young children. It appeared that most of these children did not need to grow up significantly delayed if they were provided appropriate stimulation early in life (Nave, Nishioka, & Burke, 2009). Then came research showing that intelligence was not fixed at the time of birth—not determined solely by genetics. Instead, intelligence was shown to be greatly influenced by environment and experience (Bloom, 1964; Hunt, 1961). Before that time, genetic predeterminism—heredity—was believed to be the deciding factor in the distribution of intelligence among individuals.

Evidence of the importance of the earliest years of development continues to unfold.

During this same era, Kirk (1972) began an experimental preschool for young children considered to be "mentally disabled." For several years, he provided groups of children with enriched preschool experiences. His data suggested strongly that an inadequate learning environment might well be the cause of so-called mental retardation in many young children. These research findings, among others, provided convincing evidence that children's intelligence develops most rapidly during their early years. The findings also demonstrated that the development of sound intelligence depends on appropriate stimulation from the environment.

The next move was up to public policymakers. Before long, they, too, were convinced of the need to provide enriched learning environments for young children. The outcome was the widely publicized early intervention and **compensatory education** program known as Head Start, which began in 1965. Since then, innumerable studies have demonstrated that early intervention has improved both the learning capabilities and the quality of life of millions of young, low-income children and their families (Bailey, Hebbler, Spiker, Scarborough, Mallik, & Nelson, 2005).

Evidence of the importance of the earliest years of development continues to unfold. Hart and Risley's (1995) important work on children's early experience and later communication skills and school achievement demonstrates the impact of environment during the first three years of life.

Current brain research also demonstrates the importance of experience during the early childhood years. Although this evidence is clear to educators, legislative activity has not been entirely supportive of early childhood education. Head Start has never been fully funded, and the welfare reform acts of the late 1990s required more children to be placed in underfunded child care settings. The research outcomes and related legislative efforts suggest that early childhood advocates and researchers must become more active in their attempts to convince policymakers of the need for greatly increased numbers of trained early childhood personnel and expanded services for young children and their families.

compensatory education educational programs (such as Head Start) designed for children who are disadvantaged; their purpose is to provide children with some of the opportunities (social, educational, medical) that advantaged children enjoy

2-1b ■ Civil Rights

Awareness of the impact of environment and experience on early development ran parallel to an emerging awareness of the potentials and rights of

individuals with disabilities. The civil rights movement, which began in 1954, had exposed grossly unequal—even inhumane—schooling conditions for minority children. This led to a searching of the public conscience about overall differences in educational opportunities. Civil rights advocates worked tirelessly to ensure that the constitutional rights of *all* citizens were upheld.

The right to a free and equal education received particular attention. Special-interest groups, recognizing that individuals with disabilities also represented an unequally treated minority, began speaking out. One of the earliest and most influential of the special-interest groups was the National Association for Retarded Children (NARC). Later renamed the Association for Retarded Citizens (ARC) and now referred to as *ARC for people with intellectual and developmental disabilities,* ARC continues to be a powerful **advocacy group**. Other organizations, both professional and citizens' groups, also became active on behalf of individuals with developmental disabilities. Among them are:

- the Council for Exceptional Children (CEC)
- the Division for Early Childhood (DEC) (a division of CEC)
- the American Speech, Language, and Hearing Association (ASHA)
- the American Association on Intellectual and Developmental Disabilities (AAIDD), formally the American Association on Mental Retardation (AAMR)
- TASH, formerly the Association for Persons with Severe Handicaps

The efforts of these and other organizations helped produce a number of important laws referred to as **landmark legislation**. Never before had there been such significant federal rulings on behalf of people with disabilities. What follows is a brief review of the laws that provide specifically for young children with developmental disabilities and their families.

advocacy group individuals who work collectively for a particular cause

landmark legislation a turning point in or an entirely new approach to public policy. The Education for All Handicapped Children Act is considered landmark legislation because of provisions never before written into law on behalf of the handicapped

---

Did You Get It?

What was the significance of Bloom's (1964) and Hunt's (1961) research studies?
  a. Indicated genetic predeterminism to be the deciding factor in the distribution of intelligence among individuals.
  b. Showed that intelligence was fixed at the time of birth.
  c. Instead of intelligence being fixed at time of birth or solely determined by genetics, intelligence was shown to be greatly influenced by environment and experience.
  d. Children did not need to grow up significantly delayed if provided with appropriate stimulation early in life.

Take the full quiz on CourseMate.

☀ 2-2 Landmark Legislation and People with Disabilities

Since the early 1960s, a number of laws have been passed to provide services for (and humane treatment of) individuals with developmental disabilities. These laws take many forms and have effected change for a wide range of individuals.

This chapter focuses only on mandates bearing directly on young children and their families. See Figure 2-1 for a timeline of landmark legislation from the past four decades.

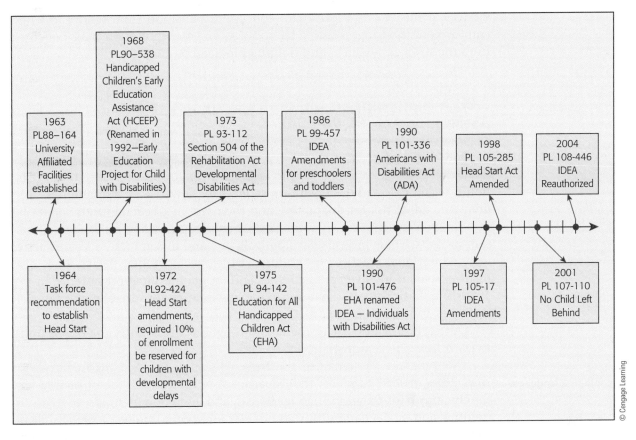

FIGURE 2-1

Landmark Legislation Timeline

2-2a ■ University Affiliated Facilities (PL 88-164)

This 1963 law provided federal funds to establish University Affiliated Facilities (UAF) for the "mentally retarded." These centers were (and are) staffed by teams of professionals from various disciplines. Their goal is to promote exemplary professional team practices related to the **interdisciplinary** aspects of early intervention to better serve infants and children with developmental disabilities.

Authorized through the Developmental Disabilities Assistance and Bill of Rights Act of 2000, PL 106-402, UAFs were renamed University Centers of Excellence in Developmental Disabilities (UCEDDs). There are 67 UCEDDs, which are located across the country, approximately one per state. Their main purposes are:

- to create, demonstrate, and evaluate intervention and educational programs for children and youth with disabilities and their families.
- to provide professional trainees with interdisciplinary training.
- to conduct research related to human development and developmental delays.
- to establish university–community partnerships to improve services for people with disabilities.

UCCEDDs have played a role in every major disability initiative over the past four decades. Issues such as early intervention, health care, community-based

interdisciplinary team refers to several different professionals working together on a common problem

services, inclusive and meaningful education, transition from school to work, employment, housing, assistive technology, and transportation have benefited from the services, research, and training provided by UCEDDs.

2-2b ■ Handicapped Children's Early Education Assistance Act (PL 90-538)

In 1968, a new law focused on the very young: the Handicapped Children's Early Education Program, often referred to as HCEEP. The major purpose of this legislation is to improve early intervention services for children with disabilities, children who are at risk for disabilities, and their families. Federal funds supported experimental centers known as the First Chance Network and model demonstration projects. These projects develop, validate, and disseminate new and better early educational practices for children with developmental delays. They also focus on parent involvement activities and program evaluation systems. In the 1980s, emphasis shifted somewhat to include funding for several major research institutes and outreach projects.

Outreach provides other programs throughout the country the opportunity to learn from the demonstration projects.

This program was renamed the Early Education Project for Children with Disabilities in 1992 to reflect the Department of Education's use of **people-first terminology**. This program no longer exists, and discretionary funds for research, training, and model demonstration projects for young children with disabilities and their families have been integrated into the general fund that finances these projects for all children, from birth to age twenty-one.

2-2c ■ Head Start Act

The Head Start Act of 2007 required that, beginning in fiscal year 2009, "not less than 10 percent of the total number of children actually enrolled by each Head Start agency and each delegate agency will be children with disabilities who are determined to be eligible for special education and related services, or early intervention services…by the State or local agency providing services under section 619 or part C of the Individuals with Disabilities Education Act" [IDEA].

Head Start had always been an "open door" policy: *all* children who met the economic requirement, regardless of their developmental status, were to be included in Head Start programs.

Head Start has been a pioneer in the field of including young children with severe disabilities in community-based programs. The newest Head Start regulations continue to stress this aspect of the program and to encourage local programs to work with other local agencies (such as public schools and universities) to provide appropriate inclusive programs for young children with disabilities.

Head Start continues to grow By 2007, Head Start was serving more than 908,412 children, with 220,000 staff in more than 18,275 centers.

Head Start continues to be one of the primary programs that include children with disabilities, with more than 12.2 percent of Head Start children having an identified disability. Since Head Start began in 1965, this important program has served more than 25 million children and their families (Office of Head Start, 2008).

Head Start has been a pioneer in the field of including young children with disabilities.

© Cengage Learning

2-2d ■ Developmental Disabilities Act (DDA) (PL 106-402)

Another set of rulings related to developmental disabilities was authorized in the Rehabilitation Act of 1973 and reauthorized in 2000. Section 504 focused on reducing discrimination against individuals with disabilities.

The law required that everyone with a disability be given access to jobs, education, housing, and public buildings. The popular name for part of this law was the *wheelchair requirement*. This law also ruled that states offering preschool services to non-disabled children must offer comparable services to those with disabilities. This law requires schools to accommodate children who have disabilities but do not qualify for special education. For example, some children with attention deficit disorder (ADD) may need accommodations such as extra time to complete work or special seating arrangements but do not need special education.

2-2e ■ Education for All Handicapped Children Act (PL 94-142)

This legislation was signed into law in 1975. Its popular title is *The Bill of Rights for Handicapped Children*. This public law is required to be reauthorized every ten years. It is now referred to as the **Individuals with Disabilities Education Improvement Act (IDEIA)**. The name was changed to reflect people-first terminology. The most recent reauthorization of the bill, PL 108-446, was signed into law in 2004. Advocacy groups hailed the legislation as a major step in upholding the constitutional rights of citizens with disabilities. It guaranteed (for the first time in our country's history) all children and youth—regardless of the severity of their disability—the right to a free and appropriate public education. Among other things, the law gives specific support to early education programs for children under five years of age. Special funds, called *incentive monies*, are authorized to encourage states to locate and serve preschool children who require early intervention services. This federally supported process of finding and identifying such children is called **Child Find**.

In addition to the early intervention component, PL 94-142 has a number of rulings that apply to all children with developmental disabilities.

Individuals with Disabilities Education Improvement Act (IDEIA) Individuals with Disabilities Education Act; federal law PL 101-476—amended as PL 105-17 Individuals with Disabilities Education Act Amendment of 1997—is the reauthorization of the original law (PL 94-142) that describes the types of educational services that must be provided to students from birth through age twenty-one who have disabilities. The Individuals with Disabilities Education Improvement Act of 2004 aligns IDEIA closely to the No Child Left Behind (NCLB) Act, helping to ensure equity, accountability, and excellence in education for children with disabilities

Child Find a program established in the 1960s to identify children with developmental problems or delays

Zero reject Local school systems must provide all children, regardless of the severity of their disability, with a free education appropriate to each child's needs.

Nondiscriminatory evaluation No child may be placed in a special education program without full individual testing. The tests must be **nondiscriminatory**, that is, appropriate to the child's language and cultural background. Assessment is to be based on several types of evaluation and is to include cognitive, adaptive, and social performance.

nondiscriminatory screening and diagnostic tests compatible with a child's native language and culture

Appropriate education Local school districts must provide educational services that are appropriate to each child. Details of the educational program are described in a child's individualized education program (IEP) or individualized family service plan (IFSP).

Least restrictive environment: inclusion To the greatest extent possible, children with disabilities must be educated alongside students who do not have identified disabilities. It is important to remember that the least restrictive environment clause assumes that children with disabilities in the general education environment will receive the specialized support necessary to optimize their development.

Including children with disabilities without adequate support does not meet the letter or the spirit of this law.

Due process Under the provisions of due process, parents must have the right to call a special hearing when they do not agree with the school's educational plans for their child. Due process further ensures that a child cannot be removed from a classroom simply because of annoying or inconvenient behavior. In brief, due process gives parents the right to:

- examine all records that pertain to their child.
- be consulted about their child's educational program before it is put into effect.
- receive written notice of any proposed changes in their child's educational classification or placement.
- demand legal representation if disagreements between themselves and school personnel cannot be resolved.

Parent participation PL 94–142 recognized the importance of parents' contributions to their child's progress. The role of parents was strengthened by IDEA 1997 and then in the reauthorization of 2004. For example, states must provide mediation to schools and parents if there are disagreements about children's educational services.

To the greatest extent possible, children with disabilities must be educated alongside students who do not have disabilities.

© Cengage Learning

2-2f ■ Education of the Handicapped Amendments (PL 99-457)

In 1986, Congress passed the most comprehensive legislation ever enacted on behalf of infants and young children, in which services were mandated for children from birth through age three. In 2004, new criteria were added in the areas of IFSP development, Child Find, transition to kindergarten, and dispute resolution. The services provided under the IFSP need to be scientifically researched, to include measurable pre-literacy and language skills, and to provide a plan for transition to kindergarten. Procedures are also in place to allow for mediation if parents have a complaint regarding services provided or not provided for their child.

The continued need for a tremendously increased number of early childhood teachers and related staff is obvious. Looking beyond young children, the law also reaffirmed its commitment to those of school age. It stresses the importance of the transition planning for children aged sixteen to twenty-one. The commitment is reflected in the long-range planning of many two- and four-year teacher training programs. Projected increases in staff are reflected also in programs that train the trainers of teachers and early childhood administrators.

Greatly increased numbers of health care providers also will be needed. Many of these professionals, from various disciplines, will be trained to work in early childhood centers. They will work with teachers in the classroom, implementing programs for individual children.

Services for children from birth to age three IDEA 2004 restructured the format of this bill, so services for infants and toddlers, formerly referred to under Part H, are now covered in Part C.

This part of the law is known as **discretionary legislation**. This means that a state may serve children from birth up until three years of age if it chooses, but it is not required by law to do so. One exception is that any state serving non-disabled infants and toddlers must serve infants and toddlers with disabilities.

discretionary legislation law is implemented by the individual state or local agency

Legislators explained the reasoning behind Part C:

Congress finds an urgent and substantial need to enhance the development of infants and toddlers with handicaps and minimize their potential for developmental delay; reduce the education costs to society, including our schools; minimize the likelihood of institutionalization; and enhance the capacity to provide quality early intervention services and expand and improve existing services. Thus creating a State Interagency Coordinating Council (SICC) which has at least one member from the following agencies:

- State agency that supports Medicaid;
- Office of Coordinator for Education of Homeless Children and Youths;
- State child welfare agency responsible for foster care; and
- State agency responsible for children's mental health.

PL 94–142 recognized the importance of parents' contributions to their child's progress.

© Cengage Learning

It is therefore the policy of the United States to provide financial assistance to states to develop and implement a statewide, comprehensive, coordinated, interdisciplinary program of early intervention services for infants and toddlers with handicaps and their families (Federal Register, 2002).

A brief summary of Part C guidelines is presented here.

- ***Individuals to be served***. Those to be served are infants and toddlers who are experiencing developmental disabilities (children who are not achieving skills as quickly as expected) or are at risk of experiencing substantial delays unless they receive early intervention services.

- ***Labeling no longer required***. Very young children no longer need to be labeled as having a particular kind of disability. They need not be put into a category such as "emotionally disturbed."

- ***Individualized family service plan (IFSP)***. According to the IFSP, each infant and toddler and his or her family must receive a **multi-disciplinary**, written assessment of his or her needs and of the services prescribed. These services will be provided by a team of qualified personnel that includes special educators, speech and language pathologists and audiologists, occupational and physical therapists, social workers, nutritionists, and other professionals as deemed necessary. Services will be coordinated by a service coordinator assigned to each family. One purpose of the service coordinator is to make sure the family has a part in planning the child's IFSP; another is to help the family obtain and coordinate services that ensure that identified needs are being met. The services also need to be provided in a natural environment, such as the home or in community settings where children without disabilities participate (Hestenes, Laparo, Scott-Little, Chakravarthi, Lower, Cranor, Cassidy, & Niemeyer, 2009).

Services for three-, four-, and five-year-olds remain much as they were under PL 94-142, except for two important changes. One was substantial increases in funding. The second was a five-year time schedule for channeling the additional money to the states. This change provided the necessary impetus to make universal early childhood special education services a reality. Beginning in the 1990–1991 school year, every state and territory in the United States provided preschool services to young children ages three to five with developmental disabilities. As noted earlier, most of the requirements of PL 94-142 are retained in the PL 99-457 amendments.

The mandate that children with disabilities be educated in the least restrictive environment (the inclusion concept) is still in effect. Due process, Child Find, and individualized education programs (IEPs) also are continuing requirements. Services for children beginning at age three are *not* discretionary.

States receiving federal funds for early intervention programs must serve young children with developmental disabilities according to the same formula and requirements as before. Furthermore, parent support services are allowable as "related services." The combination of PL 94-142 and PL 99-457 fulfills goals for young children that the early childhood profession long has advocated. Furthermore, the laws indicate that Congress is willing to accede fully to popular opinion that early identification and intervention are important. The laws also indicate a quality-of-life recognition: that early intervention is the best way to improve the well-being of young children with developmental disabilities and their families.

Now called the Individuals with Disabilities Education Improvement Act, PL 108–446, IDEIA was last updated in 2004. The law came into effect on July 1, 2005. The revision maintains the integrity of IDEA, with a few significant modifications:

1. An extensive definition of "highly qualified" special education teachers requires special education teachers to hold at least a B.A., obtain full state special education licensure or equivalent, and not to hold temporary or emergency licensure.

2. Extensive provisions aim at ensuring special education and related services for children with disabilities who are homeless or otherwise members of highly mobile populations. The provisions require the school to appoint a surrogate within thirty days of the request for placement so that there is no lapse in services for the child.

3. Significant changes have been made to procedural safeguards, including:

   - The addition of a resolution session prior to a due process hearing to encourage the parties to resolve their dispute. Within fifteen days of the parent's complaint, the **Local Education Agency (LEA)** calls a meeting with the parent and school personnel to try to resolve the issue. If it is resolved, a legally binding agreement is signed and upheld in the district court; if not, the parent can pursue the hearing within thirty days of the original complaint.

   - **Functional behavior assessment**. When a child violates the student code of conduct, a meeting is convened with the LEA, parent, and school personnel to determine whether the behavior is a result of the disability or not. If it is, then the child is removed for ten days to a separate setting and a **functional behavior assessment** is performed, if one has not already been completed. If it is not a result of the disability, then the school can impose the consequences of breaking the school code on that child and separate the child for not more than forty-five calendar days. Children with disabilities who have been expelled from school still have the right to an education, and the state must guarantee that services are still provided throughout the expulsion (Bowe, 2008).

4. Authority is granted to extend Part C services for infants and toddlers beyond the age of two. This allows states to extend services until the child enters kindergarten. Educational components on pre-literacy, numeracy skills, and language must be included in the IFSP. Parents must be notified of the differences between Part C and Part B.

5. Short-term objectives and benchmarks are no longer required sections in the IEP. States can determine "the extent to which short-term objectives and benchmarks are used" (*Federal Register*, 2006).

Discipline issues One of the major changes to IDEIA in the most recent reauthorization was in the section relating to the disciplining of students with disabilities. In general, there are different rules and limitations in the area of discipline for children with identified special needs than there are for typically developing children. A student with a disability generally cannot be suspended for more than ten school days if the misconduct was related to his or her disability, and services still

Local Education Agency (LEA) an educational agency at the local level that exists primarily to operate schools or to contract for educational services

functional behavior assessment evaluating the degree to which children's behaviors "work" to get them what they want and need

You operate a family day care and notice that a boy, age two years, seven months, does not respond to his name, has limited language for his age, and has daily tantrums lasting thirty minutes or more. Based on the information in this chapter, what laws and federal programs could help this child?

positive behavioral support strategies providing positive rather than negative feedback to children's efforts; concentrating on what the child does right

need to be provided. Although most of the provisions of these requirements may not be appropriate for young children with disabilities, one important change is. The spirit of IDEIA 2004 requires educators/guardians to deal with challenging behaviors proactively. The IEP team, including parents, must conduct a functional behavior assessment and consider strategies, such as **positive behavioral support strategies**, to facilitate appropriate behavior in the classroom.

2-2h ▪ Americans with Disabilities Act (PL 101-336)

In 1990, the Americans with Disabilities Act (ADA) was passed into law. Patterned after Section 504 of the Rehabilitation Act, ADA gives civil rights protection to individuals in private employment, all public services, and accommodations, transportation, and telecommunications.

For early childhood education, some of the most significant implications are in the area of access to child care and community recreation programs. The ADA requires that child care providers, preschools, and schools (private and public) not discriminate against persons with disabilities on the basis of their disability. In other words, they must provide children and parents with disabilities with an equal opportunity to participate in their programs and services. Specific requirements include:

- A center or school cannot exclude children with disabilities from their programs unless their presence would pose a direct threat to the health or safety of others or require a fundamental alteration of the program.

- A center or school has to make reasonable modifications to their policies and practices to include children, parents, and guardians with disabilities in their programs. The only exception is if doing so would constitute a fundamental alteration of the program.

- A center or school must provide appropriate auxiliary aids and services needed for effective communication with children or adults with disabilities, when doing so would not constitute an undue burden.

- A center or school must generally make their facilities accessible to persons with disabilities. Existing facilities must be modified to remove barriers, while newly constructed facilities and any altered portions of existing facilities must be fully accessible.

Complaints about violations of the ADA are filed with the U.S. Department of Justice. It is authorized to investigate alleged violations and bring a civil action in federal court. Activities include lawsuits, formal settlement agreements, informal settlement agreements, and mediations. Between 2000 and 2011, twenty-two formal, informal, and mediation agreements have occurred (Child Care Law, 2011).

Section 504 of the Rehabilitation Act of 1973 protects qualified individuals from discrimination based on their disability. Section 504 is widely recognized as the first civil rights statute for persons with disabilities. The law defines individuals with disabilities as persons with a physical or mental impairment that substantially limits one or more major life activities. Major life activities include such activities as caring for one's self, walking, seeing, hearing, speaking, breathing, working, performing manual tasks, and learning.

The requirements of the law apply to employers and organizations that receive financial assistance from any federal department or agency. These organizations and employers include many hospitals, nursing homes, mental health centers, and human services programs. Section 504 prohibits these organizations and employers from excluding or denying individuals with disabilities an equal opportunity to receive program benefits and services.

Did You Get It?

What was the significance of the change of name of the Education for All Handicapped Children Act of 1975 (popularly referred to as *The Bill of Rights for Handicapped Children*) to the latest title of Individual with Disabilities Education Improvement Act?

a. Reflect changes from 1975 to current day.

b. Name has to be changed every ten years.

c. Reflects focus on people-first terminology.

d. Guarantees right to a free and appropriate public education.

Take the full quiz on CourseMate.

No Child Left Behind 2-3

On January 8, 2002, President George W. Bush signed into law the No Child Left Behind Act (NCLB, PL 107-110), a reauthorization of the Elementary and Secondary Education Act. This law was intended to improve reading and math testing in public schools and to reauthorize education reform using federal funds. NCLB requires states to develop accountability standards to measure annual student progress in reading and math. It has forced states to create or adopt adequate tests to support curriculum. Graduation rates also are factored in. If states show growth in accountability, then they qualify for federal funding. If there is little or no growth, then schools and school systems are at risk of losing funding and teachers.

Specifically, states are required to bring all students up to the "proficient" level on state tests by the 2013–14 school year. Based on a formula spelled out in the law, individual schools have to meet state "adequate yearly progress" goals for both their overall student population and for certain demographic subgroups. If a school receiving federal Title I funding fails to meet the target two years in a row, it is provided technical assistance, and its students would be offered a choice of other public schools to attend. Under NCLB, schools that continue to miss their goal are subject to outside corrective measures, including possible governance changes.

The law has separate headings for children with disabilities, children with English as a second language, children of Native American or Alaskan descent, children at risk or abused, and children of migrant workers. The program works on literacy development and even has appropriations for Even Start, which serves at-risk children from birth to age two. A major focus of Even Start is to help parents develop literacy skills to work with their children.

The law does not end there. Teacher requirements and family initiatives are built in to ensure that by 2014 no child is left behind. The teacher requirements cover not only the classroom teacher but also any professional who interacts with children. These individuals must have the proper certifications required by each state. The law affects teacher assistants and new teachers the most. It includes professional development standards, and each state can choose how to enforce these standards. Professional development must:

- improve teachers' knowledge of the academic subjects they teach.
- be a part of a school-wide educational improvement plan.
- help teachers teach students to meet challenging standards.
- improve teachers' classroom management skills.
- enable teachers to maintain high-quality, sustained, intensive classroom focus.
- support teacher recruitment, hiring, and training.
- be connected to effective instructional practices predicated on scientifically based research.
- substantially increase the knowledge and teaching skills of teachers.
- be aligned with state standards.
- be developed in collaboration with K–12 educators and parents.
- assist teachers of limited English proficient (LEP) children.
- provide training in the use of technology as it relates to improving performance in core academic subjects.
- be regularly evaluated for impact.
- provide instruction in methods of teaching children with special needs.
- include instruction in the use of data and assessments.
- include instruction for working with parents.
- involve partnerships between K–12 schools and institutions of higher education to provide prospective and beginning teachers with an opportunity to work under the guidance of experienced teachers and college faculty.
- help paraprofessionals (teaching or classroom aides who assist teachers with routine activities) meet state standards.

One requirement of No Child Left Behind is to improve teachers' knowledge of the academic subjects they teach.

© Cengage Learning

Unless otherwise stated in the law, these standards apply to any professional development reference in NCLB (Trahan, 2002).

2-3a ■ Assessment of Children with Disabilities

Children with disabilities or delays in development are to be tested along with children without disabilities beginning in the third grade, with few exceptions. The major issue for early childhood special education professionals is whether these children require test accommodations. The answer is provided in the children's IEPs: If a child's IEP calls for accommodations in assessments, these must be offered; if it does not, accommodations cannot be provided. A good source for information about test accommodations, including options that you may consider, is the National Center on Educational Outcomes (NCEO) at the University of Minnesota (**http://education.umn.edu**); for preschool go to the Early Childhood Outcomes (ECO) Center at the University of North Carolina (**http://www.fpg.unc.edu**).

A few children are exempted from state and national tests. Usually this is because they have cognitive or other limitations that are so severe they cannot successfully take part in such assessments. An alternative assessment is provided, which may be observation of the child as he or she performs activities that are highlighted in the IEP. Sometimes, parent and teacher reports are used for assessment. The NCEO is a good source for information about alternative assessments (Bowe, 2008).

2-3b ■ Concerns about NCLB Lead to Changes

Since the implementation of NCLB, concerns have arisen about the rules regarding adequate yearly progress and the goal of 100-percent proficiency by 2013–14. For example, traditionally high-performing schools failed to meet their set rates of improvement. By 2010, 38 percent of schools were failing to make adequate yearly progress, up from 29 percent in 2006 (n.p., *Education Week*, 2011).

In March 2010, President Barack Obama released his plan for reform of the Elementary and Secondary Education Act, the precursor to No Child Left Behind. Specific revisions focused on states implementing a broader range of assessments to evaluate advanced academic skills. These included such skills as a student's abilities to conduct research, use technology, engage in scientific investigation, solve problems, and communicate effectively.

In addition, Obama also proposed that the strict accountability punishments to states under NCLB be lessened by focusing more on student improvement. Improvement measures included assessing all children appropriately, including English language learners, minorities, and special needs students. Measurement would be expanded beyond solely

TeachSource Video Connections

Video supplied by the BBC Motion Gallery

No Child Left Behind

This video provides a brief overview of the original requirements of No Child Left Behind, and some of the drawbacks that led to President Obama allowing states to request waivers from some of these requirements.

After watching the video discuss the following:

1. What were some of the requirements of the original No Child Left Behind?

2. What were some of the issues and concerns that led to the need for the waiver program?

3. What are the requirements of the waivers?

Watch on CourseMate.

reading and math tests. Schools would also need to develop incentives to keep students enrolled in school through high school graduation. The president's objectives also focused on lowering the achievement gap between black and white students.

In 2012, President Obama granted waivers from NCLB requirements to several states. In exchange for increased flexibility, the states developed plans designed to improve educational outcomes for all students, close achievement gaps, increase equity, and improve the quality of instruction. As of January 2013, thirty-four states have been approved for flexibility and forty-four states have submitted requests (U.S. Department of Education, 2013).

Did You Get It?

How is it determined whether children with disabilities or developmental delays require test accommodations?

    a. The teacher decides.

    b. The child decides.

    c. The school decides.

    d. The answer is provided in the children's IEPs.

Take the full quiz on CourseMate.

2-4 Inclusion and Case Law

Case laws are clarifications of existing laws that are drawn from judicial decisions. Once a law is enacted, questions concerning interpretations and applications of that law often are determined in court. These interpretations affect how the law actually impacts the lives of the people the law was meant to benefit. Case law has played an important role in school reform and in advancing the rights of students with disabilities in the public school system since the *Brown v. Board of Education* ruling in 1954, where the court found that segregated schools violated the Fourteenth Amendment of the Constitution. Although this case involved race—not ability—it is often noted as a landmark case for the inclusion of all children. It is beyond the scope of this chapter to review all the case law relevant to inclusion or early childhood special education. Rather, we present summaries of two recent cases that have been heralded as landmark cases supporting the inclusion of all children in general education classes.

2-4a ■ *Sacramento Unified School District v. Holland* (1992)

This case involved a nine-year-old girl with Down syndrome. The district court ruled that she must be fully included in a general education classroom and provided a four-part test to evaluate the feasibility of inclusion. The four-part test asks:

1. What educational benefits are available to the child with disabilities when supplemented by the appropriate supports?

2. What are the nonacademic benefits of placement in a general education classroom? (for example, social)

3. What is the effect on non-disabled children?

4. What is the cost?

2-4b ■ *Oberti v. Board of Education of Clementon School District* (1993)

This case was similar to *Holland,* except that the child involved had severe disabilities. The judge ruled strongly in favor of the child's right to receive inclusive education and said, "Inclusion is a right, not a privilege for a select few."

These cases, along with the work of parents and advocates, have been extremely important in advancing inclusive education. The decisions have helped support the interpretation of the least restrictive environment being the general education classroom.

Did You Get It?

What educational reason is cited for the relevance of the *Brown v. Board of Education* case?

a. Race.

b. Ability.

c. Landmark case for the inclusion of all children.

d. Fourteenth Amendment.

Take the full quiz on CourseMate.

Public Policy and the Gifted 2-5

Concern for the gifted has not been a major focus for public policy in this country. Currently, all fifty states have definitions of **giftedness**. These definitions are used to inform school programs and to attempt to obtain federal funds. However, states are not required to have special programs for children who are gifted or talented. This is a major difference between programs for children who are gifted and programs for children who qualify for special education.

giftedness evidence of superior or unusual ability in areas such as intellect, creativity, artistic talent, physical agility, or leadership

Special education services are mandated for students between the ages of three and twenty-one.

One challenge in providing special services to children who are gifted is identifying them in a manner that is not racially or culturally biased. A major barrier to identifying children who are gifted or talented or both is overcoming the traditional view of giftedness that relied solely on a child's intelligence as measured by IQ tests (Feldman, 1993). A more contemporary view of giftedness builds on theories of multiple intelligences (Gardner, 1993, 1999).

Interest in identifying giftedness in young children continues. For example, Gross (1999) found the precocious development of speech, movement, and reading is a powerful indicator when the skills appear at extremely early ages and particularly when they appear in tandem. Hodge and Kemp (2000) studied preschool children identified by their parents as gifted. Results suggest that a majority of these children have in common characteristics such as advanced language, strong memory, creative thinking, and interest in reading and in problem-solving activities. Finally, Haensly (2000) discussed hallmarks that can help educators identify potentially gifted young children, especially those from culturally diverse and economically disadvantaged backgrounds. These hallmarks include the self in control of its environment, purposeful behavior seeking to accomplish goals, and communicative creativity. These recent studies

Interest in identifying giftedness in young children continues.

© Cengage Learning

indicate that while definitions of giftedness in young children may vary, the study of giftedness is expanding on account of the widespread interest in exceptional development.

In 1988, the Jacob K. Javits **Gifted and Talented** Special Education Act was funded. It was reauthorized in 2001, using this definition:

> Students, children, or youth who give evidence of high achievement capability in areas such as intellectual, creative, artistic, or leadership capacity, or in specific academic fields, and who need services and activities not ordinarily provided by the school in order to fully develop those capabilities.

Federal money supporting this discretionary public program is to be used for:

- identifying and serving students who are gifted and talented.
- training and professional development for teachers.
- creating a National Center for the Education of the Gifted.

The major emphasis of the program is on serving students traditionally underrepresented in gifted and talented programs, particularly economically disadvantaged, limited English proficient (LEP), and disabled students, to help reduce the serious gap in achievement among certain groups of students at the highest levels of achievement. Because this is a discretionary program, funds are not guaranteed each year. In fact there was no funding available in 2011 and 2012.

Over the years, various advocacy groups such as the **Association for the Gifted** (TAG, part of the Council for Exceptional Children), the **National Society for the Gifted and Talented** (NSGT), and the **Gifted Advocacy Information Network** (GAIN) have worked to obtain funds for the education of the gifted. In addition, a number of states have local parent and professional groups working toward support of programs for gifted children in their communities.

No legislation has focused exclusively on giftedness in the very young child. Yet attention should be directed toward these children and early childhood programs; it is during these earliest years that "attitudes toward learning are solidified and rampant curiosity becomes either encouraged or discouraged" (Gallagher, 1988, p. 110). Support for model programs for gifted children should be part of our national agenda, and yet, as of today, this support is still not fully funded. According to Sankar-DeLeeuw (2002), the need for identification of and intervention with gifted and talented children at an early age is critical to improving opportunities for optimal development.

gifted and talented children or youth who exhibit high achievement capability in areas such as intellectual, creative, artistic, or leadership capacity, or in specific academic fields, and who need services or activities not ordinarily provided by the school in order to fully develop those capabilities

---

Did You Get It?

What are the distinguishing features between traditional and contemporary views of identifying giftedness?

a. Traditional view of giftedness relies solely on a child's intelligence as measured by IQ tests; contemporary view builds on theories of multiple intelligence.

b. Traditional view builds on theories of multiple intelligence; contemporary view relies solely on a child's intelligence as measured by IQ tests.

c. Different levels of interest in identifying giftedness.

d. States were not required to have special programs for children who are gifted or talented; states are now required to have special programs for children who are gifted or talented.

Take the full quiz on CourseMate.

In many instances, intervention services might never have been needed, had prevention been available. In the chapter on causes of disabling conditions, it is noted, for example, that the incidence of developmental disabilities could be drastically reduced if every family's most basic needs were met. The issue of prevention and its relationship to federal legislation is addressed in this section.

2-6a ■ The Timing of Prevention

Just as disabling conditions can be a threat at any point in development, preventive measures can also be called into action at any point. Prevention should begin before conception with the good health of the mother and father and continue throughout the developmental years. For all children, prevention should be an ongoing process.

Prevention before conception One source of developmental disabilities is the genetic makeup of an infant. Chromosomal mishaps account for only a small percentage of such problems; most are preventable. Many parents seek genetic counseling and chromosomal analysis if they have reason to suspect their child may inherit a disability. When the results are favorable, they can proceed with a pregnancy with a fair degree of confidence. In the case of negative results, different options must be weighed. One choice is to forgo having children; another is to adopt them. Another choice might be to proceed with pregnancy and have a prenatal diagnosis to see whether the unborn infant has a genetic disease or disabling syndrome. Information of this kind can be obtained through amniocentesis or chorionic villus sampling (CVS). If the results of either test indicate abnormality, parents have another difficult choice concerning continuing or terminating the pregnancy. Usually the decision is based on their moral and religious beliefs.

    Many couples have strong feelings that it is immoral to bring an infant with severe disabilities into the world. Others have equally strong feelings about the immorality of abortion. There are no easy answers in such situations.

amniocentesis a medical test for genetic abnormalities that can be done about the sixteenth week of pregnancy

chorionic villus sampling (CVS) a test for genetic abnormalities; can be done between the ninth and eleventh weeks of gestation

Prevention during pregnancy Ensuring the good health of a mother during pregnancy is a major preventive measure in terms of reducing developmental disabilities. Good health and adequate prenatal care go hand in hand with appropriate medical services. Most diseases in the mother are preventable with immunization or appropriate medical treatment. Damage to the unborn child also can be prevented by forgoing the use of nicotine, alcohol, cocaine, and other chemical substances.

    These substances are known to have harmful effects on the infant *in utero*. What is not known is how much of any of these substances is harmful. Each woman has a different biochemical makeup that governs how much is too much for the baby she is carrying. In some instances, even relatively small amounts of a substance can have damaging effects.

in utero unborn; literally, "in the uterus"

    Another damaging but preventable factor is malnourishment. Infants born to mothers whose diets are seriously deficient in protein and other necessary nutrients often are of **low birth weight**. A low-birth-weight infant is at risk for a variety of problems that can persist throughout the developmental years (Child Trends, 2012; Children's Defense Fund, 2012).

low birth weight an infant born weighing less than 5.5 pounds (2500 grams) regardless of gestational age

These problems are all commonplace among mothers subsisting at or below the poverty level. Legislation and preventative programs are discussed further in the section.

Prevention during and after birth Appropriate medical services, before and during birth, can prevent many developmental disabilities. A doctor or nurse midwife who has provided care throughout a pregnancy knows what to expect and how to handle problems that might arise. With modern medicine, few infants need suffer any kind of damage at birth.

The first minutes and hours after birth are crucial for identifying potential problems. Routine screening of newborns is an important aspect of prevention. The Apgar score is in widespread use for this purpose. This test is generally done at one and five minutes after birth. The Apgar score is determined by evaluating the newborn baby on five simple criteria. The resulting Apgar score ranges from zero to ten. The five criteria include **A**ppearance, **P**ulse, **G**rimace, **A**ctivity, and **R**espiration. A low score indicates the infant is likely to be at serious developmental risk and in need of immediate and constant attention. With intensive and highly specialized medical care, crippling disabilities often are prevented.

Potential problems that are not so visible also can be detected during the newborn period. Most states require that a blood sample be tested on the third or fourth day after birth (no earlier, as adverse biochemical reactions do not show up during the first few days of life). Analysis of the blood will reveal certain metabolic disorders, if they are present. The most widely known of these is PKU, or phenylketonuria (see Chapter 5 for additional information on PKU). Delays in cognitive development can be prevented if the infant is placed immediately on a prescribed diet. It should be stressed that even a few weeks' delay can result in serious brain damage—hence the need for preventive screening of all newborns.

Not all problems can be identified easily. Many have symptoms so subtle or so seemingly harmless that they are either not noticed or not taken seriously. This situation may result in wait-and-see advice that allows a problem to progress from preventable to developmentally disastrous, as in a serious hearing impairment, for example.

Other problems present at birth may not show up until later in childhood, among them sexually transmitted diseases, such as syphilis, that have been passed on to the child prenatally. By the time the symptoms show up in middle childhood, considerable developmental damage—preventable and unnecessary—already may have taken place.

2-6b ■ Prevention of Secondary Disabilities

secondary disabilities developmental problems that come about because of the primary disability

cumulative deficits adding on or layering of developmental problems; an undiagnosed hearing loss can result in an accumulation of additional problems (language, cognitive, and social)

When a disabling condition does occur—before, during, or after birth—prevention continues to be the watchword, specifically, prevention of **secondary disabilities**. These are developmental disabilities that come about because of the primary disability. A child with a hearing impairment, for example, may never develop language or adequate cognitive skills unless preventive measures to overcome the language and cognitive deficits are undertaken early in the child's life. Secondary conditions can become even more disabling than the original problem.

A child may also become more disabled than need be because of the **cumulative deficits** of a disabling condition. Untreated problems tend to snowball:

the further the child gets behind in any area of development, the more damaging it is. For example, a four-year-old who talks like a three-year-old is not necessarily disabled. It is a different story if that child is still talking like a much younger child at age twelve. It is likely the child's disabilities (in several areas of development) have increased out of proportion to those created by the initial language delay. In such cases, preventive measures might very well have reduced the cumulative deficit in the child's language skills and lessened the secondary disabilities.

Preventive measures also are needed to keep some disabilities from becoming worse, even irreversible. For example, early identification and treatment of an infant's eye problems may prevent total and irreversible loss of vision; residual vision often can be saved and strengthened. Similarly, the permanently crippling (and painful) joint contractures in a child with severe spasticity are likely to have had a good chance of being prevented if an appropriate positioning and exercising program had been ongoing.

2-6c ■ Prevention and Federal Legislation

In recent years, much of the legislation on behalf of young children has been directed toward the prevention of developmental disabilities. Inadequate nutrition and lack of medical services all too often result in developmental damage. Low-income families have the greatest numbers of children with developmental disabilities. At the same time, these are the families least able to provide themselves and their children with the kind of nutrition and health care that help prevent developmental delays. Here we provide examples of legislative acts designed to prevent developmental delays while benefiting children and families.

Society itself benefits from this legislation in at least two ways: (1) reduction of health care costs for preventable disabilities and (2) improvement in our reputation as a nation that, presumably, cares about its children and families.

Early and Periodic Screening, Diagnosis, and Treatment—EPSDT (PL 90-248)

The major focus of EPSDT is the prevention of developmental disabilities. The intention of the law is that low-income children be screened regularly during infancy and the preschool years to prevent (and treat) health problems that could interfere with development. At the time the law was passed (1967), it reflected two major concerns of Congress.

One had to do with the extreme variations among states in the number of children receiving treatment for developmental delays. Some states did a good job of caring for these children; others did not. The second concern was the issue of children with serious but under-served health problems. There were many such children in every state with problems so severe that the outcome often was irreversible developmental damage. Since the enactment of EPSDT, millions of children have received the health care necessary to prevent disabling problems. The Children's Defense Fund (2012) points out that children who receive comprehensive preventive health services have fewer health problems and developmental disabilities, resulting in 10 percent lower health care costs for taxpayers.

Vaccines for Children Program (VFC)

A measles epidemic in the United States from 1989–1991 resulted in tens of thousands of cases of measles and hundreds of deaths. The Centers for Disease Control and Prevention (CDC) discovered that more than half of the children who had measles had not been immunized. In response to that epidemic, Congress passed the Omnibus Budget Reconciliation Act (OBRA) on August 10, 1993, creating the Vaccines for Children (VFC) program. The Vaccines for Children (VFC) program helps provide vaccines to children whose parents or guardians may not be able to afford them. The purpose is to prevent childhood diseases such as rubella, mumps, measles, diphtheria, tetanus, and pertussis. The cost-effective VFC Program provides approximately 43 percent of all routinely recommended childhood vaccines in the United States and improves the lives of millions of young children.

According to the CDC, vaccines are one of the most successful and cost-effective public health tools for preventing disease, disability, and death. Vaccines reduce the economic costs resulting from vaccine-preventable diseases. An economic evaluation of the impact of seven vaccines given routinely as part of the childhood immunization schedule (DTaP, Td, Hib, polio, MMR, hepatitis B, and varicella) found that these seven vaccines prevent over 14 million cases of disease and over 33,500 deaths over the lifetime of children born in a year. Furthermore, immunization with these seven vaccines results in annual cost savings of $50 billion in direct medical costs and in indirect costs to taxpayers and society (CDC, 2007).

One of the major health goals in the United States is to eliminate health disparities among racial and ethnic populations. According to 2005 National Immunization Survey data, there is no statistically significant difference in immunization rates between black and white children nationwide, although income does seem to matter, as poor black children are less likely to be immunized than black children from higher incomes (Children's Defense Fund, 2012).

Supplemental Food Program for Women, Infants, and Children Commonly referred to as WIC, this federal program has an excellent record in the prevention of developmental delays. Passed in 1972, the law allocates nutrition money to state agencies and to certain Native American tribes. The funds are to be used to provide healthy foods to low-income pregnant and nursing mothers and to infants and young children at risk for medical problems. The program also provides nutritional counseling and education. Evaluations of WIC show that the program greatly benefits those who participate; however, fewer than half of the eligible women and children are served (Children's Defense Fund, 2008). For those families who have received the supplements, major benefits include:

WIC, a federal supplemental food program, has an excellent record in the prevention of developmental delays.

© Cengage Learning

- reduced infant mortality (fewer infant deaths at the time of birth or during the first few months of life).

- increase in the birth weight of many infants and reduction in the number of low-birth-weight infants.

- reduction in the number of premature infants.

Each of these benefits leads to fewer health problems in both mothers and their infants. Furthermore, medical research demonstrates that full-term infants of adequate birth weight are less likely to become developmentally delayed or disabled during the early childhood years. All of this adds up to a program that improves the quality of children's lives while maintaining its cost effectiveness.

Medicaid and the Children's Health Insurance Program Medicaid and the Children's Health Insurance Program (CHIP) provide coverage to more than 36 million children each year. While this is the highest coverage in over 20 years, there is still a considerable number of children who qualify but remain uninsured. This number is estimated at more than 8 million children. Two-thirds of these uninsured children are eligible under Medicaid and CHIP. Children of color are disproportionality uninsured, and, as a result, suffer from treatable and preventable diseases throughout their lives (Children's Defense Fund, 2012).

Although millions of women and children receive no medical services, study after study reports the cost effectiveness of preventive health care: Every dollar spent can save thousands of dollars over a child's lifetime.

> **Did You Get It?**
>
> **What term applies to the escalation of developmental problems related to the disability?**
> **a.** Developmental delay.
> **b.** Cumulative deficits.
> **c.** Secondary disabilities.
> **d.** Primary disabilities.
>
> Take the full quiz on CourseMate.

Summary

Intervention in the form of remedial and compensatory early childhood programs has become a popular approach to reducing both the number and the severity of developmental disabilities. The importance of early intervention came to be recognized with research related to the role of experience in determining developmental outcome.

▶ Out of the findings of this research came Head Start and then early intervention programs for young children with disabilities. Both the civil rights movement and the efforts of various advocacy groups helped advance programs for individuals with disabilities. Legislation on behalf of gifted children, especially young gifted children, has been less widespread.

▶ Significant and groundbreaking laws have been passed on behalf of young children classified as disabled or at risk for developmental delays. These include authorization for university-based interdisciplinary training programs for clinicians, development of innovative early intervention programs, and the federal mandate for special education for students age three through twenty-one (IDEIA).

▶ IDEIA also allows—but does not require—states to provide intervention services for children from birth to age three who have (or are at risk for) developmental delays. At this time, all states provide such services.

▶ NCLB mandates that all states be held accountable for student progress in reading and math. States must determine which test to use and evaluate students against their annual progress goals. Children with disabilities are not exempt from these tests, but IEP accommodations for testing are allowed.

▶ Case law has been important in promoting inclusive education for students with disabilities. Significant cases have supported every child's right to attend school in the mainstream and have reinforced the intent of the original legislation to provide free and appropriate education to all children with disabilities.

▶ Prevention of developmental disabilities has become a major focus of both children's advocacy groups and Congress. Prevention of developmental disabilities can occur throughout the lifespan (and can even start with conception). More than 50 percent of disabling conditions and crippling health problems in this nation are linked directly to poverty: substandard medical care, nutrition, and housing, as well as inadequate education about the care of infants and young children. Laws have been enacted that provide programs for the early identification of medical needs, immunization of children against the serious childhood diseases, supplemental nutrition for pregnant women and their infants, and pre- and postnatal care. All of these programs have proven worthwhile on two scores: improving the quality of children's lives and saving vast amounts of taxpayers' dollars. Nevertheless, large numbers of infants, children, and pregnant women go unserved because of the lack of funding.

Key Terms

advocacy group, 32

amniocentesis, 47

case law, 30

Child Find, 35

chorionic villus sampling (CVS), 47

compensatory education, 31

cumulative deficits, 48

discretionary legislation, 37

functional behavior assessment, 39

gifted and talented, 46

giftedness, 45

Individuals with Disabilities
  Education Act (IDEA), 35

interdisciplinary, 33

in utero, 47

landmark legislation, 32

Local Education Agency
  (LEA), 39

low birth weight, 47

nondiscriminatory, 36

people-first terminology, 34

positive behavioral
  support strategies, 40

secondary disabilities, 48

Student Activities

1. Use the Internet to find your state's department of education and search for information regarding early education programs for exceptional children in your state. Inquire about programs for gifted children and about Part C in particular.

2. Speak with a parent of a child with a developmental disability. Ask the parent to identify how the family has been able to access services authorized by public law for their child.

3. Contact your local Department of Social and Health Services (DSHS) or comparable agency to learn about the implementation of the WIC program in your community.

4. Call or e-mail one of your representatives in Congress or do a web search for an update on federal legislation related to young children with disabilities and their families.

5. Form several small groups. Select one of the pieces of legislation described in this chapter. Advocate for that law—that is, convince the rest of the class why they should have voted for that law.

6. Visit your local school administration office and ask how they are meeting the requirements of NCLB. Evaluate the plan and determine its effectiveness.

Review Questions

Define and give an example of each of the following terms.

1. people-first terminology

2. advocacy group

3. nondiscriminatory evaluation

4. zero reject

5. due process

6. discretionary legislation

7. cumulative deficit

Helpful Websites

The Child Care Law Center

http://www.childcarelaw.org

The Child Care Law Center uses legal expertise to secure good, affordable child care for low-income families and communities. They provide education and training to providers regarding child care laws and offer many online resources regarding the laws and the child care center's legal responsibilities.

The Children's Defense Fund

http://www.childrensdefense.org

The mission of the Children's Defense Fund Leave No Child Behind® is to ensure every child a healthy start, a head start, a fair start, a safe start, and a moral start in life and successful passage to adulthood with the help of caring families and communities. Their website includes updates on current legislation as well as links to hundreds of other organizations, including individual state Children's Defense Fund sites.

National Head Start Association

http://www.nhsa.org

This website has information about Head Start policy and legislation, as well as information on training and program issues.

No Child Left Behind (Federal law 107-110)

http://www.ed.gov

This website was set up by the government to provide information relating to NCLB. It divides the content into usable segments according to the written law. Once at the site, search for NCLB.

Zero to Three

http://www.zerotothree.org

Zero to Three's mission is to support the healthy development and well-being of infants, toddlers, and their families. They are dedicated to advancing current knowledge; promoting beneficial policies and practices; communicating research and best practices to a wide variety of audiences; and providing training, technical assistance, and leadership development. Zero to Three is a national nonprofit organization.

 Visit the Education CourseMate for this textbook to access the eBook, Did You Get It? quizzes, Digital Downloads, TeachSource Video Cases, flashcards, and more. Go to CengageBrain.com to log in, register, or purchase access.

Inclusive Programs for Young Children

3

OBJECTIVES

After reading this chapter, you should be able to:

3-1 describe three types of programs where inclusive early childhood services are provided.

3-2 provide examples of the individualized systems and supports a child may need to be successful in an inclusive environment.

3-3 list recommended practices for inclusive programs.

3-4 identify essential elements of an inclusive program for children from birth to age two.

3-5 identify essential elements of an inclusive program for children three to five years of age.

3-6 identify essential elements of an inclusive program for children six to eight years of age.

• • • • • • • • • • • • • • • • • • •

naeyc

The following NAEYC Standards are addressed in this chapter:

STANDARD 1 Promoting Child Development and Learning

STANDARD 2 Building Family and Community Relationships

STANDARD 3 Observing, Documenting and Assessing to Support Young Children and Families

STANDARD 4 Using Developmentally Effective Approaches

STANDARD 5 Using Content Knowledge to Build Meaningful Curriculum

STANDARD 6 Becoming a Professional

CONNECTIONS

- Tyrone, a three-year-old with significant language delays, spends nine hours every day at the child care center of a corporate building downtown where his father works.
- Leah, a toddler with Down syndrome, and her mother participate in a "Mommy and Me" exercise class three times a week.
- Sean, a four-year-old who uses a wheelchair, participates in child care, religious school, and vacation programs at his church.
- Eva, a five-year-old with autism, attends kindergarten at her neighborhood school.

All of the above programs are inclusive programs. An inclusive program is any educational, child care, community, or recreational program that provides services to children regardless of ability. Any type of program that is appropriate for young children can be appropriate for young children with disabilities. Young children (birth through age eight) may spend time in different environments throughout the day. In addition to time spent at home, many are enrolled in child care, preschool, school-based, or community recreation programs. Although these programs vary in size, location, programming philosophy, and religious affiliation, they have elements in common simply because they provide care to young children.

developmentally appropriate practices learning activities based on teachers' knowledge of developmental theory

The National Association for the Education of Young Children (NAEYC) has guidelines for high-quality early childhood programs. The dominant principle is that programs for young children should be **developmentally appropriate**. Developmental appropriateness includes two significant dimensions: age appropriateness and individual appropriateness. NAEYC defines developmentally appropriate practice as meeting children where they are and enabling them to reach goals that are both challenging and achievable. Teaching practices should be appropriate to the child's age and developmental status and be responsive to the cultures and social contexts in which the child lives. NAEYC's 2009 revision of the guidelines for developmentally appropriate practices highlights three challenges of early childhood education today: 1) Reducing learning gaps and increasing the achievement of all children; 2) creating improved, better-connected education for preschool and elementary children; and 3) recognizing teacher knowledge and decision making as vital to educational effectiveness (NAEYC, 2009). The concept of developmental appropriateness is essential for programs serving all young children. For children with developmental disabilities, these guidelines are necessary but not sufficient; they must be supplemented with specialized services. The concept of developmental appropriateness for programs serving infants and toddlers, preschoolers, and children in the primary grades is discussed in this chapter.

☀ 3-1 Types of Inclusive Early Childhood Programs

Early childhood programs exist in most communities. Some programs are large; others are small. Some are licensed by the state and are housed in buildings specially designed for that purpose; others are housed in the care provider's home.

Some are government-funded; others are privately funded. Some are designed to provide all-day care for children while their parents are at work or school; others are short in duration or specific in focus. (For example, community recreation programs may meet for one hour a week and provide only gymnastics instruction.)

All of these programs are potentially inclusive. Whatever the purpose or location, these programs should share a common goal of providing quality learning environments. Quality early childhood programs provide benefits to young children with and without disabilities. However, inclusion alone does not always guarantee a positive outcome; a high-quality environment and supports for the classroom must both be present (Cate, Diefendorf, McCullough, Peters, & Whaley, 2010; Wolery, 2007).

An essential component of any quality early childhood program is that the program makes appropriate accommodations to ensure the development of *all* children. These accommodations may be in the areas of cultural, linguistic, learning, or behavioral differences. Brief descriptions of common early childhood program arrangements are provided below.

3-1a ■ Child Care Programs

Most child care facilities provide all-day care, and many children are in care for more than eight hours every day. The availability of affordable, high-quality care is a major issue in the United States (Children's Defense Fund, 2005). Capizzano, Adams, and Sonenstein (2000) examined data from the 1997 National Survey of America's Families and determined that 76 percent of preschool children with working mothers are regularly cared for by someone other than their parents. Only 6 percent of children are regularly cared for in their own homes by a babysitter or nanny, while 32 percent of children are in center-based child care arrangements, and approximately 16 percent are in family child care. Most out-of-home child care arrangements fall into the following categories.

Family child care Child care in the provider's home is called *family child care*. Family child care programs usually consist of one provider taking care of a small number of children, usually six or fewer; however, regulations regarding the number of children vary across states. The provider may or may not be related to the child. Family child care is often preferred by families with children who are two years old and under. Child care homes can be regulated by states; however, many children are in unregulated family child care homes.

Center child care Programs that employ multiple staff members and care for larger numbers of children are called *child care centers*. These programs range in size from one classroom to more than ten. Staff–child

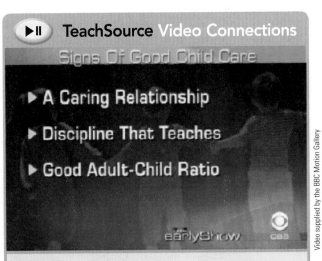

TeachSource Video Connections

Signs Of Good Child Care

▶ A Caring Relationship

▶ Discipline That Teaches

▶ Good Adult-Child Ratio

earlyShow

Video supplied by the BBC Motion Gallery

Quality of Childcare

In this video, Ellen Galinsky, from the Families and Work Institute, describes the findings of three research studies related to the importance of high-quality care and education. She discusses the characteristics of high-quality child care and warning signs parents should look for.

After watching the video, discuss the following:

1. The video lists four quality indicators of a quality program. What else would you add to the list?

2. List the warning signs provided in the video. Are there other warning signs you would add to this list? What should a parent do to determine if their child is experiencing temporary distress versus an issue of real concern?

Watch on CourseMate.

ratios are determined by state regulation; a typical ratio is approximately one staff member per ten children. Additional staff is required for infant and toddler care.

Corporate child care Corporate child care centers are run by businesses for their employees. These centers are usually on-site, and working parents are encouraged to visit their children during the day for lunch, a snack, or a quick hello. Research has shown that employees with children in on-site care have better attendance, are more satisfied with their jobs, and are more productive than employees whose children are not in company-sponsored care.

3-1b ■ Preschools

Preschool programs are usually designed for children aged three to five. Major distinctions between child care and preschool programs include the amount and type of planned activities and the length of the program day.

Preschool programs usually run for less than four hours each day, while child care programs are usually full-day programs. Although the actual programming in many child care and preschool programs may be similar, these types of programs may be viewed differently by parents and regulatory agencies. Preschool programs can be run by public or private agencies. Common types of preschool programs are described in the following paragraphs.

Public school preschool programs Public school programs are usually housed in elementary school buildings or in community centers. Most public school preschools were designed initially as special education or compensatory education programs—programs designed to provide children who are disadvantaged with some of the same opportunities (social, educational, medical) that children who are advantaged enjoy.

Some states, however, are expanding early childhood services to provide at least one year of preschool experience for all children. Approximately 35 percent of all four-year-olds are in publicly supported pre-kindergarten programs (Takanishi & Kauerz, 2008).

Community-based programs Many community centers offer preschool programs. They often rely heavily on parent participation and are sometimes called *parent co-operative (co-op) programs*. Co-ops require parents to participate in the program or to provide support in other ways. Co-op programs often are

Preschool programs are usually designed for children aged three to five.

© Cengage Learning

Public schools frequently offer on-site child care before or after school.

associated with community colleges and provide a valuable source of parent education and support.

Religious-organization-based programs Many children attend preschool programs at churches, temples, and religious community centers. In addition to early learning activities, these programs provide religious and cultural emphases.

3-1c ■ Head Start

Head Start was originally funded in 1965 under the Elementary and Secondary Education Act. It was developed as a compensatory education program for young, disadvantaged children as part of the War on Poverty. Head Start programs now serve more than 900,000 children and their families every year. Head Start and Early Head Start are comprehensive child development programs that have expanded to serve children from birth to age five, pregnant women, and their families. The programs are child-focused and have the overall goal of increasing the school readiness of young children in low-income families.

3-1d ■ School-Age Children

Children of kindergarten age and older typically attend public schools in their neighborhoods. However, some parents choose the option of private schools or home schooling. School-age children with special needs receive special education in a variety of settings, ranging from a self-contained classroom to inclusion in a public school classroom with their peers. In addition, public schools frequently offer on-site before- and aftercare programs, which provide another opportunity for inclusion.

3-1e ■ Recreation Programs

Recreation programs for young children are increasing in popularity. Many preschoolers participate in organized art, dance, gymnastics, or swim programs. As children enter elementary school, many also become involved in organized sports (e.g., soccer, T-ball) and various scouting activities. These programs offer opportunities for inclusive experiences for young children.

☀ 3-2 System of Supports and Services

One of the recommendations in the DEC/NAEYC Joint Position paper on Inclusion (2009) is to establish a system of services and supports that reflects the needs of children with varying types of disabilities. The type of service and support a child may need to participate successfully in an inclusive program will vary widely from child to child. Services and supports may include:

- staff development and education about the child's disability.

- individualized therapy such as speech, occupational therapy, or physical therapy.

- the support of a paraprofessional to help adapt curriculum or facilitate social interactions.

- the ongoing support of an inclusion specialist who provides recommendations and assists the staff with developing strategies to meet the needs of the child.

Did You Get It?

The primary recommendation of the DEC/NAEYC Joint Position Paper on Inclusion (2009) is embodied in which statement?

a. To provide ongoing support of an Inclusion specialist who provides recommendations and assists the staff with developing strategies to meet the needs of the child.

b. To provide individualized therapy such as speech, occupational therapy, or physical therapy.

c. To ensure the support of a paraprofessional to help adapt curriculum or facilitate social interactions.

d. To establish a system of services and supports that reflects the needs of children with varying types of disabilities.

Take the full quiz on CourseMate.

☀ 3-3 Recommended Practices for Programs

best practices recommended strategies agreed upon by members of a profession

Six general principles are used to identify the **best practices** for working with children who have special needs; these practices apply equally to early care programs for all children (Odom & McLean, 1996). To be considered a recommended **best practice**, a strategy must be (1) research-based or value-based, (2) family-centered, (3) multicultural in emphasis, (4) cross-disciplinary, (5) developmentally/chronologically age-appropriate, and (6) normalized. A brief description of each of these principles follows.

3-3a ■ Research-Based or Value-Based Practices

empirical information based on observation or experiment

Practices, strategies, and techniques used in early childhood education (ECE) and early childhood special education (ECSE) must be supported by **empirical** research. In some instances (e.g., inclusion), practices are driven by personal and societal values rather than empirical research. In these cases, it is necessary to work toward gathering the empirical evidence necessary to evaluate those practices.

3-3b ■ Family-Centered Practices

Family-centered intervention practices are designed with, rather than for, the child and family. This view of intervention acknowledges that the child is part of a dynamic family system and that any change in the system (e.g., intervention or change in programs) affects all parts of the system. (Chapter 9 provides additional information on Family-Centered Practice.)

3-3c ■ Multicultural Practices

Recommended practices embrace a multicultural perspective and celebrate the concept of family uniqueness. **Family uniqueness** encompasses ethnic, linguistic, cultural, and racial differences as well as the history and traditions of individual families. This is especially important as our society becomes more pluralistic and families more commonly consist of blends of backgrounds. This multicultural perspective recognizes and respects different needs and value systems of the children and families. This respect must be translated into practice by developing programs that are **culturally competent** and supportive of differences. The Linguistic and Cultural Diversity Connections box lists some aspects of a culturally competent program early childhood program.

family uniqueness perspective that recognizes that every family is different

culturally competent classroom activities, materials, and curricula that acknowledge and respect the different ethnicities that are represented in the classroom and community

3-3d ■ Cross-Disciplinary Practices

Early childhood and early childhood special education programs should involve professionals from different disciplines working as a team. In addition to education and special education teachers, early childhood teams often include specialists in speech pathology, audiology, occupational therapy, physical therapy, nursing, medicine, nutrition, psychology, and social work. (Chapter 10 provides additional information about interdisciplinary teams.)

Linguistic and Cultural Diversity Connections

Aspects of Culturally Competent Early Childhood Programs
(adapted from Moule, 2012; NAEYC, 2009; Cross, Bazron, Dennis & Isaacs, 1989).

- Acknowledge and respect the unique, culturally defined needs of children and their families.
- Acknowledge that culture has an impact on education.
- View the family and community, including churches, as primary supports for culturally diverse populations.
- Understand that culturally diverse children are usually best served by individuals who are part of or in tune with the children's culture.
- Have policies and practices that build upon the home languages and dialects of the children, families, and staff in programs, and that support the preservation of these home languages.

Developmentally appropriate practices are based on knowledge of how children develop and learn.

3-3e ■ Developmentally/Chronologically Age-Appropriate Practices

Developmentally appropriate practices are based on knowledge and understanding about how children develop and learn. Educators of young children must know about child development, about what to teach, and how to teach it. They must know how to assess learning, and, most important, they need to know the individual children and families with whom they are working (NAEYC, 1996).

3-3f ■ Normalized Practices

normalization the process by which the care and education of people with disabilities are as culturally normal as possible, with services provided in regular community facilities rather than in segregated schools and institutions

Normalization refers to providing opportunities for individuals with disabilities to go to school and participate in education experiences, as do other children and youth. For young children, these experiences may include preschool, child care, swimming lessons, play groups, movies, religious training, and dance lessons. A family with a child who has disabilities should have access to the same range of activities and services as any other family (Bailey & McWilliam, 1990). These principles are appropriate for all early childhood programs, ranging from those for infants and toddlers to those for children in the early primary grades.

Although there are many cross-age similarities in quality programming, there also are many elements that are age-specific. The rest of this chapter discusses age-specific elements of inclusive programs. The information in these sections is based primarily on the recommendations of the National Association for the Education of Young Children (Copple & Bredekamp, 2009) and the Division of Early Childhood.

Did You Get It?

The right of a child with disabilities to have access to the same experiences as all young children is incorporated in the term
  a. Normalization.
  b. Developmentally/Chronologically Age-Appropriate Practices.
  c. Quality programming.
  d. Best practice.

Take the full quiz on CourseMate.

Inclusive Programs for Children 3-4 from Birth to Age Two

The quality of early childhood programs influences child development in the short and long run. We know that "from infancy through about age 10, brain cells not only form most of the connections they will maintain throughout life, but during this time they retain their greatest malleability" (Dana Alliance for Brain Initiatives, 1996, p. 7). We also know that the quality of early childhood environments influences this development (Herschkowitz & Herschkowitz, 2004). These youngsters require more individual attention and caregivers' time. Caregivers must be knowledgeable about typical child development and how to adapt the environment and interactions to support the healthy development of infants and toddlers with special needs.

3-4a ■ Relationships among Caregivers and Children

Children develop best when they have secure, consistent relationships with adults who are responsive (NAEYC, 2009). One goal of the infant caregiver, whether at home or in out-of-home settings, is the healthy development of the infant. The caregiver's role becomes an even greater challenge when dealing with infants who are developmentally delayed. A caregiver must believe in the potential of the infant and be responsive to the infant's cues and communicative signals (Widerstrom, Mowder, & Sandall, 1997). The caregiver helps the infant "make things work," thereby increasing the infant's ability to act on the environment. The caregiver focuses on providing a setting in which daily routines, play activities, the caregiver's responsiveness, and intervention procedures are geared to the infant's responsiveness and skill levels. Such an environment is not only developmentally appropriate; it is also an **enabling environment** for the following reasons:

enabling environment (infancy) environment that supports a child's optimal development

- It encourages the infant to respond and adapt to environmental experiences by helping him or her regulate biological rhythms (sleeping, eating, eliminating) and psychological state (ability to be soothed, excitability, responsiveness).

- It helps the infant learn to maintain a balance between avoiding environmental events that deter development and approaching events that support healthy attachment and **intentional communication**. Infants accomplish this best when caregivers help them learn to respond to people and activities in mutually satisfying ways.

intentional communication gestures, vocalizations, and other communicative behavior that is directed toward a specific communicative partner and that has a specific function

- It promotes the infant's emerging abilities to select simple, more specific responses out of **undifferentiated responses** and to practice them. The interactions between caregiver and child foster the child's sense of control and use of various senses to experience the environment in selective ways.

undifferentiated response a behavior that is not directed toward a specific person or intended to communicate a specific message

- It facilitates the infant's efforts to respond in new ways to people, objects, and events.

3-4b ■ Environment and Experiences

First and foremost, a developmentally appropriate environment for infants and toddlers is a safe and healthy environment. It offers protection for children and their undertakings, wherever care is provided—in the child's home, in a family child care home, or in a center-based child care facility.

An appropriate environment for very young children is also a **responsive learning environment** (Mulligan, Green, Morris, Maloney, McMurray, & Kittleson-Aldred, 1992; Lally, 2000). A responsive environment actively engages and reacts to the child. It supports infants and young children when they interact with adults and other children. A responsive environment also supports infants and toddlers by providing a predictable routine. It supports them when they are using materials and equipment. It supports them when they are alone and engaged in calming or entertaining themselves. By its very nature, a responsive environment encourages and supports active exploration by providing opportunities for:

- accessing what is happening in the environment.
- making choices that respond to their overtures and also reflect their expressed intentions.
- engaging in experiences that evolve from simple to more complex and that are based on the interest of the children.
- causing things to happen.
- playing alone and with peers.
- making connections with the family

3-4c ■ Equipment

The extent to which infants are supported in initiating activities is largely determined by the space available and how it is divided, how materials are stored and presented, and the actual materials provided. When arranging toys and accessories (e.g., mobiles), caregivers should consider how items will be viewed and accessed from the infants' and toddlers' perspective. Caregivers should also choose play materials that are visually appealing and that invite manipulation. Safety considerations always come first when selecting materials. All objects must be large and smooth enough to be mouthed, because infants and toddlers suck, bite, or chew almost everything with which they come into contact. To prevent objects from becoming lodged in the throat, mouth, ears, or nose, a general "rule of fist" should be used: a child under three should not have access to objects smaller than his or her own fist. Figure 3-1 lists appropriate toys for very young children.

A responsive environment actively engages and reacts to the child.

© Cengage Learning

FIGURE **3-1**

Appropriate Toys for Very Young Children

- sturdy picture books
- household items such as measuring cups and unbreakable bowls
- vinyl-covered pillows to climb on
- childproof mirrors
- nesting toys
- large beads that snap together
- washable cloth squares (24 × 24 in.) of different colors and textures
- shape sorters
- squeeze toys that squeak or rattle
- rattles, spoons, and teethers
- dolls
- balls
- pull toys
- music boxes and other musical toys
- simple cause-and-effect toys (such as a jack-in-the-box)
- various types of containers (and things to put in them)

© Cengage Learning

TeachSource Digital Download Download from CourseMate.

3-4d ■ Health, Safety, and Nutrition

Promoting health and safety is a priority in planning a program for very young children. Caregivers must be sure that the environment is well prepared before children arrive and that procedures are in place to maintain health and safety measures.

Marotz (2012) points out that caregivers must rehearse fire and disaster plans for getting children to safety. In addition, they emphasize the need for emergency numbers to be posted by the telephone and for a quickly accessible file indicating what parents want done if they cannot be reached in an emergency. Guidelines for a safe and healthy environment for very young children include the following:

- Toys should be safe, washable, and too large for young children to swallow. Mouthed toys are replaced with clean ones so that the mouthed toys can be disinfected with a bleach solution (one-quarter cup bleach to a gallon of water or one tablespoon bleach to a quart of water).

- Electrical outlets are covered; extension cords are not exposed; hazardous substances are kept out of children's reach.

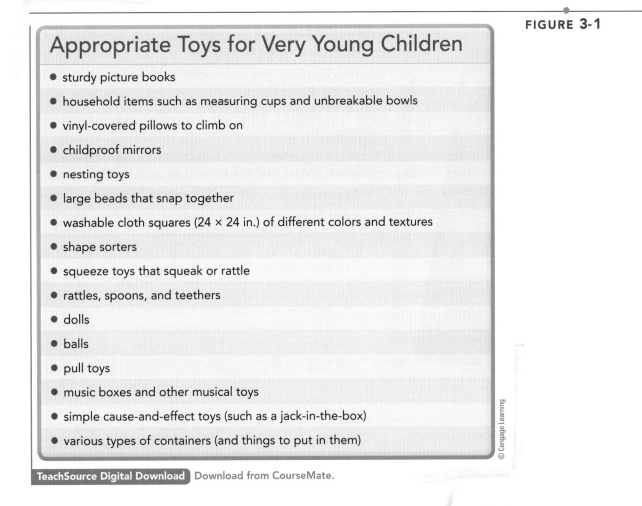

Each infant has his or her own bedding, diapers, clothing, pacifiers, and special comforting objects.

© Cengage Learning 2015

- Each infant has his or her own bedding, diapers, clothing, pacifiers, and special comforting objects. Personal items are labeled with the child's name.
- Diaper-changing areas are easily and routinely sanitized after each diaper change.
- Staff is healthy and take precautions not to spread illness.
- Caregivers wash their hands before and after every diaper change and the feeding of each infant.
- Adults are aware of the symptoms of common childhood illnesses, of children's allergies, and of potential hazards in the environment.
- Infants always are held with their bodies at an appropriate angle ("head above the heart") when being fed from a bottle.
- Children who can sit up are fed with one or two other infants with a caregiver present to help if needed.
- Safe finger foods are encouraged. Only healthy foods are offered. Eating is considered a sociable, happy time.

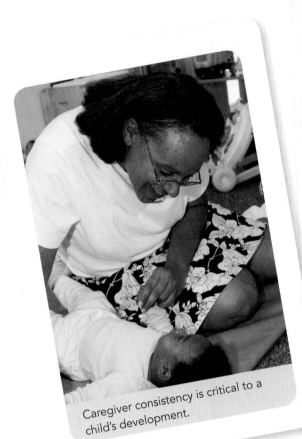

Caregiver consistency is critical to a child's development.

© Cengage Learning

3-4e ■ Reciprocal Relationships with Families

reciprocal relationship
relationship in which each member gives and receives in response to the giving and receiving of the other

Positive and candid interactions among parents and staff members—**reciprocal relationships**—are important. Staff must remember that parents are the primary source of affection and care in the child's life. Positive interaction between staff and parents can help parents feel more confident in their roles and with their child care choices (Gonzalez-Mena & Eyer, 2012). Guidelines for positive interactions with parents include:

- sharing important information with parents about their children.
- demonstrating respect for a family's culture, language, and life choices.
- having appropriate information that enables teachers to answer questions about child development and available community resources.
- responding respectfully to parents' questions, comments, and concerns.
- welcoming parents to participate in the program and participate in decision making regarding the care and education of their child.

Did You Get It?

When a staff member shares important information with parents about their children, or responds respectfully to parents' questions, comments, and concerns, what does this signify?
  a. Demonstrative relationship.
  b. Caring relationship.
  c. Sharing relationship.
  d. Reciprocal relationship.

Take the full quiz on CourseMate.

Inclusive Programs for Children 3-5 ☀
Ages Three to Five

Programs for three- to five-year-olds are often a child's and a family's first experience with a center-based program. For many children, it is their first time with a large group of children. A key to their adjustment is that teachers not expect too much or too little from the children or their parents. Clear and consistent expectations along with a well-planned learning environment result in a positive experience for young children and their families.

3-5a ■ Creating a Caring Community of Learners

A goal of all early childhood programs is to create a classroom environment—both physical and social—that supports the learning of all children. The idea of a community of learners underscores that everyone in the classroom benefits when anyone is successful (Gibbs, 2001). A community of learners emphasizes working on social relationships, collaboration between children and adults, and respect for every individual in the classroom.

The foundation of a caring community is consistent caring relationships between the adults and children, among children and teachers, and between teachers and families (NAEYC, 2009). (See the "Case Study" below for further exploration of this issue.)

This goal of early childhood programs makes sense given what we know about the importance of developing early and positive peer relationships (Hartup & Moore, 1990; Ladd, 2005).

3-5b ■ Teaching to Enhance Development and Learning

Appropriate environments for preschool children support self-directed problem solving and experimentation. Some teaching strategies will be directed to an individual child, while others will be directed at a group. Teaching strategies must be both age- and individually appropriate, so teachers use a variety of strategies to meet the needs of children in the classroom. An important component of teaching young children is preparing environments that invite and support learning.

Case Study ■ A caring community of learners ■

Hayden is a four-year-old attending a community preschool. He has a diagnosis of autism and is supported by a shadow aide who helps him participate in the curriculum. A classmate, Miles, came to school and announced that what Hayden has is contagious. For the last week, some of Hayden's classmates will not sit beside him at circle, and are teasing him during playtime. Hayden is very upset by the change in his classmates. The shadow aide has done her best to explain to the students that Hayden is not contagious and all members of the class are friends. Hayden has reported to his parents that Miles is mean, causing the parents to ask the teacher what is going on. What can the teacher do to change the class climate and create a caring community of learners?

In inclusive classrooms, teachers design learning environments that provide carefully matched opportunities and contexts for children with diverse abilities. Teachers also use incidental teaching strategies (see Chapters 11 and 17) to take advantage of teachable moments that occur throughout the day. Teaching strategies also must support children's independence, self-determination, and creativity. Children are given the opportunity and guidance—when needed—to make and carry out choices. In addition, teachers recognize that there is more than one right answer or one right way to solve a problem, tell a story, or build a tower of blocks. In other words, appropriate teaching strategies provide opportunities for young children to learn skills, problem solve, and acquire information in contexts that are relevant to their everyday lives.

3-5c ■ Constructing an Appropriate Curriculum

Young children learn by doing; therefore, curriculum goals incorporate child-initiated, teacher-supported exploration and discovery activities. Play is the medium through which children learn best and should be a primary consideration in setting up curriculum goals and classroom activities. Curriculum goals should be developed using an integrated model of child development that acknowledges the interdependence of development across domains. Individual diversity is planned, and each child's individual pattern of growth and development is supported by the curriculum. An appropriate curriculum includes opportunities for exploration and instruction in the following areas.

Social-emotional Development Developing social skills and peer relationships is a major competence that young children must acquire. Early childhood educators can play an important role in supporting children as they learn to play together, cooperate, give and receive help, negotiate, and solve interpersonal problems. Social-emotional development can be facilitated by teachers who:

- model self-control.
- encourage appropriate behaviors.
- use positive statements and other social forms of praise.
- set clear limits.

Social norms vary across cultures; the social skills taught in preschool must respect the child's culture. (Facilitating the development of social skills is described in Chapter 15.)

Communication and literacy development Functional use of language and support of children's emerging literacy are essential during the preschool years. Although most children who are typically developing will have functional communication skills when they enter preschool, many children with disabilities may still be developing rudimentary conversational skills. Functional communication skills enable children to control their environment by using speech, signs, or another form of augmentative communication to get what they need and want. (Chapter 16 focuses on facilitating communication skills.)

Literacy development is also an important goal. Though formalized instruction in reading and writing is not considered appropriate in a preschool curriculum, teachers must provide a rich literacy environment with many experiences that help children learn to read. There must be opportunities for children to see books, hear and tell stories, engage in word games (e.g., rhyming songs or recitations), play with sandpaper and magnetic letters, write, and draw (Notari-Syverson, O'Connor, & Vadasy, 2007).

As the conclusion of the joint position of the International Reading Association and the National Association for the Education of Young Children (IRA & NAEYC, 1998) elegantly states:

> To teach in developmentally appropriate ways, teachers must understand both the continuum of reading and writing development and children's individual and cultural variations. Teachers must recognize when variation is within the typical range and when intervention is necessary, because early intervention is more effective and less costly than later remediation.

Physical development Children need daily opportunities to engage in **gross motor** and **fine motor** activities. They are growing fast and need to move and use their bodies throughout the day. Gross motor activities offer children opportunities to use large muscles through jumping, balancing, and running. Activities should be fun, challenging, and noncompetitive and should take place every day, preferably outdoors. Fine motor activities are often referred to as *manipulative* or *tabletop* activities, such as writing, drawing, painting, cutting, and using pegboards, puzzles, and parquetry blocks.

gross-motor skills physical activities that require the voluntary use of large muscles, such as running, sitting, and pulling up pants

fine-motor skills physical activities that require the voluntary use of small muscles, such as holding a pencil, using scissors, and buttoning

Aesthetic development Experiences in art and music should be available every day in preschool classrooms. Emphasis is on exploration, spontaneity, self-expression, and appreciation, rather than on completing a specific product or learning a particular tune. Art and music activities should represent the cultures of the children and staff in the classroom.

3-5d ■ Assessing Children's Learning and Development

The primary goal of assessment is to gather information to help answer a question. When we think about assessment with young children in inclusive settings, our primary questions are concerned with how the child is functioning in the classroom. The answers to assessment questions can help teachers determine what types of accommodations, modifications, or instructional strategies are needed to enable the child to succeed. Assessments do not determine a child's "readiness" for a program but are the teacher's guide to planning and implementing curriculum. According to the NAEYC, guidelines on developmentally appropriate practice, assessment, and curriculum are integrated. Teachers repeatedly engage in observational assessment for the purpose of refining teaching and improving learning.

The accountability aspect of No Child Left Behind (NCLB), mandating that students pass certain tests, has brought with it some unintended consequences for preschoolers and kindergartners. The required testing, beginning with first graders, has led policymakers and parents to set unrealistic academic goals for five- and six-year-olds. As a consequence of these goals, there is

Children need daily opportunities to engage in fine motor activities.

© Cengage Learning

often growing pressure to push academics such as reading down to a younger and younger age. This pressure can lead early childhood educators to use inappropriate curricula that focus on developing specific skills rather than developing active learners (Blaustein, 2005).

3-5e ■ Reciprocal Relationships with Parents

Parents and teachers must work together to provide consistency for young children. Teachers may see some parents every day when they drop off and pick up their children; other parents are at the school less often. Teachers need to establish regular communication with all parents. This allows teachers and parents to discuss the child's progress regularly; if a problem occurs, teachers and parents already have a relationship established that will facilitate addressing the problem. Many preschools use newsletters or weekly schedule notes to keep parents connected with classroom activities. (Communicating with parents is discussed in detail in Chapter 9.)

Did You Get It?

What cause does Blaustein (2005) identify as having the detrimental effect of leading early childhood educators to use inappropriate curricula strategies?
- a. Children's readiness.
- b. Required testing that sets unrealistic academic goals for five- and six-year olds.
- c. Observational assessment.
- d. Instructional strategies.

Take the full quiz on CourseMate.

 ## 3-6 Inclusive Programs for Children Ages Six to Eight

Although these programs are part of elementary school, the recommended practices for early childhood education continue to be appropriate. The primary grades are an amazing time for children, academically and socially. They learn to read and write and to understand simple mathematics; they learn to function as part of a large and complex social institution. A developmentally appropriate primary classroom plays an important role in helping the child and family establish a positive relationship with the school.

3-6a ■ Creating a Caring Community of Learners

As children enter elementary school, the challenge for teachers is to maintain a focus on social development. In the primary grades, classroom communities have two major goals: promoting positive climates for learning, and building democratic communities. Both of these goals require teachers to set up classroom rules and problem-solving strategies that are fair, inclusive of all children, and consistent. The ideal classroom serves as a caring community in which children can develop and learn, acknowledge differences in abilities and talents, and value each member for his or her individual strengths. Teachers should also consider the impact of groupings and scheduling on classroom communities and membership (Billingsley, Gallucci, Peck, Schwartz, & Staub, 1996). For example, if classroom meetings are always held immediately before lunch, that would not be an appropriate time for a child to be removed for resource-room or speech therapy.

3-6b ■ Teaching to Enhance Development and Learning

Teachers in the primary grades create environments that support student exploration and child-directed inquiry; they also offer explicit instruction to provide children with the academic tools they need. There must be time for spontaneous play, too, because children continue to learn through unstructured activities. Although children in the primary grades can sit still longer than preschoolers, they still need to be active to ensure learning. Children continue to depend on firsthand experience to learn new concepts.

3-6c ■ Constructing an Appropriate Curriculum

In the primary grades, an appropriate curriculum is broad; it includes physical, social, emotional, and intellectual goals. Children progress at different rates; thus, individualized planning and instruction are essential in a developmentally appropriate primary curriculum. As children enter kindergarten and the early grades, they are usually just beginning their relationship with the public school system. Therefore, one goal of the primary curriculum should be to establish a foundation for lifelong learning and to create a positive school experience for the child and family. Activities that promote self-esteem and help children increase their confidence and competence as students also are important goals.

3-6d ■ Integrated Curriculum

An **integrated curriculum** teaches around themes, experiences, and projects that include skills from many areas; it resists establishing artificial boundaries between academic areas.

integrated curriculum lessons that include, in a single activity, content from more than one domain

For example, if children are working on the lifecycle of salmon, an integrated approach could include literacy skills (reading, writing, spelling), math and science skills, social studies, geography, and art. An integrated curriculum provides children an opportunity to learn and teachers an opportunity to teach academic skills in a meaningful context. Students work in cooperative groups, rather than using discrete worksheets and abbreviated individual assignments. A collaborative project for the lifecycle of the salmon could include a story for the class newspaper, a map of where salmon live during different parts of their lifecycle, charts depicting changes in the salmon population, and drawings of different types of salmon. Field trips related to the theme would be an important component of an integrated curriculum. Appropriate field trips for the salmon project could include trips to a hatchery, fish ladder, or aquarium.

3-6e ■ Guidance of Social-Emotional Development

Peer relationships continue to be important as children enter elementary school. Friendships are essential in establishing personal and social adjustment.

Children who have trouble making friends are more likely to have both academic and mental health problems as adolescents and adults (Walker, Ramsey, & Gresham 2003). Emphasis in the primary grades is on teaching young children self-control, self-assessment, and problem-solving techniques as an integrated part of the curriculum, rather than addressing those skills only when a problem occurs. Primary-grade children sometimes are taught in multiage groups (Bailey, Burchinal, & McWilliam, 1993; Geist & Baum, 2005). Such groupings add to the diversity of the classroom and provide natural opportunities for children to learn helping and nurturing roles. More competent children in the classroom should have experiences with older students so that they, too, receive as well as provide assistance.

Student assessment should include direct observation and collection of work samples.

© Cengage Learning

3-6f ■ Assessing Learning and Development

The purpose of assessment in the primary grades should be for making decisions about teaching and learning, identifying areas of concern for individual children that may require intervention, and helping improve these interventions (NAEYC, 2009). The evaluation of children's work in the primary grades needs to be **contextually based** and **formative**. Rather than viewing mistakes as indicators of what children do not know, teachers should evaluate mistakes as a way of learning about children's understanding of concepts. Further instruction then can be based on this error analysis.

Letter grades should not be used; rather, teachers should use narrative progress reports and portfolios of children's work. More appropriate strategies for student assessment include classroom-based procedures such as direct observation, collection of work samples, and portfolios and multiple sources of evidence gathered over time (Hills, 1993; Keefe, 1995; Meisels, 1993, NAEYC, 2009).

contextually based assessment and intervention practices that are embedded into naturally occurring activities of the child (e.g., teaching or assessing hand washing as children prepare for snack)

formative assessments that are ongoing and used to shape programs and interventions

3-6g ■ Reciprocal Relationships with Parents

A challenge for teachers in the primary grades is to develop good working relationships with parents. Teachers should be in regular contact with parents through visits, phone calls, e-mails, or notes. Parents should be welcome in the classroom at any time, and strategies to facilitate their comfortable participation in classroom activities should be developed. For example, parents can be invited to share their talents, expertise, interests, and cultural backgrounds with the class.

> ### Did You Get It?
>
> **What focus do teachers need to be aware of as children transition into elementary school?**
> a. Promoting positive climate for learning.
> b. Building a democratic community.
> c. Social development.
> d. Classroom with rules.
>
> Take the full quiz on CourseMate.

Summary

▶ Many types of inclusive early childhood programs are found in child care, preschool, Head Start, community recreation programs, and elementary schools.

▶ Inclusive programs are culturally sensitive and responsive to differences in language, social values, and the educational background of children and their families.

▶ Some children may require additional services to be successful in an inclusive program. This may include therapies, additional staff support, and/or consultation.

▶ Developmentally appropriate practices result in educational teams—including families—making decisions for individual children. These decisions are based on what is known about child development and instructional strategies, the strengths and needs of the individual child, and the social and cultural contexts in which children live.

▶ For programs to be truly developmentally appropriate, the educators must think about children as individuals and design programs that meet the needs of individual children.

▶ Quality programs for infants and toddlers provide a safe, healthy, and well-supervised environment filled with developmentally appropriate play materials and staffed by responsive caregivers.

▶ For children from three to five years of age, a quality program provides many opportunities to *learn by doing*. Children acquire knowledge of the world through play. Good programs provide well-planned learning environments and appropriate instruction across developmental domains, including language, literacy, science, social development, and the arts.

▶ As children enter kindergarten and the primary grades, they still need programs that adhere to the principle of developmental appropriateness. Quality primary programs provide integrated learning opportunities and instruction. Child-directed and teacher-supported active learning is the key to quality programs for children this age.

Key Terms

best practices, 60
contextually based, 72
culturally competent, 61
developmentally appropriate, 56
empirical, 60
enabling environment (infancy), 63

family uniqueness, 61
fine motor, 69
formative, 72
gross motor, 69
integrated curriculum, 71
intentional communication, 63

normalization, 62
reciprocal relationships, 66
responsive learning environment, 64
undifferentiated responses, 63

Student Activities

1. Visit at least two different early childhood programs—family child care, center-based child care, preschool, kindergarten or primary grade classrooms, or community recreation programs. List features that these programs share and ways in which they differ.

2. Find out which agency in your state regulates child care programs. Contact that agency and inquire about the child care regulations in your state. How do they relate to the best practices described in this chapter?

3. Visit a local public school and learn what they are doing to reduce the achievement gap. How do their efforts match the description in NAEYC's position paper on Developmentally Appropriate Practice?

4. Observe an inclusive program for children aged three to five. Observe one child with disabilities and one child who is typically developing. Describe the similarities and differences in their activities during your observation.

5. Interview a teacher of young children. Describe practices that he or she uses that would be characterized as developmentally appropriate.

6. Reflect on your own early elementary experiences. Describe your own experience with inclusion, or lack thereof.

Review Questions

Respond to the following items in list form.

1. List at least four types of potentially inclusive early childhood programs.

2. List the six general principles used to evaluate recommended practices in early childhood special education.

3. List the essential elements for quality early childhood programs serving children up to age two.

4. List the essential elements for quality early childhood education programs serving children aged three to five.

5. List the essential elements for quality early childhood education programs serving children aged six to eight.

6. List some ways a teacher can make her classroom an inclusive setting.

7. List some aspects of a culturally competent early childhood program.

Helpful Websites

The Council for Exceptional Children (CEC)

http://www.cec.sped.org

CEC publishes *Exceptional Children* and *Teaching Exceptional Children*. Of particular interest to early childhood education is one of CEC's affiliate groups, the Division for Early Childhood Education. (A number of other divisions also focus to some extent on issues related to young children.)

National Association for the Education of Young Children (NAEYC)

http://www.naeyc.org

NAEYC's website includes a resource catalog, professional development materials, and links to related sites. Of note is the NAEYC position statement on standardized testing of young children age three through eight (adopted 1987 by NAEYC).

Frank Porter Graham Child Development Institute

http://www.fpg.unc.edu

One of the nation's oldest and largest multidisciplinary centers devoted to the study of young children and their families. Research is occurring on over 80 projects related to developmental disabilities; early care and education; physical and social health; professional development, technical assistance, and implementation science; public policy and evaluation; and racial, ethnic, linguistic, cultural, and socioeconomic diversity.

National Early Childhood Technical Assistance Center

http://www.nectac.org

This website contains information and publications on a variety of early childhood education topics, including assessment, family partnerships, quality assurance, inclusion, and much more.

Visit the Education CourseMate for this textbook to access the eBook, Did You Get It? quizzes, Digital Downloads, TeachSource Video Cases, flashcards, and more. Go to CengageBrain.com to log in, register, or purchase access.

Early Intervention & Public Policy

Cengage Learning

WHAT IS A TEAM?

For a child to succeed in an inclusive environment, it takes a team. The team consists of family members and professionals who work together to ensure this success—as we see in the nearby photo. Interdisciplinary teamwork and collaboration are the cornerstones of successful inclusion. Collaboration in early childhood education requires that professionals and families adopt a common set of developmentally appropriate standards that guide the major activities of screening, diagnostic assessment, individualized curriculum planning, progress and program evaluation, and family-centered services. The involvement of the team will look different for every child and family. In some cases, the team will meet to develop goals and to plan placement. At other times, team members might be involved on a daily or weekly basis assisting the child as needed to learn in the classroom. In order for a team to be effective, its members must keep each other informed about changes in progress

and programming. The team must believe that all individual team members' contributions are equally valuable and must share responsibility for decision making and planning. The team must have a common goal that drives their teamwork, a goal around which they pool their knowledge to plan intervention and programming (Friend & Bursuck, 2006).

About the Special Focus Features in This Text

In each Section Wrap Up, we will include a "Special Focus" feature. The Special Focus pieces in this text are all written by members of teams. Their contributions to this text are written from each team member's viewpoint and describe how each has participated in creating an inclusive experience for a child. First you will read about a preschool teacher's experience as she describes how she makes accommodations for all her students. You will read about the experience of one parent over the years as we follow her son's progress from early intervention to his later elementary years. You will learn how an elementary school teacher creates a caring environment for her students and those who join her class from a special day class. And finally, you will hear from a Behavior Analyst/Inclusion Specialist as she describes her role supporting students and teachers in inclusive settings.

Reference

Friend, M & Bursuck W. D. (2006). *Including Students with Special Needs: A Practical Guide for Classroom Teachers.* Allyn & Bacon: Boston, MA.

Courtesy of Claire Petersen

SPECIAL FOCUS • A PRESCHOOL TEACHER'S THOUGHTS

My name is Claire Peterson and for nearly ten years I have been a teacher at a play-based, parent-participation preschool in California. Our program philosophy of a child-inspired, teacher-guided, play-based curriculum that focuses primarily on the children's social-emotional development provides me with the opportunity to teach in an environment that is inclusive of all preschoolers. Our program also provides opportunities for peer scaffolding, a realistic environment in which to practice their emerging social-emotional skills, and, above all, a place to play—all children learn through play!

Each child in our program, whatever his or her needs, requires accommodations in order to be successful. On a given day I may make any number of accommodations for my students who are typically developing. I may alter the seating arrangements to support a child who is suffering from separation anxiety. I may make curriculum accommodations for a child who needs a small-group or individual activity because the child is feeling overwhelmed by larger group play/projects. I may make sensory accommodations for a child who is particularly interested in or adverse to "messy" sensory experiences. For my students with identified needs, I simply extend my approach to provide accommodations that specifically support their independent learning plan.

All early childhood education professionals make these kinds of accommodations multiple times a day, although they may not realize it. Including preschoolers with identified needs in a classroom of children who are typically developing is a natural extension of the early educator's core strengths: knowledge of child development, enthusiasm for working with young children, and ability to be flexible and try new approaches to problem solving.

Peer-to-peer scaffolding is another key element in teaching in an inclusive environment. Each child, and each adult, for that matter, has his or her own strengths and weaknesses. Peer groups quickly identify each other's strengths and weaknesses through repeated interactions. This provides all preschoolers with the opportunities to provide assistance to and ask for assistance from their peers.

In my current class I have a student who is nonverbal but has the best letter recognition skills within the group. His name is Matthew. When working on alphabet puzzles the children who are verbal will ask Matthew for help finding specific letters—and he never lets them down! The children who are verbal also provide support to Matthew. When they are together on the tire swing and he wants to get off, or be pushed more, and they aren't able to help him, they will go and get Matthew's aide and let her know that he needs support.

Developing social skills can also be positively impacted by peer scaffolding. All students in our classrooms are asked to talk through conflict and resolve their conflicts verbally. All peers benefit from these conflicts being resolved verbally. The participants directly involved in the conflict benefit from having their conflict resolved. The children who are nearby and observe the conflict learn from seeing verbal resolution. They may also contribute to the resolution if the participants are too distraught or don't have the language skills to explain to the teacher what happened.

For example, a child becomes quite distraught after having been pushed by another child in the sandbox. A nearby peer may be able to say that the child was pushed because he was about to step on the other child's sandcastle. Peer interactions, such as these when facilitated by a teacher, provide invaluable role modeling and peer scaffolding to both the child who is typically developing and the child with developmental delays.

These types of peer interactions in an inclusive classroom provide all of my students with the opportunity to develop the social skills they will need to interact in a world full of people with differences. The early educator's job in the inclusive classroom is to provide the support and guidance that children need to leverage each other's strengths and shore up each other's weaknesses while developing strong social skills through play.

Application Questions

1. What information from the chapters in Section 1 applies to this story?
2. Describe this teacher's philosophy and why it might make for successful experiences for children with diverse abilities.

Normal and Exceptional Development

4

OBJECTIVES

After reading this chapter, you should be able to:

4-1 describe typical development and distinguish between developmental sequences and developmental milestones; give examples of each in motor, social, cognitive, and language development.

4-2 explain the terms *atypical* and *exceptional development* and relate these terms to the development of young children.

4-3 outline biological and environmental factors that can put infants and young children at developmental risk.

• • • • • • • • • • • • • • • • • • •

naeyc

The following NAEYC Standards are addressed in this chapter:

STANDARD 1 Promoting Child Development and Learning

STANDARD 3 Observing, Documenting and Assessing to Support Young Children and Families

STANDARD 4 Using Developmentally Effective Approaches

CONNECTIONS

- Jeremy is by far the biggest boy in the first grade. He looks like an eight-year-old, yet behaves like the young six-year-old that he is.
- Aki, by age three, was fluent in three languages; by age five, she was reading words and phrases in two languages. She was also producing clay figures and paintings more typical of a second grader than a preschooler.
- The twins Jennifer and Jeffrey began talking at eighteen months. At the same time, they developed a private language of their own, incomprehensible to others.

exceptional children a term coined at the 1930 White House Conference on Handicapped Individuals to refer to all children who are different from typically developing children

pathologist certified professional who focuses on diseases or impairments

atypical development any aspect of a child's physical or psychological makeup that is different from what is generally accepted as typical to early childhood

Each of the children in the introduction can be viewed as normal, or typically developing, yet each is also atypical, different from others of the same age. This is true of all young children: alike in many ways, different in others. Children with differences that alter their development often are referred to as "exceptional" or "atypical." The many ways that **exceptional children** are like other children tend to be overlooked.

Such perceptions are undergoing change, however, especially in light of recent findings of developmental **pathologists** (Cohen & Cicchetti, 2006). They argue that both typical and **atypical development** emerge from the same basic processes, that we need to learn how to respond to the diverging developmental pathways among children of essentially the same age. When working with infants and children, one must keep two significant principles in mind:

1. *First, a child is above all else a child, regardless of how smart or delayed or troubled that child may be.*
2. *Second, every child is unique, different, and therefore exceptional in one or more ways.*

In small, close-knit societies, the fact that some children are different is seldom an issue. Not so in societies like ours. Historically, the philosophy has been to keep these individuals apart from the rest of society, to exclude them from most mainstream experiences. Times have changed, however, as we discussed in Section I of this text.

Even so, the underlying issue of distinguishing between those children said to be developing normally and those who are developing atypically continues to plague us. Developmental specialists, teachers, administrators, and policymakers interpret these concepts differently. Definitions of normalcy and exceptionality vary also among physicians, psychologists, and all other professionals associated with the growth and development of young children (Bee & Boyd, 2012).

Lawyers, for example, use their own guidelines to define blindness, while educators use different guidelines. There is little consensus across professions as to which individuals are to be classified as developmentally disabled, who are the gifted and talented, or who are truly normal. The result is confusion for everyone. Confusion increases when everyday words take on connotations. For example, it is argued that *typical* is a more appropriate word than *normal* when describing development. In this text, those common words and others, such as *disabled* and *exceptional*, are used interchangeably.

This chapter will provide practical definitions of typical development and atypical development. Typical development will be discussed first. The rationale is obvious: To work effectively with infants and children with atypical development, teachers must have a thorough knowledge of normal growth and development. The main goal of all early childhood programs should be the improvement of each child's overall development. A parallel goal is the prevention or lessening of developmental problems. Thurman and Widerstrom (1990) advise: "To improve the development of children with special needs we must understand normal development, including the problems that may occur in normal developmental patterns" (p. 11).

What Is Normal, or Typical, Development? 4-1

Normal, or **typical, development** implies an ongoing process of growing, changing, and acquiring a range of complex skills. Beginning in earliest infancy, the process moves along a **developmental continuum** according to a predictable pattern common to most children of the same age. However, the term *normal development* has long been the subject of dispute. What is normal for one child may be quite abnormal for another. For example, many teachers expect children to make eye contact when spoken to, perhaps failing to understand that in the child's own community, children are considered disrespectful if they look directly at the adult who is speaking to them.

In addition to culturally defined differences, there are individual differences among children. No two children grow and develop at the same rate, even within the same family. Some children walk at eight months, others not until eighteen months. Most children begin walking somewhere between those ages. All children within this range, and even a little on either side of it, are normal with respect to walking. Typical development shows great variation and significant differences among children.

normal (typical) development
the process of growing, changing, and acquiring a range of skills at approximately the same age and in the same sequence as the majority of children of similar age

developmental continuum
the range of skills or behaviors among children in any one area of development

4-1a ■ Developmental Sequences

Despite these variations, certain principles serve as guidelines. For example, sequences of normal development are predictable. These predictions are based on detailed observations of hundreds of children at various ages. Early childhood teachers (and experienced parents) know that each child who is typically developing can be expected to progress, step by step, toward mastery of each developmental skill in every area of development.

A developmental disability may not be easy to recognize.

© Cengage Learning 2015

In this process, individual differences emerge. Each child will accomplish the specific steps, but will do so at his or her own rate. Furthermore, no matter how quickly or slowly a child is developing, each preceding step is usually accomplished before practice on the next begins: Most babies roll over before they sit, sit before they stand, and stand before they walk.

Exceptions are common. Most infants crawl before they walk, but some do not; and a few move about by sitting up and hitching forward with one foot. Others lie flat on their back and push with both feet. Such methods of getting about are appropriate, though atypical. Rarely is developmental progress smooth; irregularities and slowdowns are common. Progress in one skill area may actually slow or stop while the child is trying to learn a new skill in a different area of development. For example, the infant who talked early may quit talking for a time while learning to walk. Some children even regress—fall back—under certain conditions (the three-year-old who temporarily loses bladder control with the arrival of a new baby).

4-1b ■ Developmental Milestones

Regardless of the many variations, children acquire specific skills in a fairly predictable order. These significant junctures often are referred to as **developmental milestones**. A child who is seriously delayed in reaching one or more of these milestones needs attention from his or her pediatrician and possibly further screening and assessment, depending on the significance of the delay.

A brief overview of common milestones follows. More detailed profiles are given in the chapters on physical, cognitive, language, and social development. For a comprehensive account of developmental areas, see Appendix B for a skill profile for age 0–72 months or see Marotz and Allen (2012). This skill profile is also available as a Digital Download on CourseMate.

Infancy It was once thought that eating and sleeping were about all the newborn could do. Little or nothing was thought to be going on in the brain. Research has proven otherwise. Within the first days—even hours—of birth, experience begins to influence development. Many of today's **neuroscientists** report that stimulation from even the earliest experiences dramatically increases the number of **synapses** that develop in the brain.

This **neural** activity enables the child to engage in increasingly complex learning, a signal that healthy development is in progress. From everyday observation of very young babies, we also know how quickly they begin to react to their immediate surroundings. They follow a moving object with their eyes. They turn their heads in response to a loud noise. They make a face if they taste something unpleasant. They synchronize their body movements in response to changes in the voice of the person speaking to them. For example, when the voice speeds up, the baby's arms and legs flail about rapidly; when the voice slows, the baby's movements also slow. From earliest infancy, the human face (especially that of the mother or major caregiver) is of great interest to the baby.

Rarely is developmental progress smooth: irregularities and slowdowns are common.

© Cengage Learning 2015

developmental milestones points at which specific skills are acquired in a fairly predictable order

neuroscientists those who study the brain and the nervous system

synapse the contact point between two nerve cells in the brain and nervous system

neural involving the nerves and nervous system

Connecting Developmentally Appropriate Practice to Brain Research

EXPERIENCES AND BRAIN DEVELOPMENT

Common everyday early childhood experiences fuel brain development, often described as "experience-expectant" brain development. Without these critical early experiences, brain development can be stalled. Scientists believe that typical early experiences such as hearing, exposure to language, and coordinating one's movements with vision contribute to the infant's developing brain.

According to Thompson (2001) in his paper *The Future of Children* "the developing brain expects and requires these typical human experiences and relies on them as a component of its growth" (p. 29).

The second form of brain development occurs throughout one's life. "Experience-dependent" brain development refers to each individual's life experience and the impact of one's experiences on brain growth and brain structure. An illustration of this is the comparison of the brain of an artist and the brain of a mathematician. Both have had varied life experiences and have exercised different regions of their brain. Thompson notes these experiences influence neural connections uniquely in each individual as they account for new learning and the development of new skills.

Your Turn

Explain how "experience-expectant" brain development can be impacted by the quality of an early caregiving experience.

Source: Thompson, R.A. (2001). Developing in the first years of life. *The Future of Children*, 11(1), 20–33.

Ross A. Thompson, Ph.D., is a Carl A. Happold Distinguished Professor at the University of Nebraska.

A very young infant tries to imitate facial expressions: sticking out its tongue, pursing its lips, and opening its eyes wider, when the caregiver makes such faces (Meltzoff & Moore, 1983, 1997).

Between four and ten weeks, babies begin social or responsive smiling. The social smile is a major developmental milestone. Absence of social smiling in a twelve-to sixteen-week-old may signal a potentially serious developmental problem.

At two or three months, the infant begins to make social sounds. These sounds, mostly cooing and gurgling, are labeled "social" for two reasons. First, they are made in response to the voice of the person talking to the baby. Second, when initiated by the infant, the sounds may capture and hold the attention of a nearby adult, who usually responds vocally. Thus, the infant learns that he or she can make things happen and can get people to respond. Such **reciprocity**, or "give and take," is essential to the **attachment process**. It also is a major step toward language and social development.

reciprocity the "give-and-take" interactions between a child and others

attachment process building positive and trusting bonds between individuals, usually infant and parent or major caregiver

Learning to drink from a cup is an important milestone.

© Cengage Learning 2015

Reciprocity between the infant and others demonstrates the basic need of infants to have responsive caregivers if they are to develop well. Given a responsive environment, the infant soon is smiling readily and discovers, with delight, that most people smile back. Infants three and four months old also are smiling at objects and even at their own noises and actions.

In addition to smiling, developing infants reach for an object and sometimes manage—usually accidentally—to touch it or make it move. Reaching is a significant milestone, a sign that eye–hand coordination is developing. By five or six months, most infants show trunk control and can roll over. At seven months, many are sitting, some with support, others without. At nine months, a few infants are walking; many more are crawling or showing readiness to crawl.

Cruising (walking while holding on to a low table or other piece of furniture) comes next. Walking often begins at about twelve months, though there are great differences among children. Beginning to walk anywhere between eight and eighteen-to-twenty months is considered typical.

The baby's cognitive development is closely interwoven with motor development. Most child development textbooks present motor, cognitive, social, and language development separately. In real life, however, all developmental areas are interrelated. In early years, language, cognitive, and social skills are intertwined and mutually supportive. Furthermore, all three depend on sound motor skills.

sensorimotor Piaget's term for the first major stage of cognitive development from birth to about eighteen months; infant moves from reflexive to voluntary behavior

The importance of motor skills to healthy development cannot be overemphasized. Piaget began to analyze this relationship more than fifty years ago. He described the first twenty-four months of life as the **sensorimotor** stage: the infant learns by poking, patting, touching, banging, and tasting whatever comes within reach. The older infant is on the move every waking moment, crawling and toddling about, and so experiencing the environment. This early exploring is the foundation for sound cognitive development and intellectual functioning.

▶❚❚ **TeachSource** Video Connections

Language Development for Early Childhood, from 2–5

From ages two to five years children's language develops rapidly. This video discusses some of the changes that occur. The video includes examples of children speaking to illustrate some of the developmental stages, including Caroline, who explains her recent experience with golf and bowling.

After watching the video discuss the following:

1. Discus the term overregulation as it is applied to children's language development.

2. Given all of the changes that occur in language during the preschool years, why is it important for teachers and parents to have knowledge of child development? How could inadequate knowledge possibly lead to unwarranted concerns about a child's language development? Provide an example.

Watch on CourseMate.

Toddlerhood Between eighteen and thirty months, most children are moving about freely. Walking becomes well established during these months, and many children are running skillfully. Most learn to climb stairs but do not yet use alternating feet. Toilet training may or may not be accomplished. Toddlers also work hard at trying to feed and undress themselves, with varying degrees of success.

Toddlers are usually friendly toward others, eager for adult attention, and are becoming less wary of strangers. They are curious about people and whatever is going on, and so must be watched constantly. Property rights come into play; many a red-faced toddler can be heard shrieking, "Mine!" while clutching a chosen toy. Toddlers tend to play alone, although they often watch other children intently and imitate them.

The latter part of toddlerhood can become a major challenge for both child and parent or caregiver. The two-year-old's continuing dependence on adults conflicts with a developmental drive for independence. The result? The toddler's unwillingness to accept limits may lead to tantrums and to the adult's viewing the child as "impossible." Cooperation occurs more frequently as the child develops functional language and basic reasoning skills.

The preschool years Between three and six years of age, basic motor skills are perfected. The typical child learns to run, jump, and climb. Skill in manipulating objects and tools such as paintbrushes, pencils, and crayons grows day by day.

Creativity and imagination color everything from role-playing to telling tall tales. Vocabulary and concept development occur rapidly. The result is a dramatic increase in the ability to express ideas, make judgments, solve problems, and plan ahead. All of these combine to allow the child increasing breadth of movement and thought. This, in turn, leads to increasing independence, and yet, preschool children tend to frequently touch base with important adults.

During the preschool years physical growth is slower, resulting in a reduced need for food. Many parents and caregivers are not aware of this biological shift. They think the child is not well or has become a "picky" eater. They may try to force the child to eat more than he or she needs. Serious conflict can result, creating an unhappy effect on the parent–child or caregiver–child relationship.

Language skills are developing rapidly during the preschool years. It is not unusual, however, for children who were talking well to become less fluent for a while. They may go through a period of stammering or stuttering—a normal developmental irregularity. Usually, this early **dysfluency** disappears unless there is adult pressure to "slow down" or "say it right." Most children are talking freely by six years of age. At this time, a vocabulary of 2,500 words is not uncommon, with the child using most of the grammatical forms of the native language.

dysfluency hesitations, repetitions, omissions, or extra sounds in speech patterns

autonomy self-direction; independence

The preschool child is beginning to understand that he or she is a separate person with a separate identity. This sense of self-directing individuality is the essence of **autonomy**. Toward the end of the preschool years, most children are sharing and taking turns (at least some of the time). Children who have been in group care much of their lives may demonstrate these social skills considerably earlier. Older preschool children usually are beginning to show empathy, that is, an understanding of how another person feels. The notion of "best friends" is taking hold, too.

Skills in manipulating objects such as paintbrushes, pencils, markers, and crayons improve every day during the preschool years.

© Cengage Learning 2015

Case Study ▪ Why are they so restless? ▪

Circle time is the most challenging time of the preschool day for Lisa, a recent college graduate who is new to early childhood education. She struggles with keeping the children engaged and sitting cross-legged for the thirty-minute daily circle.

Some of the preschoolers roll around on the floor, while others can't keep their hands to themselves. Based upon what you know about typical child development, what suggestions would you give Lisa regarding circle time?

The primary-school years Children at this stage are becoming amazingly competent. They can take care of most of their personal needs: dressing, bathing, eating, getting ready for bed, even grooming. Dawdling is still an issue between many a parent and child. In most cases, the dawdling lessens with a developing awareness of time and the consequences of being late. In fact, fear of being late promotes a general anxiety about school in many children.

Learning to read is the major developmental task in the primary-school years. It requires:

- learning to sit still for longer periods of time.
- learning to listen attentively.
- learning to recognize and discriminate (tell the difference between) letter sounds and letter shapes.

Reversal of letter shapes and sounds is a common irregularity. It tends to disappear spontaneously, although a few children may need special help. What is remarkable is that most children do acquire complex literacy skills and are soon taking their ability to read for granted.

Having friends and being sought out as a friend is important. "Best friends" are seen as desirable but tend to come and go easily. By seven or eight, most children enjoy group and team activities. Again, allegiances may be short-lived.

What about a child who is developing typically in some areas but has a delay or disability in another area? What about children with physical problems who cannot walk, much less run and jump and climb? Many of these children are developing typically otherwise, and they may even be gifted in language, intellectual, or artistic development. Let us next look at these children and others with developmental differences.

Did You Get It?

What helps early childhood educators and experienced parents determine whether a child is developing typically?
a. Individual differences between children.
b. Great variation exists.
c. Guidelines drawn from predictions based on detailed observations of hundreds of children at various ages.
d. Instinct.

Take the full quiz on CourseMate.

✺ 4-2 What Is Atypical or Exceptional Development?

Classifying children as "exceptional," or "developing atypically," presents ongoing problems. At one time, the term *exceptional* was all-inclusive, referring to children with the mildest of speech differences to those who were outstandingly brilliant (but *different*) as in the case of so-called **savants**.

In the 1960s, children who were noticeably different—either physically or mentally—were referred to as "crippled" or "retarded." Society provided "homes for crippled children" and "institutions for the feeble-minded"— common terms in those days. Years later, terms that covered a broader but more individualized

savant an individual who is unusually knowledgeable about one particular subject but is lacking in other areas of cognitive skill

range of disabilities came into use. *Behavior-disordered, learning-disabled, mentally deficient*, along with *handicapped, deviant*, and so on, were common. Individual identities were locked into their differences: *he's Down syndrome; she's autistic.* Now we vigorously oppose such terms when describing a given individual.

For example, statements such as "She is a learning-disabled child" highlight the problem rather than the child. By contrast, "The child has a learning disability" puts the focus on the child. If we put the person before the disability, our statements define what the person has, not what the person is (Snow, 2009). This word order and terminology are referred to as **people-first language** (PFL).

The *people-first* approach highlights a fundamental assumption of inclusion: All children are children and our practices should reflect that reality (Wolery & Wilbers, 1994). Figure 4-1 provides examples of how to use person-first language (Snow, 2009). It should be noted, however, that the appropriateness of terms and the way individuals are described will continue to change over time. It is important for individuals in the field of education to remain aware of such changes throughout their career.

people-first language/ terminology in referring to people with disabilities, language that speaks of the person first and then the disability; for example, "a child with autism" rather than "an autistic child" emphasizes abilities rather than limitations

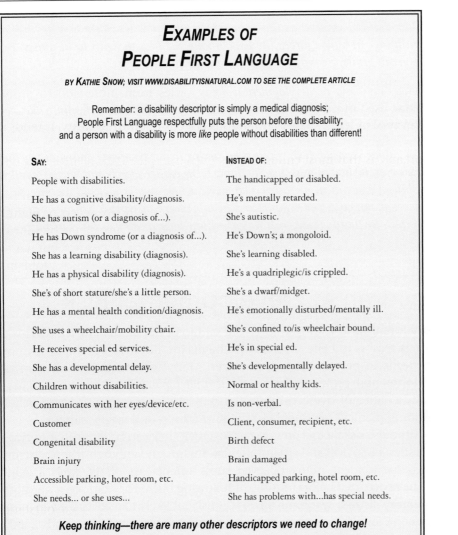

FIGURE 4-1
Examples of How to Use People-First Language (PFL)

EXAMPLES OF PEOPLE FIRST LANGUAGE

BY KATHIE SNOW; VISIT WWW.DISABILITYISNATURAL.COM TO SEE THE COMPLETE ARTICLE

Remember: a disability descriptor is simply a medical diagnosis; People First Language respectfully puts the person before the disability; and a person with a disability is more *like* people without disabilities than different!

SAY:	INSTEAD OF:
People with disabilities.	The handicapped or disabled.
He has a cognitive disability/diagnosis.	He's mentally retarded.
She has autism (or a diagnosis of...).	She's autistic.
He has Down syndrome (or a diagnosis of...).	He's Down's; a mongoloid.
She has a learning disability (diagnosis).	She's learning disabled.
He has a physical disability (diagnosis).	He's a quadriplegic/is crippled.
She's of short stature/she's a little person.	She's a dwarf/midget.
He has a mental health condition/diagnosis.	He's emotionally disturbed/mentally ill.
She uses a wheelchair/mobility chair.	She's confined to/is wheelchair bound.
He receives special ed services.	He's in special ed.
She has a developmental delay.	She's developmentally delayed.
Children without disabilities.	Normal or healthy kids.
Communicates with her eyes/device/etc.	Is non-verbal.
Customer	Client, consumer, recipient, etc.
Congenital disability	Birth defect
Brain injury	Brain damaged
Accessible parking, hotel room, etc.	Handicapped parking, hotel room, etc.
She needs... or she uses...	She has problems with...has special needs.

Keep thinking—there are many other descriptors we need to change!

Excerpted from Kathie's People First Language article, available at www.disabilityisnatural.com.

Early childhood educators were among the first to argue against the word *handicapped*. The term was virtually written out of the early intervention segment of PL 99–457. In its stead, the law uses terms such as *developmental delay* and *developmental disability*. The change in terminology promotes the concept that young children with atypical characteristics resemble all children in their *potential* for growth and development. It also emphasizes that many young children who are atypical in one way or another resemble other children more than they differ from them. With few exceptions, all children go through the same sequence of development, although at different rates.

Many infants and young children who start out with serious delays overcome them if they receive appropriate early intervention services. Low-birth-weight infants, who may also be premature, are a good example. With adequate care, by age five most are looking like and performing like all other five-year-olds.

Some impairments, even though serious, may never interfere with developmental progress. The condition may continue, but the child and family find ways to compensate and to function normally despite it.

> *Bret was born with one short arm and malformed hand. At preschool, Bret could do as well as any other child with puzzles, form boards, or block building. In kindergarten, he was among the first to learn to tie shoes. By seventh grade, he was a champion soccer player.*

The diagnosis of *developmental delay* varies from profession to profession. Delay, as used in this text, is said to exist when *a child is performing like a child of a much younger age who is typically developing*, as in the following example.

> *As a three-year-old, Josh was just beginning to put two-word sentences together. However, he had moved steadily through the earlier speech and language milestones. Clinical assessment indicated a language delay: language would continue to develop, but on a somewhat later schedule than was typical. This prediction proved correct. By fourth grade, Josh was using language as ably as his classmates.*

Did You Get It?

What is the current preferred method of referring an individual in terms of classification?

a. Exceptional or developing atypically.

b. Behavior disordered or learning disabled.

c. He or she is a learning-disabled child.

d. The child has a learning disability.

Take the full quiz on CourseMate.

☀ 4-3 Children at Developmental Risk

at risk indications (either physical or environmental) that an infant or child may develop serious problems

Many infants and young children are said to be **at risk** or *at high risk*. This means there is reason to believe serious problems are likely to develop. An important fact needs to be emphasized, however: Many infants and children at risk for developmental problems *have the potential for healthy development*. They have a good chance of overcoming initial setbacks with early intervention services, including medical treatment, ample nurturance, and family support.

Although risk factors often occur together, they can be grouped into two major categories: biological and environmental. Infants and children whose systems have undergone accident, injury, or severe stress suffer *biological risk factors*. The incident may have occurred before, during, or following birth. For example, a newborn with **respiratory distress syndrome (RDS)** is at risk but likely to recover if given immediate treatment. Similarly, premature birth or low birth weight (5.12 pounds/2500 grams or less) are risk factors that require immediate, intensive intervention. Without such intervention, many infants suffer severe developmental problems.

respiratory distress syndrome (RDS) a problem commonly found among premature infants caused by immature lung development; may also occur in about 1 percent of full-term infants during the first days of life

chromosomal disorder developmental problem that comes about at the time of conception

Other biological risk factors include genetic and **chromosomal disorders**, such as Down syndrome and Fragile X syndrome. Heart defects are present in about

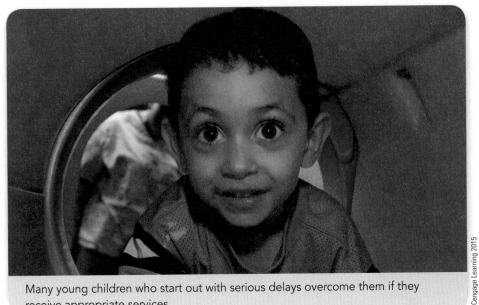

Many young children who start out with serious delays overcome them if they receive appropriate services.

© Cengage Learning 2015

cardiac problems those that involve the heart in terms of physical damage or poor functioning

resilience the ability to "come back" after a damaging or traumatic experience

vulnerability lack of resistance or ability to recover from a damaging or traumatic experience

45 percent of infants born with Down syndrome. Without correction, many of these children will die of **cardiac problems** during infancy or early childhood. Biological risk factors will be discussed further in Chapter 5.

The term *environmental risk factors* refers to things in the child's everyday world that have a negative effect on development. Poverty produces many kinds of risk conditions. However, poverty is not the only environmental situation that puts infants and young children at risk. Other conditions include child abuse and neglect, unfit living conditions created by addicted or diseased family members, religious or cultural beliefs that prohibit urgently needed medical treatment or surgery, and lack of access to medical care (as when families live in remote mountain or rural areas).

Resilience and vulnerability Biology and environment (nature/nurture) may not interact in the same way for every child. The degree of inborn **resilience** or **vulnerability** appears to make a difference. Horowitz (1990) concludes that given a facilitative environment, vulnerable children often have a good developmental outcome. Resilient children in a poor environment also may do quite well because they learn to use the resources available to them. However, the vulnerable child raised in an unfavorable environment is in double jeopardy and is almost sure to be in developmental trouble.

4-3a ■ Children with Special Gifts and Talents

Children are described as gifted or talented or both when they do exceptionally well in one or more areas of development. They often are a good fit

Chromosomal disorders include Fragile X syndrome.

© Cengage Learning 2015

with the concept of *multiple intelligences*. Gardner (2006) theorizes eight types of intelligence: linguistic, logical-mathematical, musical, spatial, **bodily kinesthetic**, interpersonal, intrapersonal, and naturalist. These gifted or talented children's accomplishments seem to appear spontaneously, as a part of their unique development. It is unlikely that these early and outstanding abilities emerge because of special training or parental pressure. Parents of especially bright or talented children often are surprised when told of their child's remarkable abilities (Robinson, 1981).

Gifted and talented students may be at risk if they do not receive adequate services to meet their needs. However, unlike the Individuals with Disabilities Education Improvement Act (IDEA), federal legislation does not require specific services for gifted and talented students. The programs that do exist vary and are determined at the state and local levels.

Characteristics of young gifted children The characteristics that identify young gifted children appear to be a combination of advanced verbal skills, curiosity, and the ability to concentrate, learn rapidly, and enjoy problem solving. In addition, researchers have identified the following characteristics (Clark, 2007; Coleman & Cross, 2005; Renzulli et al., 2002; Roedell, 1980; Rogers, 2001):

- detailed memory
- large vocabulary and experimentation with new words
- invention of songs, stories, and rhymes; play with the sound and rhythm of words
- asking intelligent questions
- learning information quickly
- use of logic in arriving at commonsense answers
- a broad base of knowledge—a large quantity of information
- understanding of abstract concepts such as time, family relationships, cause and effect, and connections between past and present
- complex classification and discrimination skills; spontaneous grouping of items such as toy cars, boats, airplanes, and trucks; arranging objects according to size and color
- finding and solving difficult and unusual problems
- curiosity, wanting to learn
- absorption in particular topics, such as dinosaurs, astronomy, animals, mechanical objects
- good orientation skills and sense of spatial relationships
- awareness of what is new and different in the environment: rearrangement of equipment, a teacher's new hairstyle
- awareness of the feelings of others; commenting when a teacher is not feeling well or another child appears withdrawn

Demonstration of complex classification and discrimination skills is just one characteristic of gifted children.

© Cengage Learning 2015

bodily-kinesthetic awareness of the body's position and movement

Children with developmental disabilities who are gifted An often-overlooked fact is that a child with a disability may be gifted. A child with a learning disability may have superior intelligence or outstanding artistic or mechanical talents. The same is true of children with hearing impairments, cerebral palsy, or any other disability. The potential for intellectual or artistic giftedness in these children seldom receives much attention. Education tends to be narrowly focused on helping overcome physical or sensory deficits. Students with both a disability and giftedness may use their talent and or intelligence to compensate for their disability. This may make both their disability and their giftedness seem less extreme (Willard-Holt, 1999).

As Gallagher (1988) points out, rarely do we search for giftedness in special populations. Identifying gifted children with developmental delays may be difficult. Wolfle (1989) suggests direct observation in a natural setting. The importance of this recommendation is underscored by the following story, told by a teacher of four-year-olds in an inclusion preschool: Benjamin, blind since birth, had developed unusual and repetitive behaviors sometimes observed in young children

Many students with impairments have high potential for both intellectual and creative achievement.

© Cengage Learning 2015

Linguistic and Cultural Diversity Connections

Gifted Minority-Language Children

It should be noted that most of the clues to giftedness are related—directly or indirectly—to language. Bright children from minority cultures and different ethnic backgrounds often are not recognized because they lack middle-class language skills. Most procedures to identify gifted and talented students were developed for use with middle-class students who are native English speakers (Cohen, 1990). The over-reliance on standardized testing, a narrow definition of giftedness, and the policies and procedures that guide local and state programs also have led to the under-identification of gifted children from culturally/linguistically diverse and/or economically disadvantaged families, as well as gifted children with disabilities (Coleman, 2003). Other influences work against the identification of gifted minority preschoolers. Karnes and Johnson (1989) note several discriminatory factors in our social-educational system:

- a prevalent attitude that giftedness does not exist among children from low-income backgrounds
- a definition of giftedness that reflects only the majority culture's values
- the use of identification procedures that are unfavorable to low-income and minority children
- the provision of few opportunities for enhancing intellectual or artistic achievement in minority children

Clearly, there are gifted children in every ethnic and racial group at all socioeconomic levels. Appropriate preschool education for children without economic advantages is an important means of identifying and nurturing those with special gifts and talents (Stile & Kitano, 1991).

It is important to fund early intervention programs that provide training in identifying and nurturing young gifted children from every socioeconomic level.

who cannot see. His preschool teachers noted, however, that the strange behaviors stopped whenever there was music in the classroom. Benjamin appeared to listen intently and always asked for more. One teacher began sitting down with Benjamin with musical instruments: a ukulele, an autoharp, a recorder. After a brief period of experimentation, Benjamin would "find" tunes on the instruments.

Next the teacher took him to a classroom that had a piano. Again, with only limited exploration, Benjamin began to improvise simple tunes. The teacher shared these experiences with Benjamin's parents, who were able to buy a piano. Benjamin spent hours at the piano and became an eager piano student. By age sixteen, he was regarded as a gifted young pianist.

Many young children with impairments have high potential for both intellectual and creative achievement. Karnes and Johnson (1989) argue that it is important for our nation to fund early intervention programs that provide training in identifying and nurturing young gifted children from every socioeconomic level. With appropriate learning opportunities, minority children and children with all kinds of impairments can be helped to realize their potential (Kirk & Gallagher, 2008).

Did You Get It?

What is Horowitz's (1990) view of resilience or vulnerability?
a. Biology and environment may not interact in the same way for every child.
b. Vulnerable children often have a good developmental outcome when given a facilitative environment.
c. Vulnerability of children living in remote mountain or rural areas.
d. There are different degrees of resilience.

Take the full quiz on CourseMate.

Summary

▶ The definition of "typical" or "atypical" development varies among communities, school districts, and professions. Typical development is a complex process and includes such a wide range of developmental skills. Guidelines are available, however. These include knowledge of developmental sequences, developmental milestones, and the interrelatedness of developmental areas.

▶ Deciding what is atypical development raises complex issues and is equally difficult. Therefore, a thorough knowledge of normal growth and development is necessary to understand and work with all children.

▶ Because young children constantly change, they should be thought of as having a developmental delay or difference—not a handicap. One reflection of this change in approach is the movement toward people-first language: giving the individual precedence over his or her disability.

▶ Children at developmental risk are likely to develop delays if they do not receive special services as early as possible. Risk factors—biological, environmental, or both—may occur prenatally, at birth, or during the early developmental years.

▶ Gifted and talented children are those with exceptionally advanced skills in one or more areas of development. Potentially gifted children from cultural minorities and low-income families often are not identified because of restricted learning opportunities and socially biased identification procedures.

▶ Many children with developmental disabilities also are gifted, but their potential may go unidentified because of cultural or educational biases.

Key Terms

at risk, 88
attachment process, 83
atypical development, 80
autonomy, 85
bodily kinesthetic, 90
cardiac problem, 89
chromosomal disorders, 88
developmental continuum, 81

developmental milestones, 82
dysfluency, 85
exceptional children, 80
neural, 82
neuroscientists, 82
normal (typical) development, 81
pathologist, 80
people-first language, 87

reciprocity, 83
resilience, 89
respiratory distress
    syndrome (RDS), 88
savant, 86
sensorimotor, 84
synapse, 82
vulnerability, 89

Student Activities

1. Provide three justifications of the following statement: To work effectively with children who have developmental problems, teachers need a thorough knowledge of normal growth and development.

2. Think about a time a friend or classmate referred to someone as "retarded." Given what you know about person-first language and sensitivity to others, how would you handle the situation if you were the teacher and heard such a statement?

3. Observe a group of preschool children. Make two lists: 1) list examples of what you believe may be atypical development or behavior; 2) list any curriculum expectations that you feel are developmentally inappropriate.

4. Have you or any of your brothers, sisters, friends, or relatives been described as gifted or talented? Describe the exceptional characteristics that led to such a label.

Review Questions

Define and give an example of each of the following terms.

1. developmental milestone
2. developmental continuum
3. normal development
4. developmental delay
5. atypical development
6. biological risk
7. people-first language
8. nurturance
9. irreversible developmental problem
10. gifted child

Additional Resources/Readings

It's Okay to Be Different
Written by Todd Parr
Little, Brown Books for Young Readers

It's *Okay to Be Different* delivers the important messages of acceptance, understanding, and confidence. The illustrations use bold and bright colors. This book designed for young children will help them learn to celebrate their own individuality through acceptance of others. This book is great for reading to a class and then asking the children to share their own uniqueness either through art or in discussion with a paired classmate. Many lesson plans using this book are available by searching on the Internet.

Helpful Websites

The Council for Exceptional Children (CEC)

http://www.cec.sped.org

The CEC publishes *Exceptional Children* and *Teaching Exceptional Children*. Of particular interest to early childhood education is one of CEC's affiliate groups: the Division for Early Childhood Education. (A number of other divisions also focus to some extent on issues related to young children.)

Disability Is Natural

http://www.disabilityisnatural.com

This website provides commonsense articles about the importance of thinking differently about individuals with disabilities. The focus is on person-first language (PFL) and developing an inclusive society.

National Association for the Education of Young Children (NAEYC)

http://www.naeyc.org

NAEYC's website includes a resource catalog, professional development materials, and links to related sites. Of note is the NAEYC position statement on standardized testing of young children ages three through eight (adopted in 1987 by NAEYC).

The Society for Research in Child Development (SRCD)

http://www.srcd.org

SCRD is an interdisciplinary organization that publishes the journal *Child Development*, as well as monographs, abstracts, and bibliographies.

 Visit the Education CourseMate for this textbook to access the eBook, Did You Get It? quizzes, Digital Downloads, TeachSource Video Cases, flashcards, and more. Go to CengageBrain.com to log in, register, or purchase access.

Developmental Disabilities: Causes and Classifications

OBJECTIVES

After reading this chapter, you should be able to:

5-1   specify several possible causes of developmental differences and give examples of causes both prior to and after birth.

5-2   describe and understand the classifications of developmental disabilities.

. . . .

![naeyc]

The following NAEYC Standards are addressed in this chapter:

STANDARD 1 Promoting Child Development and Learning

STANDARD 3 Observing, Documenting and Assessing to Support Young Children and Families

STANDARD 4 Using Developmentally Effective Approaches

CONNECTIONS

- Graham and Bart are three-year-olds with similarly diagnosed hearing loss. Graham is talking almost at age level. Bart has two distinguishable words among the songs and signs that he makes.

- As a newborn, Noah was characterized as a "floppy baby"; that is, he had little muscle tone. Therapists have worked with Noah and his parents since early infancy. His condition has not been specifically diagnosed.

- Clarrissa is four and only speaks one or two words. She communicates using signs and gestures.

Clinicians and parents endlessly ponder the causes of many types of developmental differences.

What causes developmental problems?

Should we assign a disability category to young children with atypical developmental patterns?

These two questions, of significant concern to everyone working with young children, have no agreed-upon answers. Despite years of research and discussion, lack of agreement continues because of varying professional and legal viewpoints. There are no ready answers. The best response is that the causes of developmental differences appear to be a combination of interacting events: heredity, biology (physical makeup), temperament (personality), and a long list of environmental factors, including poverty. This again raises the heredity versus environment issue. Neuroscientists have found that, throughout the entire developmental process, the brain is affected by the environment. According to Shore (2003), "A great deal of new research leads to this conclusion: how humans develop and learn depends critically on the interplay between nature (an individual's genetic endowment) and nurture (the nutrition, surroundings, care, responsiveness, and teaching that are provided or withheld). All are crucial" (p. x).

In addition, the **behavior geneticists** argue, children are born with particular types of temperaments that shape the environment around them. Some children may actually create for themselves a more responsive learning environment because of their more responsive temperaments. Deciding on a developmentally appropriate category of exceptionality in a young child is equally baffling and just as controversial. The range of both normalcy and individual differences is broad. Furthermore, most young children experience one or more developmental irregularities that may or may not require special attention. More harm than good comes from prematurely classifying or labeling a child.

behavior geneticist an individual who seeks to understand both the genetic and environmental contributions to individual variations in human behavior

Children themselves have an influence on their own environments.

© Cengage Learning 2015

Causes of Developmental Differences 5-1 ☀

Whatever the cause of a developmental disability, the harm can occur at any stage of development. (See Figure 5-1 for characteristics of typical fetal development.) A condition present at the time of birth is termed **congenital**. Congenital problems may or may not be genetic.

Let's take deafness as an example. Deafness in a child may have been caused by an infection the mother had during early pregnancy. In another child, it may be linked to deafness in the child's parents. Some disabilities are recognized at birth; others may not be detected or do not become apparent until much later. Generally, the more severe the disability, the earlier it is recognized. Exceptions are many, however. For example, a serious hearing loss may not be discovered until the child starts school.

There is indisputable evidence that biology and environment act together to produce both atypical and typical development. It is nearly impossible to isolate one or the other as the single cause of a developmental problem. In every instance, environmental factors act on inborn traits and characteristics to determine developmental outcome. Furthermore, as behavior geneticists point out, children themselves exert influence on the environment. A healthy infant virtually hooks parents into responding. Strong, early bonding is the usual result. A sickly, low-birth-weight infant may not be able to interact or may respond inconsistently.

congenital describes a developmental condition or deviation present at the time of birth that may or may not be genetically related

5-1a ■ Biological Factors

Biology plays a major role in determining both healthy and less-than-healthy development. **Biological insult** refers to interference with or without damage to an individual's physical structure or functioning. The insult may occur at the time of conception, with resulting genetic disorders. It may occur during pregnancy, often within the first trimester (initial twelve weeks of pregnancy), and it may be related to health problems in the mother. The fetus is especially vulnerable during the first trimester (D'Alton & Decherney, 1993). Insults also can happen at the time of birth or any time during childhood.

biological insult a term that describes interference with or damage to an individual's physical structure or functioning

Genetic disorders The fertilized egg has forty-six chromosomes: twenty-two pairs of autosomes (non-sex chromosomes) and two chromosomes that determine the child's gender (xx in a girl, xy in a boy). During repeated divisions and recombinations of chromosomal material, an embryo forms, containing the unique genetic combination that will determine the individual's characteristics. Physical characteristics such as size, body build, and eye and skin color have thus been decided, as have any genetically determined abnormalities.

Genetic disorders resulting in abnormal biological development may be caused by deviations in chromosomal structure or by abnormal single genes. Chromosomal abnormalities are usually biological accidents; that is, they are one-time occurrences and do not affect future pregnancies. They occur in all races with similar frequency.

Single-gene defects, on the other hand, are hereditary and often show racial variations. Many inconsequential physical deviations (such as a web between the second and third toes) pass through generations as an **autosomal dominant gene** carried on one of the 44 chromosomes. A few disorders causing serious developmental disabilities show this kind of inheritance. However, in most single-gene disorders, both parents are healthy carriers of the same abnormal gene. Statistically, one in four of their children will be affected by an **autosomal recessive gene disorder**.

genetic disorder a disorder caused by alteration in the chromosomal materials that control inherited characteristics

autosomal dominant gene disorder a gene on any chromosome except the sex chromosomes that, if inherited from either parent, results in a child with a medical condition

autosomal recessive gene disorder a gene carried by healthy parents on any chromosome except the sex chromosomes that, if inherited from both parents, results in a child with a medical condition not present in the parents

FIGURE 5-1

Typical Fetal Development

2 weeks
- Cell division results in an embryo consisting of sixteen cells.

3–8 weeks
- Structures necessary to support the developing embryo have formed: placenta, chorionic sac, amniotic fluid, and umbilical cord.
- Embryonic cell layers begin to specialize, developing into major internal organs and systems, as well as external structures.
- First bone cells appear.
- Less than 1 inch (2.54 cm) in length at 8 weeks.

12 weeks
- Weighs approximately 1 to 2 ounces (0.029–0.006 kg) and is nearly 3 inches (7.6 cm) in length.
- Sex organs develop; baby's gender can be determined.
- Kidneys begin to function.
- Arms, legs, fingers, and toes are well defined and movable.
- Forms facial expressions (e.g., smiling, looking around) and is able to suck and swallow.

16 weeks
- Weighs about 5 ounces (0.14 kg) and is 6 inches (15.2 cm) in length.
- Sucks thumb.
- Moves about actively; mother may begin to feel baby's movement (called "quickening").
- Has strong heartbeat that can be heard.

20 weeks
- Weighs nearly 1 pound (0.46 kg) and has grown to approximately 11 to 12 inches (27.9–30.5 cm) in length (approximately half of baby's birth length).
- Experiences occasional hiccups.
- Eyelashes, eyebrows, and hair forming; eyes remain closed.

24 weeks
- Weight doubles to about 1.5 to 2 pounds (0.68–0.90 kg) and length increases to 12 to 14 inches (30.5–35.6 cm).
- Eyes are well formed, often open; responds to light and sound.
- Grasp reflex develops.
- Skin is wrinkled, thin, and covered with soft hair called lanugo and a white, greasy, protective substance called *vernix caseosa*.

28 weeks
- Weighs about 3 to 3.5 pounds (1.4–1.6 kg); has grown to approximately 16 to 17 inches (40.6–43 cm) in length.
- Develops a sleep/wake pattern.
- Remains very active; kicks and pokes mother's ribs and abdomen.
- Able to survive if born prematurely, although lungs are not yet fully developed.

32 weeks
- Weighs approximately 5 to 6 pounds (2.3–2.7 kg) and is 17 to 18 inches in length (43–45.7 cm).
- Baby takes iron and calcium from mother's diet to build up reserve stores.
- Becomes less active as a result of larger size and less room for moving about.

36–38 weeks
- Weighs an average of 7 to 8 pounds (3.2–3.6 kg); length is approximately 19 to 21 inches (48–53.3 cm).
- Moves into final position (usually head down) in preparation for birth.
- Loses most of lanugo (body hair); skin still somewhat wrinkled and red.
- Is much less active (has little room in which to move).
- Body systems are more mature (especially the lungs and heart), increasing baby's chances of survival at birth.

TeachSource Digital Download Download from CourseMate.

Sometimes the mother unknowingly carries an abnormal gene on one of her two x chromosomes. If a son inherits that x chromosome, he will be affected by the inherited **sex-linked gene disorder**. Statistically, half of the woman's sons will be affected.

Syndromes Syndromes are a major class of genetic abnormalities. **Syndrome** refers to a grouping of similar physical characteristics called **stigmata**. When several stigmata are found together in a recognizable pattern, the child is said to have a syndrome. Often the syndrome is named after the person who first described its unique combination of characteristics.

Down syndrome The most widely recognized syndrome is Down syndrome, also known as Trisomy 21. The individual with this syndrome has forty-seven rather than forty-six chromosomes. On chromosome 21, there is an extra chromosome, hence the term Trisomy 21. Usually the extra chromosome is contributed by the egg, but in about 25 percent of cases it comes from the sperm. Trisomy 21 occurs with an estimated prevalence of 9.2 cases per 10,000 live births in the United States. The risk for a woman aged twenty is one in 2,000 births and increases in women over forty-five to one in twenty births (Roizen, 2002). The physical stigmata that make Down syndrome readily recognizable include:

- small round head, flattened in the back
- profile characterized by a flat mid-face
- curving skin folds at the inner corners of the eyes
- small ears
- short stature
- short fingers with little fingers curving inward
- **simian crease** on the palms of one or both hands

About 50 percent of children with Down syndrome have congenital defects. Heart and intestinal abnormalities, often life-threatening, are common. Hearing impairments owing to frequent ear infections (otitis media) also are prevalent. Cognitive delays, ranging from mild to severe, typically become apparent as the children grow older.

Fragile X syndrome **Fragile X syndrome** was first described as a structural abnormality on the X chromosome of some males with a developmental disability. Boys inherit the X chromosome from their mothers (and the Y chromosome from their fathers). This disorder, therefore, often shows a sex-linked pattern, with one mother having more than one affected son even if the sons have different fathers. The mother and her daughters are partially protected by having another normal X chromosome. The presence of a Fragile X can cause some disability in both sexes, but boys tend to be much more seriously impaired physically, mentally, and behaviorally.

An estimated 5 to 7 percent of intellectual disabilities in males may be due to Fragile X syndrome (Zigler & Hodapp, 1991). This condition is the leading known familial cause of intellectual

sex-linked gene disorder a gene carried on one of the two X chromosomes in a female; if inherited by a daughter, the gene confers an asymptomatic carrier state, as with her mother; if it is inherited by a son, the gene results in a medical condition not present in other family members

syndrome a grouping of similar physical characteristics

stigmata an identifying mark or characteristic; a diagnostic sign of a disease or disability

simian crease a single transverse crease on the palm of one or both hands (instead of the typical two creases on the palm)

Fragile X syndrome a chromosomal abnormality associated with intellectual disability, affects more males than females; behavioral characteristics often resemble autism

Biology plays a major role in determining both healthy and less-than healthy development.

© Cengage Learning 2015

disabilities in the United States. A wide range of symptoms are associated with Fragile X, including language delays, behavioral problems, autism or autism-like behavior (including poor eye contact and hand flapping), large or prominent ears, hyperactivity, delayed motor development, and/or poor sensory skills (WebMD.com, 2010).

Metabolic disorders **Metabolic disorders** cause a breakdown in the complex chemical activities needed to **metabolize** food. The breakdown can destroy, damage, or alter cells. Metabolic disorders are single-gene defects, such as PKU, described here.

PKU (phenylketonuria), which occurs about once in every 10,000 births, is a disorder caused by an autosomal recessive gene common in people of Northern European ancestry and uncommon among African Americans. The infant born with PKU lacks an **enzyme** that breaks down the **amino acid** phenylalanine, present in milk, wheat, eggs, fish, and meat. The mother's normal metabolism protects the fetus before birth, but as soon as the infant is fed milk, toxic substances build up, leading to irreversible brain damage. Today, all newborns are routinely screened for this disorder through a simple blood test. If PKU is discovered, a formula low in phenylalanine is immediately prescribed. A restricted diet (many substitute products have been developed) must be continued throughout the developmental period. It is recommended that affected females stay on the diet throughout their childbearing years. If an affected woman does not do so, any baby she carries will be severely brain damaged, having been exposed to an abnormal metabolic environment *in utero*. The control of PKU demonstrates how environmental manipulation can modify genetic disorders successfully. This breakthrough has become a model for prevention of intellectual disabilities in other metabolic disorders.

5-1b ■ Abnormal Gene Disorders

The following are some specific examples of abnormal gene disorders:

Tay Sachs Tay Sachs is a rare autosomal recessive disorder occurring most commonly in children of Eastern European Jewish descent. In this disorder, a faulty enzyme of fat metabolism is the culprit. Fatty accumulations in the brain interfere with **neurological** processes. The result is rapid degeneration, leading to death in early childhood.

Cystic fibrosis Cystic fibrosis (CF) is a common autosomal recessive disorder that causes a buildup of mucus in the lungs, digestive system, and other organs. It is a chronic health disorder that often interferes with the child's learning because of frequent absences from school. It does not, however, affect the brain directly. Although this is a fatal disorder, improved medical therapy now enables many individuals to live well into adulthood.

Sickle-cell anemia A disorder of the red blood cells characterizes this autosomal recessive disorder that mostly affects African Americans. Painful joints, ulcers, and susceptibility to infections make it a serious chronic health disorder in young children.

Duchenne muscular dystrophy Duchenne's is a sex-linked disorder that occurs in males. The muscles waste away, causing increased physical disability and eventually death. Progress has been made in identifying this and many other

---

metabolic disorder a breakdown somewhere in the complex chemicals needed to metabolize food

metabolize the chemical process within living cells by which energy is manufactured so that body systems can carry out their functions

enzyme complex protein that produces specific biological-chemical reactions in the body

amino acid the chief component of proteins; obtained from the individual's diet or manufactured by living cells

neurological referring to the nerves and the nervous system in general

genetic disorders in families identified as otherwise healthy. The fact that parents are carriers of a genetic disorder becomes evident when they have their first affected child. Such families can then be offered counseling on reproductive choices.

5-1c ■ Prenatal Infections and Intoxicants

Most developmental abnormalities, especially those that occur prenatally, cannot be explained by genetics. It is estimated that no more than 3 percent of all birth defects are purely genetic in origin. Diseases that have a negative effect on a mother's health during pregnancy are responsible for 25 percent or more of all developmental deviations.

Some of the more common prenatal diseases include the following.

- *Rubella (German or three-day measles)*. This illness can have a devastating effect on the unborn infant. If contracted during the first trimester, rubella can lead to severe and lifelong disabilities. Childhood immunizations have now drastically reduced the incidence of congenital rubella.

- *CMV virus (cytomegalic inclusion disease)*. If a pregnant woman contracts CMV, the infant can be seriously harmed. Often the pregnant woman has no symptoms. Ninety percent of CMV infants are **asymptomatic** at birth; that is, they show no abnormalities. It is only later that intellectual disability, deafness, diseases of the eyes, and other disabilities begin to show up.

  > **asymptomatic** showing no signs of a disease or impairment that nevertheless may be present

- *Herpes simplex*. This is an incurable viral disorder that can cause recurring severe-to-mild genital sores in adults. Even in **remission**, a woman can pass it on to her unborn infant. Results can be devastating, even fatal, as in cases of inflammation of the infant's brain and spinal cord. Less damaging results include periodic attacks of genital sores.

  > **remission** in reference to health problems, temporary or permanent relief from the problem

- *AIDS (acquired immune deficiency syndrome)*. AIDS interferes with the body's ability to ward off diseases such as respiratory disorders and certain types of cancer. AIDS is transmitted through sexual contact, shared hypodermic needles, or blood transfusions. An infected mother can pass AIDS to her unborn infant.

- *Diabetes*. Maternal diabetes puts the infant at high risk for serious developmental problems, even death. Today's diabetic woman has a better chance of bearing a healthy baby because of medical advances. Nevertheless, maternal diabetes must be monitored throughout pregnancy.

- *Preeclampsia (toxemia)*. This is a serious medical condition that usually occurs after twenty weeks of pregnancy. It is characterized by elevated blood pressure and the presence of excess protein in the urine. If left untreated, toxemia can lead to complications and death in both mother and infant.

Alcohol and other drugs Maternal use of any chemical substance during pregnancy, whether for medicinal or recreational purposes, can damage the unborn infant. Alcohol consumption, even in moderate amounts, has been linked to a variety of developmental problems now grouped under two headings: fetal alcohol syndrome (FAS) and fetal alcohol effect (FAE). Years of research by Streissguth, Barr, and Sampson (1990) indicate that the potential for a subnormal IQ is three times greater among children whose mothers drink during pregnancy.

These researchers report that even occasional binge drinking can be extremely damaging to the fetus. It is not known whether there is a safe amount of maternal alcohol consumption. In light of such incomplete knowledge about alcohol and fetal damage, the only safe course is for a woman to refrain from drinking during pregnancy.

A number of drugs used by pregnant women for medicinal purposes can also cause serious birth defects. *Pregnant women should take no medication without consulting a physician.* This is particularly important in terms of over-the-counter drugs. Illegal drugs (cocaine, for example, and its many variants) used during pregnancy can put the unborn infant at high risk for both short-term and long-range developmental problems. Many such infants are born prematurely, have low birth weight, or are stillborn; still others die of sudden infant death syndrome (SIDS) during their first year. Many more suffer neurological damage that may not show up until years later as a serious learning disability (Keith et al., 1989). Again, it is not known how much drug use during pregnancy is too much. As with alcohol, the best thing a woman can do for her baby while she is pregnant is to completely abstain from drug use, unless prescribed by a physician.

In the past decade, there has been a tremendous amount of attention given to understanding the effects of cocaine use by pregnant women on their unborn children. As stated earlier, no drug is completely safe for a developing fetus. Children who are exposed to cocaine prenatally are often underweight, have smaller head circumferences, and are at greater risk for developmental delays than children who have not been exposed. These delays are seen in the areas of attention, information processing, learning, and memory (Shore, 2003). Research suggests that risk is cumulative; that is, children who have more risk factors (for example, drug exposure, low birth weight, poor prenatal care, poor nutrition) are more likely to have developmental delays than children with fewer risk factors (Decoufle, Boyle, Paulozzi, & Lary, 2001; Hanson & Carta, 1996). Linda Mayes and colleagues at Yale New Haven Hospital compared sixty-one cocaine-exposed and forty-seven non-exposed three-month-old infants. Their results demonstrated that cocaine exposure is manifested at this early age by delays in motor development (Mayes, Bornstein, Chawarska, & Granger, 1995).

Poor nutrition Lack of adequate protein intake from foods such as milk, cheese, eggs, fish, chicken, and other meat often results in low birth weight, illness, and higher risk of death during the baby's first year. Stunted growth throughout childhood often is another consequence. The effects of a poor diet are particularly damaging during the last trimester of pregnancy, when significant maturing of the brain and nervous system is taking place. It is recommended that a pregnant woman gain twenty-five to thirty pounds during pregnancy—more if she is underweight to begin with.

5-1d ■ Birth Complications

Birth itself can result in trauma—that is, injury or shock. An infant, perfectly healthy until the moment of birth, can experience damage during the birth process. For example, **anoxia**, lack of oxygen to the brain cells, can occur because of labor complications. Brain damage or severe neurological problems such as cerebral palsy may result. When damage does occur, it may come from a newborn's inability to breathe immediately. However, the failure to start breathing may have been caused by earlier, perhaps unsuspected, damage *in utero*.

anoxia lack of oxygen to the brain cells

This is one example of how difficult it is to pinpoint the cause of a developmental problem.

Premature infants, especially, are subject to another kind of trauma: hemorrhaging, or bleeding, into the brain. These immature newborns also are at higher risk for breathing problems, heart failure, and infections. Even less severe problems at birth can result in trouble later. It is now thought that some school-age learning disabilities may be associated with low birth weight or seemingly minor disturbances at the time of birth (Child Trends, 2012; Hittleman, Parekh, & Glass, 1987).

Complications at birth may necessitate caesarean section delivery. Often referred to as a "C-section," this type of delivery may be required when typical vaginal delivery is impossible or when the lives of the mother, infant, or both are threatened. The most common reasons for the procedure are signs of fetal distress, such as weak infant heartbeat or **breech** presentation of the about-to-be-born infant.

breech presentation of buttocks first during birth

5-1e ■ Complications Following Birth

Once the baby is born, other events can lead to developmental problems. A discussion of some of these postnatal complications follows.

Meningitis Meningitis is considered a virus or bacterial infection that causes inflammation of the protective covering of the brain and spinal column. When meningitis-related death occurs in newborns, the cause is usually organisms found in the intestine or birth canal of the mother. The results of meningitis are unpredictable. Some children show no serious effects; others experience major neurological damage.

Encephalitis Encephalitis attacks the brain itself. The symptoms are many and so varied that the infection often is not diagnosed correctly. A range of aftereffects is possible, from no damage to identifiable neurological damage and later learning problems.

Lead poisoning Lead poisoning can cause grave damage to young children, whose bodies and nervous systems are still developing. Little children put everything into their mouths, so lead-based paint for indoor use and on children's toys has been outlawed. Today at least four million households have children living in them that are being exposed to lead. Disproportionately affected are children living in old, dilapidated housing. Recent research indicates that even low levels of lead in an infant or toddler's blood (levels classified as *safe* by federal guidelines) can be damaging. According to several long-term studies, the adverse effects on a child's IQ are still apparent at age ten (Bellinger, Stiles, & Needleman, 1992).

Because of such studies, the Centers for Disease Control and Prevention now requires

By law, play equipment and toys are no longer painted with lead-based paint.

© Cengage Learning 2015

much lower levels of lead to be classified as dangerous (Bee & Boyd, 2012). Lead poisoning affects a young child's development by causing speech delays, hyperactivity, attention deficit disorder, learning disabilities, behavioral disorders, neurological and renal damage, stunted growth, anemia, hearing loss, and cognitive deficits.

5-1f ▪ Poverty

Many developmental problems that occur before, during, or after the birth of a baby can be directly or indirectly related to poverty. Families living in poverty experience higher rates of infant death, failure to thrive, and birth defects than any other segment of our society. Children of these families also experience higher rates of intellectual disabilities, learning disabilities, and social and emotional deviations.

The Children's Defense Fund (CDF) describes poverty as a persistent and pervasive social problem in the United States and declares it "deplorable." In 2010, 16.4 million children were poor in the United States, and 7.4 million of those children lived in extreme poverty, according to the State of America's Children Handbook (2012).

Many parents find ways to cope, to raise bright and healthy children despite severely challenging circumstances. The reverse also is true: Adequate living conditions do not necessarily ensure children a good life. Families with seemingly adequate resources may abuse and neglect their children or fail to provide necessary stimulation. Nevertheless, the devastating link between poverty and developmental problems cannot be denied. Poverty undermines development in several significant ways.

Nutritional deficiency Recognizing that substandard nutrition often is associated with poverty, the Special Supplemental Food Program for Women, Infants, and Children (WIC) formed in the early 1970s. WIC provides nutritious food to women who are pregnant or breastfeeding and to their children up to age five. It also links food distribution to other health services, including prenatal care. Participation in WIC is estimated to reduce by as much as 25 percent the chance that a high-risk pregnant woman will deliver a premature or low-birth-weight baby.

An average of almost nine million women, infants, and children received WIC benefits each month during the 2011 fiscal year. During 1974, the first year of WIC, 88,000 people participated. Children have always been the largest category of WIC participants. Of the 8.9 million people who

WIC provides food to low-income children up to age five.

© Cengage Learning 2015

received WIC benefits each month in FY 2011, approximately 4.7 million were children, 2.1 million were infants, and 2.1 million were women (WIC, 2012).

By serving low-income pregnant women, many of the high costs of medical treatment, income support, and special education are averted. Despite its economic savings, WIC has never had the funds to serve more than a quarter to a third of the women who would most benefit from such services.

Inadequate health care and education A major preventive measure for developmental problems is adequate health care—yet one in ten children in America, a total of 7.95 million, were uninsured in 2010. Children of color are more likely to be uninsured. One in six Hispanic children and one in nine black children are uninsured, compared to one in ten white, non-Hispanic children (CDF, 2012). Health care must begin in earliest pregnancy, be maintained during pregnancy, and continue for mother and infant following delivery. Throughout the developmental years, it is important that children receive regular medical checkups. About 25 percent of pregnant women do not receive adequate prenatal care, and the percentage of women who receive virtually no care is increasing steadily. Pregnant women who are young, poor, unmarried, relatively uneducated, uninsured, or living in inner cities or rural areas are the least likely to have even minimal medical care. Yet these are the women who need it most, and who often bear infants at high risk for developmental problems.

Homelessness and substandard housing Significant numbers of American children are homeless. According to the 2002 United States Conference of Mayors' report data for twenty-three cities, 41 percent of the homeless are families with children, and 73 percent of these families are headed by a single parent. This same group released an update in 2008 showing that on average, the twenty-five cities now reporting data experienced a 12-percent increase in homelessness from 2007 to 2008, and sixteen cities reported an increase in the number of homeless families. The most recent data from these cities (2012) indicated that the number of families experiencing homelessness increased across the surveyed cities by an average of 8 percent, with 71 percent of the cities reporting an increase.

The primary cause of homelessness for families was lack of affordable housing, poverty, and unemployment (United States Conference of Mayors, 2008, 2012).

Single-parent families While single-parent families occur at all economic levels, they are overrepresented among our poorest families, especially those headed by teenage girls. When families cannot or do not choose to stay together, it is important to help both parents support their children emotionally and financially.

Too often, low-income noncustodial parents (usually fathers) with low wages and high unemployment rates are unable to pay child support. The child-support system traditionally has not helped such parents meet their obligations, since its focus has been on securing support from those parents who are employed and can afford to pay. Parents who cannot pay often amass such large child-support debts that they are forced to evade the system by taking jobs off the books (usually low-paying ones) and decreasing contact with their children. Studies show that nonresident fathers who pay child support tend to be more involved with their children, providing more emotional and financial support (Seltzer, McLanahan, & Hanson, 2001). One study found that 79 percent of children born to unmarried parents whose fathers have a support order and pay child support see their fathers regularly, compared with only 43 percent of those whose fathers do not have an order and do not pay support (Koball & Principe, 2002).

The need for quality child care during the developmental years has been documented repeatedly.

© Cengage Learning 2015

Child care The need for quality child care during the developmental years has been documented repeatedly. Yet decent, affordable child care continues to be in critically short supply for all but affluent families. According to The Center for American Progress (2012), without high-quality early childhood care, an at-risk child is:

- 25 percent more likely to drop out of school
- 40 percent more likely to become a teen parent
- 50 percent more likely to be placed in special education
- 60 percent more likely to never attend college
- 70 percent more likely to be arrested for a violent crime

5-2 Classifications of Developmental Disabilities

Should we categorize young children in terms of their impairment: intellectual disability, deafness, blindness, learning disability, emotional disturbance, and so on? Those in favor of categorization argue that it is key for answering questions such as:

- How many individuals have a particular problem?
- How widespread is it?
- Does it occur mostly in particular areas or among certain groups (urban, rural, immigrants, itinerant farm workers)?
- Is the problem increasing? Decreasing?
- How many teachers, clinicians, and special facilities are needed?
- Are available funds shared equitably according to the numbers of children in each disability category?
- Which individuals are eligible for Supplemental Security Income (SSI) and other legislated benefits?

Those opposed to labeling or categorizing argue that it can be harmful. The harm may be especially great where young children are concerned. The fear is that the very young may get locked into categories that are developmentally unsuitable or put into programs that compound their disability, as in the following example.

At age 3½, Jodie was talking very little, seemed incapable of following simple directions, and had few play skills. She scored low on an IQ test and was placed in a segregated preschool for children who are intellectually disabled. It was not until age 7 that a severe hearing loss was discovered. Between 3½ and 7—crucial developmental years—Jodie functioned as a child who is intellectually disabled. Why? Because she had been labeled as intellectually disabled and consequently had not been identified as a candidate for deaf education services.

Current laws recognize the many situations like Jodie's and the potential harm of prematurely classifying children under the age of six. **Categorical funding** has been discontinued in the birth-to-age-six component of the law. Instead, the more flexible concept of *developmental delay* is used to cover all developmental problems.

categorical funding public or private money assigned on the basis of type of handicap or disability

5-2a ■ Categories of Disability under the IDEIA

The Individuals with Disabilities Education Improvement Act (IDEIA) provides a guide for how states define disability and determine who is eligible for a free and appropriate public education under special education law. The specific disability terms from the IDEIA regulations are listed in Figure 5-2. It is

FIGURE 5-2

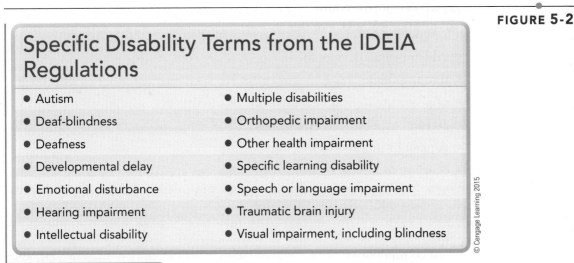

Specific Disability Terms from the IDEIA Regulations

- Autism
- Deaf-blindness
- Deafness
- Developmental delay
- Emotional disturbance
- Hearing impairment
- Intellectual disability

- Multiple disabilities
- Orthopedic impairment
- Other health impairment
- Specific learning disability
- Speech or language impairment
- Traumatic brain injury
- Visual impairment, including blindness

© Cengage Learning 2015

TeachSource Digital Download Download from CourseMate.

important to note that for all categories, in order to fully meet the definition (and eligibility for special education and related services) as a "child with a disability," a child's educational performance must be adversely affected due to the disability.

Despite controversy, categorization does exist. Among other things, the system is used to allocate federal funding for educational services. Everyone working with children of any age needs to know something about each of the impairments. The following is a brief introduction to some of the categories listed in Figure 5-2.

Specific learning disabilities Specific learning disabilities (SLDs) or learning disabilities (LDs) is defined as a disorder in one or more of the basic psychological processes involved in understanding or in using language, spoken or written, that may manifest itself in the imperfect ability to listen, think, speak, read, write, spell, or do mathematical calculations.

In the school-age child, the label is often one of exclusion—what the child is *not:*

- *not* displaying an intellectual disability
- *not* hearing impaired
- *not* visually impaired
- *not* displaying identifiable neurological problems, such as cerebral palsy

A normal or above-normal IQ is characteristic of most children with learning disabilities. Nevertheless, these children have problems learning to read, write, or do arithmetic. Trouble with reading, which affects most children with learning disabilities, is referred to as *dyslexia. Dysgraphia* is the term sometimes used to describe problems with printing and writing.

More than a hundred labels have been assigned to children whose learning problems baffle clinicians and educators. These labels, it should be noted, do little to help children with their learning problems. The reauthorization of IDEIA provides more flexibility to educators in how they identify and intervene with students with potential learning disabilities. Chapter 8 provides a description of Response to Intervention (RTI), a systematic approach to supporting all learners in the classroom that prevents overuse of the label *learning disabled.*

Speech and language impairments Speech and language impairments account for the second-largest category of educational disabilities among young people aged six to twenty-one. With young children, it is often difficult to clearly define what is and what is not a problem because of these interacting factors:

- rate of overall development
- temperament
- opportunity to hear language and talk to others
- cultural expectations and values
- general health and well-being

A number of typical or normal irregularities are common during language development. These need not become problems unless the child is unduly pressured. Speech and language problems often accompany other developmental disorders. Children with cerebral palsy may have serious speech problems, as may children with hearing loss or severe emotional disturbance. Whatever their causes, it is important that speech and language disorders receive attention as early as possible.

Disproportionality in Special Education

Historically there has been an overrepresentation of minority students under IDEIA, including English Language Learners (ELL) identified with a learning disability or other type of disability. When a minority group's numbers in special education are statistically higher than they should be, they are considered disproportionate, and thus the term *disproportionality*.

For example, statistically, about 12 percent of the language-minority population in the United States should require special education. But typically, language minorities are overrepresented in programs for the learning disabled. In California, where students with limited English proficiency make up 22.2 percent of the student population, ELL children are significantly overrepresented in special education, particularly in specific learning disabilities and speech impairment classes.

This is a problem, because it means that students have been misidentified and misplaced and thus are not receiving appropriate educational services. Disproportionality is a problem because children may be prevented from reaching their full academic potential. It also fosters negative stereotypes regarding minority groups. In addition, it hinders schools from identifying the fact that curriculum and teaching methods need to be altered to reach the instructional needs of a diverse student body.

As Artiles and Ortiz (2002) state: "Research shows that ELLs in special education with learning disabilities demonstrate lower verbal and full-scale IQ scores after placement in special education than at their initial evaluations.

"This means that even in special education, ELLs (in general) do not receive the type of instruction they need (due to the lack of ESL instructional methodology and other professional development for special education professionals)" (p. 1).

Disproportionality may be caused by several factors, including use of inappropriate assessment strategies for ELL and racial minorities, failure to accommodate cultural differences, and lack of responsiveness to these differences.

Sources: Artiles, A. J., & Oritz, A. A. (2002). *Before Assessing a Child for Special Education, First Assess the Instructional Program.* A Summary of English Language Learners with Special Education Needs. Center for Applied Linguistics: Washington, DC. Retrieved from http://www.misd.net/bilingual/ellsandspedcal.pdf

Minow, M. L. (2001). *Limited English proficient students and special education.* National Center on Accessing the General Curriculum: Wakefield, MA. Retrieved from http://aim.cast.org/learn/historyarchive/backgroundpapers/lep_sp_ed

Developmental delay According to Part C under IDEIA, children from birth to age three, and Part B under IDES, for children from ages three through nine, the term *developmental delay*, as defined by each state, means a delay in one or more of the following areas:

- physical development
- cognitive development
- communication
- social or emotional development
- adaptive (behavioral) development

Intellectual disability *Intellectual disability* is a new term in the IDEIA. Until 2010 the law and the field of education used the term "mental retardation." This change came about when President Obama signed Rosa's Law. The bill was named after Rosa Marcellino, a nine-year-old girl who has Down syndrome. President Obama noted,

> "This may seem to some people like a minor change, but I think Rosa's brother Nick put it best. He said, 'What you call people is how you treat them. If we change the words, maybe it will be the start of a new attitude towards people with disabilities.' That's a lot of wisdom from Nick" (The White House, 2010).

The long-standing term of mental retardation was very controversial and had acquired social stigma. It also was a serious disrupter in regard to its use with young children. Children change and evolve, and the term's finality failed to take this development flux into account. While the term changed, the definition remained the same, meaning significantly subaverage general intellectual functioning, existing at the same time with deficits in adaptive behavior. This delay must be manifested during the developmental period that adversely affects a child's educational performance.

According to the American Association on Intellectual and Developmental Disabilities (AAIDD), adaptive behaviors comprise three skill types:

- Conceptual skills—language and literacy; money, time, and number concepts; and self-direction
- Social skills—interpersonal skills, social responsibility, self-esteem, gullibility, social problem solving, and the ability to follow rules/obey laws
- Practical skills—activities of daily living (personal care), occupational skills, health care, travel/transportation

© Cengage Learning 2015

▶❚❚ **TeachSource** Video Connections

Kristina: Modifications for a Culturally and Linguistically Diverse Student in an Inclusive Elementary Classroom

In this video you will hear from Kristina's teacher, Ms. Lee, as she describes the steps she has taken to help Kristina succeed in her fourth-grade classroom.
After watching the video discuss the following:

1. What strategies did Ms. Lee use to foster Kristina's progress?
2. How might Kristina's educational experience have been different if she had attended a different school or had a different teacher?

Watch on CourseMate.

Emotional disturbance According to the IDEIA, an emotional disturbance is defined by an individual exhibiting one or more of the following characteristics over a long period of time and to a marked degree that adversely affects a child's educational performance:

- An inability to learn that cannot be explained by intellectual, sensory, or health factors.
- An inability to build or maintain satisfactory interpersonal relationships with peers and teachers.
- Inappropriate types of behavior or feelings under normal circumstances.
- A general pervasive mood of unhappiness or depression.
- A tendency to develop physical symptoms or fears associated with personal or school problems.

Emotional disorders are characterized by behavioral or emotional responses that are so different from appropriate age, ethnic, or community norms that the responses adversely affect educational performance, including academic, social, vocational, or personal skills (Forness & Knitzer, 1990; McClelland, Morrison, & Holmes, 2000). Children's behavior during their early years is heavily influenced by child-rearing practices, cultural values, and expectations of family and community. Parents who are aggressive, for example, tend to have children who also behave aggressively. Thus, the child's aggressiveness is perfectly "normal" in light of his or her upbringing.

The social and emotional characteristics of young children also are highly influenced by particular stages of development. (In the past, early childhood educators and pediatricians used terms such as "the Terrible Twos" to describe a toddler's struggle for independence.) Behavior difficulties often arise out of the frustrations a young child experiences in trying to master basic developmental skills: learning to feed, dress, and toilet himself or herself; learning what to fear and what not to fear; learning what is acceptable behavior and what is not. A child's behavior always should be judged by what is developmentally appropriate for his or her particular age and background.

Multiple disabilities A number of children have more than one disability. It has been estimated that 20 to 50 percent of children with serious hearing deficits have additional problems such as language delays. Many of the syndromes also are characterized by several problems occurring together. For example, children with cerebral palsy may have a speech delay, fine or gross motor difficulties or both, and feeding problems. The IDEIA specifically states that, in order to qualify for this category, the combination of disabilities must cause such severe educational needs that they cannot be accommodated in a special education program solely for one of the impairments. The term does not include deaf-blindness.

A normal or above-normal IQ is characteristic of most children with learning disabilities. Nevertheless, these children have problems learning to read, write, or do arithmetic.

© Cengage Learning 2015

Hearing impairment and deafness These are treated as two separate categories under the IDEIA. Hearing impairment means an impairment in hearing, whether permanent or fluctuating, that adversely affects a child's educational performance but is not included under the definition of "deafness."

As defined by federal regulation, *deafness* is a hearing loss so severe that individuals cannot process spoken language, even with hearing aids or other forms of amplification.

Deafness and hearing impairments often are labeled according to when the damage occurred. Individuals who have been deaf since birth experience congenital deafness. Individuals born with normal hearing who have lost it through an injury or disease experience adventitious deafness. If the loss occurs after a child has acquired some language, the developmental problems tend to be fewer.

Children who have even a short exposure to language before they lose their hearing do better in acquiring language skills than do children who were born deaf. Nevertheless, even a mild hearing loss can affect all aspects of development unless the child receives appropriate intervention services.

Orthopedic impairments Developmental problems that interfere with walking or other body movement are considered orthopedic or physical impairments. In many instances, orthopedic problems and neurological problems are closely related. According to federal regulation, **orthopedic impairments** refer to impairments caused by **congenital anomalies** and structural deformities such as club foot, absence of a limb, or paralysis; impairments caused by diseases such

orthopedic impairments developmental problems that interfere with walking or other body movements

congenital anomaly a developmental difference present at birth; not necessarily of genetic origin

as polio; neurological and spinal cord damage resulting in problems such as paralysis of major muscles; and impairments from other causes such as severely fractured bones, amputations, or burns.

It may be weeks or months (even well into the first year) before an infant gives evidence of a neurological impairment. The problem may become noticeable only when certain of the very early **reflexive** behaviors do not emerge on schedule and so interfere with the infant's acquisition of new and more mature responses. For example, most newborns automatically grasp a finger placed in their hand. Unless this primitive grasp reflex drops out between one and four months of age, infants will not be able to learn to release objects at will.

Other health impairments Young children with severe health problems often have limited strength, vitality, and alertness. They also may experience pain and discomfort much of the time. A normal childhood may be nearly impossible because of frequent hospitalizations or intensive medical treatment.

Health disorders take many forms:

- heart problems (weak or damaged heart)
- leukemia (cancer of the bone marrow)
- asthma (disorder of the respiratory system)
- sickle-cell anemia (red blood cell malformation)
- hemophilia (a bleeding disorder)
- diabetes (faulty metabolism of sugar and starch)
- cystic fibrosis (lung and digestive problems)

Health disorders may be described as **chronic** or **acute** (although a chronic problem can go into an acute state). In either event, the child's overall development is threatened. While poor health may not be the actual cause of other developmental disorders, it can create situations that lead to other problems.

A child who is physically weak, unable to run and jump and play with children of the same age, may be socially isolated. Brothers and sisters may resent having to play with the child instead of with their own playmates. They also may resent the parents' focus on the sick child.

Visual impairments As with other problems, there is no clear-cut definition of visual impairment.

A legal definition is proposed by the National Society for the Prevention of Blindness:

- **Blind**: Visual acuity of 20/200 or less in the better eye with the best possible correction; or a much-reduced field of vision (at its widest diameter, a visual arc of 20 degrees or less).
- **Partially sighted**: Visual acuity between 20/70 and 20/200 in the better eye with the best possible correction.

Vision impairments range from severe to mild. The American Foundation for the Blind offers an educational definition for visual impairments:

- **Blind**: Visual loss is severe enough that it is not possible to read print, requiring the child to be educated through the use of **Braille** and other **tactile** and **auditory** materials.
- **Partially seeing**: Residual vision is sufficient to allow a child to read large print or possibly regular print under special conditions and to use other visual materials for educational purposes.

reflexive involuntary body reaction to specific kinds of stimulation (a tap on the knee produces the knee jerk)

chronic term for a health problem of long duration or frequent recurrence

acute the sudden onset of an illness; usually of short duration; a chronic problem may have periodic acute episodes

visual acuity how well an individual is able to see; keenness of vision

Braille a system of writing for the blind that uses patterns of raised dots read by the fingers

tactile referring to touch

auditory what is experienced through hearing

residual vision whatever vision remains after disease or damage to a person's visual system

Total blindness, whether congenital or occurring after birth, is readily identified. The baby simply does not respond to people or objects with the range of a sighted person. Less severe visual disorders may be more difficult to identify. Frequently, the problem does not show up until it is time for the child to learn to read and write.

Combined deafness and blindness A combination of vision and hearing problems requires highly specialized intervention programs. Serious sensory deficits in combination usually result in problems with language and in cognitive and social development. Until the late 1960s, education for children who were both deaf and blind was available only in private institutions. In 1968, the picture changed: Federal legislation authorized eight model centers for educating children who had both deafness and blindness. More recent legislation provides states with funds for educating these children.

Autism As defined under IDEIA, autism is a developmental disability significantly affecting verbal and nonverbal communication and social interactions, generally evident before age three, that adversely affects a child's educational performance. First described in the 1940s, autism originally was blamed on lack of affectionate and responsive parenting. Subsequent research has demonstrated that parenting style is not a contributing factor for autism. Although autism still is behaviorally defined, it is now known to be a developmental disorder of the brain (Rapin & Katzman, 1998). Recent research has demonstrated that a reduced head size at birth followed by an excessive increase in head size between one to two months and six to fourteen months may be common in children with autism. This change in head size may serve as an early warning sign of autism risk (Courchesne, Caper, & Akshoomoff, 2003). In many well-known disorders (most of them genetic), autism occurs in a small percentage of the cases (e.g., Fragile X syndrome and tuberous sclerosis), but the medical origin remains unknown in most cases. Some cognitive delay is present in 75 percent of children with autism.

Traumatic brain injury This category of injuries (either open- or closed-wound) to the head cause tearing of the nerve fibers, bruising of the brain against the skull, or bruising of the brain stem. The most common consequences, as far as learning is concerned, are:

- confusion in spatial orientation and directionality
- marked distractibility and short attention span
- problems in both short- and long-term memory
- impulsivity and, sometimes, aggressiveness

5-2b ■ A Final Thought on Categories

As stated previously, each of these categories describes a condition that makes a student eligible for a free and appropriate public education under special education law. In order to fully meet the definition (and eligibility for special education and related services) as a "child with a disability," a child's educational performance must be adversely affected due to the disability. It should be kept in mind that just because a child qualifies under a specific category, the category does not prescribe the services the child will receive. There are evidence-based best practices identified for some of the categories (many of which you will read about throughout this text); however, the child's specific services and the instructional strategies a teacher or specialist uses are determined based on the child's individual needs.

Summary

▶ Determining the cause of a developmental disability is difficult. The same is true of assigning a classification of exceptionality to a young child. Both issues—cause and classification—are subject to varying definitions, depending on professional perspective.

▶ Biological and environmental factors, in combination, account for most developmental problems.

▶ Biological factors include genetic disorders, diseases, and infections that occur during pregnancy.

▶ Problems at the time of birth, as well as diseases and infections following birth, also may cause developmental damage.

▶ In young children, especially those raised in old and dilapidated housing, lead poisoning is a common problem.

▶ Poverty, in general, accounts for a large percentage of developmental problems, most of which are preventable with comprehensive early intervention.

▶ The IDEIA provides categories to help guide how states define disability and determine who is eligible for a free and appropriate public education under special education law. In order to fully meet the definition (and eligibility for special education and related services) as a "child with a disability," a child's educational performance must be adversely affected due to the disability.

Key Terms

acute, 114
amino acid, 102
anoxia, 104
asymptomatic, 103
auditory, 114
autosomal dominant gene
    disorder, 99
autosomal recessive gene
    disorder, 99
behavior geneticist, 98
biological insult, 99

Braille, 114
breech, 105
categorical funding, 109
chronic, 114
congenital, 99
congenital anomaly, 113
enzyme, 102
Fragile X syndrome, 101
genetic disorder, 99
metabolic disorder, 102
metabolize, 102

neurological, 102
orthopedic impairments, 113
reflexive, 114
remission, 103
residual vision, 114
sex-linked gene disorder, 101
simian crease, 101
stigmata, 101
syndrome, 101
tactile, 114
visual acuity, 114

Student Activities

1. Research medical recommendations for prenatal care. Develop a list of essential components. How do recommendations change based on the mother's age?

2. Discuss with your mother your own birth and that of your brothers and sisters to determine the kinds of problems, if any, that she or the infants experienced (you might also carry out this activity with any woman who has given birth and is willing to discuss the issues with you).

3. Study a copy of your state's system for funding the education of children with disabilities. Make a chart of the categories it uses, with the number of students in each category. If preschool-age children are included, indicate what percentage of the total they make up.

4. Participate in a panel discussion on the inappropriateness and disadvantages of labeling young children as having learning disabilities, intellectual disability, or emotional disturbance.

5. Make a list of the kinds of services available in your community for pregnant teenage girls. Do the same for pregnant women with alcohol- or drug-related problems. With each service, indicate availability in terms of waiting list, beds available, and so on.

Review Questions

Briefly respond to the following items:

1. What is a congenital problem? Give an example.
2. Define metabolic disorder. Give an example.
3. What is meant by *birth complications*? Give an example.
4. What is temperament and what effect can it have on a child's development? Give an example.
5. What are the possible effects of lead poisoning on children?
6. How do a family's child-rearing practices influence a child's development? Give an example.
7. Explain why even a mild hearing loss may have a negative effect on a child's overall development.
8. What is the difference between a chronic and an acute health problem? Give an example of each.

Helpful Websites

Autism Society of America

http://www.autism-society.org

This site includes information on support and advocacy and other services for individuals with autism and their families. It includes information on behavior and communication.

The Children's Defense Fund

http://www.childrensdefense.org

The mission of the Children's Defense Fund is to leave no children behind and thus to ensure every child a healthy start, a head start, a fair start, a safe start, and a moral start in life and successful passage to adulthood with the help of caring families and communities. Their website includes updates on current legislation as well as links to hundreds of other organizations, including individual state Children's Defense Fund sites.

National Dissemination Center for Children with Disabilities (NICHCY)

http://www.NICHCY.org

NICHCY is the national dissemination center that provides information on disabilities and disability-related issues. Anyone can use their services—families, educators, administrators, journalists, and students. Information is available about specific disabilities, IEPs, education rights and laws, early intervention, parent materials, and more.

U.S. Department of Education

http://www.ed.gov

The website contains publications, research, statistics, and resources on general education and special education in the United States.

 Visit the Education CourseMate for this textbook to access the eBook, Did You Get It? quizzes, Digital Downloads, TeachSource Video Cases, flashcards, and more. Go to CengageBrain.com to log in, register, or purchase access.

Sensory Impairments: Hearing and Vision

OBJECTIVES

After reading this chapter, you should be able to:

6-1   describe deafness and hearing loss as it relates to a child's overall development and what teachers can do to support the child's development.

6-2   discuss blindness and other visual impairments and outline the characteristics of an appropriate early intervention program for children who are blind or visually impaired.

· · · · · · · · · · · · · · · · · ·

naeyc

The following NAEYC Standards are addressed in this chapter:

STANDARD 1 Promoting Child Development and Learning

STANDARD 2 Building Family and Community Relationships

STANDARD 4 Using Developmentally Effective Approaches

STANDARD 5 Using Content Knowledge to Build Meaningful Curriculum

CONNECTIONS

- During a routine screening program, Matthew scored low on the mental functioning part of the test. His parent was advised to enroll him in a segregated preschool for mentally retarded children, a common practice prior to the enactment of PL 94-157. The teacher soon began to question the mental portion of the test. Matthew seemed alert and interested, even though his response was often slow. Matthew's mother was also dubious about the test results. The teacher helped her to get in touch with a pediatric audiologist. Matthew, it was discovered, had a selective hearing loss that had not shown up on the screening test: some sounds he could hear; others he could not—hence, his unpredictable responses. Matthew was fitted with a hearing device in each ear and placed in a classroom with typically developing four-year-olds.

- The twins Nadia and Yusef were born prematurely at very low birth weight. They spent their early weeks in the neonatal intensive care nursery. By the time the twins were four months old, their mother was convinced that Yusef was not able to see. Diagnostic testing confirmed her fears: Yusef was blind. Though their grieving was intense, the twins' parents began to follow up on suggestions made by the vision clinic and their pediatrician. A specially trained teacher began weekly home visits to help the family learn how to arrange their home and family life so as to accommodate the special needs of every family member. Over the next several years, the family participated in inclusive toddler and preschool programs for the twins, as well as a support group. A few months before their sixth birthday, the twins entered a regular kindergarten class.

sensory system any one of several ways individuals receive information or input from their environment

sensory impairments impairments that affect the ability to sense the environment through a specific sensory modality such as hearing or vision

From the moment of birth, we learn almost everything about ourselves and our world through a complex **sensory system**. This system is usually operational at birth and enables us to hear, see, taste, smell, and recognize what we touch. Every aspect of development depends on this system being in good working order.

The most serious and most prevalent **sensory impairments** are hearing and vision losses. Most of what infants and children are expected to learn is acquired through these two senses. A child who is both blind and deaf is at extreme developmental risk and requires highly specialized services (Malatchi, 1995).

A common belief is that it would be worse to be born blind than deaf. While both are serious, deafness has the potential for greater and more generalized interference with development. Hearing loss has the potential for devastating effects on oral language. This, in turn, has a negative effect on cognitive development. The development of cognitive skills and the development of language skills are virtually inseparable.

Children who are blind learn language with considerably less difficulty than children who are deaf. They benefit from the many incidental-learning opportunities available every day. They hear casual conversations containing bits of information that add up to valuable learning. They hear teachers' and parents' instructions and suggestions. All of this contributes to cognitive development. Because of the influence of language in forming and maintaining relationships, children who are blind also have more options for social learning than children who are deaf.

Infants and young children with severe hearing or vision losses require teachers who are trained to meet their special needs. PL 99-457 requires all children to be educated in the least restrictive environment to the degree that it meets their educational needs. The relative restrictiveness of an intensive, highly specialized program may be necessary in the very early years if the child is to have greater freedom in the long run. On the other hand, most early childhood educators argue that many of the developmental needs of children who have vision or hearing loss are the same as for all children. They, too, benefit from learning experiences provided in a quality early education program.

Both arguments have merit. A combination of programs offers the best solution for many children. Whatever the decision, it is imperative that the parents remain involved.

Deafness and Hearing Loss 6-1

Children with hearing loss may be classified in two ways: as deaf or as hard of hearing. **Deafness** refers to a hearing loss so severe that the individual cannot process spoken language even with amplification devices. *Hard of hearing* refers to a lesser hearing loss, but one that nevertheless has a definite effect on social, cognitive, and language development.

Losses may be thought of as **pre-lingual** (occurring before speech and language have had a chance to develop) or **post-lingual** (occurring after the onset of language). Lowenbraun and Thompson (1994) corroborate that children with a pre-lingual loss have greater difficulties in all areas of development throughout their growing years. The most severe developmental interference occurs when a hearing loss is congenital (when the infant is born deaf). Generally speaking, the outcome is more positive when the hearing loss occurs *after* the child has begun to learn language.

deafness a hearing loss so severe that the individual cannot process spoken language even with amplification devices

pre-lingual deafness describes hearing loss occurring before the child has acquired speech

post-lingual deafness describes hearing loss occurring after the child has acquired speech

6-1a ■ Types of Hearing Loss

Hearing losses are categorized in various ways through various kinds of assessments. To ensure valid results, pediatric **audiologists** should do both screening and testing. The results of hearing tests usually are plotted on what is called an *audiogram*. A hearing loss is classified according to where the loss occurs.

A loss in the outer or middle ear produces a **conductive hearing loss**. A loss in the inner ear (**cochlea** or auditory nerve) produces a **sensorineural hearing loss**. A loss in the **higher auditory cortex** produces central deafness. A *combined loss* refers to two or more of the above.

It should be noted that a conductive loss interferes with the ability to hear, not the ability to understand. If the sound is loud enough to be heard, the child can understand the message. Therefore, these losses can be corrected relatively easily with amplification.

Chronic or frequent ear infections, especially those with resulting fluid accumulation, can lead to intermittent hearing loss. These recurrent hearing losses can lead to delays in children's language and learning abilities. Although antibiotics were once prescribed routinely to treat **otitis media**, physicians are now more likely to wait and see whether the infection and fluid will resolve on their own. Thus, it is important to observe children closely and seek medical treatment if the condition persists, to prevent long-term developmental delays. Many children at any given time may have an intermittent loss of hearing.

Identifying an intermittent hearing loss is difficult. There are times when the condition has been missed entirely during routine screening; the child is hearing adequately and therefore responding appropriately at the time of testing. In more recent years, schools that employ screening programs have been effective

audiologist a specially certified professional who focuses on hearing testing and hearing impairments

conductive hearing loss refers to problems in the mechanical transmission of sounds through the outer, middle, or inner ear

cochlea the bony, snail-shaped structure in the inner ear that allows hearing to occur

sensorineural hearing loss malfunctioning of the cochlea or auditory nerve

higher auditory cortex the section of the gray matter of the brain that processes sound

otitis media chronic ear infection affecting hearing

in identifying hearing loss (Roeser, Valente, & Husford-Dunn, 2007). These programs usually combine methods to check for both conductive hearing loss and sensorineural hearing loss. Once the loss has been identified, the child should be referred for further diagnosis and appropriate treatment.

Unlike conductive hearing losses, sensorineural and central deafness do not respond readily to medical intervention. Sensorineural hearing losses can cause sounds to be inaudible and distorted. With a sensorineural loss, even if the sound is loud enough to be heard, the child may still have difficulty understanding speech. Those children whose loss is too severe to be helped by hearing aids may benefit from a **cochlear implant** (Discolo & Hirose, 2002). These surgically inserted devices are provided for children as young as twelve months. In the United States, there are more than 14,000 children aged eighteen or younger with implants (Smith, 2006). Research has demonstrated that children who are deaf who receive cochlear implants before the age of thirty months are better able to integrate auditory and visual information than are those who receive their implants when they are older (Schorr, Fox, van Washove, & Knudsen, 2005).

While the increased use of cochlear implants is changing education of the deaf, their use is not without problems. Cochlear implants can malfunction and are difficult to program; when they are off the individual is deaf; there is background noise and sounds are heard differently; their use impacts lifestyle, because the external portion of the device must not get wet and is easily damaged; and there are no long-term data regarding their use (U.S. Food and Drug Administration, 2010).

cochlear implant device surgically placed by opening the mastoid structure of the skull; allows electrical impulses (sound) to be carried directly to the brain

6-1b ■ Warning Signs of Hearing Loss

Soon after birth, most infants begin making a variety of responses to sounds in the environment. The whole body may move in a *startle* response: eyes may blink, arms may jerk, or a rapid increase in sucking may occur. At about four months, infants begin to *localize*, that is, turn their heads in the direction of sound. Over the next several months, they get better and better at localizing. Early hearing is so good that many infants can discriminate between voices and indicate preference for their mother's voice (Marotz & Allen, 2012).

When infants do not make such responses, hearing loss is a possibility. On the other hand, all infants make so many random movements that many infants who are hard of hearing may appear to be typical. Furthermore, if the infant has some **residual hearing**, the loss may be difficult to identify. Infants who have residual hearing may be hearing just enough to respond appropriately *some of the time*, giving the appearance of normalcy. Interestingly enough, if infants who are deaf are exposed to sign language, they babble—with their hands (Petitto & Maramette, 1991).

residual hearing refers to whatever degree of hearing is left to a person who is deaf or hearing-impaired

Hearing loss is one of the most common disabilities present at the time of birth. Often, it is not detected until a child reaches one to three years of age (Mason & Herrmann, 1998). Parents may suspect that something is wrong but not consider a hearing loss. Early identification and appropriate treatment can minimize the negative effects of hearing loss on all aspects of a child's development. Consequently, many states have now passed legislation supporting universal newborn hearing screening (UNHS) whereby a baby's hearing is tested in the hospital shortly after birth (Pickard et al., 2002).

Infant caregivers, early childhood teachers, and health care providers are in a strategic position for noting possible hearing problems or risk conditions. Persistent ear

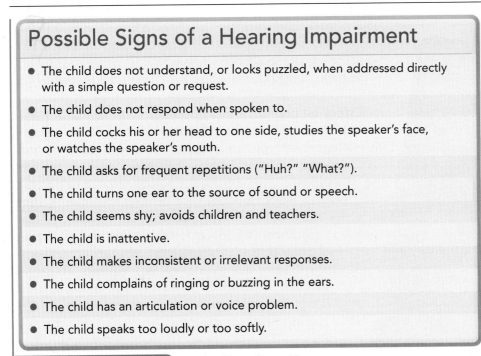

FIGURE 6-1

infections, discharge from the ears, or constant poking or pulling at the ears often indicates a problem. Children may also drop certain initial voiceless consonants: *p, h, s, f.* They simply do not hear these sounds and so do not reproduce them. As for a more severe loss, a marked delay in speech and language development is a major warning sign.

Figure 6-1 lists possible signs of a hearing impairment. Teachers should be alerted when a child who has acquired some language displays these behaviors.

When teachers become aware of a possible problem, the first step is to confer with parents about seeking clinical help.

6-1c ■ The Impact of Hearing Loss on Development

"All hearing losses are serious" (Cook, Klein & Chen 2011). The **cumulative effect** of an undiagnosed hearing loss on children's cognitive, social, and language development is clear. Many children with moderate-to-severe hearing loss are educationally delayed by as much as three to five years. They have significant social and behavioral problems. As these children grow older, some fall even further behind due to the increasing complexity of school and community expectations.

cumulative effect adding on or accumulation of consequences

Effect on language development The most serious and far-reaching effect of hearing loss is on early speech and language development. It appears that language acquisition may be tied to certain periods in a child's development (the *critical period* idea). According to this theory, a child who cannot hear sounds and verbal stimulation at certain points in development may never fully master language. Inadequate auditory input during early development almost always leads to serious problems in language acquisition and in speech production. Faulty early language development also may be caused by lack of responsiveness from family and teachers. Unwittingly, they may fall into the habit of not talking to a child with a hearing loss. It is easy to see how this happens. The child's range of responses is limited, thus providing inadequate feedback for family and friends. Consequently, the child's language skills become even more delayed.

Effect on cognitive development Once the typically developing child is beyond the sensorimotor stage, cognitive skills become intertwined with language skills. In turn, language skills, including the ability to communicate thoughts, continue to be inseparably related to adequate hearing. Thus, children with hearing loss often perform less skillfully than hearing children in cognitive activities.

Children with severe hearing problems may be several years behind educationally. Their educational delay seldom is due to poor cognitive potential. Usually the cause is the inadequate auditory input; in other words, the child has been denied a major channel for cognitive development.

Effects on social development Children with hearing loss often experience some degree of social isolation in a hearing world. They begin to be left out of things, even within the family, at a very early age. The child may be in the room where a family activity is going on, and yet often be unintentionally ignored for a very simple reason: The child is not able to enter into verbal give-and-take and so has no way of figuring out what is going on. Hearing loss in itself does not cause abnormal social development. It is the poor communication that develops between the child and others that leads to social adjustment difficulties.

Reports of impulsivity, aggression, or low self-esteem often begin during the preschool years. This social immaturity may increase with age as communication demands increase (Martin & Clark, 1996).

Luetke-Stahlman and Luckner (1991) suggest that the inability to respond to a playmate's language and social nuances during play may limit the social, emotional, and linguistic development of young children with hearing loss. Even children with moderate hearing loss may have difficulty establishing friendships and interacting with peers (Davis, Elfenbein, Schum, & Bentler, 1986). Children with normal hearing typically prefer to interact with other hearing children rather than expend the extra communicative effort to interact with children with hearing loss (Bench, 1992).

As they grow older, many children with hearing deficits tend to be less mature socially. Often they have a low frustration **threshold**, which may be related to an earlier inability to make their preferences known. At times, these children may also seem to be uncaring or unaware of the needs and feelings of others. It is unlikely that they are truly indifferent. More to the point is that they have not heard, and therefore not learned, the language of sympathizing—a language that most young children acquire almost spontaneously.

Effects on family life Having a child with a hearing loss can dramatically change the tenor of family life. The more severe the loss, the greater the impact. Both family members and the child are exposed to countless frustrations, especially in the early stages of learning to communicate with each other. A young

The most serious effect of a hearing loss is on early language development.

© Cengage Learning 2015

threshold the physical or psychological point at which an individual begins to respond to certain kinds of stimulation

child's inability to process the communicative efforts of others accurately makes it difficult for family members to establish behavior limits for the child who does not hear well (Steinberg & Knightly, 2007). It is also challenging for families to spend the time and effort required in carrying out recommended intervention procedures that will help the child learn to function in a hearing world. Supporting the family in adapting to their child's deafness involves multiple approaches, including behavior management, family therapy, and the facilitation of family communication (Greenberg & Kusche, 1993).

Methods of communication Early and easy communication between a child and the people in his or her environment is critical not only to language development but also in the areas of cognitive and social development (Malloy, 2003). Several methods of communication are available:

- In **speech reading**, a child learns to read what another individual is saying by watching face, mouth, tongue, and throat movements.

- **Cued speech** is a visual communication system that uses eight hand shapes in four different placements near the face, in combination with the mouth movements of speech, to make the sounds of spoken language look different from each other. Cued speech has been found to be effective when paired with the use of cochlear implants (Smith, 2006).

- **American Sign Language (ASL)** is a complete, complex language that employs signs made with the hands and other movements, including facial expressions and postures of the body. Refer to Figure 6-2 for a description of sign language around the world.

- Signed English is a sign language that parallels the English language. For every word there is a sign. Word order is the same as in spoken English.

- The finger-spelling system is made up of an alphabet of twenty-six hand-formed letters that correspond to the regular alphabet. One hand is held in front of the chest, and the other hand spells out the words letter by letter.

- **Total**, or simultaneous, **communication** is a system that combines both speech and a sign system. A program designed to help parents and teachers with total communication is Oral Deaf Education. See the Helpful Websites section at the end of this chapter for more information.

speech reading the more accurate term for lip reading

cued speech a visual communication system that uses eight hand shapes in four different placements near the face, in combination with the mouth movements of speech, to make the sounds of spoken language look different from each other

American Sign Language a language with its own vocabulary and grammar

total communication a system for teaching children with deafness that combines speech reading and a sign system

FIGURE 6-2

Sign Language around the World

The status of sign language varies in each country. The first country in the world where sign language was recognized and passed into parliament was Uganda in 1995 (World Federation for the Deaf, 2012). No one form of sign language is universal. American Sign Language (ASL) is one of the most commonly known forms of communication for the deaf, and many people assume that it is *a universal language*. They would be incorrect. Different sign languages are used in different countries or regions. For example, there are two sign languages in Belgium (French Belgian Sign Language and Flemish Sign Language) and in Spain (Spanish Sign Language and Catalan Sign Language). Also, there are different sign languages in countries that have the same spoken language, such as in the United Kingdom and Ireland. Some languages, such as Japanese Sign Language, incorporate more mouthing of words than other sign languages such as ASL. A person who is deaf travelling to a foreign country would not necessarily understand the sign language used there.

© Cengage Learning 2015

Bilingual Education

Being bilingual means knowing and using two languages. Children with a hearing loss who are taught sign language and a written or oral form of their home language are considered bilingual. The deaf child's other language should be the oral language used by the hearing world to which he/she also belongs—for example, the language of the child's parents and extended family as well as future friends, teachers and employers (Grosjean, 2001). Deaf individuals who speak a different first language from where they are educated would be considered trilingual, because they have learned two oral and written languages in addition to sign language. For example, in the United States, where the primary language is English, a child from a Spanish-speaking family would be trilingual if she or he learns ASL, English, and Spanish.

Which method? A long-standing controversy has to do with which system to use in teaching language to a young child. Is there a *best* way? Should the child be held to oral communication exclusively, allowed to do no signing of any kind? Is a combination method such as total communication the most effective? Those who have studied families favor the total approach. Each method has its own philosophy, methodology, and expectations (Malloy, 2003; Martin & Clark, 1996). Many professionals have formed particular biases, but there is no definitive research that proves one method of training to be distinctly superior to any other. Clearly, however, the earlier that communication can occur between the child and his or her environment, the better the outcome (Malloy, 2003; Schorr, Fox, van Washove, & Knudsen, 2005).

signing non-oral communication systems, such as finger spelling or American Sign Language

The final decision about **signing**, speaking, or combining the two must be made by the parents. Teachers need to accept the parents' decision and work with them and the deaf education specialist to provide the child with the best learning environment possible.

6-1d ■ Early Intervention

The importance of early language stimulation and training cannot be overemphasized. Language deficiencies may be the result of failure to begin language-learning activities during the infant and toddler years. The longer the delay in starting language intervention, the more difficult it is for the child to develop fully functional language. Even a mild hearing loss can result in reduced language ability if the child has not had special help.

6-1e ■ Guidelines for Teachers

Over the years, early education teachers have worked successfully with children with hearing loss. Effective programming usually incorporates the skills of a specially trained early childhood deaf education consultant. The specialist assists both teachers and parents in providing an education tailored to the child's hearing loss. Specialists often make the following recommendations:

1. Sit, kneel, or bend down to the child's level to talk. Look directly at the child. Children who are hard of hearing need to be spoken to face to face.

2. Use clear speech. Talk at a slightly slower pace with careful pronunciation. Avoid an overly loud voice and do not over-enunciate.

3. Use gestures when appropriate, but avoid over-gesturing. Too many gestures interfere with the child's efforts to speech-read.

4. Use brief but complete sentences when the child has reached that stage of language development. As with hearing children, **holophrastic** and **telegraphic speech** belong to particular stages of language development.

5. Seat the child directly across from the teacher. This gives the child the best possible position for speech-reading.

6. Face the light when talking to a child with a hearing disability. The light needs to be on the speaker's face, not the child's. Glaring light in the child's eyes interferes with bringing the speaker's face and mouth into full focus.

7. To get the child's attention, gently touch or tap her or him on the shoulder or hand. Always be aware of the possibility of startling a person who does not hear.

8. Speak the child's name when addressing him. Be sure the child is facing you before you start speaking.

9. When talking about something in the room, point to it, touch it, or hold it up. For example, if the teacher picks up the scissors and demonstrates the cutting task while giving instructions, the child has a better chance of understanding what is expected.

10. Include children with hearing impairments in all music activities. Provide many opportunities for them to participate by:
   - putting their hands on various instruments so they can feel the vibrations.
   - allowing them to play the instruments.
   - having frequent rhythmic activities such as clapping, jumping, rolling, and twirling.
   - pairing a normally hearing child with a child who is hard of hearing, for various musical games.

11. Involve all children, especially those who are hard of hearing, in story time. Choose books with bright clear pictures that "*tell*" the story. Gesture and use facial expressions that give clues to the story's moods.

12. Keep to a regular schedule of activities each day. Young children—especially children who are hard of hearing—often do not pick up on environmental signals and need to know what comes next to feel secure.

13. Some children with moderate-to-severe hearing loss make strange noises. They do not hear themselves, but their noises often bother other children. Teachers must find subtle ways to help these children be quiet when necessary (perhaps gently putting a finger on the child's lips and on the teacher's in a "Sssh" gesture).

14. In kindergarten or primary classrooms, avoid moving about the room or writing on the board while talking.

15. When a **manual interpreter** is present (unusual in an early childhood setting), allow the child and the interpreter to choose the most favorable seating.

16. Teach peers how to get the attention of the child and remind them to look at the child.

holophrastic speech a state of speech development where the child conveys meaning with a one-word utterance

telegraphic speech a stage of speech development when the child conveys meaning with two-word utterances

manual interpreter an individual who translates spoken language into sign language for the deaf

Children with hearing loss need to be talked to face to face.

© Cengage Learning 2015

6-1f ■ Assistive Technology

In addition to the cochlear implants discussed previously in this chapter, the following are some other types of assistive technology.

amplification device any instrument that augments (increases) hearing

earmold that part of an amplification device (hearing aid) that is fitted to the individual's ear

Amplification devices/hearing aids Most young children are fitted with behind-the-ear **amplification devices**. In most cases, plastic tubing carries the amplified sound to an **earmold** made especially for the child. The hearing aid may have on/off switches and volume controls.

Despite the benefits of hearing aids, problems occur in their use. A child's wearing a hearing aid does not guarantee that she or he is hearing. Teachers and parents need to be aware of minor problems in the system, such as:

- *An improperly fitting or damaged earmold*. If the earmold does not fit properly, it can cause irritation and discomfort. The same holds true if the earmold becomes chipped or cracked. A cracked earmold also can make an unpleasant feedback sound.

- *Dead or feeble batteries*. Batteries die with amazing frequency. Teachers and parents know when batteries are dead because the child stops responding. However, batteries should be replaced well before they are dead so children do not have to cope with periods of diminishing sound.

- *Feedback*. This irritating, high-pitched squealing sound can have several causes. Teachers and parents need to ensure that the earmold is properly seated in the ear and that it is not cracked.

Case Study ■ Helping a new student ■

You have just learned that a new child will be entering your preschool classroom on Monday. She cannot hear and does not speak. She knows a few signs, including "potty" and "hungry." What resources would you need to support her development in all domains? Identify local resources in your area that provide assistance to you (as the teacher) and the child's parents.

- **On and off switch**. Teachers must check regularly to make sure a child's hearing aid is turned on. Young children tend to turn the devices off, sometimes repeatedly. This happens most frequently when they are learning to wear a hearing aid. Eventually, most children become accustomed to the device and leave it turned on all the time. At this point, children can begin to check its working order themselves. Nevertheless, adults should continue to spot-check at least once a day.

- **Sore ears**. The earmold should never be inserted into a sore, cracked, or infected ear. At the first sign of irritation, the child should see a health care provider.

FM Systems Many children can use an additional amplifying system that helps reduce background noise. These devices work like miniature radio stations. They can be connected directly to hearing aids, or the child may wear a small plastic neck loop. Teachers clip a microphone and transmitter to their clothing and transmit their voices directly to the receiver worn by the child. Checking batteries and the device's on/off switches is as important with FM systems as with hearing aids.

Alerting devices Numerous alerting devices have been designed for the deaf and hard of hearing. These typically alert the individual through vibrations and/or bright lights. Examples include alarm clocks, doorbell signals, phone rings, and fire alerts.

Did You Get It?

What is the difference between hearing loss that occurs in the outer or middle ear and hearing loss that occurs in the inner ear (cochlea or auditory nerve)?

- **a.** A loss in the outer or middle ear produces a conductive hearing loss; a loss of hearing in the inner ear produces a sensorineural hearing loss.
- **b.** A loss in the outer or middle ear produces a sensorineural hearing loss; a loss in the inner ear produces a conductive hearing loss.
- **c.** A loss in the outer or middle ear produces a conductive hearing loss; a loss in the inner ear produces central deafness.
- **d.** A loss in the outer or middle ear produces central deafness; a loss in the inner ear produces conductive hearing loss.

Take the full quiz on CourseMate.

Blindness and Vision Impairments 6-2 ☀

Children with visual disabilities tend to be classified as *blind* or as having *residual* or *partial* vision. For educational purposes, the American Foundation for the Blind provides the following definitions.

- **Blind**. Visual loss is severe enough that it is not possible to read print, requiring the child to be educated through the use of Braille (a system of raised dots representing alphabet letters) and other materials using touch or sound.

- **Low vision**. Residual vision is sufficient to allow a child to read large print or possibly regular print under special conditions and to use other visual materials for educational purposes.

low vision refers to a severe visual impairment, not necessarily limited to distance vision; it applies to all individuals who are unable to read print even with the aid of eyeglasses.

- **Total blindness** is the inability to distinguish between light and dark. Few children are so drastically afflicted. Most have slight vision. Some can see the rough, general outlines of things but no details. Others can distinguish light and dark or very bright colors. It should be noted that the usefulness of residual vision will be lost unless children are encouraged constantly to exercise whatever vision they have.

6-2a ■ Types of Vision Problems

Vision losses vary as to cause, type, and severity. They are generally grouped in terms of physical abnormalities, **visual acuity**, and muscle problems.

The majority of true visual impairments are caused by physical problems. Visual acuity problems due to **refractive** errors are correctable with eyeglasses. Muscle imbalance problems, such as **strabismus** and **amblyopia**, are correctable by eyeglasses, patching, or surgery. A **pediatric ophthalmologist** who can provide appropriate treatment should follow children with visual impairment closely.

Physical abnormalities Many physical problems of the eyes that result in impaired vision develop prenatally. The cause may be an inherited disorder or a condition that results from maternal drug ingestion or infection such as rubella. Visual disorders linked to prenatal development include *cataracts* (a progressive clouding of the lens of one or both eyes) and *glaucoma* (a gradual destruction of the optic nerve as a result of a buildup of pressure caused by poor circulation of the fluids of the eye).

Sometimes damage to the eye occurs at the time of birth. One example is *retinopathy of prematurity* (ROP). Before the mid-1950s, excessive oxygen concentrations administered in the incubator to premature infants caused scar tissue, called *retrolental fibroplasia,* behind the lens. At present, ROP is found in extremely low-birth-weight infants even if oxygen concentration is ideal. Treatment is available if the condition is identified early, so ophthalmological screening of premature infants is essential.

Some types of visual impairments are caused by physical problems within the brain. Infections or injuries that occur before, during, or following birth may damage the optic nerve or the visual cortex (the portion of the brain where messages from the eyes are processed). Although vision is affected, the eyes appear normal. Other common terms related to atypical vision include the following:

- *Cortical blindness.* This term is used to describe certain visual impairments in the brain.

- *Visual acuity problems*. Normal-appearing eyes might have refractive errors, causing common problems with visual acuity. ***Refraction*** refers to the bending of light rays necessary to make a focused image at the back of the eye (Figure 6-3). Relatively minor deviations in the shape of the eye can cause refractive errors.

- ***Astigmatism***. Uneven refraction in different planes of the eye causes blurred vision; this is especially distracting when reading.

Excessive rubbing of the eyes can be a warning sign of vision problems.

© Cengage Learning 2015

visual acuity how well an individual is able to see; keenness of vision

refractive describes a visual acuity problems correctable with eyeglasses

strabismus eye muscle imbalance problems correctable with eyeglasses

amblyopia a vision problem that occurs when a child's eye does not get enough use and the visual system in the brain does not develop properly, leading to poor vision in the affected eye; it usually affects one eye but may occur in both eyes.

pediatric ophthalmologist physician who specializes in diseases and malfunctioning of the eyes during the developmental years

cortical blindness visual impairments originating in the brain

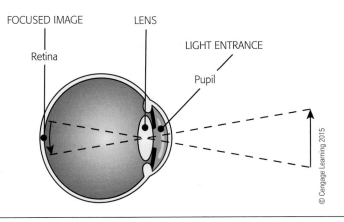

FOCUSED IMAGE   LENS

Retina   LIGHT ENTRANCE

Pupil

© Cengage Learning 2015

FIGURE 6-3
Structure of the Eye

- *Myopia*. Nearsightedness reduces the ability to see distant objects clearly.
- *Hyperopia*. Farsightedness reduces the ability to see close objects clearly.

Muscular Abnormalities Unbalanced contractions of the eye muscles can cause uncoordinated eye movements. Common problems include:

- *Strabismus*. This condition occurs when the eyes are not aligned and therefore do not work together as a unified pair. There are several forms of strabismus, including cross-eyes, wandering eyes, or one eye that turns inward or outward (wall eyes). Each variation has its distinct characteristics, causes, and treatment. In an older person, strabismus causes double vision. In young children, the brain suppresses the image received from one eye, which gradually leads to permanent loss of vision if not corrected. If the child sometimes focuses with the left eye, sometimes with the right eye (alternating strabismus), both eyes may continue to work well.

- *Amblyopia*. Marked differences in visual acuity between the eyes, or strabismus, that result in repression of vision from the same eye, can gradually cause amblyopia and loss of vision (in the affected eye) to the point of blindness. This condition is sometimes referred to as "*lazy eye*." Unfortunately, there are often no observable signs associated with amblyopia—alignment of the eyes appears normal unless the child has strabismus. Amblyopia causes a lack of normal depth perception and also increases the risk of long-term visual impairment.

- *Nystagmus*. Quick, jerky, back-and-forth or up-and-down eye movements are sometimes found in children who have poor vision. The condition is not caused by an abnormality of the eye muscles per se. Rather, neurological abnormalities may cause nystagmus and interfere with visual acuity. This condition improves with age.

6-2b ■ Identifying Vision Problems

Congenital blindness can usually be identified in the first year of life. Parents become aware that their infant does not look at them or at objects they wave in front of, or hand to, their child. Partial vision losses are more difficult to recognize. Often, they go undetected until the child is in school. Even then, many vision problems are not identified until the third or fourth grade, when the print in textbooks gets smaller, pictures are fewer, and the print becomes more condensed.

Accurately assessing the visual function of a young child with disabilities is essential in determining appropriate intervention and educational strategies (Koenig et al., 2000). Many children with visual impairments are identified through routine screening in preschools and child care settings.

The *Snellen Illiterate E* test is widely used for identifying visual acuity and amblyopia. In younger and low-functioning older children, visual acuity can be assessed with *Teller Acuity Cards* (Teller et al., 1986). Teller Acuity Cards test for pediatric visual acuity without requiring a verbal response. The professional judges an infant's attention to a series of cards showing stripes of different widths. This allows the professional to perform accurate infant vision screening and avoid the more complex, time-consuming laboratory testing that would otherwise be necessary.

Photo screening is a relatively new technique for detecting amblyopia, strabismus, cataracts, and significant acuity conditions in infants, toddlers, and children who have developmental delays or are difficult to screen (American Academy of Pediatrics, 2002). A major problem in trying to assess vision is that children with vision loss have no idea what they are supposed to be seeing; in other words, they really do not know that what they see is imperfect or different from what others are seeing. For this reason, parents and early childhood teachers often are the first to suspect possible vision problems in young children.

Warning signs The following list is adapted from material published by the National Society to Prevent Blindness. The *alerts* are grouped according to children's behavior, appearance, or verbal complaints.

- rubs eyes excessively
- shuts or covers one eye; tilts head or thrusts it forward
- has difficulty doing work or playing games that require close use of the eyes
- blinks excessively or becomes irritable when doing close work
- unable to see distant things clearly
- squints; squeezes eyelids together; frowns
- crossed eyes or eyes each turn outward
- red-rimmed, encrusted, or swollen eyelids
- inflamed, infected, or watery eyes
- recurring sties
- itchy, burning, or scratchy-feeling eyes
- inability to see well
- dizziness, headaches, or nausea following close work
- blurred or double vision

If parents' and teachers' observations or a vision screening suggest a problem, the next step is for parents to obtain medical assistance, preferably from a pediatric ophthalmologist. The ophthalmologist may prescribe eyeglasses, medication, surgery, eye exercises, **occlusion** of one eye, or some combination of these.

If a screening test does not reveal a problem, but the symptoms continue, it is still wise to refer a child for a medical workup. Marotz and Allen (2012) explain that *false positives* can occur. This means that a child with a vision

occlusion to obstruct; as used here, to prevent vision

problem (or any other kind of problem) may pass the screening test. In the case of vision screening, there may have been unintended coaching by the examiner, or the child may have peeked around the **occluder** during testing. Test results always should be regarded with caution, especially when a teacher or parent has reason to believe that a child's behaviors indicate a potential problem.

Children, especially school-age children with weak residual vision, may be referred to a low-vision clinic. Specialists can determine whether the child will benefit from using magnifiers, telescopic lenses, specific electronic devices, or closed-circuit, greatly magnified television. As children advance through the elementary grades, a number of other sophisticated reading and writing devices become available.

6-2c ■ The Impact of Vision Problems on Development

Even with average or above-average intelligence, a child who is blind from birth or early childhood is likely to have significant developmental delays (Cass, Sonkesen, & McConachie, 1994). Much of what a child learns comes from scanning the environment and then focusing on particular stimuli (Erin, 2000). Learning also comes from watching others, imitating them, and observing what follows. Poor vision affects a child's language development, motor development, and cognitive and social development. Why? Because the child's ability to interact with people, objects, and activities is curtailed. Children with vision problems may fail to recognize amusing events or may be oblivious to the consequences of their behavior. They may be unable to enter into new experiences because they have no visual grasp of what is going on. A card game such as "Go Fish" cannot be understood just by listening to players.

It is likely that the inability to play freely is as great a hindrance to development as anything else. Whereas sighted babies begin deliberately reaching for, and playing with, nearby objects, infants who are blind remain passive. Fewell and Kaminski (1994) observe:

> The cognitive, social, language, and adaptive skills that are acquired and practiced in the play of normally developing children as they prepare for higher order skills cannot be expected to arise from these natural childhood experiences for blind children. The facilitation of play in blind children appears to be a challenge for parents and teachers. (p. 152)

Children with early and severe vision loss have little idea of what they are supposed to be seeing.

An additional interference with development may be the behavioral mannerisms called **blindisms** displayed by some children with severe vision loss. These are self-stimulatory behaviors such as rolling the head, swaying the body, waving fingers in front of the face, forcibly blinking, and pressing the eyes (Good & Hoyt, 1989). These behaviors interfere with the child's acquisition of social, motor, and cognitive skills. As teachers help the blind child learn to play with

The ophthalmologist may prescribe eyeglasses.

© Cengage Learning 2015

occluder the object the eye examiner uses to prevent the child from seeing (usually one eye at a time)

blindisms a typical mannerisms displayed by some children with severe vision loss

materials and other children, the interfering behaviors can be replaced gradually with behaviors that enhance the child's development.

Effect on language development Language acquisition depends on discovering and identifying objects and actions. This is difficult for children who cannot see an object and its actions. Instead, such children must depend only on what they can touch or hear, which reduces their learning opportunities.

Once the child with a vision deficit begins to understand how to explore objects and formulate ideas about them, and when a parent or teacher models language, development of language proceeds more rapidly. It takes a child with a moderate-to-severe vision impairment at least a year longer to develop a full range of language skills. By school age, most are using language normally.

Effect on cognitive development Children who are blind or partially sighted generally lag in cognitive development and concept formation. Delays are more noticeable during the first three or four years of life (Council for Exceptional Children, 2003). With adequate nurturing and early intervention, the child with a vision deficit (if there are no other disabilities) usually catches up by age five or six.

Effect on motor development Although limited vision is not the cause of delayed and imperfect motor development, it does exert a negative influence. The greater the vision loss, the greater the delays in reaching, crawling, and walking. In fact, a child with limited vision does not develop the ability to localize sound and move toward it until the end of the first year (Fraiberg, 1979). Many children who are blind do not walk until they are two years old. Motor development is further delayed by the child's inability to learn skills related to judging distance, direction, body position, and an object's position in space. The children often develop strange ways of walking and positioning themselves because they have no visual reference points or models.

Effect on social development Often, young children with vision problems are unable to participate in interactions that build good social skills and interpersonal relationships. As infants, they tend to be quiet and passive. Nixon (1991) stresses the importance of family members and teachers providing a running commentary on what is happening. This helps to familiarize the child with everyday interactions and activities. Example: "Nikki is sitting next to you, Sarah. *She* is stringing wooden beads, and *you* are stringing wooden beads."

Most children with limited vision learn to function in a well-staffed preschool.

© Cengage Learning 2015

Play skills, as mentioned above, develop more slowly in children who are visually impaired. Toys, for example, are used less creatively, and play often is stereotyped because of the lack of visual models necessary to expand the imagination. Inclusion in an early childhood program with typically developing children is helpful, provided there are specific support strategies for promoting socialization (Warren, 1994).

Effects on family life Children who have vision impairments tend to be identified earlier than children with other impairments. Many vision difficulties are the result of prematurity, so vision tests are done on very young premature infants. As a result, the mother may experience depression related to the diagnosis. This depression is not postpartum but in addition to postpartum.

Reactions from the parents to the infant and the infant to the parents may also impact this depression. If a parent knows that their child cannot see them, they may not smile at their baby. The baby then does not coo back at the parent, because it cannot "feel" the emotion. It is like talking to your friend on the telephone. Your friend can tell you are smiling even though they cannot see you. Their tone of voice then changes and the conversation continues. The infant can sense the smiles and affectionate gazes of the parent and respond. The parent needs to be encouraged to look at, engage, and interact with their baby as if the baby could see (Hatton, McWilliam, & Winton, 2002).

6-2d ■ Early Intervention Programs

Intervention programs serving infants and toddlers usually focus on the parent as teacher. For the first year, programs tend to be home-based. A teacher, trained in working with infants who are blind and their parents, visits the home on a regular basis. The teacher provides information about the effects of vision problems on all aspects of development and coaches parents in special techniques for interacting with their infant.

Programs for older toddlers and preschoolers most often are center-based. The toddler program usually includes parents who serve as an integral part of the teaching staff. When the child enters preschool, parents continue to participate in their child's learning activities. An **orientation and mobility specialist** and a developmental therapist serve as consultants and provide support for the early childhood teacher and the parents. Young children with severe vision problems may require a segregated program that focuses on the basic adaptive strategies for learning to function in a seeing world. Most children will soon be able to progress into an inclusive classroom, although a dual placement may be required for a period of time. Most children with limited vision learn to function well in an adequately staffed preschool.

When teachers model appropriate ways to interact with a child with any kind of developmental problem, children learn to do the same. They learn to call the child's name or touch the child's shoulder to attract his or her attention. They learn to put things directly into the child's hands, naming each object. They learn to help the child move about by describing things specifically: "Here are the lockers. Jenny's locker is the second one. You can put her truck on the bottom shelf." However, assisting a classmate must never be a burden. Children who serve as helpers should enjoy the task and take pleasure in providing assistance.

orientation and mobility specialist therapist who teaches individuals with vision impairments the awareness of their position in the environment, of significant objects within the environment (orientation), and how to move safely and efficiently (mobility) by utilizing their remaining senses

In a classroom environment, the help of a consultant trained to work with children who have visual impairments is essential. This resource person can assist teachers in arranging classroom and curriculum activities to ensure effective learning experiences. The consultant can also help parents and teachers achieve the broader goal of strengthening children's intact sensory abilities through touch and sound (Pogrund, Fazzi, & Hess, 2002).

Many adults find it difficult not to overprotect children who have little or no vision. Like all young children, they need to explore their environment if they are to learn. They may bump into a wall, fall down, get up, start out again, have another mishap, and another, and another. To ensure the child does not experience unnecessary harm, the classroom and play yard must be kept safe and orderly. Pathways need to be clear of strewn toys and misplaced equipment that the child with low vision (and the teachers and other children) may trip over. Most important, children with low vision need to be helped with their mobility skills throughout the day. Learning to get about safely and efficiently is of prime importance.

Teachers must avoid the tendency to take over the rights of the child to learn self-defense and the rights of possession. One way is to refrain from speaking out prematurely on behalf of the child. However, the teacher may need frequently to supply the words: "Melinda, say, 'No! My egg beater!'" Another time, it may be necessary to tell the child that he or she is about to lose a turn: "Marcie, Tammy has been waiting for a turn on that swing. She is next." "Tammy, tell Marcie, 'My turn.'" At this point, the teacher must follow through. It is important that the sighted child yield the swing, give back the egg beater, or respond to any other reasonable request from the child. Figure 6-4 contains guidelines for teaching children with vision loss.

FIGURE 6-4

peripheral vision that degree of vision available at the outer edges of the eyes

Teaching Children with Vision Loss: Guidelines for Teachers

- Determine the degree of residual vision; find out from the child's parents and the vision specialist what the child can see. Many children can see shadows, color, and large pictures or objects. Some children's **peripheral vision** may be their best vision; thus, a turned-away head does not necessarily signal inattention.

- Make orientation and mobility skills a teaching priority. Familiarize the child with the classroom layout and storage of materials. Whenever changes occur, be sure to reorient the child.

- Put identifying materials or subtle noisemakers on the floor, doors, room dividers, and lockers. Examples:

  o a wind chime near the door to the play yard

  o tile in the creative areas, carpeting in the blocks and large-group area

  o rough matting by doors to the outside

  o a patch of velveteen glued to the child's locker

- Use specific words to tell the child what to do: "Put the book on the table," or "I'm sitting by the piano. Bring your shoes to me." Avoid nonspecific phrases such as "Come here," "Put it there," or "Be careful."

FIGURE 6-4
Continued

- Talk to the child about everything in the immediate environment. Give the names, over and over, for everyday objects: *ball, dog, cup, brush.* Naming the object is not enough; to understand *watering can*, for example, the child must hold one, feel what is inside, pour from it, and handle it empty and filled with water.

- Provide action words. Tell the child, many times over, what he or she is doing. "You are *running* in the grass." "You are *brushing* your teeth." "You are *drinking* juice."

- Help the child to localize and sort out sounds. Describe the classroom sounds and tell where they are coming from: the guinea pig squeaking *by the window;* the faucet dripping *in the sink;* the fan whirring *up on the ceiling.* Help children learn to identify the tick of a timer and the swishing of sandpaper blocks rubbing together.

- Play auditory guessing games. The teacher or another child can make the sound of one of several objects on a tray (tearing paper, closing a book, dropping a marble in a cup). The child with a vision problem locates the correct object(s) by touch. To make the game challenging for sighted children, too, the teacher can turn away from the children while making the sound, or can make the sound under a cloth or in a large box open only on the teacher's side.

- Teach sounds that may signal danger in contrast to those that are simply frightening. The sound of the power mower in the play field is something to stay away from. The drone of the vacuum cleaner signals something the child can help push. The fire alarm indicates to stop whatever is going on and stand by the door. The squeak of a chain warns a child to stay back because the swings are in motion.

- Offer several opportunities each day to learn through smelling, touching, and tasting. Actual objects, rather than plastic replicas, are best for teaching. In a session about fruit, a real banana and orange should be used for feeling, cutting, peeling, smelling, tasting, and comparing. Cooking experiences are good, too, and not just for children who are visually impaired. Sorting activities are important. Using something other than sight to tell the difference between shapes, sizes, textures, weight, and odors is a sorting and discrimination activity that provides valuable learning experiences for all children.

- Provide numerous physical prompts. Demonstrations need to take the form of subtle physical assistance and hand-over-hand "put throughs." Always work from behind the child so that the teacher's and the child's movements are synchronized. For example, when helping a child put on socks, sit behind the child, holding the sock open. If the child does not grasp the sock, gently guide his or her hands to the top of the sock to hold it open. If the child moves to pull the sock on, loosen your grasp and allow the child to do what he or she can. If a child stops or begins to struggle, move your hands back to the sock and provide only the needed amount of assistance. Gradually reduce assistance as the child masters the successive steps required to accomplish a task.

- Provide left-to-right training. Informal practice in working from left to right is a skill all preschool children need in preparation for reading. Braille and other academic activities follow the same format. When using pegboards, for example, the child can be encouraged to systematically fill the board by placing pegs in left-to-right and top-to-bottom progression.

- Show peers how to be friends, and how to be helpful. Peers should learn to identify themselves and to discuss what they are doing to help. "Hi, it's me, Abby, and I am putting a puzzle on the table for us to build" (Noonan & McCormick, 2006).

Did You Get It?

Which visual acuity problem can be corrected with eyeglasses?
a. Strabismus.
b. Amblyopia.
c. Refractive errors.
d. Physical abnormality.

Take the full quiz on CourseMate.

Summary

▶ Problems with hearing or vision greatly interfere with overall development.

▶ A severe hearing loss has a more pervasive negative effect on development than a vision loss.

▶ Infants with sensory impairments benefit from being in an early intervention program that starts in the first months of life and includes their parents. These children need to be educated in the least restrictive environment possible. This may require a segregated setting, at least in the very early years, if children are to receive the specialized education appropriate to their needs.

▶ Hearing losses are classified in three ways: conductive hearing loss, sensorineural hearing loss, and problems originating in the higher auditory cortex. Combined losses also occur. The most devastating result of a severe hearing loss is interference with early speech and language development. Chronic ear infections, especially otitis media, which may come and go, are responsible for problems with both hearing and language.

▶ Infants who do not startle or blink their eyes in response to loud noises may have a hearing impairment. A hearing loss may also be suspected in children who have acquired some language, if they begin asking frequently to have things repeated or behave in ways that suggest difficulty with understanding.

▶ Specially trained educators can teach speech as well as a variety of language systems, including American Sign Language, to children

with a hearing problem. The long-standing controversy continues: Should the child be taught to communicate *only* through speech, or should the child be allowed to use all forms of communication?

▶ Children who are partially sighted learn to function well in an adequately staffed classroom. They will be able to learn through specially presented printed or other visual materials.

▶ Screening tests are not always reliable for identifying children's vision problems. Therefore, parents and teachers must observe children closely and be alert to behavior signs associated with visual impairment. Early identification and treatment can reduce the negative impact poor vision might otherwise have on all aspects of children's development.

▶ Children with vision problems require more time, more practice, more verbal mediation, and more encouragement from adults. Early intervention programs serving infants and toddlers are usually home-based and focus on training parents as teachers.

▶ Young children, even those who are visually impaired, are readily accommodated in an early childhood classroom if a specially trained consultant is available to assist the teacher. It is important that teachers and parents refrain from overprotecting the young child who is vision-impaired. That child needs to learn self-defense and the rights of possession.

Key Terms

amblyopia, 130
American Sign Language, 125
amplification device, 128
audiologist, 121
blindisms, 133
cochlea, 121
cochlear implant, 122
conductive hearing loss, 121
cortical blindness, 130
cued speech, 127
cumulative effect, 123
deafness, 121
earmold, 128

higher auditory cortex, 121
holophrastic speech, 127
low vision, 129
manual interpreter, 127
occluder, 133
occlusion, 132
orientation and mobility
    specialist, 135
otitis media, 121
pediatric ophthalmologist, 130
peripheral vision, 136
post-lingual deafness, 121
pre-lingual deafness, 121

refractive, 130
residual hearing, 122
sensorineural hearing loss, 121
sensory impairments, 120
sensory system, 120
signing, 126
speech reading, 125
strabismus, 130
telegraphic speech, 127
threshold, 124
total communication, 125
visual acuity, 130

Student Activities

1. Locate someone with a hearing or vision loss (friend, schoolmate, grandparent). Talk with that person about the impact of the loss on everyday life.

2. Invite several people with a vision or hearing impairment to class to demonstrate the use of their amplification or magnification devices.

3. Simulate greatly impaired vision by playing blindfold games in class, such as moving about the classroom without mishap. Try moving toward one particular person based on that person's voice among several. Have several students blindfolded at one time and ask them to guess the source of sounds that you provide (closing a door, lowering a window shade, sharpening a pencil, etc.).

4. Prepare an identify-by-touch guessing game that sighted children and children with a vision problem could enjoy together. Try it out with your classmates and have them critique it. Alter your game to take account of appropriate recommendations. Now try the game with young children.

5. Devise a game such as the one you did above, but with a child with a hearing impairment in mind.

6. This text does not discuss the issue of a "culture of deafness." Do some research to learn about this topic and discuss the impact and use of cochlear implants in terms of what you learn.

Review Questions

Respond to the following items in list form.

1. List and explain the four types of hearing loss.

2. Identify seven behaviors in a child who already has language that may indicate hearing loss and what teacher strategies you would use to work with that child.

3. List ways that children who have a hearing impairment can learn to communicate and what you as the teacher need to do to engage the child in conversation.

4. List ways a teacher can support a parent in facilitating a child's understanding and lip reading.

5. Explain ways in which a hearing aid can malfunction.

6. List three common visual acuity problems and three muscular imbalance problems related to eye functioning.

7. As someone who is aware of the behaviors in young children that may indicate vision problems, explain the teacher's role in guiding such children to be active class participants.

8. What areas of development are likely to be affected by blindness or impaired vision, and what strategies would you, as a teacher, implement to minimize developmental delays?

9. What reactions do parents have to receiving the diagnosis of hearing impairment or vision impairment?

Additional Resources/Readings

Children's Books on Sensory Impairments for Preschool to Grade 3:

Brian's Bird
Written by Patricia Anne Davis
Shen's Books

Brian, who is visually impaired, enjoys taking care of the parakeet he receives on his eighth birthday. He names him Scratchy as that is how the parakeet feels on his hand. When his older brother accidentally lets the bird escape but then helps Brian get it back, the boys feel closer.

Screaming Kind of Day
Written by Rachna Gilmore
Fitzhenry and Whiteside Publishing

Scully, who is hearing-impaired, listens to her teasing brother and scolding mother only when she wants to; then she turns on her hearing aids. One rainy day when she wants to play outside, her mother sends her to her room instead. Sneaking out the back door causes Scully more problems before she and her mother reconcile.

Lucy's Picture
Written by Nicola Moon
Orchard Books

Lucy wants to make a picture for her grandpa, but she doesn't want to use brightly colored paints like the rest of her class. Lucy's grandpa is blind, so Lucy wants to make him a very special picture with twigs, feather, velvet, and sand—a picture he can feel with his fingers.

Moses Goes to a Concert
Written by Isaac Millman
Square Fish Books

This is one of several books about Moses. In this story, Moses and his classmates, all of whom are deaf, go to a concert with their teacher and enjoy experiencing music. They discover that the percussionist in the orchestra is also deaf. Includes information on sign language.

Helpful Websites

ERIC Clearinghouse on Disabilities and Gifted Education

http://eric.hoagiesgifted.org

ERIC is the acronym for the Educational Resources Information Center. The ERIC Clearinghouse on Disabilities and Gifted Education (ERIC EC) is one of sixteen federally funded clearinghouses. ERIC EC gathers and disseminates professional literature, information, and resources on the education and development of individuals of all ages who have disabilities and/or are gifted. Topics include identification, assessment, intervention, and enrichment.

National Association for Parents of Children with Visual Impairments (NAPVI)

http://www.spedex.com/napvi

NAPVI is a national organization that enables parents to find information and resources for their children who are blind or visually impaired, including those with additional disabilities.

National Dissemination Center for Children with Disabilities (NICHCY)

http://www.NICHCY.org

NICHCY is the national dissemination center that provides information on disabilities and disability-related issues. Anyone can use their services—families, educators, administrators, journalists, or students. Information is available about specific disabilities, IEPs, education rights and laws, early intervention, parent materials, and more.

Oral-Deaf Education

http://oraldeafed.org

Oral-deaf education is a collaborative, family-centered educational approach that develops a child's speech and listening abilities along with confidence and life skills to meet the challenges of the greater world. This means that parents and family play a key role right from the start. Oral-deaf education integrates the earliest and most natural intervention and the most current and inclusive education along with today's sophisticated hearing technologies, to enable children with a hearing loss to learn to listen and talk. All materials are free.

Visit the Education CourseMate for this textbook to access the eBook, Did You Get It? quizzes, Digital Downloads, TeachSource Video Cases, flashcards, and more. Go to CengageBrain.com to log in, register, or purchase access.

Physical Disabilities and Health Problems

OBJECTIVES

After reading this chapter, you should be able to:

7-1 define and give examples of physical disabilities.

7-2 recognize the various health problems an early childhood teacher may encounter.

7-3 describe the program implications and the role of the early childhood teacher when working with children with physical disabilities and health problems.

7-4 outline practices for maintaining health records and administering medication.

· · · · · · · · · · · · · · · · · ·

naeyc

The following NAEYC Standards are addressed in this chapter:

STANDARD 1 Promoting Child Development and Learning

STANDARD 2 Building Family and Community Relationships

STANDARD 3 Observing, Documenting and Assessing to Support Young Children and Families

STANDARD 5 Using Content Knowledge to Build Meaningful Curriculum

CONNECTIONS

- Beth was nearly four years old and not walking when her grandparents became her guardians. From early infancy, she had been seriously neglected by her parents and had been without adequate medical care despite her obvious physical and developmental problems. Soon after Beth moved in with her grandparents, they made appointments for her to be seen by the pediatric team at a nearby medical center, and they enrolled her in a preschool program associated with the center. Within a year and a half, Beth was showing marked improvement: walking, riding tricycles, and climbing on playground equipment along with the other children.

- Jack has asthma, which is controlled with daily breathing treatments he receives at home. His first-grade teacher, the principal, and the yard-duties and office manager have all been trained to look for signs of breathing difficulty and are familiar with his Emergency Treatment Plan. Jack's parents communicate about how Jack is doing and how changes in seasons and activities are impacting Jack's asthma. Because of this careful planning and ongoing communication, Jack's parents know he is well cared-for at school and able to participate with his first-grade peers.

Physical activity and general good health are essential for optimal early development. Infants and children who eat well, sleep well, and move about freely are likely to acquire a well-integrated range of cognitive, language, social, and physical skills. Problems with health and motor control tend to interfere with everything a child tries to do or learn. Few have described the situation better than Caldwell (1973). She noted that children with disabilities who cannot move about freely are not able to explore their environments and thus cannot access learning opportunities available to children who are typically developing. Since young children's learning is activity-based, a physical disability may affect overall development because it interferes with the ability to move about, explore, rearrange play materials, and seek out additional playthings and playmates.

A nine-month-old tires of playing with familiar toys. She crawls to the bookcase and soon discovers the fun of taking books off the shelf. That infant has found a challenge for herself and a match for her rapidly developing motor skills.

In this chapter, discussion will focus on two broad categories of problems.

1. Physical impairments that relate to problems involving skeleton, joints, and muscles. These include:

   - missing limbs, club feet, congenital hip dislocations
   - neurological disorders such as **cerebral palsy**
   - joint **contractures** caused by fractures, burns, or amputations

2. Health conditions related to limited strength, vitality, or alertness as a result of chronic or acute health problems. These include:

   - heart conditions
   - epilepsy
   - asthma
   - leukemia
   - diabetes
   - sickle-cell anemia

cerebral palsy a condition caused by injury to certain parts of the brain; usually results in paralysis and uncontrollable muscle movement in particular parts of the body

contracture permanent tightening of muscles and joints

Physical disabilities and serious health impairments frequently overlap.

© Cengage Learning 2015

- HIV/AIDS
- hemophilia
- obesity

Physical disabilities and serious health impairments frequently overlap. Neurological problems may complicate both—as in cerebral palsy, spina bifida, and other childhood conditions.

Physical Disabilities 7-1

The term *physical disabilities* (sometimes referred to as "physical challenges") refers to conditions that interfere with the normal functioning of bones, joints, and muscles. The problem is usually congenital and may be noted at birth. Club foot is an example. Other disabilities, such as muscular dystrophy, manifest themselves later in childhood.

7-1a ■ Cerebral Palsy

Cerebral palsy (CP) is the most common physical disability in children. The term is used to describe neurological disorders resulting in lack of control of muscle movements. The cause is damage to the brain that can occur before, during, or after birth. Oxygen deprivation, injury, infection, and hemorrhage might be involved, but the exact cause of this disorder can seldom be identified. The brain anomaly is static and not progressive. However, the neurological symptoms in young children change with the rapid maturation of the brain in early infancy and therefore are sometimes not diagnosed until around eight months of age. The full degree of the neurological disability is usually not apparent until about age five. CP varies in severity and type. It is classified by the type of abnormal muscle tone displayed and by the body parts affected.

Spasticity Children with CP have abnormal muscle tone. They are described as **hypertonic**, or *spastic*. Spasticity affects certain muscles more than others. When the muscles that flex a joint have a higher muscle tone than the muscles

hypertonic having abnormally high muscle tone

that extend a joint, a contracture develops. When this occurs, the joint's **range of motion** is significantly decreased, and the child's mobility is impaired. Most frequently, contractures occur in the hips, knees, ankles, elbows, and wrists.

7-1b ■ Hypotonicity

Too little muscle tone characterizes **hypotonicity**. The result is an inability to move about or maintain postural control, a "rag doll" condition. Infants of this type often are referred to as "floppy" babies. Many have difficulty with head control. This deprives them of learning experiences that most infants get from being held upright. The quantity and quality of their interactions with the environment are mildly to severely limited, depending upon the degree of hypotonicity.

Athetosis Fluctuating or uneven muscle tone is called *athetosis*. Muscle control that goes from one extreme to the other (either too low or too high) is typical. Children with this condition tend to retain **primitive reflexes** such as grasping and sucking past the normal time. This interferes with the development of **voluntary motor responses**.

Ataxia Lack of motor coordination—*ataxia*—is characterized by poor balance and a lurching walk. Children with ataxia may also have great difficulty with fine motor activities such as feeding themselves, writing, cutting with scissors, and picking up small objects. Materials may get dropped or pushed off the table as a result of involuntary movements. About 30 percent of children with CP have a mixture of spasticity and athetosis or ataxia.

Classifications based on body parts A second way of classifying CP is according to the parts of the body that are affected. Figure 7-1 lists the terms used to describe the location of involvement.

The extent of motor impairment varies. Some children have disabilities so severe they cannot hold their heads still or straighten their arms or legs. Others have control problems so slight as to be scarcely noticeable. Many children with CP, like children with other developmental problems, fail to meet major motor milestones at expected times. A distinction must be made, however. Children with general developmental problems usually have delays in all areas. In contrast, children with CP may have delayed motor skills (including speech), but many have good cognitive and receptive language skills.

Young children with CP usually benefit from an inclusive classroom experience. The success of the placement depends on the child and his or her teacher receiving adequate support. A physical therapist or occupational therapist (sometimes both) should provide ongoing consultation and therapy whenever a child has a motor dysfunction (Washington, Schwartz, & Swinth, 1994).

FIGURE 7-1

Terms that Describe the Location of the Body Affected by CP

- *Diplegia:* Involvement of all four extremities with the legs more severely affected than the arms.
- *Hemiplegia:* Only one side of the body is involved.
- *Paraplegia:* Involvement of the legs only.
- *Quadriplegia:* Involvement of both arms, both legs, trunk, and the muscles that provide head control.

© Cengage Learning 2015

Children with CP often have excellent cognitive and receptive language abilities.

Jaren Wicklund/Fotolia

myelomeningocele a congenital protrusion of the spinal cord through the vertebrae; paralysis of the lower trunk and legs often results

meningocele similar to the *myelomeningocele*, except that the protrusion contains only the covering of the spinal cord and usually causes little or no neurological impairment

hydrocephalus condition that results from undrained fluids leading to enlarged head and ultimate deterioration of the brain

shunt a tube implanted into the brain to allow proper circulation and drainage of fluids within the skull

7-1c ■ Spinal Cord Injuries

Spinal cord damage presents motor problems quite different from those associated with CP. When the spinal cord is injured or severed, muscles below the point of damage become impaired. The muscles no longer receive messages from the brain. Alternately, sensations normally experienced below the point of injury no longer are transmitted back to the brain. It is important to note that the brain itself is not affected.

Because of this interruption in neural communication between the brain and certain parts of the body, a person may have no sensation of where his or her affected limbs are positioned or what is happening to the limbs. A child may unknowingly suffer serious burns, cuts, or broken bones. Families, teachers, and caregivers of young children must learn to be the *sensory monitors* for the child's affected extremities and trunk.

The most familiar of the spinal cord injuries is spina bifida (**myelomeningocele** and **meningocele**). The damage comes from imperfect development of the spinal cord and spinal column during the first thirty days of fetal development. Children with spina bifida experience a number of problems in addition to paralysis of the affected limbs.

Two of the more common conditions are:

- **Hydrocephalus.** Blockage of the circulation of the spinal fluid in the cranial (brain) cavity.

If uncorrected, usually through placement of a **shunt**, the fluid accumulates in the cavity, enlarging the head and damaging the brain.

- ***Incontinence***. Lack of bladder and bowel control. A number of children with myelomeningocele do not receive messages from the urinary system.

Progressive weakening of the muscle structure characterizes several early childhood disabilities.

Rich Legg/iStockphoto.com

The result is the inability to hold or release urine. The same may be true of bowel activity. While this disability is difficult to overcome, many children can be helped to learn to manage their bowel and bladder needs independently. Liptak (2012) points out that competence in toileting is necessary for social growth toward independence and that prevention of soiling, wetting, and odor enhances the child's self-esteem. As the team assesses the child's developmental skills, adaptive behaviors, and emotional strengths, team members can determine the child's readiness to learn toilet skills and other everyday tasks (Lozes, 1988).

7-1d ■ Muscular Dystrophy

progressive in terms of health, a condition that gets steadily better (or worse)

juvenile rheumatoid arthritis a disorder that involves the joints, causes stiffness, swelling, and limited motion; may be accompanied by inflammation of the eyes

Progressive weakening of the muscles is the major characteristic of muscular dystrophy and related muscular disorders. There are several types of muscular dystrophy. The most common is Duchenne's disease, a sex-linked disorder that affects only boys. In Duchenne's disease, progressive muscle weakness begins at the hips and shoulders and gradually moves out to the arms and legs. Hand skills often are retained, even when the limbs are severely impaired. One child, for example, was able to string small wooden beads in complicated patterns if the beads were placed in a basket in his lap. However, when he ran out of beads he was unable to lift his arms to get more beads from the nearby table.

A child with muscular dystrophy must be encouraged to move about the classroom frequently. Prevention of muscle contractures is a major goal of both therapy and classroom activities for these children. Dormans and Batshaw (2007) advise that children with muscular dystrophy be kept out of wheelchairs as long as possible and be involved in active exercise programs.

© Cengage Learning 2015

▶❙❙ **TeachSource** Video Connections

Including Children with Physical Disabilities: Best Practices

Teachers in inclusive classrooms are responsible for ensuring that all students succeed academically as well as socially and emotionally. In this video, you'll see how elementary school teacher Lisa Kelleher, in collaboration with her classroom aide, provide an optimal educational experience for Maryanne, a student who has spina bifida.

After watching this video, discuss the following:

1. Describe the adaptive equipment/assistive technology you observed in the video. What was the positive outcome of its use for Maryanne?

2. Describe the roles of both the teacher and the classroom aide in Maryanne's education.

Watch on CourseMate.

7-1e ■ Hip Dysplasia

Developmental dislocation of the hip (DDH), once called *congenital dislocation* of the hip, occurs more frequently in girls than in boys. The dislocation can occur *in utero* or it may occur gradually after birth (Dormans & Batshaw, 2007). The head of the thigh bone (femur) may be out of the hip socket, or move in and out. The hip displacement is usually diagnosed soon after birth and treated nonsurgically. Without treatment, the child is not able to walk normally and often waddles.

7-1f ■ Juvenile Rheumatoid Arthritis

Arthritic conditions generally are associated with older people. However, young children also develop certain types of arthritis, especially **juvenile rheumatoid arthritis**. Chronic and painful inflammation of the joints and the tissue surrounding the joints is a major symptom. Prolonged sedentary activity can cause further stiffening of the joints. Children with juvenile rheumatoid arthritis need both the freedom and the encouragement to move about a great deal at home and at school. Symptoms often disappear by age eighteen.

The major goal of teachers is to help children keep their motor skills functional.

Did You Get It?

What are the significant differences between athetosis and ataxia?

a. Fluctuating or uneven muscle tone characterizes athetosis; lack of motor coordination with poor balance and a lurching walk characterizes ataxia.

b. Lack of motor coordination with poor balance and a lurching walk characterizes athetosis; fluctuating or uneven muscle tone characterizes ataxia.

c. Children with athetosis may have great difficulty with fine motor activities such as feeding themselves, writing, cutting with scissors, and picking up small objects; children with ataxia tend to retain primitive reflexes such as grasping and sucking past the normal time.

d. Involuntary movements resulting in materials being dropped or pushed off the table are particular to athetosis; the retention of primitive reflexes of children with ataxia affects the development of voluntary motor responses.

Take the full quiz on CourseMate.

Program Implications 7-2

Early and appropriate intervention has a positive effect on the acquisition of motor skills in young children with physical disabilities. Despite individual differences among children with physical impairments, they have the same basic classroom needs:

- the services of various pediatric professionals working as a team with classroom teachers
- **adaptive equipment** designed for each child's particular disability
- environmental adaptations to facilitate and support each child's learning efforts

adaptive equipment mobility devices, prostheses, and prescribed alterations of standard furnishings to meet the needs of exceptional children

7-2a ■ Team Efforts

A team approach that includes and supports teachers and families has been discussed in several other contexts. Here we present a brief review related specifically to physical disabilities. (As noted repeatedly, good motor skills are critical to every aspect of children's development.)

Physical and occupational therapists (PT/OT), trained to focus on early motor skills, often are selected as *family service coordinators* (FSCs). The FSC works closely with parents, teachers, and other team members. For example, in developing an intervention program for a child with CP who has a feeding problem, the OT/PT, as coordinator of family resources, may call upon the nutritionist, the social worker, and perhaps the dentist to provide consultation or direct assistance.

If a child also has a language or hearing problem, the services of a speech therapist and audiologist will be enlisted. A psychologist is often asked to join the team to consult on a variety of issues, including behavior problems. The various disciplines may also work or consult with the teacher and parents directly.

At other times, the OT/PT may serve as a transdisciplinary agent who blends the various recommendations into intervention activities to be carried out in the child's home and school environment.

The team coordinator needs to understand the goals of early childhood education and also needs to help teachers and families understand therapy goals. As teachers, families, and team members work together, there is greater assurance of shared implementation and integration of the child's daily therapy program into the everyday format of the home and classroom structure (Mather & Weinstein, 1988, p. 7). The ways in which a child with physical disabilities is positioned and helped to move about, at home and at school, are crucial to development.

Depending on the therapists' assessment, individual remediation activities are mapped out for each child. The classroom teacher should never be expected to put a child through stressful exercises. Nor do teachers initiate any kind of **therapeutic** activity without specific instruction and supervision from a certified specialist. Activities that are pleasant for both the child and the teacher (and often fun for other children as well) are the usual recommendations. *Under no circumstances should teachers initiate positioning exercises or remedial motor activities without specific guidance from a certified therapist.*

Children with uncertain motor skills, even though they are able to walk, fall frequently.

© Cengage Learning 2015

7-2b ■ Adaptive Equipment

therapeutic related to treatment of a disease or disability

prostheses artificial devices replacing body parts that are damaged at birth or later removed

The occupational therapist and physical therapist (OT/PT) guide teachers in the use of special mobility devices, or **prostheses**, and the adaptation of regular play equipment. The following are examples of adaptive equipment options:

Mobility devices Braces, a walker, or a wheelchair may be among the mobility devices prescribed for children who cannot move about easily. Young children with paraplegia may use a low, small-wheeled flat cart. They lie tummy-down on the cart and push themselves from one activity to another with hands and arms. Power wheelchairs are increasingly in use, even by two- and three-year-olds, to provide mobility at school and at home.

Children with uncertain motor skills, even though they are able to walk, fall frequently. The falls are likely to distress adults more than they do the child, who tends to become accustomed to falling. Children who fall frequently may be fitted with a helmet to prevent serious head injury. All children with a history of frequent falling are given training in how to fall, as well as how to get up again. The latter is especially important.

Adults must restrain themselves from rushing to the rescue, picking the child up before he or she has a chance to get up independently. Adults who restrain themselves save the child from being unnecessarily and additionally disabled through *learned helplessness*. Not rescuing the child can be painful for caring adults, as this continuation of Beth's story illustrates.

Beth glowed with triumph over every motor skill she mastered, but Grandfather had a difficult time of it. He often stayed to watch after dropping Beth off at the classroom.

Frequently, a teacher watched with him and talked about what was going on. It always pained him to see how hard Beth had to struggle. Why were the adults so uncaring, even unkind, as to allow this little child, who already had experienced such hardships, to work so hard to pull herself to a stand?

The first time Grandfather saw Beth fall and it appeared that no one was going to pick her up, he started to rush into the classroom himself to pick her up. The teacher who had been talking with him gently stopped him. Once again she explained the underlying philosophy—the threat to Beth's ultimate independence if she were not allowed to practice the survival skills she was being taught.

Positioning devices Motor problems can be accompanied by muscular weakness that interferes with head and trunk control. Maintaining a sitting position becomes a problem, as does grasping and hanging on to objects. The OT/PT can help teachers reduce the effects of motor problems by recommending or procuring specially designed equipment such as a **wedge, bolster,** or **prone-board.** It is essential that therapists help teachers identify the purpose of each device and how it applies to particular children and their particular disabilities. Teachers should be sure they feel comfortable with the use of the equipment, as the inappropriate use of adaptive equipment can do more harm than good.

Therapists also must help teachers be aware of special precautions or situations that might arise while a child is using the equipment. Teachers can help therapists by describing classroom activities and sharing with the therapist which activities are difficult for the child.

wedge, bolster therapeutic devices to help maintain a child's position

prone-board a therapeutic device to help a child maintain a standing position

7-2c ■ Adapting Materials

One framework for supporting all young learners is called **universal design for learning (UDL).** The principles of universal design were introduced in the area of architecture to address the challenges associated with designing physical spaces for all people, including individuals with physical and cognitive disabilities.

universal design for learning (UDL) a framework that guides the development of curricula that are flexible and supportive of all students; inspired by the universal design movement in architecture

The universal design of early learning "suggests that instead of creating a curriculum and then adapting it to meet the needs of individual children in the program, it is better to start off with an instructional design which provides learners with a variety of ways to access and process information and demonstrate what they have learned" (Blagojevic, Twomey, & Labas, 2007).

Teachers can help therapists by describing classroom activities that are difficult for the child.

© Cengage Learning 2015

FIGURE 7-2

The Three Principles of UDL

Multiple means of representation	Multiple means of expression	Multiple means of engagement
• Provide instructions and learning opportunities in multiple formats	• Give plenty of options to express what they know	• Provide choices that fuel student's interest and independence
• Vary level of complexity	• Provide models and feedback for differing levels of proficiency	• Teach them to risk making mistakes and learn from these mistakes
• Highlight critical features		
• Provide background information		
• Support vocabulary		

Source: UDL at a glance (2012). http://www.cast.org

A universal design approach to learning follows good practice in early education (Conn-Powers, Cross, & Traub, & Hutter-Pishgahi, 2006):

1. recognizing that a one-size-fits-all approach to education does not work
2. understanding the need to design curricula to meet the needs of all classroom learners
3. believing that all children who attend early education programs will be successful in their development and learning

The principles of the universal design for learning are not foreign to those familiar with the best practices in early childhood education. The principles require teachers to take the next step and apply what they know about these concepts to a curriculum designed to reach the greatest number of learners. UDL includes the three following principles:

1. Providing multiple means of representation.
2. Providing multiple means of action and expression.
3. Providing multiple means of expression (CAST, 2011).

Figure 7-2 provides a description of each of these principles in the classroom. The following is an example of UDL in a preschool class where the teacher adapted a classroom routine so that all students could participate, despite their varied abilities.

Krista teaches in a classroom with children ages three to five. They range in language abilities from typical to nonverbal. Some of her students use words, while others use signs or a picture exchange program (described in Chapter 16). Each morning during circle, Krista gives her students the chance to choose the closing song. On a small flannel board, she places a choice of four small cards, each bearing a symbol for one of the class's favorite songs. (She rotates the choice regularly.) Throughout the week, the children each get a turn to choose their favorite song card. The children all shout encouraging words as their peer make a selection. Children who are verbal not only pull a song card off the board and hand it to Krista, but they are also asked to tell the class which song they have chosen. Likewise, students who are nonverbal choose a card and hand it to Krista. She will then either announce the song or asks another student to announce the song. This simple strategy of a song board enables all of her students to participate in what is now the class's favorite part of circle.

Teachers should make every attempt to design their classroom universally. A UDL model establishes a foundation for success that, once done, can be adapted to meet the particular needs of individual students (Stockall, Dennis, & Miller, 2012). Examples of possible adaptations follow, and they are summarized in Figure 7-3.

Manipulative materials For children who must spend much of their time standing or in a wheelchair, materials can be mounted on a board fastened to the wall. Wall displays allow children to grasp and manipulate objects they otherwise might not be able to manage. (The arrangements give a new dimension to materials for children who are typically developing, too.) Items that are to be mounted on a play board should be the same materials all children are using. The use of wall boards should not be limited to children with physical disabilities. The following is a partial list of materials:

manipulative materials materials that children can handle and work with, such as puzzles, blocks, and wooden beads

- bolts, such as those used to lock doors
- Lego® or Duplo® boards with a bag or container to hold extra blocks
- puzzles with Velcro on the backs of pieces

FIGURE 7-3

Classroom and Material Adaptation

Classroom/Curriculum Area	Materials/Adaptations
Creative/Art Area	• Large pencils, crayons, and markers or adapted with a ball • Paper taped to table to avoid slipping
Fine Motor Area	• Wall-mounted manipulatives including puzzles with Velcro on back of pieces, Lego boards, pegboards
Snack Area	• Built-up spoon handles • Suction cups or skid-resistant shelf paper to keep plates and cups from sliding
Outdoor Play Area	• Swings adapted with safety harness • Pedal and wheel toys adapted with foot block and Velcro • Ground surface soft and resilient
Overall Classroom	• Wide aisles and space to turn around and maneuver wheelchairs or walkers • Handrails and ramps where needed • Low shelves • Clearly defined play spaces

© Cengage Learning 2015

One principal of universal design learning (UDL) is believing that all children will be successful in their development.

- pegboards with a bag or container to hold extra pegs
- towel-drying racks that are open at one end so that beads can be threaded onto the bars
- flannel, Velcro, or magnetic boards

Creative materials These materials can be adapted in various ways. Here are some examples:

- Large crayons, chalk, or paintbrushes are available. Even these may be too small for some children to grasp firmly. If so, a section can be wrapped with layers of securely taped-down plastic material, enabling the child to get a firmer grip.
- Pencils, crayons, and colored pens can be pushed through a small sponge rubber ball. The child holds the ball to scribble and draw.
- Paper can be taped to the table to prevent it from sliding away when a child is coloring, painting, or pasting.
- Magic markers or thick-tipped felt pens can be provided for children with weak hand and wrist controls. They require less pressure than crayons, but result in the rich, bright colors that please children.
- Finger paint, potter's clay, and water play can be available more frequently. These materials require minimal fine motor control but make a major contribution in the improvement and strengthening of small-muscle function.

Self-help devices Many devices (available through special education catalogs) assist children in feeding, grooming, and dressing themselves.

In addition, low-cost adaptations can be devised:

- Put a small suction device (such as a bar soap holder) under a child's plate to keep it from sliding out of reach or off the table.
- Shelf-liner paper that is skid-resistant can be placed on a table area to keep plates, papers, and the like from skidding.
- Build up a spoon handle by taping a hair roller or piece of foam rubber in place. This gives the child better control of the spoon.

- Improvise a cuff that keeps a spoon in the palm of the hand. The cuff is a wide strap that has a pocket for the spoon and is fastened around the hand with a Velcro closure.
- Use Velcro to replace buttons, zippers, and snaps. In many cases, Velcro can be put over existing buttons and buttonholes.

7-2d ■ Adaptations in the Classroom

Alterations may be needed in the classroom and play yard if children with motor impairments are to have a safe and appropriate learning environment.

Wheelchair accommodation Space to maneuver a wheelchair in and out of activities and to turn it around is essential. Toileting areas must be clear so a child can wheel in and out of the bathroom easily and pull up parallel to the toilet.

Handrails mounted on the wall are necessary so that the child can learn to swing from the wheelchair onto the toilet seat. Ramps can be constructed to facilitate movement between buildings, classrooms, and playground areas.

It is important to consider floor coverings when working with children with mobility problems.

Railings Indoor and outdoor railings attached in strategic places help children with poor balance and faulty coordination move about more independently. Railings can serve other children, too, as exercise and ballet bars.

Floor coverings Carpeting, if it is well stretched and securely nailed down, is helpful for children with mobility problems. It also provides a warm and comfortable play surface for all children. When carpeting is not possible, crutches must have non-skid tips, and shoes should have non-skid soles. Non-skid soles can be devised by gluing fine sandpaper, felt, or textured rubber onto the existing soles of a child's shoes.

Eye-level materials It is helpful for teachers to ask themselves, "How does the room appear at a child's level? Are there interesting things (such as a manipulative wall hanging) for all children to watch, touch, and work with? What is available at eye level for a child on a scooter board or in a wheelchair or for one who gets around only by crawling?

Transitions Children with physical disabilities who are using adaptive equipment such as wheelchairs and walkers or who are slower to transition from one area or activity to another may always feel like they are playing "catch up" with their

It is helpful for teachers to ask, "How does the room appear at a child's level?"

classmates. For example, during the transition from outdoor time to circle, if the child with the walker starts out last in line, she will not only be the last one in the classroom but most likely the last one to hang up her coat and get to the carpet for circle time. Teachers should be aware of these issues and change the lineup or grouping regularly so that the same children aren't always first or last.

Did You Get It?

When should a teacher be instructed to arrange for therapeutic activities for a child with physical disabilities?

a. Under no circumstances should teachers initiate positioning exercises or remedial motor activities without specific guidance from a certified therapist.

b. Teachers may initiate positioning exercises without specific guidance from a certified therapist.

c. Teachers may initiate remedial motor activities without specific guidance from a certified therapist.

d. Teachers may initiate therapeutic activity.

Take the full quiz on CourseMate.

7-3 Health Problems

Children experience a variety of health problems during infancy and early childhood. For the most part, these are relatively mild and do not interfere appreciably with growth and development. On the other hand, some children are chronically ill and live every day with serious health problems. In addition, many developmental disabilities involve significant health risks and problems. These present the child, the family, and teachers with challenges throughout the developmental years. Chapter 5 provides information regarding many of these disabilities, including Down syndrome.

7-3a ▪ Asthma

Asthma is the most common chronic childhood disease. Nearly seven million asthma sufferers are under age eighteen (Centers for Disease Control and Prevention, 2009; American Lung Association, 2012). Asthma is the most common form of school absenteeism due to chronic disease, and it accounted for an estimated fourteen million lost school days (Smart, 2004).

During an asthma attack, the child has discomfort and tightness in the chest. Breathing becomes labored and may turn to wheezing as the individual tries to expel air that has become trapped in the lungs. Attacks may be brought on by certain foods, pollens, animal furs, temperature changes (particularly cold air), strenuous exercise, and respiratory infections.

Before the actual onset of an attack the child may begin to have a runny nose and then a dry hacking cough. During an attack, breathing (wheezing) may become loud and labored. Lips and fingertips may take on a bluish tinge due to lack of oxygen. At the beginning of an attack, the child should be encouraged to (1) rest, relax, and try to stay calm; (2) remain sitting in an upright position; and (3) sip warm water. (Avoid cold liquids.)

Everyone working with children must know about emergency treatment. Many children who suffer from asthma have a medication (usually a medicated inhaler) to ease an attack and allow easier breathing. Teachers should not hesitate to call in **paramedics**, especially if the child's breathing becomes labored. A child can die from a combination of oxygen deprivation and exhaustion (Marotz, 2012).

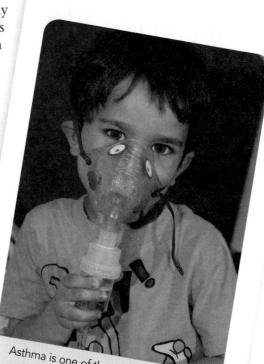

Asthma is one of the most common, yet serious, health problems in children.

© Cengage Learning 2015

7-3b ■ Cystic Fibrosis

Among Caucasian children, cystic fibrosis is the most common of the inherited chronic diseases. This is in contrast to other racial groups, among whom it occurs less frequently. The disease is incurable, but with modern medical care many people with this disorder live into their thirties and forties. From earliest infancy, children with cystic fibrosis are at high risk for severe respiratory infections (Gallico & Lewis, 2007). The disease is characterized by excessive mucus, a chronic cough, progressive lung damage, and the body's inability to absorb fats and proteins appropriately. Children have trouble gaining weight, despite an often excessive appetite. They also tend to have frequent, foul-smelling bowel movements and unusually salty perspiration.

paramedics specially trained individuals who handle emergency medical situations

The rate of deterioration varies from child to child; symptoms may be minimal in one five-year-old and severe in another. In general, teachers should encourage physical activity as long as the child is reasonably well. Both the child and the family are likely to need considerable emotional support from teachers who also may be involved in helping the child with breathing exercises and aerosol therapy to loosen secretions.

7-3c ■ Hemophilia

Hemophilia is a rare inherited disorder in which the blood does not clot properly. It is estimated that 18,000 people in the United States have hemophilia. Each year, about 400 babies are born with the disorder. Except for very rare occasions, hemophilia usually occurs in males (MedlinePlus, 2012). The condition is caused by a deficiency of certain clotting factors that result in the blood clotting too slowly or not at all.

> The chief danger is not bleeding to death from accidental injury. ... It is internal bleeding that poses the greatest threat to life and health. Bleeding into the joints, especially knees, ankles, and elbows can cause severe and constant pain, and eventually permanent crippling. ... Internal bleeding episodes, particularly in children, can be triggered by what seem to be trivial bumps, falls, and minor injuries. Often they occur without any known injury at all. (Apgar & Beck, 1973, p. 295)

Young children with hemophilia should be encouraged to be as active as possible, without exposing them to unnecessary risks. Active children seem to have fewer episodes of bleeding than inactive youngsters with a similar degree of clotting deficiency. Sometimes, an increase in physical activity results in a decrease in bleeding. On the other hand, precautions must be taken whenever necessary. Some children may need to wear a helmet or have protective padding on knees and elbows to shield them from injury from falls common to all children. At the same time, teachers and parents must avoid treating the child as so special or fragile that the child becomes excessively dependent or overly concerned about personal health and well-being.

7-3d ■ Leukemia

chemotherapy use of chemicals in the treatment of disease

The most common of the childhood cancers is leukemia. Although it was previously viewed as a fatal disease, most afflicted children now survive with aggressive treatment such as **chemotherapy** and radiation. Clinicians report that some children with leukemia may receive intravenous chemotherapy at home rather than undergo repeated hospitalizations. Wherever treatment is administered, the child will have associated physical discomfort and may have emotional problems as a result of both the disorder and the stresses associated with treatment. The teacher has a dual role:

- keeping track of the progress of the disease through frequent contacts with parents
- encouraging and supporting the child in joining as much as possible in program activities

7-3e ■ Sickle-Cell Anemia

asymptomatic showing no signs of a disease or impairment that nevertheless may be present

Found almost entirely among African American children, sickle-cell anemia is an autosomal recessive disorder (both parents are **asymptomatic** carriers).

In Africa, the carrier state of sickle-cell anemia used to be an advantage, offering protection against malaria. Affected children of carriers, both in Africa and countless generations later in this country, continue to have sickle-shaped red blood cells, which lead to chronic health problems such as severe pain in the abdomen, legs, and arms; swollen joints; fainting; and overall fatigue.

The disorder has no cure. Sickle-cell anemia is steadily decreasing in the United States, where malaria is not a threat. Therefore, according to Jorde, Carey, Bamshad, and White (2009), this genetic mutation has almost died out because of natural selection. A child with sickle-cell anemia is particularly vulnerable to infection. Teachers can cooperate with parents and the physician in preventing a sickle-cell crisis by helping the child avoid fatigue, stress, and exposure to cold, and by making sure the child has adequate fluid intake.

7-3f ■ Heart Problems

Many heart defects result in death during an infant's first year. Other defects can be surgically repaired, allowing the child to lead a normal life. Children with heart conditions who reach school age have a reduced risk of life-threatening problems. Children with heart disease may have shortness of breath. Physical activity may be more tiring than it is for other preschoolers. Some children experience *cyanosis*, a blueness of the skin, frequently the most striking on the lips and the fingernails, owing to poor oxygenation of the blood.

The child with continuing heart problems should not be pressed to participate in activities that bring on excessive fatigue. Most children with heart problems are fairly reliable monitors of their own exertion tolerance. Children who have had complete surgical correction should have no difficulty participating in all preschool activities. Teachers, parents, and health care providers need to exchange information on a continuing basis. Together, they can plan activity levels for home and school based on the current status of a child's condition.

7-3g ■ Diabetes

Diabetes is a disease in which the body does not produce or properly use insulin. Insulin is a hormone required to convert sugar, starches, and other food into energy for daily life. The body needs insulin in order to **metabolize** glucose (a form of sugar). Without insulin, cells cannot use the glucose already in the bloodstream. The result is insufficient nourishment for carrying on the body's functions. The cause of diabetes continues to be a mystery, although both genetics and environmental factors such as obesity and lack of exercise appear to play roles.

metabolize the chemical process within living cells by which energy is manufactured so that body systems can carry out their functions

Diabetes is one of the most common chronic conditions in school-age children in the United States, affecting 215,000 children and adolescents, or approximately one in every 400 youth under twenty, has type 1 diabetes (American Diabetes Association, 2012). Every year, more than 13,000 youth are diagnosed with type 1 diabetes (Evert, 2004). There are two types of diabetes: type 1 and type 2.

- *Type 1 diabetes* is caused by an autoimmune disorder—a problem with the body's immune system. In type 1 diabetes, the immune system mistakes beta cells for invaders and attacks them. When enough beta cells have been destroyed, symptoms of diabetes appear. It is estimated that up to 10 percent of Americans with diabetes have type 1 diabetes.

- *Type 2 diabetes* is the more common form of diabetes. It results from insulin resistance (a condition in which the body fails to use insulin properly) combined with relative insulin deficiency.

Children with diabetes must receive insulin regularly. Adverse reactions to insulin are a constant threat. One such threat is *hypoglycemia*, excessively low levels of sugar circulating in the blood. Another is *hyperglycemia*, too much sugar circulating in the bloodstream. Hypoglycemia and hyperglycemia can result in diabetic coma (unconsciousness).

Katz (2004) advises, "If there is doubt, the situation should always be managed as a low sugar insulin reaction, since the administration of sugar will cause no harm, while withholding sugar could have serious consequences" (p. 78). Teachers and caregivers will need to be involved in other ways, too, by:

- regulating food intake.
- monitoring the child's exercise and activity level.
- observing the child for changes in behavior and signs of infection.
- assisting in blood glucose monitoring.

Some children with diabetes do poorly in school, not because of the disease, but because of social and emotional problems resulting from it (Gallico & Lewis, 2007). It is important that teachers, parents, and health care providers communicate regularly to ensure the best possible care for the child, with the fewest complications.

7-3h ■ Seizure Disorders

The child with epilepsy should not be restricted from participating in the full program unless specific limitations are imposed by parents or physicians.

© Cengage Learning 2015

Seizures (convulsions) are caused by a disturbance of the brain's electrical activity. A burst of electrical energy results in partial or total loss of consciousness, uncontrolled muscle movements, or changes in behavior or sensory activity. Seizures may be *focal* (partial), localized to one muscle group (or sensory system), or they may be *generalized* with loss of consciousness. Sometimes focal seizures may spread and become generalized. The term *epilepsy* refers to recurrent seizures. Teachers should be aware of the following seizure types common among young children with seizure disorders.

seizures convulsions caused by a disturbance of the electrical activity of the brain

- *Febrile seizures* occur in 3 percent to 5 percent of all young children and are brought on by high fever. They are usually short, do not require treatment, and do not result in epilepsy.

- *Generalized tonic-clonic (grand mal) seizures* cause children to lose consciousness and fall to the floor with violently jerking movements. The child may stop breathing temporarily, lose bowel and bladder control, and start foaming around the mouth.

- *Absence seizures (petit mal)* are generalized seizures with momentary loss of consciousness that may occur many times a day. The child might nod, blink, or briefly stop an activity (such as eating). These lapses are so brief that they often go unnoticed. The child may be accused of daydreaming.

- *Partial psychomotor seizures* are episodes of bizarre behaviors that might resemble tantrums. The child does not lose consciousness but is unaware of behaving strangely.

Another clue that these behaviors represent seizures is that the episodes are stereotypic, repeating themselves with an identical pattern and in the same sequence on different occasions under different circumstances.

Episodes that do not represent seizures but might be confused with seizures include breath-holding spells, syncope (fainting), and facial tics. Parents should always be encouraged to consult their child's physician when teachers report unusual behaviors that might be seizure activity.

Various medications are used to control seizures in children. The medication may have an adverse effect, especially in the beginning, causing the child to be drowsy or inattentive. An important role for teachers is to *observe* and *record* changes in the child's behavior. Behavioral observations assist the child's physician in altering medication or dosage as needed. In general, the anticonvulsant medications prescribed for a child are effective in preventing seizures. Rarely does the early childhood teacher encounter a generalized tonic-clonic seizure. However, it is important to know what to do should there be an episode.

The following recommendations are adapted from material published by the Epilepsy Foundation of America.

1. Remain calm. Children will react the same way teachers do. The seizure itself is painless.

2. Do not try to restrain the child. Nothing can be done to stop a seizure once it has begun. It must run its course.

3. Clear the space around the child so that no injury from hard objects occurs and there is no interference with the child's movements.

4. Do not try to force anything between the teeth.

5. Loosen tight clothing, especially at the neck; turn the child's head to the side; wipe away discharge from the mouth and nose to aid breathing.

6. When the seizure is over, allow the child to rest.

7. Generally it is not necessary to call for medical assistance unless the seizure lasts for more than five minutes or is followed by another seizure. However, emergency medical help should always be summoned in the case of a first seizure, unless it is absolutely certain it is a febrile seizure. Many things can trigger seizures in young children: poisoning, infections, severe electrical jolts, and allergic reactions. If unsure about whether to call for medical help, it is always better to err on the safe side (Marotz, 2012). Parents often provide specific guidelines for handling their child's seizures based on input from their pediatrician.

8. The child's parents should always be informed of a seizure. Teachers and parents plan together how future seizures are best handled for that particular child.

The child with epilepsy should not be restricted from participating in the full program unless specific limitations are imposed by parents or physicians. A seizure episode can be turned into a learning experience for the children in the class.

Teachers can explain in simple terms what a seizure is. They can assure children it is *not catching* and children need not fear for themselves or for the child who had the seizure. The Epilepsy Foundation goes on to suggest that it is important that teachers help children understand but *not pity* the child so that he or she remains "one of the gang." Making sure the child receives the prescribed medication regularly and in the proper amounts is the best approach to preventing seizures. Teachers who are asked to administer medication must follow the guidelines described later in this chapter.

In concluding this section on epilepsy, it seems important to reiterate two points. The first is a repeat of the cautionary note: *Never attempt to force anything between the child's upper and lower teeth*. This procedure, once thought necessary, was discontinued years ago. Children's teeth can be damaged and adult's fingers severely bitten. The second point that bears repeating is that teachers *remain calm*. Young children rarely become unduly alarmed about anything if their teachers do not appear anxious or upset. Children's anxieties over a seizure episode are reduced almost immediately if adults are confident and matter-of-fact about assuring them that the child soon will be all right. In fact, the teacher's quiet care of the child having the seizure can be a valuable example of compassion that benefits each child.

7-3i ■ AIDS (Acquired Immune Deficiency Syndrome)

immune system that aspect of body functioning responsible for warding off diseases

AIDS stands for "acquired immune deficiency syndrome." It is a disease that leaves an individual open to contracting illnesses that a healthy **immune system** might otherwise overcome. It is caused by the human immunodeficiency virus (HIV). Individuals may be infected without knowing it and without showing symptoms of the infection.

antibody substance manufactured either by the body or artificially to help the body fight disease

AIDS is transmitted primarily through sexual contact and blood-to-blood contact (as through shared hypodermic needles) or from an infected mother to her baby. It is estimated that one-third to one-half of the infants born to infected mothers will be infected. However, all infants of HIV-infected mothers will test positive for the disease in the first year or so of life. Why? Because the infant is still benefiting from its mother's **antibody** system while its own is gearing up and getting ready to function.

In the very early years of the AIDS epidemic, there were cases where the disease was transmitted during routine blood transfusions. Today, all blood used for transfusion is routinely and systematically checked for AIDS. No evidence supports *casual* transmission by sitting near, living in the same household with, or playing with an individual with clinical AIDS (American Academy of Pediatrics, 2005). According to the Committee on Pediatric AIDS (2000):

> The spread of HIV infection in school has not been documented, and fear of its communicability must be allayed by appropriate education of all school personnel. Participation in school provides a sense of normalcy for children and adolescents with HIV infection. (p. 1358)

Some children who have AIDS are too ill to be in a child care program or preschool classroom. Also, children with AIDS are highly vulnerable to the many childhood infectious illnesses; enrollment in an early childhood group can be against their best interests. For children who are well enough to be in a program, strict hygiene procedures are required of caregivers: thorough hand washing, wearing disposable gloves when dealing with bodily secretions, and cleaning caregiving surfaces with bleach and water solution.

In an early childhood center, no individual—child or adult—should be attending or working in the program if he or she has open, oozing sores. Neither should he or she be in the program if there is any sign of bloody discharge accompanying diarrhea. This applies to everyone, those with and those without known HIV infection. Information on AIDS/HIV is changing constantly. Therefore, it is essential that everyone working with infants, young children, and families keep abreast of current findings.

7-3j ■ Obesity (Overweight)

obesity the condition of being -considerably overweight

Although **obesity** is not necessarily handicapping, it is a health problem that has reached epidemic proportions in the United States, with one in five children being overweight. Childhood obesity has more than tripled in the past thirty years. The percentage of children aged 6–11 years in the United States who were obese increased from 7 percent in 1980 to nearly 20 percent in 2008.

Connecting Developmentally Appropriate Practice to Brain Research

RECESS AND BRAIN DEVELOPMENT

During the last decade and especially with the push from No Child Left Behind, many school districts have reduced the amount of recess. Reasons cited include fears that reduced classroom time could lead to lower test scores, as well as safety and liability concerns. As stated in the NAEYC's Play, Policy, and Practice Interest Forum (2009) *Recess—It's Indispensable!*:

> *The authors found no research to support administrators' assumptions that test scores required by No Child Left Behind could be improved by keeping children in the classroom all day. There is, however, substantial evidence to support the need for recess.*

- Brain research shows a relationship between physical activity and the development of brain connections. In a study of nine- and ten-year-old children, an association between physical fitness and brain development was found. Researchers discovered that those who are more fit tend to have a bigger hippocampus and perform better on a test of memory than their less fit peers (Chaddock et al., 2010).

- Children are less fidgety and more on-task when they have recess. Children with ADHD (attention deficit hyperactivity disorder) benefit the most.

- Research on memory and attention shows that recall is improved when learning is spaced out during the day rather than concentrated. Recess provides breaks during which the brain can "regroup."

- A school system that devoted a third of the day to nonacademic activities such as art, music, and physical activity improved attitudes and fitness and slightly increased test scores, in spite of spending less time on academics.

Given the ever-increasing rate of diabetes and childhood obesity, it is critical that parents, teachers and administrators work together to provide children with ample time for physical activity. Research suggests that it will help not only with the children's weight but also with their brain development.

Your Turn

Complete some additional research on this topic. What articles/research did you find that support either side of the argument? Using the research you find, write an editorial for a local newspaper supporting the need for recess in schools.

Sources: Chaddock, L., et al. (2010). A neuroimaging investigation of the association between aerobic fitness, hippocampal volume and memory performance in preadolescent children. *Brain Research*, 2010; DOI: 10.1016/j.brainres.2010.08.049

NAEYC. (2009). *Recess—It's indispensable!* Play, Policy, and Practice Interest Forum. Reprinted from Young Children September 2009. Retrieved http://www.naeyc.org/files/yc/file/200909/On%20Our%20Minds%20909.pdf

Unchecked, obesity leads to significant long-term health problems as well as social and psychological problems. Overweight children often are teased and excluded from play activities. This leads to a poor self-image, decreasing physical fitness, and fewer opportunities to build satisfying social relationships (Marotz, 2012).

Obesity is related to chronic disequilibrium between energy output and caloric intake. Quite common among children with disabilities, obesity tends to further reduce their activity level. According to the American Academy of Pediatrics (2010), children with obesity have a high potential risk for:

- high cholesterol and blood pressure levels, which are risk factors for heart disease.

- **sleep apnea** (interrupted breathing while sleeping). In some cases this can lead to problems with learning and memory.

- a high incidence of orthopedic problems, liver disease, and asthma. In some cases there is an alarming increase in the incidence of type 2 diabetes, also known as adult-onset diabetes.

- impaired balance.

- becoming overweight or obese adults (70-percent chance).

sleep apnea condition that interrupts or may stop normal breathing during sleep

Allow children to eat only what they want, but provide healthy choices.

© Cengage Learning 2015

empty calories refers to foods in which there is high caloric content and low nutritional value

Research also indicates that children who are obese have lower self-esteem and self-confidence than thinner peers. Low self-esteem and self-confidence have been linked to poor academic performance, fewer friends, and depression. Due to all of these risks, it is important to prevent childhood obesity and identify overweight and obese children quickly so that they can receive intervention and achieve and maintain a healthy weight (American Academy of Pediatrics, 2010).

Fat babies do not necessarily become fat adults. Substantial evidence suggests, however, that overweight preschoolers are not likely to outgrow the problem. As weight increases, children tend to move slower and then continue to put on weight. This further compounds both physical and psychological problems.

The increase of obesity in children has risen dramatically. According to Brizee, Sophos, and McLaughlin (1990), and Barlow et al. (2007), the increase is thought to be associated with reduced physical activity and increased consumption of convenience foods and fast foods, which tend to be high in fat. Certainly, genetics also play a part in a child's susceptibility to obesity. Nevertheless, excessive weight itself is the result of controllable factors.

- **Overeating**: Obese individuals consume too many calories, or at least too many calories from the wrong kinds of food, often referred to as **empty calories**. Often the overweight individual eats excessive amounts of food with poor nutritional content, popularly known as junk food.

- **Under-exercising**: Lack of physical activity often leads to obesity. It has been estimated that the incidence of obesity in this country increases about 2 percent for each additional hour of television viewing nationwide.

For families who have a child with weight problems, the following are recommended areas for change (Barlow et al., 2007):

- monitoring frequency of eating outside the home at restaurants or fast-food establishments
- avoiding excessive consumption of sweetened beverages
- monitoring portion size based on the child's age
- limiting excessive consumption of 100-percent fruit juices
- monitoring meal frequency and snacking patterns
- encouraging consumption of breakfast, as well as fruits and vegetables

Many overweight children are undernourished. The early childhood teacher can work closely with parents and a nutritionist or health care provider to make sure a child with a weight problem is getting a daily intake of appropriate foods in appropriate amounts. Teachers also can focus parts of the early childhood curriculum on helping children understand the role of good nutrition and exercise in everyday life.

Some children with developmental problems require the concentrated supervision of a dietary specialist. Situations vary. Patterns of excessive food intake may have been established unintentionally by well-meaning adults. By providing an abundance of food, they may have thought to compensate for the many ordinary life experiences otherwise denied the child. Yet the amount and kind of food offered may be excessive. Often the child's dietary needs are less than other children's because their disability reduces their activity level. This in turn lessens their caloric requirements.

7-3k ■ Undernourishment

Consuming too few calories is as damaging to a growing child as consuming too many. Some children burn far more calories each day than they are able to take in. One example is the child with severe cerebral palsy. These children use up tremendous amounts of energy on constant and uncontrollable muscular reactions characteristic of their disability. Often these children are far below ideal body weight. The muscle impairment that burns so many calories also can lead to other nutritional problems. Some children have trouble holding food in their mouth, chewing, or swallowing. Parents, teachers, and caregivers need specialized help in learning to provide easy-to-swallow foods that are high in nutritional value. Nutritionists—and in some cases occupational, speech, or physical therapists—can be of assistance with feeding issues.

7-3l ■ Schools Play a Critical Role

The Healthy, Hunger-Free Kids Act of 2010 directed the USDA to update the Nations School Lunch Program's meal plans and nutrition standards based on the latest Dietary Guidelines for Americans. The new meal plan went into effect at the beginning of 2012–13 school year. Changes included increased availability of fruits, vegetables, and whole grains in the school menu, as well as new dietary specifications that set specific calorie limits to ensure age-appropriate meals for grades K–5, 6–8, and 9–12. While school lunches must meet federal meal requirements, decisions about what to serve is made at the local school level (National School Lunch Program, 2012).

Because schools play a critical role in improving the dietary and physical activity behaviors of students, the Centers for Disease Control and Prevention developed nine guidelines to help schools create environments that support students' efforts to

Monitoring portions and snacks is one way to prevent obesity.

© Cengage Learning 2015

▶❚❚ **TeachSource Video Connections**

Childhood Obesity and School Nutritions

The number of overweight children in the United States is on the rise. A Massachusetts school district has seen an 11-percent reduction in their student obesity rates. They have accomplished this by eliminating junk food and providing healthier foods to students in alignment with national nutrition guidelines.

After watching the video complete the following:

1. List the CDC guidelines listed in Figure 7-4 that you saw in action in the video? Discuss how they are having an impact on the nutrition of the children in the school.

Watch on CourseMate.

Video supplied by the BBC Motion Gallery

FIGURE 7-4

School Health Guidelines to Promote Healthy Eating and Physical Activity

1. Use a coordinated approach to develop, implement, and evaluate healthy eating and physical activity policies and practices.

2. Establish school environments that support healthy eating and physical activity.

3. Provide a quality school meal program and ensure that students have only appealing, healthy food and beverage choices offered outside of the school meal program.

4. Implement a comprehensive physical activity program with quality physical education as the cornerstone.

5. Implement health education that provides students with the knowledge, attitudes, skills, and experiences needed for lifelong healthy eating and physical activity.

6. Provide students with health, mental health, and social services to address healthy eating, physical activity, and related chronic disease prevention.

7. Partner with families and community members in the development and implementation of healthy eating and physical activity policies, practices, and programs.

8. Provide a school employee wellness program that includes healthy eating and physical activity services for all school staff members.

9. Employ qualified persons, and provide professional development opportunities for physical education, health education, nutrition services, and health, mental health, and social services staff members, as well as staff members who supervise recess, cafeteria time, and out-of-school-time.

Source: CDC, 2011.

eat healthily. The guidelines serve as the foundation for developing, implementing, and evaluating school-based healthy eating and physical activity policies and practices for students. Figure 7-4 provides a listing of these guidelines (Centers for Disease Control and Prevention, 2011).

Did You Get It?

What differentiation is made between type 1 and type 2 diabetes?

a. Type 1 diabetes is caused by an autoimmune disorder; type 2 results from insulin deficiency.

b. Type 1 diabetes is caused by an autoimmune disorder; type 2 results from insulin resistance combined with relative insulin deficiency.

c. Type 1 diabetes results from insulin resistance combined with relative insulin deficiency; type 2 is caused by an autoimmune disorder.

d. Type 1 diabetes is more common than type 2 diabetes.

Take the full quiz on CourseMate.

Health Problems and 7-4 ☀
Classroom Practices

Early childhood teachers sometimes feel anxious, inadequate, and even threatened when first asked to include a child with a serious health problem or a disabling physical condition in their class. However, teachers find that the more they work with children with special needs, the more natural it seems. The NAEYC health manual (Aronson, 2002) states:

> When children with special needs participate in inclusive early childhood settings that provide for their special needs and have teachers who know how to adapt teaching techniques and activities, they and their typically developing peers do better. (p. 162)

7-4a ■ Health Records

It is imperative that teachers maintain a complete and frequently updated health record on every child in the group. Include the following essential information:

- telephone numbers where parents and alternate emergency contacts can be reached at all times
- name of the child's regular health care provider or clinic with address and telephone numbers
- permission slips authorizing emergency health care and transportation and the administration of prescribed medications
- child and family health history
- immunization information with dates
- results of medical assessment or physical and dental examinations and treatment
- results of special testing, such as vision or hearing assessments
- dated reports, signed by the attending teacher, on all injuries or illnesses that occur while the child is in the classroom or play yard or on a school-sponsored excursion
- notations about allergies, special diets, treatment procedures, medications, prosthetic devices, or other health concerns
- notations on health-related communications with parents and health care providers, including referral recommendations and follow-up
- ongoing records of medications given to the child while at school

When leaving the school, whether for an actual emergency or simply on a field trip, teachers should be sure to take emergency contact information, lists of allergies, first-aid supplies, and adequate medication for students who require it.

7-4b ■ Administering Medication

In many states, the law or licensing agency requires that medication given in the early childhood center be administered *only on written order from a physician.*

Most states require that the package or bottle containing the medication be a child-resistant container and labeled with the following:

1. child's name
2. physician's name and phone number
3. name of the medicine
4. information on how much is to be given to the child
5. schedule for administering dosages

Teachers are not required to give medication. However, most teachers are willing to take on this responsibility if it enables the child to stay in the program. Staff members who dispense medication need to receive specific training in the procedure. Each time the medication is given, the time and date are to be recorded on the child's record sheet and initialed by the person who did the medicating. Medication must be kept in a locked cabinet or refrigerator or otherwise out of the reach of all children. An adequate supply of medications should always be kept on hand to ensure that there is enough in the event of an emergency, during which caregivers cannot reach the school in time to provide additional doses.

7-4c ■ Emergency Considerations

All programs serving young children are required to have detailed plans for emergency situations in general. When children with health problems and physical disabilities are enrolled, individual plans need to be devised for each child. These include:

- conferring with parents (or the child's doctor) to plan for an emergency health crisis.
- understanding the cause of a crisis and the frequency with which it is likely to occur.
- learning how a child may behave *before* as well as during and after a crisis.
- knowing what to do during and after the crisis and understanding when to call for additional help.

Marotz (2012) recommends that all teachers who are expected to administer first aid to children complete first aid and CPR training, preferably before they begin work.

Preventing a health crisis is important, too. For example, it is good to prepare a list of classroom activities. Give this to the child's parents or physician and ask them to indicate activities that should be avoided or modified. In addition, the other children need to be prepared for a possible health crisis of classmates. Teachers can give simple explanations. Teachers can also explain that they will be able to take care of all the children, not only the child with the problem.

7-4d ■ Confidentiality

Schools and programs must be aware of the legal confidentiality requirements in place to protect children with health-related issues and their families. Staff should be trained in confidentiality requirements and understand their importance in working with families. The importance of confidentiality and of establishing trust with families is discussed in Chapter 9.

Did You Get It?

Who specifies that medicinal bottles are required to bear specific details and packaged according to safety regulations?
a. Teacher.
b. Parent.
c. State.
d. NAEYC.

Take the full quiz on CourseMate.

Summary

▶ Physical problems in children vary, ranging from mild to life-threatening. Neurological involvement often accompanies problems.

▶ The physical disabilities that teachers are most likely to encounter were described briefly in terms of characteristics, causes, program recommendations, and the responsibilities of teachers, including crisis management as needed.

▶ Children with physical and health problems benefit from being enrolled in an inclusive early childhood classroom.

▶ Interdisciplinary team members work with teachers in planning and implementing classroom activities. A variety of disciplines play significant roles, depending on the nature of the child's problems.

▶ Teachers should never initiate any kind of therapeutic activity without specific instruction and supervision from a certified specialist. The specialist also learns from the early childhood educator how to accommodate therapeutic recommendations to the everyday activities and developmental principles of the classroom.

▶ Regular classroom activities, materials, and equipment can be adapted to meet the needs of children with special health and physical needs.

▶ A major responsibility of teachers is to help children with physical and health impairments keep active and involved. Children need to learn to do as much as possible for themselves so that their illness or disability does not dominate their lives.

▶ Another responsibility of teachers is to prepare themselves to meet emergency situations. When teachers remain calm and quietly in charge, young children do not panic.

Key Terms

adaptive equipment, 149
antibody, 162
asymptomatic, 158
bolster, 151
cerebral palsy, 144
chemotherapy, 158
contracture, 144
empty calories, 164
hydrocephalus, 147
hypertonic, 145
hypotonic, 146

immune system, 162
juvenile rheumatoid
   arthritis, 148
manipulative materials, 153
meningocele, 147
metabolize, 159
myelomeningocele, 147
obesity, 162
paramedics, 157
primitive reflexes, 146
progressive, 148

prone-board, 151
prostheses, 150
range of motion, 146
seizures, 160
shunt, 147
sleep apnea, 163
therapeutic, 150
universal design for
   learning (UDL), 151
voluntary motor responses, 146
wedge, 151

Student Activities

1. Form small groups and discuss disabilities or serious health problems that members have experienced firsthand or through association with someone who has a disability. Discuss common experiences and attitudes.

2. Observe a classroom. Think about how the room could be rearranged or redesigned with universal design in mind so that it could better serve all children.

3. Select a common preschool manipulative material and demonstrate ways it might be adapted so that a child with impaired fine motor skills could use it successfully.

4. Devise a game with balls, suitable for four- and five-year-olds, that would allow a child in a wheelchair to participate.

5. Select a possible crisis situation, such as an asthma attack, insulin shock, or grand mal seizure. Describe what you would say to a group of four- and five-year-olds that witnessed such an episode for the first time.

Review Questions

Define and give an example of each of the following terms:

1. contractures
2. chronic health condition
3. progressive disease
4. hydrocephalus
5. hip dysplasia
6. mobility device
7. adaptive equipment
8. diabetic coma
9. petit mal seizure
10. empty calories

Additional Resources/Readings

Children's Books on Physical Disabilities for Kindergarten through Grade 3:

Featherless/Desplumado
Written by Juan Felipe Herrera
Children's Book Press

Spina bifida keeps Tomasito in a wheelchair, where he often feels like his featherless pet bird, Desplumado, who cannot fly. But with a friend's encouragement, Tomasito finds freedom on the soccer field. Bilingual text in English and Spanish.

Zoom!
Written by Robert N. Munsch
Cartwheel Books

When Lauretta's mother takes her shopping for a new wheelchair, Lauretta wants one that goes really fast. The store lets her have a 92-speed dirt bike model for home testing, and then Laurette's adventures begin.

Danny and the Merry-Go-Round
Written by Nan Holcomb
Jason & Nordic Publishers

Danny, who has cerebral palsy, visits the park with his mother and watches other children playing on a playground. A friendly gesture from a child he meets provides for a new adventure.

Helpful Websites

AbleNet, Inc.

http://www.ablenetinc.com

AbleNet, Inc., strives to improve the lives of people with disabilities in every targeted setting by offering a selection of creative curricular programs and materials for teaching students with disabilities. In addition, their website contains links to many helpful resources for both teachers and families.

About Special Ed.com

http://specialed.about.com

Provides ideas and suggestions for working with students with physical disabilities in the classroom.

National Center on Universal Design for Learning

http://www.udlcenter.org

Founded in 2009, the national UDL center supports the effective implementation of UDL by connecting professionals in the field and providing resources and information about implanting UDL. The website contains multiple videos that describe and illustrate UDL principles.

National Organization for Rare Disorders, Inc. (NORD)

http://www.rarediseases.org

NORD is a federation of voluntary health organizations dedicated to helping people with rare diseases and assisting the organizations that serve them. NORD is committed to the identification, treatment, and cure of rare disorders through programs of education, advocacy, research, and service.

 Visit the Education CourseMate for this textbook to access the eBook, Did You Get It? quizzes, Digital Downloads, TeachSource Video Cases, flashcards, and more. Go to CengageBrain.com to log in, register, or purchase access.

Learning and Behavior Disorders

OBJECTIVES

After reading this chapter, you should be able to:

8-1   describe the characteristics of a child with attention deficit hyperactivity disorder (ADHD) and discuss intervention options.

8-2   identify various types of learning disabilities including risk factors and describe Response to Intervention (RTI) as it relates to learning disabilities.

8-3   provide a description of behavior disorders including depression and anxiety.

8-4   describe Autism Spectrum Disorder and discuss recent research and effective intervention strategies.

8-5   discuss elimination and eating disorders and when a teacher should be concerned.

• • • • • • • • • • • • • • • • • •

naeyc

The following NAEYC Standards are addressed in this chapter:

STANDARD 1 Promoting Child Development and Learning

STANDARD 2 Building Family and Community Relationships

STANDARD 3 Observing, Documenting and Assessing to Support Young Children and Families

STANDARD 4 Using Developmentally Effective Approaches

STANDARD 5 Using Content Knowledge to Build Meaningful Curriculum

CONNECTIONS

- Tyra is a toddler with autism. She does not make eye contact easily, but she smiles and watches attentively when her teacher produces her favorite stuffed-dog toy.
- Anthony is a second grader diagnosed with attention deficit disorder. He is better able to stay on task now that his teacher has taught him how to monitor his behavior and use a schedule to predict what is going to happen during the day.
- Ken is a kindergartner with very challenging behavior. He is aggressive and destructive when asked to participate in activities that are not his choice. Through the use of simple behavioral contracts, however, he is demonstrating more appropriate behavior in the classroom.

Disorders associated with learning and behavior have been linked to many developmental problems. In this chapter, we will discuss learning and behavior disorders that are not a result of a primary disability, such as intellectual disability (previously referred to as mental retardation) or blindness, and those that are chronic behaviors—that is, that occur over time. These behaviors fall outside the range of normal variations in the behavior of typically developing children. Behaviors such as occasionally not following directions or finding it hard to sit still for twenty minutes are typical behaviors of young children. The behaviors we will discuss in this chapter are qualitatively different from the typical ones.

attention deficit hyperactivity disorder (ADHD) short attention span accompanied by excessive activity

autism spectrum disorder (ASD) a term used to refer to a broad definition of autism, including the classical form of the disorder as well as closely related disabilities that share many of the core characteristics

In this chapter, we will examine **attention deficit hyperactivity disorder (ADHD)**, learning disabilities, behavior disorders, and **autism spectrum disorders (ASD)**. The diagnosis of all four of these types of disabilities is based on a professional's impression of a child as it relates to standard diagnostic criteria. The criteria are listed in the *Diagnostic and Statistical Manual of Mental Disorders* (DSM-5). Several types of professionals can diagnose these types of disabilities, including physicians, psychologists, neurologists, and psychiatrists. Although standard diagnostic criteria exist for these disabilities, no blood test or other physical procedure or examination confirms or refutes the diagnosis. For this reason, it is especially important that the parent or primary caretaker is involved in the assessment process; that the assessment instruments used are culturally relevant, unbiased, and in the child's home language; and that at least part of the assessment is conducted in an environment that is familiar to the child.

learning disability a condition that interferes with learning to read, write, or do math

When working with young children who present challenging or inappropriate behaviors, it is essential to keep in mind what is developmentally appropriate. Most four-year-olds do not follow all directions, do challenge adults occasionally, and can go from laughter to tears in a few seconds. The terms *behavior disorder*, ADHD, or **learning disability** should therefore be used with extreme caution when describing young children.

8-1 Attention Deficit Hyperactivity Disorder (ADHD)

What is ADHD? What are the symptoms? What can be done about it? Every day, these questions plague teachers, parents, clinicians, and researchers. ADHD has been heavily researched, particularly in the past few years. Before discussing the disorder and its ramifications for both children and teachers, we will present a brief examination of its history.

ADHD was first described by Heinrich Hoffman as early as 1845. It has been scientifically studied for more than fifty years. It has undergone numerous name changes, beginning with *brain injured* and *minimally brain damaged* (MBD). By the late 1960s, concern arose about using medical terms for a condition characterized by behavior (excessive movement) rather than by identifiable physiological evidence. The term *hyperactivity* came into use. Many **psychopathologists**, however, felt it was not excessive activity that best characterized these children as much as their inability to pay attention. Therefore, in 1980, the American Psychiatric Association (APA) changed the name to Attention Deficit Disorder (ADD) with two subcategories: ADD with hyperactivity and ADD without hyperactivity. Further disagreement among the association's members brought about the most recent name change: ADHD. Some members of the APA believed that ADD could not exist without hyperactivity; others insisted there were children with ADD who had no excessive motor activity. The compromise, in 1987, was the term attention deficit hyperactivity disorder (ADHD), accompanied by a list of behaviors intended to make it clear that hyperactivity did not necessarily coexist with ADHD.

psychopathologists individuals who specialize in viewing mental disorders from a psychological perspective

In 1994, the APA again revised the definition of ADHD and returned to the classification system that differentiates between attention problems and hyperactivity. The *Diagnostic and Statistical Manual of Mental Disorders* (DSM-IV-TR) listed three patterns of behavior indicate ADHD. People with ADHD may show several signs of being consistently inattentive. They may have a pattern of being far more hyperactive and impulsive than others their age. Or they may show all three types of behavior. This means that three subtypes of ADHD are recognized by professionals.

1. *predominantly hyperactive-impulsive type* (which does not manifest significant inattention);

2. *predominantly inattentive type* (which does not manifest significant hyperactive-impulsive behavior), sometimes called ADD—an outdated term for this entire disorder;

3. *combined type* (which displays both inattentive and hyperactive-impulsive symptoms) (Strock, 2006).

In the most recent release of the DSM-5 (2013), the diagnostic criteria for attention-deficit/hyperactivity disorder (ADHD) are similar to those in DSM-IV. The most significant change is to the onset criterion. This has been changed from "symptoms that caused impairment were present before age 7 years" to "several inattentive or hyperactive-impulsive symptoms were present prior to age 12 years. In addition, the DSM-5 allows a comorbid diagnosis with autism spectrum disorder.

8-1b ■ Current Attempts at Defining ADHD

A comprehensive evaluation is necessary to obtain a diagnosis and rule out other causes for the symptoms. A comprehensive evaluation includes a clinical assessment of a child's developmental level, as well as the child's academic, social, and emotional abilities. A detailed history should be obtained by interviewing parents, teachers, and the child, as appropriate.

Checklists and rating scales are often used by clinicians. In addition, a thorough medical exam, including hearing and vision, should be completed to rule out any other conditions that could be contributing to or causing the symptoms.

The American Academy of Pediatrics (2000) recommends the following questions be asked at all visits for school-aged children to heighten attention about ADHD and as an initial screening for school performance:

1. How is your child doing in school?
2. Are there any problems with learning that you or the teacher has seen?
3. Is your child happy in school?
4. Are you concerned with any behavioral problems in school, at home, or when your child is playing with friends?
5. Is your child having problems completing classwork or homework?

8-1c ■ Causes and Prevalence of ADHD

Parents report that approximately 9.5 percent or 5.4 million children 4–17 years of age have been diagnosed with ADHD, as of 2007. Diagnosis of ADHD increased an average of 3 percent per year from 1997 to 2006 and an average of 5.5 percent from 2003 to 2007 (CDC, 2011). In an even more recent study, researchers from the Kaiser Permanente Southern California Medical Group reviewed the electronic health records of nearly 850,000 children aged 5–11 years between 2001 and 2010. According to the new findings, the rate of children who were diagnosed with ADHD jumped by about 24 percent during the decade of 2001 and 2010 (Getahun, Jacobsen, Fassett, Chen, Demissie, & Rhoads, 2013). Boys are more than twice as likely as girls to be diagnosed with ADHD (13.2 percent versus 5.6 percent) (CDC, 2011). This means that in a classroom of twenty-five to thirty children, it is likely that at least one and most likely two will have ADHD (Barkley, 2005; Strock, 2006; Wolraich, Hannah, Pinnock, Baumgaertel, & Brown, 1996). Longitudinal data published by Barkley (2005) indicate that the mean age of onset of ADHD is between three and four years. It was once thought that children outgrew ADHD in adolescence, but it is now believed that the hyperactivity only decreases during the teen years. Many symptoms continue into adulthood, affecting approximately 2 percent to 4 percent of adults (Murphy & Barkley, 1996).

Research has yet to reveal a specific cause of ADHD. Several hypotheses have been offered, one or two of which are backed up by fairly sound evidence. One is the possible role of genetic transmission. Bee and Boyd (2012) cite a study in which one-fourth of the subjects with ADHD had parents with a history of hyperactivity. Studies of twins also show possible genetic implications. Among identical twins, both are more likely to have hyperactivity, which is not the case among fraternal twins (Stevenson, 1992; Deutsch & Kinsbourne, 1990).

Researchers continue to research the brain and its various functions to explain ADHD. A correlation also has been found between ADHD and a mother's smoking and alcohol use during pregnancy (Markussen Linnet, Wisborg, Obel, Secher, Thomsen, Agerbo, & Brink Henriksen, 2005; Wang, Samir Haj-Dahmane, & Roh-Yu Shen, 2006).

In addition, other neurological and psychological disorders may sometimes accompany ADHD. These include learning disabilities, oppositional defiant disorder, conduct disorder, anxiety disorder, and depressive disorder. Table 8-1 indicates the prevalence in children with ADHD.

8-1d ■ Intervention Strategies

Children who do not receive adequate treatment for ADHD can experience serious consequences. These may include poor self-esteem, academic failure, and

TABLE 8-1

Disorders that Sometimes Accompany ADHD

Disorder	Prevalence
Learning Disability	20–30%
Oppositional Defiant Disorder (ODD)	35%
Conduct Disorder (CD)	25%
Anxiety Disorder	18%
Depressive Disorder	18%

Source: American Academy of Pediatrics, 2000; Strock, 2006.

poor social development and interactions. Treatment plans should be developed with the parent or caregiver to best meet the individual needs of the child and family. The most effective approaches to helping children diagnosed with ADHD are medication and behavior management, often in combination. These combined treatments result in significant improvement in children's behavior, academic work, and relationships with peers and family. The effectiveness of combined treatments was demonstrated in the Multimodal Treatment Study of Children with Attention Deficit Hyperactivity Disorder (MTA Cooperative Group, 2004).

The MTA study examined 579 elementary school boys and girls with ADHD who were randomly assigned to one of four treatment programs: (1) medication management alone; (2) behavioral treatment alone; (3) a combination of both; or (4) routine community care. Three groups were treated for the first fourteen months in a specified protocol, and the fourth group was referred for community treatment of the parents' choosing. Children were reassessed regularly throughout the study. Teachers and parents rated the children on hyperactivity, impulsivity, inattention, and symptoms of anxiety and depression. Social skills were also rated.

The results of the study indicated that long-term combination treatments and the medication management alone were more effective than intensive behavioral treatment and routine community treatment used alone. In some areas—anxiety, academic performance, tendency to be oppositional, parent–child relations, and social skills—the combined treatment of medication and behavioral treatment was usually superior. A notable benefit of combined treatment was that children could be successfully treated with lower doses of medicine compared with the medication-only group.

Medication As of 2007, parents of 2.7 million youth ages 4–17 years (66.3 percent of those with a current diagnosis) report that their child was receiving medication treatment for ADHD (CDC, 2011). In assessing highly active children, it is argued that distinctions should be made between the child whose high activity level is truly **organic** and the run-of-the-mill overactive child. The reason for making the distinction is that some children in the organic group may benefit from prescription drugs such as Ritalin or Dexedrine.

organic within the individual's own body or neurological system

Psychostimulants such as these are the most widely used class of medication for the management of ADHD. When effective, these medications can lead to increased attention and concentration, and decreased levels of impulsivity and activity (Swanson & McBurnett, 1993). However, the medication may have undesirable side effects, including weight loss, insomnia, or increased blood pressure.

It should be noted that medication has been ineffective in treating one-quarter or more of children with ADHD. Even when activity level improves, the effects are short-term. In addition, medication brings no lasting benefit and can set up negative consequences for the child, especially if parents and teachers inquire, "Have you taken your medicine?" whenever the child is disruptive. According to Reeves (1990), this kind of question, associated directly with good and bad behavior, can instill in the child the idea that she or he is really not responsible for the behavior. As an aside, it is sometimes parents and teachers who come to rely on the medication; in other words, they may become "addicted" to having the child on medication because the child is much less troublesome when medicated.

Kopelwicz (1997) gives us a clear reminder about the limitations of medication when she comments, "Ritalin (the most commonly prescribed drug for children with ADHD) lets a kid pay attention more. It does not force kids to do their homework, it doesn't teach social skills, it doesn't make them smart, it just makes them more accessible to perform in these areas" (p. 15).

Special diets Special diets should be viewed with skepticism. Scientific research on ADHD diets is limited and results are mixed. The controversial Feingold diet, for example, linked artificial food coloring and food additives with hyperactivity. Feingold (1985) asserted that the behavior of many children labeled as hyperactive would improve if synthetic colors, flavors, and natural **salicylates** were removed from their diets. Studies investigating his claims found no clinically significant differences between untreated groups of children and those on the diet (Conners, 1980). True, no harm can come of feeding children foods that are nutritious and additive-free. However, even if a curative diet is nutritious (and some are not), looking for a diet to cure a behavior disorder often results in ignoring basic problems that require quite different treatments.

salicylates chemical compounds commonly known as salts

Behavior management Drugs and special diets do not teach; every intervention program must be accompanied by individually designed behavior-management strategies. Landau and McAninch (1993) point out that much of the feedback that children with ADHD get from parents, teachers, and peers is in the form of complaints or reprimands; therefore, the use of rewards for appropriate behaviors (gradually removed as the child learns more acceptable behaviors) is particularly helpful. "Rewarding positive behaviors thus not only encourages the child to continue behaving well but also

Medication doesn't teach social skills, or force kids to do their homework, it just makes them more accessible to perform in these areas.

© Cengage Learning 2015

provides the child with desperately needed success, thereby building self-esteem" (p. 55).

Behavioral procedures are discussed throughout this text, with special emphasis on hyperactivity in Chapter 18. The section on learning disabilities that follows also applies, especially to children who are diagnosed as having an attention disorder. The starting point for teachers is to examine the learning environment to make sure an appropriate match exists between the environment and the child:

> Children with ADHD benefit from the same environments that all children do; thus, designing classrooms appropriate for the child's development is an important step toward managing the behavior of a child with ADHD. (Landau & McAninch, 1993, p. 53)

Finally, it seems worthwhile to quote the *Young Children* editor's note on the Landau and McAninch article: "Most children who are diagnosed by competent mental health professionals as having attention-deficit hyperactivity disorder, do; but as early childhood educators, we must always ensure that our classrooms are developmentally appropriate and that children are not being inappropriately labeled because our classroom is inappropriate" (Landau & McAninch, 1993, p. 49).

Did You Get It?

What treatment has been shown to allow a lower medicinal rate for children with ADHD?
a. Medication management.
b. Behavioral treatment.
c. Routine community care.
d. Combination of medication management and behavioral treatment.

Take the full quiz on CourseMate.

Learning Disabilities 8-2

As many as one out of every five people in the United States has a learning disability. Almost one million children (ages six through twenty-one) have some form of a learning disability and receive special education in school (one-third of all children who receive special education have a learning disability) (*Twenty-Ninth Annual Report to Congress*, U.S. Department of Education, 2010). Children with learning disabilities have many characteristics in common, yet there are many differences among them, too. In varying degrees and combinations, learning disorders are said to include:

- constant motion and purposeless activity
- poor perceptual motor skills
- low tolerance for frustration
- frequent mood swings
- poor coordination, both large and fine motor
- distractibility, short attention span
- poor auditory and visual memory
- variety of language deficits

It is obvious that learning disabilities encompass a wide range of disorders. Efforts at clinical classification are ongoing. Some textbooks discuss learning disabilities in conjunction with attention deficit disorders. Others group learning disabilities with cognitive disorders or impaired mental functioning. Other classifications are motor dysfunction and impaired motor planning. In this text, learning disabilities will be discussed in a separate category. We base our decision on the extensive overlap of learning disabilities with other disorders and developmental problems.

What is a learning disability? Two answers come immediately to mind: first, it is many things; second, many other things it is not. The formal definition under IDEIA (2004) defines "Specific Learning Disability" as:

> a disorder in one or more of the basic psychological processes involved in understanding or in using language, spoken or written, which may manifest itself in the imperfect ability to listen, think, speak, write, spell, or do mathematical calculations. The term includes conditions such as perceptual handicaps, brain injury, minimum brain dysfunction, **dyslexia** and developmental **aphasia**. The term does not include children who have learning problems, which are primarily the result of visual, hearing, or motor handicaps, intellectual disability, of emotional disturbance, or of environmental, cultural, or economic disadvantage.

This definition often is referred to as either a definition by exclusion or as a *residual* diagnosis.

It states clearly that a learning disability is *not* the result of:

- visual, hearing, or motor handicaps
- intellectual disability
- emotional disturbance
- environmental, cultural, or economic disadvantage
- second language learning

Children with learning disabilities often exhibit poor coordination in motor control.

© Cengage Learning 2015

dyslexia an impaired ability to read and understand written language

aphasia the imperfect ability to express oneself or to comprehend spoken or written language; usually due to damage or disease in the language area of the cortex

Thus, we can say what a learning disability is *not*; what we cannot say for certain what it *is*. This ambiguity is not for lack of research. During the past forty years, hundreds upon hundreds of studies on the topic have been conducted. Competent researchers in the fields of psychology, neurology, education, and educational psychology have attempted to establish definitive answers to the elusive question of how to define (and diagnose) learning disabilities.

It is especially important to remember that students who are bilingual or learning English as a second language (ELL) should not be categorized as having a learning disability. It is important to determine a child's competence in his or her home language, even if it is different from the language spoken at school.

The federal definition of learning disabilities raises several issues. Two of these may be especially relevant to early childhood education. One is the issue of the *disadvantaged*; the other is *academic performance* as a diagnostic measure.

Nondisadvantaged ruling The legislative definition of learning disabilities automatically excludes children who are subject to environmental and economic disadvantage. Under the existing ruling, poor children are not eligible to participate in programs funded for remediation of learning disabilities because, under the definition, they cannot qualify as learning disabled.

Academic ruling As described in the formal definition, learning disabilities are related primarily to academic performance: "the ability to listen, think, speak, read, write, spell, or do mathematical calculations." Because most early childhood

FIGURE 8-1

Risk Indicators for Learning Disabilities

Perinatal conditions

1. Low Apgar scores
2. Low birth weight and/or preterm birth
3. Hospitalization for longer than twenty-four hours in a neonatal intensive care unit
4. Difficulty with suckling, sucking, and swallowing
5. Chronic otitis media that may result in intermittent hearing loss

Genetic or environmental conditions

1. Family history of LD
2. Child is adopted
3. Family history of language problems
4. Exposure to environmental toxins or other harmful substances
5. Limited language exposure in home, childcare, and other settings
6. Poverty

Developmental milestones

1. Delay in cognitive skills
   a. Not demonstrating object permanence
   b. Lack of symbolic play behavior
2. Delay in comprehension and/or expression of spoken language
   a. Limited receptive vocabulary
   b. Reduced expressive vocabulary
   c. Difficulty understanding simple (e.g., one-step) directions
   d. Monotone or other unusual prosodic features of speech
   e. Reduced intelligibility
3. Delay in emergent literacy skills
   a. Limited phonological awareness (e.g., rhyming, syllable blending)
   b. Minimal interest in print
   c. Limited print awareness (e.g., book handling, recognizing environmental print)
4. Delay in perceptual-motor skills
   a. Problems in gross or fine motor coordination
   b. Difficulty coloring, copying, and drawing

Attention and behavior

1. Distractibility/inattention
2. Impulsivity
3. Hyperactivity
4. Difficulty changing activities or handling disruptions to routines
5. Perseveration (i.e., constant repetition of an idea)

© Cengage Learning 2015

TeachSource Digital Download Download from CourseMate.

educators consider it developmentally inappropriate for preschool-age children to be spending their school hours in such pursuits, should young children ever be considered learning disabled?

"No" seems to be the logical response; yet not all teachers are comfortable with that, and for good reason. Many young children show maladaptive behaviors that have been associated with learning disabilities in older children. They may be distractible, easily frustrated, excessively active, or poorly coordinated. These behaviors already are interfering with their everyday learning activities in a variety of ways. A number of early childhood educators believe it is in children's best interests to deal with these troubling behaviors during the preschool years, before they worsen and compound a child's problems and affect academic performance in later years. A range of environmental, biological, genetic, and perinatal conditions may be associated with adverse developmental outcomes (Shonkoff & Phillips, 2000) and may be risk indicators (i.e., warning signs) for LD. Figure 8.1 is a partial listing of risk indicators for infants, toddlers, and preschoolers (National Joint Committee on Learning Disabilities, 2006).

8-2b ■ Risk Indicators

Figure 8-1 lists risk indicators for learning disabilities, which means that children with these characteristics and criteria may be more likely to have learning disabilities than other children.

Predicting learning disability Is it possible that certain behaviors in a young child may be predictors of subsequent trouble with academic tasks? The answer seems to be "Yes," provided it is understood that the judgment is based on educated guesswork. Teachers of young children frequently spot a child whose behaviors appear to put him or her at risk for learning disabilities and, perhaps, later academic problems. Is it possible that these worrisome behaviors can be eliminated, or at least reduced, before they have a serious effect on later academic performance? Again, the answer seems to be "Yes." During the past several years, early identification of young children as potentially learning disabled has gained strong support. Child developmentalists, parents, and experts in other disciplines such as medicine and psychology believe that many learning, social-emotional, and educational problems can be prevented or remediated if identification and intervention are provided before the child enters school.

Professionals need to exercise caution in identifying young children at potential risk for later learning disabilities. The first step is observing the child in a number of activities. The next step is matching the observed performance to performance expectancies in all areas of development. It must be remembered that all young children are different, and all have much development yet to come. Another point is that young children often demonstrate marked differences or delays that are still within a normal range of development. These are some of the reasons for considering learning disabilities an inappropriate diagnosis for a young child. In most instances, it is more beneficial to the child to view early problems as developmental deviations calling for learning experiences that meet individual needs. Such a decision also is a more economical use of professional energy than trying to decide whether to pin (or not to pin) the label "learning disabled" on a child.

Prerequisite skills A cue in older preschool children that learning problems may lie ahead is a lack of what are sometimes called *readiness* or **prerequisite skills**. These are skills thought to be necessary for academic success once the child enters grade school. However, simply waiting for the unready child to become ready rarely helps the child. Readiness comes through experience, learning, and the opportunity to practice and master developmental skills. What follows are examples of particular deviations or delays in various areas of development thought to be related to potential learning disabilities.

prerequisite skills skills that must be acquired before a higher-level skill can be attempted

Sensory-motor difficulties (gross motor) Many developmentalists theorize that early learning is sensory-motor based. Children about whom teachers express concern in terms of future academic performance invariably show some kind of sensory-motor problems. In addition, they often show generalized delay in reaching basic motor milestones, and they exhibit one or more of the following characteristics.

- *Imperfect body control* resulting in poorly coordinated or jerky movements; trouble with running, throwing, catching, hopping, or kicking.

- *Poor balance* that may cause the child to fall off play equipment, fall down, or fall into furnishings or other people. Inability to walk a balance beam may be a symptom in a kindergartner or a first-grade child.

- *Uncertain bilateral and cross-lateral movements* are often a sign of future problems with academic tasks. The child with a bilateral problem may not be able to use both arms in synchrony, as children do when catching a ball or jumping off a wall. Or a child may not use opposite legs and arms in harmony (cross-laterality), as seen in agile children climbing to the top of a jungle gym.

- *Inability to cross body midline* has long been viewed as a possible predictor of future academic difficulty. In such cases, the child has trouble using the right hand to work on a task where any part of the task lies to the left of the midpoint of the child's body or vision.

  The same holds true of the left hand and the right-side focus. A common example is a child painting on a large piece of paper at the easel. The child transfers the brush from the right hand to the left when painting on the left half of the paper, and back again, when painting on the right.

- *Faulty spatial orientation* interferes with children's ability to understand where they are in space, in relationship to their physical surroundings. For example, a child may walk into a wall; poor orientation interferes with the child perceiving the wall as being *right there*. Or the child may gear up for a mighty jump, only to land with frightening force because the ground was much closer than the height the child had anticipated.

spatial orientation knowing where one is in relationship to one's surroundings

Putting clothes on wrong side up or backwards, or having difficulty going up and down stairs also may indicate problems with spatial orientation.

Sensory-motor difficulties (fine motor) Problems in buttoning, lacing, snapping, cutting, pasting, and stringing beads are characteristics of older preschool children thought to be at future academic risk. Often these children are unable to draw a straight line or copy simple shapes such as a circle, cross, or square. When they manage to draw a crude imitation, the circle is seldom closed, the corners on the square are rounded or irregular, and the cross is crossed far off center.

Tasks of this kind are virtually impossible for these children to master without extensive training and practice.

Perseveration (repeating the same act and or words over and over, seemingly endlessly) is typical of many children who seem likely to develop a future learning disorder. These children appear unable to stop what they are doing. A child may scrub back and forth with the same crayon or draw the same shape for several minutes at a time until stopped by a teacher or parent. Some children chant the same words or make the same hand gestures repeatedly until someone succeeds in diverting them to something else. Even when a change is accomplished, there may be carryover from the preceding activity. For example, the child mentioned earlier may have been moved into block play. Here the back-and-forth scrubbing continues on the floor, with the child using a block rather than a crayon to make the back-and-forth motions.

Cognitive disorders Trouble organizing thoughts or processing information logically is characteristic of many young children with potential learning disabilities. They tend to operate only in the here and now, with little or no ability to deal with any kind of abstract thought. While concrete thinking is characteristic of young children, older preschoolers are able to deal with a certain amount of abstraction. For example, it is the rare four- or five-year-old who cannot relay a little information about the pet at home or the new swing set in his or her backyard.

Cognitively disorganized children also may have trouble carrying out simple directions or remembering what it was they were supposed to do, even while they are working on the task. Trouble with generalizing from one event to another is common, too. For this child, a rule about no running indoors may not generalize to no running in the classroom, halls, or library, even though all are indoors and within the same building. Especially frustrating for adults is that the same mistakes are made again and again, simply because there is no carryover from one event to the next.

Visual and auditory perception problems "The ability to interpret what is seen" is one definition of visual perception. A visual perception problem has nothing to do with blindness or impaired vision. In other words, there is no physical problem. Instead, the problem lies with how the child's processing mechanism handles the information that enters the brain visually. Various aspects of perceptual motor skills were described in Chapter 6; here, the focus will be on other aspects related specifically to learning disabilities, where the problems take several forms.

- *Visual discrimination* is the ability to look at objects or pictures and note how they are alike and how they are different. Children with visual discrimination problems may have trouble sorting objects according to color, size, or shape. They may not be able to match lotto pictures, to copy block designs, or to tell the difference between the smiling and the frowning clown pictures. Often they can be seen trying to fit a large object into too small an opening or container.

Visual-motor integration is a skill that can also be thought of as eye–hand coordination. It is as if the child's hands cannot do what the eyes say needs to be done.

© Cengage Learning 2015

perseveration repeating the same act over and over with no discernible intention (obsessive, ritualistic)

- **Visual orientation** is related to spatial orientation. The child may recognize three-dimensional objects such as a head of lettuce, a cap, or a paintbrush, but not recognize the same items in two-dimensional pictures. Another example of visual disorientation is recognizing objects in their normal or upright positions, but failing to recognize them when they are turned over or lying sideways. One child insisted an overturned wooden armchair was a cage; the moment it was turned right side up, he labeled it a chair. Even when the chair was turned over while he watched, he insisted it was a cage the moment it was turned on its side.

- **Visual memory** is remembering what was just seen, at least for a few seconds. Children with visual memory problems may not remember the name of the animal on their card, for example, even though the picture has been placed face-down for only a moment. Or, in the familiar take-away game, they cannot recall what was removed, even though there were only three or four articles on the tray when it was presented just a moment before.

- **Visual tracking** is a skill in following objects visually. Children with tracking problems may have trouble keeping an eye on the ball, following the flight of a bird, or buttoning buttons in order from top to bottom. Visual tracking is likely to be associated with reading skills, in that reading requires systematic eye movements from left to right and top to bottom.

- **Visual-motor integration** is a skill that can also be thought of as eye–hand coordination. Children with this kind of problem may have trouble with almost every motor task that requires vision: fitting appropriately shaped pieces into a puzzle box, cutting on the line, drawing around a form, or tracing a simple shape. It is as if the child's hands cannot do what the eyes say needs to be done.

- **Auditory perception problems** make it difficult for many young children to process (make sense of) what they hear. Again, this is not a physical problem; being deaf or hard of hearing is not the cause of the child's problems. Basically, it is the inability to tell the difference between sounds. *Hat* and *mat* may sound the same to these children; rhyming games are beyond them. Often, they cannot tell the difference between high and low musical tones, especially as the range between tones lessens. Localization of sound is usually a problem, too. The child may have to look in two or three directions when trying to locate a whistler or a barking dog.

Children at risk for learning disabilities frequently have trouble carrying out directions that include common prepositions such as in, on, and under.

© Cengage Learning 2015

Language delays Children at risk for learning disabilities frequently have trouble with receptive or expressive language, or both. Acquiring the more advanced grammatical forms and the ability to formulate organized sentences tends to come considerably later than for most children.

While vocabulary is not necessarily more limited, trouble can arise, for example, when the child tries to call up a well-known word to describe a familiar concept. Carrying out directions that include common prepositions such as *in, on, under,* and *over* is often baffling. If the teacher says to put the block *on top of the box*, a child may look at the teacher questioningly while putting the object *in* the box. Many of these children have trouble repeating short sentences, rhymes, and directions. In addition, they often have difficulty imitating sounds, gestures, body movements, facial expressions, and other forms of nonverbal communication.

Social skills delay Children who appear to have the potential for later learning disabilities tend to have more than their share of social problems. They may be bullying or aggressive, withdrawn, or overdependent. Their behavior often confuses other children, and so they have trouble making friends. When they do succeed in forming a friendship, they tend to have difficulty keeping it. Sometimes the child puts too many demands on the friend, or has such inadequate play skills that the friend loses interest. Moreover, their impulsiveness may cause them to say and do inappropriate things; they may not foresee the possibility of negative consequences such as hurt feelings or the unintentional destruction of a friend's favorite toy. When a child loses two or three friends (for reasons the child neither understands nor seems able to change), feelings of rejection are likely to follow. Rejection increases frustration, a sense of incompetence, and low self-esteem. These feelings, in turn, lead to a tendency to break into tears at the slightest provocation, to strike out, or to withdraw even more.

Response to Intervention (RTI) the practice of providing high-quality instruction/intervention matched to the student's needs, using learning rate over time and level of performance to make important educational decisions

▶❙❙ **TeachSource** Video Connections

© Cengage Learning 2015

Autism Therapy and Insurance

The Oldham family has two sons diagnosed with autism. Intensive, one-on-one behavioral and speech therapy called Applied Behavior Analysis (ABA) helps the boys but costs up to $7,000 a month for each child for the recommended forty hours per week. The Oldhams struggle to pay half that amount, and their insurance does not cover autism therapy. They live in a state where insurance does not cover ABA services.

After watching the video discuss the following:

1. As of July 2012, there were thirty-one states that mandate coverage for ABA therapy for certain health plans, and more states are coming on board each year. Complete an Internet search and provide an update on the number of states providing coverage for ABA services.

2. What are your thoughts on the ethical issue discussed in the video? Do you believe insurance should be required to pay for ABA services?

Watch on CourseMate.

8-2c ■ Response to Intervention (RTI)

The Individuals with Disabilities Improvement Act of 2004 (IDEIA) permits educators to use **Response to Intervention (RTI)** as a substitute for, or supplement to, the previous practice of requiring a discrepancy between ability and achievement to identify students with learning disabilities. The law does not require its use, but it provides more latitude to use either or both approaches unless a state decides to restrict the use of the discrepancy model (Zirkel, 2006). Currently, most states are engaged in some level of implementation of RTI. While the status of practice varies from emerging to fully developed, depending on regions, districts, and sites, state leadership for RTI seems strong and is growing stronger. It is the hope of policymakers that RTI will encourage educators to intervene earlier and also to provide a more valid method of LD identification—thus reducing the number of false positives; labels that are given as a result of poor instruction rather than an actual disability (Fuchs & Fuchs, 2001).

Response to Intervention (RTI) is the strategy of providing high-quality instruction/intervention matched to the student's needs. Learning rate over time and level of performance are used to monitor progress and to make educational decisions. RTI consists of a tiered approach, shown in Figure 8-2, which

FIGURE 8-2

The Response to Intervention Model

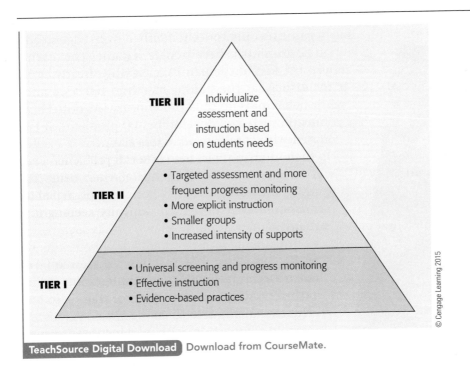

TIER III Individualize assessment and instruction based on students needs

TIER II
- Targeted assessment and more frequent progress monitoring
- More explicit instruction
- Smaller groups
- Increased intensity of supports

TIER I
- Universal screening and progress monitoring
- Effective instruction
- Evidence-based practices

© Cengage Learning 2015

TeachSource Digital Download Download from CourseMate.

begins with 1) *Screening and Group Interventions.* Students who do not make satisfactory progress when provided with high-quality instruction and support will be provided with the next tier of support, 2) *Target short-term interventions.* Target short-term intervention uses scientifically research-based interventions that are provided in addition to core instruction; data are collected and analyzed and progress is closely followed. Students not making progress in this tier move to 3) *Intensive Instruction,* consisting of academic and behavior strategies, methodologies, and practices designed for students significantly lagging behind established grade-level benchmarks. If a child does not respond to these more intensive interventions, he or she receives an individualized comprehensive evaluation that addresses all eligibility and procedural safeguards specified in IDEIA.

Pre-K RTI While RTI was originally conceptualized for K–12 students, there is a growing interest and use of RTI at the preschool level—**Pre-K RTI.** Table 8-2 lists the key components of the RTI and Pre-K-RTI. Several existing early childhood practices provide a foundation for its implementation (Coleman, Roth, & West, 2009)

- the use of tiered service-delivery models;
- instruction guided by learning standards;
- embedded learning opportunities;
- intentional planning of learning opportunities;
- use of progress monitoring measures
- data driven decision making.

Pre-K RTI a relatively new phenomenon of applying the best practices of RTI at the preschool level

TABLE 8-2

The Key Components of RTI and Pre-K RTI

High-quality instruction

Tiered instruction and intervention

Ongoing student assessment/progress monitoring

Family involvement

Source: Coleman, Roth, & West, 2009

8-2d ■ Program Considerations

In concluding this section on possible learning disabilities in young children, one concept bears repeating: Characteristics associated with learning disabilities can be observed in *all* young children at one time or another. Is there a preschool teacher anywhere who has not watched a child complete a lovely painting only to see it overlaid from edge to edge and top to bottom with endless coats of paint? The teacher may mourn the loss of the painting (having already earmarked it for display at the parent meeting) but this once-in-a-while behavior is no cause for concern. As noted before, in connection with *all* developmental problems, it is a matter of degree: Are the behaviors happening excessively? Do they interfere with the child's development and general well-being? Age, too, must be a consideration. It is always a warning sign when a problem behavior is extreme *and* persists significantly beyond appropriate age levels.

In working with children whose behaviors seem to predict future learning disabilities, it is essential to carefully re-examine the learning environment. A thorough review of effective teaching strategies is also essential. These strategies have been described throughout the text in connection with various developmental issues. Many of the strategies relate especially to working with preschool children who are at risk for future school success. They include the following reminders

- Be consistent in the use of positive reinforcement to increase behaviors that facilitate the child's development, thereby decreasing behaviors that interfere.

Provide the child with encouragement and descriptive praise for each step forward, regardless of how small.

© Cengage Learning 2015

- Provide the child with encouragement and descriptive praise for each step forward, regardless of how small.

- Provide learning activities that support the child's home language and culture.

- Remember that every child has strengths and does some things well. Concentrate attention on these, rather than on the child's weaknesses and misbehaviors.

- Break skills into small steps (task analysis) to teach whatever skills the child is having trouble with, whether learning to imitate, to focus attention, to say "No" instead of hitting, or any other inappropriate behavior.

- Give directions one at a time and allow adequate time for the child to comply. Verify the child's understanding of the request; rehearse (walk the child through) the required response as often as necessary.

- Teach new concepts and skills in short sessions with concrete materials that allow a child to use several sensory modalities: seeing, hearing, and manipulating.

- Be patient. Children with learning problems may have to be told or shown many times in many different ways how to accomplish a simple task. Do not expect learning to generalize from one situation to another. Each situation seems new to the child.

- Help parents understand that their child is not being difficult or inattentive on purpose. Tell them of their child's accomplishments, no matter how small. To enhance the child's self-esteem, describe his or her accomplishments to the parent in the presence of the child whenever possible.

Did You Get It?

What important indicator highlights the need to avoid hasty diagnosis of a child as learning disabled?

a. All young children are different, and all have much development yet to come.

b. Early problems are not merely a developmental deviation.

c. Observation of activities.

d. Observation of performance.

Take the full quiz on CourseMate.

Behavior Disorders 8-3 ☀

Children who are identified as having a behavior disorder (BD) are those whose behavior is extreme, chronic, and unacceptable. Defining and diagnosing behavior disorders are ongoing challenges in special education, and such definitions and diagnoses are extremely problematic in early childhood. Sometimes drawing the distinction between developmentally appropriate behavior and challenging behavior in a toddler or preschooler is difficult for even the most skilled teacher or parent.

8-3a ■ Definitional Issues

In 1975, when PL 94-142 was implemented, the term *seriously emotionally disturbed* was used to describe children and youth who demonstrated chronic challenging behaviors. Although this term still appears in IDEIA, experts who work with these children prefer the term **behaviorally disordered** because it places the focus on the observable aspect of the children's problems: the behavior that is causing problems in school and at home (Kaufman & Landrum, 2008). The most commonly accepted definition of BD is proposed by the National Mental Health and Special Education Coalition.

behaviorally disordered children who demonstrate chronic or pervasive behavior challenges

(I) The term emotional or behavioral disorder means a disability characterized by behavioral or emotional responses in school so different from appropriate age, cultural, or ethnic norms that they adversely affect educational performance. Educational performance includes academic, social, vocational, and personal skills. Such a disability:

A. *is more than a temporary, expected response to stressful events in the environment;*

B. *is consistently exhibited in two different settings, at least one of which is school related; and*

C. *is unresponsive to direct intervention in general education, or the child's condition is such that general education interventions would be insufficient.*

(II) Emotional and behavioral disorders can co-exist with other disabilities.

(III) This category may include children or youths with schizophrenic disorders, affective disorders, anxiety disorder, or other sustained disorders of conduct or adjustment when they adversely affect educational performance in accordance with section (I) (Forness & Knitzer, 1992, p. 13).

8-3b ■ Prevalence

Data published by the U.S. Department of Education (2005) suggests that about 1 percent of school-age children are identified with serious emotional or behavioral disorders. However, many authorities argue that children who demonstrate these types of behaviors often are drastically underserved. While behavior problems may be seen in preschool children, it is unwise to refer to young children as having a behavior or conduct disorder.

On the other hand, when aggressive and destructive behaviors threaten to become a young child's habitual way of responding to stress and frustration, intervention is imperative. The longer such behaviors dominate a child's social development, the more difficult they are to eliminate. These inappropriate behaviors become the norm for these children—the learned way to interact with others. Case histories of incorrigible juveniles make this tragically clear.

8-3c ■ Depression

Young children are seldom thought of as having severe depression. Today, experts agree that severe depression can occur at any age. Studies show that depression is a common disorder among children (younger than age eighteen). Approximately 5 percent of children at any one time may suffer from serious depression (University of Michigan Depression Center, 2007). The disorder is marked by changes in emotions, motivation, thoughts, and physical well-being.

The causes of these conditions are not clear. Some evidence suggests that children growing up with depressed parents are more likely to have bouts of anxiety and depression. This does not hold true for all children, however. In one study, more than 60 percent of the children of depressed parents showed no signs of the disorder (Dodge, 1990). Low self-esteem also seems to be associated with depression, especially among adolescents (Harter, 1990). It would be unwise, however, to completely dismiss the question of depression where young children are concerned. The possible precursors to such problems need to be recognized and addressed.

8-3d ■ Anxiety

phobias fears that result in excessive and unrealistic anxiety about everyday happenings

Young people who experience excessive or intense fear, worry, or uneasiness may have an anxiety disorder. These feelings can last for long periods of time and significantly impact their day-to-day living. If not treated early, anxiety disorders can lead to:

- repeated school absences
- impaired relations with peers
- low self-esteem
- alcohol or other drug use
- anxiety disorder in adulthood

Anxiety disorders are among the most common of childhood disorders. According to the Anxiety and Depression Association of America (2013), as many as one of every eight children has an anxiety disorder. Anxiety disorders include phobias, panic disorders, obsessive-compulsive disorder, generalized anxiety disorder, and post-traumatic stress disorder.

Fears that result in excessive and unrealistic anxiety about everyday happenings are called **phobias**. The individual with a phobia may go into a panic reaction at encountering a feared object or event, or at the mere thought of encountering it. For example, some phobic individuals take unrealistic measures (such as climbing twenty flights of stairs) to avoid riding an elevator; some walk a mile out of the way, every day, rather than pass a well-fenced yard in which a small, securely tied dog barks at passersby.

A certain amount of fear is normal. Fears are natural, adaptive mechanisms in young children and are built in for survival purposes. No child should be laughed at or shamed for his or her fears. By the same token, children's fears should not be allowed to get blown out of proportion. Normal fears can become unrealistically stressful if adults are overly attentive to the child's fearful responses. On the other

Did You Get It?

How does the term *behaviorally disordered* offer a more favorable description than *seriously emotionally disturbed* for a child presenting chronic challenging behaviors?

a. Places the focus on the observable aspect of the child's problem.

b. Focuses on the behavior at school, rather than at home.

c. It denotes something temporary.

d. Focuses on the behavior at home, rather than at school.

Take the full quiz on CourseMate.

hand, not enough attention can make the child feel insecure and rejected. These feelings can lead to other kinds of maladaptive behaviors and stressful reactions.

Autism Spectrum Disorder 8-4 ☀

Autism spectrum disorder (ASD) refers to a group of childhood disorders usually evident by age three. With the newly released DSM-5 (2013), disorders previously referred to as early infantile autism, childhood autism, Kanner's autism, high-functioning autism, Asperger's disorder, pervasive developmental disorder (not otherwise specified), and childhood disintegrative disorder are consolidated within the overarching category of Autism Spectrum Disorder (ASD). According to an APA news release (2012), the change indicates that the symptoms of these disorders represent a continuum from mild to severe, rather than being distinct disorders. The new category is designed to help clinicians more accurately diagnose people with relevant symptoms and behaviors by recognizing the differences from person to person. It was felt that previous criteria led to providing general labels that tended not to be consistently applied across different clinics and centers.

These disorders have identifiable characteristics and behaviors that can be exhibited in children to extremely varying degrees—hence the concept of a "spectrum." The primary characteristics include 1) deficits in social communication and social interaction and 2) restricted repetitive behaviors, interests, and activities. Table 8-3 shows the DSM-5 criteria for autism spectrum disorders. A child with ASD may be slightly different from his peers or extremely different, depending on the severity of his symptoms. The autism spectrum disorders can be reliably diagnosed by age three in most children.

TABLE 8-3

Criteria for Autism Spectrum Disorders

Autism Spectrum Disorder (APA, 2013)

Must meet criteria 1, 2, and 3:

1. Clinically significant, persistent deficits in social communication and interactions, as manifest by all of the following:

   a. Marked deficits in nonverbal and verbal communication used for social interaction
   b. Lack of social reciprocity
   c. Failure to develop and maintain peer relationships appropriate to developmental level

2. Restricted, repetitive patterns of behavior, interests, and activities, as manifested by at least two of the following:

   a. Stereotyped motor or verbal behaviors, or unusual sensory behaviors
   b. Excessive adherence to routines and ritualized patterns of behavior
   c. Restricted, fixated interests
   d. Hyper- or hypo-reactivity to sensory input or unusual interest in sensory aspects of the environment

3. Symptoms must be present in early childhood (but may not become fully manifest until social demands exceed limited capacities)

4. Symptoms cause clinically significant impairment to social, occupational, or other important areas of current functioning.

Autism spectrum disorder is diagnosed four times more often in boys than in girls. However, girls with the disorder tend to have more severe symptoms and greater cognitive impairment (Yeargin-Allsopp, Rice, Karapurkar, Doernberg, Boyle, & Murphy, 2003). There is much debate about prevalence and the increase in rate, as indicated by this statement from the 2006 Addendum to the Autism Spectrum Disorders NIMH Fact Booklet:

> The rate of autism found in a study published by the Centers for Disease Control (CDC) in 2003 is higher than the rates found from studies conducted in the United States during the 1980s and early 1990s, but was consistent with those of more recent studies. Debate continues about whether this represents a true increase in prevalence. Changes in the criteria used to diagnose autism, along with increased recognition of the disorder by professionals and the public may all be contributing factors. Nonetheless, it is clear that more children are being diagnosed with an ASD than ever before.

The Centers for Disease Control and Prevention estimates that one in eighty-eight children in the United States has been identified as having an autism spectrum disorder (ASD). Autism spectrum disorders are almost five times more common among boys than girls – with one in fifty-four boys identified. Study results from the 2008 surveillance year show 11.3 per 1,000 eight-year-old children have been identified as having an ASD. This latest analysis shows that autism is up 23 percent since 2006 and 78 percent since 2002. The study also shows more children are being diagnosed by age three, an increase from 12 percent for children born in 1994 to 18 percent for children born in 2000. Some of this increase is due to the way children are identified, diagnosed, and served in their communities, although exactly how much is due to these factors is unknown (CDC, 2012).

The new change in the DSM-5 may also impact these figures in the future, but how, no one knows for sure at this point. Autism Speaks is funding a three-year research project to assess the effect of proposed revisions to the criteria used to diagnose autism. The new study will be conducted at one of the sites currently used by the Centers of Disease Control and Prevention (CDC) to estimate prevalence of ASD. The study will provide important information regarding how the changes in diagnostic criteria will influence estimates of prevalence (Autism Speaks, 2012).

There is increasing evidence that the earliest signs of autism appear during the first year, after babies reach six months. Sally Ozonoff and her colleagues (2010) reported that while such babies begin life appearing relatively normal in terms of social responsiveness (e.g., eye contact, smiling), there was an observed decline in this responsiveness, with symptoms beginning to emerge between six and twelve months. This finding is of particular note, given that the average age of diagnosis is four-and-a-half years. Due to this relatively late age of diagnosis, the Centers for Disease Control and Prevention launched a campaign to stress the importance of recognizing milestones. The CDC website, provided at the end of this chapter, contains a variety of resources, including a milestones checklist, guidelines for sharing concerns with pediatricians, and resources for help.

Children with autism differ significantly in the types of skills they present. As Siegel (1998) reminds us, "Autism is a collection of overlapping groups of symptoms that vary from child to child" (p. 301). Approximately 75 percent of children with autism also have some degree of intellectual disability. Since there is currently no physical or medical test for autism, a thorough assessment completed by an interdisciplinary team is warranted. This team should include a physician, psychologist, teacher, language specialist, and parent or parents.

Lower Rates of Autism in Hispanic Children?

According to a study by Stephanie E. Bean and her colleagues, Hispanic children are diagnosed with autism at lower rates and at older ages compared with white non-Hispanic children. According to the Centers for Disease Control and Prevention's Autism and Developmental Disabilities Monitoring (ADDM) Network 2006 data, the prevalence is one in 170 children.

Ms. Bean and her associates analyzed data from a subset of the National Survey of Children's Health. The data was obtained from phone interviews with parents of children aged 3–17 years who had a current autism spectrum disorder diagnosis.

According to Ms. Bean, the higher rate of diagnosed "speech problems" in Hispanic children is not surprising, since many Hispanic households speak more than one language at home: "Because language delay is a factor of autism, it might be that the speech problem masks the autism spectrum disorder diagnosis," said Ms. Bean, a graduate student in public health at Johns Hopkins University in Baltimore.

A later, or incorrect, diagnosis can have a serious impact. Children may not receive services that appropriately meet their needs. Additional efforts are needed to provide outreach and education to this demographic to ensure timely diagnosis and access to appropriate services.

Source: Boschert, S. (2012). Comorbidities might mask autism in Hispanics. *Family Practice Digital News Network.* Retrieved from http://www.familypracticenews.com/index.php?id=2934&type=98&tx_ttnews%5Btt_news%5D=139275&cHash=da03e20e363

As listed in the criteria in Table 8-3, children with autism spectrum disorder exhibit marked deficits in nonverbal and verbal communication used for social interaction. Many children with autism do not join in shared attention with adults and do not use nonverbal communication, such as pointing, in the same way as typically developing children.

The verbal communication of children with autism (some do not develop speech) is often strange. A child may have beautifully clear speech with complex language that is so disorganized that it makes no sense. Another child may use language simply to express rote memorization. Many of these children can recite verbatim commercial jingles heard on television, but they have no communicative language. One four-year-old knew all the words to every stanza of more than forty popular songs and folk ballads. That same child had no social language except for a few stereotyped, **echolalic** phrases. To add to the mysteries of ASD, children have been known to add, divide, and multiply complicated sets of numbers as rapidly as a calculator. Others can read a newspaper, word for word, with expression; yet they understand not a word they read.

It is important to support the parents of children with autism in every way possible and work with other members of the interdisciplinary team to help parents find **respite care.** Another urgent parental need is frequent assurance that the autism was *not* caused by a lack of love or caring on their part. Parents of children with autism often have been greatly wronged. Without valid evidence, it has been implied that they (or, more often than not, the mother) were somehow responsible for their child's autism.

Evidence indicates, however, that parents are not to blame. According to Bee and Boyd (2012), children appear to be born with the disorder: "Whatever the specific origin, the evidence jointly points to the conclusion that autism reflects

echolalic language characterized by meaningless repetition of words and sentences used intelligently by others; a condition often associated with autism and schizophrenia

respite care temporary care given to provide regular caregivers (usually the mother) relief and time away from the individual who is disabled

different brain functions of some kind." For a moving and fascinating true story of a family's efforts on behalf of their children with autism, we recommend Catherine Maurice's book, *Let Me Hear Your Voice: A Family's Triumph Over Autism* (1994).

8-4b ■ Advances in Autism Research

In recent years, autism and autism research continue to reach the front pages of the news. There has been an increase in the number of publications and scientists entering the field. With this increase in research, more is being learned about genetics and the effects of the environment and their relationship to ASD.

Genetic Links Recent research has shown spontaneous mutations in the DNA of children with autism. Researchers also found that the mutations were increasingly frequent in children born to older fathers (Sanders et al, 2012). Researchers from the University of Washington in Seattle discovered that these spontaneous mutations associated with ASD come primarily from the father. They also discovered an increase in frequency with a father's age at time of conception (O'Roak et al, 2012). Scientists from Iceland similarly reported that children of older men had a greater number of *de novo* mutations than children fathered by younger men. A de novo mutation is a genetic difference that is not inherited directly but arises due to a gene alteration that appears in the father as a result of a mutation in a sperm. The researchers found that the number of mutations in a child's genome increased with the father's age—by around two per year. The study also found a slight association between a mother's age and these mutations (Kong et al, 2012).

Andy Shih, Ph.D., Autism Speaks senior vice president for scientific affairs, explained, "Taken together, these findings are starting to give us a better picture of the biology of autism, of the possible underlying disease mechanisms. They are one piece of a larger puzzle that is helping us understand the causes of autism" (Autism Speaks, 2012).

Impact of Environmental Pollutants Recent research has demonstrated that exposure to certain pollutants may contribute to the development of ASD. Scientists with the University of California's MIND Institute reviewed past research on pesticide exposure, brain development, and ASD. They concluded that evidence strongly suggests that certain pesticides can increase the risk for autism. Further research is needed to explore how the timing or dose of exposure influences risk. Research is also needed to identify the biological mechanisms involved (Shelton, Hertz-Picciotto, & Pessah, 2012).

A team of researchers from the University of Southern California's Keck School of Medicine reported some of the first direct evidence of an association between air pollution and autism. The researchers examined air pollution records associated with the geographic location of more than 500 children and their mothers. Approximately half the children were diagnosed with autism. They reported that high levels of air pollution during pregnancy and the first year of life were associated with a three-fold increase in autism risk (Volk et al., 2013).

8-4c ■ Problems that May Accompany ASD

Several problems and syndromes may accompany ASD. They include sensory problems, intellectual disability, seizures, Fragile X syndrome, and tuberous sclerosis sensory problems. Many children with ASD are extremely sensitive to certain sounds, textures, tastes, and smells. Some children find the feel of clothes touching their skin unbearable. This discomfort may result in tantrums, screaming, and other avoidance behaviors. Some children with ASD are oblivious to extreme cold or pain. A child may experience a severe injury and not cry or seek help. The following is a list of some problems that may accompany ASD.

- *Intellectual disability.* Many children with ASD have some degree of cognitive impairment. When tested, some areas of ability may be normal or even advanced for the child's age, while others may be especially weak. For example, a child with ASD may excel at completing puzzles and fine motor tasks but lag behind peers in receptive and expressive language. According to her 2006 study, Meredyth Edelson makes the case that research literature over-reports the percentage of children with ASD that have an intellectual disability. She explains that recent epidemiological surveys have shown that the prevalence rates of "MR" (intellectual disability) in children with autism is between 40 and 55 percent She adds that recent empirical studies indicate that when appropriate measures of intelligence are used—those that take into account the interference of autism—a significantly lower prevalence rate of intellectual disability is found relative to the rates typically reported in literature.

- *Seizures.* One in four children with ASD develops seizures, often starting either in early childhood or in adolescence. In most cases, seizures can be controlled by medicines called *anticonvulsants*.

- *Fragile X syndrome.* This disorder is the most common inherited form of intellectual disability. A description of this syndrome can be found in Chapter 5. Fragile X syndrome affects about 2 to 5 percent of people with ASD. If parents are considering having another child, their child with ASD should be checked for Fragile X. It has been found that when a child with ASD also has Fragile X, there is a one-in-two chance that boys born to the same parents will have the syndrome (Powers, 2000).

- *Tuberous sclerosis.* Tuberous sclerosis, a rare genetic disorder, causes benign tumors to grow in the brain as well as in other vital organs. It has a consistently strong association with ASD. Recent studies estimate that approximately 50 percent of individuals with tuberous sclerosis could be diagnosed with autism (Jeste, Sahin, Bolton, Ploubidis, & Humphrey, 2008).

8-4d ■ Other Forms of Autism Spectrum Disorder

Rett's Disorder This relatively rare disorder, also known as Rett syndrome, is diagnosed primarily in females. Incidence is one in 10–15,000 children; in the United States approximately 30,000 children and women are affected (Rett Syndrome

Case Study ■ A new student ■

Sarah is a second-year kindergarten teacher. Her principal has just told her that a student is moving into her classroom next week. The child has autism and will be accompanied by an aide. This is her first experience with a child with autism and with having an aide in her classroom. Think about the following questions: What will she need to do to prepare for the student's arrival? Should Sarah do anything to prepare the other students? If so, what? What can she do to develop an effective working relationship with the aide?

Research Trust; 2009, Morris, 1993). Parents report normal development over the first eighteen months, followed by a loss of abilities, especially in the area of gross motor skills. This regression continues in the areas of speech and hand use. Diagnosis is often made on the basis of the repetitive gestures and hand movements described as "hand wringing." Scientists sponsored by the National Institute of Child Health and Human Development have discovered a mutation in the sequence of a single gene that causes Rett syndrome. This discovery may lead to methods of screening for Rett syndrome, enabling doctors to start treating affected children much earlier, or perhaps stopping the progression of the symptoms (NIH, 2001).

Attention-deficit/hyperactivity disorder Being overly focused or easily distracted are common behaviors observed in individuals with autism spectrum disorder. Researchers at Kennedy Kriegar Institute in Baltimore reported that a third of the 162 children with autism they studied also had symptoms of attention deficit hyperactivity disorder. They also noted that the children with co-occurrence of autism spectrum disorder and attention deficit hyperactivity disorders face greater impairments (Rao & Landa 2013).

Dr. Rebecca Landa, the senior author of the study and director of the Center for Autism and Related Disorders at Kennedy Kriegar, said:

> We are increasingly seeing that these two disorders co-occur and a greater understanding of how they relate to each other could ultimately improve outcomes and quality of life for this subset of children. The recent change to the Diagnostic and Statistical Manual of Mental Disorders (DSM-5) to remove the prohibition of a dual diagnosis of autism and ADHD is an important step forward.

Dr. Landa and her team emphasize the need for further research studies on attention, social, communication and cognitive functioning of children with ASD.

applied behavior analysis (ABA) a teaching approach used with children with autism that involves observation, assessment, breaking skills down, and teaching skills systematically; progress is closely monitored through ongoing data collection

8-4e ■ Intervention

Many methods of treatment and education are available for children with autism. Some have been validated via research; others have not. Among these treatments, **applied behavior analysis (ABA)** has become widely accepted as an effective treatment. Mental Health: A Report of the Surgeon General states, "Thirty years of research demonstrated the efficacy of applied behavioral methods in reducing inappropriate behavior and in increasing communication, learning, and appropriate social behavior" (Department of Health and Human

During Discrete Trial Teaching, skills are taught in small steps.

Christina Kennedy/Photo Edit

Services, 1999). Applied behavior analysis refersto the process of systematically using interventions that are based on the principles of learning, and through this systematic process demonstrate that the interventions are responsible for learning or changes in behavior. There are several treatment strategies that fall under ABA, including discrete trial teaching (DTT), incidental teaching, and pivotal response training (PRT). Probably the best known of these approaches is **discrete trial teaching (DTT)**. This approach consists of teacher-provided antecedents (instructions), a behaviorally defined response from the child, and a consequence, either a reinforcer for a correct response or a prompt for no response or incorrect responses (Mastergeorge, Rogers, Corbett, & Solomon, 2003). Complex skills are broken down into smaller teachable steps through a process called task analysis (described in Chapter 12). The basic DTT research done by Ivar Lovaas and his colleagues at the University of California, Los Angeles, demonstrated that intensive, one-on-one child–teacher interaction for forty hours a week resulted in dramatic improvements in language and social skills and thus IQ (McEachin, Smith, & Lovaas, 1993). Many researchers agree that intensive ABA intervention can result in substantial gains (Sallows & Graupner, 2005).

The approach that works best for a child with ASD is one that is individualized to meet the specific needs of the child and family. Children with autism demonstrate highly individualized learning styles and needs (Schreibman, Koegel, Charlop, & Egel, 1990). The most successful programs build on the child's interests, teach tasks as a series of simple steps, actively engage the child's attention in highly structured activities, provide regular reinforcement of behavior, provide predictable routines, and use effective instructional strategies and developmentally appropriate curricular content. Children with ASD can make outstanding progress in high-quality, inclusive settings (Schwartz, Sandall, Garfinkle, & Bauer, 1998; Strain & Cordisco, 2008). Several suggestions for working with children with autism follow

- Keep messages simple and direct.

- Use objects and actions along with words. (Show the child a shoe and demonstrate pulling the lace through.)

- Emphasize spoken language by having the child ask for something by name whenever possible.

- Give the child opportunities to interact with children who are at a more "normal" level in terms of language and social development.

- For behavior management programs, use **tangible reinforcers** (small toys, stickers, music, favored foods) and pair these with adult attention.

- Establish a predictable environment, including teachers' language and behaviors, the daily schedule, and classroom furnishings and materials.

- Rearrange the environment (place highly desired items out of reach) and use teaching strategies that motivate the child to request these items.

- Provide opportunity for the child to generalize new skills by ensuring the opportunity to practice these skills in a variety of settings (home, school, and park) and with a variety of people (several teachers, parents, siblings, peers).

- Focus on improving the child's communication skills, perhaps using a communication device such as the picture exchange communication system (PECS) (Bondy & Frost, 1994). PECS teaches children to give a picture of a desired object in exchange for that item. By using PECS, the child learns to initiate communication.

discrete trial teaching (DTT) a teaching strategy that enables the learner to acquire complex skills and behaviors by first mastering the subcomponents of the targeted skill

tangible reinforcers material things that the individual likes; in children, favorite foods and drinks, toys, stickers, and such

Connecting Developmentally Appropriate Practice to Brain Research

EARLY INTERVENTION MODEL HELPS NORMALIZE BRAIN ACTIVITY IN CHILDREN WITH AUTISM

According to a study published in the *Journal of the American Academy of Child & Adolescent Psychiatry*, an early intervention therapy called Early Start Denver Model (ESDM), which had previously been shown to be effective in increasing language and social skills and cognitive thinking, and in decreasing symptoms in children with autism as young as eighteen months old, now also has shown to be effective in pushing brain activity to work in a "normal" way. ESDM combines developmental, play-based, and relationship-based methods with the proven teaching practices of Applied Behavior Analysis (ABA). Its core features include:

- Naturalistic applied behavioral analytic strategies

- Sensitivity to normal developmental sequence

- High parental involvement

- Focus on interpersonal exchange and positive affect

- Shared engagement with joint activities

- Language and communication taught inside a positive, affect-based relationship

Thomas R. Insel, director of the National Institute of Mental Health, said:

"This may be the first demonstration that a behavioral intervention for autism is associated with changes in brain function as well as positive changes in behavior. By studying changes in the neural response to faces, Dawson and her colleagues have identified a new target and a potential biomarker that can guide treatment development."

Forty-eight boys and girls between the ages of eighteen and thirty months who were diagnosed with autism participated in the research project. The children were randomized to receive either the ESDM therapy or referral to community intervention for two years. The Children in the ESDM group received therapy for twenty hours per week, and their parents were taught to provide therapy. The participants referred to community intervention underwent community-based interventions and also received referrals, evaluations, and resource manuals.

At the study's conclusion, the researchers monitored the children's brain activity by use of EEGs (electroencephalograms). The purpose was to evaluate brain activation when the children looked at social stimuli, such as people's faces, and non-social stimuli, such as toys.

Previous research has shown that children without autism display more brain activity when they look at social stimuli than non-social stimuli. This is the opposite for children who have autism.

The results of the ESDM study showed that twice as many children who participated in the ESDM intervention showed increased and greater brain activity when they saw faces rather than toys, which is the same as seen in children with normal brain activity. Only 5 percent of the children who participated in the community-based interventions showed normal brain activity.

The researchers also noted that the children who participated with ESDM and displayed the highest amount of brain activity when looking at faces were also found to have better communication and social skills.

Sources: Autism Speaks. (2013). *What Is the Early Start Denver Model?* Retrieved from http://www.autismspeaks.org/what-autism/treatment/early-start-denver-model-esdm

Dawson, G., et al. (2012). Early Behavioral Intervention Is Associated With Normalized Brain Activity in Young Children with Autism. *Journal of the American Academy Child & Adolescent Psychiatry*, October 2012, doi:10.1016/j.jaac.2012.08.018. Retrieved from http://www.jaacap.com/article/S0890-8567(12)00643-0/abstract

n.p. (2012, October 27). "Autism Early Intervention Can Help Regulate Brain Activity In Kids." *Medical News Today.* Retrieved from http://www.medicalnewstoday.com/articles/252079.php.

- Reduce class or group size and provide appropriate seating for the child, to help minimize distractions.

- Modify the curriculum according to the child's strengths and weaknesses. For example, many children with autism learn skills faster with visual supports (e.g., scripts for play time, photos for transitions)

- Provide frequent communication with parents and other care providers.

Parental involvement has also emerged as a major factor in treatment success. Parents are involved in intervention and work with teachers and therapists to identify the behaviors to be changed and the skills to be taught. Parents are trained to deal with behaviors and teach new skills so that intervention occurs across environments and throughout the day.

Other interventions In an effort to do everything possible to help their children, many parents of children with ASD continually seek new treatments. Although an unproven treatment may help one child, it may not prove beneficial to another (NIMH, 2009). One has only to search for treatments on the Internet to see the confusing array of treatment options and to hear conflicting reports of what is effective and what is not. To be considered proven, the treatment should undergo clinical trials (preferably randomized, double-blind studies) that compare treatment and no-treatment groups.

Table 8-4 provides a list of questions parents can use to help determine the appropriateness of an intervention for their child and family.

The following are among the interventions that have been reported to have been helpful to some children, but whose efficacy or safety has not been proven (Strock, 2004).

Dietary interventions: Some feel that food allergies and an insufficiency of a specific vitamin or mineral may cause autistic symptoms. Some parents report results from a diet that is gluten-free and casein-free. Gluten is a casein-like substance that is found in the seeds of various cereal plants—wheat, oat, rye, and barley. Casein is the principal protein in milk. Since gluten and milk are found in many of the foods we eat, following a gluten-free, casein-free diet is extremely difficult.

TABLE 8-4

Questions for Program/Treatment Evaluation and Planning

Questions for Potential Program/Treatment Evaluation and Planning

- Has the program/treatment been successful for other children?
- Will the treatment result in harm to the child?
- Is the treatment developmentally appropriate for the child?
- How will failure of the treatment affect my child and family?
- Has the treatment been validated scientifically?
- How will the treatment be integrated into the child's current program?
- Do staff members have training and experience in working with children and with autism?
- How are activities planned and organized?
- Are there predictable daily schedules and routines?
- How much individual attention will my child receive?
- How is progress measured? Will my child's behavior be closely observed and recorded?
- Is the environment designed to minimize distractions?
- Will the program prepare me to continue the therapy at home?
- What are the costs, time commitment, and location of the program?

Sources: Freeman, 1997; National Institute of Mental Health, 2009.

Vitamin B6 is a supplement that some parents feel is beneficial for their child with ASD. The result of research studies is mixed; some children respond positively, some negatively, some not at all or very little (Volkmar, 2000).

Chelation: An unproven theory claims that by removing the heavy metals from a child with autism's blood, symptoms can be reversed. Chelation is used on the premise that there is a link between the use of thimerosal, a mercury-based preservative used in the measles-mumps-rubella (MMR) vaccine, and autism. Mercury is no longer found in childhood vaccines in the United States. Many well-done, large-scale studies have failed to show a link between thimerosal and autism.

The National Institute of Mental Health (NIMH) had planned on undertaking research to address the widespread but unproven theory that autism may be treated successfully by chelation therapy. Chelation is more commonly used to treat lead toxicity, but many families seek the treatment to try to remove mercury and other metals from their autistic child's blood (NIMH, 2006). The study was called off in 2008, due to the fact that the federal review board that originally approved the study determined that there was no clear evidence for direct benefit to children who would participate in the chelation trial and that the study presents more than a minimal risk (WebMD, 2008).

Medications Medications are sometimes used to treat behaviors associated with autism, such as aggression, self-injury, and tantrums. In 2006, the U.S. Food and Drug Administration (FDA) approved the use of risperidone (generic name) or Risperdal (brand name) for the treatment of behaviors and irritability in autistic children and adolescents ages five to sixteen. This is the first approval for drug use to treat behaviors associated with autism in children.

8-5 Eating and Elimination Disorders

Eating problems associated with particular disorders, as well as with over- and underweight children, were described in Chapter 7. Incontinence associated with spinal-cord damage was also discussed. This section will look at several other eating and elimination disorders sometimes found among young children in group settings.

8-5a ■ Pica

pica craving to eat nonfood substances

Pica is the craving for nonfood substances. Early childhood teachers may encounter children who are constantly eating substances considered inedible: dirt, tar or grease, chalk, paper, or finger paint. Frequent consumption of inedible materials is a health threat.

Many young children sample materials such as paste, play dough, or clay. This should not be confused with pica. However, such actions should be discouraged, with an explanation that they can cause stomach upset. If the child continues, the problem is usually solved by removing the material with the simple statement, "I can't let you play with the clay if you eat it." Children also may go on *food jags*. They insist on eating certain foods to the exclusion of all others. Except in extreme cases (or if too much pressure is put on the child to "eat right"), the jag usually disappears in a reasonable time. There also is the occasional child who eats excessive amounts of a certain food. One four-year-old was known to eat whole heads of lettuce, almost ravenously. Whenever a teacher is concerned about a child's eating habits, the parents and appropriate members of the interdisciplinary team should be consulted.

8-5b ■ Soiling and Wetting

It is not uncommon for early childhood teachers to encounter children who are not toilet-trained, or are not reliable about getting themselves to the toilet in time. The same holds true for young children with developmental disabilities, many of whom may not be toilet-trained when they reach preschool age. The reasons vary. Often it is the result of a toilet-training impasse between child and parents. In an early childhood program, where emotional involvement is at a minimum, toilet training usually can be accomplished quickly. Effective training guides describing schedule and intensive training programs are available, including the well-known *Toilet Training in Less Than a Day* by Azrin and Foxx (1989), *Steps to Independence* by Baker and Brightman (2004), and *Self-Help Skills for People with Autism* by Anderson, Jablonski, Thomeer, and Knapp (2007). It is the rare child—even one with a severe intellectual disability—who cannot be taught to use the toilet.

Even though toilet-trained, however, young children with and without developmental disabilities may have soiling or wetting episodes on occasion. They often give clues of an impending accident by jiggling or clutching themselves. What is needed is a quiet instruction from the teacher *before* the accident occurs: "Run in and use the toilet. I'll save the swing until you get back." When a toilet accident does occur, a child should never be ridiculed or made to feel guilty. Clothing should be changed matter-of-factly and the soiled clothing rinsed out and put in a plastic bag. Every young child needs spare clothes at school, rotated from home if possible.

encopresis chronic soiling problem

enuresis chronic wetting problem

Chronic soiling or wetting sometimes occurs in an older preschool or primary-age child who has been reliably toilet-trained. It is important for teachers to be aware of the following.

- Persistent wetting, especially in girls, may be related to chronic urinary tract infection.

- A child may have a recurring, low-grade intestinal virus, causing loose or runny bowels.

- Children with diabetes may have failure of urine control at times.

- Some children are anxious about using a strange bathroom, or have been trained to greater privacy than is available at school.

- Some school bathrooms have a toilet that flushes much more loudly than the home toilet, and children become fearful of using the bathroom due to the sound.

Once in a while, even when all physical disorders have been ruled out, the child continues to have problems. **Encopresis** (chronic soiling problem) and **enuresis** (chronic wetting problem) are the clinical names assigned to such conditions.

Teachers may need to remind a child engrossed in an activity to use the bathroom.

© Cengage Learning 2015

Although a number of possible reasons can be given, earlier difficulties associated with elimination or toilet training may have become intertwined with anxiety, fear, and other emotional reactions. These can result in a child's unpredictable and hard-to-control soiling or wetting accidents. Even in these cases, the clothes should be changed matter-of-factly, without reprimand or moralizing. Working together, teachers, parents, and the appropriate team member(s) can help a child with enuresis or encopresis gain reliable control.

Did You Get It?

What is the difference between pica and a food jag?
   a. Sampling materials such as paste, play dough, or clay is associated with pica
   b. Pica is the craving for nonfood substances; a food jag is the insistence on eating certain foods to the exclusion of all others.
   c. Pica lasts for a short time; a food jag lasts for a long time.
   d. Pica is the insistence on eating certain foods to the exclusion of all others; a food jag is the craving for nonfood substances.

Take the full quiz on CourseMate.

A Final but Important Note

For early childhood educators, behavior and learning issues can raise a number of questions. For example, is it ever appropriate to diagnose a preschool-age child as learning disabled? If not, what about the many behaviors in some preschool children (distractibility, short attention span, visual perception problems, and many others) that resemble the behaviors of older children having serious problems with academic tasks? Is it not important to deal with these nonacademic behavior disorders in the early years, before they become greater problems that are likely to have a negative impact on subsequent academic learning? The answer seems to be "Yes," and the question then becomes "How?" A cautionary theme runs throughout this chapter: Behavior problems of every type are common among young children. Every child exhibits a number of them during the developmental years. It is only when problems become excessive or interfere with a child's developmental progress that they are of great concern. Even then, to prematurely label or classify a young child who has much development yet to come often does the child a grave injustice. It is not how a child is classified, but how a child is cared for and taught as an individual, that is the most important issue in addressing behavior and learning problems in young children.

Summary

▷ Teachers of young children may encounter varying types of developmental problems. Disorders associated with learning and behavior have been linked to many developmental problems.

▷ Teachers of young children may encounter a number of problems related to anxiety.

▷ Learning disabilities are classified under a variety of headings, depending on the researcher's, the clinician's, or the teacher's theoretical background.

▷ Children with autism spectrum disorders often are enrolled in inclusive preschools. It is important for teachers to work with the child's family and team of specialists to make modifications that will support the child's learning.

▷ Soiling and wetting episodes that continue long past the expected age range for children to be reliably toilet-trained may also be of concern.

Key Terms

aphasia, 180
applied behavior analysis (ABA), 196
attention deficit hyperactivity disorder (ADHD), 174
autism, 192
autism spectrum disorders (ASD), 174
behaviorally disordered, 189
discrete trial teaching (DTT), 197

dyslexia, 180
echolalic, 193
encopresis, 201
enuresis, 201
learning disability, 174
organic, 177
perseveration, 184
phobias, 190
pica, 200

Pre-K Response to Intervention (Pre-K RTI), 187
prerequisite skills, 183
psychopathologists, 175
respite care, 193
Response to Intervention (RTI), 186
salicylates, 178
spatial orientation, 183
tangible reinforcers, 197

Student Activities

1. Search on the Internet for at least two additional autism treatments not mentioned in the text. Use the questions in the text to determine the safety and appropriateness of the treatment.

2. Contact a local school district or school site and investigate how and whether they are implementing a response to intervention (RTI) strategy.

3. Visit an early intervention applied behavior analysis (ABA) program for children with autism, or find information about a program online. Make a list of what you consider the most important aspects of the program.

4. The chapter includes some of the most recent research on autism at the time of publication of the text. Complete an Internet search to learn about additional research in the area of autism.

5. The final paragraph of the chapter states "…to prematurely label or classify a young child who has much development yet to come often does the child a grave injustice. It is not how a child is classified, but how the child is cared for and taught as an individual, that is the most important issue in addressing behavior and learning problems in young children." Interview at least two professionals in the early education field. Get their opinion and experiences in relation to this statement.

Review Questions

Part 1. Define the following terms.

1. pica
2. enuresis
3. food jag
4. phobia
5. perseveration

6. echolalia
7. respite care
8. behavior disorder
9. ADHD
10. autism spectrum disorder (ASD)

Part 2. Respond to the following items in list form.

1. List three questions a teacher might ask in deciding what observations to make of a child described as having social impairments.
2. List four characteristics of autism in very young children.
3. List six characteristics found among young children with possible learning disabilities.
4. List four conditions that do not apply to children who are diagnosed as learning disabled.

5. List five large-motor problems found among children with sensory-motor difficulties.
6. List three common language delays that may indicate a learning disability.
7. List seven tips for teachers who work with young children who appear to be at risk for learning disabilities.
8. List five suggestions a classroom teacher should keep in mind when working with a child with autism.

Helpful Websites

Autism Society of America

http://www.autism-society.org

This site includes information on support and advocacy and other services for individuals with autism and their families. It includes information on behavior and communication.

Centers for Disease Control and Prevention—Learn the Signs/Act Early

www.cdc.gov/ncbddd/autism/actearly

This site provides parents and educators with information about identifying the signs of autism at an early age. There are developmental checklists and resources to assist families during the assessment and diagnosis process.

Children and Adults with Attention Deficit/ Hyperactivity Disorders (CHADD)

http://www.CHADD.org

CHADD was founded in 1987 in response to the isolation and frustration parents and adults were experiencing in dealing with and finding resources for ADHD.

Families for Early Autism Treatment (FEAT)

http://www.feat.org

FEAT is a nonprofit organization of parents, educators, and other professionals dedicated to providing education, advocacy, and support for the Northern California autism community. Their website provides information to parents of children diagnosed with autism spectrum disorders, including autism and Asperger's syndrome.

LD Online

http://www.ldonline.org

LD OnLine.org is the world's leading website on learning disabilities and ADHD, serving more than 250,000 parents, teachers, and other professionals each month. LD OnLine seeks to help children and adults reach their full potential by providing accurate and up-to-date information and advice about learning disabilities and ADHD. The site features hundreds of helpful articles, monthly columns by noted experts, first-person essays, children's writing and artwork, a comprehensive resource guide, very active forums, and a referral directory of professionals, schools, and products.

National Institute for Mental Health (NIMH)

http://www.nimh.nih.gov

The website has many fact booklets on learning and behavior disorders as well as up-to-date research.

 Visit the Education CourseMate for this textbook to access the eBook, Did You Get It? quizzes, Digital Downloads, TeachSource Video Cases, flashcards, and more. Go to CengageBrain.com to log in, register, or purchase access.

Likenesses and Differences among Children

Leslie Kowitz

Over the last several editions of this text we have been fortunate to hear of one family's journey with their child with autism and their experience with inclusion. Their story begins in preschool and continues through fifth grade. While fifth grade is outside the scope of this text, it will provide insight into the ongoing struggles and challenges which families with children with special needs, in this case autism face.

SPECIAL FOCUS • INCLUSION EXPERIENCE AT JCC—A PARENT'S PERSPECTIVE

When our son, Aaron, was first diagnosed with autism at twenty months, he was already attending the Jewish Community Center (JCC) preschool two mornings a week with his twin brother. While I had suspected that something was amiss with Aaron, I remember the sadness and fear of the unknown I felt when I finally heard it from the professionals.

We looked at a couple of early intervention programs within an hour's drive. The first one was a full-day program and consisted of all special-needs children, some with very severe disabilities. I couldn't imagine leaving my little guy there all day, even though the staff seemed very committed and caring. I spoke to the director at the JCC and shared openly about our situation. She was extremely kind and embracing and assured us that Aaron was welcome there and that they would work with us to do what was best for him. Hearing those words came as such a relief, and it made me feel like we were part of a community, not just a paying family that kept the school going.

During the time Aaron was two to three years old, he received early intervention support through the Children's Hospital Autism Intervention (CHAI) program in Oakland. The beauty of their program was that it allowed him to continue at JCC with his brother and other typical children. A variety of tutors would visit him onsite at the preschool, usually a few times a week, and work with him in his environment. He also had one-on-one sessions at the CHAI office in Oakland several days a week. Although sometimes I felt the erratic schedule and driving back and forth was an inconvenience to me, I also saw him improve dramatically over the months. When he began the program he spoke only one or two words and fixated on spinning wheels of any kind for long periods of time. If we tried to move him on to a different activity he usually had a meltdown.

After Aaron turned three, the school district took over supervision of his early intervention program. I remember feeling very insecure about his fate. Since the school district did not offer a preschool program for higher-functioning kids like Aaron, we requested that he remain at JCC with an aide. Fortunately, they agreed. We were also fortunate in that we had met a wonderful and dedicated woman, Emily, who had worked with Aaron the previous year at CHAI. They spent the next school year together and what I saw was quite heartwarming and promising. Day by day, the bond between them grew as she pushed him through many obstacles. He was resistant to so many things. On picture day, he screamed and cried for forty minutes until she was able to coax him into the photographer's area. The day I received his portrait, I got choked up thinking that he looked just like a "regular kid." Being at the JCC gave Aaron the opportunity to interact with other children continuously over the course of the year, through a variety of situations. We were lucky to have two families agree to participate weekly

in an integrated play group at home. This included Aaron, his brother, and one other child, plus a facilitator. After about six months of games and prompted conversations, as well as free play, he began interacting with these kids independently at school and in other social settings. The beauty of these interactions at this age is that children seem very innocent and accepting of each other. They haven't learned to be cliquish or exclusive.

I belong to an e-mail list of parents with ASD kids, and I often read posts asking about how to tell, or *if* to tell, other parents about a child's diagnosis. I chose early on to share this information with other parents and teachers. Initially, I think I wanted some moral support from a couple of the moms I had gotten friendly with. As time went on, though, it became just a fact of life that I mentioned at times and hoped it might educate those who had no exposure to autism. The warmth and caring from the other parents and the great staff really made our experience at the JCC a positive one.

This latest school year, Aaron's aide moved on to other opportunities. I worried how he would react to the transition. To my surprise, he warmed up quickly to his new aide, and she has become part of the JCC tapestry. In addition, his new teachers are both very open to him and his unique needs.

While things are progressing for Aaron, I don't want to paint an inaccurate picture. Today, the class took its first field trip to an educational farm. Aaron screamed for much of the time because he is so afraid of animals. The other kids didn't seem to be put off or repulsed. They will still talk with him at school tomorrow and sit next to him for lunch.

Despite the fears and meltdowns on occasion for things that could be as simple as not having a particular food in his lunch, Aaron has made tremendous strides. He can express himself in ways I wished I had been able to do at a much older age. He made a playmate all on his own when we were on vacation this summer. He and his brother continue to expand their imaginations and conversational repertoire, and he is keeping up with, if not exceeding, age expectations intellectually. The areas in which I see a dramatic difference between him and his twin are physical, gross-motor activities. Where his brother is riding a trainer bike and learning tae kwon do, Aaron is barely able to sit on the bike without fear. But that's OK. He's a beautiful, engaged child.

What would Aaron be like had we not kept him in a typical preschool environment? He would not be who he is now. It may take him longer to master some tasks, or he may go about it in a circuitous way, but ultimately he has risen to the challenges placed before him. We, as a family, believe in him and will continue to nurture his uniqueness and encourage him to succeed. Next year we will be transitioning from the womblike environment of the JCC preschool to the public school kindergarten—the unknown. However, I plan to use a similar approach in my interactions with teachers and families and know that Aaron will continue to grow, as will I as a parent. He will always have his unique ways of being in the world, but that doesn't mean he shouldn't or couldn't participate as fully as he can.

Should every child be in an inclusion-type setting with typical peers? Maybe—maybe not. But, for Aaron the answer is definitely yes. We learn so much from those around us. And not only is Aaron able to learn from his peers but also his peers get to learn from and experience the joy and uniqueness that Aaron brings to the world.

INCLUSION EXPERIENCE: UPDATED FOR SECOND GRADE

I just reread my previous writing about our son, Aaron, which describes his inclusion in preschool and my worries over the unknown with transition-

ing to public school. I realize how much he's grown and progressed in those past two-and-a-half years, yet I see the daily challenges he still faces.

Despite my initial concerns, Aaron made the transition into public kindergarten with the help of a full-time aide. She acted as an additional resource in the classroom, not someone who was there only for Aaron's benefit, which helped him socially not to be singled out as the "special" kid. He and his twin brother were together in the same class that first school year. Aaron engaged with other classmates, most of the time unprompted. Although his language was very well developed, his fine and gross motor skills needed strengthening through occupational therapy (OT), which the school provided during class time.

As first grade brought more self-awareness to Aaron and his peers, we decided it was time to remove the security blanket of an aide. Initially, I was nervous about this because he has difficulty staying on task, among other things. But I trusted my gut, as he'd already surprised us in so many ways.

During first grade, I spent time in the classroom and watched Aaron firsthand. His teacher made a huge difference in his growth. Engaging, dynamic, fun, creative, inclusive—she was everything you would want for your child, special-needs or typical. He kept up academically, and his teacher provided him and other kids some alternative lessons that were more interesting than repetitive drills, which he liked.

We had concerns about Aaron's socialization when I noticed him wandering alone near (but not playing with) other kids on the playground. An aide for another child on the spectrum gave him some support during recess by helping him join other kids, and eventually he started doing that on his own, with one boy in particular. When I heard that Aaron and this boy participated in Walking Club, often holding hands, I got choked up.

Fast-forward to today, and we're in the middle of second grade. Aaron is completely on his own in both the classroom and during recess. How's that going? Well, it's a mixed bag. Due to economic realities, the class size has increased by six kids. That may not sound like much, but with a group of energetic and noisy kids, Aaron complains almost daily about the noise levels, to which he is extremely sensitive. His teacher does not have the capacity to control the kids in a positive manner, and the class work is getting more challenging. He still has difficulty completing work in class, and he forgets to hand in homework or bring things home. But he's one of the better readers in class and loves science and sings in the chorus. At first glance, you probably wouldn't notice him as being any different from the other kids.

I don't want to paint an unrealistic picture of my son as someone who totally overcame the obstacles of autism by being included in a typical classroom. For the most part, he's doing much better than I ever would have imagined. But there are almost daily challenges once he gets home. I imagine the effort it takes for him to sit, try to focus, and keep up with the many transitions during the day that are very taxing on him. He often has meltdowns at home over simple things, which is probably his way of letting off steam from maintaining composure throughout the school day.

On the flip side, Aaron seems to be liked by his peers, and that's more important at this stage than academic success. He belongs to a group of a few boys who play together at recess. They would be considered the "nerdy" kids back in my day—the ones who prefer science and imaginative play to sports. He still has his pal from first grade, whom he hangs out with the most. We noticed that Aaron tried holding his hand when walking recently and the friend consciously avoided taking it, so my husband explained the social cues that Aaron frequently misses. But after that, he now understands that second-grade boys show they like one another by sitting next to each other or walking next to each other. He gets it once you tell him the rules.

As part of his IEP, Aaron is in a "social skills" group of two ASD boys and a psychology intern. I can't say how much this is helping him, but he seems to enjoy it. He's a very astute kid and he's begun asking questions about his development. He asked why he went to CHAI (the early intervention program) and other questions. I'm conflicted about whether or when to talk to him about the "A" word (autism), but I know that it's not the right time now.

In the two-and-a-half years that have passed since the first writing, Aaron's made progress in areas that previously terrified him. While he used to scream around animals, especially dogs, he's now pretty interested and relaxed. When our friends adopted a very calm dog from a shelter, Aaron was initially scared and wary; however, over time and through exposure he's come to really like Max and has even asked if we can get a dog for our family. Never in a million years did I think I'd ever hear that!

Aaron plans to grow up one day. He talks about when he has a wife and children, which always gives me a jolt. My dream for him is that he experience love and fulfillment in his life and that someone special (besides his family) sees the beauty in him. We have a long way to go until then, but I can't help thinking about it when he talks that way.

INCLUSION EXPERIENCE UPDATED FOR FIFTH GRADE

The time has gone quickly since my last (second) installment when our son was in second grade—he's now in fifth grade. When I first wrote about inclusion from a parent's perspective, we were just getting ready to transition from preschool into a public kindergarten. Similarly, our focus today is on another upcoming transition—moving on to middle school—which feels much more ominous and uncertain.

Before I go into that, I want to step back and look at what's gone on more recently and see what lessons have evolved.

Telling about Diagnosis

One of the most significant changes has come from telling Aaron he has autism/Asperger's syndrome. At the last writing, I discussed his asking questions about his abilities, but we didn't feel he was ready to hear or understand what it meant. This past year, as Aaron asked me "why are things so hard for me?" I made a quick decision and just told him why—a condition called autism.

In hindsight, I probably should have involved my husband in the talk or at least had agreement that the timing was right, but that wasn't how it played out. Other parents have asked me about the "to tell" or "not to tell" decision. The best advice is to trust your instinct and your knowledge of your very unique child.

For me, I felt it would do a disservice to Aaron and his sense of self to withhold the information much longer. I see that disclosure as pivotal to his development, in that it showed a respect and acknowledgement of his unique strengths and of who I believe he can become. He can harness his awareness and abilities and grow, in spite of or because of his uniqueness. I believe our relationship has gotten closer since then. Not long ago, as he was crying and feeling sorry for himself for not being able to do things like the other kids, he actually said, "Mom, I'm glad you told me I have autism. I wouldn't have

wanted *not* to know." Is there an old soul inside a 10-year-old kid's body?

Involvement with a Community

Getting involved with other parents of special kids (mainly moms) was a much-needed change for me. We came from different situations with respect to our children's challenges, but were unified in our hearts and minds to furthering the (true) concept of inclusion in our school. From our grassroots-style group, along with support and commitment from the principal, we had the first "Diverse Abilities Awareness" event in our district, with the goal of teaching empathy for kids with diverse learning styles and cognitive abilities. Inclusion as a concept sounds great, but without educating the typical population of students (as well as their parents), *inclusion* is just an empty buzzword.

How many kids on the spectrum or with other challenges are thriving emotionally and socially in the public school setting? My vision of what inclusion really means for our kids can be compared to what racial desegregation was in the 1960s. It's not enough to just have faces of different colors together in a classroom because the law states it, but for kids to grow up oblivious to those racial differences. In the decades since desegregation, at least in the San Francisco Bay area, we walk down the streets of our community and (hopefully) don't think twice about a racially mixed group of kids or parents and their biracial children. I guess in an ideal school scenario, kids who had cognitive, sensory, or physical challenges would be embraced as part of the school "family," with understanding, empathy, and encouragement for his or her accomplishments of whatever magnitude. In the same way we cheer emphatically for the runner with prosthetic legs, why don't we do the same for kids who are trying their best to learn to read or start a conversation with a classmate? We need to trade snickering and blatant teasing for accepting and encouraging.

Finding Fault with the Child

For inclusion to be successful, teachers need appropriate training and support. We had a pretty rocky fourth-grade year when Aaron was not understanding or retaining basic math concepts. Instead of looking for different modalities to teach the material, the school administration kept hunting for answers as to *why* he wasn't learning. Was it lack of motivation, defiance, depression, or emotional disturbance? Who cares why? He's a kid with autism who learns differently from the mass of other kids. All of that frustrated us immensely because we lost valuable time that could have helped our son. Finally, we made the choice to pay for a private program, which in ten weeks did more for his learning and self-confidence than a year's worth of school. While it helped Aaron, it put us in conflict with the school district, which reported us to the local attendance board for truancy. We'd taken him out of school for two hours a day during school hours. But that's a story for another focus.

Emotional Well-Being

Have you ever met someone else's autistic child and wished yours were more like that child? Maybe more verbal, more coordinated, smarter? It's natural to compare. I know I have. I sometimes wonder what it would be like if Aaron were less self-aware. I think kids who are more oblivious to their differences and challenges have an easier time in school. They don't notice others making fun of them, don't

feel excluded from a dodge-ball game; don't notice their social limitations. But having a child who does can be very painful. If only he'd believe me when I tell him that life *really* begins after high school!

My biggest worry is not that Aaron will get through school and be able to live an independent life, but rather that he has a strong sense of himself and likes who that person is. Without that core, I fear a life of depression, self-doubt and discontentment. While typical parents worry about API scores for their schools and what college their kids might go to, all I really care about is that my son comes out of his youth with his soul intact rather than crushed.

The past six months have been difficult as Aaron slipped further into a depression about his abilities and chance for a future. At ten years old, I never had a clue that anything existed beyond that day's activity and summer vacation. Aaron will comment that he worries about his future. He says he wants to be successful so he can go to college and get a good job so he can take care of his wife and family. It stuns me to hear such adult thoughts. Recently, his worries and anxieties escalated to a point at which he needed a doctor's care, but we have hope that his emotional life will find balance. Even in the span of a few months, we can see a positive change.

Parents' Critical Decision

All this discussion brings us to the looming transition to middle school. What are we going to do? Our options are a mainstream public middle school with some supports, versus a more restrictive environment for private school for ASD kids, or homeschool. Even theoretically removing the financial burden from the equation, it's a huge decision. Do we put him into an environment that represents a microcosm of what awaits out in the real world? Or do we buffer that by enrolling him in a comfortable place designed for diverse learners, but an environment that may not challenge him or may actually increase his feelings of alienation and differences? Which one will deliver the holy grail of an educated youth (albeit one with some challenges) with an intact soul and positive self-image? Looking back on my own life, I see how decisions made in the tween years have long-lasting ripples, which is why this decision weighs heavily. You may read this and think, "I wish my child was even able to attend mainstream school." But trust me when I say, it's not all it's cracked up to be. This is often a tougher road, because it's more nebulous and the risks higher for failure on many levels.

What's Going Well

Despite worries and fears, there are many things to be grateful for in Aaron's development and school life. He finally has a dedicated teacher who's a great match for him—he sees Aaron's strengths and tailors his expectations to elicit small successes rather than finding Aaron's shortcomings. I'm in close communication with his teacher, as well as the new principal, and feel we're a team working toward the best possible scenario for Aaron. I encourage parents to take the time and effort to develop rapport with willing school staff and grit your teeth and advocate hard when you're dealt some uncooperative administrators.

For the most part, Aaron appears to be comfortable in his school and extra curricular activities. He referred to the school as his "happy place," when we talked to him about switching to a smaller setting when he was having troubles last year. He has a small and friendly group of kids he talks to, and his teacher reports most classmates find him to be a nice and kind kid, even if he's a bit quirky. He rides his bike to school with his brother and a few neighbor boys and is part of a small Cub Scout den. We have a lot to feel positive about.

While having a child like Aaron in a mainstream environment means he works harder in ways others don't, due to the way he learns, it offers a constant example of the larger society outside. The more he can navigate within that environment, the greater chance of success he'll have when he becomes an adult. He can choose to engage in the realm of neurotypical people and/or chose a closer-knit community of Asperger/neurodiverse peers. But without the experience of inclusion early on, I don't think he'd have the luxury of choice.

Inclusion for kids with cognitive differences in mainstream schools is in its infancy. We have a long way to go until this these kids are truly accepted as equals and valued for their contributions to our community. However, no great change in society has come easily. We owe much to the early trailblazers who got scraped up along the way finding the right path forward. If your child is able to go into a mainstream program, consider yourselves part of the trailblazers who, over time, will change the face of our classrooms and the hearts and minds of its students.

Application Questions

1. What information from the chapters in Section 2 applies to this story?

2. What key components made Aaron's inclusion experiences successful? What made it less successful at times?

3. List some of the decisions Aaron's parents needed to make during the first several years of his life. How might have things been different if they made other decisions (e.g., placed him in a special education classroom)?

4. Aaron's family is faced with a new decision, which raises many questions including the ones listed in their story. *Do we put him into an environment that represents a microcosm of what awaits out in the real world? Or do we buffer that by enrolling him in a comfortable place designed for diverse learners, but an environment that may not challenge him or may actually increase his feelings of alienation and differences?* Discuss the pros and cons of Aaron attending a private school designed for diverse learners versus continuing to attend the public intermediate school.

Partnership with Families

9

OBJECTIVES

After reading this chapter, you should be able to:

9-1   provide a historical perspective on family involvement.

9-2   define the concept of family uniqueness and explain how this concept affects teachers' practices in early childhood education.

9-3   list the components of family-centered practice.

9-4   describe the various ways parents and families participate in their child's program.

9-5   list five or more ways for teachers to communicate with parents.

• • • • • • • • • • • • • • • • • •

naeyc

The following NAEYC Standards are addressed in this chapter:

STANDARD 1 Promoting Child Development and Learning

STANDARD 2 Building Family and Community Relationships

STANDARD 4 Using Developmentally Effective Approaches

CONNECTIONS

- Jennie, a third-grade teacher, communicates with Malik's mother every day by e-mail.
- Grace's nanny comes to the toddler play group with her every day and facilitates an art activity.
- Willie's dad comes to school once a month for the "father's group" and talks about how important this group is to him for learning to care for his child with severe disabilities.

Family involvement has been a tradition in early childhood education for many years. With the advent of intervention programs for children with developmental disabilities, family involvement now is viewed as required, as well as essential, to the progress of the child. The success of early intervention and early childhood special education programs can be directly attributed to the service providers' ability to work cooperatively with each family and each other (Noonan & McCormick, 2006).

Contrast this with much earlier times when parents were advised, almost routinely, to institutionalize a child with a disability. Shonkoff and Phillips (2000) describe this evolution: "As its knowledge base has matured, the field of early childhood intervention has evolved from its original focus on children to a growing appreciation of the extent to which family, community, and broader societal factors affect child health and development" (p. 339).

As we develop strategies and programs to facilitate family involvement, it is important to understand the families with whom we work. Our society is becoming increasingly diverse, and the families with whom we work come from different cultures and speak different languages. Service providers must strive for cultural competence. This means they must respect each family's values, traditions, and child-rearing beliefs, as well as their communication and decision-making styles and views on the assistance and involvement of individuals outside their family. Most importantly, it means demonstrating this understanding and respect by creating a program that is supportive of each family's participation (Noonan & McCormick, 2006).

According to research written by Anne Henderson, one of America's foremost authors on parent involvement, and Karen Mapp, titled *A New Wave of Evidence: The Impact of School, Family, and Community Connections on Student Achievement*, students with parents who are involved, no matter what their income or background, are more likely to:

- earn higher grades and test scores, and enroll in higher-level programs
- attend school regularly
- have better social skills
- show improved behavior and adapt well to school
- graduate and go on to postsecondary education

achievement gap the observed outperformance on a number of educational measures between groups of students, especially groups defined by gender, race/ethnicity, and socioeconomic status

Additionally, studies show that families of all income and education levels, and all ethnic and cultural groups, are engaged in supporting their children's learning at home. They suggest that supporting more involvement at school from all families may be an important strategy for addressing the **achievement gap** (Henderson & Mapp, 2002).

Federal law mandates that we educate *all* children, and the majority of children with disabilities attend classes in public school buildings. These changes have come about because of changes in the way society views people with disabilities, and as a result of the hard work of parents and advocates for people with disabilities, such as The Arc of the United States, formerly the Association for Retarded Citizens of the United States (ARC), and United Cerebral Palsy (UCP).

The role of families in the planning, implementation, and evaluation of early childhood special education programs has changed dramatically over the past thirty years, as early intervention services have moved from a child-centered to a family-centered approach. The Turnbulls and colleagues (2005) describe this shift.

> The pendulum has swung in many ways: from viewing parents as part of the problem to viewing them as a primary solution to the problem, from expecting passive roles to expecting active roles, from viewing families as a mother–child dyad to recognizing the presence and needs of all members, and from assigning generalized expectations from the professionals' perspective to allowing for individual priorities defined from each family's perspective. (p. 21)

The swinging pendulum finally came to center on two pieces of federal legislation: PL 94-142 and PL 99-457. Both laws specifically address family support as a legitimate requirement when providing intervention services for young children with disabilities. "The family dimension of the law emphasized the equal partnership role for parents and outlined certain responsibilities for parents for the purpose of enhancing services to children" (Bailey & Winton, 1994). The importance of family participation and choice was reinforced by IDEIA.

This reauthorization strengthens the role of the family in planning for special education. This chapter will review the major mandates, with special focus on the following issues:

- involvement of families in planning and implementing intervention services and educational programs for infants and young children with developmental problems

- rights and options of parents

- avoidance of professional intrusion into family affairs

- empowerment of the family

- service coordination and the family

- development of **culturally competent** early intervention services

culturally competent classroom activities, materials, and curricula that acknowledge and respect the different ethnicities that are represented in the classroom and community

As background, we will examine various aspects of family life, beginning with the diversity of families in today's society. The effect of having an infant with disabilities on parents, and on the family as a whole, will be described. The rationale and justification for family involvement will follow, with emphasis on the family as a system of interactive, reciprocal relationships. Strategies that early childhood teachers engage in when working with parents of children with disabilities will conclude the chapter. Throughout, primary caregivers will be referred to as "parents." Due to the complexity of this topic the chapter cannot be expected to address all aspects but rather is designed to provide an introduction to this critical topic.

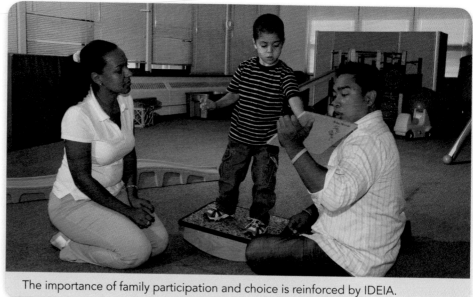

The importance of family participation and choice is reinforced by IDEIA.

© Cengage Learning

☀9-2 Family Uniqueness?

The makeup of families and their expectations regarding the behavior of family members varies across and within families and cultures. It is important to remember that membership in a cultural or ethnic group does not define a family.

There is a great deal of individual difference across African American families, Jewish families, Hispanic families, and families from other cultures. It is simplistic to assume that all members of any group view all issues in the same way. The emotional climate within families varies, too. Often it is characterized by the way parents interact with each other and their children.

9-2a ■ What Is a Family?

Families are big, small, extended, nuclear, multi-generational, with one parent, two parents, and grandparents. We live under one roof or many. A family can be as temporary as a few weeks, as permanent as forever. We become part of a family by birth, adoption, marriage, or from a desire for mutual support ... A family is a culture unto itself with different values and unique ways of realizing its dreams. Together, our families become the source of our rich cultural heritage and spiritual diversity. Our families create neighborhoods, communities, states, and nations. (Bissell, n.d.)

As the passage above reflects, today's families come in all shapes and sizes. Family members may be related by blood or marriage, or they may be connected by a commitment to common goals and priorities. Families may be headed by a teenage mother, a single mother, a married couple, a gay or lesbian couple, a single father, an interracial couple, a grandparent providing primary care for children, or any combination of these. In addition to the parents' biological children, families may include adopted children, foster children, or other relatives who are living with the family. "Family is no longer a unitary concept that describes a specific set of characteristics. Rather, it has become a generic name for a group of individuals who are affiliated with one another" (Lynch & Hanson, 2011).

Families are self-defined units whose members have made a commitment to share their lives.

As early childhood educators, we have the privilege and challenge of working with a wide variety of families. It is our responsibility to honor the personal choices and values of these families and to invite every family member to be a partner in the early intervention process (Harry, Torguson, Katkavich, & Guerrero, 1993).

The concept of family uniqueness requires that practitioners learn how to work with families as individuals, how to communicate with families effectively, and how to develop cultural self-awareness to understand the ways our own beliefs influence our work (Harry, 1992).

Many of the families with whom we work come from different cultures, speak different languages, and live in different social environments from those of the staff members in our programs. These families may have different attitudes and beliefs about child-rearing practices and early education. Our challenge as practitioners is to develop early intervention programs that are culturally sensitive and linguistically responsive to all of the children and families in the program (Gonzalez-Mena, 1992). Early interventionists must become culturally competent. One of the first steps to increase our sensitivity to the values and practices of the families who are in our care is to be aware of the ways our own culture and upbringing influence our expectations of children (Marshall, 2001). There is more information on this topic in the "Linguistic and Cultural Diversity Connections" box located in this chapter. Lynch and Hanson (2011) recommend the following steps that early interventionists can take toward being more culturally competent:

Often family members have difficulty accepting a child's disability.

© Cengage Learning

- Learn more about the families in the community you serve.
- Work with **cultural mediators** or guides from the family's culture to learn more about the culture, including interaction styles, child-rearing practices, and cultural beliefs about disability.
- Learn words and forms of greeting in the family's language.
- Allow additional time to work with interpreters and be sure to find appropriate interpreters. (For example, older school-age siblings are not appropriate interpreters for IEP meetings.)
- Use modes of communication that are acceptable and meaningful to the family. For example, if the family has limited English proficiency, notes in English from you to the child's home may not be an effective way to communicate. Families may want to communicate via e-mail, voice-mail messages, or text messages.
- Use as few written forms as possible for families who are ELL. When forms are used, be sure they are available in the family's language.
- Recognize that the collaboration assumed in family-centered early intervention programs may not be comfortable for families from different cultures.

cultural mediators individuals who help mediate between the culture of the school and the culture of the family; they share information and enhance understanding so that the family can participate fully in the assessment and education process

When early childhood educators acknowledge and respect children's home languages and cultures, ties between the family and program are strengthened. This atmosphere provides increased opportunity for learning because young children feel supported, nurtured, and connected, not only to their home communities and families but also to teachers and the educational setting.

In addition to the cultural, ethnic, and linguistic diversity represented by the families in most early childhood programs, there are social factors that affect families and add to their diversity. For example, divorce and remarriage continue to be common occurrences. The majority of divorced men and women remarry. When children are involved, the arrangement is often referred to as a **reconstituted** or **blended family**. It is not uncommon for *her* children, *his* children, and *their* children to be living under one roof.

In addition, children may talk about having two mommies or two daddies because of their relationships with their biological parents and their new stepparents by remarriage. Early childhood teachers must respect a child's family constellation and create a classroom culture that supports diversity.

Another variation in family structure is the continuing increase in dual-career families and of mothers of young children in the workforce. Babysitters, nannies, and caregivers other than parents often are viewed as members of the child's family. Children also may grow up in extended families where combinations of parents, grandparents, aunts, uncles, and cousins live in the same household. Extended family arrangements also may include living with friends. More and more children attending early childhood programs are homeless or live in transitional housing or emergency shelters (National Coalition for the Homeless, 2009; Klein, Bittel, & Molnar, 1993). Homeless children have to change schools more frequently, which often leads to disruption in education. According to the Institute for Children and Poverty (2008), homeless children are nine times more likely to repeat a grade, four times more likely to drop out of school, and three times more likely to be placed in special education programs than their housed peers.

Finally, children are the poorest Americans, living in poverty in increasing numbers. These conditions can be stressful for parents and children, and early childhood teachers should take care to offer appropriate support and demonstrate sensitivity to the situation.

reconstituted (or blended) family each parent bringing children into a new household

9-2b ■ Families of Children with Disabilities

Whatever the makeup of a family, those with children with disabilities will feel the impact on family life. Some families say they become closer as they learn to adapt to a child's disability, and that the child's disability has enhanced the existing strengths of their family (Turnbull & Turnbull, 1993). Others are less able to cope; still others are pulled apart.

The vast majority of research about families is actually research about mothers of children with disabilities. Yet there has been some research that shows that fathers demonstrate feelings similar to the way mothers do, although fathers often are more concerned about long-term care issues and less concerned about day-to-day issues.

When we talk about families, we usually mean parents. However, it is important to consider the needs of other family members in adapting to a child with disabilities. Early childhood educators may have limited contact with grandparents, but they may nevertheless serve as a support and resource for a parent who is dealing with a difficult reaction from their parents or in-laws.

Cultural Self-Awareness and Cultural Competence

To understand and fully appreciate the diversity that exists among families, individuals including service providers must first fully understand their own culture. According to Lynch and Hanson (2011):

> Anglo-Europeans may have less awareness of the ways in which their culture influences their behavior and interactions than those of other cultures. ... The melting pot to which America aspired to during the early waves of immigration took its toll on the diversity of all groups, including the diversity of groups who emigrated from Great Britain and Europe. The diminishing of these early immigrants' roots has resulted in some Anglo-European Americans feeling that they do not have a culture, that they are "just American," or that they are "cultureless." (p. 45)

In order to better understand one's own culture and heritage, one might need to begin with some research. This might include talking to older family members to garner information about the early history of the family, as well as looking through any available albums and family journals. In addition, a public document search may be necessary.

Once some knowledge is obtained about one's own culture, the next step is to examine the values and behaviors associated with that culture. For example, one can look at their family's child-rearing practice and how this might be a reflection of heritage and may differ from those of the families they are serving. For example, some families/cultures put an emphasis on the goal of independence for young children with early toilet training, independence in feeding and dressing. This approach may be opposite for cultures that place a greater importance on interdependence and do not emphasize teaching these skills until later years.

After becoming familiar with their own culture and the effect it has on their beliefs and actions, they can begin to learn about other cultures. There are many ways to accomplish this, but Lynch and Hanson recommend the following as perhaps the most effective practices:

1. learning through books, arts and technology such as websites
2. talking, working, and socializing with individuals from other cultures
3. participating in the daily life of another culture
4. learning the language of another culture

According to the National Center for Cultural Competence, cultural competence is a developmental process that evolves over an extended period. Individuals and organizations are at various levels of awareness, knowledge, and skills. This is an important point to keep in mind, and it is best summarized by Lynch and Hanson: "Skills and information are only the beginning, a first step in the never-ending journey toward cross-cultural competence; this is an area in which the head is less important than the heart. After all of the books have been read and the skills learned, and practiced, the cross-cultural effectiveness of each of us will vary. And it will vary more by what we bring to the learning than by what we have learned. Enthusiasm, openness, respect, awareness, the valuing of all people, and the willingness to take time are the underlying characteristics that support everything that can be taught and learned. These are the characteristics that distinguish those individuals who can understand the journey from those who will actually take it" (p. 487).

Sources: Goode, T. D. (2004). *Cultural Competence Continuum*. National Center for Cultural Competence, Georgetown University Center for Child and Human Development, University Center for Excellence in Developmental Disabilities: Washington, DC.

Lynch, E. W., & Hanson, M. J. (2011). *Developing cross-cultural competence: A guide for working with young children and their families*. Brookes: Baltimore, MD.

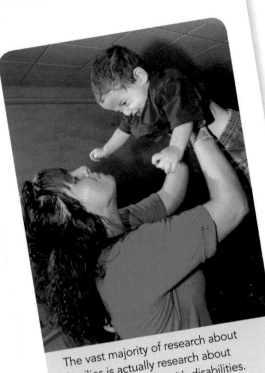

The vast majority of research about families is actually research about mothers of children with disabilities.

© Cengage Learning

Another important group of family members that must be considered are siblings. Siblings have a lifelong relationship with their brother or sister with a disability. They can benefit from special support and honest information about the disability. Meyer and Vadasy (2007) describe a program called Sibshops, which provides siblings with opportunities for peer support. Sibshops allow school-age siblings of children with disabilities to participate in recreational activities. The siblings share information and coping strategies to deal with the unusual concerns and special opportunities associated with having a sibling with a disability.

Evidence suggests that children with disabilities are more at risk for abuse than typically developing children (Grayson, 1992; Child Welfare Information Gateway, 2012). According to the U.S. Department of Health and Human Services (2010), children with disabilities are 1.7 times more likely to be abused than are children without disabilities. One explanation may be that children with disabilities are more dependent, are more difficult to care for, and may require a higher percentage of family resources (both emotionally and financially) than typically developing children.

Adequate support systems are a key factor in ensuring the well-being of families with children with developmental disabilities (Janko, 1994). Support is often taken for granted when a family has regular income, comprehensive health insurance, adequate housing, and caring family and friends. Even so, additional support is usually required. Families do not plan to have a child with a disability. They expect a healthy infant who will grow slowly but surely into an independent and productive adult. From the start, parents of children with disabilities are faced with disappointments and adjustments. These will affect every member of the family and every aspect of the family's life together.

9-2c ■ Family Adjustment

Grief is the usual reaction when parents first realize they have an infant with a disability. It is almost as if their child had died. In a way, this is so: the perfect baby or child that parents had planned for and expected will never be. "Welcome to Holland" is an essay, written in 1987 by Emily Perl Kingsley, about having a child with a disability. The piece is given by many organizations to new parents of children with special needs. The essay describes the excitement of a vacation planned for Italy, which is a metaphor for a typical birth and the child-raising experience. It then describes the disappointment when the plane lands in Holland, a metaphor for raising a child with special needs. The essay (see the accompanying box) highlights some of the changes and grief described with this change in plans.

In the process of grieving, parents may become angry, depressed, or overwhelmed. Or, they may deny that anything is wrong, regardless of the child's appearance or behavior. These reactions are normal.

Welcome To Holland

By Emily Perl Kingsley

I am often asked to describe the experience of raising a child with a disability—to try to help people who have not shared that unique experience to understand it, to imagine how it would feel. It's like this ...

When you're going to have a baby, it's like planning a fabulous vacation trip—to Italy. You buy a bunch of guide books and make your wonderful plans. The Coliseum. The Michelangelo David. The gondolas in Venice. You may learn some handy phrases in Italian. It's all very exciting.

After months of eager anticipation, the day finally arrives. You pack your bags and off you go. Several hours later, the plane lands. The stewardess comes in and says, "Welcome to Holland."

"Holland?!?" you say. "What do you mean Holland?? I signed up for Italy! I'm supposed to be in Italy. All my life I've dreamed of going to Italy."

But there's been a change in the flight plan. They've landed in Holland and there you must stay.

The important thing is that they haven't taken you to a horrible, disgusting, filthy place, full of pestilence, famine and disease. It's just a different place.

So you must go out and buy new guide books. And you must learn a whole new language. And you will meet a whole new group of people you would never have met.

It's just a different place. It's slower-paced than Italy, less flashy than Italy. But after you've been there for a while and you catch your breath, you look around ... and you begin to notice that Holland has windmills ... and Holland has tulips. Holland even has Rembrandts.

But everyone you know is busy coming and going from Italy ... and they're all bragging about what a wonderful time they had there. And for the rest of your life, you will say "Yes, that's where I was supposed to go. That's what I had planned."

And the pain of that will never, ever, ever, ever go away ... because the loss of that dream is a very very significant loss.

But ... if you spend your life mourning the fact that you didn't get to Italy, you may never be free to enjoy the very special, the very lovely things ... about Holland.

At the same time, parents need help in working through these feelings. Almost immediately, they will have to begin to make urgent decisions and solve complicated problems affecting every member of the family. These might include:

- expensive and perhaps painful or life-threatening medical treatment, surgery, or hospitalization that may occur repeatedly and for extended periods

- heavy expenses and financial burdens other than medical, such as expenditures for special foods and equipment

- frightening and energy-draining crises, often recurring, as when the child stops breathing, turns blue, or has a major convulsion

- transportation problems, babysitting needs for the other children, or time away from jobs to get the child to consultation and treatment appointments

- continuous day-and-night demands on parents to provide routine caregiving tasks (for example, feeding a child with a severe cleft palate)

- constant fatigue, lack of sleep, and little or no time to meet the needs of other family members

Did You Get It?

How do siblings of a child who is disabled benefit from programs set up on their behalf, such as Sibshops, as described by Meyer and Vadasy (2007)?

a. After-school homework assistance.
b. Provides help for parents.
c. Prevention of abuse.
d. Opportunity for peer support, and sharing of information and coping strategies.

Take the full quiz on CourseMate.

transactional relationships the understanding that children and adults influence each other in their ongoing relationships and that both children and adults learn from these interactions; future interactions are influenced by earlier interactions

family-centered practice a way of thinking that leads to a set of practices in which families are considered the central and most important decision maker in the child's life.

- little or no opportunity for recreational or leisure activities
- difficulty (and additional expense) of locating babysitters who are both qualified and willing to care for a child with a disability, especially if the child has severe medical or behavioral problems
- lack of respite-care options
- jealousy or feelings of rejection among brothers and sisters who may believe the special child monopolizes the family's attention and resources
- marital problems arising from finances, fatigue, differences about management of the child's disability, and feelings of spousal rejection
- choosing among different interventions or approaches

When these problems are further compounded by social isolation and poverty, the subsequent development of a child with a disability, as well as the growth and well-being of the rest of the family, are doubly jeopardized. Such problems further emphasize how nearly impossible it would be to provide effective intervention for a young child without including the child's family.

Bronfenbrenner (2006) convinced developmentalists of the range of environmental and family influences on a young child's development. The mother–child relationship, once thought to be the major determining factor, has proven to be but one of many. Innumerable strands of **transactional relationships**, both cultural and personal, are at work (Sameroff & Chandler, 1975). They form the system, or *ecological niche*, into which the child is born and reared. A child's ability to cope or adapt depends on understanding his or her larger social system, made up of family function, support of friends and community, and cultural beliefs.

9-3 Family-Centered Practice

There has been considerable discussion in the field regarding best practices for working with families, especially those with children with special needs. Beginning in the 1980s the early intervention field shifted its philosophy to move to **family-centered** practices.

As stated by Marilyn Espe-Sherwindt in 2009:

During the last two decades, the field of early childhood disability has successfully defined the working principles of family-centered practice for practitioners. Although research has acknowledged that the paradigm shift to family-centered practice is neither simple nor easy, a substantive body of evidence demonstrates that (a) family-centered practice can be linked to a wide range of demonstrated benefits for both children and families, and (b) families are more satisfied and find family-centered practice to be more helpful than other models of practice. (p. 136)

Family-centered practice includes three key elements:

- an emphasis on strengths, not deficits;
- promoting family choice and control over desired resources; and
- the development of a collaborative relationship between parents and professionals.

NAEYC and DEC both have their guidelines for working with and engaging families. NAEYC provides guidelines for engaging families, and they are listed in Figure 9-1. The DEC developed seventeen family-based

FIGURE 9-1

naeyc

NAEYC's Principles and Guidelines for Family Engagement and Reciprocal Relationships with Families

- **Principle 1:** Programs invite families to participate in decision making and goal setting for their child. *Teachers and families establish goals for the child together. Goals are established for learning both at school and at home.*

- **Principle 2:** Teachers and programs engage families in two-way communication. *Communication is initiated both by family and program. Communication occurs in multiple forms and reflects the family's primary language.*

- **Principle 3:** Programs and teachers engage families in ways that are truly reciprocal. *Families and programs share information. The program invites families to share their unique knowledge. The program encourages active participation in the life of the school. Teachers seek information about children's lives, families, and communities and use this information in their curriculum and teaching practices.*

- **Principle 4:** Programs provide learning activities for the home and in the community. *Families are encouraged to provide learning opportunities outside the classroom.*

- **Principle 5:** Programs invite families to participate in program-level decisions and wider advocacy efforts. *Parent input is sought regarding the program. Parent advocacy regarding early childhood education is also encouraged.*

- **Principle 6:** Programs implement a comprehensive program-level system for family engagement. *Policies regarding family engagement are adopted. Staff is given support needed to fully engage families.*

Establishing Reciprocal Relationships with Families

(Guideline 5 of NAEYC's "Developmentally Appropriate Practice")

A. In reciprocal relationships between practitioners and families, there is mutual respect, cooperation, shared responsibility, and negotiation of conflicts toward achievement of shared goals. (Also see guideline 1, "Creating a Caring Community of Learners.")

B. Practitioners work in collaborative partnerships with families, establishing and maintaining regular, frequent two-way communication with them (with families who do not speak English, teachers should use the language of the home if they are able or try to enlist the help of bilingual volunteers).

C. Family members are welcome in the setting, and there are multiple opportunities for family participation. Families participate in program decisions about their children's care and education.

D. Teachers acknowledge a family's choices and goals for the child and respond with sensitivity and respect to those preferences and concerns, but without abdicating the responsibility that early childhood practitioners have to support children's learning and development through developmentally appropriate practices.

E. Teachers and the family share with each other their knowledge of the particular child and understanding of child development and learning as part of day-to-day communication and in planned conferences. Teachers support families in ways that maximally promote family decision-making capabilities and competence.

(continued)

FIGURE 9-1

Continued

F. Practitioners involve families as a source of information about the child (before program entry and on an ongoing basis) and engage them in the planning for their child.

G. The program links families with a range of services, based on identified resources, priorities, and concerns.

Sources: NAEYC (2009). Developmentally Appropriate Practice in Early Childhood Programs Serving Children from Birth through Age 8. Retrieved from http://www.naeyc.org/positionstatements/dap.

NAEYC (n.d.). Family Engagement Principles. Retrieved January 11, 2013 from http://www.naeyc.org/familyengagement/about

"recommended practices" that are organized into four categories or themes, as follow:

1. **Shared Responsibility and Collaboration**

   Practices in this category focus on families sharing responsibility and working together with professionals. They develop appropriate family outcomes, and share information so the family can make decisions. Relationship building is responsive to cultural, language, and other characteristics.

2. **Strengthened Family Functioning**

   Families are provided with supports and resources that strengthen parenting competence and confidence. They are provided in ways that are supportive yet don't disrupt family and community life.

3. **Individualized and Flexible Practices**

   Intervention practices are individualized and based on what each family wants for their child. The supports and resources incorporate family beliefs and values into all decisions and intervention plans.

4. **Strengths- and Assets-Based Practices**

   Family-based practices that are most effective move beyond simply identifying strengths and assets to using these assets as building blocks for acquiring new information and skills.

These practices are based on evidence from early childhood intervention and other fields and are designed to help inform professionals about what is important when supporting families (Trivette & Dunst, 2005).

A recurring concern about early intervention, especially programs that are family-centered, is that it promotes the family's dependence on educational and social service agencies. Some predict that families will become less able to maintain autonomy. This prediction is without foundation. Research evidence indicates that social support has positive effects on parental well-being, and this in turn has a positive effect on parenting styles and interactions with their child, which directly impacts the child's development (Trivette, & Dunst, 2005).

Early intervention often helps families learn their rights and become effective advocates for their children. This is partially due to a major philosophical thrust of early intervention: the *enablement* and *empowerment* of families. Deal, Dunst, and Trivette (1989) suggest the following definitions of these terms.

Enabling families means creating opportunities for family members to become more competent and self-sustaining with respect to their abilities to mobilize their social networks to get needs met and attain goals. Empowering families means carrying out interventions in a manner in which family members acquire a sense of control over their own developmental course as a result of their own efforts to meet needs. (p. 33)

Enabling and **empowering** families strengthens them without taking away their ability to cope. Early intervention aims to support and build on those things the family already does well. Policymakers believe this can be accomplished by providing families with the information and skills that will enable them to solve their own problems and meet their own needs. The service coordinator plays the pivotal role of fostering and overseeing the empowerment of families. "Service coordination may be considered effective only to the extent that families become more capable, competent, and empowered as a result of the help-giving acts" (Dunst & Trivette, 1989, p. 99). Service coordinators have a legal responsibility to be sure the following components of program delivery are provided in accordance with state and federal laws (Howard, Williams, & Lepper, 2009):

- assessments
- development, reviews, and evaluation of IFSPs
- coordination of services
- informing families of services options
- coordination with health providers
- development of a transition plan

Enabling families means creating opportunities for family members to become more competent and self-sustaining.

© Cengage Learning

Did You Get It?

How does the category of sharing responsibility and collaboration facilitate enhanced therapeutic practice?

a. Provides individualized intervention.

b. Provides resources to prevent disruption.

c. Develops appropriate family outcomes, and shares information so family can make decisions.

d. Moves beyond strength and assets.

Take the full quiz on CourseMate.

empowering planning and carrying out intervention activities in ways that pass on as much control and decision making as possible to the family

---

Parent Participation 9-4 ☀

Parents and teachers are partners in the business of children's learning. They bear the ongoing and primary responsibility during the long years of a child's growth and development (many additional years when a child is developmentally disabled or delayed). Numerous studies describe the benefits of active parent involvement in a child's early intervention program. Without it, children tended to regress once the program has ended (Simeonsson & Bailey, 2000). Parent involvement has two major functions. One, it provides an ongoing reinforcement system that supports the efforts of the program while it is under way. Two, it tends to maintain and elaborate the child's gains after the program ends.

9-4a ■ Rationale for Parent Participation

Many reasons can be given for encouraging parents' involvement in their children's early education and intervention program.

1. Parents are the major socializing agents for their child, the primary transmitters of cultural values, beliefs, and traditions.

2. Children with disabilities acquire developmental skills more quickly when parents participate in home teaching.

3. Involvement in the early intervention program offers parents access to support from other parents and a better perspective on their own child's strengths and needs.

4. Consistency of adult expectations can be maintained. Young children become anxious when important adults do not agree on expectations. Confusion—even resistance—may result if, for example, teachers expect a child to put on his or her own coat while parents always do it for the child.

5. Parents know their child better than teachers or clinicians; thus, parents are a source of unique information.

6. Family members can help the child transfer learning from school to home and neighborhood.

7. Only a few hours a day are spent in school; many more hours are spent at home.

Only a few hours a day are spent in school; many more hours are spent at home.

© Cengage Learning

9-4b ■ Degree of Participation

The extent to which parents can be actively involved in their child's services depends on a number of factors:

- work schedule and job constraints
- additional young children at home who need care
- availability of transportation
- parental health (both physical and psychological)
- parental maturity and understanding of the child's needs
- attitudes toward school, teachers, and authority figures
- cultural and linguistic match with the program

It is important to recognize that simply *maintaining a child's involvement with services is a form of parent involvement.* Lack of active participation does not imply disinterest in the child or the program. Instead, as Ray, Pewit-Kinder, and George (2009) suggest, it may be a form of energy conservation:

Appreciating and respecting the extra work it takes for families to care for and educate children with special needs is important. At the age of three months, Ella began a weekly schedule of six hours of physical, speech, developmental, music, and occupational therapies. She engaged in oral-motor exercises three times daily.

We taught all of Ella's caregivers how to feed, carry, and play with her. To accomplish the innumerable daily therapy goals, we kept lengthy, detailed checklists for separate caregivers. We asked caregivers to work on occupational therapy tasks such as having Ella pick up objects with clothespins and tongs or blow bubbles or suck drinks through thin straws to work on oral-motor (speech) therapy. All play activities were tailored to meet therapy objectives, as were the toys and books we purchased. Ella is now five years old, and our lives revolve around her therapies.

Our family's life is not unique in the strain that a child with special needs can place upon family time. Whether it is a therapy session, exercises, medical treatment done at home, or an unexpected hospital stay, there are extra demands for families of children with special needs. For working parents who cannot rearrange their daily schedule to fit therapies or doctors' appointments, difficult choices between their child's care and workplace requirements cause additional stress. (p. 19)

9-4c ■ Types of Parent Participation

The ways families are involved with their child's programs can be as individualized as the family themselves. Dr. Joyce Epstein of Johns Hopkins University has developed a framework for defining six different types of parent involvement (see Figure 9-2). This framework was also used in the creation of the national PTA's Standards for Parent Involvement Programs.

Participation may range from a parent actually spending time in the classroom or center to completing projects at home at the parent's convenience. For some parents it might include an observation at the school to see how their child is doing (refer to the detailed description that follows, on observations). Other parents may take on leadership roles in the program. Hopefully, for all parents,

Epstein's Framework of Six Types of Parent Involvement

1. **Parenting:** Help all families establish home environments to support children as students.

2. **Communicating:** Design effective forms of school-to-home *and* home-to-school communications about school programs and children's progress.

3. **Volunteering:** Recruit and organize parent help and support.

4. **Learning at home:** Provide information and ideas to families about how to help students at home with homework and other curriculum-related activities, decisions, and planning.

5. **Decision making:** Include parents in school decisions, developing parent leaders and representatives.

6. **Collaborating with the community:** Identify and integrate resources and services from the community to strengthen school programs, family practices, and student learning and development.

Source: Epstein J. L., et al. (2009). *School, Family, and Community Partnerships: Your Handbook for Action, Third Edition.* Corwin Press, Inc.: Thousand Oaks, CA.

FIGURE 9-2

it will include participation in decision making regarding their child's goals and programs.

Parent observations Parents must be welcome at any time in all programs for young children. As parents are the senior partners in their child's development, they have the right to see and question everything that goes on in the classroom. Such firsthand observations provide one of the best ways of providing indirect parent education. Watching their child interacting with other children and adults, and with materials and activities, provides insights that can be obtained in no other way. Against a background of children with similar developmental levels, parents gain a better appreciation of their own children's skills and progress. Ideally, every parent observation is followed by at least a brief discussion with a teacher.

When a conversation cannot take place on the spot, a follow-up telephone call is important. The follow-up conversation serves several purposes.

- The teacher can answer questions a parent may have about what she or he observed. Also, teachers can explain why certain play or group situations were handled as they were.

- Teachers can help parents recognize the positive aspects of their child's uniqueness and developmental progress.

- Teachers can describe the appropriateness of individualized activities in enhancing the child's development and meeting the child's special needs.

Parent observations may be regularly scheduled events or impromptu. As noted, brief informal observations occur regularly as parents drop off and pick up their children. When a formal observation is planned, it is helpful for teachers to provide some type of structure. For some parents, a clipboard and simple observation form works well. Figure 9-3 provides an example. Parents are asked

FIGURE 9-3

Sample Form for Parent Observation

Notes for 15-minute Observation

Child _____ Date _____ Start time _____ Person taking notes _____

Take notes for three 15-minute blocks.	List activity/ area the child was involved in.	List other children they played with.	Was an adult involved in the play or activity? If yes, describe who, and how they were involved.	Language Sample (List one or two sentences or words you heard the child say.)	Notes
First 5 minutes					
Second 5 minutes					
Third 5 minutes					

© Cengage Learning

 TeachSource Digital Download Download from CourseMate.

to note the child's activities, playmates, special interests, and avoidances, if relevant. For others, a staff member may sit with the parent and point out certain activities and describe their importance. Focused observing helps parents note what actually is going on with their children. As with other aspects of the program, parental observations need to be tailored to meet the family's varied needs and desires.

It is important that parents be made to feel welcome and comfortable in the classroom. Teachers would do well to provide a place for the visitor to sit (preferably in an adult-sized chair) during the observation. Some parents like to visit frequently and be involved in classroom activities. Talk with parents beforehand and suggest ways that they can participate. For example, they may help with art activities, read books in the library corner, or work with children at the computer. Other parents like to visit frequently, but prefer to be less actively involved. Often these parents are pleased to help prepare materials needed in the classroom, such as cutting out figures or laminating materials. Talk with parents individually and determine strategies to make their visit to their child's classroom pleasant and beneficial.

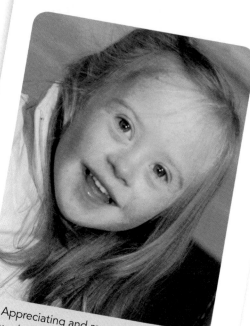

Appreciating and respecting the extra work it takes for families to care for and educate children with special needs is important.

© Cengage Learning

9-4d ■ Establishing Trust

To ensure ongoing effective communication, teachers and parents must first establish and maintain a trusting relationship. As Klein, Cook, and Richardson-Gibbs (2001) state:

> Perhaps the most important ingredient in the process of creating a true partnership with families is the development of mutual trust. Trust will not develop unless families feel safe. Their right to privacy, to confidentiality, to ask questions and to make choices for themselves and their children must be respected. (p. 254)

As stated, one key to forming this trust is maintaining confidentiality. Parents must know that information about children or their families will not be discussed with other parents or with other staff in a casual setting, such as the lunchroom, or with other community members, without the parent's written permission.

Confidentiality—in combination with acceptance of the child and his or her family, respect and value for the child's home culture, and encouragement of participation of all families—becomes a strong foundation for a positive working relationship.

Did You Get It?

How do children react without active parent involvement in early intervention programs?
   a. Reinforcement through teachers improves.
   b. Behavior tends to improve once the program has ended.
   c. Children tend to regress once the program has ended.
   d. Child's gains are maintained.

Take the full quiz on CourseMate.

✵ 9-5 Communicating with Parents

The teacher's approach to parents is the same as the teacher's approach to children: respect and appreciation for individual differences in terms of culture, values, attitude, and learning style. When mutual understanding can be established between parents and teachers, children are more likely to experience a good learning environment. Two-way communication is the cornerstone of understanding. Talking *with* rather than *to* parents is the basis for effective communication. Teachers simultaneously share knowledge and obtain feedback. They also deal with parents' expressed and unexpressed concerns. Unexpressed concerns are among the biggest obstacles to communication.

It is helpful to talk with parents about how they would like to communicate with the teacher and the school staff. For example, do they prefer phone calls, e-mail, or notes sent home? If they prefer phone calls, is there a time that is most convenient and when they will be able to give the call their full attention? How often would parents like to hear from classroom staff? Teachers must work with the family to set up expectations for ongoing communication that meet family needs and are sustainable by staff (Davern, 2004). When considering how to communicate with various families in an early childhood classroom, issues of culture, language, and literacy must be taken into consideration: Who in the family will be the primary contact? If the family is limited in speaking English, is there a member of the classroom staff who speaks their native language? Is it acceptable for this staff member to be their primary contact in the classroom? If written communication is used (e.g., newsletters, notes sent home, e-mail), these should be written in the family's primary language (Lynch & Hanson, 2011).

The key to effective communication with parents is to communicate continually, not only when there's a problem. Start from the first day of school and keep them informed throughout the year (Learn NC, n.d.).

To ensure ongoing effective communication, teachers and parents must first establish and maintain a trusting relationship.

© Cengage Learning

9-5a ■ Informal Exchanges

A tremendous amount of information can be exchanged during informal encounters. The quick conversations that occur in programs where parents pick up and deliver children are especially fruitful. To take full advantage of these, with as many parents as possible, arrival and departure time should be an extended period (twenty to thirty minutes). One teacher is assigned specifically to these program periods. These brief exchanges often focus on specific issues, such as the child's sleep patterns or on relaying the physician's reasons for increasing a child's medication. Mini-progress reports can also be given; for example,

"Laricia can point to red, yellow, and blue now."
"Jane climbed to the top of the slide all by herself this afternoon."
"Michael hung up his jacket every day this week."

Appreciative comments made by teachers to parents in the presence of the child are important. Parents come to realize that seemingly small events have developmental significance. Children learn that their accomplishments have merit; otherwise, why would the teacher pass on the news? And why would both of these important adults, parent and teacher, look so pleased? Appreciative comments have another function, too. They serve as models for parents. It helps them put into words their own recognition and appreciation of their children's efforts. Furthermore, positive reporting, within earshot of other parents and children, contributes to the self-esteem of both parent and child because the evaluation was made publicly.

Because of their public nature, arrival and departure times are *not* used to discuss concerns about a child or problems with his or her behavior or learning. These moments are not to be used to talk about anything unsuitable for the child or other parents and children to hear. If a parent brings up a sensitive issue, the teacher listens and makes a quick note. The teacher then promises to telephone the parent as soon as possible to talk it over or to arrange a conference. The teacher makes a point of asking for a specific time to make the call. This is to ensure that the child is otherwise occupied. Any serious discussion between a parent and teacher seems to get blown out of proportion in a child's mind if it appears that the adults are trying to keep the child from listening.

Parents must be welcome at any time in all programs for young children.

© Cengage Learning

9-5b ■ Telephone Calls

Telephone calls help maintain communication between teachers and parents. When children are bussed and parents work, the telephone may become the chief means of maintaining contact. It is important to keep a log of telephone

Case Study ■ Sofia's mom ■

Sofia and her mother just moved into the area and enrolled in your preschool class. Sofia's mom is a single parent who works two jobs to make ends meet. She drops off Sofia one to two times a week, but on most days Sofia is transported back and forth by a babysitter. Sofia's mom speaks primarily Spanish and some English. What are some things that you, as the teacher, can implement in order to develop a trusting relationship with Sofia's mom?

Because of their public nature, arrival and departure times are not used to discuss concerns about a child or problems.

© Cengage Learning

contacts that every staff member has with each family. These logs can be quite simple, but they should note the date and length of the call and the subjects that were discussed. Telephone calls may be used for the same kinds of casual reporting as arrival and departure contacts.

Many parents prefer that a convenient day and time be arranged in advance so they can plan to have a few minutes to talk freely. When teachers' calls become a regular event, most parents welcome them; a call from school no longer signals trouble. Usually, the focus is on routine matters, such as:

- the outcome of a visit to the audiologist

- the progress of an illness

- the reason for an absence of several days

For children who are not picked up by their own parents, the teacher should telephone to report any unusual happening at school: torn or soiled clothing; a scrape, fall, or rash; a child's refusal to eat. The teacher always tries to reach the parent *before* the child arrives home. This helps to avoid misunderstandings that occur when messages are relayed from the bus driver or a parent driving the car pool. The advance call also forestalls unpleasant surprises that may be difficult for some parents to deal with when caught off guard.

Finally, the teacher's call in advance of the child's arrival home protects the child. Young children often have difficulty explaining why something happened. They themselves may not understand it, may not perceive it accurately, or may not have the appropriate words of explanation. If the teacher is the first to reach the parent with potentially troubling news, the parent can release his or her anger or distress on the teacher, rather than on the child. In addition, the call allows teachers to find out whether parents consider it necessary to make changes in the program in order to reduce the likelihood of a recurrence of the incident.

two-way journal a notebook for questions or observations on a particular child that is passed back and forth between parents, teachers, and other team members on a regular basis

9-5c ■ Written Notes, Including E-mails

If immediate reporting and feedback are not issues, written notes sent home with the child can be useful. Written notes, either in a **two-way journal** or via e-mail, can provide a range of helpful functions (Davern, 2004).

- Provide an awareness of what happened in a child's day
- Allow parents the opportunity to contribute information from home that may increase a child's participation in activities
- Provide assurance that the child was actively participating
- Share information about instructional themes and special events
- Share health concerns
- Report progress and provide a record of communications

Once a relationship has been established between a teacher and parent, a written note or e-mail is often preferred to a telephone call. Parents can read the note at a convenient time. They are saved the sometimes aggravating interruption of a call. The note may be a duplicated reminder of a meeting or an upcoming event. It may be a request, perhaps for additional clothing to be kept at school. It may be a report of an exciting breakthrough: "Lauren laced her shoes all by herself today." Parents appreciate a teacher's personalized recognition of their children, even in the form of a one-liner such as the report on lacing shoes. Notes of this kind give parents something specific and positive to talk about with their child. In addition, notes are one more way for teachers to help parents recognize the developmental significance of a child's seemingly routine accomplishments.

While written notes, including e-mails, can be helpful, they are not without their drawbacks, nor should they be relied on as the sole form of communication. Teachers need to be aware of the following when using written notes (Montgomery, 2005; Davern, 2004):

- Teachers must be sure to provide a balance of information and not use daily notes to provide information only about "bad behaviors." If notes focus only on what the child is not doing well, parents will no longer want to read them. Not all information is appropriate to be shared via a written note. A teacher needs to determine what is best communicated via a phone call or other form of communication.
- Information needs to be provided in a jargon-free, welcoming way.
- Decide who from the classroom will write the note. While a teacher's assistant might be very familiar with the child and their day, parents also want to hear from the teacher, at least occasionally.
- Notes should be reread by the writer and looked at from the parent's perspective. Notes should be examined for tone and possible misinterpretation.
- There is no way to know if the note or e-mail is actually read unless the teacher requests a reply.
- A notebook should be only one of many forms of communication. A teacher needs to plan on developing a relationship with the parent in additional ways.

9-5d ■ Texts

For some parents, receiving a text message may be the best way to relay some information. Texts should be reserved for short updates and focus on the positive. For example, texting a parent who had to leave a crying child to let them know that their child is fine and playing happily is an appropriate use of texting.

9-5e ■ Photos and Videos

With so many teachers having access to smart phones it is easy to record significant events to share with parents. It might mean snapping a photo of a child riding a tricycle for the first time, or, for an older child, taking a video of them making a speech to the class. Care must be taken to have adequate written permission in place if photos or video are shared with individuals other than the child's family.

9-5f ■ Class Websites and E-mail Updates

A class website can provide a place for teachers to post information about activities, permission forms, the parent handbook and school calendar, and ideas for at-home activities. A website can also be a place to post student artwork (with the parent's permission). Care must be taken not to post recognizable pictures of students unless they are posted on a password-protected portion of the website, and then only with the parent's permission.

Many schools and programs maintain websites to which a teacher can post a class section. For teachers without this option, tools to create web pages, such as Google Sites and Facebook, are free and accessible from any computer.

A faster and easier way to update parents about what their child's class is doing is to send a daily or weekly update about the activities planned for the class. The format is briefer and less formal than a newsletter, described later. These updates provide the parents with information to use when talking with their child about their experiences at school.

While a website and email updates are a great way to foster communication, it can also raise an equity issue, as not all families will have access to or knowledge of how to use a computer, much less navigate a website. The following are strategies to increase access to technology for all families (Mitchell, Foulger, & Wetzel, 2009):

- Continue to provide print copies of newsletters and information posted on your website to families who are unable to access the website.

- Help families increase their comfort with technology by providing a brief orientation to your website during open house or another family evening.

9-5g ■ Newsletters

Most parents appreciate a newsletter, either duplicated and sent home with children, or sent electronically for families with Internet access. The major purpose of a newsletter is to describe the everyday events and learning activities that go on at school, from spring vegetable planting to the installation of a child-friendly computer. A newsletter also can serve as a reminder about situations that involve all families, such as the need for warm clothing during colder weather.

Newly enrolled children and families can be introduced in newsletters, as well. When the new child has a disability, emphasis can be on the many things the child can do: "Dorsey is learning to use her crutches outdoors, but there are lots of things she doesn't need them for. She goes down the slide by herself and swings in the tire swings." A newsletter must be written to fit the reading level of families receiving it. In many programs, newsletters need to be written in two or more languages.

To ensure a simple and straightforward style, children can be involved in the writing. All children learn from discussing what to include in a newsletter. Many children have fun dictating parts of it or drawing pictures to include in it. Teachers must be sure to read the finished newsletter to children before they carry it home. This enables children to talk with their parents about the contents and prompts parents to read the letter. In fact, a good rule for teachers is that they inform children of every communication with parents: telephone calls, notes, parent conferences. When a teacher says, "I called your father and told him how good you are at matching colors," the child realizes that good things truly are being reported.

9-5h ■ Parent and Teacher Meetings

The meeting has been the traditional form of parent–teacher interaction. Usually held on the school premises, meetings provide opportunities for parents to see their children's work, interact with teachers, and compare notes with other parents.

An advantage of inclusive early education programs is that the parents of children with disabilities are included in all-parent meetings. When children with disabilities attend segregated programs, parents often are not invited to PTA or other all-school functions or do not feel comfortable attending them.

Large-group meetings Group meetings usually focus on issues of general interest, such as aspects of child development or the early childhood curriculum. A recognized expert in a particular area may be invited to speak. Parent meetings that draw the best attendance are those dealing with parents' concerns. Time for questions and open discussion is an important part of any parent–teacher get-together. An informal coffee hour often precedes or follows the discussion. Casual socializing helps parents and teachers get to know each other. An open-house hour sometimes precedes group discussion. Parents visit their children's classrooms, where paintings, clay work, and woodworking projects can be on display. Toys, equipment, and teaching materials are often made available for parents to examine and manipulate. Many parents find they can talk more easily with teachers when they can focus on materials. For shy or reserved parents, looking at materials may be an avenue to talk with other parents.

Parent conferences Regular parent conferences should be scheduled two or three times a year, more often in some instances. Conferences can be helpful to parents, or they can be threatening and intimidating. A positive note must be established at the outset. Parent conferencing requires a quiet place with comfortable seating. After greeting parents cordially and exchanging social pleasantries, the teacher starts off by giving a brief progress report. The report should be interlaced with many examples of how the child is gaining or has mastered particular skills. A recent parent observation or a videotape of the child in class can be a good jumping-off point for the conference. Throughout, the teacher pauses frequently in order for parents to have opportunities to comment, ask questions, and express concerns. The conference closes with a brief summary of the discussion, a restatement of long- and short-term learning goals, and a recap of the child's unique and valuable qualities.

For some conferences, a translator may be included in the conference when the teacher and parent need help understanding each other. The involvement of a translator can reduce the stress a family feels about not being able to completely understand or communicate with the teacher. In every parent conference, the focus must be on issues related to the child's development and learning. Teachers *do not* counsel parents on deeply personal concerns, regardless of the effect on the child. Teachers may, however, attempt to help the family find the appropriate resource.

Ethical issues are a concern of many teachers in their work with parents. Ethical professional behavior means that an early childhood teacher will be the best teacher he or she can be and support others in providing quality services with the highest standards (Feeney & Kipnis, 2005; Howard, Williams, & Lepper, 2009).

What should be done, for example, when a child has serious behavior problems that parents apparently do not recognize? Before going into such a conference, the teacher makes extensive observations and takes frequency counts, when appropriate, of the behavior in question. The teacher also consults with the other teachers. This ensures staff agreement that a serious problem exists and that it cannot be handled through rearrangement of particular aspects of the program. No matter how carefully the teacher sets a positive note at the outset of such a conference, nor how tactfully the teacher brings up the problem, parents will be threatened. Inevitably, they feel that whatever is "wrong" with their child is their fault or is perceived by teachers as the parents' fault. At first mention of their child's shortcomings, parents may feel alienated or defensive. Little can be accomplished in this kind of emotional climate. Teachers, therefore, would do well to bring up major problems only when the child's present and future well-being is at stake, and they cannot assist the child without the parents' help.

It would be unconscionable for teachers not to bring up certain problems. Suspected child abuse by the parent is one such problem. Teachers are mandated by law to report suspected abuse and neglect to appropriate agencies, such as Child Protective Services. If abuse is suspected, the teacher levels with the parents immediately. After brief greetings, opening statements should relate to the frequency and seriousness of the injuries that have been observed and documented. However, if the child acts worried, fearful, anxious, or withdrawn, the *teacher does not introduce the issue.* Parents may become upset and further abuse the child for behaving in a way that indicates that abuse is happening. From the parents' perspective, it may seem their child is getting the family into deeper trouble. At no point does the teacher withdraw or back down. The teacher states that a call has immediately been made to the appropriate child protection agency. In many instances, it is advisable for the teacher to hold this type of conference in the company of the school's director or nurse or with a member of the social service agency serving the community.

Even a conference of this type must end with a positive comment or two about the child. In addition, there needs to be a brief summary statement and a commitment from teachers that they will work with the parents in every way possible. If the child involved has developmental disabilities, it is likely that a member of the interdisciplinary team

© Cengage Learning 2015

will handle the situation. At the team and parent conference, the teacher often is the major source of supporting information.

9-5i ■ Parent Support Groups

Families of a child with special needs have individual concerns and need specific information regarding their child, available services, and community resources. Parent support groups provide parents with the opportunity to talk about such issues while supporting each other. Many different parent groups have been formed, and their structure may vary according to their purpose. Some might offer education and parent training, some might help parents learn to become advocates for their child, and others might be an informal exchange of information. Almost all groups focus on developing relationships and friendships for support and exchange of resources. A group may be offered by an early childhood program or may be sponsored by a community-based organization. A listing of several types of support groups follows:

- Support groups (such as Parent to Parent) for families of children with disabilities; this may be at a local center or community-based.
- Parent training and information programs funded by the federal government, such as the Technical Assistance ALLIANCE for Parent Centers (the ALLIANCE) and Parent Information and Resource Centers (PIRCs).
- Groups concerned with a specific disability, such as United Cerebral Palsy (UCP) or ARC, The Arc of the United States (formerly the Association for Retarded Citizens of the United States).

It is important that programs also remember the fathers' needs. Some programs offer "dad-only" support groups, which give fathers their own forum to discuss issues that are specific to them.

A program deciding to offer a support group or parent meeting must consider parents' schedules when establishing a meeting time. Do parents need a nighttime group meeting, or is morning better? What about child care?

Moreover, teachers need to be familiar with the support services for parents in their area and make this information readily available to families. The National Dissemination Center for Children with Disabilities (NICHCY) provides a listing, by state, of local parent groups and resource centers. A "Parent's Guide to Accessing Parent Groups" is also available from this organization.

9-5j ■ Parent Feedback

Most feedback from parents is obtained indirectly. Much of it comes from incidental comments during informal parent–teacher exchanges.

Indirect feedback also may come from criticisms of the program made to another parent, but purposefully, within the teacher's hearing. Teachers cannot ignore such feedback. It must be noted and discussed with staff. **Direct feedback** from parents is often difficult to obtain. Many parents are afraid of alienating the staff that provides them with sorely needed child care or early intervention services. Other parents are intimidated by the teachers' expertise. Still others fear their comments or dissatisfaction will be considered trivial. On the other hand, parents who do give direct feedback often are those who are chronically dissatisfied. While their comments may be frequent, they are likely to be the least helpful.

indirect feedback covert or secondhand communication, such as one parent criticizing a teacher's methods, not to the teacher but to another parent within earshot of the teacher

direct feedback firsthand communication between parent and teacher

Questionnaires can provide feedback as well. Parents' responses are the most useful if questions relate to specific aspects of the program. In addition, questions should be designed so that parents can rate the *degree of satisfaction* on each item rather than having to give a *yes* or *no* answer. Suggestion boxes also can be helpful. Parents can make their comments anonymously if they are supplied with a form. They can fill it out at home, then bring it back and drop it in a box, unobserved. It is important to respond to all feedback from parents. The program's response may be noted in the newsletter, letters sent home, or on a bulletin board in a place that all parents will see. The best way to encourage parents to continue giving honest feedback is to always be responsive to them (Schwartz & Baer, 1991).

9-5k ■ Home Visits

In their literature review titled *Family Engagement, Diverse Families, and Early Childhood Education Programs,* Halgunseth, Peterson, Stark, and Moodie (2009) state that "home visits provide opportunities for teachers and families to connect in an informal setting, to prevent and resolve problems in a more succinct and efficient manner, and to expand the teacher's knowledge of students' home life and cultural backgrounds" (p. 9).

Home visits have a long tradition of bridging the gap between school and home. Getting to know a family in its own setting enables teachers to work more effectively with children in the school setting. A home visit by a teacher before the child's first day of school can help ease the child's transition. The teacher can obtain information about a child's personal interests; for example, a favorite toy or stuffed animal. The teacher can then refer to this information to help comfort the child during the first days in the classroom. Home visits require teachers to behave differently than they do in their own classrooms. In a child's home, teachers are no longer the central figure—parents are. The teacher is a guest who needs to conform to the social and cultural customs of the family.

If there is more than one adult in the home who shares caregiving, home visits ideally should be scheduled to involve both of them. If that is not possible on a regular basis, at least one visit should be conducted when all the caregivers can participate. Home visits are excellent opportunities to observe children's ability to function in their own environment and to observe their level of competence in daily living skills. If a teacher is interested in a specific skill, he or she plans the home visit to coincide with a time when that skill is used naturally. For example, if the parents have many questions about feeding, it would be advantageous to schedule the visit around a meal or snack time.

Much can be learned about the child's developmental opportunities from a home visit (Caldwell, 1984). For example:

- What types of materials are available for the child?
- Are there toys or household items converted into play materials readily available?
- Are there books and crayons?
- How do the children spend their time when not in the program?
- Is the home excessively neat or excessively disorganized?
- How do parents respond to their children? To a particular child? Are parents overprotective? Impatient with the child's shortcomings?

When home visits are scheduled on a regular basis, the visiting teacher usually brings learning materials, demonstrating to the child and parent how to use them. Then the parent and child use the materials together, with the teacher providing feedback. The visiting teacher also makes suggestions as to how the parent can extend and elaborate the activity during the period between visits. The emphasis of the home visit should be to enhance naturally occurring activities, rather than adding extra duties for the family to perform. Michelle Davis, a family service provider at Puckett Institute in North Carolina, summarizes this idea: "The goal is to find ways to build on what the family is already contributing to their child's learning and growth" (ERIC/OESP Special Project, 2001).

Regardless of the approach, teachers must remember the parents' roles in their child's learning. Not only are parents their child's first teacher, they also are their child's most frequent teacher. With appropriate support, parents can make their home a rich and secure learning environment. All developmental skills can be practiced over and over at home, in a real-life setting, involving those individuals who have a personal stake in the child's development.

Did You Get It?

How do children gain from appreciative comments made by teachers to parents about their child, in front of the child?

a. Realize that small events may have developmental significance.
b. Learn that their accomplishments have merits.
c. Serve as a model.
d. Helps put into words their own recognition and appreciation of his or her efforts.

Take the full quiz on CourseMate.

Summary

The family, regardless of its makeup, is a child's first and most important teacher. The family defines a child's culture and community.

▶ One of the teacher's major responsibilities is to respect cultural beliefs and practices. While early childhood teachers are partners in the teaching process, parents are always the senior partners.

▶ For children who have developmental disabilities, parental involvement is especially important. Involvement takes many forms. Simply keeping their child in the intervention program may be the only involvement some parents can comfortably manage.

▶ The teacher–parent partnership is fostered in a variety of ways. A relationship that will benefit children is based on open communication, trust, and teachers' respect of the range of individual differences among parents.

▶ Many of the most effective teacher–parent exchanges are brief and informal chats such as those that occur when a parent delivers his or her child, or observes in the classroom. Telephone calls, written notes, e-mail correspondence, newsletters, and group meetings keep the lines of communication open between teachers and parents.

▶ Formal conferences are another means of communicating with parents, as are home visits.

▶ Teachers also may seek parent feedback about the program through questionnaires and suggestion boxes.

Key Terms

achievement gap, 216
culturally competent, 217
cultural mediators, 219
direct feedback, 239

empowering (a family), 227
family-centered, 224
indirect feedback, 239
reconstituted (blended) family, 220

transactional relationships, 224
two-way journal, 234

Student Activities

1. Prepare a brief profile of three different family lifestyles found among your friends or extended family. Be specific about the caregiving arrangement for the infants and young children.

2. Select several classmates to role-play parent–child pairs during a program's arrival time. Serving as teacher, initiate brief exchanges with each parent around a sleep problem, a child's new leg braces, a special painting a child has done, or a child's reluctance to play outdoors.

3. Prepare a one-page newsletter relating events that occurred in the classroom where you observe or practice-teach.

4. Reread the "Linguistic and Cultural Diversity Connection" from this chapter, on page XXX. Make a list of other practices that may vary between classrooms in individualistic and collectivistic cultures.

5. Review NAEYC's six principals for engaging families and DEC's four categories for family-based practices. Identify how they overlap and how they differ.

6. Contact your local Parent Information and Resource Center (PIRC). Make a list of the various roles they play in helping families.

Review Questions

Define and give an example of each of the following terms:

1. extended family
2. family-centered practice
3. cultural mediators (as related to PL 99-457)
4. respite care
5. empowering families

Additional Resources/Readings

Developing Cross-Cultural Competence: A Guide for Working with Children and Their Families
Written by Eleanor Lynch and Marci Hanson
Brookes Publishing

Lynch and Hanson (2011) provide a guide to help individuals working with children and their families with this valuable resource. The book includes cultural information about a number of groups that make up the population of the United States. It provides recommendations to service providers to enhance their cultural awareness and responsiveness to all families.

Helpful Websites

The National Center for Cultural Competence (NCCC)

http://nccc.georgetown.edu

The National Center for Cultural Competence (NCCC) provides national leadership and contributes to knowledge on cultural and linguistic competency within systems and organizations. Major emphasis is placed on translating evidence into policy and practice for programs and personnel concerned with health and mental health care delivery, administration, education, and advocacy.

PACER Center

http://www.pacer.org

The mission of the PACER Center is to expand opportunities and enhance the quality of life of children and young adults with disabilities and their families, on the basis of the concept of parents helping parents. This site includes publications and many helpful resources.

Parents Helping Parents (PHP)

http://www.php.com

PHP serves children by providing information, training, and support to their families, the professionals who serve them, and the communities in which they live. Online services include a resource directory, library listings, and an equipment exchange.

Sibling Support Project

http://www.siblingsupport.org

The Sibling Support Project is the only national effort dedicated to the interests of more than six million brothers and sisters of people with special health, mental health, and developmental needs.

Visit the Education CourseMate for this textbook to access the eBook, Did You Get It? quizzes, Digital Downloads, TeachSource Video Cases, flashcards, and more. Go to CengageBrain.com to log in, register, or purchase access.

Assessment and the IFSP/IEP Process

10

OBJECTIVES

After reading this chapter, you should be able to:

10-1   list the six steps in the assessment process.

10-2   describe the process of early identification, including Child Find and screening.

10-3   discuss the family's role in the assessment process.

10-4   explain the role of the early childhood teacher in the identification of developmental problems and in the IFSP/IEP process.

10-5   summarize the major requirements of an IFSP.

10-6   summarize the major requirements of an IEP.

10-7   summarize the major requirements needed to obtain a 504 plan.

• • • • • • • • • • • • • • • • • •

naeyc

The following NAEYC Standards are addressed in this chapter:

STANDARD 2 Building Family and Community Relationships

STANDARD 3 Observing, Documenting and Assessing to Support Young Children and Families

STANDARD 4 Using Developmentally Effective Approaches

- The school nurse checks the hearing and vision of all the children in a Head Start classroom.
- The teacher uses a checklist to observe a child's play skills.
- As a result of family concerns, a kindergarten student is tested by the speech language pathologist and the school psychologist.

The scenarios above are but a few examples of assessments used to gather information about children. Such information is needed for identification, IFSP/IEP development, program planning, and evaluation.

Assessment is a process of collecting information to help answer a question. The questions that are asked determine the types of information needed. Some questions involve comparing a child's behavior to the behavior of other children of the same age. Others involve comparing the child's behavior one day to that same child's behavior at a different time (e.g., tracking progress across a school year).

This chapter describes the process of assessment—for assessing concerns about children. Assessment data can be used at a doctor's appointment to confirm diagnosis. In addition, the individual family service plan (IFSP) and individualized education program (IEP) are described and discussed in terms of how they relate to assessment.

Early identification of developmental problems has been a priority of the federal government for more than forty-five years. In 1967, the Early and Periodic Screening, Diagnosis, and Testing (EPSDT) program was initiated. Screening and subsequent referral to appropriate service providers continues to be a priority in early childhood programs.

As more is learned about the first five years of life and early brain development, the importance of early, accurate, and comprehensive identification of children at risk for developmental delays and learning problems is reinforced.

Early identification of developmental problems allows for effective intervention. It also helps in the prevention of secondary handicapping conditions through individualized programming and educational planning.

☀ 10-1 Assessment of Young Children

In all programs, assessment is a broad term that can include observing, gathering, and recording information. The type of assessment instruments used and data collected depend on the questions that teachers ask. Therefore, when a teacher is conducting an assessment, the first thing he or she must know is why it is important to collect the information. In other words, what are the questions that the teaching staff is trying to answer?

naeyc

According to the NAEYC Position Statement on Early Childhood Curriculum, Assessment and Program Evaluation (2003), the purposes of doing an assessment are:

1. to make sound decisions about teaching and learning.
2. to identify significant concerns that may require focused intervention for individual children.
3. to help programs improve their educational and developmental interventions.

Six interrelated steps have been identified in assessment of young children with special needs (Cohen & Spenciner, 2007). These steps are described here briefly and are included in the IDEIA law.

Step 1. *Screening.* The purpose is to identify children who need more thorough evaluation.

Step 2. *Determining Eligibility.* The purpose is to determine whether a child has an identifiable disability and qualifies for special education services. This decision cannot be made on the basis of a single test, nor does the classroom teacher decide it. Assessment information from multiple domains and sources must be used to determine eligibility.

Step 3. *Determine Services.* Once eligibility has been established, the services required are identified, and the appropriate personnel are convened to write the IEP or IFSP.

Step 4. *Planning the Program.* The purpose is to identify an appropriate program for a child and begin to plan what services will be delivered, how they will be delivered, and what skills and areas will be addressed.

Step 5. *Monitoring Progress.* The purpose is to determine how the child is progressing in the program. The information from these monitoring activities is used to modify the child's program.

Step 6. *Evaluating the Program.* The purpose is to make decisions about the effectiveness of the intervention program for individual children. Decisions can be made about specific activities, modifications, or the entire program.

Assessment information is collected in many different ways, including observation work samples, **portfolios**, **standardized tests**, and checklists. Often, however, when teachers hear the word *assessment*, they think about standardized instruments that have been developed to collect a specific type of information. Three common types of tests used in assessment are **criterion-referenced assessments**, **norm-referenced assessments**, and **IQ tests**.

10-1a ■ Criterion-Referenced Assessment

Some screening instruments are criterion-referenced; that is, a child's performance on each task is compared to preselected standards (*criteria*). These types of assessments have high **instructional utility**; that is, they are useful in program planning. A child's performance is *not* compared to the performance of other children. For example, criterion-referenced test items might ask:

- Can the child lace and tie his or her own shoes?
- Can the child walk seven consecutive steps on a balance beam?
- Can the child match five shapes and colors in one minute?
- Can the child play cooperatively with peers?

10-1b ■ Norm-Referenced Assessments

With norm-referenced assessments, the question becomes: How well does the child do, *compared to other children the same age?* Norm-referenced assessments provide standardized information intended to relate to children's abilities at various ages. In other words, the norm-referenced assessment provides scales that compare the performance of one child to the average performance of other children of approximately the same age. It must be recognized, however, that these assessments tend to be less than reliable with young children (Cohen & Spenciner, 2007).

portfolio a carefully selected collection of a child's work that is used to document growth and development

standardized tests assessment instruments that include precise directions for administration and scoring

criterion-referenced assessment assessment that describes a child's developmental level and progress according to a prescribed set of skills, tasks, and activities

norm-referenced assessments instrument that compares a child's developmental level to a normative sample of same-age peers

IQ tests intelligence tests are usually norm-referenced and are designed to determine how much a child knows, how well the child solves problems, and how quickly a child can perform a variety of mental tasks; IQ tests do not predict future intellectual performance

instructional utility teaching the skills that will be useful to the child in a given environment

10-1c ■ IQ Tests

Most intelligence tests (IQ tests) are norm-referenced. Tests such as the Wechsler Intelligence Scale for Children-IV (WISC-IV) and the Stanford-Binet Intelligence Scales, 5th edition, are sometimes given to young children. The avowed purpose is to attempt to determine how much a child knows, how well the child solves problems, and how quickly a child can perform a variety of mental tasks.

The scores from IQ tests must be viewed with caution, even skepticism (Neisworth & Bagnato, 1992). A number of factors may lead to poor performance on an IQ test. The child may be tired, hungry, or unwell at the time. The child may be anxious about the unfamiliar testing situation and the unfamiliar person giving the test. The child also may be answering in ways appropriate to his or her own language or culture, but inappropriate in terms of standardized test responses.

Furthermore, some children are hampered by an unidentified developmental problem. A partial vision or hearing loss, for example, can interfere with a child's ability to respond appropriately; thus, the child's IQ score falsely indicates a delayed range of mental functioning.

IQ scores of infants and young children *do not predict future intellectual performance*. In fact, they are not even useful in assessing a young child's current intellectual capabilities. The major problem with IQ scores is that they do not account for the child's learning opportunities (or lack thereof). Neither do they reflect the quality of the learning experiences a child may have had.

The use of a single test score to determine a child's intellectual competence is illegal and must always be challenged. In fact, more than one instrument should be used in any screening program to ensure a valid picture of the child's development. Teachers and parents have been told that tests have meaning, that they point out what children know and understand, and that they can help give direction to instruction (Perrone, 1990). The tests *don't* match the promise. Their contribution to the education of young children is virtually nil (p. 13). Every young child has the right to appropriate assessment. Assessment must be ongoing, developmentally appropriate, and supportive (Hyson, 2002).

The teacher's role in assessment is to help identify children for early intervention, to collect data and documentation that will be used in the development of the IEP, and to monitor the child's progress throughout the year. The rest of this chapter addresses these issues.

Did You Get It?

Which answer pertains to one of the six steps incorporated into IDEIA law, taking into account the NAEYC Position Statement on Assessment (2003)?

a. To make sound decisions about teaching and learning.

b. Determining eligibility.

c. To identify significant concerns that may require focused intervention for individual children.

d. To help programs improve their educational and developmental interventions.

Take the full quiz on CourseMate.

✹ 10-2 The Process of Early Identification

Early identification of developmental problems can take place any time from a few weeks after conception to age eighteen. These years are formally recognized as the *developmental period* of the human lifespan. Early identification of problems is not limited to young children. A child may be perfectly healthy up to age twelve or fifteen, then show first-time symptoms of a developmental disability (juvenile rheumatoid arthritis, for example). The older child is as much in need of early identification of the emerging problem as is a two-year-old. In both cases, early identification can lead to prompt treatment. Prompt treatment can reduce the severity of the problem and prevent it from affecting other areas of development.

10-2a ■ Case Finding

case finding locating children in need of special services

Case finding is the process of locating children in need of special services. Developmental problems often go undetected because many children and their families have inadequate health care or are without health care. To deal with this situation, a federal program entitled **Child Find** was established in the 1960s.

Child Find a program established in the 1960s to identify children with developmental problems or delays

Child Find The effectiveness of Child Find depends on widespread publicity. Announcements of Child Find roundups should be simply written and free of clinical jargon. They should be written in as many languages as are spoken in the community and posted in churches, synagogues, and other religious institutions, as well as laundromats, supermarkets, child care and community centers, and shelters for homeless families. The publicity should emphasize that developmental problems are often hard to recognize and that *all* young children should be screened. Child Find programs also must be easy to get to. They should be offered through pediatrician's offices, public health facilities, and social service networks. Many families—often those most in need of such services—depend on public transportation. See Figure 10-1 for an example of an effective Child Find flyer.

FIGURE 10-1
Sample Community Child Find Flyer

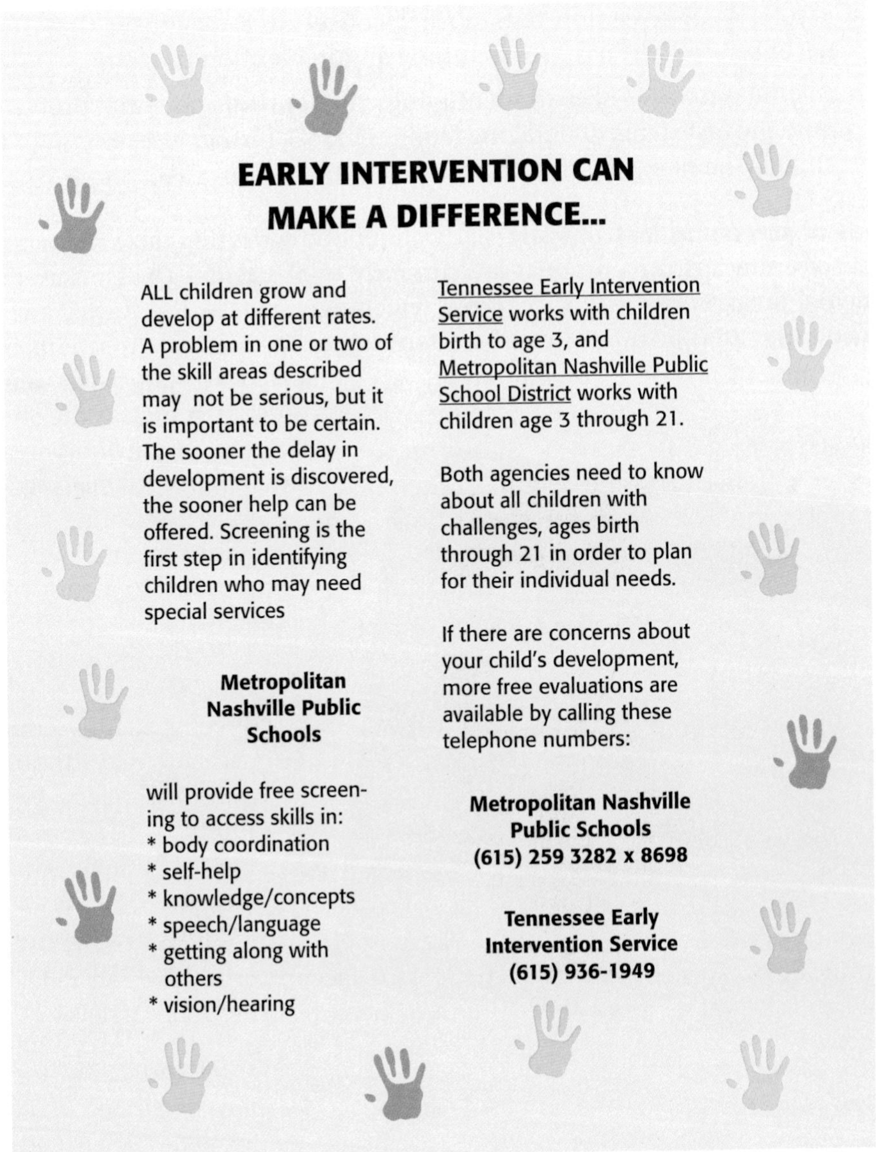

EARLY INTERVENTION CAN MAKE A DIFFERENCE...

ALL children grow and develop at different rates. A problem in one or two of the skill areas described may not be serious, but it is important to be certain. The sooner the delay in development is discovered, the sooner help can be offered. Screening is the first step in identifying children who may need special services

Metropolitan Nashville Public Schools

will provide free screening to access skills in:
* body coordination
* self-help
* knowledge/concepts
* speech/language
* getting along with others
* vision/hearing

Tennessee Early Intervention Service works with children birth to age 3, and Metropolitan Nashville Public School District works with children age 3 through 21.

Both agencies need to know about all children with challenges, ages birth through 21 in order to plan for their individual needs.

If there are concerns about your child's development, more free evaluations are available by calling these telephone numbers:

Metropolitan Nashville Public Schools (615) 259 3282 x 8698

Tennessee Early Intervention Service (615) 936-1949

Source: Tennessee Early Intervention Service and Metropolitan Nashville Public Schools.

screening the identification of developmental problems or the potential for such problems

Screening—the identification of potential developmental problems—is the major purpose of Child Find. The goal is to provide easily administered, low-cost testing for as many children as possible. The purpose of screening is to identify children who need a more detailed assessment. Children with obvious disabilities should not be put through screening procedures. They and their families need to be referred directly to the appropriate health care or social service agency.

Screening tests describe a child's level of performance, but *only at that point in time* (Marotz & Allen, 2012). **Comprehensive screening** evaluates the child's current abilities, deviations, delays, and impairments in all areas of development. If problem areas are identified during routine developmental screening, clinical diagnosis is indicated.

comprehensive screening evaluation of a child's current abilities, delays, and impairments in all areas of development

Several points should be emphasized.

reliable relates to consistency: how accurate, dependable, and predictable a test is

valid founded on truth or fact; a test that measures what it purports to measure

sensitivity ability of a screening test to identify correctly children with disabilities

specificity ability of a screening test to identify correctly children who do *not* have a disability

paraprofessional a trained person who assists a certified professional as an aide

- Accurate screening results can be achieved only with tests that are **reliable** and **valid** and developed specifically for use with young children. In the absence of valid instruments, testing is of no value (National Association of Early Childhood Specialists, 2003).

- Results from screening tests do not constitute a diagnosis; they should never be used as a basis for planning an intervention program.

- *Follow-through is essential.* Identifying children with potential problems is only the first step; encouraging families to seek further assessment for their child is the next step (Lynch & Hanson, 2011.

Types of screening instruments Early childhood screening takes many forms. Most screening instruments that are currently used attempt to assess all developmental areas. Some very specialized screenings, such as the Apgar, are used immediately after birth to assess the infant's need for medical attention. Other screening tests assess sensory functions, such as the Snellen chart for vision and pure tone audiometry for hearing.

When selecting a multi-domain screening test, it is important to consider the **sensitivity** and **specificity** of the tests. *Sensitivity* refers to the ability of a test to correctly identify children who have a disability; *specificity* refers to the ability of the test to *not* refer children who do *not* have a disability. Among the more commonly used screening instruments are the DIAL-4 (Developmental Indicators for the Assessment of Learning, 4th edition), the Denver II, and

All young children should be screened.

© Cengage Learning

the Early Screening Inventory–Revised (ESI-R) with Ages and Stages (ASQSE). All of these screening instruments rely on teachers and parents as informants. The advantage is obvious: These are the adults who know the child best. A list of screening and other early childhood assessment tools is provided on the companion website for this text.

Teachers also play a major role in screening for giftedness among young children. Although screening varies from state to state, a few items are common in most states:

- No single test identifies the younger gifted child

- Several measures must be used—IQ score, level of motivation, and creativity (which is difficult to define and measure)

- Teacher's observations and knowledge of a child are helpful as backup to the standardized assessments

Who does the screening? Screening programs may be conducted by professionals or **paraprofessionals**. Regardless of who is doing the screening, training in test procedures is important. Some screening tests— certain hearing tests or medical tests—should be administered only by members of that discipline. Other tests, such as the Denver II or the Snellen Illiterate E test, can be administered by a variety of individuals trained to use the instrument. Community screening programs generally are conducted by teams whose members are skilled in administering a number of tests.

In many communities, teachers of young children assist in conducting mass screening programs, sometimes called "roundups." Even if they are not members of a roundup team, early childhood teachers and infant caregivers/teachers are key figures in the early identification process. It is essential that they take responsibility for recognizing warning signs that a developmental problem exists or may develop.

Limitations of screening Screening is an important process in the early identification of developmental problems in children. As consumers of screening tests, however, teachers must be cautious when interpreting the data from a screening. First, remember that a screening is only a "snapshot" of a child in time. Also, this snapshot is often taken in a strange place, when the child is surrounded by new people, is tired, hungry, and being asked to do a number of activities that may be unfamiliar and seem silly (Hills, 1993). Therefore the picture of child competence (or incompetence) that begins to develop during the screening may not be representative of the child's behavior at school, home, child care, or any other setting. As a member of a screening team, a teacher can be aware of how surroundings, the familiarity of the examiner, and the physical state of the child can influence the

Several screening tests are available for assessing older infants as well as newborns.

© Cengage Learning

Teachers play a major role in screening for giftedness.

© Cengage Learning

results of the screening, and can attempt to optimize the setting in which screenings are conducted.

10-3 The Family's Role in Assessment

Parents have a wealth of firsthand knowledge about their children. They know what their child can and cannot do in everyday life. Often, they are the first to suspect a problem, even if they are unable to clearly specify its nature.

As described in the DEC's (2007) companion paper to the NAEYC position statement on assessment, it is a shared experience between families and professionals in which information and ideas are exchanged to benefit a child's growth and development. They recommend that assessment teams implement a child- and family-centered assessment process. This process should be designed to address each child's unique strengths and needs through authentic, developmentally appropriate, culturally and linguistically responsive, multidimensional assessment methods.

They recommend that assessment practices be integrated and individualized with the goal of accomplishing the following:

- answer any questions posed by the assessment team (including family members)

- integrate the child's everyday routines, interests, materials, and caregivers within the assessment process

- develop a system for shared partnerships with professionals and families for the communication and collection of ongoing information valuable for teaching and learning (DEC, 2007)

Cultural, ethnic, and linguistic differences Family customs, beliefs, and language influence a child's performance on screening tests (Lynch & Hanson, 2011). A child's responses may be scored as wrong even when they are right according to the family's values. The result may be an invalid (false) evaluation, suggesting that there is cause to be concerned about the child's development when none exists. Invalid assessment results became dismayingly apparent in the early days of special education reform, and continue to be apparent in the overrepresentation of minority students in special education. This type of invalid assessment leads to inaccurate diagnosis and labeling, often resulting in children who "were doing fine until they went to school" (Harry, 1992, p. 61). These children often function perfectly well in their own environment and in their own language, but have few skills and little background for functioning in schools designed to accommodate only the majority culture.

To avoid such errors, safeguards must be built into the screening and assessment process (Barrera, 1994). The following is a list of requirements for assessment according to the IDEIA law

- Assessment must be conducted in the child's native language.
- Assessment instruments that are designed for use in the native language must be used.
- Simply translating a test that was written in English and standardized on English-speaking students is never appropriate.
- Assessment should be conducted and interpreted by a "culture–language mediator," a person who is fluent in both the native and majority language and culture.
- Multiple forms of information should be collected, including work samples and child observations.
- Test items and procedures should be designed to measure a child's known strengths as well as document any perceived weaknesses.

For more information on this topic, read the "Linguistic and Cultural Diversity Connections" found in this chapter.

Linguistic and Cultural Diversity Connections

Avoiding Cultural Bias during the Assessment Process

Assessment instruments designed for use with children who speak English often are not appropriate for use with children and families who speak other languages. Children's and families' experiences and expectations differ from culture to culture and affect behavioral and developmental norms and expectations. These varying experiences may affect the results of an assessment and cause a concern for a delay, when in fact one does not actually exist.

Lynch and Hanson (2011) provide a vivid example.

A young child moved from Samoa to California. When an early intervention team conducted an assessment they became concerned as the child was observed to be extremely clumsy and delayed in the area of motor development. When the child was observed later in his home environment he was able to move freely and without difficulty. The home was furnished with mats and low lying furniture as found in a traditional Samoan home, rather than furniture and obstacles found in "typical" American homes. It wasn't that the child was delayed but rather had not had experience in moving around the type of obstacles found in the testing situation.

An obvious barrier to assessment is the language of the assessment. A direct translation from an assessment may not lead to valid results. Care must be taken to gather accurate information in a manner that is responsive to the families from diverse cultures. When selecting a commercially prepared assessment, select one that is appropriate for the language and the culture of the family. Use a trained interpreter who can interpret the language as well as cultural cues (including non-verbal cues).

It is equally important to conduct the assessment in an environment that is most comfortable for the family and at a time that allows for people important to the family to be present.

And as with any family, be sensitive to the number of team members that "have to" be present so as not to overwhelm the family. Be sure to gather information in the areas in which the family has expressed a concern. It is also critical to explain every step of the assessment process to the family. Following these guidelines will accomplish a great deal in showing the family respect at the same time as obtaining valid and meaningful assessment results.

Source: Lynch, E. W., & Hanson, M. J. (2011). *Developing cross-cultural competence: A guide for working with young children and their families.* Brookes: Baltimore, MD.

Did You Get It?

What pertinent requirement according to IDEIA law would be transgressed if an assessment was carried out in this manner?

a. Translate a test written in English and standardized on English-speaking students.

b. Collect multiple forms of information.

c. Test items and procedures should be designed to measure a child's strengths.

d. Conduct assessment by a culture-language mediator.

Take the full quiz on CourseMate.

☀ 10-4 Teachers' Role in Early Identification

The teacher's role in the identification of developmental problems in infants and young children is critical. It is the teacher's recorded observations of the child in many situations, over time, that provide a valid picture of that child's skills, capabilities, and special needs.

10-4a ■ Teachers' Qualifications

Since teachers work with children daily and see all types of children, they have the opportunity to identify children with developmental problems or potential problems. They understand the regularities and irregularities typical of early development that enable them to recognize developmental deviations. Teachers should also have had special training that allows them to provide infants and young children with sound developmental activities that bring out the best in each child during the assessment process.

Teachers are further advantaged in that they see children in a natural environment. In the classroom, a child is likely to be comfortable and spontaneous. Furthermore, teachers can observe children of similar age and interests and thus judge each child's development in the context of a broad display of normalcy. Teachers also have extended periods of time and many situations in which to observe children. Contrast this with clinicians such as the doctor, the audiologist, or the psychologist, who usually see the child only on brief and tightly scheduled visits in clinical settings. At these times, the child may be ill at ease and behave quite differently than in a familiar home or school environment.

The teacher as observer Observation is one of the most important skills for early childhood professionals. Often teachers are the only adults who see children in many different contexts with a variety of other adults and peers over an extended period of time. Their informal and formal observations provide a great deal of information about a child's developmental status.

The identification of developmental problems always begins with systematic observation of children as they work and play in the home, preschool, or child care center. Observers must be objective—that is, they write down only what a child actually does and says. Subjective recording, by contrast, occurs when

Observation is one of the most important skills for early childhood professionals.

© Cengage Learning

teachers put their own interpretations on children's behavior. Note the differences in the following statements

- **Objective:** Susie smiled and laughed frequently through the morning; she cried only once.
- **Subjective:** Susie was happy and carefree today.
- **Objective:** Mark stamped his feet and screamed "No" each time he was asked to change activities.
- **Subjective:** Mark gets angry all the time.

Systematic observations Most teachers are used to observing children; few, however, record their observations in an organized way. Systematically recorded observations are the key to effective identification of developmental problems. Each observation should start with these four parts.

1. child's name or initials (confidentiality of information is essential)
2. date (including year) and time of day
3. setting (and in some situations, names or number of children and teachers present)
4. name or initials of the observer

Teachers' observations take many forms. The questions that teachers need to have answered determine the observation strategy they will select. In most cases, it is preferable if more than one person observes the child, especially if there is a hint of a serious problem. When two people agree they are seeing the same thing, personal bias and misinterpretation of a child's behavior are reduced.

10-4b ■ Types of Observations

Here we discuss a sampling of the many kinds of observation tools that are useful in working with young children. For a comprehensive overview of observation strategies, see Bentzen (2009).

Checklists Checklists are a quick and effective way to collect systematic information on one or many children. Teachers, aides, parents, volunteers, and children themselves can use checklists. Many young children recognize their own names when printed in large letters. If teachers need to know, for example, which four- and five-year-olds are using particular learning centers, they can post a list of children's names close by. Most children can make a mark by their name as they enter; the teacher can do it for those who cannot. At the end of the day (or week), teachers know which children are using which centers, and which are doing a great deal of coming and going (useful information in planning individual programs).

Checklists can be as simple as the one just mentioned, or they can be designed to give much more information, as in the Teacher Observation Form and Checklist in Figure 10-2. The most useful checklists are the ones that teachers themselves design to answer their own questions about children and the program.

Frequency counts An effective way of making a recorded observation is simply keeping track of how often something happens. Teachers who are concerned about a particular behavior in a child need to know how often it takes place: Excessively? Infrequently? Only under certain circumstances? Every time the behavior occurs, a tally mark is made on a piece of paper posted on the wall or carried in the teacher's pocket. Over a period of several days, the tally marks

FIGURE 10-2

Teacher Observation Form and Checklist for Children 3–5 Years

Child's Name: _____   Birth Date: _____
Date: _____   Recording Teacher's Name: _____

LANGUAGE	YES	NO	SOMETIMES
Does the child:			
1. use two- and three-word phrases to ask for what he or she wants?			
2. use complete sentences to tell you what happened?			
*3. when asked to describe something, use at least two or more sentences to talk about it?			
4. ask questions?			
5. seem to have difficulty following directions?			
6. respond to questions with appropriate answers?			
7. seem to talk too softly or too loudly?			
8. make herself or himself understood?			

PRE-ACADEMICS	YES	NO	SOMETIMES
Does the child:			
9. seem to take at least twice as long as the other children to learn pre-academic concepts?			
10. seem to take the time needed by other children to learn pre-academic concepts?			
11. have difficulty attending to group activities for more than five minutes at a time?			
12. appear extremely shy in group activities; for instance, not volunteering answers or answering questions when asked, even though you think the child knows the answers?			

MOTOR	YES	NO	SOMETIMES
Does the child:			
13. continuously switch a crayon back and forth from one hand to the other when coloring?			
14. appear clumsy or shaky when using one or both hands?			
15. when coloring with a crayon, appear to tense the hand not being used (for instance, clench it into a fist)?			

*Question applies if child is four years or older.

FIGURE **10-2**
Continued

MOTOR	YES	NO	SOMETIMES
16. when walking or running, appear to move one side of the body differently from the other side? For instance, does the child seem to have better control of the leg and arm on one side than on the other?			
17. lean or tilt to one side when walking or running?			
18. seem to fear or not be able to use stairs, climbing equipment, or tricycles?			
19. stumble often or appear awkward when moving about?			
*20. appear capable of dressing self except for tying shoes?			

SOCIAL	YES	NO	SOMETIMES
Does the child:			
21. engage in more than two disruptive behaviors a day (tantrums, fighting, screaming, etc.)?			
22. appear withdrawn from the outside world (fiddling with pieces of string, staring into space, rocking)?			
23. play alone and seldom talk to other children?			
24. spend most of the time trying to get attention from adults?			
25. have toileting problems (wet or soiled) once a week or more often?			

VISUAL AND HEARING	YES	NO	SOMETIMES
Does the child:			
26. appear to have eye movements that are jerky or uncoordinated?			
27. seem to have difficulty seeing objects? For instance, does the child:			
tilt head to look at things?			
hold objects close to eyes?			
squint?			
show sensitivity to bright lights?			
have uncontrolled eye-rolling?			
complain that eyes hurt?			
28. appear awkward in tasks requiring eye–hand coordination such as pegs, puzzles, coloring, etc.?			

*Question applies if child is four years or older.

(*continued*)

FIGURE 10-2
Continued

VISUAL AND HEARING	YES	NO	SOMETIMES
29. seem to have difficulty hearing? For instance, does the child:			
consistently favor one ear by turning the same side of the head in the direction of the sound?			
ignore, confuse, or not follow directions?			
pull on ears or rub ears frequently, or complain of earaches?			
complain of head noises or dizziness?			
have a very high, very low, or monotonous tone of voice?			

GENERAL HEALTH	YES	NO	SOMETIMES
Does the child:			
30. seem to have an excessive number of colds?			
31. have frequent absences because of illness?			
32. have eyes that water?			
33. have frequent discharge from:			
eyes?			
ears?			
nose?			
34. have sores on body or head?			
35. have excessive bruising of arms, legs, or body?			
36. have periods of unusual movements (such as eye-blinking) or "blank spells" which seem to appear and disappear without relationship to the social situation?			
37. have hives or rashes? wheeze?			
38. have a persistent cough?			
39. seem to be excessively thirsty? seem to be excessively hungry?			
40. Have you noticed any of the following conditions: constant fatigue, irritability, restlessness, tenseness, feverish cheeks or forehead?			
41. Is the child overweight?			
42. Is the child physically or mentally lethargic?			
43. Has the child lost noticeable weight without being on a diet?			

Most teachers are used to observing children; few, however, record their observations in an organized way.

© Cengage Learning

frequency counts a system for keeping track of how often a behavior occurs; such data can provide significant information about a child's problem

duration measures how long an event or behavior lasts

can provide significant information as to whether a given behavior is actually a problem, as well as how much of a problem it is. The tally marks recorded should cover a typical child and a child experiencing difficulties, so that a range of acceptable behavior can be calculated.

Consider the following example. One teacher was concerned about John's safety because of what she thought were his frequent attempts to climb over the fence during outdoor play. The other teacher thought it seldom happened. An actual **frequency count** showed the fence-climbing attempts occurred four or five times each play period. Teachers now could agree there was a problem. They assessed the play yard and realized there was not much for John to climb on. They began to set up climbing activities several days a week. John's fence climbing dropped to one or fewer episodes per day. On days when no climbing activities were set up, John's fence climbing was again high. The frequency counts gave teachers clues to the extent of the problem as well as to their success in reducing the unsafe behavior.

Duration measures A **duration measure** indicates how long an event or behavior lasts. This type of observation, as with frequency counts, provides significant information that is easy to collect. By simply noting a start and stop time on a child's activities, teachers can gauge such things as span of attention, how much time a child spends in either appropriate or maladaptive behaviors, or under what circumstances a behavior is most likely to continue.

Consider the following example. Teachers were concerned about Lonny's poor attention span. They decided to find out how many minutes at a time he spent at various activities. Several days' observations

▶❚❚ **TeachSource Video Connections**

© Cengage Learning 2015

Progress Monitoring: Using Transitional Time in an Early Childhood Classroom

How do early childhood teachers incorporate progress monitoring into their daily routines? Watch this video to see how teacher Jessi uses transitional time to monitor the progress of her children on the topics of geometric shape and color.

After watching this video, complete the following:

1. Prepare a list of a minimum of ten curriculum topics Jessi could assess during transition time.

2. What type of assessment did Jessi use in the video? What other types of assessment, if any, can be used during this transitional time?

Watch on CourseMate.

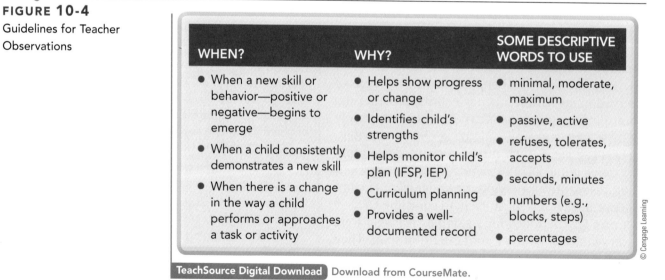

FIGURE 10-3

Example of an Anecdotal Note

> Child: Joey
> Play yard
>
> Observer M. J.
> 10/12/2013
>
> **MOTOR DEVELOPMENT**
>
> Joey climbed up eight rungs of the climbing tower. On each rung, he starts with his left foot and brought his right foot up next to it before going on to the next rung. With each step up, he grasped the bar directly above with the alternate hand (left foot, right hand). In coming down, he reversed the pattern.

indicated he spent many minutes (fifteen to twenty) with hands-on activities (painting, block building, puzzles). In contrast, he had a short attention span—only a minute or two—for activities that required listening (music, stories, conversation). These duration measures were invaluable as teachers planned Lonny's program, conferenced with his parents, and participated in the team meetings.

Anecdotal notes These are brief observations, each recorded individually on three-by-five cards or any other format that is convenient for the classroom staff. The reason for the small paper size is to ensure brevity. Anecdotal notes are recorded on each child, in each area of development, at regular intervals. An effective anecdotal note fulfills certain requirements. It refers to a specific and observable behavior. It states the level of the behavior (for example, Joey climbed up eight rungs) and it does not contain unnecessary words.

Looking back on three months of motor notes about Joey (see Figure 10-3), teachers could see how helpful the physical therapist had been. The techniques she demonstrated when working with Joey helped teachers assist Joey in improving his motor skills. Furthermore, in looking over social notes during the same period, it appeared Joey was most likely to get on the climbing frames if other children were there, too. Cognitive notes indicated he had learned most of the names of the children he climbed with and often counted how many children were on the climber. The composite picture, made up of these brief anecdotal notes, is one of a child making steady progress within and across developmental areas. See Figure 10-4 for some helpful guidelines on teacher observations and notes.

FIGURE 10-4

Guidelines for Teacher Observations

WHEN?	WHY?	SOME DESCRIPTIVE WORDS TO USE
• When a new skill or behavior—positive or negative—begins to emerge	• Helps show progress or change	• minimal, moderate, maximum
• When a child consistently demonstrates a new skill	• Identifies child's strengths	• passive, active
• When there is a change in the way a child performs or approaches a task or activity	• Helps monitor child's plan (IFSP, IEP)	• refuses, tolerates, accepts
	• Curriculum planning	• seconds, minutes
	• Provides a well-documented record	• numbers (e.g., blocks, steps)
		• percentages

TeachSource Digital Download Download from CourseMate.

Running records A running record is a factual, detailed account written over a span of time during which actions are described and quotes recorded as accurately as possible. Taken periodically, running records can create a well-rounded picture of each child's overall behavior and development. Running records are a useful form of observation; they also are the most time-consuming.

Unlike other written observations, teachers rarely can take a running record while teaching. However, a teacher can be released from direct work with children for an occasional twenty or thirty minutes to take a running record. Volunteers often are willing to relieve teachers for this purpose.

When taking a running record the teacher writes down exactly what is observed. Care should be taken not to use generic words such as "play" or "busy," but rather record exactly what the child did during "play" or while they were "busy." It is often best to only write the initial of the child being observed at the top of the paper and add the full name after the observation is completed. That way a child passing by won't notice their name and ask what you are writing about them. The running record should include the following:

- Date
- Time observation started
- Setting
- Name of observer
- Do not write names of other children involved, because you will be filing it in the target child's folder. You can use an initial or list details about the other child such as gender and age.
- Write down additional times in the margin every ten minutes or so or when there is a change in activity, so the reader can get an understanding of the length of time the child is involved in an activity.

Refer to Figure 10-5 for an example of a running record.

Logs, journals, and diaries Records of this kind are similar to the running record but less comprehensive. Written accounts may be kept in a notebook with a section for each child. (Some teachers prefer a separate folder for each child; the

---

FIGURE 10-5

A Sample Running Record

1/30/13—Kindergarten room—Roland

9:30 The teacher reminded R to move from the rug to the worktable. R got his pencil box on his own and walked to the worktable and joined the 4 other children in his work group and the parent helper who were already seated at the table. He asked the parent helper, "Can I sit here?" (Indicating the spot next to her where there was not a chair) The parent helper pointed to an empty chair. R sat down. The parent helper told the group to get a marker and trace the shapes on the paper. He picked a marker and traced the shapes on the first page. He turned to the next page and traced the shapes. He put down the marker.

9:45 He took four popsicle sticks from the table and set them on the tabletop and said, "I want to make a square." The parent helper said it was time to clean up. R did not respond. After 3 mins. he put the popsicle sticks back in the box and then began to dig through the box—flipping them into the air. The other children at the table laughed.

9:50 The teacher came over and knelt down next to R and said, "You have to stop and pick the sticks up." R smiled, flipped the sticks one more time and then put them back in the box and said, "There."

© Cengage Learning

important point is to choose a format that is convenient and easy to use.) Notes are jotted down during class time or immediately after children leave for the day. The jottings may be general notes about a child or focused notes on some aspect of the child's behavior.

For example, teachers may need to know more about a child's outdoor activities before planning an individualized program to increase play skills: With whom does Angelo play? Does he play on the climbing equipment? Ride the wheel toys? Build with outdoor blocks? Is he accepted into the play of other children? Which other children? Are some play periods better than others? Why? The answers to these questions provide clues for program planning.

Teachers should build a regularly scheduled time into their daily or weekly schedule for making entries regarding each child. This ensures that notes are taken on a regular and ongoing basis, and contain information about accomplishments as well as challenges. If there is not a regularly scheduled opportunity, too often notes are focused on challenges and problems.

Time sampling Time samplings are brief, periodic observations to determine the presence or absence of a behavior: Is Leanne engaged most of the time with play materials? Does Marty engage mostly in solitary, parallel, associative, or cooperative play? In some samplings, teachers observe the child in question for only a few seconds at regular intervals, perhaps once every two minutes, or five minutes, or fifteen minutes. In other samplings, they may take a quick look only two or three times a day, during certain periods such as circle time. If the targeted behavior is occurring, the teacher makes a mark on a tally sheet. It may turn out that Leanne, for example, was engaged with materials during only three out of the fifteen samples. Might this be an indication that she needs different materials? Or help in extending her span of attention? As for Marty, he was playing alone in 5 percent of the samples, in associative play in about 40 percent of the samples, and in cooperative play during the remaining samples—a nice balance for an almost five-year-old. See Figure 10-6 for an example of an observation sheet used during time sampling.

Language samples As noted in Chapter 5, speech and language problems account for a major portion of developmental problems. Before treatment can begin, the current level of a child's skills must first be assessed. An ideal place to get information about a child's language is in the classroom.

Here the child is doing what comes naturally: talking about familiar things with familiar people. Language samples are verbatim recordings (word for word

FIGURE 10-6

Time Sampling of Free-Play Activities

Child		Hannah	Javier	Samantha
	Time			
	9:00	D A F G	D A F G	D A F G
	9:10	D A F G	D A F G	D A F G
	9:20	D A F G	D A F G	D A F G
	9:30	D A F G	D A F G	D A F G
	9:40	D A F G	D A F G	D A F G
	9:50	D A F G	D A F G	D A F G

D = Dramatic Play   A = Art Area   F = Fine Motor/Manipulatives   G = Gross Motor

© Cengage Learning

An ideal place to get information about a child's language is in the classroom.

or sound for sound) of what the child says or what sounds the child makes. If the child says "du gul," it is written "du gul" (phonetically) even if the observer knows the child is referring to "the girl." If Billy is squealing "Eeeeee" and pointing to the juice, "Eeeeee" is what the observer writes down, not "Billy wanted juice." It is important for the observer to note the pointing along with the vocalization, to show that Billy was able to communicate his need. This type of detailed language sample is usually only conducted by a speech-language pathologist.

Portfolio assessment Another way in which teachers can collect valuable information about a child's development and progress is with a portfolio assessment. Meisels (1993) describes a portfolio as a "purposeful collection of children's work that illustrates their efforts, progress, and achievements" (p. 37). When using portfolio assessment, teachers collect work samples across activities and settings. The portfolio includes their own observations, notes from parent conferences, parent comments, and comments from other specialists.

This information, which has been collected on an ongoing basis, is then used for planning, curriculum development, and program change (Lynch & Struewing, 2001). A benefit of portfolio assessment is that it

Observation is a useful and important tool in providing high-quality education and care for all children.

© Cengage Learning

FIGURE 10-7

Teacher's Dos and Don'ts

Teachers Should:

- develop good working relationships with families.

- voice concerns to parents about possible developmental differences in their child.

- listen carefully and respectfully.

- be knowledgeable about local resources and be able to make helpful and appropriate referrals.

- make careful judgments.

- be culturally sensitive and take cultural and linguistic differences into consideration when evaluating behavior.

- work collaboratively with parents.

- remember that all children are different, and typical development encompasses a broad spectrum of individual difference.

Teachers Should Avoid:

- making diagnoses.

- using labels to describe children, remembering that all children in their program are children first.

- raising parents' anxiety.

- phrasing suggestions as orders.

- jumping to conclusions without adequate observational data.

© Cengage Learning

TeachSource Digital Download Download from CourseMate.

is an ongoing purposeful assessment, which takes place during authentic activities such as play in a natural setting, without removing a child from their natural learning environment or process. Portfolios can be a reliable replacement or supplement to standardized testing (Nilsen, 2010).

10-4c ■ Some Cautionary Notes for Teachers

Observation is a useful and important tool in providing high-quality education and care for all children. It is important to remember, however, that if teachers or other caregivers have a concern about a possible developmental difference in a child in their care, they must demonstrate caution, sensitivity, and respect in how these concerns are shared with families. Teachers should not keep concerns to themselves, but should be careful not to raise concerns based on inference rather than actual observation. Some issues for teachers to consider are listed in Figure 10-7.

10-5 Individualized Family Service Plan

The centrality of the family in providing effective early intervention services is formally recognized in PL 99-457 (the 1986 amendment to PL 94-142, the Education for All Handicapped Children Act, now called IDEIA, the Individuals with Disabilities Education Improvement Act). The law broadened the services for children three to five years of age and developed a **discretionary program** (Part C) to provide services for children birth to three years old. This program, previously Part H, was changed to Part C in the IDEA 1997 reauthorization. Part C requires development of an **individualized family service plan (IFSP)** for each infant or toddler receiving early intervention services. The purpose of the IFSP is for family members and professionals to work together to identify priorities, resources, and concerns. Although similar to an **individualized education program (IEP)**, the planning document used for children older than three, an IFSP is a more interactive, dynamic, family-friendly document.

10-5a ■ IFSP Requirements

The purpose of the IFSP is to identify and organize resources to support families in rearing children who have developmental disabilities. The IDEIA defines the requirements of the IFSP. The process must include a multidisplinary assessment, and the written IFSP must be developed in partnership with the family (Deiner, 2013). Major stipulations of the IFSP are listed here.

- Help is to be provided in ways that meet the specific needs of each child and family.
- The IFSP is to be an ongoing process that supports but *does not take the place* of parents' natural caregiving roles.
- A major function of the IFSP is to preserve the principle that infants and toddlers are best served in natural environments.
- Family-centered as well as child-centered services are to be provided through an interdisciplinary team approach.
- Family members are to be essential participants on the team.
- Dates for initiation of service, length, frequency, and duration of services should be included in the IFSP.
- The natural environment in which services will be provided. If services are to be provided in a location other than a natural environment, an explanation of the reason for this should be included.
- A **service coordinator** is to be appointed to manage services and keep the program moving.
- Specific steps assuring a smooth transition to the next intervention program are to be described.

Pre-referral and case conferencing If a parent, caregiver, or teacher decides that a child needs to be evaluated, a pre-referral process is begun. During this process, the parent is asked to answer a few questions regarding the child's behavior at home. The questions may cover verbal skills, physical skills, language skills, or cognitive skills. The caregiver is also asked similar questions on the basis of classroom behavior. The parent and caregiver then confer to determine whether their results are the same, different, or similar. At this point the child may be referred for more formal assessments.

Identification of needs Once **parental consent** is obtained, each infant and toddler with special needs is to receive an interdisciplinary assessment as prescribed

---

discretionary program implies choice or options; Part H of PL 99-457 is discretionary: states decide whether they will provide services for handicapped infants and toddlers and their families.

individualized family service plan (IFSP) similar to an IEP. The IFSP describes services for very young children with disabilities (ages 0–3) and their families. The IFSP is mandated by PL 99-457. The IFSP is written collaboratively and describes the child's current strengths and needs. The IFSP describes what services will be provided and the major expected outcomes. Plans for the transition at age three are also included in the IFSP

individualized education program (IEP) a document that is mandated for every student with a disability (ages 3–21) by PL 94-142. The IEP is the blueprint for the services the child receives and must be developed every year. It describes the child's current level of functioning and includes short- and long-term goals and objectives. All IEPs must be approved by parents.

service coordinator an interdisciplinary team member responsible for integrating services and keeping the family informed and involved

parental consent parental permission for a program, assessment, or specific activity; given after parents have been informed about choices, risks, and benefits

A service coordinator is to be appointed to manage services and keep the program moving.

in the IEP requirements of PL 94-142. The assessment's purpose is to identify the child's competencies and strengths, as well as areas of need. The assessment should look at **functional skills** and the child's ability to adapt to the environment. This process must be family-driven: that is, family members should be involved in every step of the assessment process.

functional skills skills that are useful in everyday living

Family members are essential in identifying priorities and functional skills. Families who take ownership of goals are more likely to make those goals a priority in their family routine (Winton, McCollum, & Catlett, 1997). In addition, the assessment must be conducted in a culturally responsive manner (Lynch & Hanson, 2011; Barrera, 1994). This includes conducting the assessment in the child's native language (that is, the language in which the child is most competent); using assessment instruments that are appropriate for that language and culture; and interpreting the findings in a manner that takes cultural norms and practices into consideration.

The family is also asked to voluntarily participate in an interdisciplinary and interactive family assessment. The purpose of the family assessment is to identify the family's strengths and special needs as they relate to enhancing their child's development. It is important to note that this is a voluntary activity. Family members are invited to be as actively involved as they wish; however, the family's degree of involvement does not affect the child's eligibility for necessary services.

Non-intrusiveness Constant care is needed to ensure that families are benefited, rather than weakened or demeaned, by participation in the IFSP process. The law does not give permission for any professional to intrude uninvited into a family's life or lifestyle. Family members are not to be prodded into discussing private or sensitive matters. Information gleaned from professional probing has little or no bearing on the child's problems. The out-of-family perception of a family's needs often misses the mark (Harry, 1992).

Instead, it is likely to represent professionals' own biases and values. The entire IFSP process—developing, implementing, and evaluating—must be conducted in a culturally sensitive manner, including using an interpreter whenever needed.

A parent should be provided with choices in the assessment process.

Thus, the law's emphasis is on helping families identify their own needs and recognize their own abilities. In addition, the law protects families' confidences. Family-shared information must not be discussed casually among staff. Only when early intervention programs recognize and build on the diverse and specific strengths of each family will the IFSP concept fulfill its promise as a positive force in the lives of children and their families.

Wood and McCormick (2002) offer the following recommendations for supporting the family's role in the assessment process:

- Provide the family with choices in the assessment process.
- Conduct the assessment in the child's natural environment, with everyday materials and activities.
- Avoid professional jargon and acronyms.
- Present results in a strengths-based and family-friendly manner, using interpreters as needed.
- Provide time for questions.
- Provide information to parents on such things as development, the child's disability, or legislation.
- Provide information on resources such as respite.
- Encourage participation of the extended family or other family supports in the assessment and team meetings.

IFSP evaluation The IFSP is to be evaluated at least once a year. A review of the IFSP will be forwarded to the family every six months (more often, if the family so requests). The purpose of the evaluation and review is to appraise the progress made by the child and family toward the objectives spelled out in the IFSP. If progress is unsatisfactory, program revisions are in order.

Service coordination An interdisciplinary team approach to early intervention implies that a number of individuals are dealing with the same child and family. PL 99-457 requires one particular person, designated as a service coordinator, to be in charge of each case. The service coordinator is often chosen because of professional expertise in relationship to the child's primary problem. The communication specialist might be the service coordinator when the main concern revolves around speech and hearing, the physical therapist when there are troublesome motor delays, and the nutritionist in **failure-to-thrive** cases. In addition to providing clinical skill, the service coordinator needs to be a sensitive listener, a child and family advocate, and a linkage agent to services and resources.

The service coordinator is essential to team functioning and family support. Without a liaison or go-between, both the team and the family tend to become confused. There is duplication of efforts (the family may be put through three or four intake interviews, for example), intervention services lose continuity and coherence, and whole programs can fall into chaos and disintegration.

Generally speaking, the duties of the service coordinator are decided by each team. Assigned tasks might include:

- coordinating the individual child's assessments and identification of family needs with prescribed services.

- managing team and parent conferences.

- keeping records up to date and making appointments.

- coordinating the child's transition to other programs and providing follow-up services.

- serving continuously as a source of contact, interpretation, and support for the family.

To the maximum extent possible, parents are to have the opportunity to select their own service coordinator. In some instances, family choice cannot be an option, and a service coordinator must be assigned. A family who feels that its needs are not met adequately by the assigned service coordinator must be helped to find a more acceptable one.

Parents as service coordinators Parents who wish to serve as their own service coordinators should be encouraged and supported in their efforts. The law requires that training be provided in how the system and the network of backup services operate (Bailey, McLean, & Wolery, 2004). Gathering the necessary resources and assistance should not add to the family's burdens. Instead, the family should reap positive benefits and become stronger and more capable through the course of the process. Learning

Assessments should be conducted in the child's natural environment with everyday activities and materials.

© Cengage Learning

Parents who wish to serve as their own service coordinators should be encouraged and supported in their efforts.

© Cengage Learning

Did You Get It?

What are the differences between an individualized family service plan (IFSP) and an individualized education program (IEP)?

a. An IFSP is for an infant or toddler receiving early intervention services; an IEP is used for children older than three.

b. An IFSP is used for children older than three; an IEP is for an infant or toddler receiving early intervention services.

c. An IEP is a more interactive, dynamic, family-friendly document than the IEP.

d. An IFSP was created at an earlier time than the IEP.

Take the full quiz on CourseMate.

to take the responsibility for getting required assistance is one approach to reducing over-dependence on the service system.

Program-to-program transition PL 99-457 requires support for the child and family during transition from one program to another. The hallmark of effective early intervention is the child's graduation into a more advanced program. Frequently, that program is in a different setting. The transition between programs calls for a special kind of planning and support. The focus of Chapter 19 is on planning and implementing transitions. A sample IFSP is available on the companion website.

Individualized Education Program (IEP) 10-6 ☀

The Individualized Education Program (IEP) is a blueprint for providing intervention services. Teacher input is essential throughout the IEP process, as well as in the assessment of children, in the adaptation and modification of classroom activities to implement the individualized program, and in the evaluation process. The link between classroom practice and the treatment recommendations of the child-study team is forged by teachers. Furthermore, the ongoing evaluation of the appropriateness of each child's daily program is largely dependent on the teacher. In other words, teachers are central to the entire IEP process.

10-6a ■ The IEP Team

The IEP is developed by a child-study team made up of professionals from various disciplines. The child's parent or parents (or **parent surrogates**) and the child's teacher must be included in the IEP deliberations. The type of team and

parent surrogate individual appointed to act in place of a parent

the disciplines involved vary. Several models for child-study teams have emerged over the years.

- **Multidisciplinary**—professionals working independently of each other in a kind of parallel play format: Each discipline is viewed as important, but each team member takes responsibility only for his or her own area of clinical expertise.

- **Interdisciplinary**—professionals working together to identify priorities and develop goals; professionals coordinate and collaborate across disciplines and incorporate skills from other disciplines into their own practice. All disciplines will provide services in the most natural and least restrictive setting—usually the classroom. (The term **interdisciplinary** will be used in this text.)

- Transdisciplinary—professionals teaching each other through continuous staff development; joint team functioning; role release and role substitution; determining role definition (who does what) around the characteristics of each child and family; relying on each other to build on the range of strengths found among different types of child development experts.

Changes in the IEP process mandated by IDEA 1997 and reiterated in IDEA 2004 (now referred to as IDEIA) strengthen the relationship between the IEP and the general education program. A general education teacher, or a school district representative who is familiar with the general education curriculum, is now required to attend IEP meetings. This change reminds IEP teams that the purpose of special education is to provide access to the general education curriculum for children with disabilities. This requirement may be challenging for many early childhood special education providers, since many school districts do not provide programs for typically developing children before kindergarten, even though they are required to do so by law. Teachers, families, advocates, and administrators need to find ways to be in compliance with these changes and continue to conduct IEP meetings that are family-friendly and productive.

10-6b ■ Requirements of the IEP

The IEP is to be based on developmentally valid, nondiscriminatory assessment information. The program, services, and the least restrictive environment (LRE) are to be formulated from information from multiple sources: test scores, observation in situations in which the child is comfortable and at ease, and input from significant persons in the child's life (parents, grandparents, teachers, out-of-home caregivers). While the forms used will vary from state to state and district to district, every IEP document must include the same information.

The completed IEP includes statements about:

- the child's present levels of performance and skills developed.
- long-term (annual) goals for the child and short-term objectives that will accomplish the long-term goals.
- specific services to be provided and starting dates.
- accountability (evaluation) to determine whether objectives are being met.
- where and when inclusive programs will be provided.

These requirements will be discussed one by one. (Transition plans, required by PL 99-457, will be discussed in Chapter 19.)

Assessment Before an IEP is written, a child's development skills must be assessed. As described earlier, this is an information-gathering process. It is not, however, a one-time operation; instead, it should be an ongoing process throughout the year, so that a child's progress can be tracked and programs adjusted as needed. Ongoing assessment provides a comprehensive description—a developmental profile—of a child at particular points in time.

Depending on the results of earlier screening tests, specific disciplines (audiologists, nutritionists, physical therapists, and others) conduct specialized assessments. The early childhood teacher is responsible for collecting general information and often provides the "glue" for putting together the overall developmental picture of the child. As noted earlier, it is the teacher, working with a child every day, who is especially suited to assessing that child's strengths and needs. Observing the child's play in the classroom gives teachers valuable information about his or her developmental skills and the effectiveness of intervention strategies.

Note: It is necessary to watch a child over several days and several play episodes. Consecutive observations ensure that what is observed is representative of the child's everyday behaviors (McClean, Bailey, & Wolery, 2004).

Numerous assessment instruments have been developed over the past thirty years. (The companion website for this text provides a partial list of assessment tools.) In addition, there are developmental profile forms that many teachers of young children find even more useful.

The developmental skills profiles offered in this text (Appendix B) have been used extensively by teachers for ongoing assessments of children from birth to age six. A separate chart or profile is kept on each child. Periodic observations are made of each child in several areas: gross and fine motor skills; pre-academics; self-help; music, art, and stories; social and play behaviors; and receptive and expressive language. The itemized skills on the chart are merely examples of behaviors characteristic of broad, general skills. A child may show achievement in various ways. For example, an item in the 0-to-12 months pre-academic square reads: "Puts blocks in, takes blocks out of container." The basic skill is picking up and releasing an object within a prescribed space. An infant who can pick up a cookie, drop it in a cup, and then take it out should receive a passing score.

Highlighter pens of several colors allow a quick reading of each child's status in all developmental areas. Items that the child passes in the initial assessment are lined through in one color; a different color is used for each subsequent assessment. Skills that a child does not have are left unmarked. Inconsistent successes—responses that a child displays infrequently—are especially important. They should not be lined through, but flagged, perhaps with an asterisk. These *sometimes* responses often indicate appropriate starting points for a specific intervention program.

The profile is updated periodically on the basis of observations and notes made by teachers as they work with children. The updating usually reveals that each child has acquired some of the flagged *sometimes* skills. Skills that were left unmarked in an earlier assessment often become a newly marked set of *sometimes* skills. Thus, the teaching staff has on hand at all times a current, visual profile of each child: word pictures of overall functioning in relationship to developmental expectations for children of similar ages.

Annual goals The IEP must include written statements for each child specifying expected learning outcomes for the school year. Annual goals are usually presented as broad, general statements about what can be expected of the child. Example: Erin will learn to: (1) be more independent; (2) get along with other children; (3) use nonaggressive ways to get what she wants.

Long-term goals center on priorities essential to the child's overall development. These sometimes are referred to as "functional goals" (Notari-Syverson & Shuster, 1995). As the team determines the goals for a child, care is taken to ensure that the goal fits naturally into the child's routine. If it does not, the goal should be reconsidered to determine whether that goal or skill is practical or functional for the child, family, and early childhood education setting. For every child, the number and kind of goals will vary. Goals for a child should never be so numerous or so complex as to overwhelm the child and family. Good goals address all developmental domains and progress from simple to complex. Furthermore, self-sufficiency goals, as important as they are, should not rule out goals that help to improve the child's self-esteem and enjoyment of life. For example, Melinda was a bright and lively child born with severely malformed hands. Even as an infant, it was obvious she had a talent and love for music and rhythm. While long-term goals for this child must include learning to use a **prosthesis** on each hand (a major priority), her musical development is important, too. At least one goal related to music should be written into Melinda's IEP.

prosthesis artificial device replacing body parts that are damaged at birth or later removed

Writing goals Many educators use the acronym of SMART when developing IEP goals. The term "SMART IEPs" describes IEPs that are specific, measurable, use action words, are realistic and relevant, and time-limited.

S: Specific

M: Measurable

A: Use Action Words

R: Realistic and relevant

T: Time-limited

Another way to determine the quality of an IEP goal is to be sure that it answers the following six questions:

1. **WHO?**—this refers to the student
   Expressed by noun or pronoun, i.e., the student

2. **WHAT?**—observable behavior
   Expressed in action words, verbs that are open to few interpretations, i.e., will trace the letter

3. **WHEN?**—date in time
   i.e., by _____ (date)

4. **GIVEN WHAT?**—conditions
   Describes what needs to be in place for the completion of the goal.
   i.e., When given a verbal direction …

5. **HOW MUCH?**—mastery/criteria
   i.e., 5 times weekly, with fewer than 3 prompts, or 7 out of 10 trials with 80 percent accuracy.

6. **HOW WILL IT BE MEASURED?**—data
   Include types of data such as work samples, data collection strategies, portfolios, teacher observations, and assessments—i.e., as measured by teacher observation and daily data collection.

The following are examples of "SMART IEP goals":

- When shown 10 high-frequency reading words, the student will match action pictures to the appropriate sign with 100% accuracy 3 out of 4 trials by the end of the first reporting period as measured by teacher checklist.

FIGURE 10-8
An Example of Short-Term Objective

> **Annual Goal**
> Given a three-step direction, Joseph will promptly follow all three steps, in the correct order, for 9 out of 10 opportunities.
>
> **Short-Term Objectives**
>
> 1. Given a one-step direction, Joseph will promptly follow the direction for 9 out of 10 opportunities.
>
> 2. Given a two-step direction, Joseph will promptly follow at least the first of the two steps for 9 out of 10 opportunities.
>
> 3. Given a two-step direction, Joseph will promptly follow both directions for 9 out of 10 opportunities.

© Cengage Learning

- By 2/14/14, when given child-sized scissors and a shape to cut, the student will cut along the line within 1/8 inch of it for 3 of 4 opportunities as measured by work samples.

- By March 2014, when given 10 one-inch cubes and the instruction to "build," Sam will stack the blocks to build a structure for 4 of 5 opportunities as measured by teacher observations.

Short-term objectives In IDEA 2004, Congress eliminated the requirements for short-term objectives and benchmarks in IEPs for students with disabilities, except for students who take alternate assessments. While their elimination was meant to save on resources, their use is extremely helpful in planning and assessing whether the annual goal will be achieved. They can be extremely helpful to parents in determining if their child's progress is on track. Short-term objectives break the annual goal into smaller components that can be achieved during each quarter of the year. An example is shown in Figure 10-8.

Specific services to be provided A statement of the specific intervention services, supports, and equipment to be provided for each child must be included in every IEP. In addition to a list of what services will be provided, an IEP should contain a description of how services will be provided. This is especially important with the movement toward activity-based intervention (Pretti-Frontczak & Bricker, 2004).

Activity-based or naturalistic intervention embeds the specialized instruction that the child needs into the ongoing activities of an early childhood classroom. For example, rather than removing a child from the classroom, the physical therapist will join the class during outdoor playtime and work with John on his hopping. In another example, the speech therapist might conduct a cooking activity during the free-choice time where she can address the language objectives of many children at once. This type of naturalistic intervention has been demonstrated to be more effective than **pull-out** types of therapy services (Noonan & McCormick, 1993).

activity-based intervention method of providing early intervention services in which teaching opportunities are embedded in regularly scheduled classroom activities

pull-out services a model of delivering specialized support such as physical therapy or speech therapy in which the child is removed from the classroom and taken to a special therapy setting

As the team determines the goals for a child, care is taken to ensure that the goal fits naturally into the child's routine.

© Cengage Learning

Depending on the individual needs of a child, the specific services section of an IEP might contain requirements for:

- biweekly in-class sessions with a speech therapist or physical therapist (or both).
- bus service to and from preschool.
- special educational support services provided by an **itinerant special education teacher**.
- monthly consultations with a behavior specialist to assist in behavior management issues.

itinerant special education teacher special education teacher who works as a consultant with the regular classroom teacher or directly with children with disabilities in a community-based early childhood program, such as a child care or Head Start program

Projected dates for services Projected starting and stopping dates are to be specified for each service prescribed for a child. For example, Amanda will receive orientation and mobility training at her home two afternoons a week and at school one morning a week from October 1 until the end of the semester, when it will be determined if training is to continue.

Two reasons lie behind the timeline mandate. One is to ensure that no child is left waiting indefinitely for services essential to his or her progress. The second is to prevent special services from being terminated prematurely. A reasonable length of time must be allowed for accomplishing the objectives and goals stated in the child's IEP.

Discipline IDEA 2004 reiterated mandated changes in IEP regulations related to issues of discipline and challenging behaviors. All children who demonstrate challenging behaviors should have a behavior plan as part of their IEP. The behavior plan should be based on a functional behavior assessment (FBA). The purpose of the FBA is to determine what is maintaining the challenging behavior. The behavior plan must also include positive behavior support strategies that will be used to help the child be successful in the least restrictive environment (LRE).

Evaluation (statement of accountability) At least once a year, each child's program must be reviewed to see whether objectives are being met. A program review is to be based on specifically described procedures such as test scores, data collection, and written observations. In practice, program reviews should be conducted more often than once a year. This is important, so that if changes in teaching practices are warranted due to lack of progress, these changes can be made. Every three years, a child is evaluated to determine whether placement in a special program is still necessary. Evaluation allows the team to determine whether any changes in placement or category are needed. As children mature, some learn coping skills for working with their disability and may not need services any longer. As mentioned earlier, an in-place system of ongoing assessments simplifies the procedure. The developmental skill profile, for example, provides both ongoing assessment and program evaluation (see Appendix B). Every item on the

Case Study ▪ An IEP dilemma ▪

You are a kindergarten teacher and have sent an IEP parent notification letter about a child's progress. The parent did not respond. You sent a second letter and made a phone call. The child is continuing to regress. You decide to hold the IEP meeting without the parent.

What consequences, if any, do you foresee from your actions? At what point can the teacher decide to hold the IEP meeting without the parent? Research your state's rules and regulations regarding parent contact and participation in IEP meetings.

profile describes a specific behavior; its presence or absence can be noted by a teacher. Graphs also provide program accountability. By using the skill profile to periodically assess a child and by keeping graphs of a child's progress, a convincing evaluation process is always in operation. A new parent resource available to guide parents through the IEP process and the vocabulary is the "IEP Checklist app" from iPhone. This is a free application developed by the Parent Educational Advocacy Training Center and is available from the iTunes store.

Computer-Based Information Systems Many school districts are using technology to streamline the IEP process. Programs such as SEIS (Special Education Information System), a web-based IEP/school district system developed in 2003 by the San Joaquin County Office of Education, enables all team members to have access to the same working documents. Team members can write goals, update progress, and add attachments to a student's file. Attachments might include a written assessment report or a report from an outside professional. The system even contains a goal-bank for providers to choose goals from. Changes to the IEP document can be made during the IEP meeting so that the parent can be provided with an accurate copy at the conclusion of the meeting. This use of technology makes it easier for team members to collaborate, allows them to have ongoing access to view each other's goals, progress updates and reports, and saves paper because not every team member needs to keep a hard copy of the documents. One caveat with such systems is that some school districts are choosing to project the documents on a screen during IEP meetings. While this is helpful so that all team members can see what is being written and proposed, caution should be taken to be sure that it does not interfere with the parents' and professionals' ability to benefit from the face-to-face discussion of the entire team. These give-and-take exchanges are the crux of the IEP process and should not be short-changed with the introduction of technology.

> **Did You Get It?**
>
> How would a teacher determine that what has been observed is indicative of the child's everyday behaviors?
> a. Watch the child over several days and several play episodes.
> b. Watch the child over the course of a day.
> c. Watch the child in a focused play episode.
> d. Watch the child in various play episodes over the course of a day.
>
> Take the full quiz on CourseMate.

504 Plans 10-7

The Section 504 regulations require a school district to provide a "free and appropriate public education" (FAPE) to each qualified student with a disability who is in the school district's jurisdiction, regardless of the nature or severity of the disability. Under Section 504, FAPE consists of the provision of regular or special education and related aids and services designed to meet the student's individual educational needs as adequately as the needs of non-disabled students are met (www.ed.gov, 2009).

Services under a 504 plan can be provided either in the regular classroom, a regular classroom with specialized services, and/or a resource classroom. Typically students who have a 504 plan instead of an IEP are students who qualify for services but don't need as much guidance and help as those who have an IEP. For example, students who qualify under IDEIA for services, but just need them consultatively, may be better served under a 504 plan. School systems with budget cuts do not always serve children consultatively, so the 504 plan enables the child to receive services in a more relaxed manner.

10-7a ■ Requirements of the 504 Plan

To be protected under Section 504, a student must be determined to: (1) have a physical or mental impairment that substantially limits one or more major life activities; or (2) have a record of such an impairment; or (3) be regarded as having such an impairment.

The Section 504 regulatory provision at 34 C.F.R. 104.3(j)(2)(i) defines a physical or mental impairment as any physiological disorder or condition, cosmetic disfigurement, or anatomical loss affecting one or more of the following body systems: neurological; musculoskeletal; special sense organs; respiratory, including speech organs; cardiovascular; reproductive; digestive; genito-urinary; hematic and lymphatic; skin; and endocrine; or any mental or psychological disorder, such as mental retardation,* organic brain syndrome, emotional or mental illness, and specific learning disabilities (www.ed.gov, 2009).

To qualify for a 504 plan, students still need to be assessed, using the same evaluations as those required for an IEP. States are at liberty for determining which assessments to use. The assessments generally include teacher recommendations, classroom observations, education and achievement aptitude tests, cultural norms, and adaptive behavior. Medical diagnosis from a doctor does not guarantee a child a 504 plan. The state-approved assessments must be used to determine eligibility.

Once a student has a 504 plan, it remains in place indefinitely. States need to determine how often to re-evaluate, but it is not a set time frame, like the IEP. Typically, states re-evaluate every three years. See Table 10-1, which outlines the similarities and differences between IFSPs, IEPs, and 504 plans.

TABLE 10-1

Comparative Table for IFSP, IEP, and 504 Plans

Individualized Family Service Plan (IFSP) Birth through age 2	Individualized Education Program (IEP) Ages 3 through 21 years	504 Plan Ages 3 through 21 years
Focuses on the family and parents' role in supporting the child's learning and development	Focuses on the child	Focuses on the child
Outcomes focus not only on the child, but on the family	Outcomes focus on the child	Outcomes focus on the child
Includes the concept of natural environments as places where learning occurs, such as at home, in child care, outdoors in parks, and so on (services may be provided in the home)	Focuses on school and classroom environments, with services provided in the school setting	Focuses on school and classroom environments, with services provided in the school setting
Involves many agencies in providing services because of the child's age; the IFSP integrated the services	Assigns the local school district to manage the child's services	Assigns the local school district to manage the child's services
Names a service coordinator, who assists the family in carrying out the plan	Authorizes the local school district to coordinate the program	Authorizes the local school district to coordinate the program
Involves an initial meeting with the family to offer information and resources and to define the various agencies' roles and financial responsibility	Involves a meeting with the family to develop long-term and short-term goals for the child, accommodations and modifications, services, and child placement	Involves a meeting with the family to develop accommodations and modifications
Typically includes a meeting with the family every six months	Typically includes a meeting once a year	Includes a meeting when a change is needed by either the parent or teacher

© Cengage Learning

TeachSource Digital Download Download from CourseMate.

*As noted earlier, the term is now intellectual disability.

Summary

▶ Case finding and the identification of developmental problems can take place any time after the first few weeks of conception.

▶ The earlier a problem is identified, the more likely it is that it can be treated effectively and that associated problems can be prevented. To this end, federally funded mass screening programs referred to as Child Find are regular events in most communities. All young children (except those with obvious disabling conditions) should be screened because many problems are subtle and difficult to recognize.

▶ Many kinds of screening instruments are available. Some are geared to overall development, some to specialized areas such as hearing and vision, some to particular ages or developmental domains. Whatever the test, it must be given in the child's first language with scrupulous regard for the customs of the child's family and the child's physical and psychological state.

▶ More than one instrument must be used in the assessment process. Even then, the results of many tests must be viewed with extreme caution, especially IQ tests.

▶ Most early childhood educators view standardized IQ tests as being of little value when working with young children.

▶ Teachers are major agents in the early identification process. Direct observation is a teacher's best tool in determining a child's developmental status and the suitability of specific classroom activities for the group and for individual children.

▶ Observation forms and checklists, especially those that teachers devise themselves, help teachers answer questions about children's behavior and classroom practices. Teachers must always use their information with care and in the best interests of the child and family.

▶ IDEIA provides for the individualized educational programming for children with disabilities between the ages of zero and twenty-one. Individualized educational planning occurs through the IFSP and IEP processes.

▶ IFSPs are mandated by Part C of IDEIA. They are used with children from birth to age three who are receiving early intervention services.

▶ IEPs are mandated by Part B of IDEIA and are used for students receiving special education from age three to twenty-one.

▶ There are many similarities between IFSPs and IEPs. Both require parent participation, both must be in written form and follow a number of procedural safeguards, and both include descriptions of a child's strengths, needs, and objectives to be addressed.

▶ The IFSP is more family-centered. It also requires that a family service coordinator be designated.

▶ The IEP is more school-oriented, requires the participation of a general educator on the team, and is focused toward helping the student access and succeed in the general education curriculum.

▶ A 504 plan may be developed for a child who is having difficulty, but does not meet the requirements for an IEP. A 504 plan can provide a child with the same or similar services as an IEP. The plan stays with the child until it is deemed unnecessary. It should be re-evaluated similarly to an IEP.

Key Terms

activity-based intervention, 273
case finding, 248
Child Find, 249
comprehensive screening, 250
criterion-referenced assessment, 247
discretionary program, 265
duration measures, 259
failure to thrive, 268
frequency counts, 259
functional skills, 266

individualized education program (IEP), 265
individualized family service plan (IFSP), 265
instructional utility, 247
IQ tests, 247
itinerant special education teacher, 274
norm-referenced assessments, 247
paraprofessional, 250
parent surrogate, 269
parental consent, 265

portfolio, 247
prosthesis, 272
pull-out services, 273
reliable, 250
screening, 250
sensitivity, 250
service coordinator, 265
specificity, 250
standardized tests, 247
transdisciplinary team, 270
valid, 250

Student Activities

1. Arrange to observe an early childhood classroom. Take a frequency count of how often the teacher initiates conversation with children. Do the same on another day with a different teacher. Compare the observations.

2. Select a partner. Independently of the other, take a half-hour running record of the same child. Compare your observations to see whether you were seeing the same things. Critique each other's running records for objectivity.

3. Contact a local early intervention provider or the state Part C coordinator and request a copy of an IFSP form. Contact a local school district or your state educational agency and request a copy of an IEP form. Compare and contrast these forms to each other and to the requirements as explained in the text.

4. Make a copy of the Skill Profile which can be found in Appendix B. Observe the same child for 30 to 45 minutes on three different days. Draw a horizontal line through the chart, indicating the child's age. Using a highlighter pen, color through the skills that you see the child engage in during your observations. (The skills may be on either side of the line.) Show the completed profile to the child's teacher. Ask the teacher to discuss with you how well your profile assesses the observed child.

5. Go to a nearby park and complete a running record for a child for a minimum of 20 minutes. When done, review your record and determine if you used words that described what happened rather than words that summarized. What judgments could you make about the child's development based on your running record?

6. Obtain the IFSP and IEP forms used by a local district. Compare the various components. Using Table 10-1, provide specific examples of how the forms and processes vary between the two.

7. Write SMART goals for a child who needs to learn to write their name, and put their belongings in their cubby independently.

Review Questions

Briefly respond to the following items.

1. What is Child Find?
2. What is the purpose of screening programs?
3. Who conducts diagnosis?
4. What is an IFSP?
5. What is the difference between a norm-referenced and a criterion-referenced test?
6. What is the referral process?
7. Who develops the IEP?
8. Define long-term IEP goals and short-term objectives.
9. Why graph behavioral data?
10. What is meant by a *statement of accountability* as related to the IEP?

Helpful Websites

National Association for the Education of Young Children

http://www.naeyc.org

NAEYC's website includes a resource catalog, professional development materials, and links to related sites. Of note is the NAEYC position statement on standardized testing of young children aged three through eight (adopted in 1987).

National Dissemination Center for Children with Disabilities (NICHCY)

http://www.NICHCY.org

NICHCY is the national dissemination center that provides information on disabilities and disability-related issues. Anyone can use their services—families, educators, administrators, journalists, students. Information is available about specific disabilities, IEPs, education rights and laws, early intervention, parent materials, and more.

U.S. Department of Education Office of Civil Rights

http://www.ed.gov

The U.S. Department of Education is the agency of the federal government that establishes policy for, administers, and coordinates most federal assistance to education. It assists the president in executing his education policies for the nation and in implementing laws enacted by Congress. The department's mission is to serve America's students —to ensure that all have equal access to education and to promote excellence in the nation's schools.

Wrightslaw

www.wrightslaw.com

Wrightslaw provides accurate, reliable information about special education law, education law, and advocacy for children with disabilities. It is designed to be used by parents, educators, advocates, and attorneys. It contains numerous articles on IDEIA and the IEP process.

 Visit the Education CourseMate for this textbook to access the eBook, Did You Get It? quizzes, Digital Downloads, TeachSource Video Cases, flashcards, and more. Go to CengageBrain.com to log in, register, or purchase access.

Characteristics of Effective Teachers in Inclusive Programs

OBJECTIVES

After reading this chapter, you should be able to:

11-1   discuss the role of the early childhood teacher as a member of a team.

11-2   highlight the applied developmental approaches and discuss developmental principles.

11-3   list eight or more characteristics found among effective teachers of young children in inclusive programs.

• • • • • • • • • • • • • • • •

naeyc

The following NAEYC Standards are addressed in this chapter:

STANDARD 1 Promoting Child Development and Learning

STANDARD 2 Building Family and Community Relationships

STANDARD 3 Observing, Documenting and Assessing to Support Young Children and Families

STANDARD 4 Using Developmentally Effective Approaches

STANDARD 5 Using Content Knowledge to Build Meaningful Curriculum

STANDARD 6 Becoming a Professional

CONNECTIONS

- Mary Sims, an experienced early childhood educator, volunteered to teach in an inclusive preschool in her community. Murphy was the first child with overall delayed development and several challenging behaviors to be enrolled in her classroom. His mother reported that by age three-and-a-half, he had been seen by seventeen specialists. The next two years were both challenging and rewarding for Mary and her assistant teacher as they worked with and learned from Murphy's mother and several members of an interdisciplinary team. When Murphy was seven years old, his carefully planned and executed transition to a public school first grade was accomplished.

- Kindergarten teacher Joanna began the art activity by explaining to the children that she was going to close her eyes and give them each a dot marker to use on the class mural. She went on to explain that if they wanted a color different from what they had received, they had to use their first color to make five dots on the mural, and then they could ask to trade with a friend.

Teachers are the most significant element in early childhood classrooms. Program quality is determined by teachers' skills in managing the learning environment. Quality is further determined by teachers' personal attitudes about children and about themselves, and by their philosophical beliefs on how children learn.

Cartwright (1999) reminds us that good teachers are approachable and friendly. They listen well, give support as needed, and share in laughter with, not at, the child (p. 5). In the inclusive classroom, the need for quality teaching is critical.

Developmental diversity among children calls for skilled and sensitive teachers who will respond to children's special needs with a range of individualized programs. At the same time, inclusive classrooms call for teachers who recognize that young children with developmental disabilities are more like typically developing children than they are different from them.

All children need learning activities that are geared to their individual levels of development and interests. Typically developing children need such experiences; gifted children need them; children with developmental delays and disabilities need them. Effective teachers use the developmental approach in every aspect of their teaching. They recognize that all children have basic needs and that all children have special needs. They recognize further that special needs cannot be met unless basic developmental needs also are met.

This chapter focuses on teaching skills and general principles that apply to all young children and all early childhood teachers. The point to be emphasized is this: *If children with developmental problems are to benefit from special approaches, learning activities must take place within a developmental framework.*

This chapter will focus on a brief review of basic developmental principles of greatest significance in early childhood education. These principles apply to every type of early childhood program. The principles apply, also, to every type of child—developmentally disabled, typically developing, and gifted.

11-1 Teachers as Members of a Team

Teaching in an inclusive early childhood program is both challenging and rewarding. Skilled teachers enjoy the diversity once they are convinced of the underlying developmental similarities among children. Children reflect the ethnic,

Preparing Teachers to Work with Culturally and Linguistically Diverse Children

NAEYC's position statement "Responding to Linguistic and Cultural Diversity" (1995) states that it is critical for teachers to have the skills to recognize that all children are cognitively, linguistically, and emotionally connected to the language and culture of their home. These skills should be learned beginning in their teacher preparation programs. Although many programs require students to take some coursework related to diversity issues, there is evidence that many teachers do not feel prepared to support the learning of the diverse children they find in their classrooms.

Ray and Bowman (2003) conducted a study in Chicago and found that the majority of the teachers surveyed had learned how to work with culturally diverse children and families from other teachers and from their own firsthand knowledge, not from their teacher preparation programs.

Lim and Able-Boone (2005) stated that simply having a culture-specific class or two is not sufficient to prepare teachers to meet the needs of today's diverse young children and their families. After conducting a literature review, they identified the following four strategies as promising key features of programs that effectively address cultural diversity.

- Infusion of cultural diversity throughout the curriculum
- Field experiences providing opportunities to work with diverse children and families
- Learning experiences designed for students to confront their biases, values, and culture
- Community–university partnerships

Sources: Daniel, J., & Friedman S. (2005). Preparing teachers to work with culturally and linguistically diverse children. *Beyond the Journal, Young Children on the Web*, November 2005. NAEYC: Washington, DC.

Lim, C. I., & Able-Boone, H. (2005). Diversity competencies within early childhood teacher preparation: Innovative practices and future directions. *Journal of Early Childhood Teacher Education, 26*, 225–238.

Ray, A., & Bowman, B. (2003). Learning multicultural competence: Developing early childhood practitioners' effectiveness in working with children from culturally diverse communities. Final report to the A.L. Mailman Family Foundation. Initiative on Race, Class, and Culture in Early Childhood. Erikson Institute: Chicago, IL.

racial, linguistic, and cultural diversity of their community. Every child comes from a family with its own traditions, beliefs, and life ways. "Life ways consist of a family's cultural customs, courtesies, beliefs, values, practices, manner of interacting, roles, relationships, language, rituals, and expected behaviors" (Luera, 1993). This diversity adds both richness and challenge to the program. The richness comes from the opportunities that children, families, and teachers have to learn from and about each other.

The challenge comes in creating learning experiences that are culturally sensitive to all the children and their families in the classroom. Teachers must be especially aware of the interplay of language, culture, and disability and its effect on young children and their families (Hanson & Brennan, 1997). For children with disabilities, not speaking the dominant language may further erode positive social interactions and learning opportunities unless adequate supports are provided.

The children will vary greatly in their abilities and needs. Most will be typical in their development. Some may have physical disabilities, health impairments,

Skilled teachers enjoy the diversity found in working with children of varying abilities.

or sensory impairments, but will be developing normally in the cognitive domain. Others may have language delays and cognitive delays, but be developing typically in the motor domain. A few children may have multiple or severe disabilities.

No single professional can meet the needs of all the diverse learners in an inclusive program. Early childhood teachers can make their job much easier if they seek the assistance of specialists (Klein, Cook, & Richardson-Gibbs, 2001). Teachers become members of a team of professionals who work together to meet the needs of all the children. Team members may include the parents, a speech pathologist, an early childhood special educator, an occupational therapist, an applied behavior analyst, a psychologist, and an inclusion specialist.

Each member brings specialized knowledge to planning and implementing individualized programs for children with special needs. Teamwork is especially important in providing the systematic instruction that is necessary to meet the needs of children with challenging behaviors or severe disabilities.

The expertise that the early childhood educator brings to the team is the ability to create a classroom environment and learning activities that are fun, motivating, safe, interesting, responsive, and supportive for every child.

11-1a ■ Teachers' Concerns

At the mention of inclusion, many teachers are concerned about having to work unassisted with children with challenging behaviors or disabilities. While early childhood teachers are generally positive about including children with disabilities in their classrooms, researchers have found that teachers worry about their ability to implement inclusive practices, and they need support to meet the requirements of children with disabilities (Buell, Hallam, Gamel McCormick, & Scheer, 1999; Forlin, 1995; Watson & McCathern, 2009). Odom (2000) reported similar findings with preschool teachers, who were concerned about their lack of knowledge of children with disabilities. This unease is understandable; however, in many cases support services are available to the teacher. Support may be related services such as occupational therapy, physical therapy, or speech therapy; instructional assistance from an early childhood special education teacher; or extra assistance in the classroom provided by an aide.

Insights about teachers' anxieties in relation to inclusion are provided by Blasi and Priestley (1998), who were concerned about including a child with a severe hearing loss in their classroom. They recount their experiences and report that the year was rewarding for them as well as for the child. One of their conclusions is that teachers must be willing to educate themselves. They urge teachers to seek out information and resources that will help them understand the special challenges the child faces. Armed with the information they acquire, they can, in turn, help other children understand the challenges faced by the child with special needs.

Blasi and Priestley's experience is confirmed by a research study conducted among twenty-two early childhood educators working in school settings with children three to seven years of age. Kilgallon (2003) found that as teachers got to know a child with special needs, they were better able to plan for and teach the child. She found that the teachers did have an understanding of the child's needs and effective teaching strategies, but that factors such as lack of resources, access to information, support and opportunities for collaboration, training, and time affected the teachers' perceived competence as well as their attitudes and ability to include children with disabilities in their classrooms successfully. This research confirms that in many cases it may be the teachers' responsibility to seek out the knowledge they need.

11-1b ■ Supplemental Professional Development

To provide effectively for children with developmental disabilities, teachers do not need extensive retraining. What teachers *do* need is additional knowledge about specific developmental disabilities before each child with a particular problem is about to be enrolled. Teachers also need on-the-job experience with special children, but always with help from support staff and the parents of the child. The kinds of information offered in this text provide a useful and comprehensive starting point. Additional training options are available.

Many teachers are concerned about working with children with challenging behaviors or disabilities without support.

© Cengage Learning

- All states have a designated lead agency for implementation of PL 99-457. These agencies provide community-based, in-service training for professionals working with young children.

- Most states have regional and local chapters of NAEYC that provide annual conferences and other educational programs.

- Two-year colleges and vocational/technical schools often are sources of early childhood and special child teacher-training programs.

- Nationwide, Head Start provides training for their staff on how to include children with disabilities.

- Many local, state, and regional child care organizations now offer training on how to include children with disabilities in child care programs.

- Workshops and seminars sponsored by agencies such as United Cerebral Palsy and ARC are available in many communities.

Agencies and service organizations that focus on specific developmental problems can recommend or provide videos, DVDs, articles, books, and other kinds of information. These materials describe disabilities and the associated problems that confront the child, family, and teachers. For example, the American Association for the Blind will provide helpful materials to the families and teachers of children with visual disabilities. Such materials are used in conjunction with information provided by the family.

Teachers need information about specific developmental disabilities before the child is enrolled.

© Cengage Learning

Finally, parents are the best source of information about their children's disabilities. No special coursework or training can take the place of the information that parents have to offer.

11-1c ■ Teacher and Program Self-evaluation

As mentioned previously, teachers may have concerns about welcoming a child with special needs into their classrooms and programs. Individual accommodations may be necessary to meet a child's needs and remove barriers that prevent the child from fully participating. Program staff must be willing to examine the various components of their program to evaluate where changes might need to be made. Components for examination include both the physical environment, communication with family, assessment, curriculum, and strategies for promoting positive behavior, as well as their own personal biases and experiences. Watson and McCathren (2009) developed a "Preschool and Kindergarten Inclusion Readiness Checklist" that provides a series of questions to assist teachers in the process of examining their classrooms.

☀ 11-2 The Applied Developmental Approach

11-2a ■ A Child Is a Child

It is true that early childhood teachers do not need extensive special training to teach in an inclusive early childhood setting. They do, however, need a particular mind-set: seeing each child first of all as a child, rather than as a stutterer, a behavior problem, or a child with low vision. By first viewing every child as a child, teachers come to realize that many behaviors are not related necessarily to a child's disability. Blaming a child's tantrums, excessive shyness, or aggressiveness on his or her disability is seldom justified. More accurate and more helpful to the child is to view the problem as a developmental irregularity or cultural diversity seen in many children to a greater or lesser degree.

Children's speech is a prime example. Individual children speak differently, just as communities speak differently. Consider the many ways the English language is used in this country; obviously, there is no one *right* use of the language. Difference does not imply a developmental disorder.

11-2b ■ Review of Developmental Principles

Teachers who work with children with developmental disabilities need, first and foremost, a thorough foundation in normal growth and development. To recognize and evaluate developmental deviations, teachers must have an understanding of the range and variations of behaviors and skill levels found among both normal and special populations.

Developmental sequences As emphasized in earlier chapters, the sequence of development rather than chronological age is a key factor in working with young children. Effective teachers operate on the principle that it is more useful to know that a child is moving steadily forward than to know that the child is above or below the "norm."

Example: A thirty-nine-month-old child with a central nervous system (CNS) disorder is just beginning to pull up to a standing position. The child's teachers are predicting that she soon will be walking and are planning her program accordingly. How can the teachers be so confident? Easy. They know this child has passed, in order (though late), each of the preceding large motor milestones.

Interrelationships among developmental domains Understanding the interrelatedness of developmental areas is important, too. Recognizing that each area of development affects, and is affected by, every other area, is essential when teaching young children.

Example: A developmentally delayed four-and-a-half-year-old had refused solid foods throughout his life. Clinical findings indicated that the prolonged soft diet, requiring little chewing, had contributed to poorly developed muscle tone, hence poorly controlled movement of the mouth and tongue. One result was almost unintelligible speech that, in turn, played a part in delayed cognitive and social development.

Developmental inconsistencies As noted again and again, development is an irregular process, even among typically developing children. **Developmental inconsistency** is to be expected. A period of rapid development often is followed by an unsettled period known as **developmental disequilibrium**. During such periods, children seem to be developmentally disorganized: calm and capable one moment, screamingly frustrated (and frustrating) the next. Some children may even regress—appear to go backward—for a while.

Example: A three-year-old with a nine-month-old sister beginning to compete for attention may revert to babyish ways. He may have a tantrum for no apparent reason, lose bladder control that seemed to be well established, or demand a bedtime bottle that had been given up months before. His teachers help his parents to understand that their child is continuing to progress well in every other aspect of development, and therefore it is unlikely that the current problems will persist. Both parents and teachers agree to continue to observe the child carefully in the event the situation does not right itself within a reasonable period.

developmental inconsistency learned behavior that may "come and go" before a final consolidation into the child's overall behavior pattern

developmental disequilibrium a period of inconsistent behavior that often follows a spurt of rapid development

The transactional process Continuous transactions occur between children and their environment. Children are dynamic individuals who are affected by, and have an effect upon, almost everyone and everything they come in contact with (Horowitz, 1987). Learning of some kind is going on in every child every day. These **transactional learning** interactions can be both positive and negative; they are the consequence of direct and indirect (or unintended) teaching.

> **transactional learning**
> interactions between a child and the environment that facilitate new learnings

It is easy for teachers to recognize their role in promoting intentional teachings: They set up appropriate curriculum activities, respond to children positively, and allow children to explore and experiment. Teachers are seldom aware of the unintentional teaching that goes on in a classroom. Having only one large tricycle or a meager number of unit blocks for a large group of four-year-olds may teach more about shoving and pushing, waiting endlessly, or doing without than the fine and gross motor skills the materials were intended to promote.

The following excerpt from a frequently cited case study (Allen & Goetz, 1982) focuses on efforts to help a child extend his attention span. The situation illustrates how a problem behavior may be maintained because of teachers' well-intentioned efforts to correct it.

> *James was a five-year-old who seldom stayed with an activity more than a moment or two. Teachers were constantly trying to settle him down and get him interested in something. But James continued to flit—more than ever, it seemed. What was he learning from the teachers' efforts? Certainly not to focus his attention, which was their goal. Instead, he was learning, at some unrecognized level, that flitting about was a sure way to get the teacher attention he needed and could not seem to get in any other way.*

Fascinating accounts of a similar process are found in a number of studies. One example is Fraiberg's (1974) account of transactions between blind infants and their mothers. The infant's inability to see the mother's face interferes with his or her ability to respond to her smiles. The unresponsiveness often is perceived by the mother as rejection. Without her realizing it, her behavior changes, and she smiles less and less. Both mother and baby, through no fault of their own, promote mutual unresponsiveness. This comes at a critical developmental period when both need to be engaging in the reciprocally reinforcing behaviors that lead to a strong parent–child attachment, an essential early step in acquiring social skills. A reminder: though negative examples were cited, positive adult–child transactions have an equally powerful potential for promoting healthy development.

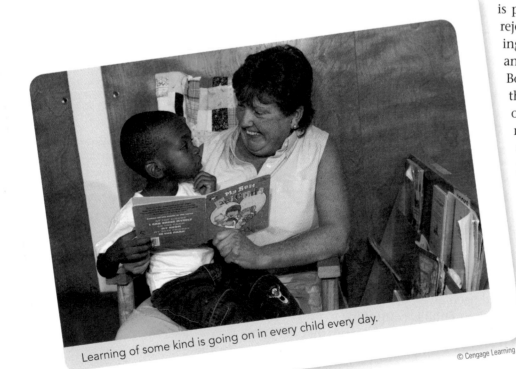
Learning of some kind is going on in every child every day.

© Cengage Learning

Contingent stimulation A closely related process is **contingent stimulation**. New learning comes about because of the prompt responses of others. Adults who react to an infant's cooing, gurgling, and babbling stimulate the infant's continuing efforts to communicate. This process is readily observable in the simple give-and-take games that parents and their babies take such delight in: peek-a-boo, pat-a-cake, chase-and-hide, toss-the-toy-out-of-the-crib. When adults respond to what the infant or child says and does, specific benefits result. Language development is earlier and better. Cognitive development is accelerated and richer. Self-esteem is much more evident, attachments are more secure, and overall development is smoother.

Readiness to learn School readiness begins in the early months and years of life. It is a major thrust of the current educational reform movement. The first goal is that all children in the United States will start school ready to learn. **Readiness** is viewed as a **multidimensional, holistic** concept, incorporating the physical, emotional, social, motor, and cognitive well-being of the child (Boyer, 1994). This concept is helpful in thinking about the multiple influences on a child's life and the effects they have on schooling. Readiness to learn is facilitated by quality infant and early childhood programs.

School readiness can seldom be accurately assessed with the readiness tests used by many school districts throughout the nation. These tests often label the child as "immature," which tends to further delay the much-needed early intervention services the child needs. The label also denies the child inclusion in a kindergarten or first-grade classroom. May et al. (1994) argue that if these practices continue, children with special needs will have an increasingly difficult time being accepted into general education classrooms.

> **contingent stimulation** responding to a child in a way that prompts further learning

> **readiness** a child's ability to learn that takes into account prerequisite physical, cognitive, language, or social skills

> **multidimensional** the relationship among the many factors that comprise a learning sequence

> **holistic** an approach to understanding the child that focuses on the interrelationship and interdependence of all developmental domains

11-2c ■ Teachable Moments

Teachable moments are those naturally occurring opportunities when a child is most likely to learn something new. Such moments are a combination of maturation, motivation, and opportunity. When these variables come together, an infant or child is often ready to learn a new skill. Consider the following examples:

> **teachable moments** points in time, perhaps associated with critical periods, when a child is highly motivated and better able to acquire a particular skill

An infant reaches for the spoon while being fed, a cue that he or she is ready—that is, is mature enough and has acquired the necessary perceptual-motor skills—to reach for and hold a spoon. The reaching also indicates readiness to begin to explore the difficult business of self-feeding. What is needed now is opportunity. Opportunity tends to come in the form of a patient adult who is willing to scrub the floor, the high chair, and the child after every meal.

Toddlers often get to the point where they hold their wet diapers away from their bodies, they demand to be changed, or they step out of their wet diapers by themselves. These children are giving clear cues that they are moving toward the idea of learning to use the toilet.

A young preschooler painting at the easel discovers that mixing yellow and blue together creates a new color. This child is ready to experiment with a variety of colors and materials to learn more about how to make new colors.

The concepts of readiness and teachable moments are easily translated into classroom practice by observant teachers attuned to developmental differences. Every day, in many ways, every child shows interest in working at new learnings.

- A two-year-old tries to put on a shoe, heel-to-toe.
- A three-year-old struggles to make an upside-down coat stay on the hook.

Teachable moments are those naturally occurring opportunities when a child is most likely to learn something new.

© Cengage Learning

- A four-year-old asks, "Where did the ice go?"
- A five-year-old tries to balance a teetering block structure.
- A six-year-old wants to write his own "book."
- An eight-year-old wants to make the cupcakes for her birthday.

In each case, on the basis of knowledge of the individual children, the teacher makes decisions about how to use the moment to the child's best advantage.

11-2d ■ Milieu Teaching

milieu (incidental) teaching
a teaching opportunity based on the child's initiation; the child approaches the teacher for assistance, information, or materials, thereby ensuring the child's interest and eagerness

First described as *incidental* teaching (Hart & Risley, 1982), **milieu (incidental) teaching** provides a strategy for making the best use of teachable moments. The distinguishing feature of such a teaching episode is that it is child-initiated and not to be confused with teacher-structured learning activities. The child approaches the teacher asking for help, materials, or information. Because the contact is child-initiated, the teacher knows the child is interested and therefore likely to be receptive to a brief learning activity about whatever it is that prompted the contact. This style of teaching represents the systematic application of principles compatible with both a developmental and a behavioral approach to early learning (Warren & Kaiser, 1988; Kaiser, 2000). It also exemplifies quality teaching practices that include:

- meeting a child where his or her interests lie.
- responding in a way that matches the child's skill level.
- introducing the element of novelty that provides challenge for the child.
- providing desired materials as a natural consequence to the child's response.

Effective milieu (incidental) teaching depends on teachers' efforts at:

- providing an interesting classroom where children can be busy, active, and inquiring.
- setting up the environment so that a child initiation is required to obtain additional materials or toys that are out of reach.

- selecting appropriate objectives for each child that match his or her skill levels and interests.

- answering a child's initiation with a request for an expanded or more sophisticated response (often related to one of the child's IEP objectives).

Did You Get It?

How would an early childhood teacher view a child from the perspective of the applied developmental approach?

a. See the child as a child.
b. See the disability first.
c. View a child's behavior as symptomatic of the disability.
d. See difference as a developmental disorder.

Take the full quiz on CourseMate.

Characteristics of Effective Teachers 11-3 ☀

In addition to a thorough knowledge of child development, other traits characterize effective teachers in an inclusive setting. As stated in the NAEYC position statement on **Developmentally Appropriate Practice** (2009):

> Teachers possess an extensive repertoire of skills and strategies they are able to draw on, and they know how and when to choose among them, to effectively promote each child's learning and development at that moment. Those skills include the ability to adapt curriculum, activities, and materials to ensure full participation of all children. Those strategies include, but are not limited to, acknowledging, encouraging, and giving specific feedback, modeling, demonstrating, adding challenge, giving cues or other assistance, providing information, and giving directions. (p. 18)

developmentally appropriate practices learning activities based on teachers' knowledge of developmental theory

Effective teaching is based on developing positive teacher–child relationships. These relationships are developed over time as teachers use developmentally and individually appropriate strategies that take into consideration children's differing needs, interests, styles, and abilities (Ostrosky & Jung, 2006). Teaching styles and interactions with children reflect a teacher's own personality; nevertheless, good teachers have a number of characteristics in common. Figure 11-1 lists the characteristics, which are described in this chapter.

FIGURE 11-1

Characteristics of Effective Teachers

Enthusiasm

Sense of Humor

Patience

Consistency

Flexibility

Trustworthiness

Provides Limits

Facilitates Experiences

© Cengage Learning

TeachSource Digital Download Download from CourseMate.

11-3a ■ Enthusiasm

Teachers of young children need unlimited enthusiasm for each child's accomplishments, great and small. This is especially important for children who may learn at a slower rate and in smaller steps. A teacher's enthusiastic support becomes a major motivation to wanting to learn more. Every child, regardless of his or her capabilities, is quick to catch enthusiasm for almost any activity from a patient, skillful teacher who rejoices with the child over each step forward.

task analysis the process of sequencing developmental tasks into small, incremental steps

incremental steps a series of small steps that lead to the eventual learning of an entire task

Enthusiasm is a mutually supportive process. The teacher's enthusiasm stems from the child's accomplishments, small as they sometimes are. The child's accomplishments, in turn, depend on the teacher's skills and enthusiasm in promoting the child's learning. It is imperative, therefore, that teachers of young children know how to carry out **task analysis**, the process of sequencing developmental tasks into small, **incremental steps**. Small-step successes give both child and teacher many opportunities to enthuse together about their work.

11-3b ■ Sense of Humor

Young children need to know that learning is fun. Teachers best convey this through their sense of humor and playfulness. Effective teachers enjoy what they are doing and are willing to laugh at things that are funny even when they are laughing at their own mistakes or when the joke is on them (Colker, 2008).

11-3c ■ Patience

Working with children, families, and systems requires patience. Children require varying amounts of repetition to learn. Some exhibit behaviors that are challenging. An effective teacher remains calm in trying situations. He or she recognizes what behaviors and situations "push their buttons" and develop strategies to remain calm.

11-3d ■ Consistency

The effective teacher is consistent and can be depended on to provide a predictable and stable environment. Young children need to know what comes next in classroom routines. They need to know what the limits are. Most important, they need to know their teacher will not behave unreasonably (for example, allowing children to climb up

Teachers must have unlimited enthusiasm.

© Cengage Learning

the front side of the slide one day and the next day banning the same children from playing on the same slide for doing exactly the same thing). Consistency is especially important for children with challenging behaviors.

In addition to being consistent, expectations also need to be communicated in ways that all children can understand. The teacher then can be confident about maintaining expectations, knowing they are developmentally and individually realistic and understood by all. Consistency provides security for children. Children who feel secure tend to be more self-confident. They learn to make sound judgments when they are sure of what is expected of them. Consistency does not rule out change. Children change throughout the developmental years.

Teachers' expectations also change. What remains consistent is the developmental appropriateness of the changing expectations and the teacher's care in communicating those changes to the children. Consistency must never be confused with rigidity or inflexibility. An inflexible teacher is not an effective teacher.

Teachers need to be flexible and follow the children's lead.

© Cengage Learning

11-3e ■ Flexibility

The ability to be flexible, to improvise, to adapt an activity to individual or group needs at any given moment is a hallmark of effective teaching. A flexible teacher knows when to cut an activity short if it turns out to be too difficult or if it fails to hold children's interest. The opposite also is true: a flexible teacher knows how and when to extend and elaborate on an activity that has developed into an especially absorbing and worthwhile experience. *Flexibility does not rule out consistency.* Truly effective teachers are a blend of consistency and flexibility.

They are good judges of when to bend the rules. They know when to overlook a minor transgression, as when a child is trying to cope with frustration or work through any other kind of learning experience. An example:

> *Jana's physical attacks on children were frequent. Never had she been heard to tell anyone what she wanted; instead, she hit, grabbed, or shoved. One day, however, she stunned teachers by shrieking, "Get out, you stupid!" The rudely shouted command and name-calling was directed at an approaching child who obviously meant no harm. The teacher, though regretting the verbal assault on a well-intentioned child, ignored the inappropriateness of Jana's response. Instead, the teacher supported Jana for talking, not hitting. This was done in the presence of the other child to promote the child's understanding that Jana was learning to replace hitting with talking.*
>
> *The teacher's flexibility indicated responsiveness to the most urgent priority for Jana as well as to the child who had been rebuffed. It let the child know classroom expectations were operating despite occasional exceptions. As for the unacceptable verbal behavior, even should it accelerate for a while, teachers should not be unduly concerned. When verbal requests dependably replaced physical assaults, a new goal—polite requesting—could be written into Jana's IEP.*

11-3f ■ Trustworthiness

Children who can trust the consistency of teachers' expectations become more trustworthy themselves. This enables teachers to be even more flexible. Teachers who respect children and their need to develop autonomy can give them even greater freedom to explore and experiment. The consistent teacher knows that children know what is expected of them. The teacher knows, too, that most children can be trusted to stop themselves before a situation gets dangerously out of bounds. DeVries and Kohlberg (1990) summarize these ideas more formally within a Piagetian context.

> In a relationship of cooperation characterized by mutual respect, the adult minimizes his authority in relationship to the child and gives him as much opportunity as possible governing his own behavior on the basis of his interests and judgments. By exercising his ability to govern his own beliefs and actions the child gradually constructs internally coherent knowledge, morality, and personality. (p. 37)

▶❚❚ **TeachSource** Video Connections

Teaching as a Profession: An Early Childhood Teacher's Responsibilities and Development

One of the goals of instruction for the preservice early childhood teacher is to help the aspiring teacher understand the breadth and depth of the early childhood teaching profession. In this video, teacher Samantha Brade details the many aspects of her job, including teaching children and keeping them safe; record keeping; and communicating with parents and her teaching team.

After watching the video, do the following:

1. List the teacher characteristics that Samantha describes.

2. Read the interview that accompanies the video case and list additional characteristics that Samantha illustrates through her description of her class and daily routine.

Watch on CourseMate.

© Cengage Learning 2015

11-3g ■ Provides Limits

Everyone needs limits, especially young children who are trying hard to learn the many things expected of them. Limits, in the form of classroom rules, allow children to relax, knowing that they can depend on someone else to make some of the decisions. For the most part, rules for the early childhood classroom focus on safety, care of property, and the well-being of the group. Rules should be stated in positive language, but unambiguously: *One child at a time at the top of the slide; wheeled toys stay on the path.* Whatever rules exist must be enforced. Therefore, the number of rules should be kept to a minimum because enforcing rules is not a productive role for teachers. Children can follow rules and instructions more easily if they are specific and tell the child what to do in a particular situation. Rules that tell the child what *not* to do leave the child still not knowing what the expected behavior is. In general, teachers can consistently enforce no more than six classroom rules. Teachers need to interact positively with children rather than police them.

The rules that adults agree on often are stated in terms of what *cannot be allowed* to avoid misunderstandings among teachers. When guiding children, however, rules are translated into positive statements.

> *"The sand stays in the sandbox."*
>
> *"Books are to read and look at."*
>
> *"Those are the teachers' cupboards; children's cupboards are down here."*

Teachers only need to give negative and emphatic commands when a child continues to ignore a reminder or redirection: "Kelly, I can't let you throw sand." Rules apply to every child in the group. "No sand throwing," means *no sand throwing*. This includes children with developmental delays and limited cognitive abilities. There can be no double standards. Double standards do the special child a disservice by not helping him or her learn acceptable behavior. Furthermore, double standards can lead to resentment and dislike of the erring child among children who try to abide by the rules. Fortunately, there is no need for double standards. Every child can learn to abide by the few and necessary rules required in a classroom.

On many occasions, children truly do not understand what is expected of them from teachers' efforts at positive **redirection**. When a teacher advises, "The sand stays in the sandbox," a child may continue to throw sand while carefully keeping it within the boundaries of the sandbox. Clearly, the child is not getting the message the teacher had intended; neither are the other children in the sandbox receiving the protection they deserve. In these instances, specific statements of rules and expectations may be more appropriate right from the start. Clear and indisputable limits offer security to children who may not grasp the subtleties of positive redirection.

Teachers who respect children and their need to develop autonomy can give them even greater freedom to explore.

© Cengage Learning

redirection a teaching strategy that directs the child's attention and energy from a behavior that is less than desirable by introducing a more appropriate behavior or activity

11-3h ■ Facilitates Experiences

A major role of an effective teacher is that of facilitator. A good teacher finds ways to help children help themselves in discovering ways to make good things happen. A facilitative teacher recognizes that experiences, not teachers, are the best instructors for young children. Therefore, the facilitative teacher is careful to:

- provide a range of interesting and appropriate materials and activities.
- present learning opportunities in ways that are attractive and conducive to children's learning.
- offer a balanced amount of assistance (not too much, but never refusing to assist).
- be aware of what the next step is for each child on each developmental task.
- respond to children with appreciative feedback.

Facilitation and support are especially important during children's play. As Gordon and Williams Browne (2010) point out, it can be difficult for teachers to decide when to join children at play and when to remain outside the activity. The important question is whether their presence will support what is happening or whether it will inhibit the play. In an inclusive classroom, teachers tend to find it appropriate to join in more frequently, but as unobtrusively

Case Study ■ One preschool teacher's inclusion experience ■

Last fall, a four-year-old boy with Down syndrome enrolled in our program. An aide, who also worked with him at home, initially accompanied him to the program. With the exception of a few biting incidents in the beginning (something we might witness in any young child regardless of whether or not they have special needs, because it often depends upon their language skills), he thrived in our setting. And once he was acclimated and comfortable with the routine, he began attending independently. He participated in everything with the typical zest of a four-year-old, was in every way an integral member of the class, and was gentle and loving.

Although I originally had concerns about how to deal with our students' questions about him, I quickly realized that I had underestimated their ability to accept the differences between themselves and other children. I also discovered that as long as we kept our answers truthful and simple ("Jacob is screaming because he does not know how to use his words yet"), it seemed to be enough for them. In fact, their immediate response was usually in the form of self-reassurance: "I know how to use my words" or "My legs work."

This experience was not without challenges, however. The greatest liability was that our teachers did not have backgrounds in special education. Although we had special education teachers on campus, I often felt ill-equipped when dealing with some behaviors such as tantrums. And truthfully, there were moments when it felt too disruptive, given my lack of experience in special education. It was at these times that I enlisted the help of the parent or the child's core teacher, or sometimes it was simply a matter of changing the time of day during which the child joined us.

- What aspects of this teacher's experience relate to the characteristics of an effective teacher?
- What did this teacher do to meet the challenges she faced?
- What else could she have done?"

---

as possible. Low-key teacher participation can go a long way toward fostering play relationships between children with and without disabilities, especially when the teacher quietly fades in and out, depending on the progress of the activity (Kontos & Wilcox-Herzog, 1997).

Teachers in an inclusive setting also facilitate (and *integrate*) the individualized intervention programs prescribed by the various disciplines. They translate clinical recommendations into interesting classroom activities that can be carried out in ways that benefit all children.

Rules that tell the child what not to do leave the child still not knowing what the expected behavior is.

© Cengage Learning

The speech therapist was working with a five-year-old on beginning B, M, and P sounds. At the small-group breakfast table, the teacher improvised a riddle game based on the therapist's objectives. The teacher described and gave the beginning sounds of various foods the children had encountered over the year. Children supplied the words or labels. The cues for the child in speech therapy had to do with such things as bananas, milk, and pears; butter, muffins, and plums. Everyone at the table participated, learned from the game, and had fun with it. No one was the wiser (including the special child) that speech therapy was going on.

Facilitating classroom activities of this kind provides a bridge that allows the child to practice, **generalize**, and **consolidate** what is learned in therapy sessions to functional, everyday situations.

11-3i ▪ The Teacher as Mediator

According to Vygotsky (2006), Feuerstein, Rand, Hoffman, and Miller (1980), and the NAEYC (2009), it is essential that teachers of young children serve as **mediators** between the child and the learning environment.

These constructivist theorists emphasize the role of the adult in helping children learn to solve cognitive and social problems. The strategy is to provide decreasing levels of support while placing higher demands as the child progresses toward the goal of independent problem solving. Vygotsky refers to this part of the teaching/learning process as **scaffolding**.

> Scaffolding can take a variety of forms; for example, giving the child a hint, adding a cue, modeling the skill, or adapting the materials and activities. It can be provided in a variety of contexts, not only in planned learning experiences but also in play, daily routines, and outdoor activities. (NAEYC, 2009 p. 19)

Example: An objective written into Maya's IEP was that she learn to talk to other children. She had the prerequisite language skills, but was not using them with peers. The teacher began the scaffolding process by bringing children together in a group and asking Maya to say "Hi" to each child (high support, low demand). When Maya became accustomed to this kind of interaction, the teacher arranged opportunities away from group time for Maya to greet peers (higher demand). Gradually the teacher reduced the amount of assistance and support. Before long, Maya was spontaneously saying "Hi" (and a good deal more) when she encountered other children.

The **mediated learning** model theorizes that cognitive and social development are intertwined. The teacher's role is to foster children's awareness of their own thought processes by asking them to *predict outcomes, test reality,* and *communicate their thoughts.* Most important, the teacher emphasizes **generalization** by encouraging children to think about how a given skill could be used in a different situation: "What might you say to Julie when she doesn't want to play with you?"

According to Mills and Cole (1999), teachers who practice mediated teaching create an environment that is conducive to learning by:

- thinking through the purpose of an activity.
- assessing the current skill levels of each child.
- providing support and placing demands that reflect the appropriate developmental goals for a child.
- demonstrating intentionality; that is, organizing the experience in ways that clearly communicate what is to be learned.

generalize to learn a specific skill so well that a child can use it in a variety of situations

consolidate behaviors are so well learned that they become an integrated part of the child's repertoire

mediator the teacher or other adult who facilitates learning by bridging the gap between the child and the learning environment

scaffolding introducing new learning built on skills already acquired

mediated learning based on the teaching premise that cognitive and social processes are interdependent factors in all learning

generalization the spread of a learned response from the training situation to real-life situations

- helping children generalize new learning to situations beyond the immediate setting.

- taking cues from children's interest and responding to child-initiated learning situations.

- providing activities that have meaning or function in the everyday life of the child.

Fundamentally, the role of the teacher as mediator is to highlight significant aspects of the environment, emphasize the social context, and encourage the child to explore the options.

The foregoing discussion of the attitudes and attributes of effective teachers in an inclusive early childhood program is by no means complete. It is critical for early childhood educators to also know how to:

- integrate behavioral and developmental principles when teaching young children.

- work with parents and members of other disciplines.

- arrange and present materials and equipment.

- schedule the daily program to provide children with an appropriate balance of child-initiated and teacher-structured learning experiences.

The remaining chapters in this text elaborate on these and many more of the skills needed to be an effective teacher of young children.

Did You Get It?

Within whose theoretical framework do DeVries and Kohlberg (1990) raise the concept of trust, expectation, and judgment?
a. Freud.
b. Feuerstein.
c. Piaget.
d. Vygotsky.

Take the full quiz on CourseMate.

Summary

▶ In an inclusive classroom, the need for quality teaching and appropriate learning experiences is critical.

▶ Children with developmental disabilities are especially in need of learning experiences adapted to their special needs.

▶ Teachers work in the classroom with a team of specialists to meet the needs of children with disabilities.

▶ Early childhood teachers in an inclusive classroom do not need extensive retraining, but rather a comfort level with their knowledge of typical child development and an extensive knowledge and experience in working with young children in general.

▶ Information about particular disabilities is available through various training programs, organizations, resource centers, and the parents of children with disabilities.

▶ Milieu (incidental) teaching is an effective approach to teaching all children; it is especially effective when working with children with developmental problems.

▶ Because milieu (incidental) teaching is child-initiated, it signals a teacher that the child is ready and interested in learning whatever it is that he or she has contacted the teacher about. The teacher's responsibility is to be always *at the ready* to take advantage of a teachable moment.

▶ Other characteristics of effective teachers in an inclusive early childhood program include enthusiasm, sense of humor, patience, consistency, flexibility, trustworthiness, setting limits for children, integrating therapy-prescribed activities into the regular classroom program, and mediating children's learning opportunities.

Key Terms

consolidate, 297
contingent stimulation, 289
developmental disequilibrium, 287
developmental inconsistency, 287
developmentally appropriate
    practices, 291
generalize, 297

generalization, 297
holistic, 289
incremental steps, 292
mediated learning, 297
mediator, 296
milieu (incidental)
    teaching, 290

multidimensional, 289
readiness, 289
redirection, 295
scaffolding, 297
task analysis, 292
teachable moments, 289
transactional learning, 288

Student Activities

1. Observe in a preschool or kindergarten classroom. Examine the physical environment and determine if the classroom and staff would be able to effectively meet the needs of a child in a wheelchair. Or a child with a hearing disability.

2. Talk with teacher(s) in an inclusive preschool or child care center about working with children with developmental disabilities and their families. Record their comments, concerns, and general attitudes about the children and their parents.

3. Observe a preschool session. Count the number of child-to-teacher contacts. Briefly describe those the teacher responded to in a way that allowed the child to expand his or her learning.

4. Interview the director of a preschool regarding his or her experience of or process for working with children with special needs. What type of support is available to the classroom teachers?

5. Role-play each of the following classroom situations.
   a. a teacher being consistent about a rule
   b. a teacher being flexible about a routine
   c. a teacher being both consistent and flexible about the same rule or routine

Review Questions

Part 1. Define and give an example of each of the following terms.

1. developmental inconsistency
2. developmentally appropriate practice
3. generalization
4. applied developmental approach
5. disequilibrium
6. readiness to learn
7. the facilitative teacher
8. functional situation
9. milieu teaching
10. mediated learning

Part 2. Write a short essay in response to the following question.

If extensive retraining is not required to teach in an inclusive preschool or child care classroom, what do teachers need to do to ensure that children with developmental disabilities have a good learning experience?

Additional Resources/Readings

Including Children with Special Needs. Are You and Your Early Childhood Program Ready?

Written by Amy Watson and Rebecca McCathern
National Association for the Education of Young Children

See the "Preschool and Kindergarten Inclusion Readiness Checklist." This tool helps teacher evaluate their classroom and program's readiness for inclusions.

Twelve Characteristics of Effective Early Childhood Teachers

Written by Laura Colker
National Association for the Education of Young Children

In addition to several of the characteristics discussed in the chapter, this article includes some more.

Helpful Websites

Early Childhood Educators' and Family Web Corner

http://users.stargate.net (Search: Teacher Pages)

This website contains articles and links to sites of interest to early childhood educators and parents. Topics include assessment, curriculum, and family issues.

National Association for the Education of Young Children (NAEYC)

http://www.naeyc.org

NAEYC's website includes a resource catalog, professional development materials, and links to related sites. Of note is the NAEYC position statement on standardized testing of young children aged three through eight (adopted in 1987).

National Early Childhood Technical Assistance Center

http://www.nectac.org

This website contains information and publications on a variety of early childhood education topics, including assessment, family partnerships, quality assurance, and inclusion.

The Early Childhood Education CourseMate website for this text offers many helpful resources. Go to **www.CengageBrain.com** to preview this chapter's Concept Maps and Chapter Themes.

Visit the Education CourseMate for this textbook to access the eBook, Did You Get It? quizzes, Digital Downloads, TeachSource Video Cases, flashcards, and more. Go to CengageBrain.com to log in, register, or purchase access.

Planning for Inclusion

© Morgan Lane Photography/Shutterstock.com

SPECIAL FOCUS •
CREATING A COMMUNITY OF CARING LEARNERS

My name is Kim Crane, and I am a third-grade teacher. For years, I have started my school year by reading books that inspire conversations about tolerance and creating a caring community. Over the years, I have found that when children are in a safe environment and are supported for their openness, they will feel more comfortable about sharing their personal perspectives and taking risks.

Some of the resources I have used over the years to build a caring classroom community come from children's literature. I recommend a book called *The Rag Coat* by Lauren Mills and a short story titled "Slower Than the Rest" by Cynthia Rylant. My suggestion is to select an appealing picture book that can be read in one or two sessions. The story has to be one that

touches you (the adult) in an almost visceral way so that the emotion is in the air and the students can embrace the feeling inspired by the words and pictures.

During discussions of both of these stories, some of my students have tearfully shared their own experiences with feeling put down or left out. One year, one of the more macho boys, with teary eyes, described a time when he felt really lonely because of his newness to the school. Another boy, who was equally tough, patted him on the back and told him, "It's OK!" We all grew in that moment. Anytime during our discussions that anyone in class became sad and weepy, there was a support system that understood the necessity to get out the sadness, share, and then move on.

One year, I had the pleasure of hosting a student with significant special needs in my classroom during math time. Although this child needed the emotional support of a special class, he was a brilliant math student. The key to his successful inclusion in my classroom was the preparation of my students prior to his arrival. Since my students were already tolerant of different learning styles and speeds, introducing them to someone who was coming to class because he was very good in math, but a bit shy, was nothing unusual. This student added a quiet and serious presence, blending with my classroom students in a very positive way. In no time, he raised his hand to answer complicated problem-solving questions. He participated in group work with some hesitation. I don't think my students ever knew that he was in a "special" class for the majority of his day. They knew he was someone who answered correctly most of the time and didn't like to say much when working in a group. He gained their respect and we all enjoyed his addition to our classroom community.

As a regular classroom teacher, I have found over the years that encouraging tolerance is a process. I feel so lucky to be in an elementary school where our students are exposed to students with special needs as a matter of their daily routine. When we hear someone walking down the hall making a lot of noise we often turn to one another and say, "Oh, everything is OK. That's just John. Sometimes he needs to make loud noises to communicate." And we return to our lesson without any judgment or additional comments. I am sure that my students and those who get the opportunity to see a variety of abilities are more accepting as they move through their lives, because of this exposure.

References

Mills, L. A. (1991). *The Rag Coat*. Little, Brown Books for Young Readers: Boston, MA.

Rylant, C. (1988). Slower than the rest. In C. Rylant, *Every Living Thing*. Atheneum Press: New York.

Special Focus Application Questions

1. What information from the chapters in Section 3 applies to this story?
2. What characteristics of effective teachers does this third-grade teacher demonstrate?
3. Visit a library, local bookstore, or search online for additional examples of children's literature that might help classroom teachers build a community of caring learners.
4. What other ideas do you have that could be implemented to help create a community of caring learners in any classroom?

The Developmental-Behavioral Approach

OBJECTIVES

After reading this chapter, you should be able to:

12-1 provide examples of changes in children's behavior that are a result of teachers' learning how to blend both developmental and behavioral principles.

12-2 define a behavioral approach to early intervention including use of reinforcement.

12-3 describe the difference between discipline and punishment.

12-4 explain step-by-step learning and the use of task analysis and how they are important when working with children in general and with children with developmental problems in particular.

12-5 provide examples of learning by imitation and explain its significance in early childhood education.

· · · · · · · · · · · · · · · · · ·

naeyc

The following NAEYC Standards are addressed in this chapter:

STANDARD 1 Promoting Child Development and Learning

STANDARD 3 Observing, Documenting and Assessing to Support Young Children and Families

STANDARD 4 Using Developmentally Effective Approaches

STANDARD 5 Using Content Knowledge to Build Meaningful Curriculum

- Two weeks ago, Miriam was still refusing to get into the rocking boat if there were other children in it. Today, she watched Marna and Stacy as they were getting into the boat, then climbed in and sat next to Stacy. They rocked together for several minutes.
- Starting on Tuesday, Joel pointed to each letter in his name and named it correctly.
- Avron brought in his homework every day last week without being reminded.

These examples of changes in children's behavior are essential testimony that developmental progress is taking place. From earliest infancy, behavior changes in every area of development are critical benchmarks—conclusive evidence of development.

The changing behaviors of infants and children in early childhood programs attest to the quality of the program and the effectiveness of the teaching. For Miriam, Joel, and Avron, the accomplishments their teachers were reporting in a staff meeting represented achievement of short-term objectives written into the child's IEP. In other words, teaching has been considered effective as indicated by positive changes in the three children's behaviors. It must be emphasized that healthy developmental progress does not occur unless there are changes in a child's behavior.

Developmental/behavioral changes range from the simple to the complex. They occur because of physical growth, maturation, experience, observational learning (modeling), and practice. These changes are orderly. They take place in accordance with specifiable laws of behavior and predictable biological sequences.

Basic developmental principles have been discussed specifically in Chapter 4 and elsewhere throughout this text. This chapter will provide a brief analysis of behavioral principles, especially those that have particular relevance for teachers and parents of young children. The major focus is on **reinforcement** procedures, with emphasis on positive social responsiveness from teachers and other significant adults. **Punishment** *also* will be discussed, not because it is a recommended practice, but because of its widespread and inappropriate use in attempting to discipline children. Many adults fail to recognize the ineffectiveness of punishment; others seem to be unaware of alternative ways of managing children. In this chapter, positive reinforcement practices are emphasized as the first and preferred approach to effective guidance and discipline.

Step-by-step learning (task analysis) and learning through modeling (imitation) are additional principles that play a major role in early childhood teaching and learning. The discussion of these topics includes the timing of teacher's attention, the role of praise, and the inappropriateness of competitiveness in presenting early learning experiences. The chapter starts with a brief overview of early behavioral research and the gradual merging of developmental theory and reinforcement/behavioral principles.

reinforcement general term for a consequence, event, or procedure that increases or maintains the behavior it follows

punishment technically, the presentation of an aversive event, or the removal of a positive event, contingent upon a response that decreases the probability of a behavior's occurrence

☀ 12-1 Developmental and Behavioral Principles: A Blend

Effective and caring early childhood teachers who want to ensure the progress of the children in their programs rely on *both* developmental and behavioral principles when deciding how and what to teach children. They know that the best measure of the effectiveness of their teaching is change in children's behavior. The examples of behavior changes in Miriam's, Joel's, and Avron's physical, social, cognitive, and language skills demonstrate the results of teachers facilitating each child's learning by combining the two principles. In each instance, behavioral objectives (new skills to be learned) were selected on the basis of each child's individual learning needs and the teacher's knowledge of child development. Decisions also were made about preparing the environment to assist each child in learning the new skills through play activities. Pretti-Frontczak and Bricker (2004) refer to these procedures as an activities-based approach to early intervention and education.

12-1a ■ Historical Influences

A developmental-behavioral approach to teaching has been evolving for more than fifty years. At mid-century, **maturationists** were in the majority. Researchers such as Gesell et al. (1993) believed that development was very nearly independent of experience. It was a natural unfolding of innate or inborn abilities. The role of teachers (and parents) was to neither unduly restrict nor push the child. Then theorists such as Hunt (1961) argued that development was *not* independent of external influences. Rather, it was controlled to some unknown extent by environmental experiences. Hunt had been greatly influenced by Piaget (1992), who theorized that changes in a child's thinking (cognitive structure) were a direct result of a child's exploration of the environment. Hunt went one step further. He suggested that learning depended on a good match between each child's developmental level and the experiences available to the child.

maturationist one who believes that human development is a natural unfolding of innate abilities and nearly independent of environmental influence

The problem of the match In early childhood education, the *problem of the match* became a central issue. Teachers were trained to provide play materials and learning opportunities that attracted and held children's attention. At the same time, the materials were to include new and intriguing elements. The newness was to be just a bit beyond the child's current skill level. Providing exactly the right match was the way to produce rewarding feelings of pleasure and continuing eagerness (motivation) to learn. There was no need for teachers or parents to push or prod the child. The joy of learning, often referred to as **intrinsic motivation**, would take over. Children would seek out additional learning of their own accord simply because they wanted to and because it made them feel good about themselves.

intrinsic motivation motivation that comes from inside the individual, rather than from any external reward such as praise or grades

Decisions must be made about how to best prepare the environment to assist each child in learning new skills through play activities.

© Cengage Learning

Learning from success The role of environmental influences also was central to the developmental ideas of Bijou (1959, 1993). He believed the results (consequences) of a child's behavior were the crucial element. According to Bijou, children tend to learn whatever brings feelings of success and positive outcome. They avoid behaviors that result in failure or negative consequences.

Teachers were trained to present tasks step by small step and to include positive feedback as the child moved through the steps. The result: a learning environment in which children had frequent success and were motivated to learn more.

Environmental arrangements Arranging the learning environment to help a child take a next step in skill development is a fundamental principle in early childhood education. Today, we often read about the **ecology** of early learning. Three examples from different periods in the history of early childhood education point to the importance of the learning environment.

Friedrich Froebel (1782–1852), hailed as the founder of the kindergarten movement, was probably the first to propose that early learning experiences be broken down into their smallest components. Froebel also argued that young children need hands-on experiences with concrete materials to enjoy, examine, and manipulate.

Maria Montessori (1870–1952), a gifted physician, was a champion of the educational potentials of children with developmental delays and disabilities. She spent her career designing and demonstrating systematic and sequential learning activities based on what she called **didactic materials**. Many of these materials, as well as her ideas about a prepared environment, are central to today's early education practices.

John Dewey (1859–1952), a major proponent of the *progressive education* movement, also put strong emphasis on the learning environment, especially the teacher. It was the teacher who made the difference, the teacher who was to respond, support, and guide children's exploration of everyday materials.

In each of these approaches to early education, the route to sound learning reflects a developmental and behavioral blend that includes:

- a prepared learning environment matched to each child's current skill levels

- materials and activities sequenced in small enough segments to provide both success and challenge

- emphasis on learning through play and active involvement with appropriate materials

- responsive teachers who serve as guides and facilitators rather than instructors

☀ 12-2 Behavior Principles and Practices

Misinformation and abuse of behavioral principles, according to Wolery (1994), has led to a knee-jerk negative reaction in many early childhood educators. He asserts:

> The behavioral perspective, although often seen as stressing the impact of the environment, in fact proposes that learning occurs from dynamic interactions between children and their environment. ... Particularly beneficial are those child–environment interactions that are initiated and directed by children and in which they are highly engaged. (pp. 98–99)

The behavioral approach to early intervention consists of arranging the environment and implementing teaching strategies in ways that enhance children's learning opportunities (Chance, 2006). While this approach is important in working with all children, it is particularly important in facilitating learning among children with developmental delays.

12-2a ■ Every Child Can Learn

In an inclusive classroom, the most significant and useful behavioral principle deserves repeated emphasis: *Every child can learn.* Some children learn faster than others. Some children learn more than others. Some children learn some things easily, other things only with great effort. Some children learn from one kind of teaching, others from a different method. But all children can learn. This well-established concept is documented by several decades of behavioral research. Bijou and Cole (1975) summarize:

> Traditionally, an individual who did not learn what was presented was considered incapable, indifferent, unmotivated, or lacking. The behavioral view on the other hand is if the student does not learn, something is lacking in the teaching situation. (p. 3)

To make the *teachability* of all children a day-by-day reality, teachers need to be knowledgeable about child development and understand and practice basic behavioral principles. In the inclusive classroom, the procedures are especially important. Each child must be provided a **responsive learning environment** matched to his or her developmental level and special interests. Gifted children can be provided with learning opportunities that neither push nor hold them back, but instead foster their interests and talents. Children with developmental problems, though some may learn more slowly or with greater effort, should be provided a responsive learning environment matched to *their* developmental skill levels. The essence of the behavioral approach is to start where the child is—developmentally—and build from there, step by step.

Children who have severe impairments may have few behaviors to build on. Observant teachers and child care providers, however, pick up on subtle cues that indicate a child's possible interest and awareness. In some instances, teachers, parents, and caregivers themselves may have to decide the starting point. One example is a child with multiple disabilities who

responsive learning environment environment that supports a child's efforts to explore and discover through interactions with other individuals, play materials, and activities

© Cengage Learning

Some children learn from one kind of teaching, others from a different method.

displays few behaviors of any kind. Simply getting the child to look in a given direction may be a first priority. Even to accomplish this, a teacher often has to structure the environment to evoke (trigger) an attending response such as eye contact or head-turning: the sight or fragrance of a favorite food or the sound of a favorite song—whatever will attract the child's attention and give the teacher a behavior to respond to and expand on.

12-2b ■ Reinforcement Procedures

Reinforcement procedures come from research related to **operant conditioning**, **behavior modification**, and **learning theory**. Numerous studies with individual children and with groups of young children demonstrate that behavior is triggered by antecedent events. These events, either internal or external, lead to increases or decreases in a behavior, according to its consequences, or **reinforcers**. These principles can be put into a simple ABC format:

A. *Antecedent* event (something that precedes or comes before a behavior)

B. *Behavior* (response of the individual)

C. *Consequence* (that which follows a behavior)

Start with what a child can do.

© Cengage Learning

operant conditioning (also instrumental conditioning) type of learning that results from the consequences of a person's behavior; operating intentionally on some aspect of the environment to produce change

behavior modification a system by which particular environmental events are systematically arranged to produce specified behavior changes

learning theory emphasizes the dominant role of environment and reinforcing experiences in learning

reinforcers increase the behaviors that they follow and are specific to individuals (candy is a reinforcer for many children, but for many it is not)

Antecedents and consequences are environmental events, planned or unplanned, that both precede and follow a behavior. Example:

A. Mother opens a bag of cookies.

B. Child, watching, says, "I want a cookie."

C. Mother hands child a cookie.

The child's request (B) was triggered by seeing her mother open a package of cookies (A). It is likely the child will ask for a cookie every time her mother opens a package because the request resulted in a cookie (C). Unwanted behaviors often are reinforced through these same procedures, but too often unrecognized. In the cookie example, the mother could have said (C), "No cookie until after lunch." This might have set off clamoring and whining (B) in the child. Mother might refuse several times, and with each refusal the whining gets more insistent until finally she gives the child a cookie. The child is likely to learn from this and similar exchanges that asking does not always pay off, but insistent whining does. The moral of this story: If mother intended to allow a cookie, she should have done it on the first request, rather than inadvertently teaching the child that whining usually pays off.

If specific learning, B, is to occur (or not occur, as in the case of inappropriate behaviors) then A and C must be decided on and systematically arranged. In simple terms, A is what teachers and parents do *before* they would have a child respond. This includes the selection, arrangement, and presentation of activities and materials. C is what adults do immediately following a child's response: such actions as providing or withholding reinforcers. Whatever adults do in A and C affects the child's behavior and learning (Allen, 1974; Chance, 2006).

Reinforcement may be either positive or negative. It also may be intrinsic. In this text, the focus will be mainly on positive reinforcement because of its value in working with young children. First, however, several other forms of reinforcement will be discussed briefly.

Negative reinforcement The strengthening of a behavior by the removal of an unpleasant consequence is called **negative reinforcement**. Negative reinforcement is a confusing concept that has been explained in a variety of ways. Bee and Boyd (2012) give one of the more easily understood definitions:

> Negative reinforcement occurs when something unpleasant is stopped. Suppose your child is whining and whining at you to be picked up. What happens when you pick him up? He stops whining. So your picking up behavior has been negatively reinforced by the cessation (stopping) of the child's whining and you will be more likely to pick him up the next time he whines. At the same time, his whining has been positively reinforced by your attention and picking up, so he will be more likely to whine on other occasions. (p. 289)

Chance (2006) defines negative reinforcement even more simply: "Negative reinforcers: A reinforcing event in which something is removed following a behavior" (p. 102). *Note:* Negative reinforcement is not the same thing as punishment, which will be discussed later.

negative reinforcement the strengthening of a behavior by the removal of an unpleasant consequence

Intrinsic reinforcement Intrinsic reinforcement provides feelings of pleasure and personal satisfaction derived from working on or accomplishing a task, discovering something new, or solving a problem. Poor readers, who have to work hard at figuring out words and meanings, find little or no intrinsic reinforcement in reading: it is taxing, something to be avoided. In young children, the same holds true whether it is tricycle riding, block building, or working with puzzles. Most children try to avoid activities that are too stressful or frustrating for them.

intrinsic reinforcement feelings of pleasure and personal satisfaction derived from working on or accomplishing a task, discovering something new, or solving a problem

positive reinforcement something that follows a response and results in the increase of that particular response

Positive reinforcement In technical terms, **positive reinforcement** is something that follows a response and results in the increase of that particular response. In simpler terms, a positive reinforcer is a pleasant consequence; therefore, it has a high probability of increasing whatever behavior preceded it. For example, Carla always asks her father rather than her mother for certain privileges. Why? She has learned that her father is likely to grant (reinforce) her request, and her mother to deny it.

Antecedents are what the teacher does before the child responds.

© Cengage Learning

Intrinsic reinforcement: a sense of pleasure, satisfaction and self-esteem.

▶❚❚ TeachSource Video Connections

Guidance for Young Children: Teacher Techniques for Encouraging Positive Social Behaviors

It is important to guide each child's social behavior so that each child understands the consequences of his or her behavior. This is best accomplished in the context of a positive, nurturing classroom environment. Watch this video to see how early childhood teacher Linda Rudolph guides her students' behaviors while engaging them in interesting activities.

After watching the video discuss the following:

1. Provide examples of Linda engaging in everyday teacher behavior that serve as reinforcers for children.

2. What other aspects of a developmental-behavioral approach did Linda incorporate into her teaching?

Watch on CourseMate.

Different children like different things. A reinforcer for one child may be of little value to another. Candy is a good example. It is generally assumed that all children like candy, but this is not true. A number of children do not like candy.

One reinforcer that is both powerful and universally appealing to almost all young children of every culture is *adult social reinforcement:* the attention of significant adults such as parents, teachers, family members, and nurturing caregivers. Generally, adult attention is readily available and potentially plentiful. Research provides conclusive evidence that adult attention is likely to increase those behaviors which it immediately and consistently follows. The opposite also is true: When adult attention is consistently withheld, the behavior decreases. The following excerpt from a classic case study (Allen, 1974) points up the appropriate and systematic use of teachers' attention in helping a child acquire a needed behavior: improved span of attention.

> Concerns about James's limited attention span led teachers to make a series of observations. It was obvious that James was getting a great deal of attention from teachers, yet there was no increase in his attention span. Teachers agreed, therefore, to focus their attention on James only on those moments—no matter how brief—that he was engaged with a material or activity. They further agreed not to interact with him just as he was leaving an activity or when he was flitting about. That is, they refrained from doing what they usually did at those times, which was

to attempt to steer the child into an activity. Teachers consistently held to their plan. James's span of attention soon began to increase.

For a complete discussion of the practices used with James and with many children whose behaviors cause concern, see Allen and Goetz (1982). Their studies demonstrate how powerful teachers are as sources of reinforcement for young children. Most important, the studies indicate how simple reinforcement procedures bring out the best in each child.

Following are brief descriptions of everyday teacher behaviors that may serve as powerful reinforcers for almost any young child:

- **Verbal responsiveness**—relevant comments, interested questions, answers to children's questions, exclamations of approval such as "Great!"
- **Descriptive praise**—comments that focus on some aspect of what the child is accomplishing: "Paula, you laced your shoes all by yourself!"
- **Physical proximity**—quietly standing or sitting close to a child and showing genuine interest by watching, nodding, smiling, or listening.
- **Physical contact**—touching, hugging, holding a child's hand, tussling with, rocking or otherwise physically comforting a child. (Teachers must note and discuss the occasional child who avoids or shrinks from adults' touch.)
- **Physical assistance**—providing support on the climbing frame, pushing a swing, helping a child achieve balance on a walking beam.
- **Providing things that children want**—play materials, activities, mini-excursions such as a ride in the elevator or crossing the road to watch a construction worker, a favorite snack, reading a story.

natural consequence a consequence that would occur without a parent's or teacher's intervention

logical consequence a consequence determined by an adult that is related to the child's original inappropriate behavior

Natural and logical consequences An effective way to teach children about their behavior is to allow for **natural consequences**—consequences that would occur without a teacher's or parent's intervention. For example, the natural consequence for Henry, who chose not to eat what was served for dinner, is that he goes to bed hungry. A natural consequence for Callie, who refuses to keep her room clean, is that she is unable to find a favorite toy that is lost in the mess.

Logical consequences are consequences that an adult determines but are related to the child's behavior. For example, a logical consequence for Jake, who purposely spills his juice at snack time, is to have him wipe his table and the other snack tables.

12-2c ■ Withdrawing or Withholding Reinforcers

Another, less pleasant form of adult social reinforcement is taking away (withdrawing or withholding) something: a favorite toy, activity, playmate, or the attention of an important adult. Withholding reinforcement is used when an inappropriate behavior is not decreasing despite teachers' efforts. (Recall the staff's attempts to

Showing genuine interest in what the child is doing is a powerful everyday teacher behavior.

© Cengage Learning

redirect James, with the resulting increase in flitting about.) The withholding of reinforcers (properly carried out and accompanied by positive attention to the desired behavior) has proven to be a highly effective form of child guidance. *Not* attending to inappropriate behavior cuts down on the emotional conflict between adult and child.

In early childhood settings, withholding attention and other reinforcers can be accomplished in several ways. Teachers may:

- ignore an incident, or act as if they do not see the undesirable behavior (as long as the child is not endangering him- or herself or others or destroying property).
- remove materials or equipment if a child continues to misuse them.
- remove the child from play with other children or from an activity.

In a well-arranged and developmentally appropriate early learning environment, the need for any kind of negative procedure is rare. A word of caution is warranted about withholding or withdrawing reinforcers, especially in terms of withholding attention and thus ignoring a behavior. It is important to be sure that anyone who is being asked to implement this type of procedure, whether it be a parent, teacher, or babysitter, is comfortable with it. A child's behavior will get worse if attention that used to follow it is withdrawn. Very often the child will engage in stronger, more persistent, and more frequent behavior. The team implementing the procedures must be willing to ride out this burst in behavior. If they are not able to be consistent, the child will learn that engaging in more persistent, stronger behavior will get the desired reinforcer.

incompatible behaviors two or more responses that cannot occur together

Incompatible behaviors Incompatible behaviors are two or more responses that cannot occur together. In other words, an inappropriate behavior cannot occur at the same time an appropriate behavior is occurring. For example, it is impossible for children to walk and run at the same time. Therefore, if the rule is *no running in the classroom*, teachers should turn their attention to children who are remembering to walk. The child who runs, after a first reminder, receives no further teacher attention until the running stops. Figure 12-1 lists other examples of incompatible behaviors.

Whenever a child is not being inappropriate, he or she is engaging in some kind of *appropriate behavior*, even if it is only standing and watching for a moment. This gives teachers and parents the opportunity to respond to something appropriate rather than wasting time and emotional energy on inappropriate behaviors.

Case Study ▪ Marie's behavior ▪

Marie is a four-year-old child with autism. Her language has improved significantly in the past year, but she still exhibits inappropriate behavior on occasion. Marie is eating lunch at home while watching her favorite television show. Her mother asks her to take one more bite. Marie says no and dumps her remaining lunch on the floor. Her mother keeps her cool, walks over to turn off the television, hands Marie a paper towel, and calmly requests that Marie clean up the food. What makes this an effective strategy? What does Marie's mother need to do after Marie cleans up the food? What if Marie whines and says no?

FIGURE 12-1

Examples of Incompatible Behaviors

- Listening is incompatible with talking out of turn;

- Making a neutral comment is incompatible with teasing;

- Throwing sand is incompatible with keeping sand in the sandbox

- Sitting at circle is incompatible with running around the classroom;

- Waiting for the cookie basket to be passed is incompatible with snatching cookies.

© Cengage Learning

TeachSource Digital Download Download from CourseMate.

Withholding attention need not (and should not) result in a child getting less adult attention. Misbehaving children tend to be attention seekers; ignoring their inappropriate behaviors often results in more varied and even greater inappropriateness as they increase their efforts to get attention. The strategy is for teachers to attend to other, more appropriate (or at least, less objectionable) behaviors the child engages in. The best behaviors for teachers to attend to are those that are incompatible with the inappropriate behavior. James, once again, will be the example.

James's constant flitting about the classroom prevented him from focusing on any one activity because flitting and focusing are incompatible behaviors. Teachers therefore gave up attending to his flitting and instead paid attention to those moments (brief as they might be) when he focused on an activity. The teacher in charge of the activity provided interest and support as long as James was engaged. When he left, that teacher and the others immediately turned their attention elsewhere, until such time as he lingered again, even briefly, with another activity. As noted earlier, James's attention span soon began to show marked improvement.

Catch the child being good Florence Harris, a remarkable teacher of young children (as well as a teacher-trainer and researcher) used to counsel teachers and parents: "Catch the child being good" (Harris, Wolf, & Baer, 1964). She urged adults to freely and spontaneously respond to (reinforce) the many *appropriate* things that children do all day long. Harris's counsel is significant; it is almost impossible for a child to be good and bad at the same time. Appropriate behaviors, therefore, have the potential of crowding out inappropriate behaviors. The strategy is to focus very little attention on what adults have agreed are inappropriate acts. The same amount of attention is directed instead to almost anything else the child does. Adults need spend no additional time on the child. They simply spend the time in ways that are more effective and certainly more pleasant for all.

Catching a child being good is contrary to what usually happens. Adults tend to remain fairly neutral until a child does something the adult considers inappropriate. Then the child is likely to get a great deal of attention, which will do little to eliminate the unacceptable behavior. "Catch the child being good" is the essence of **preventive discipline**, discussed in Chapter 13.

preventive discipline arranging the classroom environment in ways that promote children's appropriate behavior and forestall behaviors teachers consider inappropriate

12-3 Punishment

According to its common definition, punishment consists of those adult behaviors that most children find unpleasant: scolding, nagging, yelling, ridiculing, criticizing, isolating, slapping, shaking, spanking. As noted earlier, punishing children is *not* an effective way of managing them. True, punishment often stops an undesirable behavior for the moment. However, the victory is usually short-lived. Yelling at children is an example. Most children will stop, for the time being, whatever they are doing that is causing them to be yelled at. That behavior, however, is almost sure to return, again and again, under various circumstances.

12-3a ■ Side Effects of Punishment

Punishment has undesirable side effects. In the yelling example, the behavior the adult does not like is stopped momentarily. This reinforces the adult for yelling at the child. Result? The adult yells at the child all the more. (This, by the way, is an example of negative reinforcement.) In addition, the adult, according to Bee and Boyd (2012), is modeling yelling, literally teaching inappropriate yelling behavior to the child:

> Children who are yelled at yell back on other occasions. So, to a considerable degree, you get back what you give. (p. 499)

The same holds true for spanking or other forms of physical punishment. In a classic study by Bandura (1973), it was found that children who are spanked frequently, or are otherwise physically punished, become highly aggressive. Other children subjected to punishment may react very differently. Some behave as though they were tightly coiled springs. They often behave well at home or school, but away from adult supervision they seem to explode into a range of forbidden behaviors. Still other children appear troubled, turn inward, hold back, or become passive. It is as if they fear that whatever they do will result in ridicule, criticism, or some form of physical punishment. In general, punishment leads to loss of self-confidence and self-esteem. Frequently punished children seldom feel good about themselves or their world. Such feelings have a negative effect on all aspects of their development.

12-3b ■ Discipline versus Punishment

Punishment, while it may temporarily stop a behavior, does nothing to teach a child what is expected or appropriate behavior. Discipline provides appropriate expectations and consequences for the child. It teaches the child self-control and how to behave. As mentioned throughout the text, teachers must take care to arrange the learning environment in such a way as to encourage appropriate behavior. This is also referred to as preventive discipline (Harris & Allen, 1966). By observing the classroom and children, teachers can prevent problem behaviors by rearranging the things in the classroom that trigger the behavior (antecedents). Preventive discipline communicates to the child how to behave according to developmentally appropriate expectations. It teaches a child the skills or behavior needed. And finally, it creates a positive environment for children and teachers.

All children must be stopped on occasion. A child who is endangering self or others, or causing serious disruptions at home or in the classroom, must be controlled. There are occasions in the classroom when preventive discipline is not enough to address every problem behavior. On these occasions, teachers must use care in choosing a consequence for the behavior that will effectively reduce the behavior, while, at the same time, treating the child with respect and teaching the child what is appropriate.

Teachers have several options available to use as consequences.

- reminders
- redirection
- verbal reprimands
- "sit and watch"
- time-out

These consequences are presented in a continuum. For behaviors that are less severe in nature it is important to start with reminders—the beginning of the continuum. These consequences must be paired with the strategies that teach appropriate behavior, as discussed in Chapter 18.

Reminders, redirection, and reprimands For many children, a reminder, a redirection, or a mild verbal reprimand is enough. When a mild rebuke does not work, a sharp "No!" or "Stop!" may be needed, followed by a *short* and *specific* statement of the potentially harmful act. The statement must be delivered directly to the child at eye level: "No! Janie, I *can't* let you push Tammy off the tricycle." When these measures do not work, the child may have to be removed, briefly, as described here.

redirection a teaching strategy that directs the child's attention and energy from a behavior that is less than desirable by introducing a more appropriate behavior or activity

Sit and watch "Sit and watch" is a mild form of time-out used with children who have a hard time understanding expectations. The procedure calls for children to sit briefly (not more than a minute or two) at the edge of an activity and watch the appropriate play of other children. Two learnings can occur. One helps children learn the consequences of repeatedly overstepping the limits. The second is the opportunity to observe appropriate play of other children. The goal—as it should be with all forms of discipline—is to help children become self-managing.

Children often realize they have made a mistake in self-management the moment they are asked to sit and watch. To help the child remember, the teacher

"sit and watch" a mild form of time-out in which the teacher asks a misbehaving child to sit at the edge of an activity for a minute or two to observe the appropriate play of peers

asks the child to say what the appropriate alternative behavior is: "Keep the sand in the sandbox." If a child does not remember, the teacher states the expectation and then has the child repeat it. Children who are significantly lacking in self-management skills may have to be removed from play several times. Each time, the teacher removes the child matter-of-factly, without scolding or chiding, and the child is helped to restate the appropriate behavior. The child is returned to the activity to try again, with the teacher nearby, ready to respond to the child's efforts to play appropriately.

time-out the extreme form of withdrawing reinforcement

Time-out The extreme form of withdrawing reinforcement is **time-out**. Time-out involves removing all reinforcement, including teacher attention, other children, materials, and equipment. Let it be stressed at the outset: *Time-out should be used only as a last resort.* It should be reserved for seriously inappropriate behaviors that recur—behaviors that teachers have not been able to deal with effectively by redirecting, ignoring, or reinforcing behaviors incompatible with the undesirable behavior.

On those occasions when time-out has to be used, the time-out period should be short. Never should it exceed three minutes; one minute is usually enough. An important reminder: Children do not learn *what to do* in time-out; they only learn *what not to do*. If children are to learn how to work and play with each other and with materials, they need to be involved (Schickedanz, Schickedanz, & Forsyth, 1982). It is in the classroom, *not in time-out*, that teachers can help children learn appropriate ways of responding. Teachers seldom need to use time-out or any other punishment procedure when children receive adequate amounts of positive attention. It must be remembered, however, that what is an adequate amount of positive attention will vary from child to child.

If a teacher finds she is using time-out on a daily basis with a child, it is time to take an in-depth look at the child, the behavior, and why it is occurring. For some children, their misbehavior may actually be helping them to get out of doing something they don't want to do. For example, a child who disrupts consistently at the end of playtime and is placed in time-out for three minutes avoids clean-up. Information on how to determine the function or purpose of behavior can be found in Chapter 18.

A few final words about punishment: On those occasions when punishment cannot be avoided, it should come early in the sequence of misbehavior and at the mildest level possible (Patterson, 1975). It is important to immediately take the toy from the child who has ignored the reminder about not banging it on her sister or the television. Bee and Boyd (2012) put it this way:

If a teacher finds she is using time-out on a daily basis with a child, it is time to take an in-depth look at the child, their behavior, and why it is occurring.

© Cengage Learning

Consistently withholding small privileges will "work," especially if the parent is also warm, clear about the rules, and consistent. It is far less effective if the parent waits until the screams have reached a piercing level or until the fourth time a teenager has gone off without saying where she's gone—and then weigh in with yelling and strong punishment.

Step-By-Step Learning 12-4 ☀

Step-by-step learning, or **task analysis**, is a major teaching strategy. It has proven particularly useful when teaching children with developmental problems. In analyzing any kind of a task—tying shoes, counting bears, printing letters, defending possessions, making friends—the first requirement is to break the task down into small and logical steps. The steps must be in sequence, progressing from the simple and easy to the more difficult and complex. The smaller the steps, the better. Small steps provide frequent opportunities for success. The process consists of responding positively to the accomplishment of each successive small step that eventually results in learning a complex skill or behavior. Many small steps, *and therefore many small successes*, help the child avoid unnecessary frustration. Too many frustrations are defeating to young learners, and even more defeating for children with developmental problems.

task analysis the process of sequencing developmental tasks into small, incremental steps

12-4a ■ Observation and Task Analysis

To analyze a task, early childhood teachers find it helpful first to watch a young child perform the task, especially a child who has only recently mastered a particular skill. The child's motor coordination and general approach to the problem are likely to be more finely sequenced and developmentally appropriate than those of an older child or an adult performing the same task. During the observation of the task, the teacher should make a list of the individual steps a child must perform to complete the task. When developing a list of steps, make sure that each step requires a similar amount of effort on the part of the child. The overall number of steps should be manageable, usually not more than twenty-five (Anderson, Jablonski, Thomeer, & Knapp, 2007). If the task analysis is too long the skill may need to be taught as two separate skills. An example of a task analysis for hanging a coat appears in Figure 12-2.

The ability to break a task down into small steps and teach it in a systematic manner is a critical skill for early childhood teachers. This is especially valuable when working with children with special needs. A teacher can use the task analysis to collect information (data) on the progress a child is making. These data

FIGURE 12-2

Task Analysis for Hanging a Coat

1. Child walks to cubby
2. Child removes coat (able to do this)
3. Child finds loop in coat
4. Child puts finger in loop
5. Child puts loop onto hook

© Cengage Learning

Child: Ricky

Prompts: V = verbal   G = gesture   P = physical   I = independently

STEPS	DATES	1/12	1/14	1/20	1/22
Child walks to cubby		V	V	V	V
Child removes coat (able to do this)		I	I	I	I
Child finds loop in coat		P	P	P	P
Child puts finger in loop		P	P	G	I
Child puts loop onto hook		P	G	G	I

© Cengage Learning

FIGURE **12-4**

Blank Task Analysis Data
Sheet

Child: _____

Prompts: V = verbal   G = gesture   P = physical   I = independently

STEPS	DATES			

© Cengage Learning

TeachSource Digital Download Download from CourseMate.

can be used to determine the level of prompting the child needs to complete the task. This allows the teacher to plan effectively how to move the child toward completing the task independently. See Figures 12-3 and 12-4 for an example of a data sheet that can be used both for listing the steps of a task as well as for collecting data. Information about data collection for inappropriate behavior is covered in Chapter 18.

When adapting a procedure to an individual child, the starting point is determined by observing that child. The rule is to start where the child is developmentally, with what the child *can do*. This provides a successful experience from the outset. It also enables the teacher to make positive comments immediately, thus getting the new learning off to a good start.

True, the first step may be far removed from the final objective. Many times it is nothing more than a child standing and watching an activity that has been targeted as a developmentally necessary skill for that child. This, however, often proves to be an important first step to learning a more complex skill.

12-4b ■ Prompting, Fading, and Cueing

Step-by-step learning often needs to be accompanied by physical and verbal assistance referred to as **prompting** and *cueing*. Prompts and cues help all children—and especially children with developmental problems—acquire a skill they may be having trouble with. **Fading** is the process of gradually and systematically reducing assistance (the prompting and cueing) as much and as soon as possible while still maintaining correct responding. Fading of instructional prompts is critical in order for the child to respond to the natural conditions of the environment (Noonan & McCormick, 2006).

prompting verbal, gestural, or physical assistance that helps the child to learn a skill or participate in an activity

fading gradually reducing prompts, cues, and physical assistance when teaching a particular skill

During the fading process, it is important to observe the child frequently to make sure that progress continues. (Demchak, 1990, offers a good discussion of prompting and fading.) The goal is for the child to learn to perform the task as independently as is feasible. To illustrate these procedures, learning to hang up a coat is described below.

> The teacher accompanies the child to the cubby or locker and gives verbal cues: "Here is the hook for your coat."
>
> The teacher explains and demonstrates: "This is the loop that keeps your coat on the hook. It goes over the hook like this."
>
> Taking the coat off the hook but holding it open, the teacher cues: "Can you find the loop?"
>
> When the child finds it, the teacher says, "Right. Now you can put your finger in just like I did."
>
> "Now, slip it over the hook." If the child cannot yet coordinate the necessary movements, the teacher guides the child's hand.
>
> After a few tries, the teacher is able to withdraw physical assistance the instant before the loop goes over the hook, and so can say to the child, "Look at that! You hung up your coat. Good for you!"

In this example, physical assistance was gradually reduced while verbal cues and positive comments were continued. As the child got better at the task, verbal help was also reduced, but only as the child had nearly accomplished each step. Some tasks and some children need even smaller, more specific steps and special kinds of assistance. **Manual prompting**, also referred to as physical prompting, is a common form of special assistance. The strategy is to place the adult's hand around the child's and actually put the child through the motions. Once the child has the feel of the movements, manual prompting gradually is faded.

manual prompt positioning the teacher's hand around the learner's and putting the learner through the motions required for performing a particular act

Teachers must guard against overwhelming children with directions. Directions should be kept to a minimum and given only if the teacher is prepared to carry through with additional prompting and cueing. Directions are most effective when worded briefly, specifically, and positively. It is more informative and helpful to say, "Hold tight with both hands," than it is to say, "Be careful.

Don't fall." The latter statements provide no information about what the child should be doing. A primary goal is to encourage children's independence.

Therefore, teachers should provide just enough assistance to ensure success, but not so much as to promote over-dependence. Adults most effectively promote children's independence by *waiting*. Children need time to figure out what they are going to do and how they will do it. All too often the adult says, "Put on your sock," and while a young child is still trying to figure out which is the open end of the sock, the adult grabs it and expertly puts it on the child's foot. What message does this convey to the child?

12-4c ■ Amount and Timing of Reinforcement

How much reinforcement is enough? The answer varies from child to child and task to task. Almost continuous reinforcement (feedback) may be needed when a child is beginning to learn something new. Every time the new behavior occurs (or an approximation to the new behavior), the adult tries to respond in some way. At times, smiling and nodding may be all a teacher need do. In all instances, adult attention is gradually reduced as the child becomes more able. The goal, always, is that the child's success (intrinsic motivation) takes over, keeping the child eager to continue learning. To accomplish this, a balance must be achieved: not so much adult attention that the child becomes dependent, but enough so that learning continues until the skill is well-established and intrinsically reinforcing.

12-4d ■ Praise

Praise, because it is so central to children's learning, is discussed frequently in this text. It is mentioned here because of its relationship to step-by-step learning. Praise statements, like prompts and cues, need to be specific. It is of little value, in terms of children's learning, to make statements such as "Good boy," "Good work," "That's nice," "What a pretty picture." In contrast, **descriptive praise** (saying what it is that is good) gives the child specific feedback, which is always an aid to further learning. When the teacher says, "You're putting all the red blocks on the red squares," the child knows exactly what it is that he or she is doing well. Such information is useful to the child in learning the rest of the color-matching task. Furthermore, the focus is on the child's efforts and accomplishments.

Rarely, if ever, should teachers make statements such as "*I like the way you tied your shoes*" (or patted the baby, or shared a cookie, or any of the other good things children learn to do). Contrast the statement about shoe-tying with this one: "Risa, you tied both shoes all by yourself! That makes you feel good, doesn't it?" The first statement implies that a child should be working to please others and needs to depend on external sources as measures of personal worth. The second praise statement recognizes the accomplishment in a way that encourages the child to feel good about him- or herself. A child's confidence, self-esteem, and love of learning are thus nurtured.

In recent years, articles and books have been published on the issue of too much praise and too many rewards (Hitz & Driscoll, 1989; Kohn, 2001). The issue has been raised as to whether we are causing children to become dependent on adults to measure their worth, rather than children doing things for their own pleasure. The phrase "good job" has been overused in many classrooms, and as stated previously, is of little value. Teachers have gotten into the habit of using this phrase in response to many children's behaviors so much that it means little

descriptive praise
feedback that lets children know specifically what it is they are doing well

Descriptive Praise—"You put your shoes on by yourself."

Did You Get It?

How do the methods of step-by-step learning help the child with developmental problems?

a. Prompting and cueing helps children acquire a skill they may be having trouble with; fading of instructional prompts is critical in order for the child to respond to the natural conditions of the environment.

b. Prompting and fading helps children acquire a skill they may be having trouble with.

c. Prompting and cueing is critical in order for the child to respond to the natural conditions in the environment; fading helps children acquire a skill they may be having trouble with.

d. Prompting helps children acquire a skill they may be having trouble with; cueing is critical in order for the child to respond to natural conditions in the environment.

Take the full quiz on CourseMate.

or nothing to the child and may actually interrupt what they are doing. When giving attention in the classroom, two things should be kept in mind.

- Keep your words descriptive. A simple statement, free of evaluation ("You hung your coat up by yourself;" "You helped your friend get the book"), tells the child you noticed.

- Ask questions and let the child talk. Instead of telling a child how much you like his painting, why not ask, "How did you get that color?" "What do you like most about your painting?"

12-4e ■ Shaping

When positive reinforcement is provided, and is contingent on an approximation of a desired response, it is referred to as **shaping**. This often occurs naturally when a child is developing language. A parent might accept "ookie" for cookie but later expect the child to say "cookie, please" as the child gets older and language develops. Shaping can also be implemented on a more systematic basis. For example, when a child is having difficulty sitting for circle they may only be expected to sit for the first five minutes and then allowed to go play. After they are able to sit for five minutes for several days the expectation will be increased to six minutes, and so forth, until the child is eventually able to sit for the entire fifteen minutes of circle time.

Learning By Imitation 12-5 ☀

Many kinds of learning take place in natural settings, such as the home or classroom. Children watch and then imitate: That is, they model their behavior after others. They seem to require little or no direct reinforcement from anyone or anything. The involvement and self-feedback the child experiences result in learning. Specific labels for this kind of learning are **observational learning** or **modeling** (Bandura, 1977).

Children learn both appropriate and inappropriate behaviors by watching what is modeled on television, in the classroom or neighborhood, and by parents and family members. Teachers of young children are powerful models for classroom behavior. For example, teachers who believe that children should not sit on tables should not sit on tables themselves. Teachers who believe that

shaping positive reinforcement provided contingent on an approximation of a desired behavior

observational learning learning by watching and imitating another's actions; also called modeling

modeling learning by watching and imitating another's actions; also called observational learning

Connecting Developmentally Appropriate Practice to Brain Research

IMITATION AND MIRROR NEURONS

During the late 1980s and early 1990s several Italian neuropsychologists observed the behavior of Macaque monkeys who were hooked up to brain monitoring machines. They saw how the monkeys imitated their instructor. For instance, when the neuropsychologists ripped a piece of paper, or ate a piece of food, the monkey imitated the exact same thing.

Brain research on brain imaging using functional magnetic resonance imaging (fMRI) has shown that the same portions of the human brain, the inferior frontal cortex and superior parietal lobe, are activated similarly if a person is actually performing an action or if they are just observing someone else performing that action. These have been called Mirror Neuron Networks.

Mirror neuron networks throughout the brain confirm the importance of the teacher's actions, including nonverbal body language. The child's neurological synapses "mirror" not only the teacher's actions but also their reactions. How a teacher presents learning experience both verbally and nonverbally are critical. This research indicates that the child's neurons are responding to both the verbal instructions but also to the adult's nonverbal behavior, including body language and emotions. A child's system can get confused if they are observing an adult who's body language indicates they are not interested in the topic or perhaps not prepared to present the lesson. The child's interpretation at an unconscious level may be one of confusion and anxiety due to the mixed signals his or her system is receiving.

Your Turn

1. How does this research relate to the idea of learning by imitation?
2. How does this impact not only behaviors a teacher is modeling but also nonverbal behavior that children are observing?

Source: Rushton, S. P., Rushton, A. J., & Larkin, E. (2010). Neuroscience, play and early childhood education: Connections, implications and assessment. *Early Childhood Education J, 37*(351–361).

children should not yell at them should in turn not yell at children themselves. "Do as I say but not as I do" is poor and ineffective teaching.

The skills spontaneously modeled by older or more skilled children serve as motivation. Young children are eager to learn. It is almost inevitable they will try things they see more mature children doing. To facilitate imitation learning in less skilled children, teachers can provide descriptive praise or feedback to the more skilled child: "Marilee, you are getting down all by yourself, one foot and one hand at a time." An approving statement of this kind serves several purposes.

- Marilee is encouraged to appreciate her own individuality and to value her own skills and capabilities.

- An indirect lesson is provided for children within hearing distance who may not yet have achieved Marilee's level of climbing skills.

- The teacher's words, "slowly and carefully, one foot and one hand at a time," are clues to what they might try, in their own way, as they work at becoming proficient climbers.

Not all children know how to imitate, however. Many children with special needs require specific instruction. In other words, they must first learn *how* to imitate before they can learn *through* imitation. In these instances, teachers need to provide specific kinds of assistance.

12-5a ▪ Competition Is Inappropriate

Descriptive statements, such as those about Marilee's climbing, carry no implications that one child is better than another. Promoting competition among young children establishes an uneasy learning environment. Children cannot appreciate the process of learning or their own uniqueness if adults imply they should try to

Did You Get It?

What type of statement would elicit a positive sense of competition?

a. A descriptive statement suggesting a child can do better than another.

b. An approving statement measured against the child's own earlier performance.

c. An approving statement measured against another child's earlier performance.

d. A statement promoting competition.

Take the full quiz on CourseMate.

be better than someone else. The only competition that enhances development is when a child's progress is approvingly measured against that child's own earlier performance (Brophy, 1981). Example: "You are really learning colors. Now you know all the color names on this new card, too." The foregoing is a much-abbreviated sketch of learning through modeling. The practice will be further examined in subsequent sections where the focus will be on teaching particular skills.

Summary

- Developmental concepts and behavioral principles have become blended into well-articulated early childhood teaching practices.

- The effectiveness of an early education program is demonstrated by changes in children's behavior. To have healthy development, ongoing changes in behavior must occur.

- The blend of developmental and behavioral principles and practices is good for all children and particularly important in inclusive programs where the range of skill levels among children is extensive. The blend of practices demonstrates that all children are teachable; if a child is not learning, the blame is on the program, not the child.

- From the behavioral perspective, systematic reinforcement procedures, if imposed on a developmentally appropriate structure, account for children's learning. The principles can be put into an ABC format: A stands for what happens first (the antecedent that precedes the child's behavior); B stands for the child's behavior; C stands for consequences, or reinforcement (that which follows the behavior).

- Reinforcements (consequences) can be either positive or negative. Positive reinforcement is the teacher's best tool. It is readily available through the teacher's assistance, genuine interest, and positive reactions to each child and each child's activities. Positive reinforcement also resides in the interesting and appropriate materials and activities provided by teachers.

- In some instances, reinforcers must be withheld or withdrawn so a child does not get attention for behaviors that are detrimental to his or her development. When teachers must withhold reinforcement for an inappropriate behavior, it is important they double their efforts to give the child positive attention for useful behaviors incompatible with the inappropriate behavior. By so doing, inappropriate behaviors are likely to be crowded out by more appropriate ones.

- Withdrawing attention may mean, in extreme cases, withdrawing the child. This is referred to as time-out; a milder version is termed sit-and-watch.

- Time-out is used in those infrequent situations where systematic positive practices have failed to produce necessary behavior changes. Periods of withdrawing the child from play must be brief, not more than a minute or two. A child does not learn appropriate skills when isolated.

- Punishment is the least desirable and least effective of all forms of child management. Though the punished behavior may stop for the moment, it usually returns again and again. Frequent punishment has many undesirable effects, including heightened aggressiveness and diminished self-esteem.

- Preventive discipline is the recommended strategy for teachers and parents. This strategy involves arranging the environment to prevent problem behaviors and to teach developmentally appropriate skills and behavior. On occasion, when a consequence is needed for a child's behavior, options include a brief reminder, redirection, a verbal reprimand, "sit and watch," or time-out.

- Other educational practices related to reinforcement procedures include task analysis and learning through observation (modeling). Task analysis is the process of breaking a learning task into small, sequential steps for those children who need special help in the form of reduced frustration and more frequent successes. Step-by-step learning is further facilitated with prompting, shaping, and cueing.

- Children also learn by watching others and by modeling their behavior on that of a more skilled child. In every kind of learning situation, teachers provide encouragement and descriptive praise to the degree that is appropriate for individual children.

- Never, however, do teachers promote competition; competition among children has no place in early childhood education.

Key Terms

behavior modification, 310
descriptive praise, 322
didactic materials, 308
ecology, 308
fading, 321
incompatible behaviors, 314
intrinsic motivation, 307
intrinsic reinforcement, 311
learning theory, 310
logical consequence, 313

manual prompt, 321
maturationist, 307
modeling, 323
natural consequence, 313
negative reinforcement, 311
observational learning, 323
operant conditioning, 310
positive reinforcement, 311
preventive discipline, 315
prompting, 321

punishment, 306
redirection, 317
reinforcement, 306
reinforcers, 310
responsive learning environment, 309
shaping, 323
"sit and watch", 317
task analysis, 319
time-out, 318

Student Activities

1. Observe, for one hour each, two early childhood classrooms that have different teaching philosophies and approaches. Write down every example of adult social reinforcement that you see and hear.

2. Imagine a child engrossed in painting at the easel or at a table. List ten positive statements you might make that recognize the child's worth and efforts.

3. List six examples of inappropriate behavior in young children. List a possible logical consequence and a possible natural consequence for each of the examples.

4. For several days, watch an older child brush his or her teeth. Complete a task analysis of the activity, using a copy of Figure 12-2, starting with the child's approach to the sink.

5. Visit a classroom and ask the teacher what the class rules are. Make a list of the ways you see the rules reinforced and enforced. How are the students reminded of the rules? What are the consequences for not following the rules?

6. Identify three different behaviors that could be taught by shaping. Write a plan to systematically reinforce approximations of the target behavior.

Review Questions

Respond to the following in list format.

1. List four early education practices common to both developmental and behavioral theory.

2. List three possible sources of intrinsic reinforcement.

3. List five types of teacher behaviors that are likely to be positively reinforcing for most young children.

4. List five pairs of behaviors that are incompatible with each other.

5. List three possible negative effects of frequent punishment on young children.

Additional Resources/Reading

What to Do When: Practical Guidance Strategies for Challenging Behaviors in the Preschool
Written by Eva Essa
Wadsworth Publishing

This book includes information on developmentally appropriate guidelines for working with challenging behaviors; exploration of effective preventive techniques through setting up an inviting and supportive environment; discussion of children with special needs; and a focus on the importance of working with parents. Each chapter presents a step-by-step approach to changing such behaviors to more socially appropriate ones. Also included is a CD-ROM that contains additional resources, including guidelines for careful observation and record keeping, scenarios for use in practicing applying the techniques presented in the book, and a listing of books, articles, and websites for further study.

Helpful Websites

Technical Assitance Center for Social Emotional Interventions

http://challengingbehavior.org/

The Technical Assistance Center on Social Emotional Intervention for Young Children (TACSEI) takes the research that shows which practices improve the social-emotional outcomes for young children with, or at risk for, delays or disabilities, and *creates free* products and resources to help decision-makers, caregivers, and service providers apply these best practices in the work they do every day.

The Council for Children with Behavioral Disorders (CCBD)

http://www.ccbd.net

The CCBD is the official division of the Council for Exceptional Children (CEC) committed to promoting and facilitating the education and general welfare of children and youth with emotional or behavioral disorders. The goals of the CCBD include promoting quality education services, encouraging research and professional growth, providing professional support, and advocacy. The website includes research and information relevant to these goals.

ERIC Clearinghouse on Disabilities and Gifted Education

http://www.ericec.org

ERIC is the acronym for the Educational Resources Information Center. The ERIC Clearinghouse on Disabilities and Gifted Education (ERIC EC) is one of sixteen federally funded clearinghouses.

ERIC EC gathers and disseminates professional literature, information, and resources on the education and development of individuals of all ages who have disabilities and/or who are gifted. Topics include identification, assessment, intervention, and enrichment.

Positive Parenting

http://www.positiveparenting.com

The website includes articles on, and links to, positive discipline for parents and teachers. There is also an online bookstore.

 Visit the Education CourseMate for this textbook to access the eBook, Did You Get It? quizzes, Digital Downloads, TeachSource Video Cases, flashcards, and more. Go to CengageBrain.com to log in, register, or purchase access.

Arranging the Learning Environment

OBJECTIVES

After reading this chapter, you should be able to:

13-1 highlight the importance of arranging the environment in an inclusive classroom.

13-2 define preventive discipline, describe the procedure, and explain its value in guiding young children with and without challenging behaviors.

13-3 explain how types of learning are impacted by the physical arrangement of the classroom.

13-4 understand the key elements in planning early learning environments, which include safety, visibility, matching children and equipment, ease of movement, promoting independence, teachers' availability, offering choice, novelty versus familiarity, and structured flexibility.

13-5 discuss the major issues in planning a program schedule for children in an inclusive setting.

13-6 describe smooth transitions and the learnings available to children during transitions.

. . . .

naeyc

The following NAEYC Standards are addressed in this chapter:

STANDARD 1 Promoting Child Development and Learning

STANDARD 3 Observing, Documenting and Assessing to Support Young Children and Families

STANDARD 4 Using Developmentally Effective Approaches

STANDARD 5 Using Content Knowledge to Build Meaningful Curriculum

CONNECTIONS

- Tina had a congenital orthopedic problem requiring ongoing physical and occupational therapy. An IEP objective for Tina, both at home and at school, was to decrease the amount of time she spent in her wheelchair and on crutches. One aspect of the plan was to increase her tolerance for weight bearing, especially standing. Tina's therapists were delighted with the teachers' offer to arrange the classroom environment to facilitate a variety of stand-up play activities so that Tina would not be set apart from the other children.

- Gabe, a three-year-old, went to preschool at Parent Cooperative Preschool in his hometown. Each morning began with the children breaking up to form smaller circle groups with their lead teachers. Gabe often had difficulty paying attention during circle time. He would turn his back on his group, turning around to see what the other groups were doing. His lead teacher Carrie noticed this and began using a portable divider to provide a wall around her circle area. Gabe was better able to attend to his circle group with this new arrangement.

The learning environments provided by early childhood programs will influence, even determine, the development of countless numbers of children (Gordon & Browne, 2010; Prescott, 1994). Those environments also will determine how effectively teachers teach and the kinds of messages that children receive about themselves and others. According to Swim (2006):

> Taking time to reflect on the physical environment is imperative as it is considered the "third teacher" in the classroom. In other words, the environment provides guidance to the children and adults about appropriate behavior. (p. 101)

☀ 13-1 The Inclusive Classroom Environment

In an inclusive classroom, environmental arrangements assume special importance because of the range of abilities among children. Teachers who arrange play spaces and activities so that children with special needs are included easily and naturally convey a powerful message about human values: *All children can play together and have fun.* Having fun together promotes genuine integration and creates a community of caring and learning.

Wolfensberger, best known for his concept of *normalization* (1996), recommends bringing as few pieces of special equipment as possible into the classroom. He argues that special equipment brands children as too different.

Nevertheless, many children with developmental disabilities cannot function without certain types of special equipment, and Wolfensberger would agree that whatever equipment is essential to the child's inclusion in classroom activities should always be on hand.

Therapeutic equipment is available that is fun for all children: huge therapy or exercise balls, tumble tubs, balance beams, portable stair-climbing apparatus, and the like. Effective early education is based on the principle that children are children, regardless of their capabilities. All children have the same needs, though the needs may be more pronounced in some. For example:

- loud and distracting noises are difficult for most children. For hearing-impaired children, such noise may be intolerable.

Taking time to reflect on the physical environment, considered the "third teacher" in the classroom, is imperative.

© Cengage Learning

- moving about safely—in an environment free from clutter, slippery floors, or rumpled rugs—contributes to the safety and security of every child. For children with limited vision or physical problems, an environment free of obstacles protects against serious injury.

- minimizing clutter and confusion enhances the ability of all young children to concentrate on the tasks at hand. For children with attention or learning disorders, reducing distractions may be the best way to promote learning.

- a consistent routine, with warning prior to transitions, and expectations as to what the children should be doing, helps all children feel comfortable because they know what to expect next. For children with autism spectrum disorders, having a consistent routine is critical to preventing behavior problems that are often the result of not knowing what is coming next or not being well prepared for a change in an activity or routine.

Regardless of special problems, meeting developmental needs requires a well-planned learning environment. It is unacceptable to provide one kind of environment for children who are typically developing and a different kind for children with disabilities. As stated in the NAEYC Position Statement on Developmentally Appropriate Practice (Copple & Bredekamp, 2009), it is desirable that all children

> experience an organized environment and an orderly routine that provides an overall structure in which learning takes place; the environment is dynamic and changing but predictable and comprehensible from a child's point of view. (p. 17)

Preventive Discipline 13-2 ☀

Children with developmental differences and challenging behaviors need guidance procedures (discipline) that reduce prejudice and promote positive outcomes (Neilsen, Olive, Donovan, & McEvoy, 1998). Helping children learn to behave appropriately reduces the differences that often set them apart and produce unfavorable attitudes toward them. An effective and caring way for teachers to deal with such situations is to arrange the learning environment in ways that promote acceptable behavior in all children. Discipline is most effective when it is based on adult anticipation. Through their observations of children and their knowledge of child development, teachers can anticipate potential trouble and avert it before it occurs. In other words, adults prevent mishap; hence the term **preventive discipline** (Harris & Allen, 1966).

preventive discipline arranging the classroom environment in ways that promote children's appropriate behavior and forestall behaviors teachers consider inappropriate

Preventive discipline depends on what teachers do and say to forestall trouble. In a way, this entire unit on arranging the learning environment is about discipline. Placing the drying rack next to the easel helps children avoid the problems associated with carrying a dripping painting across an area. Providing a parking place for wheel toys instead of letting children abandon them mid-road helps children avoid injuring others or getting into angry exchanges as to which child really owns a piece of equipment. The point to be underscored is this: *Environmental arrangements are major determinants of children's behavior.* Preventive discipline accomplishes the following:

- It communicates to children how to behave, and then facilitates children's efforts.

- It makes it easy for children to learn the vast number of behaviors and skills necessary for growing up confident and competent in a world that expects much of young children.

- It helps children avoid unnecessary and ego-deflating errors that squander children's time.

- It assures a positive climate in which teachers enjoy teaching, and children of different developmental levels enjoy learning together.

Did You Get It?

In what way do guidance procedures reduce prejudice and promote positive outcomes?

a. Helping children learn to behave appropriately reduces the differences that often set them apart and produce unfavorable attitudes toward them.

b. Arranging the learning environment in a conducive way.

c. Facilitated by adult anticipation.

d. Through caring and effective teaching.

Take the full quiz on CourseMate.

13-3 Arrangements for Learning

Early learning environments are as varied as the programs they represent and the buildings that house them. Facilities range from multimillion-dollar child care centers, to storefronts, church or home basements, public school classrooms, or semi-renovated warehouses. The setting—even the newest or most lavish—does not guarantee quality learning experiences, however. The physical plant may contribute to quality, but it does not ensure it. As Gordon and Williams Browne (2010) point out, the environment is more than a plant; it includes the physical and human qualities that combine to create a space in which children and adults work and play together.

Setting up and maintaining an effective early learning environment puts teachers' knowledge of child development to the test. Classroom and play yard

An environment free from clutter contributes to the safety and security of every child.

arrangements must be sensitive to developmental sequences and individual differences.

Teachers must know what to do when one child is experiencing learning difficulties, another is not making developmental progress, and a third is hampered by challenging behavior. Teachers must recognize that the first move is to step back and observe the child in the context of the daily program. Necessary changes in the environment can then be made. Almost always, it is the environment that needs fixing, not the child.

13-3a ■ Types of Learning

The first step in planning an inclusive early childhood program is specifying the kinds of learning that will be offered. Most of this section will address preschool programs. A brief discussion regarding infant/toddler and early elementary years follows. Most preschool programs plan three broad types of experiences: learning through self-help routines, through teacher-structured activities, and through discovery learning periods (also referred to as *free-play* or *child-initiated activities*). Each of these will be discussed in terms of physical arrangements.

Self-help or independence skills These are independence-promoting skills related to socially prescribed routines such as toileting, dressing, eating, cleaning up, and doing one's share. Learning to perform these tasks is closely tied to the child's emerging independence and competence. During the toddler and early preschool years, teachers systematically guide children through each step of each routine until the skills become automatic. Some children need additional help in learning basic **self-help skills**. Help can be provided indirectly by arranging the environment so that all types of children can work and play together throughout the program day. This social blend assures a variety of good models. Children who are working at acquiring a skill can observe their peer who has already mastered the same developmental task.

To promote independence, children must have appropriately sized furnishings and accessories. Hooks, washbasins, toilets, and drinking facilities that can be reached and operated by children allow them to help themselves. Visual cues such as pictures illustrating the steps of hand-washing and toileting routines

self-help skills the ability to take care of one's own needs: self-feeding, toileting, dressing, and other socially prescribed routines

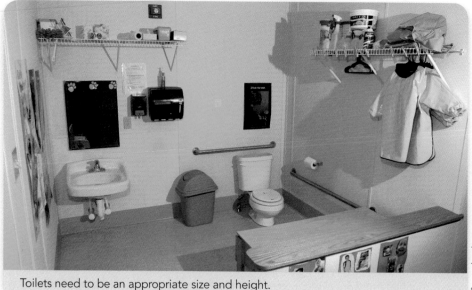
Toilets need to be an appropriate size and height.

posted near the toilet or sink can help children remember what they need to do next. With appropriate classroom adaptations, children can learn to take care of their own special needs. Examples:

- *A child in a later stage of toilet training can be given a preset timer that will go off as a reminder to get to the bathroom.*
- *A child who has difficulty remembering where his cubby is can be given a card with his name on it to match to his name on his cubby.*
- *A prearranged comfortable and secure place to go to remove leg braces as needed frees a child from having to wait for an available adult.*
- *Teaching a child to adjust the volume on his or her hearing aid reduces the time the child is uncomfortable or not "tuned in."*
- *Having everything in the classroom and play yard in good working order reduces frustration and increases children's initiative and independence.*

The latter point is especially important. Few situations make a child feel more incompetent than a doorknob that spins aimlessly, a faucet that will not turn off, or a drawer that will not open.

The experiences are especially devastating for children with developmental disabilities. When something cannot be made to work, children often do not realize it is the equipment that is at fault. To the child, it seems yet one more unsuccessful attempt to accomplish an everyday task. **Induced incompetence** is a term used to describe the effects of poorly functioning equipment on children with developmental disabilities.

induced incompetence term used to describe the effects of poorly functioning equipment on children with development disabilities

Toilet facilities Learning to use the toilet by themselves is a major developmental task for most children. A first requirement in toilet training is that toilets are of appropriate size and height. Another consideration is adequate space for maneuvering crutches or a walker or pulling a wheelchair parallel with the toilet. A handrail is needed so the child may steady him- or herself. A hollow block or footstool may be provided for a child's feet to rest on, thereby reducing insecurity and fear of falling off the toilet. In programs for toddlers or children needing help with toilet training, teachers need to be immediately available in the children's bathroom. Accessibility from the outdoor play area is especially important

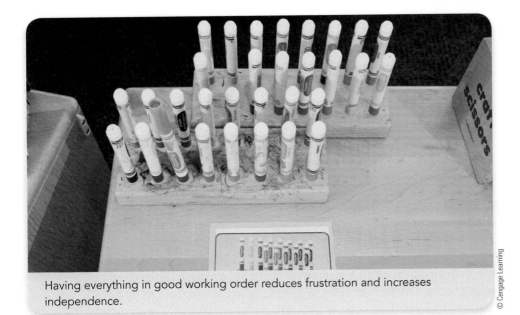

Having everything in good working order reduces frustration and increases independence.

© Cengage Learning

so that children can get to the bathroom in a hurry, as they often need to do. School-age children can be expected to use a bathroom out of sight of teachers, even down the hall.

Cubby areas Each child should have a space or cubby in which to keep his or her personal belongings. This increases responsibility and organizational skills and ensures that children have a safe place to keep their special things from home. This not only confirms the importance of both home and school environments; it also teaches the importance of respecting each other's property (Swim, 2006). The space should be labeled with their name and their picture so that each child can easily locate his or her cubby, especially at the start of the school year. The cubby or locker area should be as near as possible to the outdoor exit and the bathroom. This arrangement may put the lockers at some distance from the door through which children arrive and depart for home. This may be a problem for children who find it difficult to walk to the opposite side of the building to store their belongings. Some children prefer to ease into the classroom. Having the cubbies some distance from the entry door can be less of a problem if the traffic lane from entry door to lockers is free of obstacles, clutter, and extremely loud activity.

Sleeping area The sleeping area in all-day programs must be carefully planned and free of distractions. If a separate room is not available, a nap area can be partitioned off with low barriers. A rug or some other kind of clearly indicated space should be near the entrance to the nap area. This space should be out of visual range of the lunch area, where other children and teachers are likely to be finishing up and clearing away. In this particular spot, children remove their shoes and relax

It is important for each child to have a place to keep his or her belongings.

© Cengage Learning

before entering the nap area. Creating an environment conducive to resting might include closing the shades or blinds, turning on a small lamp or night light, playing classical music, and encouraging children to bring something to cuddle (a stuffed animal or blanket) from home. Swim (2006) also suggests providing alternatives for children who require less rest, such as small baskets of books and quiet toys. Another consideration is the location of storage for cots and bedding. It should be located such that children can help set up for nap time or perhaps even do so independently. Teachers' time and energy is too valuable to be spent fetching and carrying; it should be reserved for helping children learn the routines related to moving into a relaxing rest time.

Teacher-structured activities Teacher-structured activities (also referred to as large- and small-group activities, one-to-one tutorials, or instruction periods) are interspersed throughout the day to provide a balance of child-directed and teacher-directed activities. The teacher's intent is to impart knowledge and skills that children need but cannot learn solely through self-guided exploration of the environment. Stories, songs, finger plays, care of materials, control of paint drips, gentleness with animals, names of objects, and concept information are but a few of the content areas that might comprise a teacher-structured activity. These activities may be formally planned learning experiences, or they may arise spontaneously out of a child's immediate interest or need. Some children in the inclusive classroom need more (but perhaps shorter) teacher-structured activities. They also may need teacher-structured activities related to skills that other children seem to acquire spontaneously. For example, most children need no help in learning to point; usually they have to be taught *not* to point. Children with perceptual-motor or cognitive limitations often need direct instruction in learning to point.

Easy transition between activities is a first consideration when arranging the location for formal, teacher-structured activities such as pre-academic tasks, stories, music, and rhythms. Children respond more readily if activities can be approached from all other areas. Seeing that an activity is starting often serves as a cue. Children still in the process of cleaning up a play area may be prompted to finish up quickly and get to an activity such as stories. Placing large-group activities within easy access of all other activity areas helps teachers, too. The teacher conducting the group can be subtle when shifting a child with a shorter attention span to a teacher in another activity area. Disruption of the group experience is avoided for the children still involved.

Discovery learning *Free play, child-initiated activities*, and *free-choice periods* are other names for **discovery learning**. These are uninterrupted blocks of time, both indoors and outdoors, that are fundamental to early learning. It is through play that children discover their world and themselves. Play allows children to apply their own ideas as well as the learning they have acquired in teacher-structured activities. At every developmental stage, children need opportunities to play and to have access to play materials. Some children do not play of their own accord, or even know how to play; they must be helped to learn play skills.

Not all children benefit from large blocks of unstructured time. They may spend too much of their time unengaged or inappropriately engaged because of their limited skills or short span of attention. For these children, brief teacher-structured activities are easily interspersed during discovery learning periods. Learning to point, mentioned earlier, will be used as an example.

Baillie's IEP specified learning to point as a needed developmental skill. During a free-play period, the teacher in the immediate area noticed Baillie

Individualism versus Collectivism—What a Teacher Learned

Johanna is a first-year teacher in a school serving primarily English language learners from Latino families.

When first setting up her kindergarten classroom, Johanna took time to set up individual supply boxes for each child. She carefully labeled each marker, pencil, and scissor with the name of each child in her class. This took a great deal of time and she was quite proud of her efforts and the setup for her classroom. A colleague who had been teaching in the school for several years came into her room to welcome her to the school. Upon seeing all the individually set-up boxes she explained to Johanna that the majority of the families in her classroom would not see a need for this and that the children would be more comfortable with supplies placed in a collective bin on each work table.

Individualism and collectivism are terms used to describe different cultures. An individualistic culture is one in which an individual's goals and interests take priority over those of the group or larger society. They are responsible for themselves and perhaps members of their immediate family. In a collectivistic culture, individuals are more concerned with the group as a whole, including the extended family. Examples of individualistic cultures include: France, Netherlands, Nordic countries, Czech Republic, Hungary, Poland, Italy, German-speaking countries, the U.S., and Anglo countries. Examples of collectivistic cultures include: Thailand, Korea, Costa Rica, Chile, Russia, Bulgaria, Portugal, Spain, China, Japan, and Mexico.

The school Johanna was working in served students primarily from a collectivistic culture. She realized quickly that she needed to change some of her practices and views to better meet her students and their families' needs.

standing about, seeming not to know what to do with herself. The teacher took her by the hand and said, "Let's go pointing," an improvised game Baillie enjoyed. While keeping her eye on the other children, the teacher walked around the area with Baillie for a minute or so, having her point to well-known objects. The teacher then helped Baillie point to what she would like to do next and helped her settle in.

The location of a discovery learning area is determined by furniture, storage, and the cleanup requirements of each area.

- Tables that are used for lunch and for pre-academics are likely to determine where puzzles and other fine motor materials are to be used during alternate periods.

- A large rug in the manipulative area often is suitable for group activities such as music and rhythms.

- Placing carpet squares on the rug in a circle or semicircle as place markers for individual children can ease transitions from small-group to large-group activities.

- The unit block area needs to be clearly separate from the rug and manipulative areas. Ideally, it is a large open space, free of furniture or equipment except for shelves with materials related to block play. Shelves and a floor marker such as tape or a painted line can mark off the block play area. Photographs of simple block structures can be provided to help the child who is unsure of what to do in the block area (Sandall & Schwartz, 2008).

- When a dramatic play center is offered, it usually is set into a corner with another set of low shelves serving as third-side dividers. Partially enclosed in this way, the area is distinct from other areas.

- In some classrooms, two sets of low, open shelves can be placed back to back. One set faces one center of interest, the other a different center, thus defining two distinct areas. A sink in the classroom usually determines where children will use paints, clay, and other wet and messy materials. If there is no classroom sink, the creative area should be placed as near the bathroom as possible. It is advisable to have a tub of water and paper towels always available in the creative area. Children then can remove excess finger paint or clay before moving into the bathroom. The area where paints and clay and other messy materials are used should be set well away from traffic lanes between activity areas. This forestalls wet materials and children's dripping products being carried into other areas. The location of the creative or sensory area may also be determined by flooring surfaces. Placing this area over tile or linoleum can ease cleanup. If the only flooring available is carpeting, a shower curtain can be taped to the floor, as long as it does not become a tripping hazard or prevent those in wheelchairs from entering the area. A small hand broom and dust pan can be provided alongside a sensory table filled with rice or sand to help children maintain a clean area.

In the creative area, the availability of easel painting is made visually distinct by the large easel paper, paint containers and brushes, aprons, and drying rack, all grouped together. These are separate from containers of crayons, paper, scissors, and collage materials that are displayed on shelves.

Teachers must also determine the location of activities and centers based on noise levels. Activities that are louder, such as block play and dramatic play, should be placed next to each other. The noise level of some areas will vary depending on the materials planned for the day. For example, offering hammers, nails, and wood in the manipulative area will certainly increase the noise level over an activity such as pegs and pegboards. Care should be given to ensure children always have a quiet place to go if they need to be alone or take a break from the action. The manipulative area or book corner may serve this purpose.

Teachers' selection and grouping of materials indicates clearly how each area is to be used. A child may believe it to be all right to color in the library books if crayons are left on the bookshelves. In contrast, the examples that follow offer environmental signals dictating appropriate behaviors.

Teacher-structured activities can be interspersed throughout the day.

© Cengage Learning

- *The block area contains only those items related to block play. Accessory items to be incorporated into block play (cars, trucks, dollhouse furniture, zoo animals) are grouped, rotated regularly, and displayed in the same area on shelves separate from but adjacent to the block storage shelves.*

- *Manipulative materials are displayed only in the manipulative area. Each material is given a distinct place with related parts grouped together (hammer, individual cans of nails, and hammering board; pegs and pegboards; large, unstrung wooden beads and rigid-tipped string) in containers. The display not only tells the child what to expect of the material and how to use it but also facilitates cleanup. (Never put out a broken or incomplete set of materials for children. It is better to have no puzzles than puzzles with even one missing piece.)*

The ability to see between centers often facilitates children's play as they make connections among materials in different centers and around the room. Therefore, even though teachers carefully plan learning centers, they must be flexible in allowing children to move materials from one center to another when it allows them to expand their play and creativity. The clear line of vision across centers also supports the teachers' ability to supervise. Care must be given so that the boundaries of the center are clear enough and do not create wide-open areas and pathways that become runways or rough-and-tumble areas.

Did You Get It?

What is the significance of ensuring that everything in the classroom and play yard is in good working order, in relation to the child's needs?

a. Time efficiency.

b. Reduces teachers' frustration.

c. Avoids induced incompetence, reduces frustration, and increases children's initiative and independence.

d. Aesthetically pleasing.

Take the full quiz on CourseMate.

Planning Early Learning Environments 13-4 ☀

Incorporated into all aspects of environmental planning are certain basic principles that we will now review. These include safety, visibility, matching children and equipment, ease of movement, promoting independence, teacher availability, offering of choices, novelty versus familiarity, and structured flexibility. Figure 13-1 also provides a listing of quality indicators for inclusive programs.

13-4a ■ Safety

Safety in classrooms and play yards is a major consideration in preventing accidents and fostering independence. Independence comes about only in a safe and secure environment. Children must be able to trust adults to protect them from harm and from harming themselves. For example, rugs should have non-skid backing or be glued or tacked down. A skidding rug is a hazard for all children and teachers, and it is especially hazardous for children who are blind or physically impaired.

Teachers should also make sure that material and equipment are nontoxic, free of cracks and splinters, and in good working order. It is frustrating for any child to try to steer a wheel toy that has a bent axle; for a child with limited motor skills, it may lead to a serious accident. This can frighten the child from further efforts to join in outdoor play. If the accident involved other children, avoidance of the child may follow. The children who were hurt (and their parents) usually do not understand it was the equipment—not the child—that was at fault.

Order and organization Clutter and disorganization are incompatible with safety. Teachers must make sure that everything has a place, and, when not in use, everything is in its place. A child with seriously limited vision needs to know

Indicators of an Inclusive Early Childhood Program

The following is a list that can be used by parents when looking for a program or by program staff to determine if their program is effectively including every child.

- Each child is welcomed on arrival and wished well on departure in a way that suits them.

- Each parent/caregiver feels welcome and valued as an expert on their child.

- Teachers look for the reasons for a child's behavior and teach the child appropriate ways to express their needs and feelings.

- Furniture is stable and at varying heights to meet the needs of the children.

- Floors are even and free of tripping hazards such as rugs.

- Information is presented to children in a variety of formats (e.g., visual supports, support of gestures, and eye contact).

- All areas of the classroom are accessible to all children.

- The program includes a social skills component that emphasizes kindness, empathy, and cooperative play.

- Teachers plan for and facilitate peer interaction.

- Teachers encourage children to use their language to request materials and to label items.

- Teachers give children cues before transitions and describe how to complete activities.

- Teachers use developmental observations to collect information, and use the information to plan the curriculum.

- Teachers individualize teaching and use opportunities for repetition for children who may need more time or experiences to learn new skills.

- Teachers', children's, and parents' attitude reflect an acceptance of all children regardless of need or ability. Activities are led by the interests and enthusiasms of each child who attends.

- Pictures, equipment, and resources reflect the differing background and experiences of the children.

- The person in charge is committed to the active participation of children, parents/caregivers, team members, and others, to ensure each individual's needs are met.

- Teachers participate in ongoing training in special needs and inclusion.

- The teachers use consistent positive language in describing children, including person-first language.

- With the parents' permission, the program communicates and collaborates with other service providers working with a child (e.g., a speech therapist, an occupational therapist).

Sources: All of Us—Inclusion Checklist for Settings. KIDSactive: London. http://www3.hants.gov.uk/inclusion_checklist.pdf

Watson, A. & McCathren, R. (2009). Including children with special needs. Are you and your early childhood program ready? *Beyond the Journal. Young Children on the Web.* March 2009.

FIGURE 13-1

that the dough, cookie cutters, and rolling pins are always found in the lower-left corner of the housekeeping cupboards, for example. Logical arrangements contribute to the child's independence; they enable the child to put materials away when finished, the responsibility of every child. The ongoing restoration of play areas is especially important in inclusive classrooms. The child with limited vision needs to be confident that a rolling pin that rolled off the table earlier will not be left there for him or her to fall over later. Teachers who routinely help children restore play areas after each use provide valuable lessons in common courtesy as well as regard for safety.

Children who use special equipment should be equally responsible. A child needs to learn how to position his or her crutches when they are not in use so they do not fall, endangering others. A child who uses a wheelchair only part of the time must learn to park it in an agreed-upon place, not abandon it haphazardly.

Safe outdoor environments Outdoor play, in a safe and carefully arranged play yard, is essential for young children (Rivkin, 1995). It is here that children practice physical skills such as running, jumping, ducking, climbing, and kicking. They learn to throw, catch, and bat, and to combine these skills into games. The outdoors also provides opportunities for children to learn voice and tone modulations—shouting, chanting, whistling, imitating a siren—all without causing discomfort to others.

Outdoor equipment needs to be simple yet versatile. It should include ladders, planks, jumping boards, and simple climbing frames. There should be walking boards of various widths placed at different heights and combined with small, portable climbing frames, ladders, and gangplanks with side rails. Equipment of this type can be arranged and rearranged to meet the needs of children with delayed motor skills as well as advanced children. Children just beginning to try out their gross motor coordination can be as well-served as daring children in need of constant challenge. According to Frost (1986), "The best playgrounds are never finished."

Between 2006 and 2008, an average of 218,851 preschool and elementary children received emergency-room care for injuries that occurred on playground equipment. Fifty-one percent of the injuries happened on public playground equipment. The top three pieces of playground equipment associated with these injuries are swings, slides, and climbers (O'Brien, 2009).

The National Program for Playground Safety (NPPS) believes there are four areas that make a playground safe for children. They refer

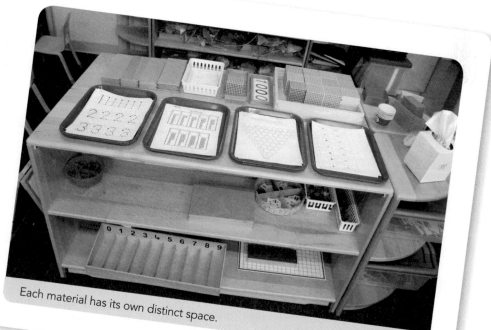

Each material has its own distinct space.

© Cengage Learning

Age-Appropriate Design for Outdoor Play Equipment

The following factors should be considered when selecting equipment:

- *Outdoor play areas should help ensure positive emotional development*
- *Outdoor play areas should help provide social development*
- *Outdoor play areas should provide intellectual development*
- *Outdoor play areas should provide accessibility and play opportunities for all children*
- *Outdoor play areas should foster appropriate physical development*

Children are developmentally different in size and ability. Outdoor play areas can facilitate physical development if developmentally appropriate.

Ages: 6 months–23 months
Provide places to crawl, stand, and walk.

Ages: 2–5 years
Provide play areas to crawl; low platforms with multiple access such as ramps and ladders; ramps with pieces attached for grasping; low tables for sand, water and manipulation of materials; tricycle paths with various textures; flexible spring rockers; sand areas with covers; and shorter slides (usually no taller than 4 feet).

Ages: 5–12 years
In addition to places to run and play ball, play areas could include: rope or chain climbers on angles; climbing pieces; horizontal bars; cooperative pieces such as tire swings, slides, and sliding poles.

Source: NPPS. Age Appropriate Design. /http://playgroundsafety.org/safe/age-appropriate-design

FIGURE 13-2

to this program as **SAFE**. The areas include adequate **S**upervision, **A**ge-appropriate design, suitable **F**all surfacing, and **E**quipment and surface maintenance (Thompson, Hudson, & Olsen, 2006). Teachers can influence safety on the playground by developing a plan that incorporates these four components. NPPS provides pamphlets and other tools such as planning videos and an evaluation tool to assist with the process of creating a safe outdoor learning environment. Figure 13-2 provides some considerations for selecting playground equipment.

13-4b ■ Visibility

A major function of early childhood education is encouraging children to explore and experiment with materials and equipment. Partial enclosure of learning activities so that children can see what is available is important. It also helps avoid distractions and allows children to function in small groups rather than feeling like they are always in a large group (Maxwell, 2004). Children will be taking risks as they try out new skills; therefore, every child needs to be visible to teachers at all times. Some of children's experiments will work; others will not. But all provide teachers with opportunities to teach. A child who decides to try jumping off a swing in motion, for example, presents a teaching opportunity. A teacher may make suggestions concerning speed and a jumping-off point suitable for a first attempt. Also, the teacher is alerted, ready to catch the child who does not heed suggestions or whose timing goes awry.

Children with developmental problems cannot always gauge their own limitations. At the first indication that a child is about to attempt something dangerously beyond his or her capabilities, the observant teacher can intervene immediately in a supportive manner. The child's efforts can be redirected to provide encouragement for continued work on the skill, but in ways more suited to the child's ability level.

While visibility is important, children also need a place to go to be alone and/or to recover when they are upset. Privacy places should be provided that let children enjoy solitude but also allow them to observe the actions of others, so that they can join in when they feel comfortable doing so (Maxwell, 2004).

13-4c ■ Matching Children and Equipment

A critical aspect of safety has to do with matching equipment and materials to the skill levels of children. As mentioned previously, this is true for outdoor playground equipment and is also true for other materials and equipment within an early childhood program. Wheel toys, for example, pose a safety hazard for younger, smaller children. They also are a hazard for children who may not be able to exercise good judgment in selecting suitable equipment. In many instances, poor judgment is simply lack of experience. Children with developmental problems often have been overprotected by well-meaning adults. All children, if they are to develop independence, must learn to take risks. Learning to take risks, however, can be accomplished only when children are protected from becoming frightened or seriously harmed.

The type of equipment and toys can also encourage or discourage play and influence the engagement levels of children. If a particular child is frequently observed to engage in low levels of play, the teachers should take a look at the available activities. Are there materials at the child's play ability and level? Does the child need individual instruction to learn how to use the materials?

One final note about matching play materials with children has to do with the amount of play materials available. Research has shown that fewer toys can lead to increased conflict among children, while an adequate amount can reduce these conflicts

Teachers can influence the safety of outdoor learning centers by developing a plan.

(Odom & Bailey, 2001; McWilliam, Wolery, & Odom, 2001). If a classroom has only one of a very popular toy, the teachers can be sure that there will be problems with sharing. While sharing is a critical skill for young children, teachers must find a balance between the amount of time they must intervene in "toy battles" and the best way to teach sharing. Teachers must determine that the class has an adequate amount of materials so children can use a desired toy within a reasonable amount of time. At the same time, be sure there are not so many toys and materials that the classroom is cluttered, or that children do not have the opportunity to learn to share or wait their turn.

13-4d ■ Ease of Movement

The classroom with clearly defined play spaces allows and encourages children and teachers to move about freely. Movement is enhanced when traffic lanes are unobstructed and adequate for maneuvering trucks and doll carriages or wheelchairs and crutches. Traffic lanes free of obstructions and unpleasant surprises (puddles of water on the floor, an abandoned doll carriage, an upturned rug edge) are essential, especially for children with limited vision. Play is enhanced if children have adequate individual space to play and interact, without other children running into their space and interrupting their play. Ease of movement within interest centers is important, too. Crowded activity areas, where children's movements are restricted, inevitably lead to conflict, lack of sharing, and aggression. Problems are prevented by providing several attractive interest centers. Small groups of children with varying developmental levels then have space to play together or side by side. On the other hand, too much open space can cause children to wander rather than become engaged in the activities.

TeachSource Video Connections

© Cengage Learning 2015

Preschool: Appropriate Learning Environments and Room Arrangements

This video describes how the setup of the classroom environment can impact children's play and learning. Miss Sheila, who is new to teaching, sets up her classroom without understanding the impact it has on her students. She learns from veteran Miss Salazar how to better arrange her classroom. Both are pleased with the reaction of the children.

After watching the video, discuss the following:

1. Describe five changes that were made to the classroom environment.

2. Why was making these changes important to the play and learning of the children?

3. What are some of the positive outcomes that were observed after these changes were made?

Watch on CourseMate.

13-4e ■ Promoting Independence

An early childhood education environment must be arranged to encourage independence. As mentioned previously, teaching children that there are established places for things and how to put things away after use fosters independence. Children should be able to get to toys easily. They should be able to transition from one activity to another with as little teacher direction as possible. For example, coats should be easily obtained by the children prior to outside time. Lunches and cups should be easily accessed so children can find a place at the table without adult assistance. A helpful strategy for teachers is to make a quick note each time they have to help a child complete a task or transition. Notes across several days and from different teachers should be reviewed. As a team, teachers will be able to identify times during the day that they are performing tasks that children could be accomplishing independently. They can then rearrange the environment and routines accordingly.

13-4f ■ Teachers' Availability

The ready availability of teachers is the key to a safe and comfortable early learning environment. Young children are learning something each of their waking moments. To facilitate appropriate learning, teachers must be where they are most needed throughout the day. When children can move independently between activities, without unnecessary distractions, teachers can teach rather than police. A teacher often can bridge two areas, being available to children both in the locker area and in an adjacent discovery learning area.

An effective way to be sure the entire early childhood environment is adequately supervised is **zone teaching**. During zone teaching, each teacher is assigned an area of the classroom for which he or she is responsible. This supervision includes monitoring materials, as well as interacting with children in the area. Zone teaching can be flexible. If there is one area of the classroom that is especially popular, a teacher from an empty area can come assist a co-teacher. To the benefit of teachers and children alike, teachers should exchange assignments to maintain variety and challenge their interactions with children (Allen & Hart, 1984).

zone teaching a strategy in which each teacher is responsible for an area of the classroom

13-4g ■ Offering Choice

One of the most effective and most often overlooked forms of preventive discipline is the strategy of offering choice to children. Offering choice is empowering to children because it allows them to decide such things as what they want to do or what color they want to use. The following are some examples of how offering choice can prevent problems as well as provide additional learning opportunities:

- *Offering choice works effectively with children who frequently say "no" when offered only one option.*
- *Offering choice provides an opportunity for a child developing language to practice requesting either with words, pointing, sign language, or an augmentative communication system.*
- *Offering choice of color, size, or quantity provides an opportunity to practice naming the desired attribute while at the same time providing the teacher with an opportunity to assess a child's knowledge.*
- *Offering choice can prevent a child from having a tantrum because they feel they have some control of the situation.*

There are many ways to offer choice in the early childhood classroom. Discovery learning times naturally lend themselves to providing choice, as there are typically several options from which the children can choose. Providing several colors or types of materials in the art area allows children to choose how they want to be creative. Offering two different types of crackers at snack times is another way to incorporate choice. Choice can also be used when difficulties arise. For example, a child who is unwilling to share in the block area can be given the choice to take turns with the truck or move to another area.

13-4h ■ Novelty versus Familiarity

While children thrive in environments that are familiar and consistent, it is important also to provide new materials, displays, and perspectives throughout the year. For example, one week a teacher might create a display of different types of seeds and the plants that grow from them. This provides the children with an opportunity

Case Study ■ Preventive discipline in action ■

Michael is a lead teacher in a pre-K classroom that serves twelve students, half of whom have special needs. After the children finish lunch, they can play in one of several areas while they wait for their classmates to finish lunch and get ready to head outdoors. These areas include train table, fine motor area, housekeeping, and reading corner. As the children finish lunch, some of the staff move from the lunch tables and help facilitate play in the play areas. Almost every day, at least two children begin chasing each other around the train table and then in between the two lunch tables. One child is usually in pursuit of the other, who has taken a preferred toy and run off with it. A staff person usually redirects them back to the play area and facilitates turn taking or appropriate requesting of a toy from a peer. Things typically settle down for a few minutes and then another similar interaction occurs. The staff has reported that they find this time of the day frustrating, as they feel like all they are doing is putting out fires and counting the minutes until they can take the children outside.

What options do Michael and his staff have to prevent this daily occurrence? Consider suggestions related to the schedule and physical layout of the classroom.

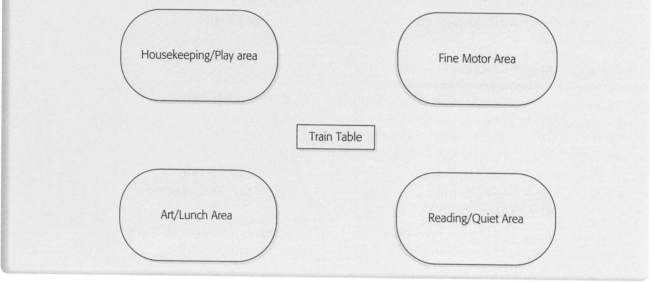

to examine and explore the seeds and guess which seed might yield which plant. Another week the teacher might bring in a poster-size print by a famous artist for the children to examine and discuss. Still another time the sensory area may be moved outside. All of these changes can lead to increased use of language, critical thinking, and problem-solving skills on the part of the children. Another way to create familiarity is to provide areas that are similar to what is found in a home. Providing a small couch, table, and lamp in the reading area replicates a living room (Swim, 2006).

13-4i ■ Structured Flexibility

structured flexibility
a well-structured early learning environment that also is adaptable to children's individual needs and preferences

To meet the range of developmental levels within a group of young children, the learning environment must possess **structured flexibility**. It must be well structured and, at the same time, flexible and adaptable. A structured environment, where rules and expectations are consistent, provides a secure framework that supports children's freedom. They can explore and test limits, and teachers can react spontaneously to the infinite variations in children's learning. Systematic advance planning and logical revision of arrangements are essential to both program structure and program flexibility. Both are based on teachers' periodic assessments of their programs. A widely used assessment instrument

A structured environment provides a secure framework that supports children's freedom.

is the Early Childhood Environment Rating Scale (ECERS) (Harms, Clifford, & Cryer, 2004). It is designed to give an overall picture of space, materials, activities, daily schedule, and supervision. A school-age care environment rating scale is also available (Harms, Jacobs, & White, 1995). Another instrument, the Preschool Assessment of the Classroom Environment (PACE) (McWilliam & Dunst, 1985) is also useful, having been tested in inclusive classrooms.

Much more could be said about arranging appropriate learning environments for young children. Softness, aesthetics (beauty), privacy, lighting variations, built-in lofts, and display of children's work at their eye level—these are some of the additional dimensions that characterize quality early childhood settings.

Scheduling 13-5 ☀

In the inclusive classroom, learning opportunities based on appropriate arrangements of space, material, and equipment are heightened by an organized schedule. Systematically structured transitions between program activities also are critical. Teachers need to know where each child is to be and what each child is to be doing at each point in the program. Scheduling decisions are based on the type of program. The number of hours children spend in the setting, their age and ability range, and the ratio of adults to children are major considerations. Full-day programs have quite different constraints on both schedule and organization than half-day programs.

In this chapter, types of schedules will not be described. The focus, instead, will be on principles related to scheduling. However, to illustrate application of the principles, a sample schedule based on a half-day program is included. This is followed by a discussion of transitions.

13-5a ■ Principles Related to Scheduling

Specific principles apply when planning daily, weekly, seasonal, and yearlong activity schedules. Individual differences among children, and their changing skill levels over time, are major scheduling factors.

Accommodating individual differences In determining the sequence of activities, teachers must be sensitive to children's special needs and preferences. Teachers strive to maintain a global outlook of the day as a whole, including sequence of activities, use of indoor and outdoor space, and opportunities to promote children's learning. This view varies throughout the year as teachers get to know children better and as children become more skilled. The length and type of classroom activities and amount of outdoor time are often different from fall to spring and from spring to summer. In the fall, for example, children may need longer active play periods out of doors as they adapt to new children, new adults, and a group experience. In the spring, the time spent in small groups and independent activities may be much extended. By spring, many children will have a longer attention span and increased self-management skills. A summer schedule, in most climates, should provide more outdoor time. Easel painting and work with clay take on entirely different dimensions out in the fresh air. Basic activities moved out of the classroom and onto outdoor tables give teachers and children a refreshing change of pace.

Children need to be alerted to a forthcoming change in activities.

© Cengage Learning

Varying activity levels Periods of high physical activity are planned to alternate with periods of quiet activities. Most children are subject to energy spillover from active play periods. Learning experiences that require children's concentration should not be scheduled immediately following vigorous free play. A brief cooling-down period needs to be built into the schedule. For example, as children gather by ones and twos, they look at books until most of the children have assembled and the teacher-structured activity begins. *Note:* Books should always be available to children, even during free-play periods. If children are taught the proper care of books from the start, their misuse is unlikely.

Ensuring orderly sequences Activities need to follow an orderly and predictable sequence. Most young children have trouble accepting any departure from what they are used to. Change in routines may be even more difficult for very young children and children with developmental problems. Children with autistic-type behaviors or attention disorders frequently become obsessively attached to the daily schedule. Commonplace routines become rituals that must be held constant; the unexpected may drive the child into a frenzy. Most children, however, feel more secure knowing what comes next. A fixed sequence of activities builds confidence in children. They can predict the order of the day. The order need not be rigid; it should be flexible so that children can learn readily to accept an occasional trip to the zoo that could not be preplanned or an unscheduled visitor who can provide an especially worthwhile experience.

A visual schedule may be needed for some children, such as children with autism. The visual schedule can help the child transition independently and assist with sequential memory, organization, and understanding of time.

Transitions in which children and teachers are busy but interacting comfortably are the hallmark of a quality program. A smooth transition appears effortless. The effortlessness is deceptive; it is the result of considerable planning, knowledge about each child, and attention to a multitude of details. Transitions should be used for teaching and for helping children learn about their own capabilities (Sainato & Carta, 1992). At no time should children be waiting about idly or in enforced silence.

The underlying principle of smooth transitions is that each child moves individually, at his or her own pace, from one activity to the next. The individual differences among children provide the gradual movement between activities for the group as a whole. Different children, because they use materials with different levels of involvement, will finish cleanup at different times. The diverse learning needs of children in various pre-academic activities prompt teachers to hold children for differing lengths of time. Arrangements such as these are ideal for all children—the very young, those with developmental disabilities, and typically developing and gifted children.

Effective transitions require detailed planning. Teachers must know who is supervising which areas and activities. Effective transitions, like all quality programming, require an adequate ratio of teachers to children. This is especially true in inclusive programs, where the ratio of teachers to children must be increased as the number of children with developmental disabilities increases. NAEYC supports this position in the following statements:

> Implementation of developmentally appropriate early childhood programs requires limiting the size of the group and providing sufficient numbers of adults to provide individualized and age-appropriate care and education. Even the most well-qualified teacher cannot individualize instruction and adequately supervise too large a group of young children. ... Younger children require much smaller groups.
>
> Group size, and thus ratio of children to adults, should increase gradually through the primary grades (Copple & Bredekamp, 2009).

13-6a ■ Procedures

A teacher puts on the same music every day at the start of cleanup. The way a teacher signals a transition is one example of the many procedures teachers use in their classrooms to teach children expected behaviors, help the class run smoothly, and thus be able to teach content (Smith, 2004). Procedures include such things as how children enter the room, how they clean up, how a teacher gains their attention, how children use the bathroom, and how they leave at the end of the day. Procedures, like behavior and skills, need to be taught. Before procedures can be taught, teachers need to identify which ones will be used. For example, is cleanup announced with music or a song or the ringing of a bell? Whatever the signal, it needs to be used consistently throughout the year. It also has to be taught through explanation and practice. Figure 13-4 lists procedures that might need to be taught in a classroom. There are several steps to teaching procedures effectively, and they are similar to steps used to teach any skill or content (Smith, 2004).

- Determine what procedures are needed.
- Break them down into simple steps.

FIGURE 13-4
Procedures That May
Need To Be Taught in
a Classroom

- Students entering the classroom
- Using cubbies
- Turning in homework (elementary)
- Getting students' attention
- Cleanup
- Using the bathroom
- Using the drinking fountain
- Passing out supplies or snack
- Sharpening pencils (elementary)
- Fire drills/safety drills
- Field trips
- Exiting for recess
- Gathering belongings to take home
- Dismissing class

© Cengage Learning

- Teach them visually, orally, and/or kinesthetically.
- Check for understanding.
- Practice them.
- Reinforce them.
- Periodically review them.

The age of the children will determine the number and complexity of the procedures a teacher would use.

13-6b ■ Considerations for Infants and Toddlers

In an infant/toddler program, the children learn concepts such as hard and soft, rough and smooth, and wet and dry. Everything in the environment, from the flooring to the lighting, provides learning opportunities. Programs need to be safe and interesting. They should engage large and small muscle groups, stimulate children's senses, and foster their curiosity (Lally & Stewart, 1990).

High-quality care for infants and toddlers must be in small groups with appropriate ratios. Zero to Three (Lally, Torres, & Phelps, n.d.) recommends that a group size be no larger than six group members. The overall caregiver to infant ratio should be no more than 1:3. For children who are crawling and up to eighteen months, the group size should not exceed nine, with ratios of no more than 1:3. For children eighteen months to three years, group size should not be more than twelve, with a ratio of 1:4. The environment affects the relationship caregivers have both with children and with parents. The amount and arrangement of space and the choice and abundance of play materials can either increase children's interaction and appropriate play or lead to biting, fighting over toys, or wandering (Lally, Torres, & Phelps, 1993). The environment also has an impact on the caregiver. If the environment makes a caregiver nervous about children's safety, the caregiver will not be able to relax and play with the children. If the room is disorganized, caregivers waste time and get frustrated looking for things (Lally & Stewart, 1990). The environment must be a place that is comfortable for both the caregiver and the child, so that both can relax and enjoy each other. The environment should also provide a place where parents can sit comfortably at the end of the day. This will provide increased opportunity for conversation and communication.

A key component of quality infant/toddler programs is continuity of care. Using one caregiver over a longer period of time rather than switching caregivers every six to nine months is critical to developing trust and expanding the child's overall development.

Providing a flexible schedule is another component that contributes to a program's ability to meet the individual needs of an infant/toddler. A flexible schedule allows a sleepy baby a chance to nap, hungry toddlers a chance to have a snack, and energetic toddlers a chance to play.

In summary, appropriate group size and ratios, an adequate physical environment, continuity of care, and a flexible schedule are all aspects of a quality infant/toddler environment.

13-6c ■ Considerations for Early Elementary Years

Teachers of children in the early elementary years must continue to design the physical and learning environment carefully. The basic principles of safety, visibility, matching children and equipment, ease of movement, promoting independence, teacher availability, offering of choices, novelty versus familiarity, and structured flexibility discussed in the previous section apply to this age group, as well.

Provide areas that allow students to be engaged in various activities and with a variety of materials. The environment must be safe and allow for the increasing responsibility that develops at this age. Opportunities and areas should allow students to work both individually and in small groups. The schedule should be balanced to allow time for physical activity, plus plenty of time for engaging fully in discovery and investigation. Teachers of children in this age group should continue to give ample warnings for upcoming transitions and, when possible, allow students to complete whatever they are working on (Copple & Bredekamp, 2009). Teachers can write the schedule on the board daily, providing a visual picture of the day. This practice can benefit students who have difficulty with changes in routine by providing advance notice and opportunity for discussion and questions.

The curriculum shifts during these early elementary years to focus on expanded literacy and writing. Choice can still be a component of the classroom as teachers differentiate the curriculum. Teachers who differentiate are ready to engage students in instruction through different learning modalities, by appealing to differing interests, and by using varied rates of instruction along with varied degrees of complexity (Tomlinson, 1999). This practice of **differentiation** is effective not only with students with learning delays but also with students who are gifted and talented. Materials and activities are offered at different levels, and choice is provided to the students by teachers offering a range of topics, projects, and products.

As with any quality program, elementary teachers should continually look at their physical environment and schedule and make changes to improve student learning and to enhance their own ability to provide students opportunities for individualization.

differentiation materials and activities are offered at different levels and choice is provided by teachers offering a range of topics, projects, and products to the students

Did You Get It?

What are the comparative ratio rates of overall caregiver to infant or child in the crawling up to eighteen months category, and the eighteen months to three years category?
a. 1:2; 1:3.
b. 1:3; 1:4.
c. 1:2; 1:4.
d. 1:3; 1:12.

Take the full quiz on CourseMate.

Summary

- The arrangement of inclusive early childhood environments determines how well children learn and how well teachers teach. Adaptations are made for special needs.

- A well-arranged learning environment communicates to children what they can do in any given area. Children are less likely to behave inappropriately in a planned and well-structured environment.

- The environment is planned in terms of types of learning that go on throughout the program day: self-care skills, teacher-structured activities, and discovery learning. Teachers arrange the activity areas that support the various kinds of learning in terms of nine basic principles: safety, visibility, matching children and equipment, ease of movement, promoting independence, teacher availability, offering of choices, novelty versus familiarity, and structured flexibility.

- Periodic assessment of all aspects of the environment is critical to advancing each child's development.

- A daily schedule based on children's individual needs and differences furthers the benefits of the well-arranged classroom and play yard.

- Each segment of the daily schedule provides valuable opportunities for teaching and learning throughout the program day. Children are given advance notice when activity changes are scheduled. Some children need advance warning and special help in dealing with departures from established routines.

- Regularly scheduled staff meetings, brief though they may be, allow teachers to teach more effectively.

- Transitions are designed to enable children, from the most delayed to the most advanced, to move at their own pace between program activities. Transitions characterized by idle waiting or enforced quiet are developmentally inappropriate and detrimental to children's learning and self-esteem.

- Procedures include such things as how children enter the room, how they clean up, how a teacher gains their attention, how children use the bathroom, and how they leave at the end of the day. Procedures, like behavior and skills, need to be taught.

Key Terms

differentiation, 357
discovery learning, 336
embedded learning opportunities (ELOs), 353

induced incompetence, 334
mobiles, 351
preventive discipline, 332
self-help skills, 333

stabiles, 351
structured flexibility, 346
zone teaching, 345

Student Activities

1. Observe a discovery learning period. Make notes on the following: Was there evidence of preventive discipline in terms of environmental arrangements? Describe. Were there other ways the environment might have been altered to provide more effective discipline? Describe.

2. Observe a preschool classroom and draw a rough sketch of the floor plan. Indicate location of furnishings, activity areas, doors, and windows. Indicate which areas will accommodate a child in a wheelchair or walker. Which will not? Sketch the floor plan again, showing possible modifications that might better accommodate these children.

3. Observe a playground during outdoor time or recess. Using the concept of SAFE (see http://www.playgroundsafety.org/ for detailed descriptions), describe the playground in terms of supervision, age appropriateness, and fall-safe surfacing. Ask staff how safety and maintenance are evaluated. If there is no process in place, develop a plan for safety evaluation.

4. Consider a first- or second-grade classroom. Develop a daily schedule, outlining procedures that would be used for transitions. Identify times during the day when differentiation could occur.

5. Observe classrooms at two different age levels. Compare and contrast the environments and schedules, including transitions and procedures.

6. Make a list of five classroom procedures one might observe in a preschool class. Describe how a teacher can teach and reinforce these procedures to increase independence of all children.

Review Questions

Briefly define and give examples of each of the following concepts as they relate specifically to environmental arrangements and scheduling of activities in early childhood inclusive programs:

1. safety
2. orderliness
3. visibility
4. ease of movement
5. novelty versus familiarity
6. area restoration
7. structured flexibility
8. varied activity levels
9. activity sequences
10. advance notice
11. offering of choice
12. promoting independence

Additional Resources/Readings

Creating Environments for Learning: Birth to Age Eight

Written by Julie Bullard
Pearson Publishing

This book is organized by chapters on learning centers (literacy, manipulative and sensory, science, mathematics, etc.), and also covers information such as the role of the teacher, the importance of the environment, design principles, and health and safety. The book provides information for all age groups in early childhood education (infants and toddlers through third grade.

Helpful Websites

The Division for Early Childhood (DEC)

http://www.DEC-sped.org

DEC is a division of the Council for Exceptional Children. The website contains position statements on a variety of issues ranging from inclusion to interventions for challenging behaviors. The site includes reproducible checklists for parents and administrators, plus a professional's self-assessment for child-focused interventions.

Early Childhood Educators' and Family Web Corner

http://users.stargate.net/

(*Search:* Teacher Pages) This website contains articles and links to sites that are of interest to early childhood educators and parents. Topics include assessment, curriculum, and family issues.

The National Program for Playground Safety (NPPS)

http://www.playgroundsafety.org/

This agency is a recognized national clearinghouse for playground safety information. The group conducts ongoing research in the area of injury prevention and sponsors a National Playground Safety Week. The website offers valuable resources, including statistics and safety report cards by state, safety evaluation kits, and a newsletter.

 Visit the Education CourseMate for this textbook to access the eBook, Did You Get It? quizzes, Digital Downloads, TeachSource Video Cases, flashcards, and more. Go to CengageBrain.com to log in, register, or purchase access.

Facilitating Self-Care, Adaptive, and Independence Skills

14

OBJECTIVES

After reading this chapter, you should be able to:

14-1   describe self-care skills as part of a curriculum.

14-2   describe when and how teachers can help children learn self-care skills.

14-3   outline the five components of a systematic approach to teaching self-care skills.

14-4   list skills that can be taught during snack/mealtime, and strategies to teach them.

14-5   explain why maturation is an important aspect to self-care skills, specifically toilet training.

• • • • • • • • • • • • • • • • • • •

naeyc

The following NAEYC Standards are addressed in this chapter:

STANDARD 1 Promoting Child Development and Learning

STANDARD 2 Building Family and Community Relationships

STANDARD 3 Observing, Documenting and Assessing to Support Young Children and Families

STANDARD 4 Using Developmentally Effective Approaches

STANDARD 5 Using Content Knowledge to Build Meaningful Curriculum

CONNECTIONS

- Alex is a three-year-old who has difficulty remembering the sequence for washing his hands. He is learning to follow a picture schedule to remember the steps.
- Esther is a two-year-old who is having trouble learning to drink from a cup. Her teacher places her hand over Esther's and guides her through the motions. The teacher's physical prompts will be reduced as Esther becomes more independent.
- Rosa's teachers and parents are collaborating with her respite-care provider to work on toilet training across all the environments in which Rosa functions.
- Teddy, a five-year-old, is learning to tie his shoes with the help of his kindergarten teacher and the classroom's paraprofessional.

The above vignettes are all examples of adaptive skills that you will be called upon to teach as an educator of young children. Adaptive skills include those behaviors that we think of as self-care, self-help, and independence skills. In the case of young children, adaptive skills are also those skills that make a child easier to care for (Wolery, McMillian, & Bailey, 2005). Common examples of adaptive skills for young children include toileting and dressing. Just as important are independent play skills and the ability to make and implement choices.

A major goal of inclusive early childhood programs is balance: *ensuring that children do things on their own (without help) and ensuring that they are not left out because they cannot do something* (Wolery, 1994b, p. 154). Two basic principles guide quality programs, according to Wolery: (1) the principle of independence—that children be encouraged and allowed to do as much as possible for themselves in learning environments designed to support their endeavors and (2) the principle of participation—that children with special needs be a part of all activities and that adaptations be made to encourage a child's participation to the maximum extent possible. Although these two principles apply to all early childhood curriculum areas, they are especially relevant in helping children with special needs acquire the self-care or self-help skills that are the focus of this chapter. These skills, when adequately learned, enable individuals to manage personal needs and to *adapt* their behaviors to social expectations.

adaptive skills the social, self-management, and communication skills deemed necessary for maintaining order in the community or culture in which a child lives

The specific **adaptive skills** that children need to learn are determined by the culture in which they live. Though patterns differ, all cultures prescribe ways of eating, toileting, dressing, grooming, behaving sexually, and keeping public places orderly. Families from different cultures may also have different beliefs about what age children should be when they are expected to begin to develop independence in the area of adaptive skills. For example, in some cultures, parents often dress their children long after the children are able to dress themselves, while in other cultures, where diapers are not used, parents expect their children to be toilet-trained as infants and young toddlers (Neville, 2007). Communicating with families regarding their practices at home and being knowledgeable and sensitive about these differences can reduce possible conflicts (Neilsen, 2010).

self-determination teaching and providing children with opportunities to take a more active role in stating their individuality and independence

An area of adaptive skills that has received much attention in recent years is **self-determination** (Powers, Singer, & Sowers, 1996). Self-determination refers to allowing people with disabilities to take an active role in making choices about their own life. Although it might seem premature to talk about self-determination for young children, it is precisely in early childhood that teachers and parents must begin to teach children with disabilities how to make choices about important issues in their lives. In early childhood, these choices may be related to how to spend free time, what outfit to wear, or what to have for snack. These minor decisions are the foundation that children need to make more important decisions as they get older.

Self-Care Skills and the Curriculum 14-1 ☀

Competence in self-care leads to greater independence. Therefore, helping young children develop a full range of self-care skills is a major curriculum goal for early childhood programs. The goal holds for all children, especially for those with developmental delays who need to learn to live as independently as possible with their disability. The more proficient a child is in caring for personal needs, the less adult support will be required for the child to be successful in an inclusive setting.

Self-care skills are learned behaviors. This means they can be taught. Traditionally, the family had major responsibility for teaching self-care skills, with early childhood programs providing assistance. As infants and children are enrolled at ever-younger ages in all-day child care programs, the pattern is reversing. Now families and early childhood programs are partners in teaching adaptive skills to infants and young children. Owing to the special nature of adaptive skills and the importance of teaching the skills consistently across environments, families and teachers must work together.

Early childhood programs can be a comfortable place to learn self-care skills. Teachers can use the same types of instructional skills they use in other domains to teach self-care skills and to work with families to develop a teaching program that can be implemented reliably at home. Teaching self-care skills requires teachers to provide clear instructions and maintain appropriate levels of support. They also need to offer multiple opportunities throughout the day to practice the skills being taught.

Eating, dressing, toileting, and care of the classroom and play yard are significant program areas in the early childhood curriculum (Figure 14-1). Self-care activities occur throughout the program day. They take up a significant portion of both teachers' and children's time and energies and therefore require systematic planning.

14-1a ■ Assessment

In teaching any self-care skill, adults must know exactly what each child is capable of doing independently in that particular skill sequence. Skills in these areas are generally assessed through checklists, developmental profiles, and the professional judgment of teachers and clinicians. Expectations vary according to age level. In infancy and early childhood, the expected behaviors are those associated with typical developmental processes.

The purpose of assessment of adaptive skills is to obtain a measure of the child's typical functioning in familiar environments such as the home and the school. Such measures provide teachers with knowledge about how a child can meet the demands of daily life and respond appropriately to environmental demands (Lord & McGee, 2001).

The information obtained from assessment can be used by the teacher and family to identify adaptive skills to teach. Priority should be given to age-appropriate skills that allow the child to have more independence and thus access to the greater community. For an example, many preschools do not enroll children who are still

naeyc

FIGURE 14-1
Examples of Self-Care Skills for Various Age Groups

	DRESSING	FEEDING	TOILETING AND WASHING	GENERAL
2 to 3 years	Can take clothes off to put on other articles of clothing but tires easily and gives up. Generally cooperative when helped.	Can use a fork, but still prefers spoon or fingers. Will feed self-preferred food. Drinks from glass.	Verbalizes toilet needs in advance. Retention span for urination lengthening—can "hold" longer.	Can open some doors with easy latches or low knobs. Goes up and down stairs, usually holding rail. Can push chair or stool around to climb on and get what is wanted.
3 to 4 years	Undresses self. Can put on most articles of clothing and can manipulate buttons and zippers, depending upon their size and place. Can put clothes away in drawers or hang them up, given right height hooks.	Usually eats with fork. Can pour from pitcher into glass with few mishaps. Enjoys eating with family, but may dawdle.	May insist on washing self in tub but does it imperfectly. Very few toilet accidents. Often wakes up at night and asks to be taken to toilet.	Can tell own age, sex, and first and last name. Can follow two- and three-step directions. Able to stay at preschool without parent.
4 to 5 years	Laces shoes; some children learning to tie. Dresses and undresses with little or no assistance, especially if clothes are laid out. May dawdle excessively over dressing. Can tell front from back but may still have trouble getting some garments on properly.	Uses fork and spoon appropriately; often needs help to cut "tough" meat. Likes to "make" own breakfast and lunches (dry cereal, peanut butter sandwiches).	Can bathe and dry self, at least partially. Can perform toileting, hand washing and drying. May forget sometimes.	Plays with peers with less supervision. Can put toys away but usually needs reminding. Can help with many household chores: set table, empty trash, feed pets. May "forget" some steps.
5 to 6 years	Ties own shoes. Can manage almost any article of clothing. Can assist younger brother or sister in getting dressed.	Can use all eating utensils but is sometimes messy. Aware of appropriate table manners but tends to forget them.	Bathes and dries self with minimal supervision. Usually does not wash own hair, but may help. Totally self-sufficient in toilet routine.	Can make own bed, put soiled clothes in hamper. Learning to distinguish left from right.

TeachSource Digital Download Download from CourseMate.

in diapers. So targeting toilet training would allow a child to participate in a program with age-equivalent peers.

14-1b ■ Embedding Self-Care Learning

Opportunities for learning self-care skills need to be integrated or embedded with every other part of the curriculum. Mealtimes, for instance, can be arranged to work toward a variety of curriculum goals in addition to those directly associated with eating. If conversation during meals is acceptable in the culture, several small tables may be set up to promote child-child and child-teacher conversations. Pre-academic as well as self-care learning can be carried out at mealtimes as teachers and children informally discuss names, colors, and textures of foods, their origins, and nutritional value.

Mealtimes provide opportunities for the **generalization** of cognitive skills presented in pre-academic activities. Knowledge about the concept *green*, for example, can be extended by drawing attention to foods such as peas, broccoli, and lettuce, or by asking children to think of other foods that are green.

Perceptual-motor skills can be practiced: lifting and pouring from a pitcher, filling a glass to a certain level, spreading jelly on a cracker, cleaning up spills, presenting the pitcher handle-first to the adjacent child.

Early childhood programs can be a comfortable place to practice self-care skills.

© Cengage Learning

Self-care routines such as eating provide a variety of opportunities for learning. A child might learn about sequence—what comes before and after eating—and how to estimate how much food to take relative to one's own hunger or the amount of food available.

Opportunities to practice language are plentiful during self-care routines. Some opportunities to learn the names and functions of the objects and actions are a part of everyday lives: clothing, furnishings, and working parts of equipment, such as toilets that flush and sinks that drain. Learning to comprehend and follow directions given by the teacher are additional language skills that can be practiced during self-care routines. Still another is the opportunity for verbal expression, as when children are encouraged to state their preferences, seek help, or explain to another child how to hang up a coat. In addition, self-care activities provide occasions for children to hear and use language that is unrelated to the activity at hand. A child telling the teacher about what happened to Grandmother's dog is an example of this important kind of activity.

Additionally, opportunities for social awareness and interactions are provided during self-care routines, such as snack. A teacher can start a conversation about who has the same snack or who has bigger crackers or smaller crackers. These types of conversation starters promote peers awareness of each other.

generalization the spread of a learned response from the training situation to real-life situations

14-1c ■ Individualizing Self-Care Programs

Effective self-care programs are designed to allow children to participate individually. Young children, as noted repeatedly, operate at different levels of motor, social, and cognitive ability. They need differing amounts of time and assistance in completing self-care tasks. Some children, with or without special needs, learn self-care skills early and with ease; others have varying degrees of difficulty. Inconsistent levels of competency may exist within the same child. Depending on the skill, a child may master some self-care skills well in advance of the normally expected time, others much later. Example: Melissa was a bright and healthy child. At thirty-four months, she still wore diapers during the day because of fairly frequent wetting incidents, yet she did not require diapers at night. For some indiscernible reason, she had remained dry at night from an unusually early age—shortly before her second birthday.

Building independence The early years are the prime time for children to learn self-care skills. Children are striving for independence during these years. They are eager to help themselves. They work hard at it if adults allow them to operate at their own pace. They constantly watch and attempt to imitate the self-care efforts of older children and adults. Furthermore, they are willing to practice, practice, practice—indeed, they insist on doing so. Think about older babies learning to walk. They take a few steps, fall down, get up, take a few more steps, and fall down, over and over again. Once the falling-down period is past, they are even more insistent about practicing their walking. A young child's perseverance and physical energy seem limitless:

- *The discovery of how to unlace shoes leads to—for days straight—the child taking the laces out of his or her shoes twelve to fifteen times a day. The perseverance of a two-year-old in pushing, pulling, tugging, shoving, dragging a kitchen chair over to the kitchen sink. Why? To get a drink of water, "all by myself."*

- *The three-year-old's struggle, twisting and turning in a mighty effort to get an undershirt on without help. The shirt, of course, may end up inside out or back to front, but that is all right. Learning that shirts have a right and wrong way of being worn comes later and requires much finer discrimination skills than the child possesses at this point.*

Building in success All children need to experience the joy and self-esteem that come from mastering self-care skills. Pride in accomplishment can be seen on the face of a two-year-old who finally gets the chair in position to get a drink of water or the five-year-old who finally learns to tie his shoes. It can be heard in the gleeful shout of the three-year-old: "I got

The early years, when children are striving for independence, is the prime time to learn self-care skills.

my shirt on all by myself!" It can also be seen in the self-confidence of the six-year-old who learns to make peanut butter sandwiches not only for himself but for his little sister. Such experiences help children feel successful and in more control of their lives. In these instances, the teacher joins in the child's enthusiasm and rejoices with that child. "Look at that! You put your shirt on all by yourself!"

Although children with severe impairments may sometimes be the exception, most children with developmental disabilities can learn self-care skills. Like children who are typically developing, they feel good about themselves simply by getting the shirt on, inside out or back to front. Not all children with disabilities are able to verbalize their accomplishment. They may not be able to say, "Look what I did!" but their facial expressions leave little doubt as to their feelings of satisfaction.

Did You Get It?

What changes can be seen in the teaching of self-care skills?

a. Traditionally, the family had major responsibility for teaching self-care skills; now the early childhood programs do.

b. Traditionally, the schools had major responsibility for teaching self-care skills; now families have major responsibility.

c. Traditionally, the family had major responsibility for teaching self-care skills, with early childhood programs providing assistance; now families and early childhood programs are partners in teaching adaptive skills to infants and young children.

d. Traditionally, the early childhood programs had major responsibility for teaching self-care skills; now families and early childhood programs are partners in teaching adaptive skills to infants and young children.

Take the full quiz on CourseMate.

When and How to Teach 14-2 ☀
Self-Care Skills

As noted earlier, teaching self-care skills is an integral part of the early childhood program. Parents and educators of young children look for opportunities for each child to demonstrate success. As with all other curriculum areas, specific principles and guidelines determine when and how to facilitate such learning.

14-2a ■ Let the Child Do It

"ME DO IT! ME DO IT!" What parent or teacher has not heard that refrain from a red-faced, frustrated, struggling three-year-old? The urge to do for oneself is strong in young children who are typically developing. Although not expressed as aggressively, perhaps, the urge is also there in children with developmental delays. The efforts of children with special needs to do for themselves often go unrecognized. Adults tend not to expect children with disabilities to even try to learn self-care skills. Also, the earliest strivings for independence may have been stifled by well-meaning family members and caregivers who could not bear to watch the child struggle.

14-2b ■ How Much Assistance?

Not all adults know how to effectively help a child with developmental disabilities. Misguided kindness leads many adults to take over. They do things for a child that the child could do, given enough time and opportunity. What happens when a teacher or parent steps in and expertly zips up the zipper the child has been working on so intently? Or reties the shoe the child has just tied with so much effort? Or whips off the wrong-side-out sweater the child is crowing about having gotten on "all by myself"? Such "assistance" often sets up patterns of conflict between adult and child, or may teach the child to be passive, sitting or standing around while the adult does more and more for her or him. This can lead to **learned helplessness**, another way a child can become unnecessarily dependent.

In early childhood programs, such adult "helping" may be the result of understaffing. Teachers may have too many children to look after. They feel they cannot take the time to let a child make repeated efforts to fasten a jacket while other children are waiting to go outdoors. More frequently, however, such helping comes from teachers' lack of confidence in their students' skills. It is also common among inexperienced teachers who do not know what to do in many situations. By doing things *for* the child, the teacher feels busy and needed, more competent, more successful. It is not only the inexperienced who feel obligated to help, however. Many adults feel uncomfortable or hard-hearted if they let a child struggle.

To prevent learned helplessness, even the kindest and most well-meaning assistance must not be pressed on a child unnecessarily. Kindness to children with developmental disabilities lies in finding ways to help them help themselves.

- Kindness is guiding a child's arm and hand so he can reach all the way down into his wrong-side-out coat sleeve. It is demonstrating how to grasp the edge of the cuff. It is helping the child learn that *he* can pull the cuff through, discovering that *he* can turn a coat sleeve right-side-out.

- Kindness is putting a rubber suction cup under the plate of a child with cerebral palsy so the plate stays in place while he works at feeding himself.

- Kindness, in the case of a six-year-old just learning to walk with a walker, is laying her clothes out within easy reach. When everything she needs for dressing herself is at her fingertips, she manages on her own.

Another aspect of kindly assistance is to provide ample encouragement and positive feedback to children who are trying to take care of their own needs. The best way to do this is to tell children exactly what they are doing right (descriptive praise). Children need encouragement in the form of immediate feedback when they are successful or getting closer to a successful performance.

They need to know, too, that their efforts are appreciated. Children thrive when a teacher offers verbal reinforcement:

- "You poured your milk nice and slowly. Not a drop spilled on the table!"

- "Look at you! You've already buttoned three buttons. Only two to go."

Children watch and imitate the self-care skills of older children and adults.

© Cengage Learning

learned helplessness excessive dependency, often induced by well-meaning parents or caregivers because they cannot bear to see the child struggle (or feel they do not have the time to let the child work at learning a particular self-help task)

- "You remembered *again* today to rinse the soap off your hands and to turn the water off. You are getting good at washing your hands all by yourself."

At the same time, kindness is *not* expecting children to do what they are not yet able to do, or to perform tasks that are too complex for their developmental level. No child learns efficiently when frustrated or confronted with frequent failure. Teachers, therefore, must know when to help, how to help, and how much to help.

14-2c ■ When to Help

Knowing when to help depends on several teaching skills discussed earlier. Among these are an understanding of developmental sequences, readiness, and the interrelatedness of developmental areas. In addition, it is critical for early childhood educators to know the abilities of each of the children in their program. Because a two-year-old managed to get a chair to the sink to get a drink of water does not mean the child can turn the faucet on. Large motor skills (in this instance, shoving a chair into place) generally precede fine motor skills (here, the eye-hand-wrist control needed to turn on the water). The adult needs to anticipate the possible outcome of the less than fully developed fine motor skills. Assistance, if needed, should be offered *before* the child becomes frustrated at not being able to get a drink.

It is important to let the child do as much as possible.

© Cengage Learning

Many children, at an early age, are able to grasp a spoon and get it to the mouth. That is no guarantee, however, that a filled spoon will remain right-side-up and so deliver the food into the mouth. Usually, adult help is needed at this point so the child can learn to keep the spoon upright, loaded, and on target.

Least intrusive assistance Assistance should be given as subtly as possible to preserve children's pride in their own efforts. In the example of the toddler at the sink, the adult might loosen the faucet just to the point where the child can make the water flow. In the second example, a teacher

© Cengage Learning

Children need to experience the joy and self-esteem that come from mastering self-care skills.

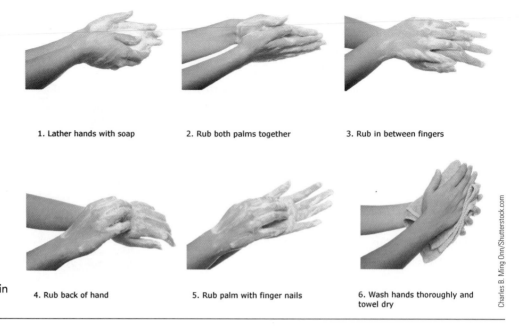

FIGURE 14-2

A Visual Cue for the Steps in a Hand Washing Routine

1. Lather hands with soap

2. Rub both palms together

3. Rub in between fingers

4. Rub back of hand

5. Rub palm with finger nails

6. Wash hands thoroughly and towel dry

Charles B. Ming Onn/Shutterstock.com

might quietly place a hand around the child's hand after the spoon has been loaded, then remove the helping hand as the spoon enters the mouth. This unobtrusive assistance gives the child a sense of accomplishment while learning a difficult task.

Excessive demands for assistance Occasionally, a child will give up without trying, or make excessive demands for adult assistance. It is likely that such a child is in need of extra attention. Teachers must find ways to give the needed attention while avoiding giving in to excessive demands. The solution is to watch for times when the child is doing a task independently and then give warm and positive attention: "You remembered where you left your hat! Looks like you're all ready to go outdoors. Do you want to help me take the new balls out?"

Visual cues and supports Visual cues and supports can often increase a child's independence with self-care routines. One type of visual cue or prompting involves providing pictures of the various steps of a self-care routine. The pictures are presented in a strip, laminated, and displayed at the child's eye level in the location where the self-care task is completed.

Figure 14-2 shows an example of a visual cue for hand washing. Initially a child's attention may need to be directed to the visual support. This should be done nonverbally by pointing to each picture. Verbal instructions are much more difficult to fade and can inhibit independence (Anderson, Jablonski, Thomeer, & Knapp, 2007). Visual cues can also be used to remind a child to begin a task—for example, if a child needs reminders to use the bathroom. Rather than telling the child to go, the teacher can show the child a photo of the bathroom.

When children can't It is true that children need to be encouraged to do as much as possible for themselves; nevertheless, teachers must make exceptions. A child may ask for help with a task long since mastered. Children, too, have their off days. Like adults, they become tired or upset or feel unwell. All children can be expected to be dependent at times. They need to know that it is all right to ask for help, to say, "This is too hard. I can't do it by myself." A child should never be ridiculed or belittled for asking for help, no matter how simple the task. Children who have been helped to feel competent most of the time will ask for assistance only when they truly feel that the task is too much for them to do by themselves.

Zack is a four-year-old in your preschool class. You recently noticed that he is not eating very much at lunchtime. When you talk to his mother about this, you discover that the mother has gone back to feeding

him with a spoon because she feels he will not eat enough unless she helps him. What might you say to Zack's mother?

In such situations, it is important that help be given immediately, in just the right amount. The adult should never take over. Instead, the adult helps the child find a way to resolve the impasse. The child always should feel more help is available if the problem is not solved on the first attempt or even on the second or third.

14-2d ▪ Game-Like Assistance

One way to keep a child involved and successful in a self-care situation is to create a game-like atmosphere. The exchange that follows is focused on Robert, born with cerebral palsy. He had recently turned six years old and was finishing up his third year in an inclusive early childhood program. Throughout the sequence, the teacher can be seen giving just the right amount of appropriately timed assistance and feedback in order to keep Robert involved. Interactions between the teacher and the child are followed by interpretive comments.

I

Robert put his foot in an unlaced shoe in the teacher's lap.

TEACHER: "Hi, Robert! What do you need?" Robert pointed to his shoe.

TEACHER: "Tell me what you need."

ROBERT: "Tie my shoes."

Children need practice using language. The teacher, therefore, required Robert to ask for what he needed. In working with children with no language or delayed language, the teacher likely would have settled for one word, or even the simple gesture of raising the foot and pointing to the untied shoe. In the latter case, the teacher might respond while tying the shoe: "You are showing me that your shoe needs tying." Because Robert had the ability to verbalize his need, he was asked to do so.

One way to keep a child involved and successful in a self-care routine is to create a game-like atmosphere.

Rachel Anne Seymour/AP Photo

II

TEACHER: "All right, but first you need to lace them."

The teacher began to sequence the task for Robert by reminding him the shoe first had to be laced. Another time, the teacher might ask Robert to tell what needed to be done before the shoe could be tied. Stating the order in which a complex task is to be accomplished is a skill that gives the child experience in thinking through ordered sequencing for all tasks. Note that the teacher did not require Robert to stop and say, "Please." The teacher chose to focus the child's efforts on the self-care task itself rather than on social etiquette.

III

ROBERT: "No, you lace them. I don't know how." As he said this he kept his eyes on two favorite playmates who seemed ready to transition to outdoor play.

With Robert's refusal to lace his shoes, the teacher reassessed the situation. It was immediately obvious that Robert did not want to be left behind when his friends went out to play. Yet the teacher knew they would be gone long before Robert, with his less-well-developed fine motor skills, could lace his shoes by himself. What to do?

IV

TEACHER (SMILING): "Robert, you are kidding me. Every day I see you lacing your shoes. Sit down here on the floor and I will help you."

The teacher knew Robert could lace his shoes and felt it was not good for him to get away with saying he was not able to do it.

On the other hand, his eagerness to be ready to play with his friends was important, too.

The teacher decided, therefore, to make a joke out of telling him she knew he could tie his own shoes, but still to give him assistance.

V

Robert sat on the floor. The teacher inserted the tip of one lace partly through an eyelet, while instructing: "Robert, you pull it through."

Having Robert sit on the floor gave him a firm base and the necessary balance for lacing the shoe. The teacher did the part of the job that would have given Robert the most difficulty, getting the lace started into the eyelet.

The tasks the teacher held Robert to could be done quickly and with immediate success, thus giving promise that the shoe was much closer to being laced.

VI

As Robert pulled the first lace through, the teacher said, "Great! You got that one through. Now hand me the other lace." The lacing continued in this fashion until only the top pair of holes was left.

With each step, the teacher gave Robert encouragement, positive feedback, and a cue for the next step in the sequence. ("Now hand me the other lace.")

VII

TEACHER: "I'll bet you can do the last two by yourself. Here, I'll hand you the laces this time."
ROBERT: "I know which ones. I can do it."

With the task almost completed, the teacher sensed it would not be difficult for Robert to finish. Hence, the friendly challenge to Robert to take the responsibility.

VIII

TEACHER: "Look at that, Robert. All done! You finished the lacing all by yourself. Here, let me tie your shoes and you will be all ready to play."

The teacher then called to Robert's friends: "Robert's ready to go out, too. Wait while he gets his coat on, okay?"

Because task completion is important to children's learning, the teacher gave specific praise: "Robert, you finished the lacing all by yourself." Then the teacher made sure Robert's efforts really paid off by having his friends wait for him. Also, no suggestion was made that Robert work on shoe tying, even though it was a task on his IEP. That would be saved for another time. Instead, the teacher tied the shoes quickly so there would be no further delay.

Robert made good progress in acquiring self-care skills despite his disabilities. Other children with developmental delays may have learned to do much less for themselves. Many cannot put on their own coats. They cannot feed themselves or take care of their own toilet needs. Some children cannot ask for what they need. In these cases, the teacher's job is more demanding. Teaching children with more severe disabilities requires ongoing assistance and support from relevant members of the child study team. The specifics of such assistance must be written into the IEP or the IFSP and implemented by the school district. Collaboration and communication among various settings (e.g., preschool, occupational therapy, speech therapy) and the home are critical to ensure individuals in each environment teach skills in the same manner and with similar expectations of independence.

Did You Get It?

What would constitute verbal reinforcement?
  a. Describing a task well done, indicating that the child's efforts are appreciated.
  b. Indicating not only what had been done, but what had not been done.
  c. Praise combined with reproach.
  d. Reprimanding regarding a task that was forgotten.

Take the full quiz on CourseMate.

A Systematic Approach to Teaching Self-Care   14-3 ☀

There are several published manuals that provide detailed descriptions of how to teach self-care skills. These include *Steps to Independence* (Baker & Brightman, 2004) and *Self-Help Skills for People with Autism* (Anderson, Jablonski, Thomeer, & Knapp, 2007). The latter specifies five steps of a systematic approach to teaching self-care skills. While designed for children with autism, these steps (when followed) will help any young child develop increased independence over time. The steps include: 1) Specifying a goal for learning, 2) Breaking the skill into small steps, 3) Using a systematic teaching approach 4) Using data to evaluate progress, and 5) modifying the teaching as needed.

14-3a ■ Specifying a Goal for Learning

It is important to know what the teaching goal is for each child. A goal should be achievable and based on what is developmentally appropriate for the child's age. The goal should be specific and include the same information as *short-term objectives* described in Chapter 10: *who, what, where,* and *when.* For example, it is not enough to state that you want Cyrus to be toilet-trained, as not everyone may agree on when he has achieved this. Does this mean he has to be accident-free for hours?

Weeks? Days? If the goal is stated as, *"When offered the opportunity to use the toilet at least 4 times each school day, Cyrus will have no more than one accident every two weeks,"* it will be very clear to all involved when he has achieved this goal.

14-3b ■ Breaking the Skill into Small Steps

Task analysis, or breaking a skill into small teachable steps, is described in detail in Chapter 12. The best way to write a task analysis is to perform the skill yourself and write down all the steps you do to complete the task (Anderson et al., 2007). The number of steps you actually need to include, and later teach, will vary greatly depending on the child's present ability.

14-3c ■ Using a Systematic Teaching Approach

Chapter 12 discusses several teaching strategies that are also effective for teaching self-care skills. These include shaping, prompting, fading, and cueing. Chaining is another teaching technique that is very effective for teaching self-care skills. Many self-care tasks can be thought of as chains of individual steps. Toileting, shoe lacing, feeding oneself—all are examples of a skill composed of a set of smaller behaviors chained together and organized into what seems to be a single skill. When adapting the chaining concept to teaching self-care skills, the adult helps the child learn one response, one link of the skill chain at a time. Once the child is performing the first component in the chain, the next step, or link, is introduced. Single components of the chain are added one by one until the child can perform all of them, in order, from start to finish. Step-by-step learning can be made easier if the child can see the entire chain being performed.

On many tasks, **forward chaining** and **backward chaining** are equally successful. The choice depends on the particular task and level of skill the child displays. In forward chaining, the teacher helps the child learn the first step in the chain, then the child is prompted, hand over hand, through the remaining steps. Once the child has mastered the first step, then the second step is taught, and so on, until the child is able to do the all of the steps in the chain with little or no assistance. In backward chaining, instruction begins with the last step and progresses backward to the first component. In both cases, as the teacher guides the child through the remaining steps of the chain, the teacher uses only the amount of pressure or prompting needed to help the child succeed (Anderson et al., 2007).

The child, in the zipping activity that follows, has fairly well-developed fine motor skills; the teacher, therefore, has broken the task into only six components. The steps are suitable for teaching the task with a forward chaining approach. Throughout, the teacher will demonstrate or provide manual prompts as needed.

forward chaining breaking a task down into a series of small steps and teaching the first step first, in contrast to *backward chaining*

backward chaining the opposite of *forward chaining*; teaching starts with the last step of a learning sequence—sometimes referred to as *reverse chaining*

Step 1. *Using both hands, the bottom front edges of the coat are brought together at the bottom.*
Step 2. *The zipper pin is inserted into the housing.*
Step 3. *The zipper pin is seated in the housing by pushing up and down with opposing movements of each hand.*
Step 4. *The tab on the zipper is grasped between thumb and forefinger.*
Step 5. *The bottom of the coat at the zipper housing is held with one hand while the zipper tab is pulled to the top with the hand holding the zipper tab.*
Step 6. *The zipper tab is pushed down and firmly into locked position.*

With a backward chaining approach, the adult zips the coat but leaves the final step for the child to do. As the child locks the zipper tab into place, the teacher can then say, "Good job! You finished zipping your coat!" This gives the child the satisfaction of task completion.

14-3d ■ Using Data to Evaluate Progress

Chapter 18 details several data collection methods. Data can be used both to monitor problem behaviors and to track the effectiveness of teaching strategies on the acquisition of new skills. The best way to ensure success for each child is for everyone involved to be aware of each child's level of independence for each of the major self-care routines throughout the day. One effective means to achieve this awareness is discreetly posting data sheets around the classroom in places where the self-care routines are likely to occur. For example, a sheet in the bathroom posted above the children's eye level lists the current abilities for all the children in the program for both hand washing and toileting (see Figure 14-3 for an example of a data sheet for toileting). When individuals assisting in that area observe changes in ability, they update the data sheet. The information is shared regularly with the parents so that the school and family work toward the same goal. The information can be used not only to increase consistency but also to monitor progress. For example, if staff members are monitoring whether children are wet or dry prior to diaper changing or toileting, they can determine which children are remaining dry for extended periods of time and who thus may be ready to move out of diapers.

14-3e ■ Modifying the Teaching as Needed

By regularly reviewing the information collected on the data sheets, educators can determine whether a change in teaching strategy is warranted. If teachers do not see progress toward the identified goal within two to three weeks, they should change the teaching approach.

▶︎❙❙ **TeachSource Video Connections**

© Cengage Learning 2015

Preschool Health and Nutrition

In this video, children's acquisition of self-care skills forms a foundation for developing additional skills related to health, safety, and nutrition. The teacher helps the children learn about proper care of teeth through a variety of activities. When preschoolers are actively involved in learning, they are more likely to remember what they are taught.

After watching the video, discuss the following:

1. Make a list of the health and self-care skills the teacher is helping the children learn.

2. If the teacher were teaching tooth brushing using a systematic approach as described in this chapter, what else might she do?

Watch on CourseMate.

FIGURE 14-3
Classroom Toileting Data Sheet

WEEK OF ___	MONDAY		TUESDAY		WEDNESDAY		THURSDAY		FRIDAY	
Becky	am	pm	am	pm	am	pm	am	pm	am	pm
	W	W	W	W	W	W	W	W	W	W
	D	D	D	D	D	D	D	D	D	D
	V	V	V	V	V	V	V	V	V	V
	BM	BM	BM	BM	BM	BM	BM	BM	BM	BM
Bryan	am	pm	am	pm	am	pm	am	pm	am	pm
	W	W	W	W	W	W	W	W	W	W
	D	D	D	D	D	D	D	D	D	D
	V	V	V	V	V	V	V	V	V	V
	BM	BM	BM	BM	BM	BM	BM	BM	BM	BM
Dante	am	pm	am	pm	am	pm	am	pm	am	pm
	W	W	W	W	W	W	W	W	W	W
	D	D	D	D	D	D	D	D	D	D
	V	V	V	V	V	V	V	V	V	V
	BM	BM	BM	BM	BM	BM	BM	BM	BM	BM
Courtney	am	pm	am	pm	am	pm	am	pm	am	pm
	W	W	W	W	W	W	W	W	W	W
	D	D	D	D	D	D	D	D	D	D
	V	V	V	V	V	V	V	V	V	V
	BM	BM	BM	BM	BM	BM	BM	BM	BM	BM
Drew	am	pm	am	pm	am	pm	am	pm	am	pm
	W	W	W	W	W	W	W	W	W	W
	D	D	D	D	D	D	D	D	D	D
	V	V	V	V	V	V	V	V	V	V
	BM	BM	BM	BM	BM	BM	BM	BM	BM	BM
Henry	am	pm	am	pm	am	pm	am	pm	am	pm
	W	W	W	W	W	W	W	W	W	W
	D	D	D	D	D	D	D	D	D	D
	V	V	V	V	V	V	V	V	V	V
	BM	BM	BM	BM	BM	BM	BM	BM	BM	BM
Kelly	am	pm			am	pm			am	pm
	W	W			W	W			W	W
	D	D			D	D			D	D
	V	V			V	V			V	V
	BM	BM			BM	BM			BM	BM
Matthew	am	pm			am	pm			am	pm
	W	W			W	W			W	W
	D	D			D	D			D	D
	V	V			V	V			V	V
	BM	BM			BM	BM			BM	BM

Key: W = wet; D = Dry; V = Voided in Toilet; BM = Bowel Movement in Toilet

TeachSource Digital Download Download from CourseMate.

© Cengage Learning

Snack Time: An Opportunity 14-4 ✹
to Teach so Many Skills

Snack time not only provides an opportunity to learn basic self-feeding skills, it also provides a time to practice social and communication skills as well as other self-help skills for all children. Figure 14-4 provides a list of skills to be taught and some strategies to use to teach these skills.

FIGURE 14-4

Skills and Strategies for Snack and Mealtime

Self-Help Skills	Social Skills/Communication
• Hand washing • Setting the table • Pouring from a small pitcher • Using a straw • Unzipping/Opening a lunch box • Spreading with a knife • Wiping up spills • Putting away their belongings • Throwing away trash • Cleaning the table	• Waiting one's turn • Making choices • Requesting help • Passing out items (place mats, napkins, cups, food) • Counting out items • Asking questions and engaging in a conversation • Making comparisons (Who has a snack that is the same/different?)
Strategies • Establish a snack/meal routine • Provide a place mat or nametag that indicates where each child should sit • Create an area where supplies needed (cups, napkins, plates) are easily accessed	**Strategies** • Assign daily/weekly jobs related to the routine • Provide visuals to remind children about how much food to take • Create topic pictures or a list of questions to ask to keep the conversation going • Seat children who are nonverbal next to children who are verbal • Let the children pass the container of food to each other

Source: Klein, Cook, & Richardson-Gibbs (2001).

Did You Get It?

Which example provides the opportunity for a child to practice social and communication skills in the first instance, and self-help skills in the other?

a. Wiping up skills; waiting one's turn.
b. Putting away belongings; making choices.
c. Requesting help; unzipping.
d. Throwing away trash; counting out items.

Take the full quiz on CourseMate.

As noted at the outset, all self-care skills are learned. It follows, then, that all self-care skills can be taught. Starting on toilet training too early dooms both child and adult to failure. Success depends, in part, on physiological maturity, especially of the **sphincter muscles.**

Toilet training, once thought to be totally dependent on **maturation**, can be task-analyzed and taught in its component parts to children who are physiologically mature enough but need additional and direct support. With some children, each part, in turn, may need to be task-analyzed and taught step by step. Ordinary toilet training includes twelve to fifteen steps. It starts with getting into the bathroom, pulling the pants down, and getting up onto the toilet. It concludes with getting off the toilet, wiping, pulling the clothes up, and flushing. What could be simpler? Yet, for many young children with and without developmental problems, one or more of the steps may present great difficulty. Even the seemingly simple task of getting on and off the toilet may need to be broken down into smaller steps. And using toilet tissue effectively is a challenge for all young children.

Consistency in toilet training will decrease the time it takes a child to become independent in toileting skills.

© Cengage Learning

sphincter muscles muscles that contribute to bowel and bladder control

maturation developmentally, maturation is often defined as an internal process that governs the natural unfolding of innate ("preprogrammed") skills and abilities

nonambulatory describes the inability to move oneself about; usually the inability to walk

14-5a ▪ Toilet-Training Programs

Commercial toilet-training programs have been developed for children with disabilities (Baker & Brightman, 2004; Foxx & Azrin, 1973), but toilet training a child with a disability is similar to toilet training a child who is typically developing (Figure 14-5). The Foxx and Azrin program, first published in 1973 and later reissued in 1989 by Azrin, is still considered one of the most effective and comprehensive programs available. The program involves similar procedures to those discussed here, with even greater emphasis on small steps. Toilet training children with disabilities requires teachers and parents to work together to implement a consistent plan across all the environments in which the child spends time. Consistency in toilet training will decrease the amount of time it takes a child to use the toilet independently. The Foxx and Azrin program also provides information on toilet training children who are **nonambulatory** and those with other special problems. (Children who are on seizure medication, for example, must not be given quantities of liquids.)

14-5b ▪ Special Considerations

In the zipping task (and in many other dressing and self-care tasks), it is most effective if the adult works from behind the child. This ensures that the teacher is performing the hand and finger movements in the same way that the child will be expected to reproduce them. Young children do not have well-developed

FIGURE 14-5
Toileting Sequence

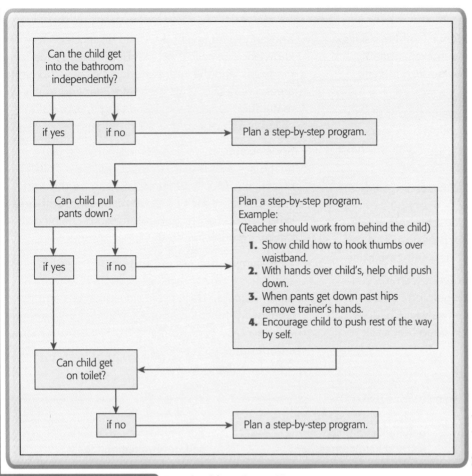

Can the child get into the bathroom independently?

if yes | if no → **Plan a step-by-step program.**

Can child pull pants down?

if yes | if no →

Plan a step-by-step program.
Example:
(Teacher should work from behind the child)

1. Show child how to hook thumbs over waistband.
2. With hands over child's, help child push down.
3. When pants get down past hips remove trainer's hands.
4. Encourage child to push rest of the way by self.

Can child get on toilet?

if no → **Plan a step-by-step program.**

© Cengage Learning

spatial orientation, nor do they understand reversibility. Teachers' demonstrations therefore must be conducted from the child's perspective. For this reason, the use of lacing, buttoning, and zipping boards for children to practice on has been questioned. It is confusing for many children to try to reverse and transfer the motions learned in practice sessions to their own bodies. Cook, Klein, and Tessier (2007) report that some teachers have been most ingenious in overcoming this problem. They attach the form boards to a pillow on which they have sewn elastic loops that are slipped over the child's arms, up to the shoulders. This holds the pillow at the upper torso position, allowing children comfortable practice sessions.

A word about the importance of suitable clothing when learning self-care skills: children who are being toilet-trained need underpants (and outer pants) with elastic at the top so they can be pulled down easily. Children who are learning to dress themselves can learn more readily if their clothing has big, sturdy zippers that work, large buttons and unrestricted buttonholes, and simple fastenings on belts and overalls. When children are having prolonged difficulty in learning to dress themselves, temporarily providing clothing a size or two too big is sometimes a help. Teachers never presume to tell parents how to dress their children, yet parents often welcome suggestions that help their children learn more easily.

Did You Get It?

How would a teacher position him- or herself to reproduce the child's movements in the most effective way?

a. From child's perspective (such as by standing behind).

b. Reverse motion position.

c. Transfer motion position.

d. By standing in front of a board.

Take the full quiz on CourseMate.

Summary

▶ The terms *self-care, independence, self-help skills,* and *adaptive skills* can be used interchangeably to mean taking care of one's personal needs in socially acceptable ways.

▶ Traditionally, families had the major responsibility for teaching self-care skills to children; in recent years, early childhood teachers and programs have become much more involved.

▶ Opportunities for learning and practicing self-care skills should be embedded with every part of the curriculum. Throughout the day, children need to experience the independence, pleasure, and self-esteem that result from mastering self-care skills.

▶ A child's disability need not prevent learning self-care skills. Genuine kindness is helping children learn ways to do things for themselves. Children trying to master a self-care skill need feedback about what works well.

▶ Knowing when and how to help depends on teachers' knowledge of each child, developmental sequence, readiness, and the interrelatedness of developmental areas. Many skills once thought to depend totally on maturation can and should be taught, especially to children with developmental problems.

▶ Specific step-by-step planning—that is, task analysis—is necessary to teach self-care skills effectively. Most self-care tasks can be thought of as chains of many smaller responses. Self-care skills can be taught through forward chaining or backward chaining.

▶ To maximize success, educators and parents should use data to evaluate progress and must communicate about the child's progress and ability. Consistent teaching strategies across environments will decrease confusion and frustration and increase independence.

Key Terms

adaptive skills, 362

backward chaining, 374

forward chaining, 374

generalization, 365

learned helplessness, 368

maturation, 378

nonambulatory, 378

self-determination, 362

sphincter muscles, 378

Student Activities

1. Observe an inclusive preschool or child care center during arrival or departure time, a toileting period, or a meal or snack time. List ten or more self-care skills and adaptive behaviors you see children engaging in.

2. The next time you shampoo your hair, think about the steps you complete. Then, write down what you did, step by step, starting with the decision to wash your hair and ending with it styled as you typically wear it. Think about which steps could be completed in a different order and which cannot.

3. Select one of the major steps in the toileting sequence (or any other self-care skill) and analyze it into its component parts. Write a three-to-five-step program for teaching that sub skill to a four-year-old.

4. Ask a fellow student to role-play a child who cannot tie a shoe. Teach the task to the "child."

5. Assume that *learning to count five or more objects* is written into the IEP of a four-year-old. Give examples of how teachers might embed this learning task into several self-care routines.

6. Make a list of all the self-care activities a first grader would be expected to complete independently during a typical school day.

Review Questions

Respond briefly to the following items.

1. Why are self-determination skills important for young children?

2. The text states that self-care skills should be integrated with all parts of the curriculum. Explain.

3. How much help and what kind should be given to a child who is trying to learn a self-care skill?

4. What are the five key steps in teaching a self-care skill?

5. What is the role of maturation in toilet training?

6. What is chaining? What is the difference between forward and backward chaining?

7. It is suggested that buttoning, zipping, and lacing boards may not be appropriate for a young child trying to learn those skills. Why not?

8. Why is specifying a goal for a child important when teaching self-care skills?

Additional Resources/Readings

Self-Help Skills for People with Autism: A Systematic Teaching Approach

Written by Stephen R. Anderson, Amy L. Jablonski, Vicki Madaus Knapp, and Marcus L Thomeer
Woodbine Publishing

Learning self-help skills (eating, dressing, toileting, and personal hygiene) can be challenging for individuals with autism, but it is critical for their independence. This manual describes a systematic approach that parents and teachers can use to teach basic self-care to children, ages twenty-four months to early teens, and even older individuals.

Helpful Websites

American Occupational Therapy Association (AOTA)

http://www.aota.org

The American Occupational Therapy Association advances the quality, availability, use, and support of occupational therapy through standard setting, advocacy, education, and research on behalf of its members and the public. The website contains information about the field of occupational therapy as well as information on special topics.

Family Village

http://www.familyvillage.wisc.edu

This website integrates information, resources, and communication opportunities for people with cognitive and other disabilities, for their families, and for those who provide them with services and support. The site includes informational resources on specific diagnoses, communication connections, adaptive products and technology, adaptive recreational activities, education, worship, health issues, and disability-related media and literature.

Pediatric Services

http://www.pediatricservices.com

An intervention team working to serve children with developmental delays provides a reference sheet for teaching self-care and daily routines, as well as developmental tips for young children with vision loss. Most of the suggestions work with all young children. Retrieved from **http://pediatricservices.com/prof/prof-09.htm**

 Visit the Education CourseMate for this textbook to access the eBook, Did You Get It? quizzes, Digital Downloads, TeachSource Video Cases, flashcards, and more. Go to CengageBrain.com to log in, register, or purchase access.

Facilitating Social Development

15

OBJECTIVES

After reading this chapter, you should be able to:

15-1   explain how social development is related to other areas of development.

15-2   provide an example of why it is difficult to define appropriate social skills.

15-3   describe how social skills are developed and the impact a developmental problem can have on their development.

15-4   outline the role early learning programs play in the development of play skills.

15-5   list strategies that teachers use to structure and support peer interactions.

15-6   describe the process teachers might use if children need additional support in the area of social development.

· · · · · · · · · · · · · · · · · ·

The following NAEYC Standards are addressed in this chapter:

STANDARD 1 Promoting Child Development and Learning

STANDARD 2 Building Family and Community Relationships

STANDARD 3 Observing, Documenting and Assessing to Support Young Children and Families

STANDARD 4 Using Developmentally Effective Approaches

STANDARD 5 Using Content Knowledge to Build Meaningful Curriculum

STANDARD 6 Becoming a Professional

CONNECTIONS

- An infant with hearing impairments smiles as her father dribbles water on her, and they both giggle.
- A child in an inclusive classroom helps a child with Down syndrome figure out how to put together a floor-sized puzzle.
- Wayne is sitting on a tricycle watching others play. A teacher approaches him with a wagon carrying Melissa, who has muscular dystrophy. "How about if I tie this wagon to your trike and you give Melissa a ride?"
- A small group of second-grade students are writing a poem together, using facts from a story they read as a class. Teddy, a student with autism, needs adult support to participate as a member of the group.

Children with developmental delays often need systematic help; appropriate social behavior may have to be taught directly.

© Cengage Learning

These are examples of social interactions that occur in early childhood settings and of how teachers, parents, and other children can facilitate the social development of children with diverse skills. Social development depends on the individual's acquisition of the many behaviors that help people live together in a family and in society. Gordon and Browne (2010) suggest four categories for the wide range of skills children learn in the early years: The "Four Hows" are (1) *how to approach*, to get in and be included; (2) *how to interact*, through sharing and cooperating; (3) *how to deal with difference*, such as teasing, bullying, including, and helping others; and (4) *how to manage conflict* by problem solving and handling aggression. All children must learn these skills: those with developmental differences, those who are developing typically, and those described as gifted. How well social skills are learned depends on the quality of the interpersonal relationships in the child's everyday life. Through interacting with others, infants and young children learn the social skills (as well as the accompanying language and intellectual skills) necessary for healthy development. It is through interacting with others that young children get the necessary feedback about their social competence.

Interpersonal relationships are reciprocal; that is, there is mutual responding or *turn-taking*. During the early months and years, social interactions depend on the child's ability to give and receive social messages. Children with developmental problems may fail to respond to social signals, or they may give too few appropriate signals. Either situation reduces feedback and may lead to negative responses; both situations will interfere with emerging social development. It is not unusual for the social delays in children with disabilities to become greater than the problems associated with their primary disability (McLean, Bailey, & Wolery, 2004).

No child should be excused from learning acceptable social skills. Children who are typically developing seem to acquire social skills spontaneously or with only brief episodes of informal coaching. Children with developmental problems, however, often need systematic help; appropriate social behaviors may have to be taught directly, often over a considerable period of time. How teachers help these young children acquire appropriate social skills is the focus of this chapter. First, however, social skills will be examined from a developmental perspective.

Social Skills and Overall Development 15-1 ☀

Though discussed as an independent topic, social skills are never truly separate from other areas of development. Each influences all others. The following example, representative of social activities of four-year-olds who are typically developing, illustrates the close interrelatedness of skills.

> *Omar ran to Aaron, who was sitting on the edge of the sandbox filling cake tins with sand.*
>
> **OMAR:** *"Let's decorate cakes. Here's some decorations."* (He poured some small plastic rings into Aaron's cupped hands)
>
> **AARON:** *"Too many."* (He handed a few back) *"That's plenty."*
>
> *Omar smiled at Aaron and began alternating rings around the edge of his sand cake while singing, "Now a blue one, now a yellow one." Aaron stuck twigs in his sand cake and pulled a ring down over the top of each twig.*
>
> *Then he sang "Happy Birthday" several times, each time naming a different classmate.*

A number of developmental skills can be identified in this play interaction. Both large and small motor skills are evident: running, pouring, picking, and placing. Cognitive skills include math concepts of *some, too many*, and *plenty*, as well as recognizing colors, naming colors, and understanding such concepts as *decorate* and *alternate* (now a blue, now a yellow). Memory was obvious, too, with Aaron singing "Happy Birthday" and recalling several classmates' names. Both children demonstrated effective communication skills in the form of verbal exchanges, listening to each other, and smiling. These developmental skills were in addition to, and blended with, high-level social skills such as:

- each child initiating his own ideas
- following suggestions from each other
- sharing materials
- role-playing (cake decorators)

The above exchange shows the developmental complexities that work for some children, but against others. In the Omar and Aaron example, each child was helping the other to learn; each was spontaneously reinforcing the other's skills and responses. Spontaneous peer reinforcement may not always happen for children with developmental disabilities; instead, their poorly developed play skills often lead to rejection.

A negative cycle is set in motion: a continuing lack of skills shuts out further opportunities to learn; lack of learning opportunities results in little positive feedback. The combination sometimes sets up emotional reactions that may cause as much developmental interference as the disability itself (as McLean et al., 2004, noted earlier). It is important, therefore, that young children with (and without) developmental problems be helped to learn appropriate social skills.

> **Did You Get It?**
>
> **What developmental skills are evident when a child runs, picks up an item, and puts it on the table?**
> a. Cognitive skills.
> b. Large and small-motor skills.
> c. Memory.
> d. Communication skills.
>
> Take the full quiz on CourseMate.

✺ 15-2 Defining Appropriate Social Skills

Appropriate social skills are rules and *expectations* prescribed by particular groups as to how group members will conduct themselves in private and in public. Prescriptions for what is socially appropriate vary from community to community, society to society, and culture to culture.

Variations exist even within the tight circle of home, preschool, and neighborhood. Confusing choices often result, especially for young children, as in the following examples:

Social skills learned in the early years include sometimes initiating play ideas with children, and other times, following other children's leads.

© Cengage Learning

- *Five-year-old Darryl had learned he could get almost anything he wanted from his parents and teenage brothers by throwing tantrums. The same behavior in the neighborhood and preschool did not pay off. Children taunted, "Crybaby, crybaby," and ran off, leaving him shrieking.*

- *Rebecca painted with obvious enjoyment during the first week of school. One day she began to cry, pointing to a small paint smudge on her sleeve. The teacher assured her it would wash out and that the apron protected most of her dress. Rebecca would not return to the easel, even on subsequent days. What emerged were confusing social expectations between home and school: Teachers had assured Rebecca it was all right if paint got on her clothing; at home, she was scolded if her "good school clothes got all dirty."*

- *Chandra spent much of her time playing in the streets with older, aggressive children. There, she learned to hit, run, dodge, grab, and kick—the social skills necessary to that particular street setting. In the preschool, these same behaviors were considered socially unacceptable. Chandra had to learn to restrain aggressive behaviors at school, but to keep them ever ready when playing in the street.*

These examples, described by teachers, are from real life. They point out how difficult it is to specify what is appropriate. In each instance, children were exhibiting social skills relevant to given situations in their lives. Yet they also were receiving contradictory signals about the inappropriateness of those same behaviors in another context.

Most children learn to deal with such contradictions. They find ways to adapt their behavior to various situations—a social skill necessary for all of us at every life stage. Such adaptations tend to be more difficult for children with developmental problems. They are likely to have trouble learning to discriminate between a behavior that is appropriate and one that is inappropriate. Trying to understand, for example, why it is all right to hug family members but not every peer in a child's first-grade class can be confusing.

Consider the major social skills to be learned during the early years, all of which relate to getting along with others:

- interacting with children and adults, in a variety of ways, at home and away from home

- trusting and enjoying known adults outside the immediate family

- recognizing and protesting inappropriate advances from known or unknown adults within or outside the family

- sometimes initiating play ideas with children; other times, following other children's leads

- participating in group activities through listening, taking turns, and contributing to group effort

- sometimes putting aside individual needs and interests so the needs and interests of the group can be met

- working and playing independently as well as cooperatively; learning to be alone without feeling isolated or rejected

- using language as the powerful social tool it is for persuading, defending, reasoning, explaining, solving problems, and getting needs and preferences attended to

Learning social skills is a complex task involving a wide range of values, knowledge, and skills. Kostelnik, Whiren, Soderman, Stein, and Gregory (2008) describe the necessary ingredients.

- Cultural competence—knowledge of, comfort with, and respect for people of varying ethnic or racial backgrounds

- Planning and decision-making skills—the ability to make choices, solve problems, and plan ahead

- Self-regulation—the ability to monitor self, reflect on feelings, and resist temptation and peer pressure

- Interpersonal skills—maintaining friendly relationships, and communicating needs, ideas, and feelings

- Positive self-identity—demonstrating sense of competence, purpose, and worth

- Social values—exhibiting caring and demonstrating responsibility, honesty, and flexibility

Did You Get It?

How is it more difficult for a child with developmental problems, as opposed to a child without developmental problems, to deal with contradictions pertaining to appropriate and inappropriate behavior?

a. All children learn to deal with contradictions; the difference is in the length of time.

b. Children find ways to adapt their behavior to various situations; the difference is in the length of time.

c. Children without developmental problems adapt easily to contradictions; children with developmental problems do not.

d. Children with developmental problems have greater trouble learning to discriminate between a behavior that is appropriate and one that is inappropriate.

Take the full quiz on CourseMate.

Acquiring Social Skills 15-3

Social skills are learned behaviors. Learning a full range of social skills—the socializing process—cannot be forced or hurried. Learning such skills is a major occupation of the developing child. Refinement of previously learned social skills and the learning of new ones are ongoing throughout the lifespan.

15-3a ■ Temperament and Emotions

The development of social skills, as noted earlier, is influenced by home, school, culture, and community expectations and by the interpersonal relations within these environments. A child's emotional reactions, or, more precisely, **temperament**, also exert influence. Thomas and Chess (1977) described three types of infants: *easy, difficult,* and *slow-to-warm-up.*

Easy babies tend to be lively but not excessively so; they are fairly calm in their reactions to the unexpected and are open to new experiences such as trying out unfamiliar foods. They tend to be regular in their eating and sleeping habits. In general, they are happy and contented.

temperament the individual's psychological makeup or personality traits

Difficult babies are likely to be irritable, easily upset, and vigorously resistant to the unfamiliar. They cry more frequently, and they cry in a way that grates on parents' and caregivers' ears (and nerves). Biological rhythms (eating, sleeping, and elimination patterns) are difficult to regulate; the child is often labeled as "spoiled."

Slow-to-warm-up infants show few intense reactions, either positive or negative. They seldom are outright resistant to new experiences, but neither are they eager to sample the unknown. For example, instead of fighting off a new food, they may simply not swallow it. They store it in one cheek or let it quietly slide out of their mouth. *Passive resistant* is a term used to describe this type of behavior.

These personality or temperament traits may have genetic linkage. However, this is difficult to demonstrate and also relatively unimportant. What is important is that babies respond differently to similar circumstances. These personal behavior patterns appear to persist into childhood, affecting how others respond. Parents and caregivers play a role in the persistence of personality traits. One caregiver might regard a child as distractible, impulsive, and hard to manage, while another might perceive the same child as an eager, active, happy-go-lucky runabout.

Granted that every child's social responses are influenced by temperament, the fact remains that all social behaviors are learned. They can be seen and heard and sometimes felt, as when one child pats or strikes another. Social skills are observable ways of behaving. Like all behaviors, they can be eliminated, strengthened, or modified. This is true even if those responses are labeled *emotional*. We know children's emotional state through their behavior:

- three children jumping on a jumping board, smiling and talking
- two children laughing while they divide cookies
- a five-year-old running from a snarling dog
- two children walking together with arms entwined

Such behaviors provide specific clues to which children are feeling happy, frightened, loving. They provide clues, also, to how well the children's social skills are developing. Each of the responses was *learned* through social interactions with the child's physical and interpersonal environment. By carefully observing children's behaviors (facial expressions, body posture, gestures, verbalizations), emotions can be recognized and dealt with in ways that strengthen both emotional development and social skills.

15-3b ■ Social Reinforcement

The development of appropriate social skills depends almost entirely on the amount and type of social responsiveness available to a young child. All children need opportunities to interact with others in a give-and-take fashion. Most newborns come equipped with social behaviors that attract and hold the attention of significant adults. In the typical situation, the baby cries, and someone

Learning social skills is a complex task involving a wide range of values, knowledge, and skills.

© Cengage Learning

comes and provides comfort. The baby is soothed and stops crying. The caregiver is pleased. This puts in motion a reciprocal system that is socially and mutually reinforcing for both infant and adult.

From Neurons to Neighborhoods: The Science of Early Childhood Development (Shonkoff & Phillips, 2000) lists the following key elements required of early relationships of young children:

- reliable support that establishes confidence in the adult
- responsiveness to the child
- protection from harm
- affection that develops self-esteem
- opportunities to solve problems and resolve conflict
- support for growth of new skills
- reciprocal interaction by which children learn the give-and-take of relationships
- mutual respect

Adult responsiveness **Social reinforcement** is a crucial factor in determining a child's development. Following is an excerpt from a 1980 U.S. government pamphlet, *Infant Care*. Even though this information was published more than thirty years ago, it remains pertinent today.

> When your baby first smiles, you pay attention to him and smile back. When he smiles again, you smile back and pay attention to him again, talk to him, and cuddle him. He soon learns that when he smiles good things happen to him, so he learns to do a lot of smiling when you are around. In just the same way, when you pay attention to his first cooing and gurgling sounds, your smile, your voice, and your fondling reward him. He coos and gurgles more and more frequently. The same holds true for all kinds of social behaviors in the infant and young child. When you respond to something your child does by giving attention, a smile, a kind word, or by fondling or joy, your baby will do that thing more and more frequently. If you ignore it, it will happen less and less. (p. 11)

The process of adult reinforcement is sometimes referred to as **contingent stimulation**. When there is at least partially contingent stimulation (responding) from significant adults, infants and young children develop better. They have earlier language, more advanced cognitive abilities, greater self-esteem, and more durable attachments.

social reinforcement the positive or negative feedback that children receive from adults and peers that leads to further learning, either appropriate or inappropriate

contingent stimulation responding to a child in a way that prompts further learning

A child's temperament influences social development.

© Cengage Learning

15-3c ■ Impact of Developmental Problems

A responsive early environment cannot guarantee a child will develop the necessary and appropriate social skills. Through no fault of parents or

Children need give-and-take interactions.

© Cengage Learning

caregivers, children with developmental problems often are deprived of stimulation and reinforcement because of their own limitations. Consider these examples.

An infant who is deaf cannot hear the crooning, loving sounds that its mother makes during bathing, dressing, and feeding routines. Thus, the infant does not make the lively responses typical of an infant with normal hearing. The infant's lack of responsiveness reduces the mother's efforts to interact. To further compound the situation, an infant's hearing loss often goes undetected during the developmentally crucial early months. Not realizing her infant has an impairment, the mother may take the infant's lack of interest in her conversation as rejection; unwittingly she may respond less positively to the child as well as less often. Social reciprocity, the give-and-take of the system, goes awry. This puts the child's social development as well as cognitive and language development at risk.

*Infants who are blind also are at high risk for poorly developed social skills. They do not engage in the **mutual gaze** interactions that appear to be crucial to the attachment process between parent and child. Mothers of babies who are blind often report they feel rejected when their infants do not look at them. Interestingly enough, Fraiberg (1974) noted that four-week-old babies who were blind did begin to smile, just as sighted babies did. At about two months, however, when sighted babies were smiling with increasing delight at their mother's face, babies with visual impairment were smiling less frequently and more tentatively. Gradually, the mothers in Fraiberg's studies on infant blindness seemed to withdraw psychologically from their babies, even though they continued to give physical care. Fraiberg's compelling example continues to hold up today.*

These examples do not imply that infants and children with special needs cannot learn appropriate social skills. Quite the contrary: They can and do. With the help of relevant members of an interdisciplinary team, parents learn to recognize alternative kinds of signaling and responding behaviors.

An infant who is blind, for example, may begin to thrash about at the sound of mother's approaching footsteps. The mother comes to value this response in the same way she would value a welcoming smile from a sighted infant. Consider another example: The infant who is deaf may snuggle in when picked up. Mother learns to respond by stroking the child rhythmically; better yet, by stroking *and* singing or crooning. Though the baby does not hear the singing, it usually gives pleasure to the mother. Singing also may transmit subtle vibrations

mutual gaze the steady looking at one another's faces that goes on between healthy newborns and their mother or primary caregiver

from the mother's chest or throat that further stimulate the infant's responsiveness.

Overstimulation and over-responding may also interfere with an infant's ability to make use of a responsive environment. Overstimulation often occurs among fragile infants: those who are premature or very low birth weight. They are easily overloaded with too many signals coming in from the environment. Their underdeveloped nervous systems simply cannot handle the rush, and so the infant shuts down, withdraws, and may become rigid and even reject loving pats and cuddling. In a sense, the infant is "unavailable to its environment, unable to obtain information or give feedback, causing the parents and other caregivers to feel less competent and effective" (Bennett, 1990, p. 36). The opposite is true of the over-responding infant. In some instances, an infant with a central nervous system (CNS) disorder, for example, may have an involuntary rigid arm extension when attempting to turn its head into nursing position. The infant's strong-arming may be perceived by the parent or caregiver as rejection or obstinacy, a reaction that interferes with establishing a warm relationship.

These illustrations point out, once again, the need to identify a developmental problem as early in infancy as possible. Early identification, followed by appropriate intervention, is a key factor in preventing other problems that invariably compound the original problem.

Social reinforcement is a crucial factor in determining a child's development.

© Cengage Learning

15-3d ■ Social Skills in Sequence

In inclusive programs, teachers will encounter children who are functioning at many levels of social competence. To work effectively with these children, some of whom will have developmental problems and others of whom will not, teachers must have a thorough understanding of the sequence of social development during the early years.

During the first year of life, infants' social responding is directed to parents, siblings, grandparents, and caregivers. If all goes well, strong **affective** bonds are established between the infant and significant individuals in the first year of life. At around nine months, children who are typically developing begin to engage in **joint attention**, an early developing social communicative skill in which two people use gestures and gaze to share attention to interesting objects or events (Jones & Carr, 2004). A child might look toward an interesting object and then to their parent and back to the object.

Somewhere in the middle of this period, a child may begin to show **separation protest**, and then fear of strangers. The stranger anxiety may last until eighteen months or so. Generally speaking, this shyness disappears of its own accord if the child is not unduly pressured. During this reluctant period, infants appear to be somewhat interested in outsiders and to have moments of responsiveness to strangers. From the safety of the grocery cart or the pack on Father's back, many babies will smile at a smiling stranger. From the security of a high chair in the restaurant, infants often follow each other with their eyes. They even laugh at each other's antics. Hammering on the high chair tray or throwing spoons to the floor appears to be a hilarious and mutually enjoyable pastime for a pair of infants, total strangers though they may be.

affective social-emotional responses that influence the behavior of others

joint attention an early social communicative behavior in which two people share focus on an object or event

separation protest displeasure the infant displays between eight and twelve months (approximately) when mother or caregiver leaves

Between the ages of one and two, interactions among toddlers and adults and among toddlers and other toddlers become longer and more involved. Episodes of turn-taking and imitation indicate that, at least at some level, toddlers are aware of the intentions of others and are developing **theory of mind** (DiLalla & Watson, 1988). As children enter the preschool years, play becomes very different as their social skills and language expand. Play becomes more complex, focusing on more pretense and social interactions with peers. Friendships develop. This change continues into the early elementary years, when children's role-plays and interactions become even more complex and involve a greater number of other children.

theory of mind the ability to infer other people's mental states and to use this information to interpret what they say, make sense of their behavior, and predict what they will do next

> ### Did You Get It?
>
> **How does the observation of children performing an action facilitate developing skills?**
> a. Opportunity for learning to take place.
> b. Provides clues as to children's preferences.
> c. By carefully observing children's behaviors (facial expressions, body posture, gestures, verbalizations), emotions can be recognized and dealt with in ways that strengthen both emotional development and social skills.
> d. Ability to detect emotional response.
>
> Take the full quiz on CourseMate.

15-4 The Role of Early Learning Programs

Early childhood education programs play a crucial role in the development of appropriate social skills. A variety of activities provide opportunities to learn social skills, such as self-help routines. Toddlers need opportunities to gain the skills required to be a member of a group. Therefore, a group story time is scheduled, but it involves only brief periods of sitting, in a loosely structured group. The toddlers are allowed to participate spontaneously and are free to chime in with their own comments and exclamations, relevant or otherwise.

Older preschool children, on the other hand, need to begin to learn how to identify with a group: sitting with others and following directions. At the same time, they need to learn how to function as individuals within a group by making contributions of general

During the preschool years, play becomes more complex, focusing on more pretense and social interactions with peers.

© Cengage Learning

FIGURE 15-1

Social Development Timeline
(Special thanks to Gay Spitz)

INFANT-TODDLER	PRESCHOOLER	PRIMARY-AGE CHILD
Response to Other's Distress		
• Reacts emotionally by experiencing what the other seems to feel	• Begins to make adjustments that reflect the realization that the other person is different and separate from self	• Takes other's personality into account and shows concern for other's general condition
Peer Interaction		
• First encounters mutual inspection • First social contacts • (18 mo) growth in sensitivity to peer play • (2 yr) able to direct social acts to two children at once (beginning of social interaction)	• Adjustment in behavior to fit age and behavior of other • (3+ yr) friendship as momentary • (3–5 yr) beginning of friendship as constant	• Friend as someone who will do what you want • Beginning of friend as one who embodies admirable, constant characteristics
Social Roles		
• (10–20 days) imitation of adults • (3 mo) gurgle in response to others • (6 mo) social games based on imitation • (18 mo) differentiation between reality and pretend play • (2 yr) make doll do something as if it were alive	• (3 yr) make a doll carry out several roles or activities • (4–5 yr) act out a social role in dramatic play and integrate that role with others (mom and baby) (theory of mind)	• (6 yr) integrate one role with two complementary roles: doctor, nurse, and sick person • (8 yr) growing understanding that roles can influence behavior (doctor whose daughter is a patient)

© Cengage Learning

interest and by practicing ways of interrupting tactfully. School-age children learn to organize and influence group activities. This includes responding in positive ways to the ideas and suggestions of others, both when agreeing and disagreeing. These patterns in the development of social skills can be guidelines as teachers work with all types of children in the inclusive setting.

According to Shore (2003), early interactions directly affect the way the brain is wired. Good early learning programs provide the kind of meaningful activities and social stimulation that support the brain's growth through repetition and practice. This provides the brain with the patterns of social skills it needs to ensure growth. Figure 15-1 is a timeline of social development for the typically developing child, and it provides additional details about the sequence of development of social skills.

Teachers can arrange the environment and teach skills that are critical to positive relationships. According to Sandall & Schwartz (2008) these skills can include:

- Being aware of others
- Helping others

- Sharing
- Making efforts to maintain social interactions
- Organizing play with others
- Giving compliments
- Negotiating
- Solving conflicts

15-4a ■ Play

Through play, young children become interested in one another. At first, they do not see each other as personalities or playmates. A fellow eighteen-month-old, for example, is something to be pushed or poked, prodded or ignored. It is not unusual to see one toddler shove a doll buggy directly into another toddler. It is as if the first child regards the other as just one more obstacle to be gotten out of the way. When the second child falls down and cries, the first child may look surprised, appearing not to connect the pushing down and the crying.

A next step in the development of early social skills and play comes out of interest in the same materials. Often, this leads to shrieks of "Mine!" as each child tries to hang on to the same toy. Following is an amusing example of evolving social skills and use of the same play materials.

Two boys, just under two years, were playing in the housekeeping area. One child was busily taking cups and plates from the cabinet and putting them on the table. The other child was just as busy, taking them off the table and returning them to the cabinet. It took several alternating trips back and forth before either noticed they were at cross purposes. The discovery led to mutual fury and clamor: "Mine! Mine! Mine!" almost in unison.

The next stage continues to focus on materials and equipment rather than on other children. There is, however, some independent *interacting* on common projects such as raking leaves, heaping them into piles, and hauling them off in separate wagons. At this stage, young children also begin to run, jump, climb, and ride wheel toys in small packs. These spontaneous groupings seem to be based on common activities rather than friendship. Then comes a cooperative stage: Children actually play together and engage fairly regularly in a give-and-take of materials and ideas.

Cooperative play leads into the next higher order of social skills, that of forming more or less durable friendships. Other children now are valued both as personalities and as companions in play. Friends are preferred playmates and are first on the birthday invitation list. Friends are also for quarreling with, making up with, and threatening to *not* invite to your birthday party.

Mildred Parten (1932) was one of the earliest researchers to describe the social interactions between children during play activities. She described play in terms of six types. Her categories are not necessarily sequential, but, as described in the previous examples above, younger children's play tends to fall into the first three types, with older children's play becoming more social, as described by the later three types of play. Depending on the situation, children may engage in the many different types of play described below:

1. **Unoccupied behavior** The child isn't engaging in any obvious play activity or social interaction. The child may watch anything that is of interest at the moment but shows no interest in any particular child or group of children.

2. **Onlooker behavior** The child spends most of his or her time watching other children play. The child is within speaking distance and may talk to

the playing children, ask questions, or give suggestions, but doesn't participate in the play. This onlooker behavior indicates a strong interest in a group of children.

3. **Solitary play** The child's play is independent of what others are doing. The child plays with toys that are different from those used by other children in the area. No efforts are made to get closer to or speak to the other children. The child is focused entirely on his or her own activity and is not influenced by other children or their activities.

4. **Parallel play** The child is playing close to other children, but beside, rather than with, the other children. The child uses toys like ones being used by others, but uses them as he or she wishes. The child is neither influenced by nor tries to influence the others.

5. **Associative play** The child plays with other children. Play material and equipment are shared; the children may follow each other around. The children engage in similar but not necessarily identical play, and there is no organization of activity or individuals. Each child does what he or she essentially wants to do.

6. **Cooperative play** The play occurs in a group, which is established for a particular purpose. There are different roles for the children (e.g., playing store or restaurant).

Teaching children to play Often described as "the breath of life" to children, play is the most common way young children learn appropriate social skills. Even in infancy, most children seem to play spontaneously and apparently effortlessly. Research indicates that children learn best in play-oriented early childhood programs that allow them to explore, discover, and practice. Play is interconnected with the development of cognitive, social, emotional, language, and physical behaviors (Fox, 2010). Children learn new skills and practice them in the course of self-initiated play activities. They participate in group activities and join eagerly in teacher-initiated play opportunities. Almost every skill that children master is mastered through play.

Such may not be the case for children with developmental disabilities. The play of children with a hearing impairment is less likely to be social and is more solitary (Anita & Kreimeyer, 1992). However, children with severe hearing loss, even those with serious language deficits, have been reported as having imaginary playmates. As for children with severe vision impairments, Skellenger, Hill, and Hill (1992) report significant delays in their symbolic play (make-believe, pretend, or using one object to represent another, as when a doll blanket becomes a magic cape). Children with autistic behaviors or limited cognitive skills also tend to be lacking in symbolic play skills. Developmental problems of this kind may lead to inappropriate use of materials, such as hammering the cookie cutters with the rolling pin or breaking the crayons into pieces.

▶❚❚ **TeachSource** Video Connections

© Cengage Learning 2015

Young Children's Stages of Play: An Illustrated Guide

Play is the medium through which young children learn. Early education teachers should understand the stages of play so that they can create curriculum opportunities for all stages.

After watching the video, discuss the following:

1. Plan a dramatic play activity that will foster cooperative play.

2. The video discusses the importance of a teacher entering a child's play by engaging in parallel play. Why is this important?

Watch on CourseMate.

Cooperative play leads to a higher order of social skills: that of forming more or less durable friendships.

Children with developmental disabilities often have fewer play skills. They may hang back, not knowing how to enter play; or they try to gain entry in inappropriate ways, for example, crashing a truck into housekeeping play, which leads to rejection.

It is essential that children who do not know how to play be taught. Teaching children to play may seem contrary to tradition. However, no child should be deprived of this powerful avenue for learning and the many enjoyable experiences that come with it. Children for whom play does not develop naturally and who need to be taught to play and interact need many opportunities to practice the skill. The goal is that the child will eventually demonstrate the play skill independently and with ease in new situations and with new materials. Play behaviors can be taught by:

1. Arranging for the child to be near other children in a given activity, enabling the teacher to describe what other children are doing to promote imitation.

2. Physically guiding the child to a play activity and helping him or her to settle in. Walk with Jenny to the housekeeping area and say, "Everybody's trying on hats. Let's go find one for you to wear."

3. Handing material to the child to establish physical contact: "Here's a ball of clay for you," as you place it in the child's hands.

4. Putting an object (a clothespin, for example) in the child's hand and moving the hand so it is directly above a container.

5. Verbalizing to the child what he or she is doing: "You have a clothespin in your hand. You can drop it in the can."

6. Rejoicing over the smallest accomplishments: "Look at that!" (or "Did you *hear* that!"); "*You* dropped the clothespin in the can."

7. Gradually helping other children join in activities, once the child has acquired a semblance of a play skill (two children might drop clothespins into the same can): "Here, Damon, you can put your clothespin in, too."

8. Providing social reinforcement for the play: "It looks like *you two* are going to fill that can full of clothespins."

9. Moving the child slowly but steadily toward group play by building small groups of two, then three, nonthreatening children who participate with the child in simple play activities.

As a child with special needs begins to play more spontaneously, teachers continue their assistance, but in less directive fashion. For example, when helping a group of children decide where to play after music time, the teacher reviews the options for each child. The child with the developmental problem is helped to choose after several other children have made their choices. Because the child has heard the choices reviewed several times and has heard several children choosing, making a choice becomes easier. It is helpful, too, for the teacher to pair the child with another who has chosen the same activity. This provides a good model for the less-skilled child in both locating the activity and in getting off to a good start.

Activities must be planned carefully so that children with developmental problems can experience maximum success. When a child with severe vision loss is participating in an art activity, the teacher might describe and physically help the child locate materials by guiding his or her hand.

> *"Here is the big circle to paste the little circles on. The little circles are here in the basket. Here is the paste, by your right hand. The sponge to wipe your fingers is next to it. Corliss is working across the table from you. Ask Corliss to help you if you need it." (This promotes the activity's social aspect.)*

Along with helping the child with developmental problems, teachers also need to help all children learn to be explicit about what they are doing in certain situations. For example, it can be disconcerting for a child who cannot see to have materials moved from the rehearsed location. Yet, telling the other children not to touch his or her materials may cause the special child to be regarded negatively. Instead, children should be taught the simple social skill of stating what they are doing whenever they use or change another person's materials: "Sophie, I need some of your paste. I'm going to move it over here (guiding Sophie's hand) so we can share, okay?"

Gentle insistence Not all children with developmental problems are eager to play, nor do they want to be taught to play; they may even avoid play materials and would-be playmates. These children sometimes need to be gently pushed to try a play activity that teachers know will be of developmental benefit to them.

> *Jolene was a somewhat solitary three-year-old with cerebral palsy. An objective written into her IEP by the interdisciplinary team was that Jolene learn to ride a tricycle. The physical therapist adapted a tricycle by adding a trunk support and stirrups. Jolene, however, would not get on. Teachers' coaxing intensified her resistance until just the sight of the tricycle set her to crying. Her teachers were ready to give up. Not so the physical therapist, who impressed on them the therapeutic value of tricycle riding for Jolene. The therapist maintained that it would promote more general development, as well as motor coordination, than any number of clinic sessions.*

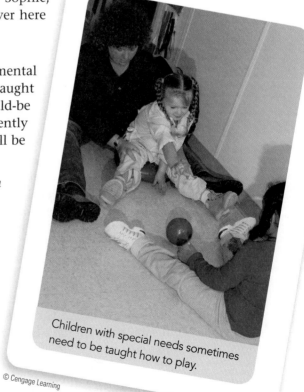

Children with special needs sometimes need to be taught how to play.

© Cengage Learning

After talking it over with Jolene's parents, a plan was agreed on: one teacher would lift Jolene onto the tricycle and support (and comfort) her while the therapist put Jolene's feet in the stirrups and pulled the tricycle from the front. This they did, with Jolene crying louder and louder at first. The teacher continued to support her physically and to comfort her while the therapist moved the tricycle gently forward, talking quietly to her and describing what was going on. Gradually, Jolene quieted.

Within a few days she stopped resisting the riding sessions. Furthermore—and much to the teachers' relief—she appeared to be enjoying the sessions. Six weeks later, Jolene was riding her specially fitted tricycle independently, in the company of other children. Giving in to Jolene's anxieties would have been to deprive Jolene of learning a play skill central to both her mobility and her social development.

15-4b ■ Incidental Social Learning

There are times when it is not only appropriate but even urgent to teach social and play skills directly. Most of the time, however, teachers can promote social interactions fairly easily by being alert to what goes on naturally among children. More frequently than adults often realize, brief, positive interactions are occurring between children with and without developmental disabilities: smiling, handing materials, moving aside, helping to pick up the pieces of a dropped puzzle, and so on. Teachers can quietly draw attention to these commonplace interactions: "Keanna, when you held the door open for Corey, it was easy for him to get his wheelchair through. See how he is smiling at you?" When the teacher makes similar comments to Corey, both children are introduced to another level of socialization. The result may be interaction between the two.

Children's concern or anxiety about another child's disability also offers opportunities for incidental social learning. A teacher may notice a child looking obliquely at the patch over another child's eye; witness one child's reluctance to hold another child's malformed hand; overhear a child expressing fear about catching the paralysis of the wheelchair-bound child. The children's concerns are genuine, not to be shushed or ignored. They provide opportunities for teachers to promote social learning and interaction. Often the teacher and the child with the disability can respond together. Using the child with an eye patch as an example, the teacher might first acknowledge the one child's concern and then help the second child explain. If the child with the eye patch is not at a verbal stage, the teacher can explain and ask for the child's corroboration.

"The doctor put the patch on one eye so your other eye can learn to see better, right?" The explanation can be expanded further, depending on the interest and comfort level of both children. Always the teacher reassures the concerned child that the disability is not catching, that there are many, many things the other child can do. Often the two children can be guided into a joint activity at that point.

Derman-Sparks (1988–1989) has noted that young children become aware of differences and similarities in people; they notice and ask questions about disabilities. Children are curious about what a child with a disability can and cannot do, about the devices or equipment they need, and what effect the disability might have on them. Derman-Sparks offers some cautions about these issues:

- Do not deny differences in physical abilities; find some area in which the children are similar: "Jackie can't see as well as you can, but he likes to paint, just like you."

Arranging for a child to work or play near another child facilitates social development.

- Do not criticize a child for noticing and asking questions about physical differences. Use the opportunity to encourage the children to talk with one another about the disability or the eye patch.

- Do not belabor the response to children's questions; children need simple, accurate answers. Use the correct terminology for the disability or device.

- Do not lightly dismiss children's expressions of fear or anxieties about disabilities, because it may lead to rejection of the child with special needs. Help the anxious child talk about the fears, then encourage further interactions between the two children.

An inclusive early childhood program provides ways for all children to develop the ability to interact comfortably and fairly with people of various disabilities (Derman-Sparks, 1988–1989).

A child's first tentative steps toward joining a play situation is another form of incidental social learning that teachers need to note and reinforce. The child who stands and watches may be nearly ready to interact. A teacher might watch with the child for a moment or two at a time, while commenting on the activity: "It looks like Bart is making cookies, and Cami's making a pie." Another time, sensing the child's readiness, the teacher might help the child actually get into play: "Matt is bringing more cookie cutters for everyone to use." The teacher also can prompt the other children directly or indirectly.

Josh, a child with Down syndrome, had a drum in his hand but was standing apart from a small group of children who were experimenting with rhythm instruments. Teacher: "It sounds like you need a drummer in your band." (pause) Teacher: "You could ask Josh. He has a drum." If Josh joined in, the teacher could then provide reinforcement to all, as a group: "What a good band! Rikky and Maria and Rocco and Josh and Shantrell, your music really sounds good." (It is advisable not to make specific mention of the children having invited Josh into the group; this could make Josh stand out unnecessarily as so different as to need special treatment.)

Incidental social learning can be expanded even further through play activities already in progress. Teachers need to reinforce the interaction in

incidental social learning
appropriate interactions promoted by a well-arranged early childhood program; for example, an adequate number of Legos reduces conflict

subtle ways to avoid distracting either child. Depending on the situation, the teacher might:

- move closer, kneel down, watch with interest, but avoid eye contact to keep from interrupting the children's mutual focus
- smile and nod if either child turns toward the teacher, but keep the focus on the activity, not the child with special needs
- bring additional materials to extend the play, placing them close to the activity with or without comment, depending on the situation
- make encouraging comments that further promote joint effort: "Missy and Sam, you are building a long, long road. It looks like it's going to go all the way to the gate!"

Frequent episodes of social interaction among children with and without disabilities characterize quality inclusion programs. Such intermixing is most likely to occur, according to Wolery (1994a), "when children with special needs are in small groups, when competent peers are in the group, when the group includes mixed ages, and when teachers encourage and support exchanges and imitation" (p. 115). Shonkoff and Phillips (2000) state:

> Finding settings in which children play competently with others, monitoring play to avert disasters, coaching children in what works, attributing their failures to situations and not to flaws in the children themselves, and searching for creative solutions that build on what they can do well seem to build social competence in most children. Good child care and preschool programs do these things, effectively providing universal interventions for all children who attend them. (p. 175)

egocentric in reference to young children, implies a view of the world from one perspective only—the child's own

Sharing and turn-taking Sharing and taking turns are the foundation for mutually satisfying play between children. Yet these skills are the most difficult to learn. Why? Because they involve giving up something, and giving up anything is contrary to the young child's perfectly normal, **egocentric** view of the world.

"MINE! MINE! MINE!" is the call of many children at one stage of development. With adult support, patience, and many unpressured opportunities to learn, most children eventually cooperate when a teacher says, "Kim, two more turns around the driveway, and then it is Sara's turn." The teacher can say this in many different ways to each child, over the weeks and months: "Sara, watch. Kim is going around the driveway

Sharing and taking turns are the foundation for mutually satisfying play between children.

© Cengage Learning

two more times; then it will be your turn. Let's count." Or, "Kim, Sara waited a long, long time for the tricycle you were riding, so she gets a long turn, too. I'll call you when she's through." Gradually reducing the amount of available material is another way to teach sharing. As always, it is the teacher who makes this happen. Conflict among children is avoided when the teacher plans such a step carefully, monitors the situation, and helps children work it through.

- *A teacher might put out fewer but larger portions of play dough to encourage children to divide their dough with latecomers to the activity. With a teacher's help, some children will be able to break off a part of their dough; when two or three children do this, the newcomer has an adequate amount to work with. The teacher then can reinforce the acts of sharing. Children who did the sharing have provided good models for the children not yet able to share.*

- *Several individual baskets of colored wooden cubes might be poured into one larger basket. The children must then share common, but plentiful, material. Again, the teacher must be there to teach, partly by assuring the children there is plenty for all. If one child is accused of taking more than his or her share, the teacher might suggest that each child take no more than five cubes at a time (thus concurrently teaching counting).*

- *A child who has great difficulty sharing may be put in charge of a plentiful but uncontested material, perhaps tickets for snacks or for a train ride (chairs lined up). The tickets may be nothing more than a quantity of small squares of colored paper—irresistible to most young children. As the child passes out the tickets, the teacher can comment what a good job he or she is doing of giving away tickets, but remarking also, "You have a lot left."*

It is always the teacher's job to promote and respond to friendly interactions between children, thereby making spontaneous sharing easier. When two children decide to work a puzzle together, the teacher might reinforce the friendly interaction by sitting down briefly and watching the children work. When two children are using a wagon together, the teacher spends some time pulling them around. Teachers also can point out situations that involve friendly interactions: "Jesse and Jay, you really have a long train now that you have hitched all your cars together." In addition, teachers help children wait for a turn or a material by offering alternates until the preferred material is available.

Self-assertion The problem may be the reverse with some children. They may give up too easily or fail to defend themselves or their possessions.

All children need to learn to stand up for their rights. It is especially important that teachers find ways to help children with disabilities fend for themselves; otherwise, some may resort to trading on their disabilities to get what they want: "You shouldn't take my doll because I can't walk as good as you." Following is an example of how a teacher might help a child with severely limited vision assert her rights.

Five-year-old Lisa, blind since birth, was playing with an interlocking floor train. Leon took one of her cars. Lisa, touching her train, realized a car was missing. She began to rock back and forth, whining and poking at her eyes. The teacher said, "Lisa, Leon has your car. Tell him to give it back." The teacher turned to Leon: "Leon, I want you to listen to what Lisa is saying to you. You took her car and she wants it back. Hand it back to her when she asks for it." By not retrieving the car, the teacher helped both children: Lisa, to learn about the rights of possession; Leon, to recognize that all children have rights that are to be respected.

Materials and equipment The materials and equipment available to children greatly influence their learning of social skills. Materials that have proven to be good socializers include:

- housekeeping and dress-up play materials
- mural-painting or collage supplies
- unit blocks and large hollow blocks
- trucks, cars, and airplanes
- Lotto and other simple board games
- musical instruments

When small groups gather, there should be sufficient material to go around, thus inviting each child's participation. It is also good to have some duplicate material. A child with a developmental problem then has the opportunity to use the same material as another child and therefore learn appropriate usage through imitation. On the other hand, too much or too many different materials, such as crayons and paints, tend to promote solitary play.

For example, a wheel toy for every child defeats a major goal of most programs: promoting sharing and turn-taking. About one wheel toy to every three or four children is a practical ratio. All kinds of inventive doubling-up games and cooperative ventures can be the result.

15-4c ■ Imitation and Modeling

Young children learn many behaviors and skills by watching other children and imitating what they do. Providing models for appropriate behaviors—especially social behaviors—to children with developmental problems, is a major argument in favor of inclusion. It must be stressed, however, that including children does not automatically lead to their learning appropriate play behaviors and social skills. From the start of the inclusion movement, it has been apparent that spontaneous social interactions between children with and without developmental problems occur infrequently (Schwartz, Billingsley, & McBride, 1998). Teachers play a central role in promoting the interactions. They make it happen by (1) arranging the environment to ensure interactions between children who are disabled and children who are not; (2) reinforcing children, in general, for playing together; and (3) reinforcing children with developmental problems when they imitate appropriate behaviors.

Each of these practices is discussed in detail in various sections of this text. Here we stress that if children with special needs are to learn from children who are developing typically, they must be involved in a wide range of play activities. Once again: *Teachers make it happen*. Teachers set up activities designed specifically to facilitate play interactions, often through small-group experiences. Children learn by watching.

15-5 Teacher-Structured Peer Interactions

At times, teachers decide which children will play together in which activities. This ensures the inclusion of a child with disabilities in an activity with children best suited to that child's skill levels. The groupings can be made on the basis of mutual interests, temperament, or abilities. Wagon trains—several wagons and tricycles hitched together in separate pairs—can be introduced. This game (and many others that teachers devise) allows a child who cannot walk the excitement of being involved—being towed in a wagon also occupied, perhaps, by a typically developing child. The child with the disability is an integral part of a spirited outdoor social activity. A rocking boat also promotes closeness and interaction, as children synchronize their efforts to make it rock. A note of caution: Children who are just beginning to interact with other children usually should not be paired with rambunctious children.

Discovery learning periods are especially good times for promoting social learning through imitation and **modeling**. Teachers need to provide several interest centers and several attractive activities where interaction is almost automatic: the water table, the dough table, a simple cooking experience. Easily conducted science and math experiences promote interactions, too, as when a few children go into the yard together to pick up leaves to sort by size, type, or color. The key issue is that *interactions occur and are pleasurable* for all the children. Play experiences that are fun and enjoyable are likely to lead to happier and more satisfying peer relationships.

modeling learning by watching and imitating another's actions; also called observational learning

15-5a ■ Peer Tutoring and Peer Mediating

Considerable research has addressed intervention strategies in which peers are taught to interact with children with disabilities in such a way that the social behaviors of the focus children are increased and improved. The socially competent peer is provided with ongoing coaching and support to promote interactions with the focus child (Dunlap & Powell, 2009).

Peer-mediated strategies take a variety of forms, yet all have certain elements in common, according to Wolery (1994a).

- Children who are typically developing are taught specific ways of engaging less competent children in social interactions.
- Mediating children are taught to keep trying to engage the less competent children in social interactions.
- Children with special needs and the other children have ongoing opportunities to play together and practice skills together.
- Teachers provide children with support and reinforcement for working and playing together.

Children who are developing in typical fashion may also occasionally act as teachers for children with disabilities. Sometimes these episodes occur spontaneously.

- One child helps another to rearrange and separate his or her fingers when putting on mittens.
- Another child at the table shows the child pouring from a pitcher how to steady it with the other hand, so as to pour slowly and avoid the juice overflowing the cup.

Teachers also can plan child-teaching-child events. Such peer-teaching episodes are appropriate to any part of the program.

- During music, two similar instruments might be provided, with a hearing child designated to help the child with a cochlear implant to recognize when and with what force to join in.
- During pre-academics, the teacher could have two children work together, asking the sighted child to help the child who is visually impaired learn to put the wooden shapes into a form board.

Case Study ■ Extra practice ■

Simon is a three-year-old with autism. Simon was supported when he attended his community preschool by a shadow aide responsible for helping facilitate social interactions with peers and classroom teachers. Simon had limited peer interaction skills. He watched his peers play. He would greet them enthusiastically upon entering his preschool. He would play chase games with them at recess. However, each day he would push or hit any peer that came close to or touched a toy that Simon wanted. The frequency of his hitting peers increased as the number of peers in the play area increased. This led to several peers being fearful of him. His shadow aide started

"Friend Time." During this time, Simon would invite a friend to join him. Initially, the shadow aide had to prompt this. Simon and the peer would go with the shadow aide to a quiet corner of the room and practice social interaction skills that Simon could use later in the classroom.

1. What social skills should the shadow aide target for teaching?

2. What types of activities do you think the shadow aide might use to facilitate these skills?

3. How might the shadow aide evaluate progress and determine success?

peer tutoring one child instructing or assisting another

In every instance, teachers pair children carefully to ensure an appropriate match of skills and temperament. It is important that the child with a disability and the other child enjoy and benefit from the interaction. Never should either child feel burdened; never should either child's learning opportunities in any other area be curtailed. Carefully managed **peer tutoring** is of benefit to both children. The child with developmental problems has the opportunity to learn through play from someone who is a master at play: another child. The child-models practice and refine their own developing social skills and learn a new and higher-order social skill, that of teaching or imparting knowledge. The tutor gains in self-esteem because of the increased status that comes with being teacher. The tutor also gains in sensitivity, in that a certain amount of nurturing is required when teaching a less able peer. Furthermore, it appears that child tutors undergo positive behavioral and attitudinal changes toward the children with disabilities who are being tutored (Franca, Kerr, Reitz, & Lambert, 1990).

15-5b ■ Additional Ways Teachers Can Structure and Facilitate Learning

In addition to choosing peer groups or providing materials and activities likely to foster interactions, teachers can identify key times of the day and alternative strategies for practicing and teaching social skills. The following are just some of the possibilities:

- Choose stories to read at circle time that focus on similarities and differences between individuals or that require the characters to solve problems. Ask questions that prompt discussion about sharing, turn-taking, and so on.

- Develop and implement a snack routine that focuses on practicing manners as well as conversing with each other. Adults should view snack and lunch as an opportunity to facilitate conversations between peers, rather than as a break.

- Be sure seating arrangements during circle time, snack, and small-group activities place children with special needs next to strong models. Also be sure that adults are not always sitting between the child with special needs and their peers.

- Prompt peers to look at each other when they are uncertain what to do next. For example, if all the children are lining up to go outside and one is wandering, prompt the child to look at his peers, "What are your friends doing?"

- Provide group art projects (e.g., group sculpture building, murals, papier-mâché, tower building) so that children take turns working in small groups to add to the group effort.

- Ensure that adults do not become translators between children with special needs and their typical peers. If a peer asks an adult a question they could be asking a peer, prompt that child to ask the peer.

- Provide a buddy center or friendship activity where the focus is on finding out what peers have in common or where projects must be completed cooperatively.

- For nonverbal children or children using augmentative communication such as a Picture Exchange Communications System (PECS) (see Chapter 16), have the child request an activity or item by giving the picture to a peer rather than a teacher.

- Change classroom songs to include social interactions such as giving a high five, saying "hi" to a peer, or shaking hands. For example, when singing "If You're Happy and You Know It," include a verse where children give their neighbor a high five. "When you're happy and you know it, give a high five."

- Assign two children to complete a task or classroom job together. For preschoolers this might include putting away a puzzle, and for school-aged children it might mean taking a note to the office.

- Arrange for children to be close to each other, and/or actively bring children together, especially those who may have trouble moving around independently (Goldman, 2009).

- Help children join ongoing group activities like dramatic play by finding appropriate roles for them (Goldman, 2009).

- Present interesting objects or activities that children are likely to flock to (Goldman, 2009).

Fair play Children who are developing typically also are good models for the simple, everyday *fair play* behaviors expected of children in an early childhood program. Appropriate use of materials and equipment is a good example. All children need to learn to use community property responsibly. No child can be allowed to paint on the walls, crash a tricycle repeatedly, deface books, or waste materials. It is especially important for children with developmental problems to learn respect for materials and equipment and to learn it in the company of other children whenever possible. Otherwise, they may be viewed as unwanted playmates, disrupters of play activities, or someone to be disliked or avoided. Remember that classroom rules (whatever they may be) apply to all children. There can be no double standards. To allow any child repeatedly and unduly to disturb or distress other children is not fair to anyone in the classroom.

Connecting Developmentally Appropriate Practice to Brain Research

COGNITIVE, EMOTIONAL, AND SOCIAL CAPACITIES

The following is an excerpt from "The Science of Early Childhood Development." Detailed information on these concepts can be found in a companion document produced by the National Scientific Council on the Developing Child entitled "The Science of Early Childhood Development: Closing the Gap Between What We Know and What We Do":

Cognitive, emotional, and social capacities are inextricably intertwined throughout the life course. The brain is a highly interrelated organ, and its multiple functions operate in a richly coordinated fashion. Emotional well-being and social competence provide a strong foundation for emerging cognitive abilities, and together they are the bricks and mortar that comprise the foundation of human development. The emotional and physical health, social skills, and cognitive-linguistic capacities that emerge in the early years are all important prerequisites for success in school and later in the workplace and community (p. 8).

1. After reading the final sentence in the above passage, make a case for the importance of teaching social skills in school.

2. What might be the impact for a child who, for a variety of reasons (poverty, repeated abuse, severe maternal depression), may not fully develop a solid foundation as described above?

For more information, see "The Science of Early Childhood Development" and the Working Paper series from the National Scientific Council on the Developing Child. www.developingchild.harvard.edu/library/

15-6 When More Intervention Is Needed

Much of this chapter has focused on identifying times within the day for teachers to facilitate and reinforce social and play skills. For some children, more systematic intervention and planning are required in order for their skills to develop. In some cases, children may find the noise and activity levels of the classroom too overwhelming to learn new skills and may benefit from the opportunity to practice or learn play skills with one peer in a quieter setting or corner of the room. Some children may require an additional step, such as practicing a play skill or dramatic play scenario with an adult, before inviting a peer to join. In all cases it is important for the early childhood educator to be aware of each child's abilities. Complex skills are required to succeed in a classroom setting. Figure 15-2 provides a checklist containing some of the critical social skills preschoolers should demonstrate. Teachers can use this checklist to determine which social skills a child might be missing. Once classroom staff are familiar with the various strengths and weaknesses of each student, they can work as a team to identify which skills can be taught and learned incidentally and which require more systematic intervention.

The tiered framework for intervention (also discussed in Chapter 18) provides a model for supporting the social and emotional development of all children and providing the systematic intervention described above. The first two levels of the framework include the development of nurturing and responsive relationships as well as providing high-quality environments. These universal practices depend upon the development of responsive, engaging relationships between the teachers, children, and their families. High-quality environments are ones that provide a developmentally appropriate and child-centered curriculum. Level two also is described as the classroom's preventative practices and includes many of the practices described throughout this text. Universal practices are typically enough to promote the social-emotional development of most of

naeyc

Social Interaction Skills during 15-minute observation

Date _____ Child _____

SKILL	FREQUENCY	NOTES
Observes peer		
Approaches peer		
Greets peer		
Responds to peer's greeting		
Plays next to peer with different toy (parallel)		
Play next to peer with same toy (associative)		
Plays with same toy and interacts		
Imitates peer's play with toys		
Imitates peer's play with toys and paired verbalizations		
Offers toy to peer		
Takes toy from peer		
Requests item from peer		
Takes turns back and forth		
Comments about own play		
Comments about peer's play		
Reciprocates comments about play		
Invites peer to play		
Asks peer's questions		
Responds to peers invitation to play		
Answers peer's questions		
Follows peer's instructions		
Provides peer's with instructions		
Reciprocates social questions/information in an exchange		
Directs others' in play		
Uses others' suggestions in play		
Offers assistance to peer		
Requests assistance from peer		
Follows peer's gestures		
Asks permission to use peer's toy		
Appropriately refuses and defends during play		
Responds to peer's refusals		
Expresses empathy		
Other		

Source: 2008 Copyright G.E. Cowdery

© Cengage Learning

the children in a classroom. From time to time a teacher may work with a child who requires more specific attention. This child may frequently not follow instructions, have difficulty regulating her or his emotions, and difficulty developing relationships. This child is a candidate for the third level of the framework: social and emotional teaching strategies. These teaching strategies emphasize planned instruction and target teaching of specific social and emotional skills for children considered at risk for developing more challenging behavior (Fox & Lentini, 2006). The final level of the framework is intensive intervention and provides for individual intervention plans designed specifically for the child, as described in detail in Chapter 18.

15-6a ■ One-to-One Shadowing

shadow aide a person who provides support to a child in an inclusive setting, which includes encouraging independence in following the routine and interacting with peers and other teachers

It is becoming increasingly common that when a young child with autism participates in their first preschool experience or even in later inclusion experiences, they are accompanied by a **shadow aide**. How much support is needed depends on several variables: where the child and peers are developmentally, how large the group is, how structured the program is, and how able the child is to follow the routine. The role of the shadow aide, or *shadow,* includes identifying potentially compatible playmates and peers, creating activities in which the child they are supporting is involved, such as initiating a game of hide-and-seek on the playground, and helping the child to follow the routine and to communicate with peers and teachers. The shadow should not serve as a translator or get between the child with autism and his or her peers. Shadows should sit behind, rather than between, the children. If a peer asks the shadow a question that is really directed to the child with autism, the shadow should support the peer in asking the question directly to the child as well as supporting the child with autism to respond. The shadow aide should try to interact with all the children in the classroom so that it does not appear that they are there only for the child with autism. It is also critical that the early childhood education teacher is also interacting with the child with autism and not leaving that responsibility primarily to the shadow. The shadow's most important role is to make the child with autism independent. Shadow aides can actually do the child a disservice if they allow the child to be too dependent on their prompts and presence. As autism expert Bryna Siegel (2008) states, "Shadows should be just that—shadows staying as much in the background as possible and not serving as personal handmaidens" (p. 201).

Learning to play nicely, make friends, and sustain friendships are not easy tasks, and children who do them well tend to have well-structured experiences with peer interactions starting in toddlerhood and preschool (Shonkoff & Phillips, 2000, p. 180).

> ### Did You Get It?
>
> **According to the tiered framework of intervention, how would one deal with a child who has difficulty following instructions, regulating her or his emotions and developing relationships?**
> a. Focus on the first level of the framework to include the development of nurturing and responsive relationships as well as providing high quality environments.
> b. Focus on the second level of the framework which includes classroom preventative practices.
> c. Focus on the third level of the framework: social and emotional teaching strategies.
> d. Intensive intervention as a final level of the framework.
>
> Take the full quiz on CourseMate.

Summary

- Like all young children, children with developmental delays need to learn how to get along with others. To do this, they must learn appropriate social skills. Such learning may be more difficult for children with developmental problems.

- Even though affected by each child's temperament, all social skills are learned behaviors. They depend largely on reciprocal responsiveness between the child and significant adults, starting within the first hours and days of life. However, children with certain developmental disabilities may not be able to engage in the give-and-take characteristics of typically developing children.

- Participation in an inclusive early childhood program can help to advance social-skill learnings for children with developmental problems.

- Play is a major medium in early learning, especially in learning social skills. Not all children know how to play; some may even be reluctant to try. In such instances, the children should be taught.

- Learning social skills through imitating and modeling is a major argument for inclusive classrooms. For modeling to take place, children with disabilities and those without must interact, which they do not always do spontaneously; teachers must make it happen.

- Teachers promote interactions among all types of children by arranging both the physical and the social environment. They also encourage peer tutoring, sometimes planned in advance, more often incidental in occurrence.

- Both the child who is typically developing and the child with developmental problems can benefit from peer tutoring and various kinds of peer mediation.

- While the majority of social skills can be taught incidentally, some children may require a more structured or systematic intervention to learn certain skills.

- Shadow aides are often used to support children with autism in inclusive settings. The shadow needs to be aware of how best to support the child without oversupporting, which can cause the child, and other teachers, to become dependent on the shadow.

Key Terms

affective, 391
contingent stimulation, 389
egocentric, 400
incidental social learning, 399
joint attention, 391

modeling, 403
mutual gaze, 390
peer tutoring, 404
separation protest, 391
shadow aide, 408

social reinforcement, 389
temperament, 387
theory of mind, 392

Student Activities

1. Observe in a child care center that serves toddlers to kindergarten-age children. Record anecdotal notes on three different children of three different ages displaying three different but developmentally appropriate social skills.

2. Observe an early childhood setting. During your observation, make notes about the types of play you observed, using Parten's six types of play. Also make notes about any inappropriate types of play. Explain why you consider it inappropriate.

3. Visit a preschool, public school, or child care center that serves children with developmental disabilities. Observe one of the children who has a disability for thirty minutes. Record the social skills the child displays. Analyze your observations and list the social skills you believe the child lacks in terms of his or her age and developmental level. Use Figure 15-2 as well as Gordon and Browne's (2008) "Four Hows," discussed at the beginning of this chapter, to help you analyze your observations.

4. List at least eight strategies or activities a teacher can implement to promote sharing and turn-taking with young children.

5. Work with another student or two as a teaching team and plan several activities or materials you might present to promote sharing among three-year-olds, some of whom have developmental delays.

6. Assume you are working with a four-year-old with a cognitive delay and few play skills. You believe it is important that this child learn to play with blocks. How might you go about teaching block play to this child? Be specific. Select a classmate to be the child and demonstrate your teaching strategies in class. How might you include another child to help in teaching block play? Demonstrate.

7. Review the example of Teddy, the second-grader at the beginning of the chapter. Make a list of social skills the second-graders need to complete the assigned task of writing a poem in a small group. How might the classroom teacher and paraprofessional work together to ensure Teddy has these skills?

Review Questions

Part 1. Respond to the following in list format.

1. List three developmental areas that are related to and support the acquisition of social skills.
2. List five skills that both define and are a part of learning to get along with others.
3. List three types of infant temperament, according to Thomas and Chess (1977).

4. List five strategies that a teacher might use to promote social development in young children.
5. List five steps a teacher might take in helping a child with a developmental delay learn play skills.

Part 2. Define the following terms.

1. reciprocal (in terms of social development)
2. peer mediation
3. temperament
4. contingent stimulation
5. mutual gaze

6. symbolic play
7. incidental learning
8. modeling
9. peer tutoring
10. egocentric viewpoint

Additional Resources/Readings

101 Life Skills Games for Children
Written by Bernie Badegruber
Hunter House Press

This book contains games designed to teach children ages 6–12 years tolerance, self-awareness, responsibility, cooperation, and communication.

Improving Social Behaviors in the Classroom: An Easy Curriculum for Teachers of Young Children with Autism, Developmental Disability, and Typical Children
Written by Stephanny Freeman, Gazi Begu, Kristin Hayashida, and Tanya Papara
DRL Books

This book focuses on social behaviors in the classroom. The curriculum is a sequence of activities but allow teachers to select their own starting point if they feel their students already know some of the skills. Skills include assertiveness, ownership, initiation, turn-taking, and simple social play and cooperation.

Helpful Websites

Association for Childhood Education International (ACEI)

http://www.acei.org

ACEI provides information such as articles, book titles and reviews, and resources on many topics related to early childhood education.

The Center on the Social and Emotional Foundations for Early Learning
University of Illinois at Urbana-Champaign

http://www.csefel.uiuc.edu

This is a five-year project designed to strengthen the capacity of Head Start and child care programs to improve the social and emotional outcomes of young children. The center develops training and technical assistance (T/TA) materials that reflect evidence-based practices for promoting children's social and emotional development and preventing challenging behaviors. The center works with professional organizations and Head Start and child care T/TA providers to ensure the use of the evidence-based practices in local demonstration sites.

Child Development Institute

http://www.cdipage.com (Search: social development)

This site contains a wealth of information for parents and teachers. Topics include child development, learning, safety, and disorders.

ERIC Clearinghouse on Disabilities and Gifted Education

http://www.ericec.org

ERIC is the acronym for the Educational Resources Information Center. The ERIC Clearinghouse on Disabilities and Gifted Education (ERIC EC) is one of sixteen federally funded clearinghouses. ERIC EC gathers and disseminates professional literature, information, and resources on the education and development of individuals of all ages who have disabilities and/or who are gifted. Topics include identification, assessment, intervention, and enrichment.

Facilitating Speech, Language, and Communication Skills

OBJECTIVES

After reading this chapter, you should be able to:

16-1   define *language* and explain how it develops according to the theories discussed in the chapter.

16-2   describe the theories of language acquisition.

16-3   trace the sequence of language development from birth through age five or six.

16-4   describe alternative language systems.

16-5   highlight the key features of a naturalistic language-learning environment.

16-6   discuss speech irregularities among young children and describe appropriate responses from teachers and parents.

16-7   discuss the similarities and differences of language development for single language speakers and English language learners.

· · · · · · · · · · · · · · · · · ·

naeyc

The following NAEYC Standards are addressed in this chapter:

STANDARD 1 Promoting Child Development and Learning

STANDARD 3 Observing, Documenting and Assessing to Support Young Children and Families

STANDARD 4 Using Developmentally Effective Approaches

STANDARD 5 Using Content Knowledge to Build Meaningful Curriculum

CONNECTIONS

- Nine-month-old Monet was eating her applesauce with apparent enjoyment. After a while, she began turning her head away each time she was offered another bite. When her mother persisted, Monet clamped her mouth shut and swiped at the spoon, sending the applesauce flying in all directions.
- Karla, almost two years old, pleaded: "Me go? Me go?" as her father picked up the car keys.
- Robin, an older four-year-old, was painting at the easel. The teacher remarked about the beautiful shade of purple he had created. Robin, the only child of a poetry professor, turned to her and said, "It's not really purple. It's more like violet; no, maybe amethyst."
- Erik, a second-grader, is very quiet in class, but when the teacher talks with him at recess or after school he speaks with great excitement about his Lego creations.

These children are "right on target" in terms of their communication skills. They are communicating effectively in a developmentally appropriate manner for their respective ages. How do the above language skills develop? How do we provide a learning environment that will ensure the optimum development of language skills? This chapter is about answering questions such as these.

16-1 Defining Speech, Language, and Communication Skills

Learning their native language is a complex developmental task, yet most children accomplish it easily. As Flavell and associates (2001) suggest, it would be virtually impossible to prevent typically developing children from learning to talk. Language can be defined as a complex symbol system. Symbols can be thought of as *signals:* words, signs, gestures, and body movements that either stand for something else or represent ideas. Another way to define the process of learning to talk is by its three interrelated components: communication, speech, and language.

Communication is the exchange of thoughts and ideas, feelings, emotions, likes, and dislikes. While speech is a major form of communication, there are other forms we use frequently. *Nonverbal communication* such as gestures and body language may be used alone or with speech. Holding up a hand with fingers upright and palm facing another individual almost universally indicates "Stop." To make the oral command doubly emphatic, the action may accompany the spoken word. Touching conveys messages such as irritation or caring, as when an adult grabs a child's arm forcibly or gently brushes the hair out of a child's eyes.

Printed words—books, letters, and directives—allow communication without speech or one-to-one contact. The same can be said of art forms such as music, dance, paintings, and sculpture, as well as the many electronic systems now used so extensively.

Speech is the *sound system* of a language, the way we communicate verbally. Speech depends on articulation: the ability to produce sounds distinctly and correctly, which is essential if speech is to be intelligible.

Language, as noted above, is a *code* or *symbol* system that enables individuals to express ideas and communicate them to others who use the same code. The code of every language is based on informally transmitted rules about grammar (syntax) and word meaning (semantics). (See Hoff, 2008, for an in-depth discussion of all aspects of language development.)

Communicating with others is the essential purpose of language. It functions as both a social and a cognitive activity. Allen and Hart (1984) describe the interrelationship: Language serves as a social skill for interacting with others, for expressing needs and ideas, and for getting help, opinions, and the cooperation of others. It serves also as a cognitive skill for understanding, inquiring, and telling about oneself and one's world.

Did You Get It?

How would the concepts of speech and language be defined?

a. Speech is the exchange of thoughts and ideas, feelings, emotions, likes, and dislikes; language depends on articulation: the ability to produce sounds distinctly and correctly.

b. Speech is verbal; language is the printed word.

c. Speech is the sound system of a language, the way we communicate verbally; language is a code or symbol system that enables individuals to express ideas and communicate them to others who use the same code.

d. Speech is a code or symbol system that enables individuals to express ideas and communicate them to others who use the same code; language is the sound system, the way we communicate verbally.

Take the full quiz on CourseMate.

Language Acquisition 16-2 ☀

Theories about language acquisition change or evolve as research reveals more about environmental input and the complex connections between the brain and language (Pinker, 2007). Here we will take a brief look at current theories about language acquisition in the very young.

16-2a ■ Environmental Perspective

A once popular theory of language development focused almost exclusively on the environment: The child learned to talk by imitating words and then receiving feedback (reinforcement) for saying them (Skinner, 1957). Today, most **psycholinguists** dismiss this explanation as simplistic, citing evidence that genetics and other factors play important roles as well. However, we cannot discount the role of environment and the input it provides. Children have to hear—or see—the language they learn. Learning to talk depends, in part, on imitation and feedback. Hart and Risley (1995) found significant differences in the amount and quality of interactions between parents and children from different economic groups. The more highly educated the mother, the more she spoke to her children. Children of professional parents heard an average of thirty million words by the time they reached three years of age, while children of working class parents heard twenty million, and children of parents on welfare heard ten million words. These differences in interactions appear to have led to significant

psycholinguist one who studies and analyzes the acquisition and production of language

differences in intellectual accomplishments being identified when these children were examined in third grade—once again emphasizing the importance of environment. Moreover, children learn very early that language has *function:* words help them get what they want and need. Words also promote social interactions and provide explanations and conversations about things a child is interested in (Hart & Risley, 1999).

Infant-directed speech Another fact that we cannot discount: The environment adapts itself to the language-learning infant. Infant-directed speech, popularly called **motherese**, refers to the particular speech patterns that adults use with the very young. Parents and caregivers, apparently the world over, speak more slowly and in higher-pitched voices when talking to infants. They use short sentences and a simplified, repetitious vocabulary that usually refers to something in the immediate environment. It is not that parents have figured out that these speech adaptations make language learning easier for their children; instead, experience has taught them that it is the best way to get and hold their child's attention and to get the child to understand what is being said. Cooper and Aslin (1994) note that babies only a few days old prefer to listen to motherese.

motherese infant-directed speech patterns that adults use with the very young

16-2b ■ Innateness Perspective

According to this viewpoint, language is said to unfold or emerge as a part of the developmental process, with the environment playing a far less dominant role. Theorists with a cognitive bias, such as Seidenberg (1997), believe that general principles of learning and cognitive development also contribute to language development, just as they do to such processes as perception and memory. Similarly, *constructivists* (theorists who believe that children construct their own knowledge through engagement with the environment) propose that the words a child hears will be learned if they connect with what the child is thinking and feeling (Bloom, 1995).

Integrated explanation How do we put this information together as we work with infants and young children? As Bee and Boyd (2012) point out, explaining how children learn language is one of the most difficult challenges facing developmental psychologists. What seems most likely and more readily

Learning to talk depends, in part, on imitation and feedback.

© Cengage Learning

understood is the three-part concept suggested by Kaczmarek (1982). Language acquisition is:

1. the maturationally determined mechanism for learning language.

2. the *input*, or quality and timing, of the child's early language experiences.

3. the use the child makes of input; the strategies the child devises for processing spoken language and then reproducing it.

There now is general agreement that healthy newborns arrive with a potential for language. They come equipped to learn to talk, and the environment shows them how. There is no dispute that language skills are developed through participation in language activities. Early language activities are informal and spontaneous. They occur during daily routines, casual play, and impromptu social exchanges. Such interactions, in the everyday world, are the main ingredients of language development. When language is not developing properly, the child is put at developmental risk. Failure to acquire normal language can have educational and social consequences that may persist for years (Warren & Kaiser, 1988).

Did You Get It?

What are the different perspectives between the older and current theories of language acquisition?

a. Previous theories of language development focused almost exclusively on the environment; today genetics and other factors are seen to play important roles as well.

b. Previous theories of language development focused on genetics; today the environment is seen to play the most important role.

c. Previous theories of language focused on genetics and other factors as playing an important role; current theory focuses almost exclusively on genetics.

d. Both focus on genetics, with the current view focusing on the environment as well.

Take the full quiz on CourseMate.

Sequences in Language Acquisition 16-3

Language acquisition, like all development, is a sequential process. The flow is from early primitive sounds and movements to the complex language and fluent speech characteristic of native speakers.

16-3a ■ Pre-Linguistic Communication

Language development begins in early infancy, long before first words appear. **Pre-linguistic communication** is characterized by body movements, facial grimaces, and vocalizations. During this period, the foundation of communicative language is established in the form of crying, then cooing, then babbling.

pre-linguistic communication body movements, facial expressions, and vocalizations used by infants before the first words are learned

Crying Healthy newborns spend most of their time sleeping. When they are awake, crying is a major form of communication. They soon learn that crying is a sure way to get the attention they need, assuming they are in a caring and responsive environment. Infant cries vary. Many parents are able to distinguish one cry from another and become skilled at discriminating hunger, discomfort, or their infant's need for company.

Cooing By two months of age, most infants are cooing, making a string of single vowel sounds such as "eeeeeeeeee" or "aaaaaaaaaa." Characteristically, the sounds indicate well-being or pleasure. Cooing increases as parents and caregivers respond with smiles and similar sounds. These early "conversations" between infant and parent seem to promote the infant's awareness of turn-taking as a way of interacting vocally with others (Bloom, Marquis, Tinker, & Fujita, 1996).

Babbling At about six months of age, infants begin to combine consonant and vowel sounds. They repeat these over and over: Bu-bu-bu-bu, gu-gu-gu-gu, da-da-da-da, ma-ma-ma-ma. "Ma-ma-ma" and "da-da-da" are purely coincidental, despite parents' jubilation that their infant is now calling them "by name." Babbling, like all other aspects of language, is readily affected by adult attention. In a classic study, Rheingold, Gewirtz, and Ross (1959) demonstrated that when adults smiled at a babbling baby, patted its tummy, or responded with similar sounds, the babbling increased.

Intonation Babbling soon begins to be marked by *intonation*, rising and falling variations in pitch that resemble adults' speech. "Learning the tune before the words" is the way Bates, O'Connell, and Shore (1987, p. 299) describe this period.

Language acquisition, like all development, is a sequential process.

© Cengage Learning

16-3b ■ First Words and Sentences

Every aspect of language development is exciting. Major milestones are first words and then sentences. Once these are mastered, language development progresses with giant strides.

Vocabulary During the latter part of the babbling period, the baby appears to be practicing various vowel and consonant combinations. The first recognizable words appear around the first birthday (Fenson et al., 1994). These are mainly nouns: names for people, animals, and favorite foods. Few verbs (action words) are uttered. Early vocabulary growth generally follows this sequence. (See Figure 16-1 for additional information about sequences of language acquisition.)

- During the three or four months after the first words, the child may acquire fewer than a dozen new words.

- Between fourteen and eighteen months, the child's vocabulary increases rapidly—up to about fifty words.

- Between eighteen months and the second birthday, a typically developing child is likely to have learned between 250 and 300 words.

- After the age of two, children acquire hundreds of new words a year.

- After the age of three, children typically use 1,000 words.

- At age five, more than 2,000 words are used.

- At age six, many children have a vocabulary of 14,000 words.

FIGURE 16-1
Sequences in Language
Acquisition

CHRONOLOGICAL AGE	LANGUAGE	SOME ACCOMPLISHMENTS
Newborn	Crying	Used to getting needs met
2 months	Cooing	Increases as parents and caregivers respond
6 months	Babbling Responds to own Name	Combines consonant and vowel sounds
Around 12 months	First recognizable words Understands simple instructions	Mainly nouns
18 months	5–50 words	Still mainly nouns
24 months	250–300 words	Can name a number of common objects Uses at least two prepositions Combines words into a short sentence
36 months	1,000 words	Can use three words, is able to use plurals and some past tenses Uses three prepositions About 90% of what the child says is intelligible
48 months	1,500 words	Knows names of familiar animals Uses four prepositions Follows simple commands even for objects not in view Asks many questions 4–5 word sentence length
60 months	2,000 words	Uses many descriptive words spontaneously—both adjectives and adverbs Knows common opposites Speech should be completely intelligible, in spite of articulation problems Able to repeat sentences as long as nine words Should be able to follow three-step commands given without interruptions

© Cengage Learning

Receptive and expressive vocabulary Language is described as having two dimensions: *receptive* and *expressive*. These dimensions are interrelated, but they are evaluated separately. **Receptive language** refers to the words an individual understands or recognizes; **expressive language** refers to the words the individual actually speaks or signs.

receptive language language that is understood

expressive language spoken words or signs that individuals use in communicating with others

Receptive language Throughout life, we understand more words than we use when speaking. While typical six-year-olds know approximately 14,000 words, they are likely to have many fewer words (about 2,500) in their expressive vocabulary.

Receptive language *precedes* expressive language. Before speaking his or her first words, an infant obviously understands much of what is said. Most infants squeal with delight when a parent says, "Let's go bye-bye," or a caregiver says, "Time for applesauce."

Expressive language Words and sentences that an individual speaks (or signs) come under the heading of *expressive* language. Gestures, grimaces, body movements, written words, and various art forms are included under the same heading.

A child's vocabulary is directly related to the materials and activities the child is engaged with at the time. The more interesting the materials and the more the child is encouraged to talk with someone about them, the larger will be the child's expressive vocabulary.

16-3c ■ Early Sentences

Progress in putting words together to form sentences is as rapid as vocabulary growth during the early years. Learning to combine words in a particular order pays off: It enables the child to convey more complex thoughts. This aspect of language acquisition is known as the development of **syntax**. It has several stages, beginning with the **holophrastic**.

syntax the way in which words are put together to form phrases, clauses, or sentences

holophrastic speech a state of speech development where the child conveys meaning with a one-word utterance

Holophrastic speech At this stage, the child uses a single word to convey an entire thought. The intended meaning is as unmistakable as a complete sentence. Holophrases usually occur in reference to something the child sees, hears, smells, tastes, or touches. The child's intonation or inflection also contributes to meaning, as do gestures such as pointing. The single word "doggie," depending on context, voice inflection, and the child's behavior, can readily be understood to mean:

"I want to play with this dog" (while toddling after the dog).
"See the dog" (while pointing to a dog).
"Where did the dog go?" (while looking outside).

Often, however, parents and caregivers have to work hard to figure out what the child wants. They say, "Show me," or offer various objects until the child selects the "right" one.

telegraphic speech a stage of speech development where the child conveys meaning with two-word utterances

Telegraphic speech Toward the end of the second year, the child begins to speak in simple, two-word sentences. These sentences convey meaning, even though many words are left out. Hence the term **telegraphic**, because of the way telegrams are written. Few parents or caregivers mistake the intent of abbreviated sentences such as "Mama's purse?" or "Daddy bye-bye." or "All done!" These two-word utterances are an important milestone in language acquisition. They indicate that the child is learning the word order (syntax or grammar) of the language (Pinker, 2007).

During the holophrastic speech stage, children use a single word to convey an entire thought.

Without appropriate order, words cannot convey meaning, especially as sentences get longer. The following example has all of the correct words for a reasonable request: "Can door you the so come open will up I?" Without conventional word order, it is going to take a while to figure out what the child wants.

Private speech Between the ages of three and six, children often make use of a strategy of talking to themselves, frequently referred to as **private speech** (Herschkowitz & Herschkowitz, 2004). Private speech serves a number of important functions for children. It helps them direct their behavior as they work things out. It helps them organize their thoughts and ideas. And it focuses their attention on what they are doing. When children master a task, the need for private speech decreases.

private speech children's strategy of talking to themselves to direct their behavior as they work things out

16-3d ■ Language Complexity

Between two and five years, language acquisition progresses rapidly. Most children learn to:

- use all of the "W" questions: ***Who? Where? What? When? Why?***
- transform positives to negatives: ***can/can't, will/won't, is/isn't***
- change verb forms, as required, to convey particular meanings: ***run/ran; will go/went; is raining/has rained***
- indicate "more than one" through the use of plurals: boy/boys, kitty/kitties, toy/lots of toys
- convey ownership: hers, ours, theirs, Daddy's, mine

(See Appendix B: Skill Profile, and Allen & Marotz & Allen, 2012, for more detailed age-by-age analysis.) This skill profile will also appear as a downloadable file on the companion website.

Overregularizations The years of rapid language development are characterized by several kinds of grammatical misconstructions. They represent not errors so much as children's *best efforts* to apply the complex rules of the language to the

overregularization language irregularities that occur because the child is applying previously learned rules of grammar; for example, "the mouses runned"

situation at hand. Often they are trying to regularize the irregular, and this leads to **overregularization**. Many children will say *digged* instead of *dug* for a while. When they say *digged*, they are relying on an earlier learning that called for adding *ed* to a verb to indicate action in the past. These children, as yet, have no understanding of irregular verbs. In a sense, *digged* is right. The child is applying the rule correctly. He or she is wrong only in not having learned when *not* to apply it. According to Rathus (1988), such errors aid rather than hinder language learning:

> Overregularization does represent an advance in the development of syntax. Overregularization stems from accurate knowledge of grammatical rules—not from faulty language acquisition. In another year or two, mouses will become boringly transformed into mice, and Mommy will no longer have sitted down. (p. 277)

When misconstructions occur, the adult, without emphasis or comment, simply uses the correct form: "Yes, the mice ran away." The child should not be criticized or corrected. Neither should a child be made to feel self-conscious or cute, regardless of how charming or amusing an adult may find the misconstructions. Unless undue attention is focused on the situation, these perfectly normal usages will self-correct in good time.

By the end of the fifth year, the development of syntax is nearly complete. Most children will be using compound and complex sentences and will have a minimum of 2,500 words in their expressive vocabulary. They will continue to add new words throughout their lives. Teachers can expect five- and six-year-olds to understand most of what is said to them, but only if they have the vocabulary and understand the several meanings that can relate to a specific word. For example, a child who knows color names may fail to perform a color-matching task. Why? Because the child may never have heard the word *match* refer to anything except a stick that produces a flame. Teachers may have to teach the vocabulary related to given tasks. Without such awareness on the part of the teacher, some children are unable to catch on to what is expected of them and may come to be labeled "slow" or "dull."

Did You Get It?

What is the difference between cooing and intonation?

a. Cooing is an attempt at combining consonant and vowel sounds; intonation consists of single vowel sounds.

b. Cooing is a string of single vowel sounds made by an infant of approximately two months; intonation is a form of babbling occurring at about six months.

c. Cooing is a string of single vowel sounds made by an infant of approximately two months; intonation is the rising and falling variations in pitch, and is a progression from babbling which occurs at about six months of age.

d. Cooing is the repetition of sounds; intonation is the rising and falling variations in pitch, and is a progression from cooing.

Take the full quiz on CourseMate.

☀ 16-4 Alternative Language Systems

An alternative language system is a method of communication that does not require spoken language. We will now review some alternative language systems used by young children and the adults who interact with them.

16-4a ■ Nonverbal Communication

Children's efforts to communicate nonverbally are important. Adults need to be aware of what children do, as well as what they say. A child who shrugs, scowls, smiles, flinches, or looks off into space is communicating. However, children do need to learn to express their needs and their likes and dislikes verbally. To facilitate this learning, the adult can respond to the body language (perhaps a flinch) while modeling words the child might use: "When Jason pushes you, say, 'Stop it!'"

16-4b ■ Augmentative and Alternative Communication Systems

Children with severe disabilities may not acquire speech easily; others may articulate so poorly that their speech is largely unintelligible. For these children, an **augmentative and alternative communication system (AAC)** using gestures, signs, symbols, or pictures is helpful. These systems can be relatively simple—only a few gestures—or they can be complex, using a **voice synthesizer** connected to a computer. There are two types of AAC systems: *unaided* and *aided*.

Unaided communication systems depend on the user's body to communicate or relay the message. Examples include gestures, body language, and/or sign language. *Aided* communication systems involve the use of tools or equipment in addition to the user's body. Examples include simple tools such as paper and pencil, as well as communication books, picture exchange systems, as well as more high-tech devices that produce voice output (speech generating devices or SGDs) and/or written output. Some devices can be programmed to produce different spoken languages. The newest devices include computer tablets, which provide the user with the opportunity to access special apps that use picture symbols, letters, and/or words and phrases to communicate. Watch the TeachSource Video Connection to see Jamie using several types of AAC devices. In most cases, an augmentative communication system is developed and introduced by the speech therapist, incorporating input from the family and teacher.

For preschool children, most augmentative systems use either sign language (Zeece & Wolda, 1995) or a picture/symbol exchange (Bondy & Frost, 1994). Intelligibility is important: Will the people in the child's environment be able to understand and communicate with the child using the system? Many young children with severe disabilities do not have the fine motor skills necessary to use sign language effectively. For these children, a picture- or symbol-based system may be a better choice.

When introducing augmentative communication, it is important to choose signs or symbols that occur frequently in the child's environment: on the playground, during circle time activities, and during free play (Reichle, Mirenda, Locke, Piche, & Johnson, 1992). Using the system across activities will improve communication skills and be useful to the

augmentative and alternative communication system (AAC) communication system that is used to supplement a child's verbal language; the system may be sign language, picture symbols, or a sophisticated computer system such as a voice synthesizer

voice synthesizer computer that can produce spoken words; type of assistive technology often used by people with severe communication disabilities

Teachers provide materials that interest children and result in talking.

© Cengage Learning

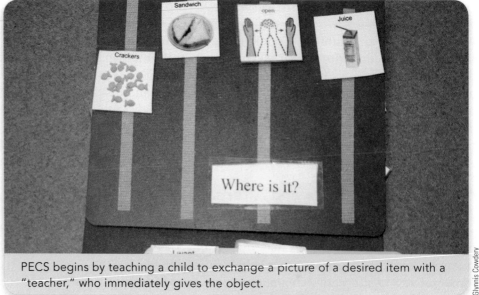

PECS begins by teaching a child to exchange a picture of a desired item with a "teacher," who immediately gives the object.

Glynnis Cowdery

Picture Exchange Communication System (PECS) an augmentative communication system that focuses on child initiation; the child exchanges symbols and pictures to communicate desires and ideas

child throughout the day. The **Picture Exchange Communication System (PECS)** is an augmentative communication system introduced by Bondy and Frost (1994). The system was the first to focus on the important issue of getting children to initiate a communication exchange. PECS begins by teaching a child to exchange a picture of a desired item with a "teacher," who immediately gives the object. Because no verbal prompts are used during the initial teaching, the child does not become dependent on an adult to begin a communication exchange. The system goes on to teach discrimination among symbols and then how to put them all together in simple sentences. More advanced individuals learn to comment and answer direct questions. Many preschoolers using PECS also begin developing speech. An important aspect of PECS is that it teaches the child to hand a picture or symbol to someone else. This request is difficult to ignore. Augmentative communication systems that involve the child pointing to pictures are often less effective, because an adult may not see a child pointing and thus may unintentionally ignore the potential interaction. Repeated episodes of not being able to communicate effectively can often lead to an overall reduction in a child's attempts to communicate. View the TeachSource Video Connection of Tyler to see him using PECS to communicate.

It is important that an augmentative communication system be used across settings. Professionals such as speech therapists, special educators, or early interventionists

Case Study ▪ Communicating with Tommy ▪

Tommy, a four-year-old in your preschool class, uses a Picture Exchange Program to communicate. He loves building with Legos and chooses this activity on a daily basis during free play. He says one- or two-word phrases, but primarily communicates using PECS by creating a sentence strip and handing it to you, the teacher. He is able to create up to a four-word sentence—including using colors and size attributes when requesting items—for example,

"I want the big, red Lego." To date he has not communicated with the other staff in the classroom or with his peers.

1. What can you do so that he communicates with the other classroom staff?
2. What activities can you plan that will increase the opportunities for Tommy to communicate with peers?

can assist teachers and families to use the system during routines and play activities. Children who use AAC are more likely to communicate with the adults in their environment because adults are more likely to meet their needs than their same-aged peers. Peers need to be educated about how to communicate effectively with their peer who uses AAC. Teachers can help the other children understand the system and use it to communicate with the child within the daily classroom activities (Hanline, Nunes, & Worthy, 2007). King and Fahsl (2012) explain that not only do peers need to understand how the systems work, but the teachers also need to actively plan for interactions to occur. Here are a few of their suggestions:

- Assign students who use AAC a classroom job that would require them to ask questions of peers.
- Teach students to count to 10 to make sure they are providing plenty of time for a response from the peer using AAC.
- Show the class YouTube videos of AAC communication devices, sign language, and picture exchange communication systems.
- Have a child who uses AAC demonstrate to the class.
- Provide all students an opportunity to interact using AAC devices. Discuss the barriers that might occur.
- For older students, read a play and assign each student a role to facilitate turn-taking

▶⏸ TeachSource Video Connections

Assistive Technology in the Inclusive Classroom: Best Practice

This video features five-year-old Jamie, a kindergartener with cerebral palsy who uses assistive technologies to help her learn the same curriculum content as the other students in her class. Jamie's teacher and inclusion facilitator share their insights about how best to teach Jamie and how assistive technologies can enhance her learning.

After watching this video, discuss the following:

1. According to Jamie's teacher, why is it helpful to everyone in the classroom to have a child who uses assistive technology?

2. What guidance does the teacher have for teachers new to working in an inclusive classroom?

Watch on CourseMate.

▶⏸ TeachSource Video Connections

Tyler: Augmentative Communication Techniques for a Kindergarten Student with Autism and Language Issues

This video shows Tyler using a Picture Exchange Communication System (PECS). His teacher and speech therapist describe several strategies they use in the classroom to help Tyler learn and communicate.

After watching this video, discuss the following:

1. What strategies did the teacher and speech therapist describe that are designed to help Tyler?

2. The PECS system Tyler is using is a low-tech AAC system. What are the advantages and disadvantages of a low-tech versus high-tech (e.g. iPad) system?

Watch on CourseMate.

© Cengage Learning 2015

© Cengage Learning 2015

Signing Signing is both functional and fun for children who are preverbal or non-verbal, learning a second language, gifted and in need of ongoing challenge, or shy about speaking up.

> Signing is a natural part of communication in an early childhood setting. Short expressive gestures, songs, and finger plays have been used successfully with young children for years. Think about the hand gestures used with such nursery classics as "The Eensie Weensie Spider," "Head, Shoulders, Knees, and Toes," or even "Old McDonald Had a Farm." (Zeece & Wolda, 1995, p. 4)

According to Zeece and Wolda (1995), teachers can teach beginning signing with very little training if they are willing to learn along with the children. They offer guidelines for teachers.

1. Observe the classroom to see what signs are already being used and build on these. Well-known nursery rhymes and songs are recommended as good starting points.

2. Introduce a sign at the children's level of understanding, making adaptations for individual differences and a child's willingness and ability to participate.

3. Move slowly and incrementally, picking favorite, familiar activities that both teacher and children enjoy. By watching adults who enjoy signing, children learn that signing serves a valuable and useful function.

4. Speak and act naturally when signing; avoid speaking louder than usual or using exaggerated speech. Natural speech patterns convey that this is an accepted, everyday way of communicating.

Zeece and Wolda (1995) conclude that signing can be an exciting and valuable component in inclusive early childhood programs: "Differences are not only accepted, they are fostered" (p. 8). A comprehensive list of resources for those interested in exploring signing in early childhood education has been compiled by Zeece and Wolda.

☀ 16-5 The Naturalistic Language-Learning Environment

Teachers play a major role in facilitating language development in infants and young children. The foundation for building children's language and communication skills, according to Schwartz, McBride, Pepler, Grant, and Carta (1993), is the social and communicative context of the environment. In the inclusive classroom, teachers will create a social climate where adults are sensitive to children's attempts to interact. The physical environment and the people in it make communication easy and enjoyable. Teachers and children become partners and share responsibility for selecting and maintaining communicative interaction.

16-5a ■ Arranging a Language-Learning Environment

Teachers arrange the learning environment so that every child has many opportunities to talk. Teachers also make sure there is plenty to talk about. Activities are arranged so that both activities and teachers are responsive to children's language efforts. The basics of arranging an effective early learning environment are covered in Chapter 13. Teachers' skills and attitudes are discussed in Chapter 11. Concepts specific to language acquisition are reviewed in this chapter.

Teachers' expectations Classroom experiences should be consciously arranged so that children are both expected to communicate and have reasons for communicating. Using language then becomes a casual yet integral part of all classroom activities. Teachers can provide a relaxed atmosphere in which children are allowed plenty of time to say what they want to say. Highly verbal children are helped to learn to listen (a skill that many talkative children need to practice). This gives less assertive or less verbal children a chance to talk. Teachers themselves can work at being good listeners and alert responders. They answer children in ways that indicate they are interested and want to hear more. They convey interest by responding with open-ended questions: they avoid questions that can be answered with a simple *yes* or *no*.

When a child says, "We went to Grandma's yesterday," the teacher might reply, "And what did you do at Grandma's?" Contrast that response with, "Did you have a good time?" While teachers need to be good responders, it is important they not talk too much. Rarely can children maintain interest in long and wordy responses. Nor can they remain interested in a response limited to the adult's perception of where the conversation should go. Children learn language by engaging in language. In a quality early learning program, talking is going on all of the time, but it is children who are doing most of the talking. Teachers are facilitators, sometimes prompting, sometimes questioning, sometimes reflecting a child's thoughts back to the child—a sure signal to the child that the teacher is really listening.

The role of questions Questions, asked or answered, are an important part of language acquisition. Care should be taken to ask open-ended questions that require more than a "yes" or "no" response from the child. When teachers ask questions, they should expect, and be willing to wait for, answers. If an answer is not forthcoming, the child is helped to formulate one. It may be a simple verbalization or gesture originated by the child, or a response modeled after one the teacher provides.

Children, including those with developmental problems, soon fall quite naturally into the routine of responding if teachers' expectations are realistic and consistent. A child who turns away without responding quite effectively ends the exchange.

Children need to have many things to talk about.

© Cengage Learning

If this happens frequently, teachers, family, and playmates may quit trying to communicate. The child loses out on two important sources of learning:

- language play and practice
- necessary information that most children get through everyday verbal exchanges

It cannot be overemphasized that teachers should not talk at children excessively; on the other hand, they do need to be responsive when children initiate interactions. In a study of children's efforts to communicate (Allen & Ruggles, 1980) in free-play situations, 65 percent of children's questions and adult-directed comments got no adult response on the child's first attempt. Some children gave up, and didn't try again. Others kept trying, getting louder and more insistent. When a teacher finally did respond, it was often impatiently or with a reprimand about the child's insistence. In either event, both teaching and learning opportunities were lost.

Activities Children need to have many things to talk about. They need novel materials to ask questions about. They need excursions, preferably simple ones, such as a visit to the house under construction across the street, so they can practice remembering and describing experiences. They need easily managed picture books that enable them to "read" the story. Certain toddler books can even become a foundation for language learning throughout the classroom (Rosenquest, 2002). They need songs, rhymes, chants, and wordplay. Long-term studies show that children who participate in turn-taking games, word/sound imitation, and pretend-play understand more and express themselves better than those who don't (Beveridge, Loader, Northstone, & Roulston, 2002).

Children need active play for prompting language of every kind. For children in need of special help with language skills, Kaczmarek (1982) emphasizes the importance of materials and equipment that require physical activity:

Gross and fine motor activities can be pleasant and powerfully reinforcing contexts for systematic language/communication intervention. Manipulating materials in fine motor activities and exercising large muscles in gross motor activities are frequent favorites of many children, ... since the language required in such activities is appropriate to the activity, linking the two is apt to aid in rapid skill acquisitions. (p. 22)

16-5b ■ Direct Assistance

Many children with developmental problems require direct and specific assistance in order to develop language and communication skills. Direct assistance is used to augment—not replace—the rich and responsive communication environment of a quality inclusion program. Schwartz et al. (1993) offer a hierarchy of direct teaching strategies.

- *Choice-making:* The teacher presents two options and asks the child to make a choice.
- *Mand-model:* The teacher uses the focus of the child's interest (e.g., toy car) and mands a response from the child (e.g., "tell me what you want"). If the child makes an incorrect response (e.g., "boat!"), the teacher models the correct response (e.g., "say car").
- *Topic continuation:* The teacher follows the child's conversational lead.
- *Time-delay:* The teacher looks expectantly at the child (for a request) before providing the desired material or activity.

- **Incidental teaching:** The teacher waits for a child to initiate and then responds immediately in such a way as to prompt a response from the child.

The degree of teacher assistance will vary according to the child's developmental needs and familiarity with the tasks. The child's relationship with the care provider and motivation are further considerations.

Milieu teaching This term refers to language-learning activities that go on throughout the day, across all activities, in the natural environment. Hepting and Goldstein (1996) offer a comprehensive review of naturalistic language intervention. Milieu teaching (Warren & Kaiser, 1988) incorporates the incidental teaching principles described in the research of Hart and Risley (1982). The child may be seeking information, assistance, materials, feedback, or reassurance. This means the adult can use a naturally occurring reinforcer such as the child's request for a material, information, or adult attention, to promote a brief but immediate learning episode. The teaching opportunity is a perfect match because the child is initiating the lesson based on an interest and a need. The more frequently a child contacts a teacher, the more opportunities there are for the teacher to teach and for the child to learn. It is important, therefore, that each child make frequent contacts. To ensure such frequency, teachers need to be:

- readily available and eager to foster learning according to each child's skill level.
- interested in what the child is offering or inquiring about.
- prompt and positive in making a response, whether verbal, giving physical assistance, or giving additional materials and equipment.
- conscious of keeping the contact brief and focused on the child's expressed interest.
- sure the contacts are pleasant—even fun—for both the child and the teacher.

During a milieu teaching episode, the teacher never tells a child, "No, that's wrong," never criticizes, reprimands, drills, or lectures. The teacher's objective is to make the encounters so pleasant and rewarding that the child will return again and again for more teaching and more learning.

Emily, a four-year-old with a language delay, held a paint apron up to the teacher. The teacher knelt down, smiled, and waited, giving Emily time to make a request. Emily remained silent. After a moment the teacher said, "Emily, what do you need?" (The teacher did not anticipate Emily's need by putting the apron on for her.) When Emily did not answer, the teacher asked, "Emily, do you want help with your apron?" Emily nodded. "Tell me 'apron'," prompted the teacher. Emily made a sound somewhat similar to "apron," and the teacher said, "Yes, *apron; that's right." When the teacher put the apron over Emily's head, she said, "Apron on," modeling what she would ask Emily to say once she had learned to imitate and could say the word *apron*.

Had Emily not said *apron*, the teacher would have put the apron on and tied it anyway. The teacher also would have described the procedure in simple language. Never should a child be scolded, nagged, or coaxed. If teachers introduce pressure into spontaneous teaching opportunities, many children stop making the contacts. Some do without. Others turn to communicating their needs less appropriately through whining, crying, or sulking. Children who are most in need of the highly individualized help that makes milieu teaching so effective are usually the first to be put off at any sign of pressure.

Did You Get It?

Through what means would a teacher provide continuous opportunities throughout the day to engage in language learning?
a. Direct assistance.
b. Indirect teaching.
c. Incidental teaching.
d. Milieu teaching.

Take the full quiz on CourseMate.

Connecting Developmentally Appropriate Practice to Brain Research

PARENT'S USE OF TECHNOLOGY AND ITS IMPACT ON THEIR CHILD'S DEVELOPMENT

(The issue of children's use of technology is discussed in Chapter 17 of this text.)

Parents today juggle and multitask through their busy days in a way previously unprecedented. Technology allows them to be ever-connected but possibly also distracted from their role of parent. Consider the following example: A parent is at a park with his child and turns to check his phone, and in that second an accident happens.

Child safety experts had previously reported a decline in child-related injuries since the 1970s, but most recently there has been an increase. Nonfatal injuries to children under age five rose 12 percent between 2007 and 2010, according to the most recent data from the Centers for Disease Control and Prevention. Since no studies have been completed that show this increase is due to distracted parenting, and parents don't tend to report that an accident occurred because they were distracted, the data only suggest an association. As Dr. Gary Smith, founder and director of the Center for Injury Research and Policy of the Research Institute at Nationwide Children's Hospital states, "What you have is an association. Being able to prove causality is the issue. … It certainly is a question that begs to be asked."

While the need for formal studies exists, psychologist Kathy Hirsh-Pasek of Temple University recently had students observe thirty parents and their children in public places. Her students found that in almost every case, a parent interrupted an activity with the child to use a device.

The question of whether parents being distracted by devices impacts children's language and social development is another area that begs for research. One needs only to walk the aisles of a store to see parents talking on phones or texting rather than engaging with their child. Shopping, while considered a chore by many, provides so many opportunities for parent–child interactions that foster language and math skills.

Over the past decade, Dr. Sherry Turkle from M.I.T. has explored the issue of whether parents' involvement with technology can affect their social and emotional connections to their children. While her research yields no definitive conclusions at this time, she reports there is a rationale for heightened concern. Dr. Turkle has previously stated that children often feel hurt and may be reluctant to discuss it when their parents are preoccupied with devices. Meals, sporting events, and afterschool or extracurricular activities are some examples of where parents may be distracted by a device rather than be present in the moment. Emotional connectivity and language development are two areas where many psychologists have expressed concern. They are asking if it is possible for excessive use of smart phones and social media to negatively affect the social bond a parent has with their child.

There is no way to avoid the fact that future generations will be raised with technology, and that the individuals doing the raising are going to be avid users of technology and social media. It is important that research continue to investigate the impact of parenting with technology can have both on children's safety and in the areas of language and social-emotional development.

Your Turn

1. Do your own research, observing parents with their children at a park or in a store and record your observations about the parents' use of technology. Does it interfere with a parent–child interaction or present a safety concern?
2. What are your thoughts on the use of technology both by parents and children?

Sources: The Perils of Texting while Parenting, *Wall Street Journal.* September 29, 2012.

Texting while Parenting. What Effect Can It Have on Your Children? *Forbes,* September 30, 2012.

✺ 16-6 Speech Irregularities

Irregularities, or dysfluencies, are typical of early speech development. Most children, 80 percent or more, will show some kind of dysfluency during the early years. For a time, the ability to formulate thoughts and ideas is greater than the child's ability to pronounce words correctly or to get them in the right order. The irregularities that early childhood teachers are most likely to encounter will be discussed briefly.

Many factors can affect the rate of language acquisition. For example, developmental disabilities can affect the production of language. The oral-structural abnormalities associated with Down syndrome and clefts of the lips or palate can affect speech sounds. Cerebral palsy can affect both speech sound and production. Autism affects a child's ability to acquire both receptive and expressive speech.

Evidence has also been found that many children inherit their language delays. Spitz and Tallal (1997) found that children with a family history of language impairments scored lower on receptive and expressive language tasks than those in a control group. At the same time, performance on a number of tasks that did not rely on language abilities did not differ as a function of family history. These results indicate that children with a positive family history for language impairments are at risk for language delay.

16-6a ■ Articulation Errors

Articulation refers to the production of speech sounds. Perfectly normal **articulation errors** are likely to occur as young children work at mastering the complex sounds that make up everyday speech. Misarticulations usually are classified as omissions, substitutions, additions, or distortions.

Omissions. Sounds are left out, often at the beginning or end of words: "That's my *agon* (wagon)," "Here's the *boom* (broom)."

Substitutions. Interchanging sounds such as **b** and **v**: "Put the *balentines* on the *vack* seat," or replacing one sound with another: *wabbit* for *rabbit*.

Additions. Inserting sounds not part of a word: *warsh* (for *wash*) or *Notta now* (for *Not now*).

Distortions. Deviations in speech sounds often occur because of tongue misplacement or missing teeth. Many six-year-olds with missing front teeth will say *schwim* for *swim* or *tink* for *think*.

articulation refers to the production of speech sounds

articulation errors speech sounds that are inconsistent with the native language (usually a temporary developmental irregularity)

dysfluency hesitations, repetitions, omissions, or extra sounds in speech patterns

16-6b ■ Lisping

Rarely is lisping (pronouncing *s* as *th*) a worrisome problem in preschool children. Seldom does it persist. Exceptions may be those few cases where the child's lisp has been showcased by adults who think it is cute. If lisping should continue beyond the primary grades, parents are usually encouraged to seek consultation.

16-6c ■ Dysfluency

Repetition of particular sounds or words, noticeable hesitations between words, extra sounds, or the undue prolonging of a sound are types of **dysfluency**. These kinds of speech irregularities are common, even normal. However, to label a young child as a stutterer is unwise, in part because the label may have a self-fulfilling effect. On the other hand, there are those few children who develop abnormal dysfluencies during the

Classroom experiences should be consciously arranged so children are both expected to communicate and have reasons for communicating.

© Cengage Learning

preschool or primary school years. According to Zebrowski (1995), specific features of a common dysfluency such as stuttering distinguish it from a developmentally typical dysfluency. These include:

- frequency
- type and proportion
- duration
- associated non-speech behaviors such as excessive frustration or grimacing

These children should be referred to a speech and language pathologist for evaluation. Let it be emphasized: *Teachers do not make referrals directly*. However, when teachers are concerned about any developmental variation in a child, it is their responsibility to share their concerns with parents and to listen attentively to parents' responses and concerns.

Guidelines A developmentally common speech irregularity seldom needs to turn into a major problem. Teachers and parents can help by practicing preventive measures, as shown in Figure 16-2.

These suggestions are well summarized by what one group of speech and language specialists call **benevolent neglect** (Rieke, Lynch, & Soltman, 1977). Benevolent neglect is based on accepting common errors. To correct a child unnecessarily undermines the child's confidence. If children are to improve their language skills, they must keep talking. Children who fear they will be criticized each time they speak tend to speak less and less. Rieke and her colleagues offer adults an important rule: *Never force a child to repeat anything that you have understood.*

benevolent neglect paying no attention to minor speech and language errors that usually self-correct as the child's communication skills mature

---

FIGURE 16-2

How to Keep Common Speech Irregularities from Becoming Major Problems

What adults should do

- Make sure the child is getting good nutrition, adequate rest, and many more hours of active play than television viewing each day.
- Provide comfort, care, and support; reduce tensions as much as possible.
- Have fun with the child and with language; inject humor, simple rhyming activities, and songs into everyday routines.
- Discipline with calmness, firmness, and consistency; avoid harshness, ridicule, or teasing.
- Offer activities where the child can be successful and develop self-esteem.

What adults should not do

- Do not correct or nag the child; avoid saying, "Slow down," "Take it easy," "Think before you speak."
- Do not call attention to dysfluencies directly or indirectly; the child becomes all the more tense when an adult focuses with exaggerated patience, a forced smile, or a rigid body, waiting for the child to "get it out."
- Do not interrupt a child or act hurried; young children need plenty of time when trying to put their ideas into spoken language.
- Do not compare a child's speech unfavorably with another child's.
- Never attempt to change a child's handedness. (It is a myth that hand dominance and speech disorders are related.)

© Cengage Learning

The importance of not overreacting to perfectly normal speech and language irregularities cannot be overemphasized (Berglund, Eriksson, & Johansson, 2001). On the other hand, if a genuine problem exists, it needs to be identified as early as possible and an intervention program put into effect immediately. The early childhood teacher may be the first to suspect a problem. Whenever a teacher has concerns, parents should be counseled (and assisted, if need be) to seek help. Parents often have the feeling that *something* may be wrong. On the other hand, they can become so accustomed to their child's speech that they do not realize how poor it actually is. Speech, language, and hearing clinicians who specialize in young children provide the most reliable testing and consultation for families at all income levels.

Early warning signs Knowledge of normal development and skill in observing children helps teachers recognize signs of a possible problem. The Speech-Language-Hearing Division of Kansas University suggests that parents seek a professional evaluation if a child displays any of the following behaviors:

- is not aware of sounds or noise
- is not talking by two years
- leaves off beginning consonants after three years
- uses markedly faulty sentence structure after five years
- uses mostly vowel sounds in speech
- is noticeably non-fluent after six years
- regularly uses a voice that is monotone, too loud, too soft, too high, or too low for the child's age and sex
- sounds as if he or she were talking through the nose or has a cold when none exists
- has frequent ear infections *and* signs of possible delay
- is a year late in acquiring any speech and language skill

16-6e ■ Intervention

Children with speech and language problems need an individualized intervention program. For best results, the early childhood teacher and the therapist work together in designing, implementing, and evaluating the

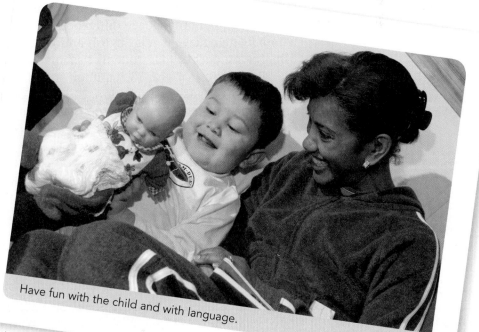

Have fun with the child and with language.

© Cengage Learning

Did You Get It?

How does cerebral palsy affect a child's speech ability, in comparison to the effect on speech of a child with autism?

a. CP can affect speech sound; autism affects production of speech.

b. CP can affect both speech sound and production; autism affects a child's ability to acquire both receptive and expressive speech.

c. CP affects a child's ability to acquire both receptive and expressive speech; autism affects both speech sound and production.

d. CP affects a child's ability to acquire receptive speech; autism affects a child's ability to acquire expressive speech.

Take the full quiz on CourseMate.

intervention. The speech therapist may work with the child directly in the classroom or take the child out for short, individual sessions. It is becoming commonplace for the therapist to move with the child in the classroom, using the ongoing activities as the context for specialized instruction (Kaiser, Yoder, & Keetz, 1992).

Treatment may be largely ineffective unless therapy activities are coordinated with classroom and home activities. This allows practice throughout the day in situations that can be both fun and rewarding for the child. Therapists can promote home and classroom cooperation by informing teachers and parents regularly about the particular skills the therapist is working on and the progress the child is making. Therapists also can demonstrate specific strategies for the natural setting, where the usefulness of language is obvious to the child.

The foregoing does not imply that teachers (or parents) are expected to become language specialists. They can, however, readily learn simple procedures for facilitating individual children's speech and language development. A classroom application of a corrective strategy might be helping a child practice making the initial *b* sound. As a demonstration for the teacher, the therapist helps the child make the sound. The teacher and child practice several times in the presence of the therapist. The teacher then works with the child whenever an opportunity presents itself. The teacher uses milieu teaching strategies, and the child learns quickly because making the *b* sound always is related to something the child wants or is interested in. Example: "You want to play with the big ball. Tell me '*big b*all.'"

16-7 English Language Learners (ELL)

 It is vitally important that teachers discriminate between delays or deficiencies and cultural or language differences. English language learners are children whose first language is not English and who are in the process of learning English. The number of ELL students has increased by 51 percent from 1997–98 to the 2008–09 school year (3.5 million to 5.3 million) (National Clearinghouse for English Language Acquisition, 2011). These rapidly increasing numbers of English language learners present challenges for educators. Teachers are trying to ensure that their students get access to the core curriculum while at the same time learning English language skills.

The federal government requires districts to provide services to English learners, but it offers states no policies to follow in identifying, assessing, or instructing them. Due to this lack of policy, practices vary widely among the states.

It cannot be emphasized enough that everything in this chapter about facilitating language acquisition applies to helping children acquire a second language. Children learning a second language progress through the same language development stages and with the same predictability as any other child learning a language (Nilsen, 2010). The importance of not pressuring, reprimanding, or correcting a child's efforts must be underscored. At the same time, teachers must expect children to talk, both in their own language and in the language they are learning, as much as they are able. Teachers must plan an environment that

What Is the Most Effective Method for Improving ELL Achievement?

There is ongoing debate and discussion about which instructional method most effectively improves achievement for ELLs—bilingual education or English-only instruction. The following is a description of several different methods.

- **English immersion:** Instruction is entirely in English. Sometimes referred to as the sink-or-swim or submersion method of instruction, it can cause stress and feelings of being overwhelmed for the students.

- **Structured English immersion:** Students are taught entirely in English by teachers who have specialized skills in language instruction and possess a bilingual education or ESL teaching credential and/or training, and strong receptive skills in students' primary language. California successfully passed the Proposition 227 initiative, which mandates "Structured English-Immersion Instruction" for non-native speakers of English. Some current educational research results seem to indicate that immigrant students who are non-native speakers of English perform much better in "mainstream" classroom settings after one or more years of "structured English-immersion instruction" than students who were subjected to traditional "bilingual education."

- **English as a second language:** May be the same as immersion but also may include some support to individuals in their native tongue. Typically, classes are composed of students who speak many different languages but are not fluent in English. They may attend classes for only a period a day, to work strictly on English skills, or attend for a full day and focus both academics and English.

- **Transitional bilingual education:** Instruction for some subjects is in the students' native language, but a certain amount of each day is spent on developing English skills. Classes are made up of students who share the same native language.

- **Two-way bilingual or dual-language education:** Sometimes also called dual-immersion or dual-language. Instruction is given to students in two languages, usually in the same classroom, who may be dominant in one language or the other, with the goal of the students' becoming proficient in both languages. In this model there are typically team teachers with each one responsible to teach in only one of the languages.

Slavin and Cheung (2005) analyzed research on the topic of bilingual education and reached a conclusion that favors bilingual education instead of English-immersion programs. They reviewed seventeen research studies and found that twelve showed positive results of bilingual education on a child's academic performance. None of the studies supported English-immersion programs, while five studies found no differences between English-immersion and bilingual education classes. While some research has concluded that bilingual education and English-only methods work equally well to teach English literacy, authors in the journal *The Future of Children* (2011) report that "the quality of instruction is what matters most in educating English-learners."

Researchers Calderon, Slavin, and Madden (2011) list the individual components of effective models, which include integration of language, literacy, and academic content instruction, cooperative learning, professional development, parent and family support teams, and monitoring implementation and outcomes.

(continued)

Continued

In April 2011, the White House released a report on improving Hispanic education. The following statement nicely summarizes the current state of the education of English learners: "While there are certain practices that have been shown to benefit ELs, more research and evaluation are needed on the types of language-instruction programs that are most effective for English-learners" (White House, 2011).

Sources: Brookings Institution and Princeton University. (2011). *The Future of Children.*

Calderon, M., Slavin, R., & Sanchez, M. (2011). "Effective instruction for English learners," *The Future of Children.*

English Language Learners (2004). *Education Week.* Retrieved from http://www.edweek.org/ew/issues/english-language-learners/

The National Clearinghouse for English Language Acquisition. (2011). The growing numbers of English learner students, 1998/99–2008/09.

Slavin, R. E., & Cheung, A. (2005). A synthesis of research on language reading instruction for English language learners. *Review of Educational Research, 75*(2), 247–284.

The White House. (2011). "Improving Latino Education to Win the Future."

gives English language learners plenty of reasons and opportunities to talk.

With young children, drill and direct instruction are counterproductive. A second language is learned most easily in the natural environment of the preschool classroom. Teachers often put labels on various things about the room: *chair, blocks, sink, easel.* This and other teaching strategies related to developmentally appropriate activities are discussed in Chapter 13. For now, let it be emphasized that children first must learn that they can get what they want (powerful motivation) through language interactions with an adult who can be trusted to accept whatever responses the child can make. Here is an example:

> *A child looks at the teacher and says: "Agua."*
> *Teacher responds: "Agua. Water."*
> *Child imitates: "Water."*
> *Teacher responds: "Water, that's right. Agua. Water."*

There is evidence that bilingual children may be advanced in cognitive development, compared to children who speak only one language (Hakuta & Diaz, 1985). It is true that bilingual children may have a temporarily lower IQ score. However, this seems to occur only while they are learning the second language. Think for a moment about how difficult it must be for a child to be thrust into a culture where teachers do not even know how to say his or her name properly. Because much of an individual's self-esteem is centered on being addressed appropriately, it is critical for teachers to use both the child's and the parents' names appropriately. This establishes from the start a more effective home–school relationship. For further information, Bennett (2010) presents approaches to facilitating language and literacy in children who are bilingual and bicultural.

A second language is learned most easily in the preschool classroom.

© Cengage Learning

Total Physical Response (TPR)

Total physical response (TPR) is a language-teaching method developed by James Asher, a professor emeritus of psychology at San José State University. He developed TPR after observing young children learning their first language. He noted that interactions between children and their parents often involved the parents speaking to the child followed by a physical response from the child. For example, a father says to a baby, "Look at your mommy," and the baby turns to look at her. Asher made three hypotheses based on his observations:

1. language is learned primarily by listening;
2. language learning must engage the right hemisphere of the brain;
3. language learning should not involve any stress.

Asher's work is based on these theories:

- Second-language learning is parallel to first-language learning and should reflect the same naturalistic processes.

- Listening should develop before speaking.

- Children respond physically to spoken language, and adult learners learn better if they do that, too.

- Once listening comprehension has been developed, speech develops naturally and effortlessly out of it.

Thus, TPR is based on the coordination of language and physical movement. In TPR, teachers give commands to students in the target language, and students respond with whole-body actions. For example, "Hand the red crayon to Malia."

The method is an example of the comprehension approach to language teaching. Listening serves two purposes: it is a means of understanding messages in the language being learned, and it is a means of learning the structure of the language itself. Grammar is not taught explicitly with this method but rather, grammar is learned through exposure.

Total physical response is used alongside other methods and techniques. It was developed for use with beginners and young learners.

Sources: Asher, J. J. (2003). Learning Another Language through Actions (6th edition). Sky Oaks Productions, Inc.: Los Gatos, CA.

Cook, B. S. (2013). What is TPR? Retrieved from http://www.tprsource.com/asher.htm

Did You Get It?

What are the comparative rates of English Language Learners (ELL) between the years 1997–98 and 2008–09?

a. 2.7 million to 16.7 million.
b. 3.5 million to 5.3 million.
c. 5.3 million to 3.5 million.
d. 5.1 million to 51 million.

Take the full quiz on CourseMate.

Summary

▶ Learning to speak and use the native language is the most complex developmental task mastered by infants and young children.

▶ Explaining how children acquire language has been the subject of thousands of studies and has yielded conflicting theories. Despite disagreement about how children accomplish this difficult task, most children do learn to talk with little apparent effort.

▶ Without specific instruction, children move through the developmental sequences in speech and language acquisition, from crying, cooing, and jabbering to producing complex sentences and multisyllabic words in their first five or six years. Speech and language irregularities come and go and appear to be self-correcting, for the most part, unless the child is pressured.

▶ Although relatively few children have problems speaking or learning the language, some have trouble with both. Problems may range from developmentally normal delays and dysfluencies to serious problems requiring the services of a speech and language specialist.

- An undiagnosed hearing loss is always a possibility and needs to be ruled out first in diagnosing a language delay or impairment in a young child (see Chapter 6).

- A stimulating classroom environment with interesting materials and activities coupled with milieu teaching practices have proven effective in enhancing the speech and language skills of all children at all levels of language development.

- Teachers' knowledge of normal development and their skill in observing children are essential in identifying language problems.

- It is important that teachers discriminate between language that is developmentally delayed or deviant and language that is culturally different.

- Some children may need to use an alternative communication system (AAC) to get their needs met.

- An increasing number of children in our schools are bilingual, even trilingual. These children, in an appropriate learning environment, experience no serious disruption in language or cognitive development.

Key Terms

articulation, 431
articulation errors, 431
augmentative communication
  system, 423
benevolent neglect, 432
dysfluency, 431
expressive language, 420

holophrastic speech, 420
incidental teaching, 429
motherese, 416
overregularization, 422
Picture Exchange Communication
  System (PECS), 424
pre-linguistic communication, 417

private speech, 421
psycholinguist, 415
receptive language, 420
syntax, 420
telegraphic speech, 420
voice synthesizer, 423

Student Activities

1. Observe at least two sets of parents and their preschool-aged child in a grocery or department store. Make notes about the different observations: What do you see the parents doing that fostered language? Make a list of other language opportunities that the parents missed.

2. Write down or record at least fifteen verbal responses of adults while they are caring for a child (or children) between one and three years of age. Is there evidence of motherese? Specify which responses.

3. Select a partner to role-play a three-year-old who approaches you, the teacher, and silently holds out

a sweater. You want to increase this child's language skills in general. Demonstrate ways to do this by using milieu teaching strategies.

4. Observe a child who is using AAC. Record your thoughts as to how the system enables or prevents the child from interacting with peers and adults.

5. Select a partner to act as the parent of a three-year-old who says to you, the teacher, "I'm really concerned. Ryan has been stuttering for the past two weeks." How do you respond to this parent?

Review Questions

Part 1. Briefly respond to the following items.

1. Explain the difference between speech and language.

2. What is motherese?

3. What is the difference between receptive and expressive language?

4. Give five examples of nonverbal communication.

5. List four types of articulation errors.

6. Define benevolent neglect as related to speech and language development.

7. List five indications that a child should be referred for speech and language assessment.

8. How might technology help or hinder a child's communication and language development?

Part 2. Arrange in appropriate sequence (from earliest to most complex) normal language development.

1. telegraphic speech
2. grammatical overregularizations
3. crying
4. vocal intonation
5. holophrastic speech
6. complex sentences
7. babbling
8. first words
9. cooing
10. private speech

Helpful Websites

American Speech-Language-Hearing Association

http://www.asha.org

This website offers resources for professionals, prospective students of speech and language pathology, and the general public on communication behavior and disorders.

Early Childhood Research Institute on Culturally and Linguistically Appropriate Services

http://clas.uiuc.edu

The CLAS Early Childhood Research Institute collects and describes early childhood/early intervention resources that have been developed across the U.S. for children with disabilities and their families and the service providers who work with them. The materials and resources available on this site reflect the intersection of culture and language, disabilities, and child development. The site is designed to inform practitioners, families, and researchers about materials and practices that are available. Parts of the site can also be read in Spanish.

The Council for Exceptional Children (CEC)

http://www.cec.sped.org (Search: communication disorders)

Division for Children with Communication Disorders (DCCD). This is an affiliate of the Council for Exceptional Children. The DCCD is an organization for professionals and parents interested in promoting a better understanding of children with communication disorders. The site provides access to three journals: *Journal of Child Language*, *Journal of Communication Disorders*, and *Journal of Speech and Hearing Research*.

Pyramid Educational Consultants

http://www.pecs.com/index.php

Pyramid Educational Consultants, Inc., offers a wide range of consulting services and products for educators and parents of children and adults with autism and related disabilities. The website provides a description of the Picture Exchange Communication System (PECS) as well as abstracts, research articles, webcasts, and products related to the system.

 Visit the Education CourseMate for this textbook to access the eBook, Did You Get It? quizzes, Digital Downloads, TeachSource Video Cases, flashcards, and more. Go to CengageBrain.com to log in, register, or purchase access.

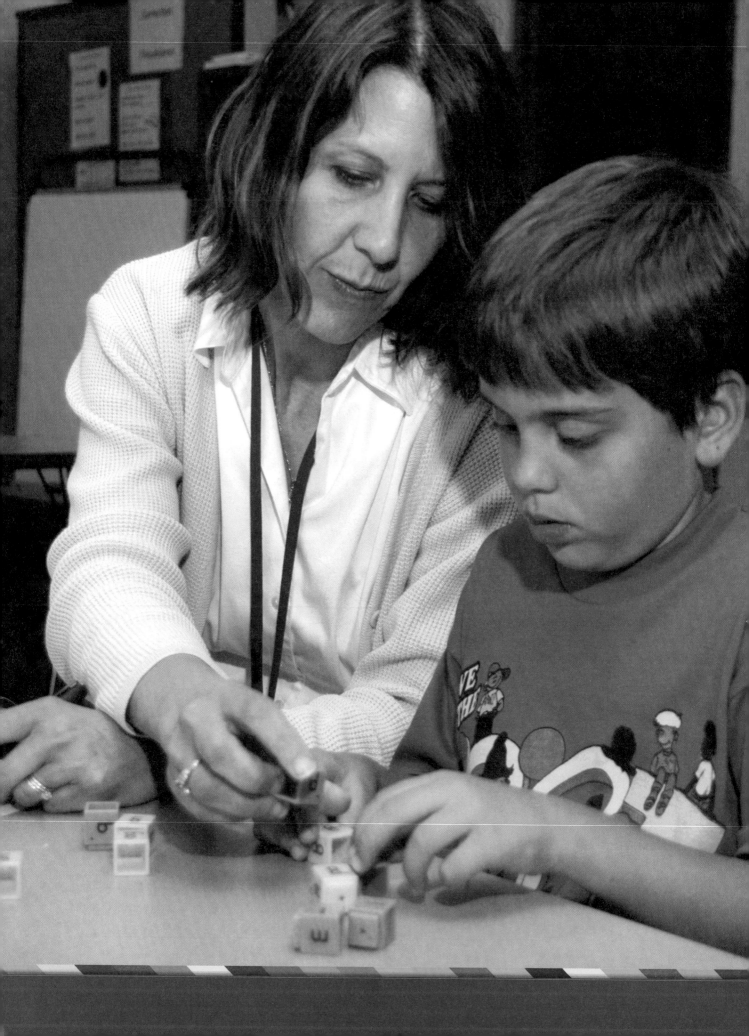

Facilitating Pre-Academic and Cognitive Learning

17

OBJECTIVES

After reading this chapter, you should be able to:

17-1 describe how cognitive development and emerging literacy are interrelated.

17-2 highlight what brain research tells us about children's development and how this can be used to design teaching activities.

17-3 understand why it is important to provide academic opportunities for preschoolers.

17-4 develop an understanding of what developmentally appropriate pre-academic activities look like.

17-5 explain how to design an early childhood classroom's pre-academic curriculum, including grouping of children, setup of tasks, and types of materials.

· · · · · · · · · · · · · · · · · ·

naeyc

The following NAEYC Standards are addressed in this chapter:

STANDARD 1 Promoting Child Development and Learning

STANDARD 2 Building Family and Community Relationships

STANDARD 3 Observing, Documenting and Assessing to Support Young Children and Families

STANDARD 4 Using Developmentally Effective Approaches

STANDARD 5 Using Content Knowledge to Build Meaningful Curriculum

CONNECTIONS

● The children in Miss Ruiz's small group—Sara, Shauna, Martin, Roberto, Lamont, and Sabrina—range in age from three years and seven months to four years and eleven months. Like most early childhood educators, Miss Ruiz believes that children need to learn to recognize, name, and match colors. She considers it an appropriate developmental task and a building block in emerging literacy. Today she is using one-inch colored cubes as the teaching material. Before the children arrived, she arranged individual baskets containing cubes and design cards geared to the varying skill levels of the children in her group. Martin's cubes and model designs are limited to red and blue. It is a starting task for the day's activity that would ensure his success, but could be readily extended if need be. Shauna's design cards are complex and call for many cubes of every color. The other children's tasks with the colored cubes vary accordingly, based on their skill levels and interests.

Activities labeled as *academic* or *pre-academic* tend to generate mistrust among some early childhood educators. Their concern is that the use of such terms might put a stamp of approval on developmentally *inappropriate* paper-and-pencil tasks and sanction a *pushed-down* elementary curriculum for young children. An alternative term, **emerging literacy**, has been gaining favor. In this text, we use terms such as pre-academic, cognitive, intellectual, and emerging literacy as related concepts.

emerging literacy the diverse skills that help children become successful in reading, writing, and other academic tasks

✸ 17-1 Cognitive Development and Emerging Literacy

Emerging literacy involves diverse skills that help children become successful in reading, writing, and other academic tasks. The process of becoming literate begins in early infancy and continues throughout the lifespan. Primarily, it involves exposure to activities and people who read, write, and use language in a variety of ways.

Interest in emerging literacy is based on several issues that affect our entire society. One is the enormous number of Americans who are **functionally illiterate**. Another is the growing concern over increasing numbers of children who start school without the early experiences and communication skills that enable them to participate in an academic curriculum. The No Child Left Behind (NCLB) Act (PL 107-110) and its program Early Reading First and Early Reading (Title 1, Part B, Subparts 1 & 2) continue the interest in emerging literacy by promoting reading competency in kindergarten through third grade. Figure 17-1 describes the goals of these programs. Later in the chapter, we will discuss specific approaches and strategies that foster emergent literacy in early childhood programs.

functionally illiterate not possessing reading and writing skills used in day-to-day tasks

17-1a ■ Defining Pre-Academics

A growing number of preschool teachers and administrators have come to embrace the concept of *pre-academics*. They see it as more descriptive of the

Goals of NCLB Early Reading First and Early Reading Programs

1. Early Reading First

Early Reading First (Title I, Part B, Subpart 2) focuses on preschool-age children. It supports local efforts to:

- Enhance children's development of knowledge necessary for successful reading development in kindergarten and after.
- Enhance children's early language and literacy development.

The program targets (1) districts serving high percentages or numbers of preschool-age children living in poverty, (2) public or private organizations serving preschool-age children located in these districts, and (3) partnerships of such districts or organizations.

2. Reading First

Reading First (Title I, Part B, Subpart 1) focuses on students in kindergarten through grade 3. The program:

- Identifies the five essential elements of reading programs: phonemic awareness, phonics, fluency, vocabulary, and reading comprehension strategies.
- Requires reading programs to be based on scientifically based research.
- Requires classroom-based screening, instructional, and diagnostic reading assessments.
- Provides funding for professional development.

This program targets eligible districts and schools with (1) a high percentage or number of K–3 students reading below grade level, and (2) a high percentage or number of students living in poverty.

Source: Learning Points Associates. (2007). *Quick Key 1: Understanding the No Child Left Behind Act: Reading.*

FIGURE 17-1

Goals of NCLB Early Reading First and Early Reading Programs

---

many types of learning activities that characterize the well-rounded preschool program and that are relevant to young children's ongoing learning experiences. Nevertheless, the issue of pre-academics is far from resolved.

A **pre-academic** curriculum includes the components that reinforce the concept of the whole child: physical activities, social interactions, and creative and affective development. Each area of development contributes to the child's cognitive learning.

"Identity crisis in the field of early childhood education" is the way Wolery and Brookfield-Norman (1988) refer to the differing viewpoints educators hold in regard to children's emerging literacy. They point out that terms such as *preoperational* and *readiness* are commonly used to describe the cognitive skills and abilities of children who are no longer infants, but are not yet reading, writing, and doing arithmetic. These skills are pre-academic skills, necessary for young children to acquire during the preschool years if later they are to engage in formal academic activities.

Many parents, striving for what they perceive as best for their children, believe that early, formal instruction in reading, writing, and math will help their children succeed in school. Preschools and child care centers are pressured to demonstrate that children are doing more than playing, that they are learning

pre-academics prerequisite skills that provide the foundation for the formal academic training that usually starts in first grade

Did You Get It?

What outcome has emerged out of the need to introduce preacademic skills into early education, in the opinion of Parlakian (2010)?

a. Identity crisis in the field of education.

b. Learning something worthwhile.

c. A reduction in children's natural curiosity, enthusiasm, and interest in learning.

d. An increase in children's enthusiasm and interest in learning.

Take the full quiz on CourseMate.

"something worthwhile." The pressure has led to many early childhood programs emphasizing paper-and-pencil tasks and workbook exercises. Such activities represent an inappropriate and ineffectual teaching format for the majority of young children. Drill-and-practice activities may actually reduce children's natural curiosity, enthusiasm, and interest in learning (Parlakian, 2010). They also are contrary to the philosophy of this text and to the statement of Developmentally Appropriate Practices (DAPs) put forth by Copple and Bredekamp (2009). However, a quality early childhood program cannot be all free play. As Copple and Bredekamp point out, children benefit from engaging in self-initiated, spontaneous play and from teacher-planned and structured activities, projects, and experiences (p. 23). Blaustein (2005) expands on this position in the following statement:

> A developmentally appropriate curriculum helps channel a child's intrinsic motivation into learning activities through interactions and the child's need to relate to others; through the use of imagination and the child's need to wonder, question, and understand; and through integration and the child's need to combine new knowledge with earlier experiences. Early childhood curricula that embrace these intrinsic motivations—the basic three I's—(interaction, imagination, integration) and combine them with hands-on learning environments help children build a solid knowledge foundation. (p. 3)

17-2 What Brain Research Tells Us

Recent research on brain development has important implications for cognitive growth and learning. Only one-quarter of its potential size at birth, the brain is particularly sponge-like in the first few years. It is during this time that the brain forms a "network of neural pathways," and young children form twice as many as they need (Shore, 2003). A major developmental task at this age is to form and reinforce these links (called synapses) so that they become a permanent part of the brain's wiring. These connections happen through continual and repeated use, primarily as a child experiences "the surrounding world and forms attachments to parents, family members, and other caregivers" (Shore, 2003, p. 17). Alison Gopnick expands on this in the following statement:

> The hypothesis is that babies and very young children are using very powerful techniques for learning about the world … actually the same techniques that adults use to find out about the world around them. That is, children have the capacity to make theories, formulate hypotheses, make predictions, test predictions, even do experiments to test those predictions. (Brain Connection to Education Spring Conference, 2000)

If it is not used, the brain begins a process of discarding excess synapses after the first decade of life. Fully half have been eliminated by the teenage years. Simply stated, the growth of the brain operates on a use-it-or-lose-it principle. This means that children's brains need to be stimulated in order for the network of connections to grow and be protected from elimination. This process is of great importance to early childhood teachers, caregivers, and parents of young children. As the research implies, young children are biologically ready to learn. The question that arises, however, is, "What best supports early brain development?"

Shore (2003) writes that a decade or more of brain research has given us some answers to these questions. She cites five major points to consider:

1. There is a complex interplay between nature (genes) and nurture (environment) in the development of the brain. *Implication:* What children experience in the first few years may matter as much as their genetic makeup.

2. Early care (both positive and negative) has a "decisive and long-lasting impact" on a child's ability to learn. *Implication:* A daily helping of warm and responsive care by parents and caregivers helps a child's emotional development and self-control.

3. The brain has a great capacity to change, but some critical time periods (such as when developing vision, language, emotional controls) are more crucial than others. *Implication:* Teachers and parents can learn to take advantage of the appropriate time period for learning certain intellectual tasks.

4. Negative experiences or lack of stimulation are likely to have serious and sustained effects; the parts of the brain associated with emotion (affect) seem to show the most effect. Stress affects the brain's function in memory and critical thinking. *Implication:* Parents, teachers, and caregivers should nurture young children to lessen the effects of poverty and neglect on their lives.

5. The value of timely, well-designed, and intensive intervention is of utmost importance in brain development. *Implication:* Research provides proof that early intervention reduces developmental delays and the number of students requiring special education.

Drill-and-practice activities may actually reduce children's natural curiosity, enthusiasm, and interest in learning.

© Cengage Learning

 Connecting Developmentally Appropriate **Practice to Brain Research**

LEARNING AND THE BRAIN

Jensen (2008) summarizes some additional principles of brain-based research:

- Each brain is unique; children's brains develop at varying rates, each age- or grade-level learner should not be held to the same standards.

- Emotions run the brain: good ones create an excitement for and love of learning; bad ones affect all attempts at learning.

- The brain is run by patterns, not facts. We learn best with themes, patterns, and contextual experiences. The brain is poorly designed for formal instruction or rote memorization.

- Each of us learns through simultaneous styles, such as visual, auditory, and kinesthetic. We do not learn as well when tasks are linear or if information is presented out of context.

- All learning is mind–body. Posture and breathing affect learning.

- The brain is stimulated by challenge, novelty, and feedback in our learning environments.

Your Turn

Based on the research findings above, plan a circle time that would target the skills of matching colors and shapes. Highlight how the different activities and their formats relate to the research findings. After considering the final research finding from above ("The brain is stimulated by challenge, novelty, and feedback in our learning environments"), outline how providing a developmentally appropriate learning environment is related to this finding.

Brain research has also had an impact on those who work with children who are developmentally delayed, neurologically impaired, or both. Greenspan's work (1992; with Wider, 1997) focused on children with autism and other children with developmental delays or impairments. Through specifically designed experiences, children developed new capacities in verbal, emotional, and social functions. Benasich and Tallal (1996) worked with infants and toddlers who had a specific language disorder. Through brain imaging studies, early detection of an auditory processing problem allowed the researchers to intervene at a much earlier age.

Clearly then, information about brain research is of critical importance to parents and educators for all children, no matter their abilities or disabilities.

Did You Get It?

What is the relationship between brain size and brain development in terms of the impact on cognitive growth and learning?

a. From preschool to school age the brain forms a network of neural pathways; a major developmental task at this age is to form and reinforce these links so that they become a permanent part of the brain's wiring.

b. From the time of birth to the first few years the brain forms a network of neural pathways; a major developmental task at this age is to form and reinforce these links so that they become a permanent part of the brain's wiring.

c. Brain development occurs through continual and repeated connections.

d. The pattern for cognitive growth and learning is set within the brain during the first few weeks of life.

Take the full quiz on CourseMate.

☀ 17-3 Banning Academics: Ill-Advised?

While the integration of child-initiated play with teacher-structured activities is important for all children, it is especially so for children from low-income or academically disadvantaged families.

Schickedanz (1999) agrees and questions if the movement to ban academics in preschools is not ill-advised in that it further delays those children who need it most. These children are denied opportunities to get the same kind of academic foundation that the majority of children get as a part of everyday family life. "For children who do not get academic learning at home, academically stimulating preschools are an opportunity equalizer" (p. 12).

Drawing on extensive research, Schickedanz asserts that "Preschoolers *are* ready for academic content—lots of it" (p. 11). Her conclusion is that teaching methods—not academics per se—are the preschool problem; that academic learning *can be embedded* in experiences that are appropriate for young children.

To conclude this discussion, let's emphasize once again: *Learning experiences should never be presented in the form of workbooks, prescribed paper-and-pencil tasks, or* **rote memorization**. Such activities are not appropriate in any early childhood curriculum or for any young child. Most early childhood educators now accept that cognitive and intellectual activities and spontaneous play are not incompatible. Quality programs can embrace both and continue to "preserve childhood" (Greenberg, 1990).

rote memorization refers to memorizing without understanding

Developmentally Appropriate Pre-Academic Experiences 17-4

Emerging literacy and early concept development can be observed in most infants.

A nine-month-old infant with a serious hearing impairment reached for the therapist's earring. The therapist took it off. The baby then grasped the therapist's chin and turned her head so he could see and then reached for the other earring. It seems obvious this infant already was exploring rudimentary math concepts of twos and pairs as well as the spatial concept of symmetry and balance.

Children with disabilities function all along the developmental continuum in cognitive skills. A child who has severe motor disabilities may be advanced in her intellectual ability. The infant mentioned above was off to a good start in understanding math concepts. How well this infant's lead would be maintained depends on the intervention services and learning opportunities available to him.

Many children with developmental disabilities never realize their cognitive potential; others excel beyond their typically developing peers. This chapter, therefore, will not approach cognitive learning for children with disabilities (or the gifted) as being somehow different from intellectual learning for all other children. Instead, the emphasis will be on *starting where the child is* and working from there, step by step.

In early childhood programs, the teacher's role in facilitating cognitive development is to set the scene and then follow the children's lead. On the basis of those leads, teachers guide children into needed learning. A first criterion is that teachers respond to children's interest, questions, and readiness for further information, then guide and prompt children to use skills and information they already have. This is an important concept of developmentally appropriate practices.

17-4a ■ Direct Teaching

During pre-academic activities, the teacher is likely to engage in limited direct teaching. Teachers may suggest to children what to do and say, but mostly they blend direct teaching with an indirect and facilitative approach.

A child asked, "What's that?" and pointed to a picture of a little-known animal. The teacher engaged in direct teaching by reading the caption, "okapi."

The teacher's role in facilitating cognitive development is to set the scene and then follow the child's lead.

© Cengage Learning

After reading the name, the teacher immediately asked the child to name it, too. The teacher then reinforced the correctness of the child's response: "That's right; it is an okapi." The child (and the other children) still seemed interested, and so the teacher took advantage of this teaching opportunity. He opened another book with pictures of familiar jungle animals and helped the children find a somewhat similar animal (a giraffe) and discover the likenesses and differences between it and the okapi.

17-4b ■ Embedded Learning

embedded learning opportunities (ELOs) the intentional incorporation of specific learning objectives into play and routine classroom activities

While some early childhood programs present cognitive tasks in structured settings at specified periods, opportunities for learning actually occur throughout the day. **Embedded learning** is an effective approach for providing additional practice of new skills (Daugherty, Grisham-Brown, & Hemmeter, 2001). Embedded learning is defined as a procedure in which children are given additional opportunities to practice and learn individualized goals (IEP) within the context of a regular classroom activity. The activity is expanded or modified so that the learning opportunity is meaningful and interesting to the children (Pretti-Frontczak & Bricker, 2004).

Embedding instruction into developmentally appropriate activities is recommended practice for early childhood programs. It provides children with opportunities to acquire and practice skills within a variety of settings and activities, and with a variety of individuals and materials (Sandall, McLean, & Smith, 2000). For embedded learning to be effective, opportunities must be planned and implemented.

The planning steps for embedded learning opportunities (ELOs) follow:

- Clarify the learning or IEP objective. Make the objective appropriate to the classroom or playground context.

- Determine the child's current level of performance of the particular objective. Do this by observing and recording.

- Determine the times and places during the classroom day when ELOs will be inserted.

- Use the classroom schedule to identify times and activities where instruction is feasible. (Refer to Figure 13-3 in Chapter 13 for an example.)

- Include the use of transition times from one activity to another.

- Design the instructional interaction. Decide what you will say and do.

- Implement the instruction during the planned times and places. Implement instruction many times during the day. Remember the child has not been successful with just the usual opportunities. The child needs extra practice.

- Establish an easy-to-use data collection method to monitor the child's performance. (See Chapter 18 for information on data collection.)

Consider the following example: A child with limited cognitive skills is trying to count blocks while putting them on the shelf. A responsive teacher makes a game of it, teaching the two skills together. This is the essence of embedded learning: spontaneous and informal, in the context of an activity that has meaning for the child (Lieber, Schwartz, Sandall, Horn, & Wolery, 1999; Schwartz, Garfinkle, Joseph, & McBride, 1999). In such an approach, cognitive development often goes unlabeled and unrecognized as real learning or real school work. Thus, the work-play argument persists, despite decades of research indicating that children's work and play are inseparable.

17-4c ■ Computers and Assistive Technology

Increasingly young children have computer experience before they enter an early childhood program. Computers can be important additions to inclusive classrooms. For children with significant disabilities, computers and other types of **assistive technology** can foster independence by providing help with mobility and communication. When technical support is provided in the classroom, teachers and the assistive technician work together to plan and implement the program for a given child.

assistive technology
various kinds of equipment, such as a computerized Braille system or voice synthesizer, designed to facilitate learning and communications for individuals with disabilities

Parents and educators have been cautioned about the use of technology and screen time for young children. There is conflicting evidence as well as opinion on the value of technology in early childhood education settings. One thing is certain, technology is a part of everyday life for many children and their families, and that number is increasing. It is important for early childhood educators and parents to make informed decisions about its use both at school and in the home.

According to the joint position paper prepared by the NAEYC and the Fred Rogers Center (2012), technology and interactive media can foster effective learning and development when early childhood educators use them intentionally. The use of these tools must be within the framework of developmentally appropriate practice and must support learning goals established for individual children. Figure 17-2 lists the guiding principles described in their position paper.

Computers have tremendous potential as teaching tools for all children if children's interactions with them are monitored and supported by adults (Davidson, 1990; Deiner, 2004). The value of computers in the classroom is directly related to the quality and appropriateness of the software that is used.

Principles to Guide the Appropriate Use of Technology and Interactive Media as Tools in Early Childhood Programs Serving Children from Birth through Age 8

- Above all, the use of technology tools and interactive media should not harm children.

- Developmentally appropriate practices must guide decisions about whether and when to integrate technology and interactive media into early childhood programs.

- Professional judgment is required to determine if and when a specific use of technology or media is age-appropriate, individually appropriate, and culturally and linguistically appropriate.

- Developmentally appropriate teaching practices must always guide the selection of any classroom materials, including technology and interactive media.

- Appropriate use of technology and media depends on the age, developmental level, needs, interests, linguistic background, and abilities of each child.

- Effective uses of technology and media are active, hands-on, engaging, and empowering; give the child control; provide adaptive scaffolds to ease the accomplishment of tasks; and are used as one of many options to support children's learning.

- When used appropriately, technology and media can enhance children's cognitive and social abilities.

- Interactions with technology and media should be playful and support creativity, exploration, pretend play, active play, and outdoor activities.

- Technology tools can help educators make and strengthen home–school connections.

- Technology and media can enhance early childhood practice when integrated into the environment, curriculum, and daily routines.

- Assistive technology must be available as needed to provide equitable access for children with special needs.

- Technology tools can be effective for dual language learners by providing access to a family's home language and culture while supporting English language learning.

- Digital literacy is essential to guiding early childhood educators and parents in the selection, use, integration, and evaluation of technology and interactive media.

- *Digital citizenship* is an important part of digital literacy for young children.

- Early childhood educators need training, professional development opportunities, and examples of successful practice to develop the needed technology and media knowledge, skills, and experience.

- Research is needed to better understand how young children use and learn with technology and interactive media and also to better understand any short- and long-term effects.

Source: National Association for the Education of Young Children and the Fred Rogers Center for Early Learning and Children's Media (2012). *Technology and Interactive Media as Tools in Early Childhood Programs Serving Children from Birth through Age 8.* Retrieved from http://www.naeyc.org/files/naeyc/PS_technology_WEB.pdf

The software market for children's programs is enormous and changes constantly. Programs can teach visual perceptual skills, eye–hand coordination, reaction speed, and attention.

While there are many positives to the use of computers, some drawbacks need to be considered. As Herschkowitz and Herschkowitz (2004) point out in their book *A Good Start in Life*, when children are spending time on the computer they are not spending time engaged in other important activities such as reading books, drawing, exercising their muscles, and interacting by using language and social skills. They go on to note that young children's visual systems are still developing and that they need to practice all types of eye–hand coordination, not just pushing buttons.

Finally, careful consideration must be given to the types of programs. Many video games contain violent or inappropriate themes for young children. Parents and caregivers need to monitor content to ensure it is developmentally appropriate. (See the Children's Software Review website listed at the end of this chapter for examples of available programs.)

17-4d ■ Fostering Eagerness to Learn

Children are born ready and eager to learn. Preserving and promoting this eagerness has long been a goal of early education. The teacher's role is to help children observe, ask, and find out about things that interest them. Children of all developmental levels, from the most delayed to the most gifted, need activities that support awareness, curiosity, and the urge to question. Activities that involve sensory experiences—touching, seeing, hearing, tasting, and smelling—are essential. In other words, children need a learning environment in which they are free to experience materials and activities through their senses in their own way and at their own pace. That is developmentally appropriate practice in a nutshell. Children with sensory losses such as blindness need such experiences, too, if their eagerness to learn is to be preserved. However, they often need teachers' help in learning to use their functioning senses to the best possible advantage.

17-4e ■ Engaging Children's Minds

As Katz and Chard (2000) put it, "Children's minds should be engaged in ways that deepen their understanding of their own experiences." At the same time, preschool teachers can indirectly but significantly advance children's anticipation of learning to read, write, and do math. Teachers accomplish this by writing out a child's questions, reading the question back to the child, and helping the child find the answer or make a measurement. They help children keep a log by writing down what each child dictates about observed changes (a plant's growth, perhaps). With these kinds of activities, most children, when they reach the primary grades, are ready and eager to learn to read about, tell about, write about—even measure—their experiences. The responsibility of early childhood teachers is to make convincing arguments on behalf of these important embedded learning practices. It is the teacher's willingness to articulate this philosophy that often sways parents, administrators, and policymakers who may be pushing for workbooks and other paper-and-pencil tasks (Wolery & Bredekamp, 1994).

17-4f ■ Valuing Today's Learning

An important goal in teachers' pre-academic planning is recognizing that today's living and learning are important dimensions in overall development. Enjoyable and challenging activities contribute to children's everyday sense of well-being and competence as well as to their long-term, school-related accomplishments. Everything that is recommended for infants and young children—good nutrition, quality child care, medical attention—has the same dual purpose: fostering everyday well-being and long-term development.

Expecting children to engage in activities that do not relate to their interests or developmental level can snuff out eagerness to learn and interest in school. Children seldom enjoy or master tasks that are a poor developmental match. True, countless numbers of children survive the mismatch during their early years, but countless others experience extremes of frustration, resulting in a poor opinion of themselves and their ability to learn; a dislike of school, school work, and teachers; and school-related avoidance behaviors such as crying, acting out, daydreaming, and chronic stomachaches.

17-4g ■ Readiness Skills

Intellectual and emerging literacy skills are a mix of social, cognitive, language, and motor skills, as well as accumulated experiences and acquired knowledge (Adams, 1994). These emerging literacy skills often are referred to as *readiness skills*, prerequisites to ongoing and future academic accomplishments. Let us now look more closely at the **readiness** concept. In the traditional sense, readiness consists of built-in patterns of change. These account for the development of progressively more complex skills.

readiness a child's ability to learn that takes into account prerequisite physical, cognitive, language, and social skills

This theoretical position led to the *readiness-as-maturation*, or "ages and stages," approach to development: each child *unfolds* (matures) automatically, at his or her own pace, very nearly independent of experience.

The *readiness-as-learning* theory attributes changes in children's skills to experience and the step-by-step learning of developmental tasks. For example, if an infant has learned to recognize food, find her own mouth and hold a spoon right side up most of the time, that child is likely *ready* to begin the more complex behavior of self-feeding. In other words, children are ready to learn a new and more complex skill when they can perform and synchronize the necessary, though less difficult, skills that precede the more complex skill.

From the unfolding (maturation) point of view, it is assumed children will learn what they need to learn simply by growing up in a safe, nurturing environment. When a child shows developmental irregularities or delays, the cause often is cited as immaturity: "The child is not ready. Let's wait and see." This puts many children on hold during a critical developmental period (Graue, 1998). The result may be further delay in development and a worsening of the child's problem. Often that is the case with infants with an undiagnosed hearing loss, whose language and cognitive skills become extensively but unnecessarily impaired.

The learning theory approach emphasizes experience: Children must have opportunities to learn. Many home and community environments do not (or cannot) support essential early learning experiences. In such settings, children may have little opportunity to master the necessary readiness skills that seem to come naturally to most children. Learning theory also demonstrates that all developmental tasks and all readiness skills can be taught through a sequencing or task-analysis approach. These teaching strategies have proved especially useful in working with young children with developmental problems who often have difficulty acquiring readiness skills on their own. The teacher's task is to identify missing skills in each child and then teach him or her, step by step.

Readiness skills likely to be missing include:

- adequate attention span
- ability to imitate
- perceptual motor efficiency
- fine motor controls (eye–hand–wrist coordination)
- ability to formulate concepts
- short-term and long-term memory
- ability to follow instructions

Each of these skill areas, as well as specific pre-reading, pre-writing, and pre-math skills, will be discussed separately in this chapter, although, in reality, they are inseparable. Academically related skills are intertwined with each other and with all other areas of development. This interrelatedness is the essence of the *whole-child* concept of development. As an example, when children are recalling a trip to the zoo, all skills come into play, even overlap, as the teacher helps them talk about, paint, draw, or dramatize what they saw, heard, and did. This interrelatedness of developmental skills also makes a convincing argument against an academic, subject-matter approach to the education of young children.

Learning readiness develops over years, as young children are exposed to multiple social experiences with socially competent adults and peers, as they have the opportunity to participate in regular routines in a safe and predictable environment, and when they have ongoing opportunities to play with and learn about various materials that stimulate their exploration and imaginations (Blaustein, 2005).

Attention span The length of time that an individual is able to concentrate on an activity is critical to all learning. Attention is critical to problem solving and performing tasks. Children have to focus on the most relevant parts of a situation while filtering out all irrelevant background noise, and they have to be able to keep this up for a sufficient length of time (Herschkowitz and Herschkowitz, 2004). When working a puzzle, a child needs to be able to focus on the frame board and the puzzle pieces while ignoring other children's play activities. Children's ability (or inability) to focus their attention depends largely on classroom arrangements.

Keisha, a typically developing three-year-old, picked up and put down puzzle pieces from several puzzles that were mixed and scattered about the table. She looked at the puzzle frames, put the pieces down, wandered around, took a much-too-difficult puzzle off the shelf, dumped it out, looked at it briefly, tried to take a completed puzzle away from another child, and then left the area.

Keisha's short attention span—at least for puzzle work—can be related directly to a poorly arranged environment. A child cannot be successful when materials are too difficult or haphazardly presented. Attractive materials and an orderly presentation go a long way in determining children's concentration. Even so, there are children who have trouble becoming involved on their own. They need help in getting started.

Manipulative materials matched to children's skill level provide informal but fun practice for fine motor skills.

Once their attention is engaged, they, too, learn to focus. Bailey and Wolery (1992) suggest several ways that teachers can help children focus their attention.

- Provide materials that are appealing and colorful, that can be manipulated, and that have built-in feedback, such as many of the Montessori materials.

- Offer participation as a privilege rather than a responsibility: Children who finish putting blocks away will then be *allowed* to come to story time.

- Give children an immediate role: "Jimmy has the punch to punch the train tickets."

- Instruct or prompt an activity: "I'll help you start a fence at this end. Where shall I put my first block?"

- Identify children's preferences for materials; preferred materials result in longer engagement.

Imitation and modeling As noted in several other chapters, the ability to imitate is essential. When trying to learn a new skill such as playing a game, jumping rope, or pronouncing a new word, the first step is to try to model the behavior that was observed. This process—observing and modeling—is repeated until the learner is satisfied with his or her performance or decides to abandon the effort. Most infants and young children imitate spontaneously. They do not have to be taught, but they do need good models and ample opportunity to practice. Peek-a-boo games, finger plays, action songs, chants, and rhyming games found in most cultures probably were devised unintentionally to motivate imitation. Such activities, popular in most preschool programs, exist for the same reason.

A distinction should be made between *learning through imitation* and *learning to imitate*. Children who do not imitate spontaneously must be taught, if they are to learn other developmental skills. However, the inability to imitate often goes unrecognized and so becomes the cause of continuing learning difficulties. When a child enrolls in a group, an informal assessment of imitation skills should be a priority. (A simplified version of a game such as do-as-I-do can tell a teacher a great deal about a child's ability to imitate.) If imitation skills are lacking, initial teaching priorities should be concentrated in that area. Bailey and Wolery (1992) offer the following suggestions.

- Imitate the child. Imitating the child's vocalizations and gestures often stimulates the child and also reinforces the child's further efforts.

- Provide models appropriate for the child's level of development. If a child at seven years of age is functioning more like a three-year-old, then behaviors typical of the younger age should be the starting models, with special concentration on those behaviors the child already has.

- Provide whatever assistance is needed to help the child learn to imitate. Placing a mirror in front of the child, for example, allows the child to judge the accuracy of his or her imitations.

- If necessary, be directive in teaching the child to imitate. Physically put the child through an imitative response. (A teacher singing "Head, Shoulders, Knees, and Toes" would stop singing at the point he modeled the motor movement; if the child did not imitate, the teacher would guide the child's hands to the correct locations.)

- Make imitating a rewarding and playful experience. Learning to imitate should be fun.

- Provide positive feedback and encouragement for approximations (first efforts) to an imitative response. When a child finally points to an object, even though it may not be the one requested, the teacher responds positively: "You're *pointing* to a blue truck. Good for you! Now let's find the red one, and you can point to it, too."

perceptual-motor skills movement generated by sensory messages, by what is seen, heard, touched, tasted, or smelled

sensory integration more than one sense working together to understand a sensory message and to translate the message into appropriate action

Perceptual-motor skills Perceptual-motor skills are made up of two closely related processes. One has to do with understanding sensory messages: what is seen, heard, touched, tasted, or smelled. The second is the translation of the messages into appropriate actions. Generally, more than one sense is involved in a response; this is referred to as **sensory integration**. Following are three examples of perceptual-motor sensory integration.

Children who do not imitate spontaneously must be taught.

© Cengage Learning

- *A two-year-old stops her play and turns at the sound of an engine. She looks up, moves her eyes back and forth, and then points to an airplane. This child is exhibiting integrated visual (seeing) and auditory (hearing) skills resulting in the appropriately matched motor responses of turning, scanning, and pointing.*

- *A four-year-old picks up a bar of cocoa butter, smells it, bites off a corner, and then spits it out while making a wry face. The child is expressing appropriate smell and taste perceptions and responding with relevant perceptual motor responses. The cocoa butter smelled like candy, and she took a bite. It tasted more like soap than candy, so she spit it out while making a face indicating an unpleasant taste.*

- *A five-year-old, during group time, reaches into the mystery bag and verbally identifies unseen objects by touch.*

Every preschool activity involves various forms of perceptual-motor activity: climbing, jumping, riding wheel toys, watching a caterpillar creep, splashing in puddles, block building, playing with table toys, painting, working with clay, coloring, cutting, and pasting. Music, stories, and dramatic play provide opportunities to pantomime and pretend and thereby practice the perceptual motor skills essential to everyday living.

Children with delayed perceptual-motor skills often receive incomplete or distorted sensory messages. In some instances, children have become nearly immobilized because they are so distrustful of moving about. For example, children with poor depth perception are sometimes hurt and badly frightened by stepping off into unanticipated space. Thus, children with sensory problems often need special activities, adapted materials, and additional support in using their intact senses.

Every preschool activity requires perceptual-motor skills.

© Cengage Learning

17-4h ■ Fine Motor Skills

Fine motor skills include eye–hand coordination and efficient use of fingers, hands, and wrists. These skills are closely related to perceptual-motor skills. Both are essential in learning self-care skills as well as learning to use all kinds of tools: paintbrushes, hammers, crayons, and pencils. Practice in fine motor control is provided by several common enjoyable developmentally appropriate activities.

- water play—pouring, squeezing, measuring
- block building—stacking, bridging, balancing, putting away
- creative arts—painting, stitchery, hammering, woodworking, modeling, cutting, pasting, crayoning
- housekeeping—dressing dolls, pouring "tea," stirring "soup," and setting the table

Manipulative materials, sometimes referred to as *table toys*, are especially good for promoting perceptual-motor skills. These developmentally appropriate examples include some children's favorites.

- wooden beads and strings with metal tips
- puzzles and parquetry blocks
- picture dominoes and Lotto
- nesting and stacking cups, kitty-in-the-keg, form boxes
- pegs and pegboards, hammer-and-nail sets
- Montessori graduated cylinders and color boards
- paper and crayons, or whiteboards with markers

When appropriately matched to children's skill levels, manipulative materials ensure practice sessions that are informal and fun. All children can use them successfully because they are so readily adaptable to children with varying levels of development. The following are just a few of the possible ways teachers can adapt manipulative materials.

- Teachers might offer only the largest wooden beads with a stiff wire on which to string them. (A straightened coat hanger, ends wrapped with tape, works well.)

- They might provide select puzzles with few pieces, each piece a recognizable object. When a child has mastered the simple puzzles, but the next ones seem too complex, teachers need to be inventive. Several of the inside pieces of more difficult puzzles can be taped down from underneath with a strip of tape doubled back on itself. These pieces remain in the frame when the child turns the puzzle out. Fewer pieces have to be replaced to complete the task, and the job is simplified because finding the fit for border pieces is usually easier. The task gradually can be made more difficult by taping down fewer and fewer pieces. The advantage to this procedure is that each time the child completes the task, she is rewarded by seeing the completed puzzle.

- Teachers can present only four or five of the largest nesting cups (in order), hand them to the child one by one to ensure successful nesting from the outset, and then let the child begin to pick up the cups and nest them. As the teacher gradually randomizes the order of presentation, the child becomes more proficient, and more cups can be added, one at a time.

Concept formation Concepts and concept formation are difficult terms to define without becoming too technical. In this text, concepts will be defined as *internal images or ideas* (mental activities) *that organize thinking*. Concepts enable us to make sense out of our world. By continuously formulating new concepts, children impose order on the many things they must learn during their early years. A number of subskills related to concept formation are described here.

Discrimination Concept development depends on the ability to *discriminate*, that is, perceive likenesses and differences among related objects and events. Put even more simply, it is the ability to tell things apart, to specify same or different, or to match objects, sounds, and ideas in terms of one or more attributes (characteristics). Opportunities to practice making both simple and complex discriminations are found throughout the school day.

- At music time, the teacher introduces an improvised song asking, "Who is wearing sandals? Boots? Running shoes? Blue socks? Striped socks? No socks?"

- During story time, a teacher asks children to identify how the story is the same as or different from a previous story read by the class.

- At the science table, children are asked to sort rocks by size and texture.

- During cleanup, children replace unit blocks according to the size and shape drawn on the shelf.

- As part of a pre-academic activity, children copy a patterned string of wooden beads—a small, round, blue bead, a big, square, red bead, a long, green bead—repeated several times. This task is complex in that the beads vary on three attributes: shape, size, and color.

Concept development includes the ability to perceive likenesses and differences.

© Cengage Learning

The fine motor and perceptual-motor skills are demanding, as well. It might be that a child could make the necessary discriminations but not have the motor skills for stringing the beads. This is an instance where the teacher would need to make an adaptation in materials, perhaps providing a wire rather than a string for the child to thread the beads onto.

Discrimination tasks can be adapted to fit any developmental level. For gifted children, the bead-stringing task can be made more complex by introducing number concepts as well as color, space, and shape: repeats of three small, round, blue beads; two large, square, red beads; one long, green bead. Or it can be made very simple: a square, red bead alternating with a square, blue bead; or simpler yet, having the child select and string only large blue beads (with only large red beads in the basket as distracters). Adaptations for individual differences are unlimited.

Classification The process of imposing order on objects and events is another characteristic of concept formation. It is the ability to classify; that is, to form *categories*. Children learn that cats, dogs, and squirrels have certain characteristics in common: fur, four legs, a tail, and so on. On the basis of these shared attributes, the creatures all fall into the category of *animal*. Each category is subject to further breakdown as the child's experiences broaden. *Dog* becomes a category by itself. Then the child learns to discriminate among different kinds of dogs—poodles, collies, Airedales.

Seriation *Seriation* is the process of arranging objects and events along orderly and related dimensions. Everyday examples include:

- tall, middle-sized, shortest, and eventually, "These tall ones are taller than those tall ones."

- first, last, next-to-last

- happy, sad, saddest of all

- the daily schedule of activities

Many early childhood activities are designed to help children learn to make comparisons about quantities, time and space, and affect (feelings). Learning to tell about what happened in the order of occurrence is another seriation skill that many older preschoolers begin to master.

"Yesterday we went to Grandma's. We got to play in the attic. Then we had dinner, but first Grandma made us wash our hands and face 'cause we got so dirty. After dinner, Grandpa read to us, and then it was time to go home."

Other activities lend themselves to seriation practice and to endless adaptations. Children can retell a story that has just been read, or teachers can ask, "What comes next?" when reading a familiar story. Sequenced picture cards (commercial or teacher-made) are useful. The cards tell a story when arranged in proper order: the first card may show a child digging a hole in the ground, the second may show planting a seed, and the third pulling up a carrot. For more advanced children, the series can be longer and more complex, including pictures related to watering, weeding, and sprouting. For a child who finds this task challenging, the teacher might use just two pictures: a child climbing up on a stool and then jumping down.

Spatial and temporal relationships Learning how objects and events are related to space, to time, and to the child is another aspect of concept formation. Spatial and temporal (time) concepts include:

- on, in, under

- in front of, behind, next to

- between, in the middle, second from the end

- yesterday, today, tomorrow
- soon, after a while, later, not yet

Many children seem to learn such concepts automatically. However, some children need direct instruction. Spatial and temporal concepts are best taught as children themselves are moving about in space and time. For example, each child must learn to recognize his or her body-occupying space in relationship to the body space of others. This may not come easily, and certainly it does not come early. Toddlers may plow through other toddlers as if they did not exist.

Active play is especially good for developing spatial awareness. Outdoors, a teacher might comment, "Tony, you climbed *so high*. You are *on top of* the ladder box." If the child is having difficulty forming spatial concepts, the teacher should do an immediate follow-up: "Where are you, Tony?" and wait for the child to respond. If the child does not respond, the teacher models the words, "High. On top." When the child repeats the statement, the teacher corroborates: "That's right, Tony. You are *high*; you are *on top*." Learning to understand time is difficult for most children. As with spatial concepts, time concepts are best learned in relationship to play and everyday activities. Young children better understand short and more immediate time intervals.

"Time to come in after you run around the track two more times." "Snack comes when we finish this story." "We will get back in time for lunch."

17-4i ■ Memory

The ability to remember is necessary to all new learning. Two kinds of memory are required: long-term and short-term—remembering what took place a while back as well as what happened in the immediate past. Tasks requiring rote memorization are seldom appropriate for children. Research shows that if a child is able to describe an event at the time it occurs, the child will be more likely to recall the event later (Herschowitz & Herschkowitz, 2004). Activities that encourage children to practice remembering within their everyday work and play activities are the kind that foster learning, such as the following developmentally appropriate activity:

1. Conversational questions *of interest to the child* (with teacher prompts, after a suitable pause):
   - What did you have for breakfast? ... (orange juice? cereal? anything else?)
   - Where does your kitten sleep? ... (in a basket?)
   - What was the caterpillar doing on the leaf? ... (crawling? chewing on the leaf?)
2. Remembering each other's names and teachers' names, and using these names appropriately.
3. Remembering where materials are stored, so as to get them out and put them away properly.
4. Telling what objects have been removed in games such as cover-the-tray.
5. Story and picture-reading activities as described earlier.
6. Leaving the bathroom in prescribed order for the next children who will be using it.

For children with cognitive, neurological, or related problems, the teacher often begins memory training by telling the child what comes next: "The paper towel goes in the waste basket." The teacher follows up immediately: "Where does the paper towel go?" (The child only has to remember long enough to repeat the information *or comply*. It is important to give adequate time to respond. In teaching towel disposal, for example, the teacher must allow time for the child's memory to become charged and produce action. The time lag varies from child to child.)

17-4j ■ Following Directions

All children need to learn to follow directions and carry out requests. Whenever a child has repeated difficulty in following directions, teachers ask themselves:

- Does the child hear (or see) well enough to know what is expected?
- Does the child have the necessary vocabulary to understand the request?
- Does the child understand the concepts (understand *match* when the teacher says, "Match circles of the same color")?
- Is the child able to imitate the behaviors expected, as when the teacher demonstrates how to fold a paper in half?
- Are the instructions too complicated or given too rapidly?

Three- and four-step directions, spoken in rapid sequence, are more than most young children can manage. It is true that a few older preschoolers might be able to carry through on, "Would you go to the sink and wet a sponge—I think there's one under the sink or in the bathroom—and then wipe up all that messy paint on the floor and the table legs?" Many others would be completely lost. A few might try to carry out the last step in the direction (the only thing they remember) by rubbing at the paint on the table leg.

The younger or less capable the child, the simpler the directions should be. *It is important that teachers take nothing for granted about what children understand.* For some children, directions need to be given one at a time. The process works best when a teacher gets down to a child's level and speaks directly to the child. Language needs to be clear and free of unnecessary words or explanations.

> *"Marty, we're going to have to get this paint wiped up. Would you come to the sink (pause) and find a sponge?" When the child has sponge in hand, the teacher gives the next direction: "Now wet the sponge." If the teacher wants to make sure the child does not cross the room dripping water all the way, an intermediate instruction should be given: "Squeeze the water out of it." Some children might not know what the teacher expects, so the teacher says, "Like this," pantomiming how to squeeze a sponge.*
>
> *"Now let's go over and wipe up the paint on the floor." When that is accomplished, the teacher can draw the child's attention to the paint on the table legs.*

Most children can learn to follow directions if they are allowed to begin with one-step directions. When the child has mastered one-step directions, it is logical to move to two- and then perhaps three-step directions. It is a good idea to pair a child with a developmental disability with a child who is developing typically: "Tina and Marcos, will you get the chalk and the small chalkboards and put them on the big round table?"

17-4k ■ Emerging Literacy

As we discussed at the beginning of this chapter, emerging literacy refers to what children know about reading and writing *before* they can actually read and write. It includes all of the experiences, good and bad, that children have had with books, language, and print from birth onward (Parlakian, 2010). Emerging literacy skills are often cited as the most important academic skills for school readiness.

Research has demonstrated the link between language development and literacy (Strickland & Shanahan, 2004). The development of language and literacy skills is social. Parents play the most critical role in language development. The more time parents spend talking to the child, the larger the child's vocabulary becomes and the faster it develops (Hart & Risley, 1995). In addition to language development, alphabetic knowledge, print knowledge, and phonological knowledge have all been identified as key to children becoming successful readers.

Effective early literacy instruction provides preschool children with developmentally appropriate settings, materials, experiences, and social support that encourage early forms of reading and writing to flourish and develop into conventional literacy. Roskos, Christie, and Richgels (2003) break teaching of literacy into eight specific strategies:

- Rich teacher talk
- Storybook reading
- Phonological awareness activities
- Alphabet activities
- Support for emergent reading
- Support for emergent writing
- Shared book experience
- Integrated content focused activities

Emerging literacy refers to what children know about reading and writing before they can actually read and write.

© Cengage Learning

Rich Teacher Talk As stated previously, talking to children is the most effective way to help them develop language and to increase their vocabularies. Children should be engaged in conversations both individually and as members of groups. Talking should include topics and vocabulary that are new and unfamiliar, but interesting to the child. The teacher should expand on what the child says, providing models for more descriptive and mature statements.

Storybook Reading The language and illustrations of high-quality children books depict rich stories that excite and surprise children, make them laugh, make them wonder, and make them think. Picture books should be a part of every day in the early childhood years (Strasser & Seplocha, 2010, p. 194). As the *Becoming a Nation of Readers Report* (Anderson, Hiebert, Scott, & Wilkerson, 1985) emphasized, "The single most important activity for building knowledge for their eventual success in reading is reading aloud to children." While the report was written three decades ago, the statement is still very much true today.

Reading aloud helps children make sense of what they hear and see. By reading aloud, parents and teachers serve as reading role models. If the adult is enthusiastic about reading, then children are sure to catch their enthusiasm. Not only

FIGURE 17-3

Strategies for Reading to Children of All Ages

(Adapted from *Reading Is Fundamental* and *Derry Korelak Reading Aloud with Children of All Ages*
http://www.naeyc.org/files/yc/file/200303/ReadingAloud.pdf)

Babies

- Very young babies love to hear familiar voices.
- Hold the baby in your lap; make sure the baby can see the pictures.
- Play with words, sing, and make up rhymes; include the baby's name.
- Offer the baby a toy to hold and chew while listening to you read.
- Read one or two pages at a time; gradually increase the number of pages.
- Point to and name pictures in the book.
- Stay on a page for as long as they baby is interested.
- Allow the baby to help turn the pages.

Toddlers

- Toddlers feel competent when they participate.
- Read books with rhymes and predictable words they can remember.
- Read the same books again and again, if asked. A toddler will let you know when he or she has had enough of a book.
- Change your voice to fit the characters and plot.
- Find and use puppets and other props related to the story.
- Repeat interesting words and phrases.
- Stop to comment, ask questions, and look closely at the pictures.
- Encourage a toddler to join in: turn pages, name things in pictures, make sounds, repeat rhymes and phrases, and think about what might happen next.
- Talk about the pictures and point out details a toddler might miss.
- Relate the story to a toddler's real-life experiences.

Preschoolers

- Read stories with simple plots children can retell in their own words.
- Before you begin a book, read the title, author, and illustrator; look at the cover; talk about what the book might be about; suggest things to look and listen for.
- Run your finger under the text; pause at the end of sentences.
- Use information from the book to answer children's questions.
- Ask children to look closely at the pictures to help them understand the story and make predictions about what might happen next.
- Repeat interesting words and rhymes while reading a book and at a later time.
- Pause and wait so children can say the word that ends a repetitive or predictable phrase.
- Ask thinking questions, such as "What might happen next? Where did he go? Why did she do that?"

Kindergarten and School-Age Children

- Set the stage before you begin reading. Review and discuss what you read yesterday and ask about what might happen next.
- Defer questions until after you finish reading—unless the answer is critical to understanding what's happening.
- Summarize, adapt, or skip parts of books that are too far above a child's level of understanding.
- Relate a book you are reading to one read in the past. Ask the children to discuss how they are alike and how they differ.
- Provide materials and activities that let children expand their understanding of a character, historical event, or situation.
- Stop reading the book at a suspenseful point so children will be eager for tomorrow's read-aloud time.

does reading out loud help to increase vocabulary, but also the repeated reading of favorite books builds familiarity, increasing the likelihood that children will attempt to read those books on their own.

Derry Korelak (2003) stresses the importance of reading to children of all ages. Figure 17-3 contains several of her suggested strategies for reading to young children of all ages.

Phonological Awareness Activities Phonological awareness is the ability to hear and identify the sounds of spoken and written language. Phonemes are the building blocks of words (Strasser & Seplocha, 2010). Phonological and phonemic awareness can be increased when teachers select books that focus on sounds and are based on familiar songs. In addition to reading books, other important activities include playing games, listening to poetry, and singing songs. Activities should focus on rhyming, alliteration (words starting with the same sound), and sound matching.

Alphabet Activities Activities can include playing with letters, singing the ABC song and reading ABC books, pointing out letters children see in the environment, and focusing on the letters in the children's own names. Labeling areas and materials in the classroom with printed signs can further help children become familiar with the alphabet.

17-4l ■ Support for Emergent Reading

Children should be encouraged to look at and read books on their own or with friends. Every classroom should provide a comfortable place to sit and read, filled with interesting and developmentally appropriate books. Functional print linked to class activities (e.g., daily schedules, helper charts, toy-shelf labels) and play-related print (e.g., signs, menus, employee name tags in a restaurant play center) provide another opportunity for reading. Pointing out labels on snack and food items and assisting the children in reading them also provides support for the emergent reader.

17-4m ■ Support for Emergent Writing

Children should be encouraged to use emergent forms of writing, such as scribble writing, random letter strings, and invented spelling. Do this by providing a well-stocked writing center, which includes pens, pencils, markers, a variety of kinds of paper, and book-making materials. Teachers should demonstrate how adults use writing by writing notes in front of the children or by providing shared writing demonstrations in which the teacher writes down words dictated by a child. Writing activities connected to the classroom routine, such as signing

▶II TeachSource Video Connections

© Cengage Learning 2015

English Language Learners: Partnering with Parents to Promote Oral Language and Early Literacy

Watch this video to see teacher Marie Mona meet with parents of children who are English language learners. Watch to see the relationship between the teacher and parents and to see the information shared about early language and literacy development when English is not the home language.

After watching the video, discuss the following:

1. What techniques did Marie encourage parents to use at home to strengthen their children's literacy skills? How are these different from or similar to recommendations she might give to a parent who speaks English at home?

2. What did the program do to embrace each family's home language?

Watch on CourseMate.

in for attendance, signing in to enter a play center, and providing play-related writing materials (e.g., pencils and notepads for taking orders in the restaurant play center) also provide another opportunity for the emergent writer.

17-4n ■ Shared Book Experience

Using big books and other enlarged texts with children enables the teacher to point to the print as it is read. The teacher can also draw the child's attention to the difference between the pictures and print, as well as how the pictures can support and add more to what the story is saying. Adults can model the skills of a good reader, including what they look for when reading, such as clues on the cover as to what the book might be about or clues in the text and pictures about what might happen next. The adult can also model the left-to-right and top-to-bottom sequence, as well as teach the components of the book, including cover page, title page, artist, illustrator, and publisher.

17-4o ■ Integrated Content Focused Activities

Teachers should take the children's lead, providing opportunities for children to investigate topics that are of interest to them. Literacy-based activities focused on their area of interest provide numerous ways for children to develop skills. Activities can include listening to and looking at books on the topic of interest, and assisting the children to gather more information about the topic through observations, questioning, and interviews. Information that is gathered should be recorded, either by the teacher or the child, depending on the child's age and ability. Play activities related to the theme should also be provided.

> As a result of such projects, children's language and literacy skills are advanced, and they gain valuable background knowledge. (Roskos, Christie, & Richgels, 2003, p. 4)

Literacy teaching opportunities available for teachers of young children are endless, but they require careful planning and consideration. Teachers should examine the types of literacy activities they are providing to their students, both daily and throughout the year. Neuman, Copple, and Bredekamp (2003) provide an easy-to-use tool to help teachers examine their curriculum and classroom environment to determine what they are doing to support children's reading and writing. "Taking Stock of what you do to promote literacy" is available on the NAEYC website.

Did You Get It?

How would a teacher adapt his or her teaching style during preacademic activities?

a. Engage in direct teaching.
b. Mostly give instructions as to what children need to do and say.
c. Mostly blend direct teaching with an indirect and facilitative approach.
d. Use an indirect and facilitative approach only.

Take the full quiz on CourseMate.

Case Study ▪ Supporting emerging literacy ▪

Selma, a preschool teacher, has observed that the recent science unit on seeds has fascinated her class. The class grew beans from seeds as part of the lesson. She wants to follow their interest and expand on it while focusing on literacy skills. She has already filled the book area with new books on the topics of seeds, growing plants, and spring. She has introduced more plants into the classroom. Over the upcoming weekend, a group of parents are building a raised-bed garden for the class to plant in. Tomorrow, in

the art center, each child is decorating the cover of a journal in which they can draw pictures of seeds and plants.

1. List additional ways that Selma can integrate her class's interest in growing seeds and plants with their emerging reading and writing skills.

2. Visit a library or look online and find some books that Selma might include in her library and read to her class.

Planning and Presenting 17-5 ☀ Pre-Academics

Many pre-academic skills are closely associated with reading, writing, and math. Teachers are advised to refer to Schickedanz (1999) and Greenberg (1994, 1998) for comprehensive coverage of developmentally appropriate ways of promoting early reading, writing, and math skills. Listed here are samples of such activities.

- "Reading" a series of pictures on a page from left to right and top to bottom. Many picture books and board games are set up to promote this kind of visual, pre-reading organization.

- Scribbling large, swirling circles upon circles; making marks children often describe as *writing*.

- Free-style cutting with scissors. (Some children spontaneously try to cut on the line.)

- Counting a row of objects from left to right by touching each in turn (one-to-one correspondence).

- Grouping objects in sets of two, three, or four.

- Identifying groups of objects as *the same, more,* or *less*.

- Recognizing that different but similar sounds are not the same. (Numerous songs, finger plays, poems, and teacher-improvised games contribute to this learning.)

None of these tasks is simple. They require at least minimal competence in the underlying skills discussed earlier. However, all readiness skills can be taught, and all can be sequenced to facilitate children's learning. Learning to cut on the lines will be used as an illustration of first steps in teaching a complex skill.

Julio was a seven-year-old with uncertain fine motor skills. Using a pair of specially designed scissors that allowed him to put his hand over Julio's, the teacher helped Julio learn to hold the scissors and then to "cut" the air with them. Next, the teacher prepared strips of paper 3/4-inch wide with heavy lines drawn across them at one-inch intervals. The teacher held up a strip and instructed Julio to open his scissors.

Functional print linked to class activities and play-related print (for example, signs) provide another opportunity for reading.

© Cengage Learning

The teacher then inserted the strip between the scissors blades, in contact with one of the black lines, and said, "Cut." It was a simple matter for Julio to close the scissors. Success was immediate and evident: A cleanly cut piece of paper came off with each contact. To add interest to the task, the teacher soon switched to strips of brightly colored paper, believing that Julio would not now be distracted from his cutting task by the variations in color. Julio's cuttings were put in an envelope to take home, play with, or paste into a picture at school.

A successful pre-academic program depends on careful planning, whether spontaneous and informal, teacher-initiated and conducted at group time, or assigned as table work. Choice of materials, how they are presented, and how children are grouped also determine how successfully children will learn.

17-5a ■ Grouping Children

A class of fifteen to twenty children is best divided into three or four small groups for structured activities. The number of teachers, aides, and volunteers who are available usually determines the number of groups. Group size can be increased as children become more skilled and more experienced. The closer children get to their kindergarten year, the greater is the need to have opportunities to work in larger groups. When they enter a program, children tend to be grouped according to age and experience at the time of entry. After children's skills have been assessed, they can be regrouped according to abilities, interests, or special talents. Each child's group placement needs to be reviewed every three or four months. (See Appendix B for use of the Skill Profile.) Reassessment is especially important for children in the middle-ability range. Reorganization of these children's programs often is overlooked. Teachers tend to concentrate on the brighter children and on the slower children. A child's social development also may be a factor in deciding on group placement. A shy child with high-level pre-academic skills might be placed with children who are less skilled. This provides the shy child with opportunities to practice both cognitive and social skills in a low-key, noncompetitive situation. It also allows the shy but intellectually competent child opportunities to tutor other children, thereby increasing the child's self-confidence and sense of worth (Katz & Chard, 2000). Social interactions are easier when they grow out of a child's competencies.

17-5b ■ Arranging Pre-Academic Group Activities

An overall goal for group activities is to help children stay interested, comfortable, and appropriately challenged. To ensure that children participate actively, the following arrangements are suggested. These are especially important with children who are new to the program, who are developmentally delayed or overactive, or who have trouble staying on task.

Advance preparation Before children arrive, all materials should be assembled and placed near where the group will meet. Once children are engaged, it is important that their attention not be distracted if the teacher needs to leave to search for materials. This absence may prompt inappropriate behavior, making it difficult to get the group back on task.

Familiar and preferred materials and activities To help children feel comfortable and competent from the start, begin with materials that children enjoy and are familiar with: crayons; simple puzzles and manipulatives; and pictures of well-known objects to talk about, match, and group. Note the materials and activities that are preferred by individual children. These can be presented several days in a row as a source of comfort and competence, as an indicator to increase the complexity of the task, and as reinforcers or motivators. Example: "Jolene, once you finish matching the circles, you can work the train puzzle."

Individual workspace with name cards Clearly identify each child's workspace at the table or on the floor. This promotes independent work habits and respect for personal space of others. Food trays, vinyl place mats, small rugs, and pieces of felt can be used to identify individual workspaces. Each workspace should be clearly labeled with the child's name on a card lettered in large primary print. A name may be printed in glue and sanded while wet to give it a raised texture for a child with a visual impairment.

Individual setups Manipulative or collage materials and matching tasks are best presented in individual setups. Small, shallow baskets or discarded produce or meat trays work well. Such an arrangement reduces the tendency of many young children to grab and hoard materials. It also reduces conflict while children are learning to work in a relatively confined space.

Short periods Start with short periods of time, perhaps from three to five minutes at the beginning, depending upon the age and interest level of the children. Gradually lengthen the time. One of the first restructurings of group membership may be based on children's span of attention. Activities should always be concluded *before* children lose interest. As children get ready for kindergarten, and, later, for primary grades, increasingly longer work periods should be provided.

Moving about Young children can sit still and be quiet for only brief periods of time. To expect otherwise can lead to behavior problems. Preacademic activities need to include tasks where moving about is made legitimate by the teacher. For example, children might be asked to retrieve or return materials or participate in a game of

Before children arrive, all materials should be assembled and ready for them to use.

© Cengage Learning

Clearly identify each child's workspace.

© Cengage Learning

Pre-academic time needs to include tasks where it is all right to move about.

"Find the ... ." They may be invited to stand, clap, jump, spin around, hop from one colored square to another, or walk around the table or circle to observe or help another child.

Changing tasks If a child is inattentive or frustrated, the teacher should first examine the immediate learning situation. Almost without fail, the problem lies not with the child, but in the learning environment. Materials and activities may need to be changed so they more closely match the child's interests and ability level. It is helpful to have additional materials handy to present as alternatives or to offer to children who finish early.

Transition activities From the start, children should be introduced to the idea of self-directed transition activities, or **holding activities**. These are activities that children can work on independently while waiting for group activities to begin. Holding activities are open-ended with no particular starting or stopping points: coloring, stringing beads, working with form boards, looking at books. They require little supervision or assistance. Just before the planned activities are to begin, the teacher gives a warning that it will soon be time to put those materials away. Putting them aside is just one more of the routines that underpin the program day. All children can and should learn about classroom routines. Occasionally a child is truly reluctant to relinquish a transition activity. In that case, the teacher helps the child put the materials aside, often with the promise that the child can go back to it during the next discovery-learning period. The material must be held for the child and the promise honored.

holding activities activities children can work on independently while waiting for group activities to begin

17-5c ■ Enjoying Teacher-Directed Activities

All learning activities should be enjoyable. When teacher-directed sessions are engaging, children will be eager to participate. Eagerness promotes successful learning. Children's successful learning is enjoyable for teachers: It represents a teacher's success as a teacher. With that kind of reward (motivation), teachers devote more time, effort, and creativity to their teaching. The result? Their teaching gets ever better, and their enjoyment increases proportionately. A positive and mutually reinforcing system is created for both children and teachers.

Summary

▶ *Pre-academics* is a term that is defined in various ways among early childhood educators. *Emerging literacy* describes the diverse skills that help children become successful in reading, writing, and other academic tasks.

▶ In this text, both terms are used to refer to a range of cognitive, language, and perceptual-motor tasks that are a part of most developmentally appropriate early childhood programs.

▶ Pre-academics do not include drills, workbooks, or paper-and-pencil tasks that some policymakers argue are the way to enhance a child's future school success. It is true that appropriate experiences do contribute to future school learning, but that is a secondary function.

▶ Promoting children's day-by-day acquisition of developmental skills and fostering their eagerness to learn are the major values of pre-academic activities throughout the early years.

▶ A decade of brain research provides new insights into a child's early development, indicating the brain's high level of activity and complexity. Early experiences shape the brain in partnership with the child's genes. Through repetition and use, the brain's network system retains early connections; by the teenage years, half are discarded.

▶ The brain's plasticity, as well as the critical time periods for learning, have great implications for appropriate and timely early intervention.

▶ There is conflicting evidence as well as opinion on the value of technology in early childhood education settings. Because technology is a part of everyday life for many children and their families, it is important for early childhood educators as well as parents to make informed decisions about its use both at school and in the home.

▶ Pre-academic skills and emerging literacy often are equated with readiness skills; both can be taught if they do not come about in due course through experience and everyday opportunities to learn.

▶ A child's short attention span or inability to imitate or follow instructions is not ascribed to immaturity. Instead of a wait-and-see approach, the specific skills are taught step by step, thereby avoiding further developmental delay.

▶ In addition to attention span, imitation skills, and following instructions, other specific foundational skills include perceptual-motor skills, memory, and the ability to formulate concepts.

▶ Pre-reading, pre-writing, and pre-math skills may also be subsumed under pre-academics; but these are child-initiated activities—not teacher-directed, seat-work activities.

▶ Small-group activities based on a variety of academically related, developmentally appropriate learning opportunities are offered in most early childhood programs. When such activities are matched to children's interests and ability levels, attractively arranged, and appropriately presented, most children enjoy them.

▶ Always, it is the teacher's job to be alert to helping individual children acquire whatever prerequisite skills they may lack.

▶ The most important aspect of all pre-academic activities is that they be enjoyable to both children and teachers.

▶ Enjoyment leads to success, and success leads to further enjoyment in learning and in teaching.

Key Terms

assistive technology, 449

embedded learning, 448

emerging literacy, 442

functionally illiterate, 442

holding activities, 468

perceptual-motor skills , 455

pre-academic, 443

readiness, 452

rote memorization, 446

sensory integration, 455

Student Activities

1. Observe a preschool or child care program during a pre-academic period. Describe the activities that were offered, the amount of time spent in various activities, and the level of the children's engagement and enjoyment. If the program does not have a structured pre-academic period, describe activities that might qualify as pre-academic.

2. Observe one child in a group, preferably a child with a developmental delay. Describe the kinds of adaptations that teachers made to enhance this child's pre-academic learning. If you saw no such adaptations, suggest what might have been done.

3. Review the guidelines listed in Figure 17-2 from the NAEYC and the Fred Rogers Center on use of technology. List examples of the use of technology that would and would not meet the intent of these guidelines.

4. Observe a teacher reading a book with a group of children or an individual child. Using the table of suggestions for reading to children, watch for which of those the teacher does. Make a list of additional things the teacher could do to support emerging literacy both when reading and within the classroom.

5. Observe a teacher for twenty minutes. Write down everything the teacher does that relates to facilitating children's pre-academic learning.

6. Obtain the kindergarten learning standards from your local school district or state department of education. Given what you know about developmentally appropriate practice and reading, what is your opinion of the expected standards?

Review Questions

Respond to the following items in list format.

1. List five ways that teachers can help children get started or become interested in pre-academic materials.

2. List three ways a teacher can help a child learn to imitate.

3. List seven types of manipulative materials that promote perceptual-motor skills.

4. List two spatial and two temporal relationships.

5. List five possible reasons that might explain a child's repeated failure to follow directions.

6. List three reasons that recent brain research is important.

Additional Resources/Readings

Curriculum for Young Children
Written by Eve-Marie Arce
Cengage Learning

This introduction to curriculum provides a straightforward and useful understating of early childhood curriculum. The text includes a chapter on cognitive development.

Helpful Websites

Pre-academics, emerging literacy, embedded learning opportunities, and arranging pre-academic and cognitive learning activities for young children are featured frequently in many of the websites previously listed in this book.

Access Center: Improving Outcomes for All Students K-8

http://www.k8accesscenter.org

The Access Center proposes that access to the general education curriculum occurs when students with disabilities are actively engaged in learning the content and skills that define the general education curriculum. Their website provides articles and resources across all areas of the curriculum, including teacher training modules.

Beyond the Journal

http://www.journal.naeyc.org

Beyond the Journal is an online supplement to *Young Children*, the journal of the National Association for the Education of Young Children.

Beyond the Journal offers readers of *Young Children* a number of articles, resource lists, and other documents online that are not included in the print issue. Typically, the online pieces in *Beyond the Journal* are useful and timely resources for the early childhood community and for others interested in the education and development of young children. The articles, which can be downloaded and printed, are designed to be shared with colleagues and used for staff development purposes.

KIDS FIRST!®—The Coalition for Quality Children's Media

http://www.kidsfirst.org

The Coalition for Quality Children's Media is a national not-for-profit organization founded in 1991. This is a voluntary collaboration of media industry companies, educators, child advocacy organizations, and families that believe that media profoundly affect children. Its mission is to (1) teach children critical viewing skills and enable them to make their own good media choices and (2) increase the visibility and availability of quality children's programs. KIDS FIRST!® is the coalition's program that evaluates and rates children's films, videos, DVDs, audio recordings, software, and television. The website provides reviews of over 2,500 titles.

 Visit the Education CourseMate for this textbook to access the eBook, Did You Get It? quizzes, Digital Downloads, TeachSource Video Cases, flashcards, and more. Go to CengageBrain.com to log in, register, or purchase access.

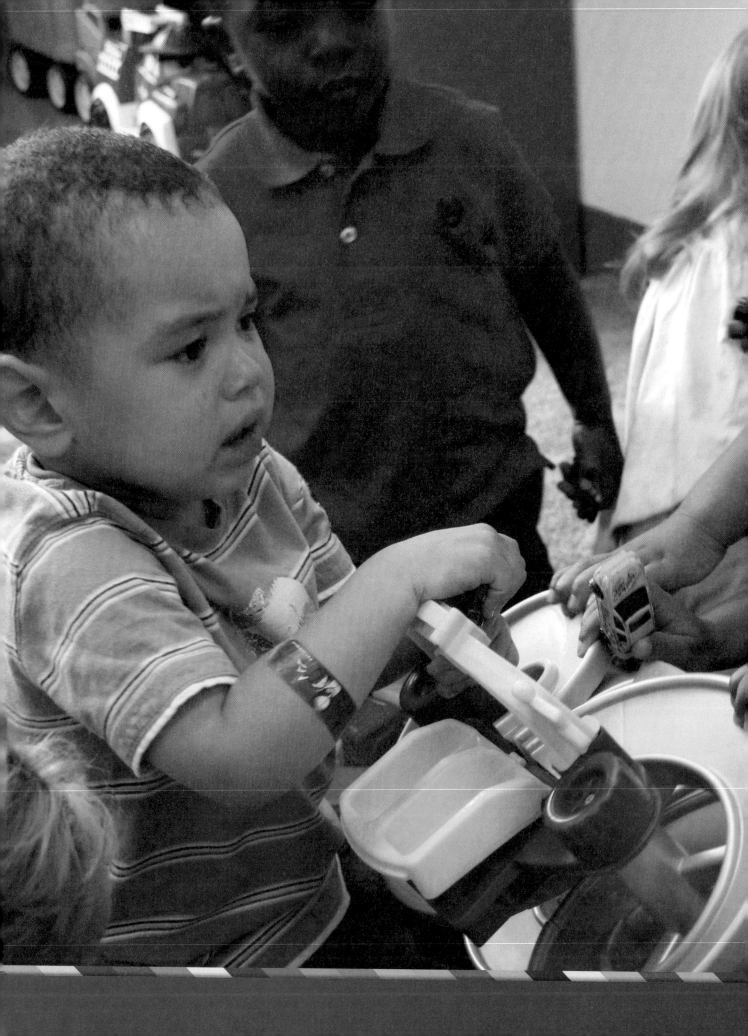

Managing Challenging Behaviors

OBJECTIVES

After reading this chapter, you should be able to:

18-1 describe developmentally appropriate behavior problems; explain the factors that determine whether a behavior problem requires special attention.

18-2 describe The Teaching Pyramid, a tiered model for supporting social competence and preventing challenging behavior in young children.

18-3 identify the steps to completing a Functional Behavior Plan.

18-4 choose an appropriate data collection method to monitor a child's behavior.

18-5 list behavior problems common to early childhood settings and strategies for preventing and reducing these behaviors.

• • • • • • • • • • • • • • • • • • •

naeyc

The following NAEYC Standards are addressed in this chapter:

STANDARD 1 Promoting Child Development and Learning

STANDARD 2 Building Family and Community Relationships

STANDARD 3 Observing, Documenting and Assessing to Support Young Children and Families

STANDARD 4 Using Developmentally Effective Approaches

CONNECTIONS

- Michael is a three-year-old boy with severe seizure activity. He has made friends in his inclusive preschool classroom and is usually very happy there. He has limited receptive communication skills, and when there are unexpected changes in the routine, he often reacts with disruptive or aggressive behavior. Through careful planning and the use of a picture schedule, Michael is learning to react more appropriately to schedule changes.

- Ginger, a five-year-old with autism, has long, curly hair. She has tantrums whenever her mother attempts to brush her hair. Through practice, carefully arranging the environment, and providing Ginger with favorite toys (preferred materials) during this time, hair brushing has become a fun time for mother and daughter.

- Connor, a first-grader with limited attention during class meetings, showed increased attention and participation when he was seated in the center front of the group.

Challenging behaviors happen. They happen at school and at home. It would be difficult to find a child who has not been accused of having a behavior problem by someone at some time. All young children engage in challenging and inappropriate behaviors, at least once in a while. It is one way that children learn the difference between appropriate and inappropriate ways of behaving. It is how they learn what to do (and not to do), where, and when. In this text, we use the terms *challenging behaviors* and *problem behaviors* interchangeably to refer to behaviors that are of concern to teachers and parents or that violate classroom rules or cultural norms.

18-1 When Is a Behavior a Problem?

At what point is an inappropriate behavior a problem behavior? There is no easy answer because so many factors influence a child's development. Cultural norms, parental expectations and reactions to the behavior, and environmental arrangements such as too many distractions or too few are among the factors that influence challenging behaviors. The range of individual differences among children further complicates matters.

It is unlikely that there is a typically developing child who has never had a tantrum or an irrational fear, who has not balked at being separated from a parent, a pacifier, a security blanket, or a favorite stuffed animal. Rarer still are children who are never moody or withdrawn, aggressive or antisocial, argumentative or oppositional. It is typical of young children to retreat or respond negatively or aggressively to situations that are new, frightening, or beyond their understanding.

A stranger replacing a long-time favorite caregiver may trigger a run of problem behaviors. The reactions usually are temporary; the untoward behaviors disappear once the child gains understanding and confidence about the new situation. A child also may exhibit unusual behaviors when overtired, hungry, or coming down with an illness. These are **normal deviations** and are not likely to become fixed patterns of behavior unless they are the only way a child can be sure of getting adult attention.

normal deviations minor irregularities that often occur in young children; the irregularities are usually self-correcting in typically developing children

goodness-of-fit when the learning opportunities are appropriate to the child's developmental status

18-1a ■ Temperament

Behaviors viewed as inappropriate may be a reflection of the child's basic personality. Some children seem to be born with a temperament that makes them easy to manage; others with a temperament that makes them more difficult. An interesting approach to understanding temperament is what Thomas and Chess (1986) call **goodness-of-fit**. These authors suggest that it is not the child's temperament itself that determines behavioral outcome. Instead, it is how the child's personality characteristics match the demands of the environment—especially the expectations of parents and caregivers. Consider, for example, a child who is active, independent, constantly curious, and into everything. This child may be seen as troublesome, a behavior problem, and a candidate for frequent punishment by overworked parents who hold high standards for order and routine. On the other hand, energetic, adventuresome parents might view this active, into-everything child as highly rewarding. They might go out of their way to reinforce, nurture, and respect the child's efforts at exploration and experimentation.

Young children who exhibit behavior problems are too often labeled as having an intellectual disability or emotionally disturbed. A common reaction is for adults to excuse these behaviors, explaining that the child "can't help it" or "doesn't know any better." Making such excuses is neither fair to the child nor sensible. All young children, regardless of their developmental level, can be helped to learn basic socially acceptable behaviors. Early childhood programs that fail to provide such learning opportunities do these children a serious injustice. Other children and adults will come to dislike and reject them. This may result in more acting-out episodes, or lead to excesses of aggression or withdrawal.

Occasional episodes of challenging behavior are seldom cause for concern.

© Cengage Learning 2015

18-1b ■ How Much Is Too Much?

Occasional episodes of challenging behaviors are seldom cause for concern. Only when a behavior or a pattern of behaviors becomes excessive is it a problem. This raises the question: How much is too much? For classroom purposes, it is useful to define excessive behavior as that which interferes seriously with a child's (or other children's) ability to learn and to engage in normal, everyday activities.

A four-year-old who has a brief tantrum once or twice a month is not likely to be a worry. The four-year-old who tantrums several times every day over minor frustrations is cause for concern. Similarly, thumb sucking is seldom a problem, except for the occasional child whose thumb sucking is so continuous that the child rarely engages in activities that require two hands. Biting others is a fairly common but unacceptable behavior, even among toddlers. In the interest of safety, the biting must be stopped, but the toddler seldom is viewed as having a serious behavior disorder. On the other hand, a five- or six-year-old who bites others, even infrequently, is of concern.

Throughout this text, there has been an emphasis on the need to provide an environment that promotes appropriate behavior and learning. In other words, this means providing support for appropriate behaviors and preventing challenging or inappropriate behaviors from happening. The teacher's first strategy should be to examine the role of the environment itself and make any changes possible to prevent a behavior. This may include strategies such as offering choice, eliminating wide-open spaces, planning developmentally appropriate activities, providing appropriate structure during transition times and being sure learning groups do not have too many children. A well-planned learning environment is one component of preventing challenging behaviors. Of course, even the best-planned learning environment cannot prevent all challenging behaviors from occurring. Fox and colleagues (2003) describe a model that provides a tiered intervention framework that promotes the social, emotional, and behavioral development of young children. This framework includes preventive classroom interventions as one of its tiers.

Figure 18-1 depicts the levels of the framework—the foundation of which (Tier 1) is *building positive relationships*. Building relationships is key to any effective early education program. The time spent developing a sense of security, self-esteem, and confidence with children is well spent and often requires less time implementing elaborate interventions (Fox, Dunlap, Hemmeter, Joseph, &

FIGURE 18-1

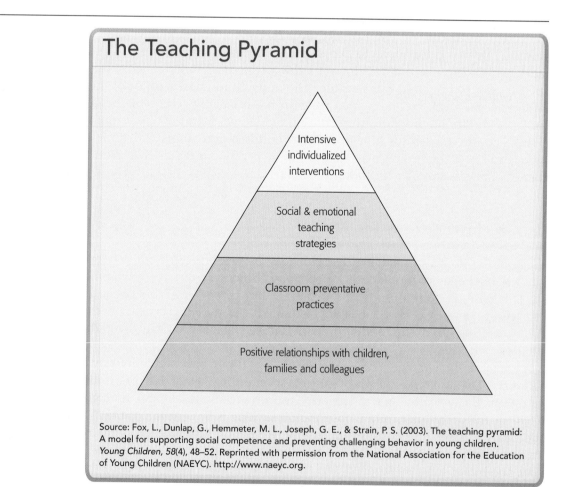

The Teaching Pyramid

Intensive
individualized
interventions

Social & emotional
teaching
strategies

Classroom preventative
practices

Positive relationships with children,
families and colleagues

Source: Fox, L., Dunlap, G., Hemmeter, M. L., Joseph, G. E., & Strain, P. S. (2003). The teaching pyramid: A model for supporting social competence and preventing challenging behavior in young children. *Young Children, 58*(4), 48–52. Reprinted with permission from the National Association for the Education of Young Children (NAEYC). http://www.naeyc.org.

Strain, 2003). The second tier of the framework is the one previously mentioned; *preventative classroom interventions.* The third tier is *social-emotional teaching strategies.* Children need to learn vocabulary related to feelings and need to be able to recognize these feelings in themselves and others. Strategies include modeling on the part of teachers, and games involving vocabulary, such as "Emotions Lotto." Children also need to learn problem solving and friendship skills such as giving compliments, helping others, turn-taking, and sharing. The final tier is *planning intensive individualized intervention.* When the lower levels of the pyramid are in place, only about four percent of children will require intensive individualized intervention (Fox et al., 2003; Sugai et al., 2000). The following example illustrates the Pyramid Tiered Framework in action.

Tier 1: *Penny, a preschool teacher of three- to five-year-olds, spends time each day reaching out to parents and children at arrival time. She greets and connects with each child during the morning free-play time and then once again at circle. At the end of the day, she sends an e-mail to all the parents letting them know about the daily activities so that they can ask their children questions and discuss their day with them when they get home.*

Tier 2: *Penny and her classroom assistants carefully plan each day's activities. When problem behaviors arise, they look to change the environment first. For example, they recently made a change during the transition to recess. The change was made because they observed that the children who were ready to go outside would often grow restless and sometimes push each other when waiting for the rest of the class to get ready. The staff decided that it would be better if a teacher took the first group of children outside when they were ready, rather than making them wait for the stragglers. This resulted in fewer behavior problems. It also motivated the children who were taking longer to get ready to move faster.*

Tier 3: *Penny noticed that several children in her class need help in learning to deal with disappointment and sharing. She is working with her staff to develop additional activities that focus on discussing feelings, practicing turn-taking, and modeling problem solving.*

Tier 4: *Penny is worried about one student in the class, Arthur. Arthur pushes friends down at recess daily. She contacts the family and begins working with them to develop an individualized behavior support plan that can be implemented at home and school.*

The next section of this chapter is about behavior problems and the individualized strategies for dealing with them (Tier 4). The focus is on troublesome behaviors that teachers are most likely to encounter among toddlers and young children with and without developmental problems. The behaviors discussed range from occasional to very nearly constant in terms of their occurrence. The urgent message in this chapter is for teachers to help children avoid or overcome these problems so they do not become fixed during the developmental years.

▶❚❚ **TeachSource** Video Connections

© Cengage Learning 2015

Emotional Development

When designing interventions for challenging behaviors, adults must also keep in the mind the third tier of the teaching pyramid (refer to Figure 18-1). The third tier is *social-emotional teaching strategies.* Children need to learn vocabulary related to feelings and need to be able to recognize these feelings in themselves and others. In this video you can see how parents and child care providers can demonstrate to children appropriate ways to express emotions and feelings.

After watching this video, discuss the following:

1. Discuss the strategies the teacher used to help children learn how to express their emotions and feelings.

2. Describe other strategies a teacher might use.

Watch on CourseMate.

18-2a ■ Designing Interventions

Teachers, family members, and other interdisciplinary team members must work together to identify the challenging behavior, identify the settings in which it occurs, and use this information to design interventions that all team members are comfortable with and able to implement. This process is called **positive behavior support**. Positive behavior support offers a strategy for understanding why a child engages in problem behavior and looks at ways to prevent the occurrence of problem behavior while teaching the child new skills.

The Division for Early Childhood, in their 2007 position statement, emphasize that it is essential that families and early educators work together to address challenging behavior. They recommend the following:

- Using comprehensive assessment approaches, including screening and identification of the triggers, maintaining consequences, and the function of the behavior.

- Implementing a variety of evidence-based strategies and services designed to prevent challenging behavior, at the same time teaching appropriate communicative and adaptive behavior and social-emotional competence.

- Providing support to team members as they develop and implement intervention plans in natural environments.

Positive behavior support offers a strategy for understanding why a child engages in problem behavior.

© Cengage Learning 2015

positive behavioral support strategies providing positive rather than negative feedback to children's efforts; concentrating on what the child does right

Did You Get It?

How does the second tier compare with the third tier in the tiered intervention framework?

a. The second tier comprises preventative classroom interventions; the third involves social emotional teaching strategies.

b. The second tier comprises social emotional teaching; the third is preventative classroom interventions.

c. The second tier is building positive relationships; the third is social emotional teaching.

d. The second tier is building positive relationships; the third is preventative classroom interventions.

Take the full quiz on CourseMate.

☼ 18-3 A Functional Approach to Managing Problem Behaviors

The best way to deal with problem or challenging behaviors—those that cause concern to teachers and families—is to prevent them (Walker, Stiller, & Golly, 1998). For there to be effective prevention, teachers and caregivers must examine their own behavior and identify factors that might be contributing to the

TABLE 18-1

A Functional Approach to Managing Problem Behaviors

1. Identify the problem situation.

2. Assess the child and the environment.

3. Specify an objective for the intervention.

4. Assess the function of the behavior.

5. Identify a replacement behavior.

6. Plan the intervention. Ensure that meaningful curriculum activities, frequent reinforcement, choice, and a predictable schedule are in place.

7. Implement the plan and ensure that it is carried out as planned.

8. Monitor the child's progress and continue to monitor implementation.

© Cengage Learning 2015

TeachSource Digital Download Download from CourseMate.

child's behavior. In Chapter 13, we discussed ways the early childhood environment can be arranged to prevent challenging behavior. Teachers should first examine their environment to determine whether changing something there could alleviate the problem. We now know that challenging behaviors have a communicative function (Koegel, Koegel, & Dunlap, 1996). The task of parents and educators is to figure out what the child is attempting to communicate, and teach him or her a more appropriate way to get the message across.

In this section, we will introduce **functional behavior assessment (FBA)**—an approach to managing problem behaviors—using the example of a child who cannot stay with an activity, to illustrate the process. The key element of the functional approach is to determine why the child is engaging in the problem behavior. Refer to Table 18-1 for the steps of the process.

functional behavior assessment (FBA) evaluating the degree to which children's behaviors work to get them what they want and need

18-3a ■ 1. Identify the Problem Situation

First, teachers need to identify and describe the challenging behavior in observable terms. For example, it is not very helpful to say a child is hyperactive; this observation is not descriptive enough to help plan an intervention. It is more appropriate to say that the child "does not stay at any activity during free choice for longer than a minute on average." Identifying the behavior in a specific manner will also be useful when teachers begin to gather specific information about the problem behavior (data collection). By having an agreed-upon definition or description, teachers can be assured they are all recording, treating, and talking about the same behavior(s).

18-3b ■ 2. Assess the Child and the Environment

It is important to know how long or how often the child demonstrates the challenging behavior. It is also important to know the events in the environment that are contributing to the behavior. These are known as *antecedents* and *consequences*. Every behavior has them. **Antecedents** are things that happen before the behavior that may serve as a trigger. Antecedents may be a certain time of the day, certain area of the room, toys or materials, or perhaps a peer. **Consequences** are events that follow the behavior. Consequences may be such things as gaining

antecedents events that come before a behavior

consequences events that follow a behavior

access to a preferred activity, getting out of an activity, or getting a reaction from teachers or peers. It can be extremely helpful for teachers to collect data; in other words, record antecedents and consequences to a specific behavior across several days or weeks (depending on the frequency of the behavior). By recording the antecedents and consequences, teachers can identify patterns and gain information about why the behavior is occurring.

This is also the time to assess the environment to see whether changes can be easily made to facilitate more appropriate behavior. In our example, we need to know how long the child stays at each activity. Could it be that he stays at the block area for fifteen minutes and then flits through the other areas? This may suggest that he knows how to play with blocks, but his play skills in other areas are limited.

18-3c ■ 3. Specify an Objective for the Intervention

What is the desired behavior at home or in the classroom? Teachers, parents, and other members of the intervention team must decide what the child should be able to do. For example, an appropriate goal may be for the child to be able to play independently for fifteen minutes in three different areas of the classroom.

18-3d ■ 4. Assess the Function of the Behavior

By carefully observing the child's behavior and identifying antecedents and consequences, the teacher can often identify the function of the behavior. Research has demonstrated that children engage in the same challenging behavior for different reasons, and they can also exhibit different behaviors for the same reason or function (Carr & Durand, 1985). To design and implement an effective behavior-reduction program, teachers must figure out what the child gains from the behavior (the function).

Research suggests that the function of a child's behavior can be broken down into three categories: (1) behavior that occurs to gain attention or a desired item from an adult or peer, (2) behavior that allows the child to escape or get out of a less-than-desirable task or activity, and (3) behavior that occurs for self-pleasure (such as object spinning) (Iwata, Dorsey, Slifer, Bauman, & Richman, 1982).

It is important for teachers to take the function of the behavior into account when developing an intervention strategy. For example, if a child throws materials each day during fine motor time and the teachers develop a plan that includes removing the child from the situation, they may have in fact chosen a strategy that will make the problem worse. A child who regularly throws materials during fine motor time is most likely engaging in this behavior to get out of doing the task. Therefore, teachers would be better off using a preferred activity as a reward or reinforcement once the child completes a fine motor task, or a portion thereof.

18-3e ■ 5. Identify a Replacement Behavior

replacement behavior a behavior that is taught to a child to replace an inappropriate one; a replacement behavior should serve the same function as the inappropriate behavior

When developing a strategy to decrease a behavior, it is critical for teachers to teach the child an appropriate behavior that serves the same function as the problem behavior. This new skill or behavior is called a **replacement behavior**. This strategy provides the child with a skill that can gain him the same or similar thing his inappropriate behavior did. For example, a child who pours his juice on the table when finished needs to be taught to pour the juice down the drain or tell a teacher he is finished.

18-3f ■ 6. Plan the Intervention

Ensure that meaningful curriculum activities, frequent positive attention, choice, and a predictable schedule are in place. This is the step of the process that focuses on prevention.

Prevention means that the important adults in the child's life look at their behavior in the classroom, home or community setting that might be maintaining the child's challenging behaviors. The first changes that are implemented are those that facilitate the appropriate behavior. In our example, some changes could be:

- helping the child make choices and plan his or her day through the use of pictures.

- making sure that there are preferred activities in different areas of the classroom.

- teaching the child how to use different materials.

- catching the child being good; that is, praising the child, encouraging him, and paying attention to him when he is actively engaged in appropriate behavior.

Teaching a child to raise her arm for a break can reduce the behavior of throwing materials on the floor to end a task.

© Cengage Learning 2015

During this step, teachers also plan what they will do when their prevention efforts do not work. For example, the teacher may decide simply to redirect the child to an appropriate activity when he is off-task. More serious behaviors, such as aggression, may need a more serious consequence such as time-out. Whatever the teacher chooses to do, the teacher should be sure that the entire educational teams, including the family, are in agreement and comfortable implementing the intervention.

18-3g ■ 7. Implement the Plan and Ensure that It Is Carried Out as Planned

This step puts the plan into action. Make sure that everyone in the environment understands the plan and knows how to implement it. If the plan is not implemented correctly and consistently, it will not work. Teachers need to be patient. It is difficult to change behavior. At first, the child may exhibit more of the problem behavior, and it may take two weeks or more before significant changes can be detected in a child's behavior. However, if teachers are consistent, change will happen.

18-3h ■ 8. Monitor the Child's Progress and Continue to Monitor Implementation

The purpose of this step is to make sure the plan is working. Teachers need to collect data about the child's behavior to determine whether the goal has been achieved. Chapter 12 provides a data collection system for monitoring the acquisition of a new skill. The **data collection** in this chapter focuses on monitoring the child's behavior and determining whether a specific intervention strategy is effective. If progress has been observed, teachers may start **fading** (i.e., slowly discontinuing) some components of the intervention. In this example, the teacher may praise the child less frequently or discontinue the teaching sessions on how to use different toys. Teachers need to continue to be consistent with consequence procedures such as time-out or ignoring until the behavior disappears. Teachers should be prepared to implement this aspect of a plan if the behavior recurs. Continuing to monitor the child's behavior is important in order to determine whether fading has occurred too quickly or too early.

☀ 18-4 Data Collection and Monitoring Progress

data collection information collected to determine whether an intervention or teaching strategy is effective and/or to learn more about a behavior

fading gradually reducing prompts, cues, and physical assistance when teaching a particular skill

A reliable and easy-to-use data collection system is essential to monitoring the success of any intervention plan (Kaiser & Rasminsky, 1999). Data indicate whether the intervention plan is working. Data can provide information about the environment and what influences the child's behavior. Data collection systems are helpful only when they are easy to use and provide an accurate picture of the child's behavior.

18-4a ■ Types of Data Collection

frequency (counts) a system for keeping track of how often a behavior occurs; such data can provide significant information about a child's problem

duration measures how long an event or behavior lasts

interval a specified period of the day that is broken into segments to record the occurrence, frequency, or duration of a behavior

Three types of behavior data are most commonly collected in an early childhood setting: **frequency**, **duration**, and **interval**. Frequency refers to the number of times during the day or the specific time the behavior occurs. This type of data collection is used to measure behaviors that have a distinct beginning and end. Hitting and biting are two examples of behaviors that can be effectively measured using a frequency count. Duration is the measure of how long each episode occurs. This measure would be used for behaviors that have a distinct beginning and end but last for at least a minute. Tantrums are typically measured this way. Interval measurement can often be an easier way to track behaviors and can be used for behaviors both long and short in duration.

During interval measurement, a specified time of day or the entire day is broken into equal segments. The length of these intervals is determined by both the behavior and how frequently adults can record the data. For example, teachers who want to measure a child's ability to share might divide the free-play period into five-minute segments. At the conclusion of each five-minute segment, a "+" would be placed in the interval if the child was able to share for the entire time, and a "–" would be recorded if there was any occurrence of inability to share.

Before establishing any data collection method, a mutually agreed-upon definition of the behavior must be written. This will increase the likelihood that all individuals recording the data are recording the same behavior.

18-4b ■ Collecting Data

Once the behavior has been identified and defined, data are collected for at least three to five days before any systematic plan is formulated to reduce the target behavior. This period of data collection is referred to as **baseline**. Baseline data provide a picture of how often or for how long the behavior is occurring. This information can be used to compare to later data to evaluate the effectiveness of the behavior plan. A vertical line should be drawn on the data graph to indicate the end of baseline and introduction of the behavior intervention plan. Once the behavior intervention plan is determined to be effective, data collection can be reduced or eliminated.

Some data collection methods can be time-consuming and impractical for a teacher to use. It is best to find a simple yet accurate way to measure the behavior. Several simple methods are available.

baseline data that are collected on a behavior prior to a systematic plan being introduced; these data provide a base against which later behavior can be compared

Frequency methods

- Drop a bead or poker chip in a jar each time the behavior occurs. Count the beads or chips at the end of a designated time.
- Wear a strip of paper around your wrist like a bracelet. Put a tally mark on the strip each time the behavior occurs.
- Use a golf counter or score keeper and push the button at each occurrence.
- Record on a frequency data sheet (see Figure 18-2).

Duration methods

- Use a stopwatch.
- Wear a strip of paper around your wrist and record the beginning and end time of each episode of behavior.
- Record on a duration data sheet (see Figure 18-3).

Interval methods

- Use a timer programmed to beep at a predetermined interval to remind you to record data.
- Record on an interval data sheet (see Figure 18-4).

FIGURE 18-2

An Example of a Frequency Data Sheet

	MONDAY	TUESDAY	WEDNESDAY	THURSDAY	FRIDAY
Frequency of Hitting Peers	ЖІ ІІІІ	ЖІ І	ІІІ	Ж ІІ	ІІІІ

© Cengage Learning 2015

FIGURE 18-3

An Example of a Duration Data Sheet

	MONDAY	TUESDAY	WEDNESDAY	THURSDAY	FRIDAY
Begin Time	9:30	11:05	8:30	9:36	
End Time	9:40	11:08	8:36	9:38	
Begin Time	10:05				
End Time	10:07				
Begin Time					
End Time					

© Cengage Learning 2015

Data collection is the first step to obtaining useful data. Data need to be graphed so that changes in behavior can be viewed and evaluated. One of the easiest methods is a data sheet that forms a pictorial image of the behavior. This approach works best for frequency behaviors. Figure 18-5 is an example of this type of data sheet. A simple graph can also be used to depict interval or duration data (see Figure 18-6).

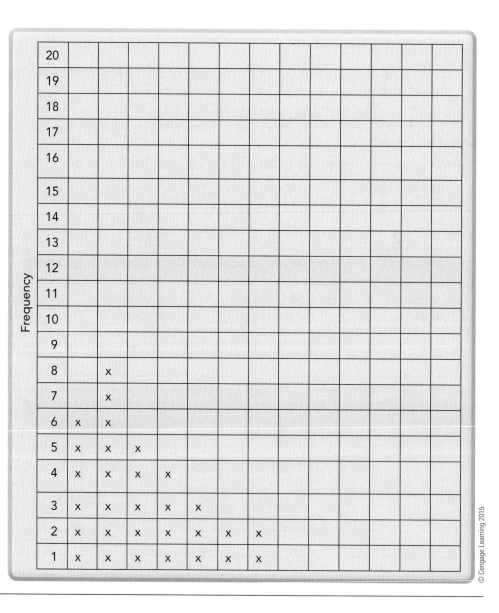

	MONDAY	TUESDAY	WEDNESDAY	THURSDAY	FRIDAY
9:00–9:15	+	–	+	–	+
9:15–9:30	–	–	–	–	–
9:30–10:00	–	–	–	–	–
10:00–10:15	+	+	+	+	+

FIGURE 18-4

An Example of an Interval Data Sheet

© Cengage Learning 2015

FIGURE 18-5

Self-graphing data sheet. An x is placed on the chart at each occurrence of the behavior. Changes in behavior from day to day are easily viewed using this method.

© Cengage Learning 2015

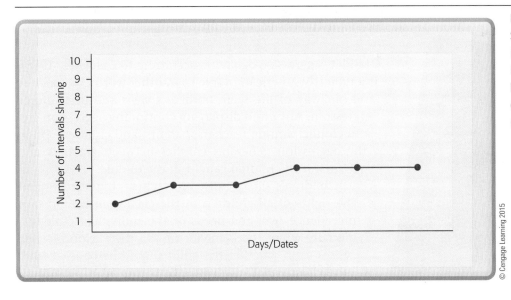

© Cengage Learning 2015

FIGURE 18-6

Sample Graph for Intervals, Frequency or Duration Measures. Measurement can be changed to match need (for example, number of minutes of tantrums).

The number of intervals in which a behavior occurred or the total number of minutes can be used as the measurement. Data should be graphed and reviewed frequently. Decisions about changes in the behavior plan should be made only after looking at the data. Data records should be saved. They can be useful in parent conferences and IEP meetings.

Did You Get It?

Why would "duration" be an effective method of data collection for a tantrum?

a. It measures the number of times during the day or specific time the behavior occurs.

b. The measure is used for behaviors that have a distinct beginning and end but last for at least a minute.

c. It measures the number of intervals the behavior occurs across.

d. Effective frequency count.

Take the full quiz on CourseMate.

Common Behavior Problems and Solutions 18-5

The remainder of this chapter deals with behavior problems that are common to early childhood settings. For each of these behaviors, specific strategies are described for reducing or preventing them. These strategies are based on the developmental-behavioral principles described in detail in Chapter 12. When selecting a strategy, teachers must base their decision on the function of the problem behavior, as discussed earlier in this chapter.

18-5a ■ Aggression

Aggression, like many other terms we apply to children, is difficult to define. What is considered aggressive by one group of people, one parent, or one teacher may seem unimportant to another group, another parent, or another member of the teaching team.

Conflict Aggressive behavior, according to Caldwell (1988), is a typically American problem. In other words, our society and our way of life seem both to spawn and to reinforce aggression. Any child displaying continuing aggression creates conflict among teachers, parents, and children. Often the aggression generates conflict between teachers and parents, with children caught in the middle.

Children's safety must be teachers' highest priority. The rights of all children in the classroom should take precedence over the needs of the individual child, especially when the behavior hurts others. Conflict also arises as to whether the child should be banned from the classroom. Caldwell suggests it is probably a tactical error to insist the child leave the group until his behavior improves. No matter what the underlying causes, some of the elicitors of outbursts are sure to be found in the group experience. Reducing aggressive behavior and maintaining the child in the group are not easy. However, it can be done, and done safely. Furthermore, problem behaviors need not become out of hand if they are dealt with at the outset, before they reach crisis proportions.

It is critical to give attention to children when they are behaving appropriately.

Managing aggression An individualized program based on behavioral procedures is imperative in situations where aggressive behaviors are truly troublesome. Always, *the behavior management program is in addition to and concurrent with teachers' best efforts at understanding the child's current feelings.* It is in addition to finding legitimate ways for the child to blow off steam. It is in addition to working with parents to help alleviate the child's stress, frustration, anxieties, or lack of self-esteem. The child who verbally abuses, kicks, hits, and knocks children around invariably needs more adult attention. However, the attention never should be given at the moment the child is hurting another child. At a different time, the teacher encourages the child to talk about the situation, the angry feelings, and what to do next time. They might even rehearse alternative and more acceptable responses.

Young children often behave aggressively because they feel left out or do not know acceptable ways of getting into play. Many children with developmental delays lack the play skills or the verbal courtesies that make them desirable playmates. The teacher's responsibility is twofold: (1) to take the initiative in helping the child acquire the necessary play and social skills and (2) to watch for approximations to more appropriate play and then interact with the child pleasantly.

When a child with a history of excessive aggression hurts another child, the teacher turns full attention to the child who has been hurt or attacked. *The child who did the hurting receives no adult attention at that time.* It is never necessary for the teacher to explain how much it hurts another child to be hit or pushed down. The child who behaves aggressively has been given that information innumerable times. Furthermore, the behavior of the injured child conveys the message eloquently. Should the teacher believe explanations about not hurting other children are needed, they should be given at another time, as noted earlier.

A child who is frequently and severely aggressive may need to be removed from the group temporarily for each aggressive episode. This step is taken when other forms of working with the child are not having the desired effect. No child can be allowed to hurt other children repeatedly. When more positive methods have failed, time-out is a nonaggressive way to help a child learn that he or she absolutely cannot hurt other children. The use of time-out should be decided jointly with teachers, a consultant from the interdisciplinary team, and the child's parents. State regulations also need to be reviewed. If the use of time-out is agreed upon, the child is shown the time-out area and told about time-out procedures; specifically, when and why he or she will be removed. From then on, the child is removed from classroom contacts as a consequence of every aggression against another child. It is best if a second teacher removes the child to the time-out area; the original teacher then can comfort and calm the child who has been hurt.

Moving a child into time-out should be done with a minimum of adult attention. The teacher accompanies the procedure with a firm "No," followed by a brief but equally firm statement: "I cannot let you hurt children." No other attention is given to the child at that time. One, two, or three minutes later, depending on the situation (but never more than five minutes, even in the most distressing cases), the teacher goes to the child with a matter-of-fact statement: "Let's try again. Where would you like to play?" When returning the child to play, the teacher does not lecture, moralize, or try to extract promises from the child to be good. What does seem to work is making a suggestion regarding a next activity: "There's room for you at the water table. I'll help you get started." A successful start is often the key to a successful play experience, especially if a teacher checks in frequently with favorable and interested comments.

On occasion a child may be aggressive toward a teacher. When this occurs, care must be taken to ensure that the reason for or function of the behavior is not escaping or getting out of the task at hand. For example, if a child hits a teacher when asked to help clean up the block area in which the child was playing, time-out can still be used. Once the time-out is complete, the child should be returned to the block area to pick up the blocks that have been left there for her return.

It is important to note that whenever time-out is used, the adults' foremost role is to still teach the child how to interact appropriately with peers and get their needs met. For example, if the aggression is occurring primarily due to a conflict over sharing, the child must be taught to problem solve with her or his peers. Using time-out alone may have a short-term effect, but for long-term gains the child most also learn self-regulation and effective strategies to deal with conflict.

18-5b ■ Disruptive and Destructive Behaviors

Every early childhood classroom, at one time or another, has a child who seems bent on upsetting the program. These children interfere with teacher-directed activities and with other children's projects. Music periods are interrupted by the child making inappropriate noises, faces, and comments, or running aimlessly about the room. Books are tossed around recklessly, and toys are unnecessarily damaged. The child tramples other children's sand structures, topples their block towers, or wets their clothes and hair at the water table. The list of possible misdeeds is long.

Case Study ▪ Reading time in Jessica's classroom ▪

Jessica is a first-year, first-grade teacher who has twenty-five students in her class. During reading time, she has divided the class into three groups. Parent volunteers assist her with the two groups she is not working with. She struggles to keep the students focused. There is at least one group that is always arguing or being disrespectful to the parent volunteers. One student in particular has been sent to the office on a weekly basis due to her outbursts and a lack of respect.

1. What steps can Jessica take to regain control of this time of day?
2. Identify some possible approaches that fall into each tier of the teaching pyramid.
3. What type of data might Jessica use to measure improvement?

Need for attention Children who behave in these ways have learned that their misdeeds are a sure way of getting adult attention. These are children who often have stress in their lives and low self-esteem. Like overactive children, they are greatly in need of large amounts of attention from important adults. These children often appear to feel that when they are being good, they are ignored, and when they misbehave, they get immediate attention. Young children are seven times more likely to get teachers' attention when they are behaving inappropriately than when they are behaving well (Strain, Lambert, Kerr, Stagg, & Lenker, 1983). Therefore, it is of critical importance to *give attention to children when they are behaving appropriately.*

The problem is that teachers and parents often feel the child is getting a great deal of attention, much more than is given to other children. This is likely to be true: Adults *are* giving large amounts of time-consuming attention but squandering it on the very behaviors that are bothering them. They also are spending large amounts of unproductive time correcting the havoc created by the child. Half as much of that time directed toward the child when not misbehaving would go twice as far toward producing a more constructive environment. Remember: "Catch the child being good." Efforts to emphasize this to parents or teachers often lead to the assertion that the child "never does anything right (or good)." This, of course, is not true of any child. If adults make several observations of the child, they are invariably amazed at how much of the time the child is appropriate and how rarely appropriate behavior draws adult attention and approval.

Mastering routines Many of the techniques for helping the overactive child apply equally to children with disruptive behaviors. Always, underlying causes must be studied; part of the cause may be stresses of one kind or another. Often, the reason for a disruptive behavior may be quite simple. Many disruptive children have never understood or mastered classroom routines and expectations. They need to be *walked through* routines, one step at a time. At the easel, a child may need to be shown and then asked to practice returning each paintbrush to its own color paint pot. A first step may be for the teacher to remove all paint containers but two. This makes it easy for the child to succeed. It also allows the teacher to give specific, descriptive feedback: "Great! You remembered to put the red paintbrush back in the red paint pot." Lengthy verbalizations must be avoided, or the important message will be lost. Expectations can be discussed in small-group sessions when necessary. As the child paints, the teacher makes appreciative comments about the brightness of the colors or how beautifully the child combined red and blue on the paper to make another lovely color.

Time-out is always reserved for serious situations.

Redirection Behaviors that damage equipment or hinder other children's learning experiences cannot be allowed. With most young children, simple, positive redirection is best. Statements such as "Paint on the *paper*," "Walk *around* Mark and Judi's launching pad," and "Tricycles stay *on the path*" are adequate.

Other children, especially those with a history of disruptive behavior, may pay little heed to subtle redirection. When the child ignores redirection, what is needed is a clear and firm statement about limits as well as expectations: "I cannot let you paint on the walls. The paintbrushes stay at the easel." If the child persists, either the material or the child is removed, depending on the situation.

Time-out Before resorting to time-out for disruptive behavior, teachers must have done everything possible to modify both the classroom environment and their own responses. Only then do teachers consider the temporary use of time-out to break the pattern of disruptiveness and to assure the child that teachers follow through when they say, "I can't let you …" Time-out is always reserved for serious situations. It provides *temporary relief* from an uncontrollable problem and helps the child learn to respond to more desirable guidance procedures such as redirection.

18-5c ■ Noncompliance

Refusing to do what an adult asks or ignoring an adult request is a frequent and typical behavior among young children. Seldom is this a serious problem unless it becomes habitual. In those instances, the child often is labeled *noncompliant* or as showing **oppositional behavior**. Following are three episodes, recorded in less than an hour, characteristic of one four-year-old's habitual noncompliance:

oppositional behavior patterns of child behavior that adults consider excessively negative, troublesome, or challenging

> **FATHER:** *"Michael, hang up your coat."*
> **MICHAEL:** *"No, you do it."*
> **FATHER:** *"All right, but you pick it up off the floor and hand it to me."*
> **MICHAEL:** *"You pick it up."* Michael started playing with a truck in the cubby next to his. Father hung up the coat, said good-bye, and left.
> **TEACHER:** Michael, let's pick up the blocks." Michael ran to his locker and sat in it, looking at a book he had brought from home.
> **TEACHER:** *"Michael, it's time to come in."*
> **MICHAEL:** *"Not coming in,"* while continuing his climb to the top of the climber.

When giving directions, look at and speak directly to the child.

The first step in dealing with noncompliance (or any other problem behavior) is to collect specific information through several systematic observations. Then, teachers should consult with parents and appropriate intervention team members. It must be determined that the child does not have a hearing loss or a problem with receptive language. Many children with these kinds of undiagnosed problems have been wrongly labeled noncompliant or disobedient and have received unjust punishments as a consequence.

Prevention strategies Oppositional children frazzle teachers' and parents' patience. However, most noncompliance (as well as other behavior problems) can be reduced to manageable proportions through **preventive discipline**. Basic to this form of discipline is systematic observation of the child to determine what triggers the inappropriate responses. Once trouble spots are identified, teachers can plan ways to handle the situations *before* a problem develops. The essence of the strategy is to determine what it is about the environment—including adults' behavior—that prompts a child's resistance.

> **preventive discipline** arranging the classroom environment in ways that promote children's appropriate behavior and forestall behaviors teachers consider inappropriate

We devoted considerable discussion to preventive discipline in Chapter 13. That information should be reviewed whenever planning for and dealing with children who are oppositional.

A number of related strategies also are effective with all kinds of behavior problems and with all kinds of children:

Give advance warning. It is important to give children ample warning before bringing an activity to an end. This is especially true of highly preferred play activities. Provide a clue as to what comes next: "Soon it will be time to come in and get ready for snack." To the child who always resists coming indoors: "Sara, you can be the *last* one in today." The offer, however, is made before the child has lined up her oppositional arguments.

Reduce overload. Check frequently to make sure the child is not overloaded with directions, expectations, and picky rules. Even a compliant child may develop some noncompliance if overwhelmed with rules and instructions.

Make requests and give directions clearly and briefly. Adults tend to say things such as: "We're going in to get washed for snack, so don't forget to hang up your coat when you take it off, but first put your truck in the shed and shut the door." (This was an actual word-for-word recording of what one teacher said in a child care classroom.) Such a jumble of directions is confusing to any child and sets up even greater opposition in a noncompliant child. The way to help a child through such a routine is to give advance warning about going indoors. When the time comes, give directions one or two at a time in the order they are to be carried out; in this case, parking the truck and then shutting the shed door.

Provide choices. All children, and particularly noncompliant children, need opportunities to make choices as often as possible.

- Do you want to sit here with Bobbie? Or over there with Paul?
- Would you like to put the cups *or* the napkins on the table?
- Who are you going to ask to help you decorate the window?
- It's a warm day. You can decide whether you want to wear your sweater outdoors.

Choosing and making decisions helps a child develop a sense of responsibility and independence. It also reduces the child's feeling that he or she is always being told what to do.

Beware of choices that are not choices. Adults must be careful of the choices they offer young children. Whenever a choice is offered, the adult must be prepared to honor it. The teacher does not ask, "Would you like to park your wagon and come in for music?" unless it is all right for the child to stay outdoors and play with the wagon during music. If the child is offered an option that the teacher has no intention of honoring, what follows is argument, confusion, or a power struggle, depending on the child. The more appropriate approach, once the earlier warning has been given, is for the teacher to say, "Time to come indoors for music. You can park your wagon by the door or in the shed."

Focus the child's attention. Teachers can reduce confusion for all young children by making sure each child is paying attention before giving instructions. To ensure the child's attention:

- Precede every request by speaking the child's name: "Gail, the pegs go in the basket."
- Get down to the child's level (the half-kneel, an almost automatic posture among preschool teachers, works well).
- Look into the child's face and speak directly to him or her. Check the child's understanding by getting verification: "Where does the puzzle go?"
- Demonstrate and rehearse as needed: "Jon, turn the pages like this. Now you try it."

Allow time to comply. An instruction should not be repeated until the child has had ample time to comply. A good rule of thumb is to give the child ten to twenty seconds to begin following the instruction. Too often, teachers repeat the instruction a second or third time while the child is gearing up, getting ready to comply with the initial request. When enough time has been given and it becomes obvious the child is not going to comply, the direction should be offered a second time. The teacher's voice quietly conveys the expectation that the child surely will comply this time. Never does the teacher coax, nag, bribe, or offer a reward. Following the second request, if no compliance occurs after a reasonable time, the teacher turns away to do whatever else needs doing. The child does not go on to another activity, however, until the coat is picked up or the book is put away. This may mean making sure some toys are left out at cleanup for the child who dawdles or avoids cleanup, even if this has to happen at the end of every cleanup when the rest of the class has already gone off to wash their hands for snack.

Practice consistency and firmness. Teachers need to be matter-of-fact, firm, and consistent when giving directions to children who are noncompliant. They also must be quietly confident of their own authority. If a teacher says, "Raoul, you may go to the woodworking table as soon as your blocks are picked up," Raoul must do just that—pick up the blocks before going to woodworking. The teacher in the block area alerts the other teachers that Raoul has a job to do in the block corner before he can play elsewhere. If other children are busy putting blocks away, the teacher pushes a fair share aside for Raoul to take care of. At this point, the contingency can be restated clearly and simply: "Raoul, this is your share of the blocks to put away. You can go to woodworking as soon as you finish." In many cases, the teacher offers to help the child: "As soon as you get started, I will help you put the blocks away."

Make sound judgments. Because consistency is important, teachers must not set a requirement they may not be able to carry out. In the Raoul example, it would be unwise to tell the child he could not go home until the blocks were picked up, especially if he were in a carpool or being bussed. Drivers cannot spare that kind of time. In such instances, the teacher provides an option: "Raoul, the driver will be here in a few minutes. How about getting your blocks picked up before he comes?" If the child says "No" or ignores the request, the teacher does not comment. The teacher's authority is not undermined, and an argument was avoided that the teacher could not have won.

18-5d ■ Temper Tantrums

Young children who have frequent, full-blown temper tantrums require special help. The advice often given is for adults to ignore the tantrum. Although that is good advice, it may prove nearly impossible to carry out. Parents repeatedly report that they tried ignoring their child's tantrums and that "it didn't work." It did not work because most adults give in long before the child gives in.

A child with a history of tantrums that are suddenly ignored may go to even greater extremes, having tantrums of even greater fury and duration. As a tantrum becomes more violent, the adults trying to ignore the tantrum get increasingly anxious; finally they can no longer restrain their concern for the child. They provide attention in one way or another. As this pattern is repeated, the tantrums become worse.

The child learns two damaging lessons from such experiences: (1) it takes ever greater and more prolonged fury to break down adults' defenses and (2) those defenses invariably do break down, and the adults eventually will provide some kind of attention. This leads to deeper trouble for both the child and the adults. Therefore, while ignoring tantrums is the surest way of ridding the child of such behavior, most adults need help and support in carrying out such a measure. Several professionals on the interdisciplinary team are qualified to work with parents and teachers in managing a child's tantrums.

Management of tantrums Difficult as it may be, tantrums can be handled at school. It takes careful planning among teachers, parents, and a psychologist, nurse, or other member of the developmental team. It is best if one teacher is designated to handle the tantrum and is coached and supported by the specialist.

At the start of the tantrum, the child needs to be removed to a separate place where injury or destruction is not likely to occur. Always, the child is shown the space in advance and given an explanation of its purpose. The teacher withholds all attention while the child is having the tantrum.

The teacher (or another adult) remains close by, but does not make eye contact or appear to be watching the child. When the tantrum stops, the teacher waits a moment and then returns the child to a play activity with no lecturing or moralizing.

Tantrums first get worse but then disappear within a week or less if adults can be totally consistent in carrying out these procedures. Lesser tantrums often are handled by teachers in the classroom. These, too, are likely to worsen briefly when attention is first withheld. Again, it is advisable that one teacher is designated to manage the tantrum to provide consistency of procedure. The other teacher focuses on the rest of the children, who may become uneasy as the tantrum worsens. A special story, game, or other activity can be presented to keep the children occupied and diverted. Sometimes children can be taken on a walk around the building or to the gym or library while the tantrum is going on. Always the children are assured that the child who is upset will be all right and is being well cared-for by the other teacher.

Teachers and parents must recognize that tantrums are always an indication that the child is experiencing stress, anxiety, or frustration. Underlying causes must be sought. The preschool or child care program must be studied for changes that can help the child. Meanwhile, tantrums must be brought under control. Otherwise, the tantrums themselves prevent the child from benefiting from the changes being made on his or her behalf. At the same time the child is being taught that tantrums are not okay, they must be taught other skills to get their needs met. For example if the tantrums are a result of anger over wanting to play with a toy longer, then the teacher can model for the child how to ask for the toy.

18-5e ■ Separation Problems

It is quite normal for infants and young children to be both fearful of strangers and unwilling to separate from a parent or major caregiver. The behavior tends to peak between twelve and fifteen months and then to lessen gradually. No consistent relationship has been found between the number of caregivers a child has had and the intensity of a child's protests over separation. In other words, a child who has had multiple caregivers is no less anxious about strangers than a child cared-for by a very few caregivers (Thompson & Lamb, 1982). In families where there is general instability, children may be especially fearful of strangers and have trouble separating throughout the preschool years and beyond.

Entering preschool or a child care center for the first time can be intimidating for children. Young children with developmental problems may experience even more anxiety. They are likely to have had fewer play experiences away from home. They often have been the focus of intensive adult care and concern that are inappropriate in a school situation; separation anxieties are common. In general, they need not become a major problem if the first days of school are carefully planned by teachers and parents.

In a few instances, a child and parent may have prolonged and severe separation problems. At the least hint that the parent may leave, the child embarks on a full-blown tantrum. The severe reactions may have come about because the parent, after agreeing to stay, had tried to slip away without saying good-bye. In these cases, teachers must involve parents in a plan to help the child learn to separate. Discussions of the problem should take place away from the classroom and out of the child's earshot. The situation can only worsen if the child is further burdened with the parents' and teachers' concerns. The focus of any separation program is on the parent's gradual withdrawal, usually over several days. The amount of time required depends on the child and the severity of the problem. Throughout the parent's separation efforts, teachers encourage and appreciate the child's participation and active use of play materials. Gradually, teacher support replaces parent support.

Children who actually enjoy coming to the program may use protest as a way to keep their parents at school. Such children engage in every activity and play happily as long as the parent stays. As soon as the parent tries to leave, the child creates a scene. These parents often complain about the child's behavior. Yet, after saying good-bye, they tend to pause and look back, as if waiting for the child to begin a tantrum. In these cases, the teacher may have to assist the lingering parent in leaving swiftly with only a brief and matter-of-fact good-bye. The child almost always settles back into play after a token protest.

18-5f ■ Over-Dependence

The early childhood teacher may be the target of a child's efforts to get extraordinary amounts of attention. The over-dependent child may cling to a particular teacher, hang on to the teacher's clothing, and shadow the teacher's every move. Complaining, whining, and tattling may be accompanying problems. Working with a child like this requires teachers to walk a fine line between giving too much and too little attention. Too much is likely to increase the dependence; too little may lead the child to feeling uncared-for, even rejected.

To receive full benefit from the program, a child must be helped to relate to all teachers and eventually to other children. Once the child is familiar with the program and the routines, the weaning process can begin. The teacher's major concern is not reducing the amount of attention given; it is making decisions as to *when* to give attention in order to help rather than hinder the child's progress. These scenarios illustrate positive attention giving:

- The teacher watches for moments when the child is not clinging and immediately gives attention: "It looks like you are enjoying the book. Let's read the pictures. What do you suppose is going to happen to the kitten?"

- When a child is pulling at a teacher's clothing or person, the teacher resists the impulse to react or respond. As always, *preventive measures are best:* as the child approaches, the teacher can reach out and put an arm around the child or take the child's hand *before* the clinging or clutching starts.

- Teachers support the child in taking personal responsibility, beginning with nonthreatening situations: "If you want to play in the rocking boat, I'll go with you while you talk to Sherri. If you ask, I know she'll stop rocking so you can get in."

- Finding ways to get the child to allow other teachers to respond to his or her needs is another step in solving the problem. The teacher chooses times when the child really wants something, as when one teacher says to another: "Miss Jane, Charles wants the red truck. Will you get it out for him?" Or to the child, "I can't read your book because I have to set up finger painting. Let's ask Mr. John to read it to you."

The occasional teacher finds it flattering to be singled out for undivided devotion and unintentionally reinforces the child's dependent behaviors. In these instances, both child and teacher need the help of other staff members.

Over-dependent, anxious children may also complain of headaches, stomachaches, or nearly invisible cuts and scrapes. Although the hurt is real to the child, it also has become a sure way of getting focused attention from an important adult. Most young children can be expected to have this kind of complaint on occasion. When the complaints go on day after day, it is cause for concern. Teachers should first check with parents to make sure there are no physical problems. Classroom procedures then become the same as for other problem behaviors: minimum attention to the aches and scrapes and additional attention when the child is actively engaged in play. This helps the child to focus on the fun times at school.

18-5g ■ Withdrawal

Some children seem to be alone most of the time.

© Cengage Learning 2015

Some children seem to be alone most of the time. They turn away when other children approach. In structured large-group activities, they may be there in body but are remote, not there in spirit. Teachers seldom express the degree of concern over these children that they do with children who act out. The behaviors of the withdrawn child are easily overlooked; those of the disruptive child seldom go unnoticed. Yet the withdrawn child may be in greater developmental jeopardy than the child who acts out.

Withdrawal problems and their causes can be so complex as to require clinical treatment and a therapeutic classroom. The children teachers encounter in early childhood programs are likely to have less serious problems with less obscure origins. The cause may be a recent upheaval at home (such as a parent's leaving) or a serious illness in the family. It may be a change of neighborhood where the new children's ways seem strange, even frightening or bullying. It may be the first venture of an only child, or a child with a developmental disability, into a play setting with other children. These children may have been overprotected unwittingly by parental efforts to keep them from getting hurt or catching a childhood disease. Some withdrawn children are simply shy. All children experience occasional shyness, but in some, shyness becomes habitual. Whatever the cause, teachers usually can help these children become more involved.

Careful observation, as always, is the first step. Specific questions need to be addressed.

● Does the child engage in particular activities when playing alone?

● Are there materials and equipment that the child appears to enjoy or prefer?

● Does the child spend time watching certain children or certain activities more than others?

● Is the child likely to leave an activity if certain children approach? Does the child avoid these children consistently?

● Are some children less threatening for the child to sit next to in group activities? to play next to in parallel play situations?

When a child's preferences (and avoidances) have been noted, plans can be made to reduce the child's isolation. "Start small" is the rule of thumb. Following are three examples of first approximations to social interactions for Jeanine, a child whose isolate behaviors were of concern.

- On several occasions, the teacher had observed Jeanine watching housekeeping play with apparent interest. The teacher arranged that he and the child together deliver additional materials to the activities in progress. Teacher: "Jeanine and I have brought more birthday candles. We'll put some of them on the cake, too, okay?"

- Jeanine seemed fascinated by the rocking boat. A quiet but friendly child asked the teacher for another ride. The teacher responded, "Yes, Jon, but let's give Jeanine a ride, too. Here, Jeanine, you sit across from Jon." Another time, a third child is invited, who also is seated across from Jeanine; then, a fourth who sits *next to* Jeanine. In each of these early steps, the teacher selected quieter, less rambunctious children to share the ride.

- Jeanine was watching two children working with pegboards. Teacher: "Jeanine, I'll put a pegboard down here for you." (The teacher placed the pegboard at the end of the small table, near—but not between—the other children.) "All three of you can reach the basket of pegs." Having Jeanine take pegs out of a common basket was a step forward from the week before. At that time, the teacher had seated her near the other children but had given her a small basket of pegs of her own.

Occasionally, a shy child will focus almost exclusively on one or more of the adults in the program. Over-dependence does not seem to be the problem; it is simply that the child prefers the company of adults. This child will find ways to sit next to the teacher, linger during transitions to help the teacher clean up, or engage in long, one-to-one conversations with the teacher. This may be pleasant for the teacher, but it does not promote the kind of social development that comes with learning to interact with other children. The teacher's job becomes one of consciously involving another child or two in the conversation or the cleanup. If no other children are about, the teacher responds to the child pleasantly but briefly. Then he or she moves to an area where there are other children. Usually, the shy child follows. This increases the teacher's chance to involve other children.

18-5h ■ Inability to Share

It is questionable whether the inability to share and take turns is serious enough to include it in a discussion of behavior problems. Many of today's children, in group care since infancy, learn to share early and readily. However, the issue continues to be of concern to many early childhood teachers. Sharing and taking turns are learned behaviors. It is suggested that, developmentally, the **egocentric** young child needs to establish a sense of *mine* before accommodating to the concept of *thine*. For many young children, this learning does not come easily. Suggestions for helping all types of young children learn to comply with these social expectations are discussed below.

egocentric in reference to young children, implies a view of the world from one perspective only—the child's own

- Providing plentiful materials is one key to helping young children learn to share. In all early childhood programs, there should be duplicates of the most popular materials. Large sets (Legos, for example) can be divided into two or three smaller sets. These are distributed among individual baskets or boxes, enabling several children to have their own supplies. Spontaneous trading of particular pieces often emerges.

- Interest centers need to be attractive and located in various parts of the classroom and play yard. With several attractive setups, children do not need to stand around waiting. The teacher can advise: "You could play at the water table or the woodworking bench for a while. I'll call you when there is room on the bouncing board." The teacher must remember to alert the child when space becomes available. By that time, the child may not want to change activities, but the teacher's part of the bargain has been kept.

- A game-like atmosphere can help children learn to wait and take turns. The teacher might use a kitchen timer and advise: "When the timer bell rings, it is Bart's turn," or "It will be Bart's turn with the big rolling pin when the timer goes off." Older preschool children can look at the clock with the teacher and understand, "When the big hand gets to five it will be your turn," or "There's no room at blocks right now, but you can go there first, right after music." Children and teachers can also count turns: "Josh, you can have two more turns around the track. Then it will be Susie's turn. She has waited a long time. . . . Susie, you and I will count."

Children must be stopped when they knock other children off equipment because they want a turn or when they use force to get or keep the toys they want. As during other instances of aggression, the teacher states the case clearly and firmly: "I cannot let you take Maria's doll," or "I cannot let you knock Jerry off the swing." At the same time, the teacher helps the other child hang on to a possession by encouraging specific verbalizations such as "Tell Nonie, 'That's my doll. Give it back,'" or "'You can't have the swing 'til I'm through.'" At that point, the teacher makes sure the doll is returned or the place on the swing is recovered. If necessary, the teacher physically assists in the return.

18-5i ■ The Family's Involvement

Families must play a central role in addressing challenging behaviors. Challenging behavior typically occurs across places, people, and time; thus, families are critical members of the intervention team. A family's culture can affect a family's participation in the assessment and intervention process. Cultural differences can account for differences in agreement about what is or is not considered a

Sharing comes easily for some children.

© Cengage Learning 2015

Connecting Developmentally Appropriate Practice to Brain Research

EXECUTIVE FUNCTION SKILLS AND SOCIAL PROBLEM SOLVING

Executive functions consist of those skills that enable a child to engage in independent, purposive, self-motivated behavior.

These skills include development of:

- attention and impulse control
- information processing
- cognitive flexibility and purposeful behavior
- initiative
- engagement and persistence, and
- reasoning and problem solving.

Children's executive function skills are the foundation for learning and social interaction and provide the link between early school success and social-emotional development.

Elementary school teachers tend to be experts in the area of executive function skills. It is often within the classroom setting, with the demands of school work, that delays in the development of executive function skills are first noted. When asked to choose, teachers often state that it is far more critical for children to come to school prepared with a base of executive functioning skills rather than knowledge of numbers and letters. According to the Center on the Developing Child at Harvard University (2011), teachers identify problems with paying attention, managing emotions, completing tasks, and communicating wants and needs as major contributing factors of whether a child is ready to succeed in school.

The center also notes that research indicates that young children who demonstrate difficulty staying focused and controlling impulsive behavior are at increased risk of exhibiting behavior problems.

The good news is that research is also showing that intervention targeted at teaching executive functions skills can make a difference. Recent evaluations of several preschool interventions designed to strengthen children's use of executive function skills in the classroom (as opposed to programs that focus on teaching cognitive skills such as letters and numbers) are demonstrating that these skills are open to improvement during the early childhood years. The interventions found to be effective tend to focus on one of three strategies: (1) fostering emerging executive function skills such as the ability to retain and use information, focus and resist distraction, as well as to make plans and revise these plans when needed; (2) training and supporting teachers in the use of effective classroom management strategies such as described throughout this text (e.g., use of positive reinforcement and redirection), as well as the support of a mental health consultant who helps with both overall

classroom challenges and the needs of particular children; and (3) modeling, coaching, and training children to develop problem-solving skills, the ability to understand and express emotions, and the ability to control impulsive behavior and organize themselves to accomplish goals.

Preschools and elementary schools are increasingly implementing programs that include a common vocabulary to describe emotions as well as a consistent strategy for problem solving. The problem-solving strategy typically includes the following steps:

1. Identify what the problem is;
2. Think about solutions;
3. Think about what will happen if I do this and how the other child will feel if I do this; and
4. Try the solution.

For children to become independent in the problem-solving process, adults model it throughout the school day, adults assist students in its use both individually and when in conflict with others, and parents support the use at home. Children as young as two or three can be supported in the use of the process and become independent in its use. A mom who fully embraced this model with her own children reported that it did take some effort upfront to teach her three- and four-year-old how to use the steps. She explained, "Within a month after we started, when I heard them beginning to disagree I would begin to count to ten to myself, and before I got to six they were usually beginning to work on solving the problem themselves. Of course there were times when I had to step in, but they became very independent in solving social conflicts both with each other as well as with friends." Her children are now young adults, and she and her husband both attest that is one of the best things they did as parents.

Given the importance of young children's executive function skills and emerging evidence that these skills can be improved through focused intervention such as that described above, efforts to support the development of these skills deserve greater focus. They should be part of the curriculum in the early childhood education programs and teacher training programs.

Your Turn

1. Make a list of five or more times during the school day that a teacher could model the use of the problem-solving steps. Give specific examples for each time of the day you identified.
2. Design a circle activity that models the steps for problem solving.
3. Discuss some other strategies a teacher or parent might use to strengthen executive functioning skills.

Source: Center on the Developing Child at Harvard University (2011). *Building the Brain's "Air Traffic Control" System: How Early Experiences Shape the Development of Executive Function: Working Paper No. 11.* Retrieved from www.developingchild.harvard.edu

challenge or problem. Throughout the process, it is essential that professionals respect the family's perspective (Noonan & McCormick, 2006).

As stated by the DEC (2007), a coordinated effort between family members and professionals is needed to assure that interventions are effective and efficient and address both child and family needs and strengths. All decisions regarding the identification of a challenging behavior, possible interventions, placement, and ongoing evaluation must be made in accordance with the family through the IEP, IFSP, or other team decision-making processes.

Did You Get It?

What would be the short term as opposed to the long term benefit of using time-out?

a. Gives teacher a break; gives the child strategies to work on.

b. Provides temporary relief; creates quiet in the environment.

c. Breaks the pattern of disruptiveness; creates quiet in the environment.

d. Breaks the pattern of disruptiveness; helps child learn to respond to more desirable guidance procedures such as redirection.

Take the full quiz on CourseMate.

Summary

The focus of this chapter was on a variety of behavior problems found in young children.

▶ A functional approach to problem behaviors, to provide teachers with a systematic way to address these behaviors in the classroom, was described.

▶ When you are dealing with challenging behaviors, it is important to remember that they serve a communicative function: that is, children—especially those with severe communication problems—are trying to tell us something. It is important that we help children find a more appropriate way to get their message across.

▶ Many challenging behaviors in preschoolers are perfectly normal. They tend to be trial-and-error responses, a part of children's efforts at learning to discriminate between acceptable and unacceptable ways of responding to the expectations of their home, school, and community. Seldom are acting-out behaviors cause for serious concern unless they become excessive to the point of threatening the child's well-being or the rights and safety of others.

▶ Most behavior problems can be managed through careful arrangement of the environment—materials, activities, space, routines, expectations, and adult attention.

▶ Positive adult attention should be focused on all of the good things each child does each day. When a child's behavior causes damage or injury, the child must be stopped; it is unethical to do otherwise.

▶ In extreme cases where the child has not responded to careful rearrangement of the environment, temporary use of time-out may be needed. Brief time-out periods always are used in conjunction with other procedures, including acceptance and understanding of the child's stresses and special attention to the child's appropriate behaviors.

▶ When any intervention is used, adults must also take care to teach the child a replacement behavior. The child must be given skills to use, in place of the problem behavior.

▶ When using an intervention such as time-out, a reliable and easy-to-use data collection system is essential. Data will help indicate whether the intervention is working and can also help teachers learn about what is influencing a child's behavior.

▶ All decisions regarding the identification of a challenging behavior, possible interventions, placement, and ongoing evaluation must be made in accordance with the family through the IEP, IFSP, or other team decision-making processes.

Key Terms

antecedents, 479
baseline, 483
consequences, 479
data collection, 482
duration measures, 482
egocentric, 496

fading, 482
frequency (counts), 482
functional behavior assessment
  (FBA), 479
goodness-of-fit, 474
interval, 482

normal deviations, 474
oppositional behavior, 489
positive behavior support, 478
preventive discipline, 490
replacement behavior, 480

Student Activities

1. Observe an early childhood program for at least sixty minutes. Identify things within the classroom that fall under the tiers of the teaching pyramid discussed in this chapter. List at least one other recommendation or idea for Tiers 1–3, and Tier 4 if appropriate.

2. Select a partner; one of you plays the role of teacher, the other, a noncompliant child. Demonstrate several ways the teacher might work with the child to obtain compliance *before* the child balks at a request. Reverse roles and play out several ways of helping a child share a wagon.

3. Divide a sheet of paper into five columns. Head each column with terms commonly used to describe children's acting-out behaviors: aggressive, destructive, disruptive, noncompliant, tantrum. Observe during a free-play period and put a mark in the appropriate column each time one of the behaviors occurs. Circle the mark if a teacher responds in any way. Figure out the ratio of teacher responses to child behaviors. Analyze whether certain behaviors draw more teacher attention than others.

Review Questions

Briefly respond to the following items.

1. Describe how *goodness-of-fit* is related to problem behaviors.

2. What are the basic components of an intervention plan to help an overaggressive child?

3. What can teachers do to help prevent noncompliance in young children?

4. Extensive research indicates that ignoring tantrums decreases them. The problem is that this advice often backfires. Why?

5. How can teachers reduce a child's overdependence?

6. What is meant by preventive discipline?

7. What has recent research taught us about the importance of executive function skills?

8. Put the following table in the proper sequence for developing a plan to manage a problem behavior.

Identify a replacement behavior.

Plan the intervention. Ensure that meaningful curriculum activities, frequent reinforcement, choice, and a predictable schedule are in place.

Specify an objective for the intervention.

Implement the plan and ensure that it is carried out as planned.

Assess the function of the behavior.

Identify the problem situation.

Assess the child and the environment.

Monitor the child's progress and continue to monitor implementation.

Additional Resources/Readings

Practical Guidance Strategies for Challenging Behaviors in Preschool
Written by Eva Essa
Wadsworth Publishing

This book is designed to help teachers work effectively with young children whose behaviors are challenging. It offers a series of chapters that provide developmentally appropriate guidelines for working with challenging behaviors. The book includes a discussion of preventative techniques, as well as the importance of working with families. There are additional chapters that present very specific guidelines for handling a range of common behavioral concerns. Each chapter presents a step-by-step approach to changing such behaviors to more socially appropriate ones. A CD-ROM is included that contains additional resources such as guidelines for careful observation, data collection, and record keeping.

Helpful Websites

Office of Special Education Programs (OSEP), Technical Assistance Center for Positive Behavioral Interventions and Supports

http://www.pbis.org

The TA Center on Positive Behavioral Interventions and Supports has been established by the Office of Special Education Programs (U.S. Department of Education) to give schools capacity-building information and technical assistance for identifying, adapting, and sustaining effective school-wide disciplinary practices. This website disseminates information on research-based practices, including effective disciplinary practices, interventions for social skills, and using behavioral assessment to design interventions.

The Technical Assistance Center on Social Emotional Intervention for Young Children (TACSEI)

http://challengingbehavior.org

The Technical Assistance Center on Social Emotional Intervention for Young Children (TACSEI) takes evidence-based practices shown to improve the social-emotional outcomes for young children with, or at risk for, delays or disabilities, and creates free products and resources to help decision makers, caregivers, and service providers apply these best practices in the work they do every day. The website includes information about the Pyramid Model of Intervention.

 Visit the Education CourseMate for this textbook to access the eBook, Did You Get It? quizzes, Digital Downloads, TeachSource Video Cases, flashcards, and more. Go to CengageBrain.com to log in, register, or purchase access.

Planning Transitions to Support Inclusion

OBJECTIVES

After reading this chapter, you should be able to:

19-1 describe two program transitions that occur in early childhood and discuss how they differ.

19-2 outline the steps in the transition process, including the roles of the family and sending and receiving programs.

19-3 discuss the transition from early intervention to preschool, including the legal requirements.

19-4 highlight the strategies that help ensure a successful transition to kindergarten.

• • • • • • • • • • • • • • • • •

naeyc

The following NAEYC Standards are addressed in this chapter:

STANDARD 1 Promoting Child Development and Learning

STANDARD 2 Building Family and Community Relationships

STANDARD 4 Using Developmentally Effective Approaches

☀ 19-1 Transitions During Early Childhood Services

Each year, thousands of children and families move from one type of early childhood program to another. Perhaps it is from an early intervention home program to a preschool, or from an early intervention preschool to kindergarten in their neighborhood public school. Transitions occur for a variety of reasons. The most common is the child's age. Other reasons include the child's developmental needs, a family relocation, or a newly identified diagnosis (Minor, 2002). Planning any of these transitions is critical, but such planning is often neglected. It is as though we expect all children and their families to be resilient, bouncing like balls from one set of services to another. Children with special needs require more attention and planning than their typical peers. They may take somewhat longer to adjust to new people and environments. They may experience separation problems from their families during the first few weeks or even months of school, especially if this is their first group experience away from home (Haymes, Fowler, & Cooper, 1994). Entry into a new program may require accommodations on the part of the service providers, the family, and the child (Bohan-Baker & Little, 2004; Rice & O'Brien, 1990). The child may need to play and work more independently. The family may need to alter its before- or after-school child care arrangements to fit the schedule of the new program. Child care, preschool, or kindergarten staff may need to redesign some activities or routines to meet the needs of the new child. If the child does not meet program expectations, or if accommodations made to assist the child are only short-term, the result can be an unsuccessful placement, creating stress and unhappiness for all involved. The consequence is yet another transition. Thus, planning both the changes required by the transition and ways of maintaining these changes over time are critical factors in ensuring a successful entry to a new program. Carefully planning a transition will prevent interruption in service to the child, ensure parents have an opportunity to participate in the process, ease the adjustment of the child and family, and reduce the likelihood of duplication of testing, planning meetings, and services (Conn-Powers, Ross-Allen, & Holburn, 1990). In this chapter, we will address basic elements of planning and implementing successful transitions. Specifics regarding transition at age three, as well as transition from preschool programs to elementary school, will also be provided.

Each year, thousands of children and families move from one type of early childhood program to another.

© Cengage Learning 2015

Steps in the Transition Process 19-2

According to the Individuals with Disabilities Act (IDEA), transition planning for both infant and toddlers and children aged three and up should begin at least six months, but preferably between nine and twelve months, before the child's birthday or move to a new program. Regardless of the age of the child or program being transitioned to, several steps in the transition process are critical to ensuring success (Minor, 2002). These steps include:

1. developing a planning team

2. setting goals

3. defining roles for the family and sending and receiving programs

4. writing the transition plan and procedures

5. reviewing the outcome of the transition and the child's adaptation to the new program

19-2a ■ Developing a Planning Team

Developing a planning team is possibly one of the most critical components of a successful transition. Team members include the parents, representatives from the receiving school district or school, and current service providers. An individual from the receiving program may not be present if the placement has not been identified. This team will discuss several issues, including the type of programs to consider on the basis of the child's individual needs and whether the child should receive services in a special day class, a typical preschool or kindergarten, or an early intervention clinic. The planning team should also determine when and how the transition will take place. During the initial stages of planning it is also helpful to identify other families with a similar child who can share their transition experience (Smith, 1993).

19-2b ■ Setting Goals

Before setting goals, team members should have a good understanding of the curriculum and expectations of the receiving program. If current service providers and parents are not familiar with the receiving program, they should observe and note the differences between the two programs. The information they obtain will be used in combination with the child's current levels to write goals. In addition to goals, the team should identify possible challenges and solutions.

Challenges may include the difference in adult/child ratios or the amount of time a child will be expected to sit and attend at circle time.

19-2c ■ Roles of Team Members

The role of the sending program The sending program is the major support system for the child and family during the transition. It assists the family in gathering information about the new program(s) and provides recent reports and evaluations to the receiving program. One critical component of transition planning is for the sending program to work with the child and family to identify any skills the child may need to learn to succeed in the new program (see the following section on preparing children for transitions). This might include experience with sitting on a carpet square for circle versus a chair, being able to attend for longer periods of time, being able to write his or her name, or walking down a hall to use the bathroom. When these skills are identified before the transition, current service providers can spend time preparing the child for the receiving program's expectations. Figure 19-1 lists the role of the sending program.

The role of the receiving program The receiving program may or may not have much experience with a child with special needs. Depending on their experience, they may be anxious about being able to meet the needs of the child. To ensure a successful transition, the receiving program should meet with the family and child before the child begins. The family should be provided with brochures, tours, and program times. Before the child starts, it is important to hold a meeting with the parents, teachers, program director (if applicable), and current providers. The purpose of this meeting is to answer any questions, identify potential problems, and share strategies found to be effective in working with the child. If an aide or paraprofessional will be shadowing the child, his or her role in relation to the other adults in the room should be clarified. It is also important for the receiving program to identify the parents' desires with regard to how to handle questions from other parents. Parents of children with special needs have varied wishes, ranging from wanting no one to know that their child has special needs to wanting to share all they have learned with fellow parents. According to parent wishes, staff should have a plan on how to handle questions when they arise.

Before the child's start date, the receiving program should ensure that all staff, including volunteers, have the information they need to work effectively with the child. Ongoing consultation from specialists or additional in-service trainings may be required throughout the year. Finally, the receiving program, in collaboration with the parents, should determine how to provide ongoing feedback and communication. This is key, because very often a transition can result in a change from parents having daily contact and communication with their child's provider to seeing them only on an occasional basis. Figure 19-1 lists the role of the receiving program.

The role of parents Throughout their children's early intervention years, families are taught to become their advocates. When the shift in services occurs from family-centered to child-centered, it can be difficult for parents (Johnson, 2001). Family involvement is a critical component of transition planning (Bruder & Chandler, 1996; Hains, Rosenkoetter, & Fowler, 1991;

FIGURE 19-1

Role of Service Providers and Parents during Transitions

Role of Sending Program	Role of Receiving Program	Role of Parents
• Gather information about the new program (i.e., contact person, telephone numbers, and population of children attending the program)	• Make arrangements to meet the family and child before the child begins	• Learn about the transition process:
• Provide copies of recent reports and evaluations	• Provide pictures, brochures, tours, times for observation for the family and/or previous service providers	○ How are children evaluated?
• Support the family during the process	• Identify physical barriers that may impede the child's access	○ When will my child make the transition?
• Determine if the child needs to learn a new skill prior to the transition	• Identify and supply special materials and equipment needed (adaptive seating, eating utensils, colorful and musical toys, trikes)	○ When will decisions be made? ○ What are the differences between early intervention and preschool?
• Determine if the new program has special materials that the child might need	• Arrange the classroom environment so that children feel safe to explore and socialize	○ What are my child's and family's legal rights related to special education?
• Provide a contact person and telephone number from the sending agency to maintain contact and provide assistance as needed	• Provide the staff information about the child's specific diagnosis and needs	• Be an active member of the transition planning team • Participate in evaluating the child
• Share information about the child that will help the new program understand the child's previous services and his ways of communicating and interacting with the environment	• Learn strategies used in previous program • Provide ongoing in-service training and information on young children with special needs	• Help amend the IFSP to include a transition plan • Work on goals to prepare the child and family for change • Help identify goals for the IEP • Visit potential programs
• Provide the new program with adaptations and supports needed to support the child's play (i.e., materials used to keep toys within the child's reach, adaptive utensils, visual schedules, communication systems)	• Work with family to develop system for ongoing feedback and communication • Evaluate the child's adaptation to the new program and participation in classroom activities	• Participate in placement decisions • Share information about the child with the new program staff • Prior to transition: ○ Visit the new program with their child ○ Arrange play dates with children from the new program

Source: Adapted from Minor, L. (2002, Summer). Effective practices in early intervention planning transitions to preschool. *See/Hear Newsletter*. Retrieved from http://www.tsbvi.edu/seehear/summer02/planning.htm.

Johnson, Chandler, Kerns, & Fowler, 1986). There are many ways that families can participate in their child's transition. Families may choose to gather information about potential programs, share important information about their child with new providers, or arrange for their child to have experiences that will help him or her get ready for preschool. Professionals should not assume that all families have the capacity, desire, or ability to participate in the same ways. A number of factors may influence how the family participates in the transition planning. These include characteristics of the family, the nature of the child's disability, the family's culture and beliefs, and the family's priorities and concerns (Lynch & Hanson, 2011).

Family involvement is a critical component of transition planning.

Families define their roles in transition planning in a variety of ways. In some instances, one parent may take the lead in making decisions for the child. In other instances, both parents may take equally active roles. An aunt or uncle who has expertise in special education may be a major player in some families, while a single parent may elect to bring a close friend to all planning meetings. For transition planning to be successful, it is critical that professionals accept the roles that families create for themselves.

It is equally crucial that providers acknowledge and respect families' preferences based on their cultural beliefs and values. Some families may believe that professionals are the experts and that it would be a sign of disrespect to question them. At the same time, other families may be offended by communicative mannerisms (e.g., gestures or touches) that are considered to be acceptable in the mainstream culture but not in their culture.

For example, an Asian family may interpret direct eye contact as a sign of disrespect on the part of the service provider (Hyun & Fowler, 1995). Service providers who understand or recognize the influence that culture may play in a family's involvement in their child's transition will be better able to support the family in identifying their priorities for transition.

Figure 19-1 presents an outline of information that families may find helpful to share in a meeting with their child's new teachers. For many families, participation in the transition planning process helps reduce the stress that they may be feeling regarding the change in programs. Just as transition plans should be individualized for each child, each family's role in the transition planning process should be individualized to meet members' needs and expectations. Some families may choose to be more involved than others. As noted earlier, their involvement may be influenced by a variety of factors such as culture, history with schools, employment hours, and child care options. Figure 19-2 presents a list of ways that families may choose to be involved in the transition planning process.

19-2d ■ Writing the Transition Plan and Procedures

Once the goals have been identified, the team is ready to develop a list of steps needed for the transition. The team works together to identify specific activities, strategies, and responsibilities. These should be put in writing and include a timeline for completion. Written transition plans help keep the team focused and prevent steps from being overlooked or forgotten (Minor, 2002).

Whether a child makes a transition to an early childhood special education program in a neighborhood public school or to an integrated community-based program, it is critical that a system be in place to support that child's transition at both the individual and the agency level (Rosenkoetter et al., 1994). When there is **interagency collaboration**, it helps to ensure that those children and families experience a smooth transition.

interagency collaboration cooperation among members of the several service agencies involved in the case management of a child and family with special needs

FIGURE **19-2**

Information That
Families May Wish to
Share with Providers

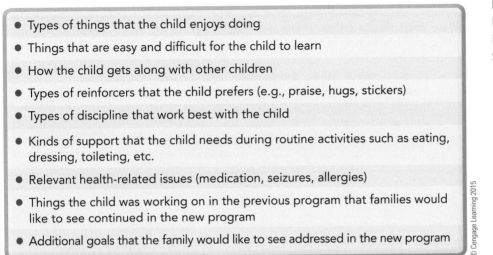

- Types of things that the child enjoys doing
- Things that are easy and difficult for the child to learn
- How the child gets along with other children
- Types of reinforcers that the child prefers (e.g., praise, hugs, stickers)
- Types of discipline that work best with the child
- Kinds of support that the child needs during routine activities such as eating, dressing, toileting, etc.
- Relevant health-related issues (medication, seizures, allergies)
- Things the child was working on in the previous program that families would like to see continued in the new program
- Additional goals that the family would like to see addressed in the new program

© Cengage Learning 2015

TeachSource Digital Download Download from CourseMate.

In addition to writing the transition plan described above, interagency collaboration may include written agreements that spell out the policies and procedures that each agency will follow as children move from one program to another (Bruder & Chandler, 1996; Fowler, Hains, & Rosenkoetter, 1990; Rosenkoetter, et al., 1994). An agreement should detail procedures, such as how the early intervention agency will share information with the local education agency, what role families may play in the evaluation process, and how the case conference to determine a child's eligibility for continuing special education will be set up (Hadden, Fowler, Fink, & Wischnowski, 1995). Research on the impact of local interagency agreements on the age-three transition suggests that a well-crafted agreement leads to improved transitions for children and families (Hadden, 1998).

19-2e ■ Reviewing the Outcome of the Transition and the Child's Adaptation to the New Program

This step is paramount, but is also probably the most overlooked step because of funding realities. The process should include addressing such questions (Minor, 2002) as:

- Is the child adjusting to the program?
- How do the parents feel about the program?
- Do the receiving staff require additional information or training?
- Are transition goals being met?

Follow-up procedures allow for the evaluation of the effectiveness of the transition process.

▶Ⅱ **TeachSource** Video Connections

© Cengage Learning 2015

Preschool: IEP and Transition Planning for a Young Child with Special Needs

This video illustrates how a preschool teacher can set the tone for a positive transition meeting. A strong collaboration between teachers and parents, with a commitment to what is best for the child, is absolutely critical.

After watching the video, discuss the following:

1. In the video, Mark's preschool teacher Ann has planned for his successful transition to kindergarten. List the critical steps you see in the video.

2. List other critical steps not included in the video.

Watch on CourseMate.

19-3 Transition from Early Intervention Services to Preschool Services

Sophie's third birthday is tomorrow, and her family is busy making plans for the big day. They are having a party for her to mark the special occasion. Sophie is excited about her party and is looking forward to having all of her friends there. There is another reason that Sophie is excited about turning three. She gets to go to preschool. Sophie was born with Down syndrome and has been enrolled in an early intervention program since she was an infant. Once a week, a child development specialist has come to her house to teach her parents, Lisbeth and Neal, things that they can do to support Sophie's development.

When Lisbeth and Neal enrolled Sophie in the early intervention program, they were told that when Sophie turned three, the public school would become responsible for providing her education. Three months before Sophie's third birthday, Lisbeth and Neal sat down with Shameem, their child development specialist; Sophie's speech therapist; and a representative from the public school district to formally plan Sophie's transition to preschool. Together, the group wrote a transition plan, a document that identified goals that would prepare both Sophie and her family for the change in programs.

One month before Sophie's birthday, Lisbeth and Neal met once more with Shameem and representatives from the school district. At this meeting, they reviewed the results of Sophie's evaluation for eligibility for special education services. All of the participants shared information about Sophie's strengths and needs. On the basis of the evaluation, the team determined that Sophie was eligible for continued services. The group wrote an individualized education program (IEP), outlining goals and objectives that would address Sophie's educational needs. They then identified programs that would best address these needs. The group decided that Sophie would receive services at a community preschool that Lisbeth and Neal liked and found to be affordable and convenient to their home and work locations.

Sophie had the opportunity to visit her new school several times before her first day. She visited it first when the children were absent so that she could explore the room, toys, and playground with her parents and new teacher. She made several short visits when children were present to watch and join in during free choice and snacks.

As Lisbeth is putting the final touches on the birthday cake, the phone rings. Shameem has called to wish Sophie a happy birthday and to see how the family is feeling about the change. Lisbeth replies that, although they are all a bit sad to have their time with Shameem come to an end, they are excited about tomorrow when Sophie will go to preschool "like a big kid!"

The age-three transition involves more than simply moving a child from one program to another. Children and families encounter many differences as they move at age three from early intervention services to special education services for preschoolers. With planning, the impact of these differences can be minimized.

19-3a ■ Changes in Service Delivery Models and Plans

One of the most obvious differences between early intervention and preschool has to do with the **service delivery model**. Early intervention programs typically provide a home-based program. Child development specialists and therapists visit the child and family in the home, or perhaps in the child care setting. Professionals work with children on an individualized basis and often spend time showing families and other care providers how to support the child's development.

service delivery model a formal plan devised by the various agencies involved in providing services to a given child and family

In contrast, preschool programs are center-based and usually operate four or five days a week. During preschool, children learn a great deal through play, with teacher guidance to support them. Instructions or directions, when provided, may be targeted to members of a small group as well as to individual children. Many young children with special needs ride a school bus or van to school. As a result, families may not have the opportunity to observe their child at school or have direct (face-to-face) conversations with their child's teacher to learn how their child is performing. Even if families transport children, opportunities for conversation may be constrained by the arrival and departure activities.

A second major difference between early intervention and preschool has to do with the plan used to guide service delivery. When a child leaves early intervention, the IFSP (individualized family service plan) often is replaced by an IEP (individualized education program). The IFSP is developed with the family to reflect the family's resources, priorities, and concerns related to their child. As such, the IFSP typically contains goals or outcomes for the family. In contrast, most IEPs are developed with the family to reflect primarily those goals that facilitate a child's educational progress and rarely include family goals.

Other changes that families and children will encounter as they move from early intervention to preschool include differences in eligibility criteria, changes in the role of the family, changes in program philosophy, and the potential reduction or loss of service coordination (Rosenkoetter, Hains, & Fowler, 1994).

19-3b ■ Legal Requirements of Transition

Fortunately, the provisions of the Individuals with Disabilities Education Act (IDEA) require transition planning for all children turning three. Specific provisions include:

1. amending IFSPs to include transition plans

2. giving parents information about the transition process and future placement options

3. preparing the child for changes in service delivery

4. ensuring continuity in services, and

5. sending pertinent child records from the early intervention agency to the local education agency

Although parents should receive information about the transition process from the time they start to receive early intervention services, formal transition planning begins when the IFSP is amended to include the transition plan.

Developing the transition plan A meeting must take place at least ninety days before the child's third birthday to develop a plan for exiting early intervention services. Alternatively, the meeting may occur up to six months before the third birthday, at the discretion of all involved parties. If the child has been receiving early intervention services for an extended period, meeting six months before the transition will give families and providers more time to plan and evaluate appropriate options for the future. A representative from the local education agency attends this meeting along with the family and a representative(s) from the early intervention agency. Federal law also requires that transition planning take place even when a child is not expected to be eligible for continuing special education services at age three. Early intervention providers and the family can discuss community options, such as Head Start or other preschool programs, if the family wants their child to receive continued services. For children who are eligible for services, the IEP must be developed and implemented by the third birthday. This can be a challenge if the child turns three during the summer. Ensuring continuity of services from early intervention to preschool will be discussed later in this chapter.

Preparing children for transition Children display many different temperaments: Some are slow to warm to new situations, while others seem to thrive on change. The transition from one program to another may be easier when the child and parent are prepared for change (Bruder & Chandler, 1996). Children and parents are more likely to be comfortable on the first day of school if they have visited beforehand. However, parents should still anticipate some level of anxiety about separation. It is not uncommon for children to cry when parents leave them at school or help them board the bus. Parents, too, sometimes cry at this initial separation or feel anxious and worried. It can be helpful for all involved if teachers provide short notes during those first few days or even weeks of school.

Children who are able to **transfer skills** from home are more likely to succeed in the new program. For example, a child who follows simple directions given by an unfamiliar adult will have an easier time adapting to the new setting than children who only follow directions given by their parents or caregivers. Children may also benefit from learning **readiness** skills for preschool (Rosenkoetter et al., 1994). It is valuable for service providers and families to teach children skills that will help them in a group setting. Nonetheless, children with disabilities cannot be excluded from a preschool program because they have not mastered certain skills. A critical function of preschool is to accept each child at his or her developmental level and to build on the child's current skills, encouraging new growth and development. According to the Americans with Disabilities Act (ADA), preschools cannot require that children with special needs be toilet-trained or have other prerequisite skills, although they may express a preference for such readiness.

In addition to teaching children skills that they may need in the new setting, families and providers can use other strategies to prepare children for transition. These include talking to the child about the new program, taking the child to visit the new program to meet the staff and to play on the playground, reading

transfer skills the ability to generalize previously learned skills to an unfamiliar setting or a new classroom

readiness a child's ability to learn that takes into account prerequisite physical, cognitive, language, and social skills

books about preschool, riding a bus, and giving the child opportunities to play with other small groups of children.

Some children may be veterans of group child care, having attended a center since infancy. For other children, the move to preschool may be their first experience with extended group care and separation from their family. Participating in programs such as "Mom's Day Out" or library story hours may facilitate a child's adjustment to these changes.

Ensuring continuity of services Waiting lists for special education preschool entry are illegal for children who are leaving early intervention and are eligible for continued special education services. Federal law requires that there be no gaps between programs.

As we know, not all children turn three years of age during the academic school year. Ensuring that children do not lose services because their birthdays occur during the summer, late spring, or early fall may require additional forethought by representatives of the local education agency. Addressing the issue of "inconvenient" birthdays is critical for ensuring that children with disabilities do not lose services merely because their birthdays do not match local administrative calendars or because existing classes are over-enrolled.

Several options are available. If a child turns three in the summer and his or her IEP indicates that the child needs continuous services, services *must be provided*, even if formal preschool classes are not available. It is possible to continue early intervention services beyond the age of three, and it is possible for local education agencies to contract with the early intervention agency to continue services. The local education agency can also provide the services identified on the IEP through home visits or through the provision of consultant services to community programs. It is illegal to place children who have turned three on a waiting list. If a child with a summer birthday has an IEP that indicates a need for uninterrupted services, it is also illegal to require the child to wait for the academic school year to begin to receive services. Early intervention programs and local education agencies can cooperate with each other to initiate preschool special education services before a child turns three if beginning preschool a little earlier is in the child's best interest. This is particularly helpful for children who have early-fall birth dates.

Transferring records Transferring a child's records is a required step in the transition from early intervention to preschool services. The legal guardians or parents of the child have the right to review all records and must be informed about what records will be sent, to whom they will be sent, and when they will be sent. Parents may request that information no longer relevant to the child's educational program be removed from the record. They may also insert a letter noting disagreements with any information contained in the records. The following questions can serve as a guide when planning the transfer of records

- When and how does the program obtain parental consent for transfer of records?
- What information collected by the early intervention program does the local education agency and preschool program need?
- When and how will additional information (e.g., assessment or eligibility data) be obtained?
- Who is responsible for sending the records?

Case Study ■ Planning for a smooth transition ■

Conrad was turning three in early June. It was time to transition from his early intervention preschool to the public school special-day-class preschool. When observed at his early intervention program, Conrad was seen to be very attached to the lead teacher, to the point of being anxious and upset whenever she was out of his sight. His anxiety would escalate to include severe hand mouthing, tantrums, and aggression. The IEP team, including his parents, were quite

concerned about transitioning him to a new program in early June, then to a different summer school program for six weeks from mid-June to the end of July, and then back to the special-day-class preschool in late August. They wanted to develop a plan that would provide for a transition that would help reduce Conrad's anxiety. Based upon the information in this chapter, what are some possible strategies that the team could implement?

- Who in the local education agency will accept and be responsible for the records?
- How are records stored and how is confidentiality maintained?

19-3c ■ Specific Considerations for Children Moving to Inclusive Settings

Children who are eligible to receive special education services at age three should receive them in the **least restrictive environment (LRE)**, that is, the setting in which that child would be if he or she did not have a disability. However, few local school districts provide preschool programs for typically developing children (Hanline, 1992). Therefore, some educators advocate that school districts provide services in community-based programs such as Head Start, private preschool, or child care programs (Peck, Odom, & Bricker, 1993).

Careful planning must take place for children just entering group care or preschool. In some instances, this is the first time that the child with special needs has had the opportunity to interact with children who have no disabilities (Hanline, 1992. Similarly, staff in the community program may have had limited experience with children with special needs. For the experience to be successful, early childhood teachers and special education teachers must forge a new relationship. They must take the time to work out logistical issues such as the best time and manner for the special education teacher to work with children who have IEPs. They also must develop a plan that allows the early childhood teacher to address IEP goals when the special educator is not there. It often requires careful scheduling for these two groups of educators to find adequate time for communication and planning (Fink & Fowler, 1997).

Families may feel additional stress when their children move into inclusive settings (Ostrosky, Donegan, & Fowler, 1997). The transition into a community program may serve to highlight the differences in their child's development. Families may wonder how the staff will accommodate their child's special learning needs and whether the other children will accept their child (Hanline, 1992). The transition from early intervention to preschool is the first significant transition many families encounter. It is not unusual for families to report heightened feelings of stress related to transition.

Several educators have argued that families who have positive experiences with early transitions are more likely to feel confident making later transitions (Fowler, Schwartz, & Atwater, 1991). When families and professionals plan together for the changes that will take place, they help ensure that transitions are successful.

It was February, and Carlos was turning five. He was proud of his new age and delighted in telling everyone that he would soon be going to kindergarten. For the past two years, Carlos had attended the ABC Preschool program, where he also received special education services from a consultant and speech services from a therapist from the local education agency. Carlos had entered preschool with a diagnosis of developmental delay and had shown substantial gains across the two years of preschool services. His mom, Rebecca, was not excited about leaving ABC. She felt comfortable and safe with the preschool and staff. She liked their approach to teaching, which involved many opportunities for the children to choose activities and materials. She also loved the fact that in the class of sixteen children, there were two teachers and many parent volunteers. She worried about how Carlos would behave in a larger classroom with fewer adults. Would he be able to listen and participate in a large group? She knew he could be a bit loud and active in preschool and often liked to play in a rough-and-tumble way. How could she ensure that kindergarten was as supportive and nurturing as preschool? Would the program have an open-door policy for parent volunteers and observers so that she could see how he was doing? Plus, she was worried about before- and after-school care. She was able to drop Carlos at his child care center on her way to work in the morning and to pick him up at 5:15 in the afternoon. Would she find a kindergarten with a similar schedule? Finally, she wondered whether he still needed special services, and if so, what kind?

least restrictive environment (LRE) most normalized environment in which the needs of a child with disabilities can be met appropriately; often, the LRE is interpreted as the environment in which typically developing children function

The transition to kindergarten is another milestone in the lives of children and families. Typically, they are entering the formal system of schooling, which extends for the next twelve years. Unlike the transition from early intervention to preschool, no legal mandates require that the family and preschool providers develop a transition plan to kindergarten. Recent legislation recommends that planning occur but does not specify requirements or steps. Transition to kindergarten is important. The Pre-Elementary Education Longitudinal Study (PEELS), funded by the U.S. Department of Education, supports the emphasis on the importance of this transition. The study examined the characteristics of children receiving preschool special education, including the services they receive, their transitions across educational levels, and their performance over time on assessments of academic and adaptive skills. The study involved a nationally representative sample of 3,104 children with disabilities who were three through five when the study began in 2003–04. The children were followed through 2009. Findings indicate that support and involvement of schools in the process of transitioning to kindergarten was significantly associated with how easy the transition was perceived to be by parents and teachers. For example, 87 percent of parents and 86 percent of teachers reported that the transition was *somewhat easy* or *very easy* when the school initiated support to facilitate the transition. Teachers involved in the study were also asked to indicate which strategies were used to help facilitate the child's transition to kindergarten. Strategies that were used by over 80 percent of teachers included receiving the child's records from the previous program (87 percent), encouraging parents to meet the child's new staff (86 percent), and receiving information about the child from his/her previous program (83 percent) (Carlson, Daley, Bitterman, Heinzen, Keller, Markowitz, & Riley, 2009).

Nearly all states provide kindergarten services; for children to be eligible for kindergarten, states may require them to turn five by a designated date. Recently, California introduced a transitional kindergarten program, which is the first year

Connecting Developmentally Appropriate Practice to Brain Research

REDSHIRTING AND READINESS

Neuroscience has established the fact that the brain is constantly changing. This *plasticity* means that the brain is always adapting and reorganizing on a daily basis. New connections are being created by everyday experiences and learning is taking place. Brain plasticity persists into adulthood but is especially pronounced in the early stages of life. At the same time the brain is growing, it is *pruning* itself, getting rid of unused synapses in a "use it or lose it" function. If the brain is rewiring itself so extensively in the preschool and early elementary years, and requires meaningful, positive experiences to grow, it begs the question: "Why is redshirting, or keeping children back one year, still being practiced?" It would appear that redshirting is actually counterproductive because it deprives the child of a challenging and stimulating school environment. The best way to give children the greatest opportunity to learn is to put them in their age-appropriate classroom setting as soon as possible where their brains are immersed in growing, learning, and changing.

The issue of school readiness has been a hot topic for years, Early childhood professionals agree that children should be able to enter kindergarten when they are of legal age and that schools should be

prepared to meet the needs of children where they are in their development. This is supported by recent brain development research that stresses stimulation and challenges as a way to foster brain growth and learning. Instead, schools have developed a variety of methods noted earlier to create more homogeneous classes rather than address the variety of developmental stages of children of kindergarten age.

There are many reasons children enter school without the resources and tools to succeed, such as poverty, language and cultural differences, access to high-quality early education programs, and lack of effective early intervention that includes comprehensive services.

Readiness has been defined as ready children, ready families, ready communities, ready early care and education, and ready schools (Rhode Island KIDS COUNT, 2005). All of these are necessary if we want all children to be ready for successful school experiences that use their brain potential to greatest advantage.

Questions

1. When might it be appropriate to delay a child's entry into school?

2. Why do disadvantaged children have the most to lose from delayed entry into school?

Source: Gordon, A. M., & Williams Browne, K. (2010). *Beginnings and beyond: Foundations in Early Childhood Education.* Wadsworth Publishing.

of a two-year kindergarten program specifically designed for children who turn five in the fall of their kindergarten year. The curriculum is developmentally appropriate for younger children. The program is designed to provide a bridge between preschool and traditional kindergarten and is intended to help students with fall birthdays become more successful in their future years of schooling. All children with special needs and an IEP are also guaranteed access to continued school services, whether the services are delivered in a public or private kindergarten. In addition to the strategies mentioned by the PEELS study, the practices within this chapter are recommended to help families, children, and educators plan a kindergarten entry that can be successful for all involved.

19-4a ■ Transition Planning

Planning is essential. As noted earlier, the accommodations required of everyone during a transition tend to be stressful (Johnson et al., 1986). Families may simultaneously celebrate and worry about the transition to kindergarten. They may rejoice in their child's growth and development while mourning the fact that their child—due to special needs or delays—may differ from other five-year-olds. Children may show separation anxiety and other signs of stress not seen since they entered preschool. If parents and professionals can work as partners in developing a plan acceptable to all, it is more likely that everyone will agree with the outcomes (Fowler & Titus, 1999).

Planning for kindergarten entry should be an ongoing part of each child's program, beginning at least three to six months before a change in programs and extending as long as needed into kindergarten. Time must be built into the regular school schedule for staff and parent meetings, for the option to visit potential new programs, and for the exchange of information about the child's preschool program, the child's progress, and family preferences. Making time for the family and preschool and kindergarten staffs to communicate after the child has entered kindergarten may also be helpful in easing some children's adjustment. It is not unusual for children to spend the first six to eight weeks getting used to their new class. Six steps identified in the following pages can improve a child's transition to kindergarten.

Step 1: Plan the transition in the spring Children with an IEP specifying services to be received during their preschool years will have an IEP meeting to update their individual plan every year. Although it is not a legal requirement, many early childhood educators recommend that the preschool staff and special service providers conduct a spring review and identify the options that may be available for kindergarten in the fall. A representative of the local education agency, often the special education consultant, can provide this information. Some communities have open enrollment in which families can request attendance at any school in their district; other communities assign schools on the basis either of neighborhood location or of social, racial, and economic distribution of children across schools. Determining whether parents have a choice of school locations is a first step. If they do have choices, providing parents with information about each school's goals, location, hours, availability of care programs before and after school, and academic calendar is important. In our vignette, Carlos lived in a community that offered many options. These included two year-round school programs and four schools with no after-school care and the option of half-day kindergarten. Special education services were available at all schools, but two schools had a greater concentration of therapists than the others. Rebecca had the opportunity to look at a number of schools and make a request for the schools that best met both her needs for after-school care and Carlos's needs for a supportive kindergarten. If families do not have a choice about the public school assignments, it is still important to provide information about the assigned school and service options available. Some families may also wish to discuss private school options.

Step 2: Identify options by visiting future programs Children benefit when early childhood professionals are familiar with the philosophy and curriculum of each other's programs. It is not unusual for a community to have a district-wide kindergarten curriculum. It is helpful for the preschool teachers and special education service providers, including speech and physical therapists, to be aware of this curriculum. In an ideal world, kindergarten and special educators would also be familiar with the range of preschool philosophies and curricula

Providing opportunities for children to make new friends can help with transitions.

© Cengage Learning

and would recognize that preschool programs accredited by NAEYC follow a philosophy of developmentally appropriate practice (National Association for the Education of Young Children, 1998). Understanding the similarities and differences in teaching styles and child expectations can assist the team planning the transition.

Sometimes, visits to a variety of kindergarten classes can be arranged by calling the school district. More and more schools have an early childhood specialist or family specialist whose job includes arranging meetings to discuss kindergarten entry. Several things are worth observing when visiting a school and its classrooms. The observer should note ways in which the program is similar to or different from the preschool and whether those differences are likely to present challenges to the child. We recommend observing a number of classrooms to understand the variation in activities, teaching style, and curricula across a school district. It is unusual for families to pick a specific teacher and classroom, and teacher assignments may change across school years. The observations should be geared to determining general trends in a school district's kindergarten program. Observation notes can be arranged under the following headings.

- *Environment*—the physical arrangement and size of the classroom, the number of teachers, aides, and volunteers, and the daily schedule.

- *Interactions*—what children and teachers do, how they interact with one another, and how often.

- *Classroom activities and curricula*—the learning opportunities provided for the children; the degree to which the curriculum is integrated so that math, writing, and reading can be part of the same activity and not separate segments of the class schedule.

- *Management strategies*—the rules and routines used in the class to guide and support child learning, the cues and consequences used to assist children in meeting classroom expectations, and the strategies used to support and encourage.

When observing kindergarten classrooms, valuable information can be obtained regarding the academic, social, and behavioral requirements of the classrooms. These observations can provide ideas for goals and objectives for the transitioning child. It is important to note that these skills should not be viewed as prerequisites or requirements to placement in the general education setting, but rather as targets for intervention and instruction (Noonan & McCormick, 2006).

Step 3: Prepare the child On the basis of kindergarten visits, the preschool or special services staff may identify a number of strategies and activities to assist children who are making the transition. Figure 19-3 presents activities and skills that will assist children in adjusting to a new program. Many of these may have already been a part of the preschool curriculum. Just as we discussed in the transition to preschool section of this chapter, children may feel more assured about their school entry if they can visit their new school. This visit should be scheduled only after a decision has been made regarding services and the location of the program. Parents also may drive by the new school during the summer and point it out to their child as his or her new kindergarten; they may want to stop and play on the playground. A strongly recommended practice is to provide the child with an opportunity to meet his or her future teacher shortly before the start of school and to visit the classroom. The family also should have an

- Talk with the child about the impending changes; note how much the child has grown and is growing.
- Read children's books about entering kindergarten that are positive and
- encouraging. For a comprehensive list of books, visit http://center.serve.org/tt/booksfor.pdf.
- Read with the child daily, encouraging increased attention and involvement in the stories.
- Provide opportunities for the child to make new friends.
- Encourage the child to communicate with others (children may do this with gestures, spoken language, or sign language).
- Encourage the child to make simple choices (e.g., ask whether she wants to wear blue or white socks, what toys she would like to play with, or whether she wants cookies or applesauce for snack).
- Help the child to care for and be responsible for some personal belongings.
- Provide opportunities for the child to practice sharing.
- Assist the child in using toys and equipment in an appropriate, functional way.
- Support the child in acquiring as many self-help skills as possible.
- Encourage the child to ask for help when needed.
- Provide opportunities for the child to play independently.
- Teach the child to follow simple directions, both in a game-like format and through helping around the home.
- Practice with the child his or her full name, address, and, if available, phone number.
- Expose the child to colors, shapes, and school-related materials such as crayons, markers, and play dough.
- Visit the new program and meet the new teacher.
- Remember to include transition-related goals in the child's IEP.

© Cengage Learning 2015

TeachSource Digital Download Download from CourseMate.

opportunity for a private meeting with the teacher to share information about their child's likes and dislikes, learning style, and other information that they deem relevant (Chandler, Fowler, Hadden, & Stahurski, 1995). See Figure 19-3 for a list of issues parents may wish to share.

Step 4: Enter kindergarten The staff and family may find it helpful to discuss ways for the child to begin school. Should the child start with a short visit to the classroom just to meet with the teacher? Does the school have a policy of inviting half the class on the first day and the other half on the second day to give children an opportunity to meet peers in a smaller group? Are the first few days of school shorter than the regular day? Can the school individualize a schedule for the child during the first few weeks, to optimize success? In some schools, a paraprofessional or experienced volunteer is provided during the first several weeks to assist children in settling into the daily routine. Of course, if paraprofessional support is specified on the IEP, then the child begins school with individualized support. With systematic planning and cooperation among staff and family, the new experience can be made comfortable, minimizing tears, confusion, and anxiety. Teachers may wish to consider the following ideas for helping children to adjust to their new class.

- Talk about the new program with the children, how the children are growing up, how kindergarten may be different from preschool, perhaps a little scary, but also fun.

- Provide extra time for free play so that children get to know one another and receive needed guidance on sharing and interacting appropriately.

- Give simple one and two-step instructions. Gradually increase the number and complexity of tasks when children have demonstrated success.

- Vary the duration and type of activities more frequently in the beginning of the school year.

- Vary the amount of teacher help during instructional tasks according to individual needs.

- Throughout the first weeks of school, review classroom rules and routines at least once each day.

- Consider pairing children up as buddies to help each other with simple tasks, such as putting toys away and putting coats on.

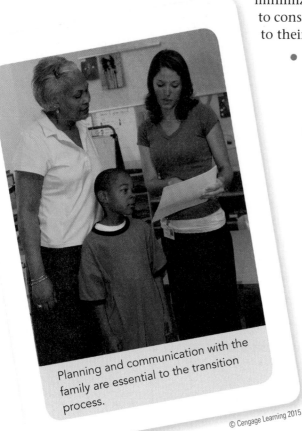

Planning and communication with the family are essential to the transition process.

© Cengage Learning 2015

Step 5: Implement informal support services During the first weeks of school, some children will need extra assistance to adjust comfortably. In some cases, the assistance can be informal and provided through an exchange of information between school staff or between school and home.

Communicating with the family A home–school notebook that is passed back and forth can provide a vehicle for a regular exchange of information. If teachers lack the time for a daily note, occasional notes paired with a weekly class newsletter assist the family in remaining informed. The child's family also can be a prime source of information for the teachers. Regular contact between the teacher and parents allows sharing of a child's progress, opportunities to express concerns, and chances to devise solutions. Crises can be avoided this way.

Communicating with the former program If parents have provided written permission for continued contact between the preschool providers and the new teachers, the kindergarten teacher or special education consultant can call the preschool. He or she may find it helpful to touch base to learn ways the child's former program responded to certain challenges, learning, or behavioral concerns.

The preschool staff may be able to suggest strategies for the kindergarten teacher that have been successful with the child in the past. They also can share information about favorite songs, rhymes, and stories, as well as toys and activities that the kindergarten teacher can use.

Step 6: Evaluate the transition and child adjustment Thoughtful and early planning are critical elements of transition. So is the evaluation of how well the child, family, and new staff have adjusted to one another. Evaluations can be formal or informal. If the child appears to be progressing well, teacher–parent conferences may be a good time to evaluate the transition. These usually occur about eight weeks into the school year and provide an opportunity for the family and staff to assess how well the child is doing and whether the accommodations made to support the child are adequate. By this time, the teacher and special services staff have had plenty of time to get to know the child and should be able to identify strengths and concerns. Families may be asked to identify concerns and any new goals they have for their child.

If the child is experiencing difficulties in adjustment, school staff should not delay in addressing the situation. Waiting for the regularly scheduled parent–teacher conference may be too late. School staff should engage in preventive planning to assess the current program and the need for additional services. If necessary—and with parent permission—additional evaluations may be in order, as may a change or increase in support services. In some cases, the family and staff may wish to consider an alternative classroom. Not all teachers and children find a good fit with one another. A more experienced or flexible teacher may be able to provide more effective support. It can also be quite helpful to ask the preschool and kindergarten staff to assess the effectiveness of the transition. A number of educators report that the most critical factor supporting successful transitions is staff time—time to visit programs, communicate with staff, communicate with the family, meet the incoming child, and plan for support services (Donegan, Ostrosky, & Fowler, 1996).

Entering kindergarten is a big step for many children and their families. Kindergarten often raises expectations for independence and for learning many new things. Children with special needs typically are included in kindergarten classes and receive support services either in the classroom or through resource rooms. There are a number of ways to optimize the adjustment of children in kindergarten. As in the transition to preschool, planning and communication among all providers and the family are essential. Children can be accommodated in the general kindergarten when teachers are flexible, willing to adjust activities and schedules, and view the child as an individual, not just as a member of the group.

Did You Get It?

The results of the study conducted by Pre-Elementary Education Longitudinal Study (PEELS) and funded by the U.S. Department of Education, indicate which of the following as significantly associated with how easy the transition to Kindergarten was as perceived by parents and teachers.

a. Children transitioning at the age of six.

b. When the school initiated support to facilitate the transition.

c. Parents are primarily responsible for the transition.

d. Showing pictures of the new school to the child.

Take the full quiz on CourseMate.

Summary

▶ This chapter has discussed two transitions that young children with special needs frequently go through: the transition from early intervention to preschool and the transition from preschool to kindergarten.

▶ Children and families must make many adjustments as they move from one program to another.

▶ Changes may be encountered, including differences in program locale, staffing, approaches to instruction, and patterns of communication between families and service providers.

▶ Planning is required to minimize the differences between programs and to ensure a smooth transition. Federal regulations clearly spell out guidelines to be followed when a child makes the transition from early intervention to preschool. These regulations address steps that early intervention and local education agencies must take to help children and families. In contrast, no such regulations govern the transition from preschool to kindergarten. Nonetheless, transition planning is considered to be best practice.

Key Terms

Student Activities

1. Obtain permission to observe an entire preschool session and an entire public school kindergarten session. Compare your two observations, listing similarities and differences between the two settings. Include information about the amount of time children spend playing, completing tabletop work, and participating in listening activities.

2. Describe various strategies that could be implemented to prepare a child for a transition from a community preschool to a kindergarten classroom at the neighborhood elementary school.

3. Interview the family of a child with special needs. Ask family members to describe the issues they faced during their child's transition. Write a summary of the issues the family members describe including parental concerns about the transition.

Additional Resources/Readings

There are an endless number of children's books written on the topic of transition, starting a new school and/or kindergarten, and being away from family. The Internet is a great source of lists of these books, many of which can be located in the public and school libraries. Here are just a few:

- Look Out Kindergarten, Here I Come, by Nancy L. Carlson
- Preparate, Kindergarten! Allá Voy!, by Nancy L. Carlson
- Mama, Don't Go!, by Rosemary Wells
- Miss Bindergarten Gets Ready for Kindergarten, by Joseph Slate
- Mouse's First Day of School, by Lauren Thompson
- My Kindergarten, by Rosemary Wells
- My Teacher Sleeps in School, by Leatie Weiss
- The Kissing Hand, by Audrey Penn
- Un beso en mi mano, by Audrey Penn
- Twelve Days of Kindergarten, by Deborah Lee Rose

Helpful Websites

Transition during early childhood services is featured frequently in many of the websites listed previously in this text. Other relevant material can be found on the following websites.

Early Childhood News

http://www.earlychildhoodnews.com

An online resource for teachers and parents of children from infants to age eight. Includes an article by Pam Devell-Gingold on successful transitions to kindergarten. It is listed under articles for Kindergarten/Primary.

The National Early Childhood Transition Initiative

http://www.nectac.org/topics/transition

The Office of Special Education Programs (OSEP) created this initiative in response to a recognized need for a systematic and strategic technical-assistance approach to support the states, territories, and jurisdictions in their implementation of the transition requirements of the Individuals with Disabilities Education Improvement Act. The website includes timelines, self-assessments, and other documents for planning and implementing effective transitions.

Visit the Education CourseMate for this textbook to access the eBook, Did You Get It? quizzes, Digital Downloads, TeachSource Video Cases, flashcards, and more. Go to CengageBrain.com to log in, register, or purchase access. Also, visit the Education CourseMate website to read an essay entitled "Inclusion in Early Childhood Education: What We Have Learned and Where We Are Going" written by Susan Sandall, researcher, author, and professor of special education at the University of Washington. She provides information about what has been learned by families and teachers and gives insight into supports that are needed to strengthen inclusive experiences for all children.

Implementing Inclusive Early Childhood Programs

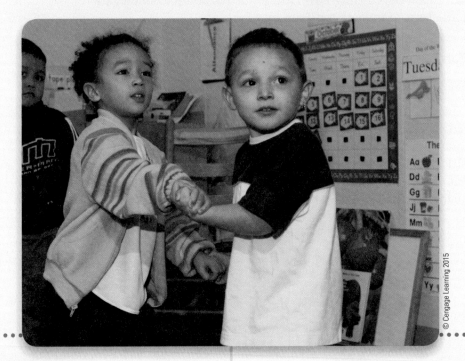

SPECIAL FOCUS •
MY ROLE IN SUPPORTING INCLUSION

What I Do

My title is Behavior and Inclusion Specialist. My job is multifaceted and I serve many roles in the districts for which I provide service. My training is in Applied Behavior Analysis and Early Childhood Education. Sometimes I am asked to complete a Functional Behavioral Assessment (FBA) and develop a Behavior Plan. Other times I provide training to aides/paraprofessionals and provide ongoing support to them as they work with children who are being fully included in a general education setting. I am also often asked to observe a child and determine what level of support they need to succeed. For instance, can they gain access to the curriculum if we adapt the environment and curriculum or do they need a staff person to help them for part or all of their day? I also work with parents to help them develop effective strategies for working with their children at home.

Behavioral Assessments and Plans

To complete a Functional Behavioral Assessment (FBA) and develop a behavior plan, I observe the child in their educational setting across various activities and times of the day. I ask the staff which parts of the day are the most successful and most challenging, to determine the times I especially want to observe. I take many notes about what the child is doing at various times, what peers are doing, and how staff are responding and supporting the child. Observing what the child's peers are doing provides a great baseline to help me determine how close or near the target the child is to meeting the expectations for the classroom. I often ask the teachers to take data about behaviors of concern, especially if I have not been able to observe it directly. The data usually includes the time of the day the behavior occurs, what happens before (antecedents), and what happens after (consequences). All of this information helps determine what function the behavior serves for the child (e.g., attention, communication, escape from a task/activity). After I gather all my notes and the data, I use them to write a plan and recommendations. Whenever a plan targets a particular behavior, I also identify an alternative behavior to teach that will service the same function for the student. For example, if a child hits a peer to gain access to a toy, I work with the staff to help the child learn how to ask for a toy. Sometimes this might be a verbal request, other times it might mean that the child gives a picture to the peer to get the toy. On many occasions, peers are involved with the intervention and may need to learn how to understand sign language or what handing a picture means. Once a behavior plan is developed, it is reviewed and revised with the staff. The staff are the ones responsible for implementing the plan, so it is critical that they understand it and agree with it. I often provide ongoing support such as modeling, providing feedback, problem solving, and revising the plan as needed.

Successful Inclusion

In my experience, behavior is the most significant variable in determining how successful a student is in a general education/inclusive environment. When a student engages in disruptive, destructive and/or aggressive behavior, it is challenging for the teacher. I have seen many a teacher give up quickly and ask that the child be placed in a different setting. In some of these cases the child

may have not been appropriately placed in the first place. The environment did not provide the support or curriculum that was appropriate to meet the child's needs.

Inclusion is an amazing experience for a child, the class, and a teacher, when it works. However, I have seen instances of inclusion gone wrong. Here is an example. A family moved to a district the week before classes start. An IEP meeting was held. The child's current IEP had expired, as he had not been in a public school the last year. The child was six years of age; he had participated for about two months in a private kindergarten and was receiving ABA services at home. The parents wanted him to be in first grade with the support of a paraprofessional. No one from the IEP team had met the child. He was placed in the first-grade class based on the parents' request and their report that he could do the work. It was quickly apparent that not only was the curriculum too advanced for him, but also he became overstimulated in the classroom and could sit at his desk for only approximately ten minutes before he became aggressive and disruptive. A behavior plan was developed that allowed him to work for breaks, and he was provided a visual schedule so he could see what he needed to do before he went on a break, and he was provided a modified curriculum. He also spent a portion of his day in the Learning Center (Resource Room) where he received 1:1 instruction. So was this inclusion? In one sense it was. He was in a class alongside his same-age peers; however, he was not able to do any of the work. He did not show any interest, even when provided with support in interacting with his peers. His behaviors were scaring some of the peers. He needed a completely different type of instruction from what was provided in the general education classroom to make progress on his goals. The school he was attending did not have a special day class (SDC). The team met with his parents to express concern over whether the placement was meeting his needs. The parents were reluctant to make any changes, as they really wanted him at his neighborhood school; however, they eventually agreed to observe other programs. After several months they found a class they were willing to try, that would provide the specialized instruction he needed.

The ideal is inclusion for every child, but, in my experience, there are some times where the general education environment is not able to meet the child's needs. Is this the fault of the child? No. Is it the fault of the education system? Probably, yes, but in reality not all general education settings are where they need to be to fully include every child.

Because of situations like I just described, my job can be very frustrating. I have seen inclusion work really well and I have seen it not work at all, as described above. What are some of things that seem to determine success? Well, that varies from case to case.

Supportive Administration and Parents

At the elementary school level it is extremely important to have an administrator who believes in inclusion and supports the teacher and staff in its implementation. Administrators work with the staff to create a caring community for all the students they serve. They create opportunities throughout the school year that celebrate the diversity of their students and help educate the community about each other. This needs to happen every day but can also happen by providing special awareness opportunities. One school I worked with had a group of parents who had children with special needs, and they really wanted to help the school community (children, parents, and teachers) understand.

They provided five activities in small settings and the classes took turns participating throughout the day. One activity provided experience that mimicked fine motor problems, one dyslexia, one sensory sensitivity, one speech problems, and an outdoor exhibit as well, which mimicked large motor. Here is a brief description of each:

- Fine motor: wearing thick gardening gloves while stringing beads.
- Speech: filling your mouth full of skittles and singing the ABCs.
- Sensory: a garage-band mix of a teacher giving out a list of complicated instructions of the kind our kids hear every day, over which was layered sounds of people talking, bells ringing, papers rustling, lights humming, etc.
- Dyslexia: a mirror activity that requires that you write a sentence while looking only in the mirror at your hand.
- Large motor: tug-of-war, sitting on the ground with legs tied together.

The parents who planned this day observed results they hadn't even anticipated. As one parent reported, "Several kids 'came out' that day and told us that they recognized that they had these problems."

In addition to the above activities, they hired a speaker. The speaker provided an hour-long talk to each grade level in the library. He spoke about 'rock stars'—and about people who have accomplished so much and who are leaders in their fields, and then he revealed that the people he was talking about had autism, Asperger's, and Tourette's. After that he asked the kids to come up and talk about what made *them* different. Some amazing things happened. A little girl in second grade got up and said she was overweight and people make fun of her and she wants it to stop. Another boy in third grade said he lives in an imaginary world and he doesn't want anyone real to come in. The fifth-graders spent the time talking about people they had made fun of and wanted to clear it all up and apologize. It was incredible. The day provided the community with some amazing awareness to build upon throughout the year.

This type of day is only possible with a supportive administration and parents.

A Caring Community

Equally important is a teacher who considers the child with special needs a part of their community and class. If you haven't already done so, read the Section 3 Wrap Up. It describes how one third-grade teacher creates a community of caring learners.

Making every child feel welcome and part of the class is one of the teacher's major responsibilities. A child who feels connected and part of the group is much more likely to be successful. As one paraprofessional pointed out to the classroom teacher, "You treat the student I work with the same; you just treat them more." This was such an accurate description. The teacher was using the same strategies with all the students in the class; she just had to do it a little differently and more frequently with the child with special needs.

When a child is provided with a paraprofessional to support them, it is also important that this adult is viewed as an adult who is there to help everyone, not just the child with special needs. This is accomplished easily if the classroom teacher provides the guidance to the adult and requests that they work with other students, especially when the student with special needs is able to work independently, or with a peer, or with the classroom teacher. I have heard the term "Velcro aide" used. It is such a perfect description of what you don't want to see in a classroom setting.

Strategies that Are Effective

There are many strategies that are effective in making an inclusive experience successful. The following list highlights a few of these:

Visuals—Providing visual supports to a child can help them to become more independent in their routine and work. It might be a picture schedule to help them remember and predict what is next. Or it might be a visual that shows different choices a student might make when they get frustrated over a work assignment.

Teaching the child to use their peer as a resource/reference—A child with special needs often needs to be taught what might come naturally to a child who is typically developing. Children in a classroom setting who miss an instruction or get stuck often observe their peers to figure out what they should be doing. It is important that children with special needs learn to observe and follow what their peers are doing. A paraprofessional or teacher can be more helpful if, rather than giving a direct instruction such as "time to line up," they ask the child to "look at what your friends are doing." The goal is for the child to be able to follow their lead.

Developing strategies that support the class rather than just one child—Very often when one child is having difficulty with something in the class, there could be several others having a similar problem. So, when looking for a strategy to support a child with special needs I try to identify strategies that would help the entire group. This can help the teacher by providing effective strategies that work for everyone, but it also helps the student with special needs, because they are not singled out. An example of this can be seen in a kindergarten class where I support a child with ASD who has a parapro-fessional providing support. His teacher used the green, red, and yellow discipline-card system I have seen in many classrooms. The first time she changed this child's card to yellow as a warning, he went out of control. He had to actually go home as he was so upset and couldn't understand that this was merely a warning to him. In talking with the para and the teacher it became very apparent that in order for this system to work for him, he needed to understand what options he had that he could use to keep him from moving to the yellow card. He was not alone in his anxiety of getting a yellow card. So we came up with the strategy of having a blue "thought bubble" card. The card listed options a student could use to keep from moving onto the yellow level, such things as ask for help, and ask for a break. The teacher introduced this to the whole class. They all shared ideas about "thought bubble strategies." Since this has been implemented, the blue card has served as an effective reminder that it is time to "stop and think" about what options to use. And the best part is that the entire class is using it.

Priming activities—Very often a child with special needs will do better with a group activity if they have learned all or part of the concept in advance. This is frequently referred to as priming. For example, the day before a teacher is reading a book to the class, a copy of the book is sent home with the child along with some questions. The parents read the book at home and practice answering the questions so that the child is able to participate as part of the whole class activity the next day.

Inclusion at most successful times for students—For students who spend part of their day in general education and part of their day in special education, it is important to carefully plan and select the time of day they are in general education. It is best for the team to determine the purpose/goal—if the goal is for the child to develop social skills and interact socially with peers, then it doesn't make sense to have them join the general education class only during math time, which is a time not typically known to provide the most opportunities for social interactions.

Get peers involved in providing support—I feel it is very important for peers to know how to interact with and support their classmate with special needs. After all, they will most likely be at the same school together year after year. This can mean everything from knowing how to remind them it's time to sit on the rug for circle, to how to get their attention to tell them something. Research has shown that children with ASD make better progress when their peers also receive training.

As I said at the beginning, my job can be frustrating but, on the other hand, it can be so very rewarding. There is nothing like watching a child who, in preschool, needed full support to have any successful interactions with peers, but who now, as a kindergartner, seeks out and plays independently with his friends at recess.

Refrence

Kasari. C., Rotheram-Fuller, E., Locke, J., & Gulsrud, A. (2012). Making the connection: Randomized controlled trial of social skills at school for children with autism spectrum disorders. *Journal of Child Psychology and Psychiatry.* *53(4): 431–9.*

Application Questions

1. Make a list of stumbling blocks to successful inclusion. What are some of the solutions to removing these roadblocks?

2. What other strategies have you learned in this text that would make inclusion effective?

3. What other activities and strategies might a school implement to develop a sense of community?

Appendix A

Culminating
Activities

© Cengage Learning 2015

Activity I

Imagine you are the director of a community preschool program. A parent of a four-year-old child with autism has decided to enroll his son in your program. His son, Benny, has participated in an intensive in-home program provided by the school district. He has not participated in a group program before. A team of specialists is involved in his program, including a shadow paraprofessional who will be accompanying Benny to your school, a speech therapist, and the Early Intervention Program Director, who is an early childhood educator and behavior analyst. She is available for consultation and training. One of your teachers is resistant to the idea of having this child in her room. Write a detailed plan, including answers to the following questions, regarding how you will ensure a smooth transition to your program.

1. What questions/information will you get from the parent and team?
2. What would you like the enrollment process to look like?
3. What will you do to prepare your staff?
4. How will you work with the resistant staff member?
5. How will you handle questions from other parents and staff?
6. How will you determine success?
7. What other issues should you plan for?

Other Activity Options

▶ Hold a mock team meeting for Benny prior to enrollment, to develop a plan. Begin by writing a description of Benny that includes his current abilities and skills/goals for his time at preschool. Have class members play the various roles of the team. Work together to develop the plan.

▶ A parent of one of your other students comes to you, the director, asking questions about Benny and expressing concern about his enrollment in the class. Role-play your discussion with this parent.

▶ Develop a sample schedule for your two-and-a-half hour preschool day or obtain a schedule from a local preschool. Make a list of skills/goals Benny will work on during each component of the day. Note how the curriculum will require modification.

Activity II

Success

Benny has been in your preschool for the past school year. He is interacting with peers, has developed some friendships, and has achieved many of his goals. Your staff has grown in their ability to provide targeted instruction. The shadow aide is a member of the classroom team, interacting with all the students so that your staff has time to interact with and teach Benny. The staff member who was initially resistant came to you last week saying that she has decided to go back to school to study special education. Benny's dad just called you to say that Benny will be attending kindergarten next fall at his neighborhood elementary school. What can you do to ensure a successful transition? What can the other team members do? Make a list of all the steps/activities to ensure a successful transition to kindergarten.

Activity III

You are a teacher of a first-grade classroom in a public school. You have been teaching for two years. The principal of the school just told you the new child starting in your class next week has a diagnosis of ADHD. This is your first experience working with a child with this diagnosis. What will you do to plan for the child's arrival? Make a list of all the information you will gather and whom you will gather it from. Consider classroom arrangements, parent communication, and curriculum modification as you make your list.

Activity IV

As the yard duty for the elementary school, you notice that several of the students from the special day class wander at recess and do not really know what to do. A parent volunteer has been assigned to recess to help you. Together you decide to develop a plan to provide some activities that would engage both the students from the special day class and other students. Describe some of your ideas and the steps you will take to implement your plan. Think about whom at the school you might use as a resource and whom you need to approve your plan.

Appendix B

Skill Profile
(0–72 Months)

Download from CourseMate.

	GROSS-MOTOR SKILLS CULMINATING ACTIVITIES	FINE-MOTOR SKILLS	PREACADEMIC SKILLS	SELF-HELP SKILLS	MUSIC/ ART/STORY SKILLS	SOCIAL SKILLS AND PLAY SKILLS	UNDER-STANDING LANGUAGE	ORAL LANGUAGE
0–12 MONTHS	Sits without support; crawls; pulls self to standing and stands unaided; walks with aid; rolls a ball in imitation of adult	Reaches, grasps, puts object in mouth; picks things up with thumb and one finger (pincer grasp); transfers object from one hand to other hand; drops and picks up toy	Looks directly at adult's face; tracks objects (follows them smoothly with eyes); imitates gestures—e.g., pat-a-cake, peekaboo, bye-bye; puts block in, takes block out of container; finds block hidden under cup	Feeds self cracker: munching, not sucking; holds cup with two hands, drinks with assistance; holds out arms and legs while being dressed	Fixes gaze on pictures in book	Smiles spontaneously; responds differentially to strangers and familiar people; pays attention to own name; responds to "no"; copies simple actions of others	Looks at people who talk to him; responds differentially to variety of sounds—e.g., phone, vacuum, closing doors; responds to simple directions accompanied by gestures—e.g., "come," "give," "get"	Makes different vowel sounds; makes different consonant–vowel combinations; vocalizes to the person who has talked to him; uses intonation patterns that sound like phrases—e.g., intonations that sound like scolding, asking, telling
12–24 MONTHS	Walks alone; walks backward; picks up object without falling; pulls toy; seats self in child's chair; walks up and down stairs with aid	Builds tower of three cubes; puts four rings on stick; places five pegs in peg-board; turns pages two or three at a time; scribbles	Follows one direction involving familiar actions and objects—e.g., "Give me (toy)," "Show me (body part)," "Get a (familiar object)"; completes three-piece form-board; matches similar objects	Uses spoon, spilling little; drinks from cup, one hand, unassisted; chews food; removes garment; zips, unzips large zipper; indicates toilet needs	Moves to music; looks at pictures in book, patting, pointing to, or naming objects or people; paints with whole arm movement, shifts hands, scrubs, makes strokes	Recognizes self in mirror or picture; refers to self by name; plays by self, initiates own play activities; imitates adult behaviors in play; plays with water and sand; loads, carries, dumps; helps put things away	Responds to specific words by showing what was named—e.g., toys, family members, clothing, body parts; responds to simple directions given without gestures—e.g., "go," "sit," "find," "run," "walk"	Asks for items by name; answers "What's that?" with name of object; tells about objects or experiences with words used together (two or three words)—e.g., "More juice"

GROSS-MOTOR SKILLS CULMINATING ACTIVITIES	FINE-MOTOR SKILLS	PREACADEMIC SKILLS	SELF-HELP SKILLS	MUSIC/ ART/STORY SKILLS	SOCIAL SKILLS AND PLAY SKILLS	UNDER-STANDING LANGUAGE	ORAL LANGUAGE
24–36 MONTHS Runs for-ward well; jumps in place, two feet together; stands on one foot, with aid; walks on tiptoe; kicks ball forward; throws ball, without direction	Strings four large beads; turns pages singly; snips with scissors; holds crayon with thumb and fingers, not fist; uses one hand consistently in most activities; imitates circular, vertical, horizontal strokes	Matches shapes; stacks five rings on peg, in order; demonstrates number concepts to two (i.e., selects set of one or two, can tell how many one or two are)	Uses spoon, no spilling; gets drink un-assisted; uses straw; opens door by turning handle; puts on/ takes off coat; washes/dries hands with assistance	Plays near other children; watches other children, joins briefly in their play; defends own possessions; engages in domestic play; symbolically uses objects, self in play; builds with blocks in simple lines	Responds by selecting correct item—big vs. little objects, one vs. one more object; identifies objects by their use—e.g., "Show me what mother cooks on" by showing stove or "Show me what you wear on your feet" by showing shoe	Asks questions; answers "Where is it?" with prepositional phrases—e.g., "in the box," "on the table"; answers "What do you do with a ball?"—e.g., "throw," "catch"; tells about something with functional sentences that carry meaning—e.g., "Me go store" or "Me hungry now"	
36–48 MONTHS Runs around obstacles; walks on a line; balances on one foot for five seconds; hops on one foot; pushes, pulls, steers wheeled toys; rides (i.e., steers and pedals) trike; uses slide without assistance; jumps over 15 cm (6 inches) high object, landing on both feet together; throws ball with direction; catches ball bounced to him	Builds tower of nine cubes; drives nails and pegs; copies circle; imitates cross	Matches six colors; makes tower of five blocks, graduated in size; does seven-piece puzzle; counts to five in imitation of adults; demonstrates number concept to three	Pours well from pitcher; spreads substances with knife; buttons/ unbuttons large buttons; washes hands unassisted; cleans nose when reminded; uses toilet independently; follows classroom routine with minimum teacher assistance; knows own sex; knows own age; knows own last name; participates in simple group activity—e.g., sings, claps, dances; chooses picture books, points to fine detail, enjoys repetition; paints with some wrist action, makes dots, lines, circular strokes; rolls, pounds, squeezes, pulls clay material	Knows phrases of songs; listens to short simple stories (five minutes); painting—names own picture, not always recognizable; demands variety of color; draws head of person and one other part; manipulates clay materials—e.g., rolls balls, snakes, cookies, etc.	Joins in play with other children, begins to interact; shares toys, takes turns with assistance; begins dramatic play, acting out whole scenes—e.g., traveling, playing house, pretending to be animals; responds to "Put it in" and "Put it on"; responds to "Put it beside" and "Put it under"; responds to commands involving two objects—e.g., "Give me the ball and the shoe"; responds to commands involving two actions—e.g., "Give me the cup and put the shoe on the floor"; responds by selecting correct item—e.g., hard vs. soft objects; responds to "Walk fast" by increased pace, and to "Walk slowly" by decreased pace	Answers "Which one do you want?" by naming it; Answers "If . . . what/when" questions—e.g., "If you had a penny, what would you do?" "What do you do when you're hungry?"; answers questions about function—e.g., "What are books for?" Asks for or tells about with grammatically correct sentences—e.g., "Can I go to the store?" "I want a big cookie"	

(continued)

GROSS-MOTOR SKILLS CULMINATING ACTIVITIES	FINE-MOTOR SKILLS	PREACADEMIC SKILLS	SELF-HELP SKILLS	MUSIC/ART/STORY SKILLS	SOCIAL SKILLS AND PLAY SKILLS	UNDERSTANDING LANGUAGE	ORAL LANGUAGE
48–60 MONTHS Walks backward heel-to-toe; jumps forward 10 times, without falling; walks up/down stairs alone, alternating feet; turns somersault	Cuts on a line continuously; copies cross; copies square; prints a few capital letters	Points to and names six basic colors; points to and names three shapes; matches related common objects—e.g., shoe, sock, foot; apple, orange, banana; demonstrates number concept to four or five	Cuts food with a knife—e.g., sandwich, celery; laces shoes; knows own city/street; follows instructions given to group	Sings entire songs; recites nursery rhyme; "reads" from pictures (i.e., tells story); recognizes story and retells simple facts; painting—makes and names recognizable pictures; draws a person with two to six parts	Plays and interacts with other children; dramatic play—closer to reality, attention to detail, time, and space; plays dress-up; builds complex structures with blocks	Responds by showing penny, nickel, dime; responds to command involving three actions—e.g., "Give me the cup, put the shoe on the floor, and hold the pencil in your hand"	Asks "How?" questions; answers verbally to "Hi!" and "How are you?"; tells about something using past tense and future tense; tells about something using conjunctions to string words and phrases together—e.g., "I have a cat and a dog and a fish"
60–72 MONTHS Runs lightly on toes; walks a balance beam; can cover 2 meters (6 feet 6 inches) hopping; skips; jumps rope; skates	Cuts out simple shapes; copies triangle; traces diamond; copies first name; prints numerals 1–5; colors within lines; has adult grasp of pencil; has handedness well established (i.e., child is left or right handed)	Sorts objects on one dimension—i.e., by size or by color or by shape; does 15-piece puzzle; copies block design; names some letters; names some numerals; names penny, nickel, dime, quarter; counts by rote to 10; can tell what number comes next	Dresses self completely; learns to distinguish left from right; ties bow; brushes teeth unassisted; crosses street safely; relates clock time to daily schedule	Recognizes rhyme; acts out stories; draws a person with head, trunk, legs, arms, and features; pastes and glues appropriately; models objects with clay	Chooses own friend(s); plays simple table games; plays competitive games; engages in cooperative play with other children involving group decisions, role assignments, fair play; uses construction toys to make things—e.g., house of Legos, car of rig-a-jig	See preacademic skills	Child will have acquired basic grammatical structures, including plurals, verb tenses, and conjunctions; following this developmental ability, the child practices with increasingly complex descriptions and conversations

The above items are selected from *The Sequenced Inventory of Communication Development*, University of Washington Press, 1975. This profile was prepared by the communication disorders specialists Linda Lynch, Jane Rieke, Sue Soltman, and teachers Donna Hardman and Mary O'Conor. The Communication Program was funded initially as a part of the Model Preschool Center for Handicapped Children by Grant No. OEG-072-5371 U.S. Office of Education, Program Development Branch, BEH: Washington, DC, at the Experimental Education Unit (WJ-10) of the College of Education and Child Development and Mental Retardation Center, University of Washington, Seattle, Washington

Appendix C

Resources for Teachers and Parents

Professional Organizations

Alexander Graham Bell Association for the Deaf *3417 Volta Pl. NW, Washington, DC 20007 Tel.: 202-337-5220 Fax: 202-337-8314* http://www.agbell.org

American Association on Intellectual and Developmental Disabilities (AAIDD) *501 3rd Street NW, Suite 200, Washington, DC 20001 Tel.: 202-387-1968* http://www.aamr.org

American Council of the Blind (ACB) *2200 Wilson Boulevard, Suite 650, Arlington, VA 22201-3354 Tel.: 202-467-5081, 800-424-8666 Fax: 703-465-5085* http://www.acb.org

American Speech-Language-Hearing Association (ASHA) *2200 Research Boulevard Rockville, MD 20850-3289 Tel.: 301-296-5700, 800-638-8255* http://www.asha.org

Autism Society of America *433 East-West Hwy, Suite 350, Bethesda, MD 20814-3067 Tel.: 301-657-0881 or 800-3AUTISM* http://www.autism-society.org

Brain Injury Association of America *1608 Spring Hill Road, Suite 110, Vienna, VA 22182 Tel.: 703-761-0750 Fax: 703-761-0755* http://www.biausa.org

Cleft-Palate-Craniofacial Foundation *1504 East Franklin Street, Suite 102, Chapel Hill, NC 27514-2820 Tel.: 800-242-5338 or 919-933-9044* http://www.cleftline.org

The Council for Exceptional Children (CEC) *2900 Crystal Drive, Suite 1000, Arlington, VA 22202-3557 Tel.: 888-CEC-SPED Fax: 703-264-9494* http://www.cec.sped.org

Easter Seals *233 South Wacker Drive, Suite 2400, Chicago, IL 60606 Tel.: 800-221-6827 (toll-free) Fax: 312-726-1494* http://www.easter-seals.org

Epilepsy Foundation of America *8301 Professional Place, Landover MD 20785 Tel.: 800-EFA-1000* http://www.efa.org

March of Dimes Birth Defects Foundation *1275 Mamaroneck Ave., White Plains, NY 10603 Tel.: 914-997-4488* http://www.modimes.org

Muscular Dystrophy Association *3300 E. Sunrise Drive, Tucson, AZ 85718 Tel.: 800-572-1717* http://www.mdausa.org

National Association for the Deaf *8630 Fenton Street, Suite 820, Silver Spring, MD 20910-3819 Tel.: 301-587-1788* http://www.nad.org

National Association for the Education of Young Children (NAEYC) *1313 L Street NW, Suite 500, Washington, DC 20005 Tel.: 800-424-2460* http://www.naeyc.org

National Down Syndrome Society *666 Broadway, New York, NY 10012 Tel.: 800-221-4602* http://www.ndss.org

National Federation of the Blind *200 East Wells Street at Jernigan Place, Baltimore, MD 21230 Tel.: 410-659-9314* http://www.nfb.org

Sickle Cell Disease Association of America, Inc. *231 E. Baltimore Street, Suite 800, Baltimore, MD 21202 Tel.: 800-421-8453* http://www.sicklecelldisease.org

Spina Bifida Association of America *4590 MacArthur Blvd. NW, Suite 250, Washington, DC 20007-4226 Tel.: 800-621-3141 or 202-944-3285 Fax: 202-944-3295* http://www.sbaa.org

TASH *1001 Connecticut Ave. NW, Suite 235, Washington, DC 20036 Tel.: 202-540-9020* http://www.tash.org

United Cerebral Palsy (UCP) *1825 K Street NW, Suite 600, Washington, DC 20006 Tel.: 800-872-5827 Fax: 202-776-0406* http://www.ucp.org

Family Organizations

The ARC *1825 K Street NW, Suite 1200, Washington, DC 20006 Tel.: (800) 433-5255* http://www.thearc.org

Children with Attention Deficit Disorder (CHADD) *(This association has many active local chapters.) 8181 Professional Place, Suite 150, Landover, MD 20785 Tel.: 800-233-4050* http://www.chadd.org

Parents Helping Parents *(This association has many active local chapters.) Sobrato Center For Nonprofits–San Jose 1400 Parkmoor Avenue, Suite 100, San Jose, CA 95126 Tel.: 408-727-5775* http://www.php.com

Sibling Support Project *6512 23rd Ave NW, #213, Seattle, WA 98117 Tel.: 206-297-6368 Fax: 509-752-6789* http://www.siblingsupport.org

Sources for Information and Other Resources

National Dissemination Center for Children with Disabilities (NICHCY) *1825 Connecticut Ave NW, Washington, DC 20009 Tel.: 800-695-0285 Fax: 202-884-8441* http://www.nichcy.org

National Institute of Child Health and Human Development (NICHD) *Eunice Kennedy Shriver National Institute of Child Health and Human Development (NICHD) 31 Center Drive, Building 31, Room 2A32, Bethesda, MD 20892-2425 Tel.: 800-370-2943 Fax: 1-866-760-5947* http://www.nichd.nih.gov

Office of Special Education Programs Office of Special Education and Rehabilitative Services *U.S. Department of Education 400 Maryland Ave. SW, Washington, DC 20202 Tel.: 202-205-5507* http://www.ed.gov *(Search: Office of Special Education Programs)*

Zero to Three National Center for Infants, Toddlers, and Families *1255 23rd Street NW, Suite 350, Washington, DC 20037 Tel.: 202-638-1144* http://www.zerotothree.org

Appendix D

Early Learning and Developmental Diversity

Young children are highly diverse in their adaptive, cognitive, language, physical, and social-emotional development. In the inclusive classroom, there are children with developmental disabilities, children who are highly gifted or talented, and children with all variations of typical development. Highlighted here are key points from the text relating to developmental diversity and the role of teachers, parents, and the developmental team.

Promoting Adaptive Development

▶ Self-care and self-sufficiency, personal responsibility, and social adjustment are examples of significant adaptive behaviors. One goal of early intervention is to help young children function as independently yet as cooperatively as possible at home, at school, and in the community.

▶ Expectations regarding adaptive behaviors are based on age-related norms and family values. Responding to what the family expects of their child is essential in maintaining an effective home–school relationship.

▶ Adaptive skills are functional skills; they enable a child to be more independent as well as easier to care for. Children with disabilities often need systematic instruction and support in learning basic developmental tasks such as self-feeding, dressing, and using the toilet.

▶ Independence is a significant adaptive skill. Parents, teachers, and caregivers must provide frequent opportunities for children to practice independence. Luckily, the very young tend to be emphatic about the need for independence. "Me do it!" is their battle cry.

▶ Functioning in a group is a necessary adaptive skill. It provides young children with many opportunities to learn appropriate behaviors by modeling after children who are sitting quietly, listening, taking turns, contributing ideas, and responding to the teacher's cues.

- Transitions from one activity to the next and from one program to another (school to child care center to home) require a variety of adaptive skills. Adults who are involved in any aspect of the process must agree upon routines and expectations that they then rehearse with the children in each setting.

- If children are to learn the necessary adaptive skills, then parents, teachers, and caregivers must jointly establish clear and simply worded expectations regarding acceptable behavior. These are stated as often as necessary and as positively as possible.

- Occupational and physical therapists on the early childhood team help children learn self-care skills (sometimes referred to as daily living skills). Children learn readily if the teaching occurs in the context of commonplace home and classroom routines. Teachers and parents can observe and work in the classroom along with the therapist to learn simple techniques for supporting children in learning to care for their own needs.

Promoting Cognitive Development

- The terms *cognition* and *intelligence* tend to be used interchangeably. Academic performance is closely related to intellectual or cognitive development and all are greatly influenced by culture, family values, and, most significant, a child's opportunities to learn during infancy and early childhood.

- Gardner describes concepts of intelligence: musical, bodily (kinesthetic), logical–mathematical, linguistic, spatial, naturalistic, interpersonal, and intrapersonal. Programs designed to effectively facilitate cognitive development have built-in ways of assessing intelligence in all of its many forms.

- Standardized IQ tests are inappropriate in the assessment of intelligence in young children. Such tests are not valid predictors of either current or future cognitive abilities in preschoolers. The tests do not take into account the opportunities a child has had (or not had) to learn the information represented by the test items. *The results of a single IQ test are always subject to challenge.*

- In a multicultural society such as ours, young children require learning opportunities that promote all types of intellectual skill. Such opportunities are essential to identify children's special talents, preferences, interests, and cultural inheritance.

- The family is often described as the child's first and most powerful teacher. Efforts on the part of the family to describe the child's strengths, as well as his or her special needs, should be supported. The family should also be encouraged to participate in ongoing evaluations of their child's developmental progress.

- Play is the major avenue for promoting spontaneous cognitive development. Play also provides developmentally appropriate opportunities to teach specific concepts to children with developmental disabilities. Teaching play skills to the special child is often a major priority in promoting cognitive development and meeting a child's individualized education plan (IEP) goals.

- When teaching new skills or behaviors, plans for generalization need to be made explicit in the IEP. Teaching is not complete without evidence of generalization, that is, until the child is able to use the new skill in a variety of settings with teachers and materials that often are unfamiliar.

- Vygotsky describes the *zone of proximal development* as skill areas where a child is ready to learn but cannot yet accomplish the task without help. Teaching within this proximal zone increases a child's motivation and participation in learning activities. The teacher's role is one of mediator between the environment and the child.

Promoting Language and Communication Development

- Communication among individuals is the purposeful exchange of ideas, thoughts, needs, and preferences. Effective communication includes speech, gestures, facial expressions, and body language. Alternative systems for individuals with developmental disabilities are available; one example is the American Sign Language system.

- Communication skills begin in early infancy (the pre-linguistic stage). Learning to communicate effectively depends on a child's everyday opportunities to hear lots of talking and to participate in language give-and-take. The quality of language that children are exposed to by age three significantly influences speech, language, and cognitive development.

- In our diverse society, most children in public schools are educated in English to varying degrees. Families should be encouraged to maintain the home language while supporting their child's efforts to acquire English. Fluency in English is imperative because children tend to have trouble learning to read in a language they do not speak.

- Young children learn to communicate best when the teaching of speech and language objectives are embedded in classroom activities and routines. An effective language learning environment provides many experiences and materials for children to talk about with other children and responsive teachers.

- Children with communication disorders are likely to need deliberate instruction in such basic skills as listening and paying attention, not talking out of turn, learning conversational give-and-take, asking and answering questions, expressing needs, and conveying choices. These skills are best taught in the context of play, using milieu teaching strategies.

- The challenging behaviors in some children often are related to their inability to communicate effectively. The teacher's role is to systematically observe the child in the context of classroom activities to determine what the child is attempting to communicate. Children who experience repeated frustration in communicating their needs and preferences must be given special help to forestall compounding problems in other developmental areas.

Promoting Physical Development

▶ Physical skills and general good health significantly influence every area of development. In the first two years, all learning—cognitive, language, and social—is based on sensory input and expressed in the infant's physical responses.

▶ During infancy and early childhood, children almost automatically master an amazing array of physical skills. Major milestones include learning to roll over, sit up, drink from a cup, walk, run, climb, and catch a ball. Children with disabilities often require a specific intervention program that includes multiple opportunities to practice new skills and abundant support from parents, caregivers, and teachers.

▶ Appropriate adaptations enable every child to engage in all types of classroom activities. Examples of low-tech, low-cost adaptations are special chairs and eating utensils, grab bars by the toilets, or Velcro fastenings on clothing. An example of a high-tech, high-cost adaptation is the voice output augmentative communication system.

▶ Play, indoors or out, should be mostly child-directed. However, some children need to be taught how to use slides, climbing frames, and other pieces of equipment and to participate in everyday activities such as playing in a sandbox, riding in a wagon, or tossing bean bags.

▶ Early childhood programs are required to meet the accessibility guidelines of the Americans with Disabilities Act (ADA). Ramps, accessible entryways, and grab bars in toilet facilities are examples of the requirements. ADA also calls for meeting individual needs; for a child in a wheelchair, materials are better placed on a table than on the floor.

▶ Assessments of an early learning environment should include the physical space itself, equipment and materials, teacher–child ratios, group size, scheduling of activities, and opportunities for peer interaction.

▶ Physical and occupational therapists are among the indispensable members of the early childhood team. They promote physical development in all types of children and help teachers and parents translate therapy recommendations into play activities within the context of everyday home and school routines.

Promoting Social-Emotional Development

▶ The major influence on social and emotional development during infancy and early childhood is the child's relationship with family and caregivers. During later childhood and the teen years, peers become a powerful and ever-increasing influence.

▶ Social interactions are *transactional:* when children and parents interact, both are influenced and changed by the behavior of the other. The tone of the transactions soon determines what will become predominantly positive or negative patterns of adult–child relationships. Teachers can help less-skilled parents acquire the interactive skills that will promote their child's social and emotional development.

▶ Developing positive peer relationships and play behaviors is a major developmental task of the preschool years. A friendly classroom promotes sound social development. It is the teacher's job to offer activities and special interest areas that facilitate comfortable peer interactions.

▶ Children with disabilities often need to be taught to interact with other children. Teachers help by structuring and supporting a child in one-to-one activities, then moving the child into small-group play, and finally helping the child transition to less structured, child-initiated situations.

▶ Learning to share toys, treats, and attention is an essential social skill that does not come easily until much later in childhood (if then!). In the very early years, classrooms should have several of each of the most sought-after toys: for example, three big *red* trucks, not one red, one blue, and one yellow truck.

▶ Part of early socialization is that children begin to learn conflict resolution and problem-solving skills. Teachers can help children work out solutions to common classroom situations: suggesting ways to negotiate trading toys; introducing a timer to facilitate taking turns; providing a model for verbalizing "No! Stop that!" when a playmate becomes bothersome (and making sure the offending child does stop).

▶ Children learn to be altruistic, helpful, and careful of the feelings of others by modeling their behavior after caring and empathetic adults and older children. Young children like to be helpers. Adults can structure opportunities so that all children, including those with disabilities, can both give and receive help.

Appendix E

Sample IFSP Form

Sample Individualized Family Service Plan

I. Child and Family Information

Child's Name Maria Ramirez   Date of Birth 12-08-10   Age in Months 30   Gender F

Parent(s)/Guardian(s) Bruce & Catherine Ramirez   Address 2120 Valley Park Place   Middletown, IN   46810

                                                           Street   City   Zip Code

Home Telephone No. (513) 555-0330   Work Telephone No. (513) 555-1819

Preferred Language English   Translator Appropriate _____ Yes X No

II. Service Coordination

Coordinator's Name Susan Green   Agency Indiana Early Intervention Program

Address 105 Data Drive   Burlington, IN   46980   Telephone No. (513) 555-0214

             Street   City   Zip Code

Appointment Date 6-10-13

III. IFSP Team Members

Name	Agency	Telephone No.	Title/Function
Susan Green	Indiana Early Intervention (EI) Program	513-555-0214	Service Coordinator
Mr. and Mrs. B. Ramirez	N/A	513-555-0330	Parents
Barbara Smith	Indiana EI Program	513-555-0215	Speech/Language Pathologist
Martha King	Indiana EI Program	513-555-0213	Occupational Therapist
Libby Young	Middletown Preschool Program	513-555-3533	Preschool Teacher

IV. Review Dates

Date of IFSP 6-10-13   Six-Month Review 12-10-13   Annual Evaluation N. A.

Source: Individual Family Service Plan, NC Early Intervention Program, Early Intervention Branch, Women's and Children's Health Section, Division of Public Health, NC Department of Health and Human Services, 2010. Reprinted by permission.

Sample Individualized Family Service Plan

V. Statements of Family Strengths and Resources

Maria's parents are well educated professional individuals with realistic goals for her educational development. The entire family unit, including her grandparents is committed and motivated to assist her in any way. Because of the family's geographic location, limited resources are available for service delivery at this time.

VI. Statements of Family Concerns and Priorities

CONCERNS

Due to Maria's medical diagnosis of Down syndrome, her parents are concerned about appropriate early intervention services to assist in ameliorating her developmental delays. Additionally, the parents have stated reluctance about a change in Maria's service delivery from her natural environment (i.e., her home) to an inclusive community-based preschool.

PRIORITIES

The priorities that Maria's parents have for her include improving her communication skills, her ability to use utensils, and her toileting skills. They desire services to be delivered at home with the eventual goal of placement with typical children who attend the local kindergarten. Her parents and grandparents want to learn ways in which they can help to facilitate Maria's development in her natural environment.

VII. Child's Strengths and Present Level of Development

Cognitive Skills (Thinking, reasoning, and learning)

Maria's cognitive abilities are commensurate with a 20-month-old child. She's extremely inquisitive and understands simple object concept skills. Imitative play is consistently observed; however, discrimination of objects, persons, and concepts continues to be an area of need.

Communication Skills (Understanding, communicating with others, and expressing self with others)

Communication/language competency skills appear to be similar to that of an 18-month-old toddler. Her receptive language is further developed than her expressive abilities. Primitive gestures are her primary mode of communication. She consistently exhibits a desire/interest to interact with others. Verbal responses primarily consist of vocalizations and approximations of single-word utterances (e.g., ma-ma, da-da, ba-ba).

Self-Care/Adaptive Skills (Bathing, feeding, dressing, and toileting)

Feeding, in general, such as drinking from a cup and finger feeding, is appropriate at this time. A great deal of assistance from caregivers is still required for daily dressing tasks and toileting.

Gross and Fine Motor Skills (Moving)
Maria appears to be quite mobile. She is adept at rambling and walking, but needs to improve muscle strength and endurance. She enjoys movement to music. She can scribble, grasp large objects, turn pages of books, and prefers using her right hand while performing tasks. She needs to work on her ability to use utensils and writing tools.

Social-Emotional Development (Feelings, coping, and getting along with others)

Maria is a very happy, affectionate, and sociable child. She enjoys being the center of attention and engaging in interactive games; however, she appears content to play alone. Temper tantrums are triggered by frustration from her inability to communicate. Sharing and turn taking continue to be difficult for Maria.

Sample Individualized Family Service Plan

Health/Physical Development (Hearing, vision, and health)

Maria's general health is good, but she has a history of chronic otitis media and upper respiratory infections. Vision and hearing are monitored frequently.

VIII. Outcome Statements

1. Participate in stimulation of all language modalities (visual, auditory, tactile) in order to increase communication competency.

Strategies/Activities	Responsible Person/Agency	Begin Date	End Date	Frequency of Service	Location	Evaluation Criteria
1.1 Maria will use word approximations combined with consistent gestures for 5 different needs across 3 different people and 2 different settings.	SLP	6-10-13	12-10-13	Once Weekly	Home	Preschool Language Scale
1.2 Maria will use words combined with signs for 5 different needs across 3 different people and 2 settings.	Mom and Dad	6-10-13	12-10-13			Observation samples

2. Maria's daily self-care skills will improve in the areas of dressing and toileting abilities.

Strategies/Activities	Responsible Person/Agency	Begin Date	End Date	Frequency of Service	Location	Evaluation Criteria
2.1 Maria will push down/ pull up undergarments with minimal assistance.	Mom and Dad Service Coord.	6-10-13	12-10-13	Once Weekly	Home	Observations
2.2 Maria will establish a consistent pattern of elimination.	Mom and Dad Service Coord.	6-10-13	12-10-13	Once Weekly	Home	Recorded data of frequency of elimination
2.3 Maria will spontaneously indicate by gestures and vocalization the need for going to the restroom.	Mom and Dad Service Coord.	6-10-13	12-10-13	Once Weekly	Home	Observation samples

3. Maria will develop improved abilities to discriminate auditory/visual stimuli.

Strategies/Activities	Responsible Person/Agency	Begin Date	End Date	Frequency of Service	Location	Evaluation Criteria
3.1 Indicate by pointing/ verbalizing whether objects are the same or different.	Mom and Dad Service Coord.	6-10-10	12-10-10	Once Weekly	Home	Observations
3.2 Sort several colors and shapes consistently.	Mom and Dad Service Coord.	6-10-10	12-10-10	Once Weekly	Home	Observation samples
3.3 Imitate words and motions in songs upon being given a model.	Mom and Dad Service Coord.	6-10-10	12-10-10	Once Weekly	Home	Observation samples

(continued)

Continued

Sample Individualized Family Service Plan

IX. Transition Plans

If eligible the followings steps will be followed to transition ___Maria Ramirez___ to preschool services on or about
___12-13-10___
PROJECTED TRANSITION DATE   CHILD'S NAME

1. The service coordinator will schedule meeting with parents to explain transition process and rationale, review legal rights, and ascertain their preferences and need for support.
2. The service coordinator will arrange for Maria and her parents (and grandparents) to visit the center and meet teachers, staff, and children.
3. The service coordinator will arrange for Maria to visit her classroom on at least three occasions in the month prior to her transition date.
4. At least 90 days prior to Maria's third birthday, the service coordinator will convene a meeting to further develop Maria's transition plan.

X. Identification of Natural Environments

The home environment is considered to be Maria's natural environment at this time.

Justification for not providing services in natural environment: Not applicable.

XI. Family Authorization

We (I) the parent(s)/guardian(s) of ___Maria Ramirez___ hereby certify that we (I) have had the opportunity to participate in the development of our (my) son's/daughter's IFSP. This document accurately reflects our (my) concerns and priorities for our (my) child and family.

We (I) therefore give our (my) permission for this plan to be implemented. ___X___ _____
                                                 YES   NO

Catherine Ramirez	6-10-10	*Bruce Ramirez*	6-10-10
SIGNATURE OF PARENT/GUARDIAN	DATE	SIGNATURE OF PARENT/GUARDIAN	DATE

Glossary

A

activity-based approach—teachers use dramatic play, art, building with blocks, and other early childhood materials to provide developmentally appropriate learning experiences

activity-based intervention—method of providing early intervention services in which teaching opportunities are embedded in regularly scheduled classroom activities

acute—the sudden onset of an illness; usually of short duration; a chronic problem may have periodic acute episodes

adaptive equipment—mobility devices, prostheses, and prescribed alterations of standard furnishings to meet the needs of exceptional children

adaptive skills—the social, self-management, and communication skills deemed necessary for maintaining order in the community or culture in which a child lives

ADHD—attention deficit hyperactivity disorder; short attention span accompanied by excessive activity

advocacy group—individuals who work collectively for a particular cause

affective—social-emotional responses that influence the behavior of others

amblyopia—a vision problem that occurs when a child's eye does not get enough use and the visual system in the brain does not develop properly, leading to poor vision in the affected eye; it usually affects one eye but may occur in both eyes

American Sign Language—a language with its own vocabulary and grammar

amino acids—the chief components of proteins; obtained from the individual's diet or manufactured by living cells

amniocentesis—a medical test for genetic abnormalities that can be done about the sixteenth week of pregnancy

amplification device—any instrument that augments (increases) hearing

anoxia—lack of oxygen to the brain cells

antecedents—events that come before a behavior

antibody—substance manufactured either by the body or artificially to help the body fight disease

aphasia—the imperfect ability to express oneself or to comprehend spoken or written language; usually due to damage or disease in the language area of the cortex

applied behavior analysis (ABA)—a teaching approach used with children with autism that involves observation, assessment, breaking skills down, and teaching skills systematically; progress is closely monitored through ongoing data collection

articulation—refers to the production of speech sounds

articulation errors—speech sounds that are inconsistent with the native language (usually a temporary developmental irregularity)

assistive technology—various kinds of equipment, such as a computerized Braille system or voice synthesizer, designed to facilitate learning and communications for individuals with disabilities

asymptomatic—showing no signs of a disease or impairment that nevertheless may be present

at risk—indications (either physical or environmental) that an infant or child may develop serious problems

attachment process—building positive and trusting bonds between individuals, usually infant and parent or major caregiver

attention deficit hyperactivity disorder (ADHD)—short attention span accompanied by excessive activity

atypical development—any aspect of a child's physical or psychological makeup that is different from what is generally accepted as typical to early childhood

audiologist—a specially certified professional who focuses on hearing testing and hearing impairments

auditory—what is experienced through hearing

augmentative communication system—communication system that is used to supplement a child's verbal language; the system may be sign language, picture symbols, or a sophisticated computer system such as a voice synthesizer

autism—a developmental disorder that appears in the first three years of life and affects the brain's normal development of social and communication skills

autism spectrum disorder (ASD)—a term increasingly used to refer to a broad definition of autism, including the classical form of the disorder as well as closely related disabilities that share many of the core characteristics

autonomy—self-direction; independence

autosomal dominant gene—a gene on any chromosome except the sex chromosomes that, if inherited from either parent, results in a child with a medical condition

autosomal recessive gene—a gene carried by healthy parents on any chromosome except the sex chromosomes that, if inherited from both parents, results in a child with a medical condition not present in the parents

B

backward chaining—the opposite of forward chaining; teaching starts with the last step of a learning sequence–sometimes referred to as reverse chaining

baseline—data that are collected on a behavior prior to a systematic plan being introduced; these data provide a base against which later behavior can be compared

behavior geneticist—an individual who seeks to understand both the genetic and environmental contributions to individual variations in human behavior

behavior modification—a system by which particular environmental events are systematically arranged to produce specified behavior changes

behaviorally disordered—children who demonstrate chronic or pervasive behavior challenges

benevolent neglect—paying no attention to minor speech and language errors that usually self-correct as the child's communication skills mature

best practices—recommended strategies agreed upon by members of a profession

biological insult—a term that describes interference with or damage to an individual's physical structure or functioning

blindisms—atypical mannerisms displayed by some children with severe vision loss

bodily-kinesthetic—awareness of the body's position and movement

bolster—a therapeutic device to keep a child in the desired position

Braille—a system of writing for the blind that uses patterns of raised dots read by the fingers

breech—presentation of buttocks-first during birth

C

cardiac problems—those that involve the heart in terms of physical damage or poor functioning

case finding—locating children in need of special services

case law—how courts interpret and implement laws

categorical funding—public or private money assigned on the basis of type of handicap or disability

cerebral palsy—a condition caused by injury to certain parts of the brain; usually results in paralysis and uncontrollable muscle movement in particular parts of the body

chemotherapy—use of chemicals in the treatment of disease

Child Find—a program established in the 1960s to identify children with developmental problems or delays

chorionic villus sampling (CVS)—a test for genetic abnormalities; can be done between the ninth and eleventh weeks of gestation

chromosomal disorder—developmental problem that comes about at the time of conception

chronic—term for a health problem of long duration or frequent recurrence

cochlea—the bony, snail-shaped structure in the inner ear that allows hearing to occur

cochlear implant—device surgically placed by opening the mastoid structure of the skull; allows electrical impulses (sound) to be carried directly to the brain

compensatory education—educational programs (such as Head Start) designed for children who are disadvantaged; their purpose is to provide children with some of the opportunities (social, educational, medical) that advantaged children enjoy

comprehensive screening—evaluation of a child's current abilities, delays, and impairments in all areas of development

conductive hearing loss—refers to problems in the mechanical transmission of sounds through the outer, middle, or inner ear

congenital—describes a developmental condition or deviation present at the time of birth that may or may not be genetically related

congenital anomaly—a developmental difference present at birth; not necessarily of genetic origin

consequences—events that follow a behavior

consolidate—behaviors are so well learned that they become an integrated part of the child's repertoire

contextually based—assessment and intervention practices that are embedded into naturally occurring activities of the child (e.g., teaching or assessing hand washing as children prepare for snack)

contingent stimulation—responding to a child in a way that prompts further learning

contracture—permanent tightening of muscles and joints

cortical blindness—visual impairments originating in the brain

criterion-referenced assessment—assessment that describes a child's developmental level and progress according to a prescribed set of skills, tasks, and activities

cued speech—a visual communication system that uses eight hand shapes in four different placements near the face in combination with the mouth movements of speech to make the sounds of spoken language look different from each other

cultural mediators—individuals who help mediate between the culture of the school and the culture of the family; they share information and enhance understanding so that the family can participate fully in the assessment and education process

culturally competent—classroom activities, materials, and curricula that acknowledge and respect the different ethnicities that are represented in the classroom and community

cumulative deficits—adding on or layering of developmental problems; an undiagnosed hearing loss can result in an accumulation of additional problems (language, cognitive, and social)

cumulative effect—adding on or accumulation of consequences

D

data collection—information collected to determine whether an intervention or teaching strategy is effective and/or to learn more about a behavior

deafness—a hearing loss so severe that the individual cannot process spoken language even with amplification devices

deficit model curriculum—focuses on a child's disabilities and delays; tries to remedy what is "wrong" with the child

descriptive praise—feedback that lets children know specifically what it is they are doing well

developmental continuum—the range of skills or behaviors among children in any one area of development

developmental disequilibrium—a period of inconsistent behavior that often follows a spurt of rapid development

developmental inconsistency—learned behavior that may "come and go" before a final consolidation into the child's overall behavior pattern

developmental milestones—points at which specific skills are acquired in a fairly predictable order

developmentally appropriate—learning experiences geared to a child's skills, interests, maturation level, and chronological age; the "goodness-of-fit" between a child and curriculum activities

developmentally appropriate practices—learning activities based on teachers' knowledge of developmental theory

didactic materials—manipulative materials in which the child's errors and successes are self-evident

differentiation—materials and activities are offered at different levels, and choice is provided by teachers offering a range of topics, projects, and products to the students

direct feedback—firsthand communication between parent and teacher

discovery learning—also known as free play, child-initiated activity, and free-choice periods; open-ended blocks of time in which children discover the learnings inherent in the play materials

discrete trial teaching (DTT)—a teaching strategy which enables the learner to acquire complex skills and behaviors by first mastering the subcomponents of the targeted skill

discretionary legislation—law is implemented by the individual state or local agency

discretionary program—implies choice or options; Part H of PL 99-457 is discretionary: states decide whether they will provide services for handicapped infants and toddlers and their families

duration measures—how long an event or behavior lasts

dysfluency—hesitations, repetitions, omissions, or extra sounds in speech patterns

dyslexia—an impaired ability to read and understand written language

E

earmold—that part of an amplification device (hearing aid) that is fitted to the individual's ear

echolalic—language characterized by meaningless repetition of words and sentences used intelligently by others;

a condition often associated with autism and schizophrenia

ecology (of early learning)—the concept of viewing the child in the context of his or her learning environment and the impact the arrangement and individuals in this environment have on the child's learning

egocentric—in reference to young children, implies a view of the world from one perspective only—the child's own

embedded learning opportunities (ELOs)—the intentional incorporation of specific learning objectives into play and routine classroom activities

emerging literacy—the diverse skills that help children become successful in reading, writing, and other academic tasks

empirical—information based on observation or experiment

empowering—planning and carrying out intervention activities in ways that pass on as much control and decision making as possible to the family

empty calories—refers to foods in which there is high caloric content and low nutritional value

enabling environment (infancy)—environment that supports a child's optimal development

encopresis—chronic soiling problem

enuresis—chronic wetting problem

enzyme—complex protein that produces specific biological–chemical reactions in the body

exceptional children—a term coined at the 1930 White House Conference on Handicapped Individuals to refer to all children who are different from typically developing children

expressive language—spoken words or signs that individuals use in communicating with others

F

fading—gradually reducing prompts, cues, and physical assistance when teaching a particular skill

failure to thrive—refers to undersized infants whose bodies do not receive or cannot utilize the nurturance necessary for proper growth and development

family uniqueness—perspective that recognizes that every family is different

fine motor skills—physical activities that require the voluntary use of small muscles, such as holding a pencil, using scissors, and buttoning

formative—assessments that are ongoing and used to shape programs and interventions

forward chaining—breaking a task down into a series of small steps and teaching the first step first, in contrast to reverse chaining

Fragile X syndrome—a chromosomal abnormality associated with mental retardation; affects more males than females; behavioral characteristics often resemble autism

frequency counts—a system for keeping track of how often a behavior occurs; such data can provide significant information about a child's problem

functional behavior assessment—evaluating the degree to which children's behaviors "work" to get them what they want and need

functional behavior management—guidance techniques that are effective and specific to the child and the situation

functional skills—skills that are useful in everyday living

functionally illiterate—not possessing reading and writing skills used in day-to-day tasks

G

generalization—the spread of a learned response from the training situation to real-life situations

generalize—to learn a specific skill so well that a child can use it in a variety of situations

genetic counseling—the process of evaluating family history and medical records, ordering genetic tests, evaluating the results, and helping parents understand them and reach decisions about what to do next

genetic disorder—a disorder caused by alteration in the chromosomal materials that control inherited characteristics

giftedness—evidence of superior or unusual ability in areas such as intellect, creativity, artistic talent, physical agility, or leadership

goodness-of-fit—when the learning opportunities are appropriate to the child's developmental status

gross motor skills—physical activities that require the voluntary use of large muscles, such as running, sitting, and pulling up pants

H

higher auditory cortex—that section of the gray matter of the brain that processes sound

holding activities—activities children can work on independently while waiting for group activities to begin

holistic—an approach to understanding the child that focuses on the interrelationship and interdependence of all developmental domains

holophrastic speech—a state of speech development where the child conveys meaning with a one-word utterance

hydrocephalus—condition that results from undrained fluids leading to enlarged head and ultimate deterioration of the brain

hypertonic—having abnormally high muscle tone

hypotonic—having too little muscle tone; "floppiness"

I

IDEA/IDEIA—Individuals with Disabilities Education Act; federal law PL 101-476—amended as PL 105-17 Individuals with Disabilities Education Act Amendment of 1997—is the reauthorization of the original law (PL 94–142) that describes the types of educational services that must be provided to students from birth through age 21 who have disabilities. The Individuals with Disabilities Education Improvement Act of 2004 (IDEIA) aligns IDEA closely to the No Child Left Behind (NCLB) Act, helping to ensure equity, accountability, and excellence in education for children with disabilities

immune system—that aspect of body functioning responsible for warding off diseases

in utero—unborn; literally, "in the uterus"

incidental social learning—appropriate interactions promoted by a well-arranged early childhood program; for example, an adequate number of Legos reduces conflict

incidental teaching—teaching in which the environment and teacher responses are arranged to prompt or encourage a child's response

inclusion—children with special needs attend preschool, child care, and recreational programs with their typically developing peers

incompatible behaviors—two or more responses that cannot occur together

incremental steps—a series of small steps that lead to the eventual learning of an entire task

indirect feedback—covert or secondhand communication, such as one parent criticizing a teacher's methods, not to the teacher but to another parent within earshot of the teacher

individualized education program (IEP)—a document that is mandated for every student with a disability (ages 3–21) by PL 94-142. The IEP is the blueprint for the services the child receives and must be developed every year. It describes the child's current level of functioning and includes short- and long-term goals and objectives. All IEPs must be approved by parents

individualized family service plan (IFSP)—similar to an IEP. The IFSP describes services for very young children with disabilities (ages 0–3) and their families. The IFSP is mandated by PL 99-457. The IFSP is written collaboratively and describes the child's current strengths and needs. The IFSP describes what services will be provided and the major expected outcomes. Plans for the transition at age three are also included in the IFSP

Individuals with Disabilities Education Act—see IDEA

induced incompetence—term used to describe the effects of poorly functioning equipment on children with development disabilities

instructional utility—teaching the skills that will be useful to the child in a given environment

instrumental conditioning—*see* operant conditioning

integrated curriculum—lessons that include, in a single activity, content from more than one domain

integrated special education—including a few typically developing children in classes where the majority of children have special needs

integration—children with disabilities and typically developing children enrolled in the same program

intentional communication—gestures, vocalizations, and other communicative behavior that is directed toward a specific communicative partner and that has a specific function

interagency collaboration—cooperation among members of the several service agencies involved in the case management of a child and family with special needs

interdisciplinary team—refers to several different professionals working together on a common problem

interval—a specified period of the day that is broken into segments to record the occurrence, frequency, or duration of a behavior

intrinsic motivation—self-feedback (independent of adult feedback) that a child feels because of having done something well; often referred to as "joy of learning"

intrinsic reinforcement—feelings of pleasure and personal satisfaction derived from working on or accomplishing a task, discovering something new, or solving a problem

IQ tests—intelligence tests are usually norm-referenced and are designed to determine how much a child knows, how well the child solves problems, and how quickly a child can perform a variety of mental tasks; IQ tests do not predict future intellectual performance

itinerant special education teacher—special education teacher who works as a consultant with the regular classroom teacher or directly with children with disabilities in a community-based early childhood program, such as a child care or Head Start program

J

joint attention—an early social communicative behavior in which two people share focus on an object or event

juvenile rheumatoid arthritis—a disorder that involves the joints, causes stiffness, swelling, and limited motion; may be accompanied by inflammation of the eyes

L

landmark legislation—a turning point in, or an entirely new approach to, public policy. The Education for All Handicapped Children Act is considered landmark legislation because of provisions never before written into law on behalf of the handicapped

learned helplessness—excessive dependency, often induced by well-meaning parents or caregivers because they cannot bear to see the child struggle (or feel they do not have the time to let the child work at learning a particular self-help task)

learning disability—a condition that interferes with learning to read, write, or do math

learning theory—emphasizes the dominant role of environment and reinforcing experiences in learning

least restrictive environment (LRE)—most normalized environment in which the needs of a child with disabilities can be met appropriately; often, the LRE is interpreted as the environment in which typically developing children function

local education agency (LEA)—an educational agency at the local level that exists primarily to operate schools or to contract for educational services

logical consequence—a consequence determined by an adult that is related to the child's original inappropriate behavior

low vision—refers to a severe visual impairment, not necessarily limited to distance vision; it applies to all individuals who are unable to read print even with the aid of eyeglasses

M

mainstreaming—enrolling children with disabilities along with typically developing children in the same classroom

manipulative materials—materials that children can handle and work with, such as puzzles, blocks, and wooden beads

manual interpreter—an individual who translates spoken language into sign language for the deaf

manual prompt—positioning the teacher's hand around the learner's and putting the learner through the motions required for performing a particular act

maturation—developmentally, maturation is often defined as an internal process that governs the natural unfolding of innate ("preprogrammed") skills and abilities

maturationist—one who believes that human development is a natural unfolding of innate abilities and nearly independent of environmental influence

mediated learning—based on the teaching premise that cognitive and social processes are interdependent factors in all learning

mediator—the teacher or other adult who facilitates learning by bridging the gap between the child and the learning environment

meningocele—similar to the myelomeningocele, except that the protrusion contains only the covering of the spinal cord and usually causes little or no neurological impairment

metabolic disorder—a breakdown somewhere in the complex chemicals needed to metabolize food

metabolism—the chemical process within living cells by which energy is manufactured so that body systems can carry out their functions

milieu (incidental) teaching—a teaching opportunity based on the child's initiation; the child approaches the teacher for assistance, information, or materials, thereby ensuring the child's interest and eagerness

mobiles—an art form made up of balanced lengths of wire or string to which pieces of various materials are attached so that air currents move them about when they are hung up

modeling—learning by watching and imitating another's actions; also called observational learning

motherese—infant-directed speech patterns that adults use with the very young

multidimensional—the relationship among the many factors that comprise a learning sequence

multidisciplinary—involving members of various disciplines who work independently but exchange their findings about a case; each concentrates on his or her own discipline

mutual gaze—the steady looking at one another's faces that goes on between healthy newborns and their mother or primary caregiver

myelomeningocele—a congenital protrusion of the spinal cord through the vertebrae; paralysis of the lower trunk and legs often results

N

natural consequence—a consequence that would occur without a parent's or teacher's intervention

negative reinforcement—the strengthening of a behavior by the removal of an unpleasant consequence

neural—involving the nerves and nervous system

neurological—referring to the nerves and the nervous system in general

neuroscientists—those who study the brain and the nervous system

nonambulatory—describes the inability to move oneself about; usually the inability to walk

nondiscriminatory—screening and diagnostic tests compatible with a child's native language and culture

normal (typical) development—the process of growing, changing, and acquiring a range of skills at approximately the same age and in the same sequence as the majority of children of similar age

normal deviations—minor irregularities that often occur in young children; the irregularities are usually self-correcting in typically developing children

normalization—the process by which the care and education of people with disabilities are as culturally normal as possible, with services provided in regular community facilities rather than in segregated schools and institutions

norm-referenced assessment—instrument that compares a child's developmental level to a normative sample of same-age peers

O

obesity—the condition of being considerably overweight

observational learning—learning by watching and imitating another's actions; also called modeling

occluder—the object the eye examiner uses to prevent the child from seeing (usually one eye at a time)

occlusion—to obstruct; as used here, to prevent vision

operant conditioning (also instrumental conditioning)—type of learning that results from the consequences of a person's behavior; operating intentionally on some aspect of the environment to produce change

oppositional behavior—patterns of child behavior that adults consider excessively negative, troublesome, or challenging

organic—within the individual's own body or neurological system

orientation and mobility specialist—therapist who teaches individuals with vision impairments awareness of their position in the environment, of significant objects within the environment (orientation), and how to move safely and efficiently (mobility) by utilizing their remaining senses

orthopedic impairments—developmental problems that interfere with walking or other body movements

otitis media—chronic ear infection affecting hearing

overregularization—language irregularities that occur because the child is applying previously learned rules of grammar; for example, "the mouses runned"

P

paramedics—specially trained individuals who handle emergency medical situations

paraprofessional—a trained person who assists a certified professional as an aide

parent surrogate—individual appointed to act in place of a parent

parental consent—parental permission for a program, assessment, or specific activity; given after parents have been informed about choices, risks, and benefits

pathologist—certified professional who focuses on diseases or impairments

pediatric ophthalmologist—physician who specializes in diseases and malfunctioning of the eyes during the developmental years

peer tutoring—one child instructing or assisting another

people-first language/terminology—in referring to people with disabilities, language that speaks of the person first and then the disability; for example, "a child with autism" rather than "an autistic child" emphasizes abilities rather than limitations

perceptual motor skills—movement generated by sensory messages, by what is seen, heard, touched, tasted, or smelled

peripheral vision—that degree of vision available at the outer edges of the eyes

perseveration—repeating the same act over and over with no discernible intention (obsessive, ritualistic)

pertussis—clinical name for whooping cough

phobias—fears that result in excessive and unrealistic anxiety about everyday happenings

pica—craving to eat nonfood substances

Picture Exchange Communication System (PECS)—an augmentative communication system that focuses on child initiation; the child exchanges symbols and pictures to communicate desires and ideas

portfolio—a carefully selected collection of a child's work that is used to document growth and development

positive behavioral support strategies—providing positive rather than negative feedback to children's efforts; concentrating on what the child does right

positive reinforcement—something that follows a response and results in the increase of that particular response

post-lingual—describes hearing loss occurring after the child has acquired speech

pre-academics—prerequisite skills that provide the foundation for the formal academic training that usually starts in first grade

preeclampsia (toxemia)—high blood pressure during pregnancy

pre-lingual—describes hearing loss occurring before the child has acquired speech

pre-linguistic communication—body movements, facial expressions, and vocalizations used by infants before the first words are learned

prerequisite skills—skills that must be acquired before a higher level skill can be attempted

preventive discipline—arranging the classroom environment in ways that promote children's appropriate behavior and forestall behaviors teachers consider inappropriate

primitive reflexes—responses the infant is born with: such behaviors as grasping, stepping, rooting, and sucking

private speech—children's strategy of talking to themselves to direct their behavior as they work things out

progressive—in terms of health, a condition that gets steadily better (or worse)

prompting—verbal, gestural, or physical assistance that helps the child to learn a skill or participate in an activity

prone-board—a therapeutic device to help a child maintain a standing position

prostheses—artificial devices replacing body parts that are damaged at birth or later removed

psycholinguist—one who studies and analyzes the acquisition and production of language

psychopathologist—an individual who specializes in viewing mental disorders from a psychological perspective

pull-out services—a model of delivering specialized support services such as physical therapy or speech therapy in which the child is removed from the classroom and taken to a special therapy setting

punishment—technically, the presentation of an aversive event, or the removal of a positive event, contingent upon a response that decreases the probability of a behavior's occurrence

R

range of motion—the direction and degree to which arms, legs, and other parts of the skeleton can move

readiness—a child's ability to learn that takes into account prerequisite physical, cognitive, language, or social skills

readiness to learn—the point at which a child has the necessary prerequisite skills to engage in specific new learning

receptive language—language that is acquired but not necessarily used in routine speech

reciprocal relationship—relationship in which each member gives and receives in response to the giving and receiving of the other

reciprocity—the "give-and-take" interactions between a child and others

reconstituted (or blended) family—each parent bringing children into a new household

redirection—a teaching strategy that directs the child's attention and energy from a behavior that is less than desirable by introducing a more appropriate behavior or activity

reflexive—involuntary body reaction to specific kinds of stimulation (a tap on the knee produces the knee jerk)

refractive—describes a visual acuity problem correctable with eyeglasses

reinforcement—general term for a consequence, event, or procedure that increases or maintains the behavior it follows

reinforcers—increase the behaviors that they follow and are specific to individuals (candy is a reinforcer for many children, but for many it is not)

reliable—relates to consistency: how accurate, dependable, and predictable a test is

remission—in reference to health problems, temporary or permanent relief from the problem

replacement behavior—a behavior that is taught to a child to replace an inappropriate one; a replacement behavior should serve the same function as the inappropriate behavior

residual hearing—refers to whatever degree of hearing is left to a person who is deaf or hearing impaired

residual vision—whatever vision remains after disease or damage to a person's visual system

resilience—the ability to "come back" after a damaging or traumatic experience

respiratory distress syndrome (RDS)—a problem commonly found among premature infants caused by immature lung development; may also occur in about 1 percent of full-term infants during the first days of life

respite care—temporary care given to provide regular caregivers (usually the mother) relief and time away from the individual who is sick or disabled

response to intervention (RTI)—the practice of providing high-quality instruction/intervention matched to the student's needs, using learning rate over time and level of performance to make important educational decisions

responsive learning environment—environment that supports a child's efforts to explore and discover through interactions with other individuals, play materials, and activities

reverse mainstreaming—special education classes that also include some typically developing children

rote memorization—refers to memorizing without understanding

S

salicylates—chemical compounds commonly known as salts

savant—an individual who is unusually knowledgeable about one particular subject but is lacking in other areas of cognitive skill

scaffolding—introducing new learning built on skills already acquired

screening—the identification of developmental problems or the potential for such problems

secondary disabilities—developmental problems that come about because of the primary disability

secondary prevention—refers to the early identification of handicapping conditions (or potentially handicapping conditions) and providing appropriate intervention services before the condition worsens or affects other areas of development

seizures—convulsions caused by a disturbance of the electrical activity of the brain

self-determination—teaching and providing children with opportunities to take a more active role in stating their individuality and independence

self-help skills—the ability to take care of one's own needs; self-feeding, toileting, dressing, and other socially prescribed routines

sensitive (or critical) period—a time when a child is especially responsive and able to learn a particular skill

sensitivity—ability of a screening test to identify correctly children with disabilities

sensorimotor—Piaget's term for the first major stage of cognitive development from birth to about eighteen months; infant moves from reflexive to voluntary behavior

sensorineural hearing loss—malfunctioning of the cochlea or auditory nerve

sensory deficit—a loss in one or more of the five senses: vision, hearing, touch, taste, smell

sensory impairment—impairment that affects the ability to sense the environment through a specific sensory modality such as hearing or vision

sensory integration—more than one sense working together to understand a sensory message and to translate the message into appropriate action

sensory system—any one of several ways individuals receive information or input from their environment

separation protest—displeasure the infant displays between eight and twelve months (approximately) when mother or caregiver leaves

service coordinator—an interdisciplinary team member responsible for integrating services and keeping the family informed and involved

service delivery model—a formal plan devised by the various agencies involved in providing services to a given child and family

sex-linked gene—a gene carried on one of the two X chromosomes in a female; if inherited by a daughter, the gene confers an asymptomatic carrier state, as with her mother; if it is inherited by a son, the gene results in a medical condition not present in other family members

shadow aide—a person who provides support to a child in an inclusive setting, which includes encouraging independence in following the routine and interacting with peers and other teachers

shaping—positive reinforcement provided contingent on an approximation of a desired behavior

shunt—a tube implanted into the brain to allow proper circulation and drainage of fluids within the skull

signing—non-oral communication systems such as finger spelling or American Sign Language

simian crease—a single transverse crease on the palm of one or both hands (instead of the typical two creases on the palm)

sit and watch—a mild form of time-out in which the teacher asks a misbehaving child to sit at the edge of an activity for a minute or two to observe the appropriate play of peers

sleep apnea—condition that interrupts or may stop normal breathing during sleep

social reinforcement—the positive or negative feedback that children receive from adults and peers that leads to further learning, either appropriate or inappropriate

socially deviant—refers to atypical behavior that is different from the social norm; behavior not expected in a given situation; inappropriate or maladaptive behavior

spatial orientation—knowing where one is in relationship to one's surroundings

specificity—ability of a screening test to identify correctly children who do not have a disability

speech reading—the more accurate term for lip reading

sphincter muscles—muscles that contribute to bowel and bladder control

stabiles—similar to mobiles, stabiles are designed to be stationary

standardized tests—assessment instruments that include precise directions for administration and scoring

stigma (pl. stigma)—an identifying mark or characteristic; a diagnostic sign of a disease or disability

strabismus—eye muscle imbalance problems correctable with eyeglasses

structured flexibility—a well-structured early learning environment that also is adaptable to children's individual needs and preferences

surrogate—a person appointed to act for another person

synapse—the contact point between two nerve cells in the brain and nervous system

syndrome—a grouping of similar physical characteristics

syntax—the way in which words are put together to form phrases, clauses, or sentences

systems-level approach—a plan devised and implemented by the several agencies involved in facilitating a child's transition to the next educational program

T

tactile—referring to touch

tangible reinforcers—material things that the individual likes; in children, favorite foods and drinks, toys, stickers, and such

task analysis—the process of sequencing developmental tasks into small, incremental steps

teachable moments—points in time, perhaps associated with critical periods, when a child is highly motivated and better able to acquire a particular skill

telegraphic speech—a stage of speech development when the child conveys meaning with two-word utterances

temperament—the individual's psychological makeup or personality traits

theory of mind—the ability to infer other people's mental states and to use this information to interpret what they say, make sense of their behavior, and predict what they will do next

therapeutic—related to treatment of a disease or disability

threshold—the physical or psychological point at which an individual begins to respond to certain kinds of stimulation

time-out—the extreme form of withdrawing reinforcement

total communication—system for teaching children with deafness that combines speech reading and a sign system

transactional learning—interactions between a child and the environment that facilitate new learnings

transactional relationships—the understanding that children and adults influence each other in their ongoing relationships and that both children and adults learn from these interactions; future interactions are influenced by earlier interactions

transdisciplinary team—team that shares the responsibilities for assessment, program planning, implementation, and evaluation across members

transfer skills—the ability to generalize previously learned skills to an unfamiliar setting or a new classroom

two-way journal—a notebook for questions or observations on a particular child that is passed back and forth between parents, teachers, and other team members on a regular basis

U

undifferentiated responses—a behavior(s) that is not directed toward a specific person or intended to communicate a specific message

universal design—an approach to the design of all products and environments to be as usable as possible by as many people as possible regardless of age, ability, or situation

V

valid—founded on truth or fact; a test that measures what it purports to measure

visual acuity—how well an individual is able to see; keenness of vision

voice synthesizer—computer that can produce spoken words; type of assistive technology often used by people with severe communication disabilities

voluntary motor responses—responses that the individual controls

vulnerability—lack of resistance or ability to recover from a damaging or traumatic experience

W

wedge—a therapeutic device to help a child maintain a position

Z

zone teaching—a strategy in which each teacher is responsible for an area of the classroom

References

Achilles, E. (1999). Creating music environments in early childhood programs. *Young Children, 54*(1), 21–26.

Adams, M. (1994). Beginning to read: *Thinking and learning about print.* MIT Press: Cambridge, MA.

Allen, K. E. (1974). Behavior modification principles. In J. C. Cull & R. E. Hardy (Eds.), *Behavior modification in rehabilitation settings.* Thomas: Springfield, IL.

Allen, K. E., & Goetz, F. M. (1982). *Early childhood education: Special problems, special solutions.* Aspen Systems: Rockville, MD.

Allen, K. E., & Hart, B. (1984). *The early years: Arrangements for learning.* Prentice-Hall Englewood Cliffs, NJ.

Allen, K. E., & Marotz, L. R. (2010). *Developmental profiles: Pre-birth through twelve* (6th ed.). Delmar Thomson Learning: Clifton Park, NY.

Allen, K. E., & Ruggles, T. (1980). *Analysis of teacher–child interaction patterns in the preschool setting.* Paper presented at the Alice H. Hayden Conference, Seattle, WA.

American Academy of Pediatrics (2010). *Prevention of pediatric overweight and obesity.* Retrieved January 30, 2010 from http://www.aap.org/obesity/about.html

American Academy of Pediatrics (AAP). (2002). Use of photo screening for children's vision screening. *Pediatrics, 109,* 524–525.

American Academy of Pediatrics. (2005). *Immunizations & infectious diseases: An informed parent's guide.* American Academy of Pediatrics: Washington, DC.

American Academy of Pediatrics. (2000). Clinical practice guideline: Diagnosis and evaluation of the child with attention-deficit/hyperactivity disorder. *Pediatrics, 105*(5), 1158–1170. Retrieved from http://pediatrics. aappublications.org/content/105/5/1158.full

American Diabetes Association. (2012). *Diabetes basics.* Retrieved October 1, 2012 from http://www.diabetes.org

American Lung Association (2012). Retrieved October 1, 2012 from http://www.lung.org/lung-disease/asthma/resources/facts-and-figures/asthma-children-fact-sheet.html

American Psychiatric Association (2013). Diagnostic and Statistical Manual of Mental Disorders (Fifth ed.). Arlington, VA: American Psychiatric Publishing.

American Psychiatric Association (2012). *Commentary takes issue with criticism of new autism definition: DSM-5 experts call study flawed.* Press Release, March 27, 2012. Retrieved January 19, 2013 from http://www.dsm5.org/Documents/12-15%20DSM%20Commentary_Autism.pdf

Anderson, S. R., Jablonski, A. L., Thomeer, M. L. & Knapp, V. M. (2007). *Self help skills for people with autism. A systematic teaching approach.* Woodbine House: Bethesda, MD.

Anderson, R. C., Hiebert, E. H., Scott, J. A., & Wilkerson, I. A. (1985). *Becoming a nation of readers.* National Academy of Education: Washington, DC.

Anita, S. D., & Kreimeyer, K. H. (1992). Social competence intervention for young children with hearing impairments. In S. Odom, S. McConnell, & M. McEvoy (Eds.), *Social competence of young children with disabilities* (pp. 135–164). Brookes: Baltimore, MD.

Anxiety and Depression Association of America (2013). *Facts and statistics.* Retrieved January 15, 2013 from http://www.adaa.org/about-adaa/press-room/facts-statistics

Apgar, V. G., & Beck, J. (1973). *Is my baby all right?* Pocket Books: New York.

Aronson, S. S. (Ed.). (2002). *Healthy young children.* National Association for the Education of Young Children: Washington, DC.

Artiles, A. J., & Oritz, A. A. (2002). *Before assessing a child for special education, first assess the instructional program. A summary of English language learners with special education needs.* Center for Applied Linguistics: Washington, DC. Retrieved from http://www.misd.net/bilingual/ellsandspedcal.pdf

Autism Speaks (2012). *Autism Speaks top 10 autism research achievements of 2012.* Press release December 19, 2002. Retrieved from http://www.autismspeaks.org/about-us/

press-releases/autism-speaks-top-10-autism-research-achievements-2012

Autism Speaks (2012). *Autism Speaks funds research on impact of DSM-5 on autism diagnosis.* Press release June 25, 2012. Retrieved January 20, 2013 from http://www.autismspeaks.org/science/science-news/autism-speaks-funds-research-impact-dsm-5-autism-diagnosis

Azrin, N. H. (1989). *Toilet training in less than a day.* Pocket Books reissue: New York.

Bailey, D. B., & McWilliam, R. A. (1990). Normalizing early intervention. *Topics in Early Childhood Special Education, 10*(2), 33–47.

Bailey, D. B., & Winton, P. J. (1994). Families of exceptional children. In N. G. Haring & L. McCormick (Eds.), *Exceptional children and youth.* Prentice Hall: Englewood Cliffs, NJ.

Bailey, D. B., & Wolery, M. (1992). *Teaching infants and preschoolers with handicaps.* Prentice Hall: Englewood Cliffs, NJ.

Bailey, D. B., Burchinal, M. R., & McWilliam, R. A. (1993). Age of peers and early child development. *Child Development, 64,* 848–862.

Bailey, D., Hebbler, K., Spiker, D., Scarborough, A., Mallik, S., & Nelson, L. (2005). Thirty-six-month outcomes for families of children who have disabilities and participated in early intervention. *Pediatrics, 116*(6), 1346–1352.

Bailey, D., McLean, M., & Wolery, M. (2004). *Assessing infants and preschoolers with special needs (3rd ed.).* Merrill/Prentice Hall: Upper Saddle River, NJ.

Baker, B., & Brightman, B. (2004). *Steps to independence: Teaching everyday skills to children with disabilities.* Brookes: Baltimore, MD.

Bandura, A. (1973). *Aggression: A social learning analysis.* Prentice-Hall: Englewood Cliffs, NJ.

Bandura, A. (1977). *Social learning theory.* Prentice-Hall: Englewood Cliffs, NJ.

Barkley, R. A. (2005). *Attention deficit hyperactivity disorders: A handbook for diagnosis and treatment.* Guilford Press: New York.

Barlow, S. E., & Expert Committee (2007). Expert committee recommendations regarding the prevention, assessment, and treatment of child and adolescent overweight and obesity: Summary report. The online version of this article, along with updated information and services, is located at http://pediatrics.aappublications.org/content/105/6/1358.full?sid=67795a9c

Barnett, W. S., & Escobar, C. M. (2000). Economic costs and benefits of early intervention. In S. J. Meisels & J. P. Shonkoff (Eds.), *Handbook of early intervention* (pp. 560–582). Cambridge University Press: New York.

Barrera, I. (1994). Thoughts on the assessment of young children whose sociocultural background is unfamiliar to the assessor. *Zero to Three, 14*(6), 9–13.

Bates, E., O'Connell, B., & Shore, C. (1987). Language and communication in infancy. In J. D. Osofsky (Ed.), *Handbook of infant development* (2nd ed.). Wiley: New York.

Bee, H., & Boyd, D. (2012). *The developing child* (13th ed.). Pearson Education: Upper Saddle River, NJ.

Bellinger, D. C., Stiles, K. M., & Needleman, H. L. (1992). Low-level lead exposure, intelligence and academic achievement: A long-term follow-up study. *Pediatrics, 90,* 855–861.

Benasich, A. A., & Tallal, P. (1996). Auditory temporal processing thresholds, habituation, and-recognition memory over the first year. *Infant Behavior and Development, 19,* 339–357.

Bench, J. (1992). *Communication skills in hearing-impaired children.* Singular: San Diego.

Bennett, C. I. (2010). *Comprehensive multicultural education: Theory and practice.* Allyn & Bacon: Boston, MA.

Bennett, F. C. (1990). Recent advances in developmental intervention for biologically vulnerable infants. *Infants and Young Children, 3*(1), 33–40.

Bentzen, W. R. (2009). *Seeing young children: A guide to observing and recording behavior* (6th ed.). Thomson Delmar Learning: Clifton Park, NY.

Berglund, E., Eriksson, M., & Johansson, I. (2001). Parental reports of spoken language skills in children with Down syndrome. *Journal of Speech, Language, and Hearing Research, 44,* 179–191.

Beveridge, M., Loader, S., Northstone, K., & Roulston, S. (2002). The speech and language of children aged 25 months: Descriptive data from the Avon longitudinal study of parents and children. *Early Child Development and Care, 172,* 259–268.

Bijou, S. W. (1959). Learning in children. *Monographs of the Society for Research in Child Development, 24*(5), 25–36.

Bijou, S. W. (1993). *Behavior analysis of child development* (2nd ed.). Context Press: Reno, NV.

Bijou, S. W., & Cole, B. W. (1975). The feasibility of providing effective educational programs for the severely and profoundly retarded: Educating the 24-hour retarded child. Paper presented at National Association for Retarded Citizens. New Orleans.

Billingsley, F., Gallucci, C., Peck, C. A., Schwartz, I. S., & Staub, D. (1996). "But those kids can't even do math": An alternative conceptualization outcome for inclusive education. *Special Education Leadership Review, 3*(1), 43–55.

Bissell, C. (n.d.) *Family-centered care.* Massachusetts Community Gateway: Palmer, MA. Retrieved from http://communitygateway.org/resources/faq/index.htm

Blagojevic, B., D. Twomey, & L. Labas. (2007). *Universal design for learning: From the start.* University of Maine: Orono, ME. Retrieved from http://www.ccids.umaine.edu/resources/facts/facts6/udl.htm

Blasi, M. J., & Priestley, L. (1998). A child with severe hearing loss joins our learning community. *Young Children, 53*(2), 44–49.

Blaustein, M. (2005, July). See, hear, touch. The basis of learning readiness. *Beyond the Journal. Young Children on the Web*. Retrieved from http://www.naeyc.org/files/yc/file/200507/01Blaustein.pdf

Bloom, B. (1964). *Stability and change in human characteristics*. John Wiley and Sons: New York.

Bloom, L. (1995). *The transition from infancy to language: Acquiring the power of expression*. Cambridge University Press: Cambridge.

Bloom, L. M., Marquis, C., Tinker, E., & Fujita, N. (1996). Early conversations and word learning: Contributions from child and adult. *Child Development*, 3154–3175.

Board of Education, Sacramento City Unified School District v. Holland, 7867, Supp. 874 (E. D. Cal 1992).

Bohan-Baker, M. & Little, P. M. (2004). *The transition to kindergarten: A review of current research and promising practices to involve families*. Harvard Family Research Project: Cambridge, MA.

Bondy, A., & Frost, L. (1994). The picture exchange communication system. *Focus on Autistic Behavior, 9*(3), 1–19.

Boschert, S. (2012) Comorbidities might mask autism in Hispanics. *Family Practice Digital News Network*. Retrieved from http://www.familypracticenews.com/index.php?id=2934&type=98&tx_ttnews%5Btt_news%5D=139275&cHash=da03e20e363

Bowe, Frank G. (2008). *Early childhood special-education birth to eight*. Thomson Delmar Learning: Clifton Park, NY.

Boyer, E. L. (1994). *Ready to learn: A mandate for the nation*. American Association of Colleges for Teacher Education: Washington, DC.

Brizee, L. S., Sophos, C. M., & McLaughlin, J. F. (1990). Nutrition issues in developmental disabilities. *Infants and Young Children, 2*(3), 10–22.

Bronfenbrenner, U. (2006). *The ecology of human development*. Harvard University Press: Cambridge, MA.

Brookings Institution and Princeton University, *The Future of Children*, Spring 2011.

Brophy, J. E. (1981). Teacher praise: A functional analysis. *Review of Educational Research, 51*(1), 5–32.

Bruder, M.B. (2000). The Individualized Family Service Plan (IFSP). www.kid needs.com/diagnostic_categories/articles/indivfamilyserviceplan.htm

Bruder, M. B., & Chandler, L. K. (1996). Transition. In S. L. Odom & M. E. McLean (Eds.), *Early-intervention/early childhood special education: Recommended practices* (pp. 287–307). Pro-Ed: Austin, TX.

Bruder, M. B., & Dunst, C. J. (1999–2000). Expanding learning opportunities for infants and toddlers in natural environments: A chance to reconceptualize early intervention. *Zero to Three, 20*(3), 34–36.

Buell, M. J., Hallam, R., Gamel McCormick, M., & Scheer, S. (1999). A survey of general and special education teachers' perceptions and in-service needs concerning inclusion. *International Journal of Disability, Development and Education, 46*(2), 143–156.

Buysee, V., & Bailey, D. B. (1993). Behavioral and developmental outcomes in young children with disabilities in integrated and segregated settings: A review of comparative studies. *Journal of Special Education, 26,* 434–461.

Calderon, M., Slavin, R., and Sanchez, M. (2011). Effective instruction for English learners. *The Future of Children*. Retrieved from http://futureofchildren.org/futureofchildren/publications/journals/article/index.xml?journalid=74&articleid=542

Caldwell, B. M. (1973). The importance of beginning early. In J. B. Jordan & R. F. Dailey (Eds.), *Not all little wagons are red: The exceptional child's early years*. Council for Exceptional Children: Reston, VA.

Caldwell, B. M. (1984). *Home observation for measurement of the environment*. University of Arkansas: Little Rock.

Caldwell, B. M. (1988). Ethic's commission member's comment. *Young Children, 43*(2), 50.

Campbell, F. A., & Ramey, C. T. (1994). Effects of early intervention on intellectual and academic achievement: A follow-up study of children from low-income families. *Child Development, 65,* 684–698.

Capizzano, J., Adams, G., & Sonenstein, F. (2000). *Child care arrangements for children under five: Variation across states (No. B-7)*. Urban Institute: Washington, DC.

Carlson, E., Daley, T., Bitterman, A., Heinzen, H., Keller, B., Markowitz, J., & Riley, J. (2009). *Early school transitions and the social behavior of children with disabilities: Selected findings from the pre-elementary education longitudinal study*. Westat: Rockville, MD. Retrieved October 13, 2012 from http://ies.ed.gov/pubsearch/pubsinfo.asp?pubid=NCSER20093016.

Carter, E. W. & Kennedy, C. H. (2006). Promoting access to the general curriculum using peer support strategies. *Research & Practice for Persons with Severe Disabilities, 31*(4), 284–292.

Carr, E. G., & Durand, V. M. (1985). Reducing problem behaviors through functional communication training. *Journal of Applied Behavior Analysis, 18,* 111–126.

Cartwright, S. (1999). What makes good early childhood teachers? *Young Children, 54*(4), 4–7.

Cass, J. D., Sonkesen, P. M., & McConachie, H. R. (1994). Developmental setback in severe visual impairment. *Archives of Diseases of Childhood, 70,* 192–196.

CAST (2011). *Universal Design for Learning Guidelines version 2.0*. Author: Wakefield, MA.

Cate, D., Diefendorf, M., McCullough, K., Peters, M. L., & Whaley, K. (Eds.). (2010). *Quality indicators of inclusive early childhood programs/practices: A compilation of selected resources*. The University of North Carolina, FPG Child Development Institute, National Early Childhood Technical Assistance Center: Chapel Hill. Retrieved from http://dpi.wi.gov/sped/pdf/spp6-qual-ind-incl.pdf

Center for American Progress. (2012). *Increasing the effectiveness and efficiency of existing public investments in* early childhood education: *Recommendations to boost program outcomes and efficiency.* Retrieved from http://www.americanprogress.org/issues/2012/06/pdf/earlychildhood.pdf

Centers for Disease Control and Prevention (2012). *CDC estimates 1 in 88 children in United States has been identified as having an autism spectrum disorder,* Press release March 29, 2012. Retrieved January 20, 2013 from http://www.cdc.gov/media/releases/2012/p0329_autism_disorder.html

Centers for Disease Control and Prevention (2012). *Childhood obesity facts.* Retrieved October 1, 2012 from http://www.cdc.gov/healthyyouth/obesity/facts.htm.

Centers for Disease Control and Prevention. (2011). School health guidelines to promote healthy eating and physical activity. *Morbidity and Mortality Weekly Report, Recommendations and Reports, 60*(5). Retrieved October 1, 2012 from http://www.cdc.gov/mmwr/pdf/rr/rr6005.pdf

Centers for Disease Control and Prevention: National Center for Health Statistics, National Health Interview Survey Raw Data. (2009). *Analysis by the American Lung Association Research and Program Services Division using SPSS and SUDAAN software.*

Centers for Disease Control and Prevention (2011). *Attention deficit hyperactivity disorder: Data and statistics.* Retrieved January 13, 2013 http://www.cdc.gov/ncbddd/adhd/data.html

Centers for Disease Control and Prevention. (2007). *Program in frief: Vaccines for children program.* Retrieved January 26, 2013 from http://www.317coalition.org/documents/vaccinebrief1.pdf

Centers for Disease Control and Prevention. (2006). *Summary health statistics for U.S. children: National Health Interview Survey, 2006.* Retrieved January 13, 2013 from http://www.cdc.gov/nchs/data/series/sr_10/sr10_234.pdf

Center on the Developing Child at Harvard University. (2011). *Building the brain's "air traffic control" system: How early experiences shape the development of executive function.* Working Paper No. 11. Retrieved from www.developingchild.harvard.edu

Chance, P. (2006). *First course in applied behavior analysis.* Brooks/Cole: Pacific Grove, CA.

Chandler, L. K., Fowler, S. A., Hadden, S., & Stahurski, L. (1995). *Planning your child's transition to preschool: A step-by-step guide for families.* University of Illinois: Champaign.

Chia, T. E., Harris, R., & Hoffman, C. (1974). Parents as identifiers of giftedness, ignored but accurate. *Gifted Child Quarterly, 18*(2), 192–195.

Child Care Law (2011). *United States Department of Justice ADA settlement summaries.* Retrieved January 26, 2013 from http://www.childcarelaw.org/files/DOJ_ADA_Settlement_Agreements.pdf

Child Welfare Information Gateway. (2012). *The risk and prevention of maltreatment of children with disabilities.* U.S. Department of Health and Human Services, Children's Bureau: Washington, DC.

Children's Defense Fund. (2005). The state of America's children. Washington, DC.

Children's Defense Fund. (2012*). State of America's children handbook.* Retrieved January 2, 2013 from http://www.childrensdefense.org/child-research-data-publications/data/soac-2012-handbook.pdf

Children's Defense Fund. (2008). *The state of America's children.* Washington, DC.

Children's Software Review. Available from http://www.childrenssoftware.com

Child Trends. (2012). *Low and very low birthweight infants.* Retrieved from www.childtrendsdatabank.org/alphalist?q=node/67

Clark, B. (2007). *Growing up gifted.* Prentice Hall: Upper Saddle River, NJ.

Cohen, D. & Cicchetti, D. (2006). *Developmental psychopathology: Theory and method.* John Wiley & Sons Inc: New York.

Cohen, L. G., & Spenciner, L. J. (2007). *Assessment of children and youth (3rd ed.).* Longman: New York.

Cohen, L. M. (1990). *Meeting the needs of gifted and talented minority language students.* Council for Exceptional Children, ERIC Clearinghouse on Disabilities and Gifted Education. (Eric CE Digest #E480): Reston, VA.

Coleman, L. J., & Cross, T. L. (2005). *Being gifted in school: An introduction to development, guidance, and teaching.* Prufrock Press: Waco, TX.

Coleman, M. R. (2003). *The identification of students who are gifted.* National Center for Research on Teacher Learning, The ERIC Clearinghouse on Disabilities and Gifted Education (ERIC EC). (ERIC EC Digest #E644): East Lansing, MI.

Coleman, M. R., Roth, R. P., & West, T. (2009). Roadmap to pre-K RTI: Applying response to intervention in preschool settings. National Center for Learning Disabilities. Available from www.RTINetwork.org/PreKRTIRoadmap.

Colker, L. J. (2008). Twelve characteristics of effective early childhood teachers. *Beyond the Journal. Young Children on the Web. March.* Retrieved from http://journal.naeyc.org/btj/200803/pdf/BTJ_Colker.pdf

Committee on Pediatric Aids. (2000). Educating children with human immunodeficiency viral infection. *Pediatrics 105*(6), 1358–1360. Retrieved from http://pediatrics.aappublications.org/content/105/6/1358.full?sid=67795a9c

Concord Special Education Parent Advisory Committee. (2001). *What is an IEP?* Retrieved from www.concordspedpac.org/WhatIEP.htm

Conners, C. K. (1980). *Food additives and hyperactive children.* Plenum Press: New York.

Conn-Powers, M. C., Ross-Allen, J., & Holburn S. (1990). Transition of young children into the elementary education mainstream. *Topics in Early Childhood Special Education, 9*(4), 91–105.

Conn-Powers, M., Cross, A. F., Traub, E. K., & Hutter-Pishgahi, L. (2006). *The universal design of early education: Moving* forward for all children. *Beyond the Journal.* Retrieved, from http://www. journal.naeyc.org/btj/ 200609/ConnPowersBTJ.pdf

Cook, R. E., Klein, M. D., & Chen, D. (2011). *Adapting early childhood curricula for children with special needs.* Pearson: Upper Saddle River, NJ.

Cook, R. E., Klein, M. D., & Tessier, A., & (2007). *Adapting early childhood curricula for children with special needs.* Prentice Hall: Upper Saddle River, NJ.

Cooper, R. P., & Aslin, R. N. (1994). Developmental differences in infant attention to spectral properties of infant-directed speech. *Child Development, 65,* 1663–1667.

Copple, C., & Bredekamp, S. (2009). *Developmentally appropriate practice in early childhood programs.* National Association for the Education of Young Children: Washington, DC.

Council for Exceptional Children, Division on Visual Impairments. (2003). Position Statement: *Family-Centered Practices for Infants and Young Children with Visual Impairments.*

Courchesne, E., Caper, R., & Akshoomoff, N. (2003). Evidence of brain overgrowth in the first year of life in autism. *Journal of the American Medical Association, 290,* 337–344.

Cross, T. L., Bazron, B. J., Dennis, K. W., & Isaacs, M. R. (1989). *Toward a culturally competent system of care.* Georgetown University Development Center: Washington, DC.

D'Alton, M. E., & DeCherney, A. H. (1993). Prenatal diagnosis. *New England Journal of Medicine, 328,* 114–118.

Daley, S. (2002). "Mom, will Kaelie always have possibilities?"—The realities of early childhood inclusion. *Phi Delta Kappan, 84,* 73–76.

Dana Alliance for Brain Initiatives. (1996). *Delivering results: A progress report on brain research.* Author: Washington, DC.

Daniel, J., & Friedman S. (2005). Preparing teachers to work with culturally and linguistically diverse children. *Beyond the Journal Young Children on the Web.* Retrieved from http://www.naeyc.org/files/yc/file/200511/DanielFriedmanBTJ1105.pdf

Daugherty, S., Grisham-Brown, J. L., & Hemmeter, M. L. (2001). The effects of embedded skill instruction on the acquisition of target and non target skills in preschoolers with developmental delays. *Topics in Early Childhood Special Education, 21,* 213–221.

Davern, L. (2004). Home to school notebooks. What parents have to say. *Teaching Exceptional Children, 36*(5), 22–27.

Davidson, J. L. (1990). *Children and computers together in the early childhood classroom.* Delmar Learning: Clifton Park, NY.

Davis, I., Elfenbein, I., Schum, R., & Bentler, R. (1986). Effects of mild and moderate hearing impairments on language, educational, and psychological behavior of children. *Journal of Speech and Hearing Disorders, 51,* 53–62.

Dawson, G., Hones, E. J., Merkle, K., Venema, K., Lowy, R., Faja, S., Kamara, D., Murias, M., Greenson, J., Winter, J., Smith, M., Rogers, S. J., & Webb, S. J. (2012). Early behavioral intervention is associated with normalized brain activity in young children with autism. *Journal of the American Academy Child & Adolescent Psychiatry,* Retrieved from *http://www.jaacap.com/article/S0890-8567(12)00643-0/abstract*

Deal, A. G., Dunst, C. J., & Trivette, C. M. (1989). A flexible and functional approach to developing individualized family service plans. *Infants and Young Children, 1*(4), 32–43.

DEC/NAEYC. (2009). *Early childhood inclusion: A joint position statement of the Division for Early Childhood (DEC) and the National Association for the Education of Young Children (NAEYC).* The University of North Carolina, FPG Child Development Institute: Chapel Hill.

DEC Task Force on Recommended Practices. (1993). *DEC recommended practices: Indicators of quality programs for infants and young children with special needs and their families.* Council for Exceptional Children: Reston, VA.

Decoufle, P., Boyle, C. A., Paulozzi, L. J., & Lary, J. M. (2001). Increased risk for developmental disabilities in children who have major birth defects: A population based study. *Pediatrics, 108,* 728–734.

Deiner, P. (2013). *Inclusive early childhood education.* Delmar, Cengage Learning: Clifton Park, NY.

Deiner, P. (2004). *Resources for the education of young children with diverse abilities.* Thomson Delmar Learning: Clifton Park, NY.

Demchak, M. A. (1990). Response prompting and fading methods. A review. *American Journal of Mental Retardation, 94,* 603–615.

Department of Health and Human Services. (1999). *Mental health: A report of the surgeon general.* Department of Health and Human Services, Substance Abuse and Mental Health Services Administration, Center for Mental Health Services, National Institute of Mental Health: Rockville, MD. Retrieved October 13, 2007 from http://www.surgeongeneral.gov/library/mentalhealth/chapter3/sec6.html#autism

Derman-Sparks, L., & The A.B.C. Task Force. (1988–1989). *Anti-bias curriculum. Tools for empowering young children.* ERIC Document Reproduction Service No. ED377255. The National Association for the Education of Young Children: Washington, DC.

Deutsch, C. K., & Kinsbourne, M. (1990). Genetics and biochemistry in attention deficit disorder. In M. Lewis & S. M. Miller (Eds.), *Handbook of developmental psychopathology (pp. 93–108).* Plenum Press: New York.

Devoney, C., Guralnick, M. J., & Rubin, H. (1974). Integrating handicapped and nonhandicapped pre-school children: Effects on social play. *Childhood Education, 50,* 360–364.

DeVries, R., & Kohlberg, L. (1990). *Constructivist early education: Overview and comparison with other programs.* National Association for the Education of Young Children: Washington, DC.

Dewey, J. (1938). *Experience and education.* Collier Books: New York.

DiLalla, L. F., & Watson, M. W. (1988). Differentiation of fantasy and reality: Preschoolers' reactions to disruption in their play. *Developmental Psychology, 24,* 286–291.

Discolo, C. M., & Hirose, K. (2002). Pediatric cochlear implants. *American Journal of Audiology, 11*(2), 114–118.

Division for Early Childhood & National Association for the Education of Young Children (2009), A joint position statement of definition of the Division of Early Childhood (DEC) and the National Association for the Education of Young Children (NAEYC). Retrieved from http://www.naeyc.org/files/naeyc/file/positions/DEC_NAEYC_EC_updatedKS.pdf

Division for Early Childhood. (2007). Concept paper on the identification of and intervention with challenging behavior. Available from http://www.dec-sped.org

Division of Early Childhood. (2007). Promoting positive outcomes for children with disabilities: Recommendations for curriculum, assessment, and program evaluation. Author: Missoula, MT. Retrieved January 28, 2013 from http://www.naeyc.org/files/naeyc/file/positions/PrmtgPositiveOutcomes.pdf

Dodge, K. A. (1990). Developmental psychopathology in children of depressed mothers. *Developmental Psychology, 26,* 3–6.

Donegan, M. M., Ostrosky, M. M., & Fowler, S. A. (1996). Children enrolled in multiple programs: Characteristics, supports, and barriers to teacher communication. *Journal of Early Intervention, 20*(2), 95–106.

Dormans, J. P., & Batshaw, M. L. (2007). Muscles, bones and nerves: The body's framework. In M. L. Batshaw (Ed.), *Children with disabilities.* Brookes: Baltimore, MD.

Dunlap, G., & Powell, D. (2009). Promoting social behavior of young children in group settings: A summary of research. *Roadmap to Effective Intervention Practices #3.* University of South Florida, Technical Assistance Center on Social Emotional Intervention for Young Children: Tampa, FL. Retrieved March 11, 2010 from http://www.challengingbehavior.org/do/resources/documents/roadmap_3.pdf

Dunn, L. M. (1968). Special education for the mildly retarded—Is much of it justified? *Exceptional Children, 35,* 5–22.

Dunst, C. J., & Trivette, C. M. (1989). An enablement and empowerment perspective of case management. *Topics in Early Childhood Special Education, 8*(4), 87–102.

Dybvik, A. C. (2004, Winter). Autism and the inclusion mandate: What happens when children with severe disabilities like autism are taught in regular classrooms? Daniel

knows. *Education Next.* Retrieved October 6, 2007 from http://www.hoover.orgblications/ednext/3344881.html

Early Childhood Community (2009). DEC/NAEYC leaders share their thoughts on inclusion. Retrieved from http://community.fpg.unc.edu/discussions/blog-speaking-of-inclusion/dec-naeyc-leaders-share-thoughts-on-inclusion

Edelson M. G. (2006). Are the majority of children with autism mentally retarded? A systematic evaluation of the data. *Focus on Autism and Other Developmental* Disabilities 21(2), 66–83. Retrieved January 18, 2013 from http://autismodiario.org/wp-content/uploads/2011/03/Focus-Autism-Other-Dev-Disabl-2006-Goldberg-Edelson-66-83.pdf

Ehlers, L. (1993). Inclusion in the lives of young children with disabilities. In S. M. Rehberg (Ed.), *Starting point: A series of definition papers* (pp. 33–43). Office of the Superintendent of Public Instruction: Olympia, WA.

Epstein, J. L., Sanders, M. G., Sheldon, S. G., Simon, B. S., Salinas, K. C., Rodriguez Jansorn, N., Van Voorhis, F. L., Martin, C. S., Thomas, F. G., Greenfeld, M. D., Hutchins, D. J., & Williams, K. J. (2009). *School, Family, and Community Partnerships: Your Handbook for Action* (3rd ed.). Corwin Press, Inc.: Thousand Oaks, CA.

ERIC/OSEP Special Project. (2001). Family involvement in special education. *Research Connections in Special Education, 9.* The ERIC Clearinghouse on Disabilities and Gifted Education: Arlington, VA.

Erin, N. J. (2000). Students with visual impairments and additional disabilities. In A. J. Koenig & M. C. Holbrook (Eds.), *Foundations of education: Instructional strategies for teaching children and youths with visual impairments* (Vol. 2, pp. 720–752). American Foundation for the Blind: New York.

Espe-Sherwindt, M. (2009). Family-centred practice: Collaboration, competency and evidence. *Support for Learning, 23*(3), 2008.

Evert, A. B. (2004). Tools and techniques for working with young people with diabetes. *Diabetes Spectrum, 17,* 8–13.

Federal Register 05-11804 July 1, 2006.

Federal Register 34CFR303.1 July 1, 2002.

Feeney, S., & Kipnis, K. (2005). Code of ethical conduct and statement of commitment. National Association for the Education of Young Children: Washington, DC.

Feingold, B. F. (1985). *Why your child is hyperactive.* Random House: New York.

Feldman, D. H. (1993). Has there been a paradigm shift in gifted education? In N. Coangelo, S. Assouline, & D. Ambroson (Eds.), *Talented development: Proceedings from the 1991 Henry B. and Jocelyn Wallace national research symposium on talented development* (pp. 89–94). Trillium: New York.

Fenson, L., Dale, P. S., Reznick, J. S., Bates, E., Thal, D. J., & Pethick, S. J. (1994). Variability in early communicative development. *Monograph of the Society for Research in Child Development, 59*(5), 1–173.

Feuerstein, R., Rand, Y., Hoffman, M., & Miller, R. (1980). *Instrumental enrichment: Redevelopment of cognitive functions of retarded performers.* University Park Press: Baltimore, MD.

Fewell, R. R., & Kaminski, R. (1994). Play skills development and instruction for young children with handicaps. In S. L. Odom & M. B. Karnes (Eds.), *Early intervention for infants and children with handicaps.* Brookes: Baltimore, MD.

Fink, D. B., & Fowler, S. A. (1997). Inclusion, one step at a time: A case study of communication and decision making across program boundaries. *Topics in Early Childhood Special Education, 17*(3), 337–362.

Flavell, J. H., Miller, P. H., & Miller, S. A. (2001). *Cognitive development* (2nd ed.). Prentice-Hall: Englewood Cliffs, NJ.

Forlin, C. (1995). Educators' beliefs about inclusive practices in Western Australia. *British Journal of Special Education, 22*(4), 179–185.

Forness, S. R., & Knitzer, I. (1990). A new proposed definition and terminology to replace "Serious Emotional Disturbance" in the Education of the Handicapped Act. *Report of the Work Group on Definition,* National Mental Health and Special Education Coalition: Alexandria, VA.

Forness, S. R., & Knitzer, J. (1992). A new proposed definition and terminology to replace "serious emotional disturbance" in individuals with disabilities act. *School Psychology Review, 21,* 29–34.

Fowler, S. A., & Titus, P. F. (1999). Handling transitions. In P. J. Beckman & G. B. Boyce (Eds.), *Deciphering the system: A guide for families of young children with disabilities* (pp. 101–116). Brookline Books: Cambridge, MA.

Fowler, S. A., Hains, A. H., & Rosenkoetter, S. E. (1990). The transition between early intervention services and preschool services: Administrative and policy issues. *Topics in Early Childhood Special Education, 9*(4), 55–65.

Fowler, S. A., Schwartz, I., & Atwater, J. (1991). Perspectives on the transition from preschool to kindergarten for children with disabilities and their families. *Exceptional Children, 58*(2), 136–145.

Fox, J. E. (2010). Back to basics: Play in early childhood. In K. Menke Paciorek (Ed.), *Annual Editions: Early Childhood Education.* McGraw Hill: New York.

Fox, L., & Lentini, L. H. (2006). You've got it. Teaching social and emotional skills. *Beyond the Journal.* Retrieved from http://www.naeyc.org/files/yc/file/200611/BTJFoxLentini.pdf

Fox, L., Dunlap, G., Hemmeter, M. L., Joseph G. E., & Strain, P. S. (2003). The teaching pyramid; A model for supporting social competence and preventing challenging behavior in young children. *Young Children, 58*(4), 48–52.

Foxx, R. M., & Azrin, N. H. (1973). *Toilet training the retarded: A rapid program for day and nighttime independent toileting.* Research Press: Champaign, IL.

Fraiberg, S. (1974). Blind infants and their mothers: An examination of the sign system. In M. L. Lewis & L. A. Rosenblum (Eds.), *The effect of the infant on its caregiver.* Wiley: New York.

Fraiberg, S. (1979). *Insights from the blind.* Basic Books: New York.

Franca, V. M., Kerr, M. M., Reitz, A. L., & Lambert, D. (1990). Peer tutoring among behaviorally disordered students: Academic and social benefits to the tutor and tutee. *Education and Treatment of Children, 13*(2), 109–128.

Freeman, B. J. (1997). Guidelines for evaluating intervention programs for children with autism. *Journal of Autism and Developmental Disorders, 27,* 641–651.

Froebel, F. W. (2005). *The education of man.* (W. N. Hailmann, Trans.). Appleton: New York.

Frost, J. L. (1986). Planning and using children's playgrounds. In J. S. McKee (Ed.). *Play: Working partner of growth.* Association for Childhood Education International: Wheaton, MD.

Fuchs, D., & Fuchs, L. (2001). Responsiveness to intervention: A blueprint for practitioners, policy-makers and parents. *Teaching Exceptional Children, 38,* 57–61.

Fuchs, L. S., & Fuchs, D. (1986). Effects of systematic formative evaluation: A meta-analysis. *Exceptional Children, 53,* 199–208.

Gallagher, J. J. (1988). National agenda for educating gifted students: Statement of priorities. *Exceptional Children, 55*(2), 107–114.

Gallico, R., & Lewis, M. E. B. (2007). Learning disabilities. In M. L. Batshaw & Y. M. Perret (Eds.), *Children with disabilities: A medical primer* (3rd ed., pp. 471–498). Brookes: Baltimore, MD.

Gardner, H. (1993). *Frames of mind: The theory of multiple intelligences* (2nd ed.). Basic Books: New York.

Gardner, H. (1996). Probing more deeply into the theory of multiple intelligences. *NASSP Bulletin, 80,* 1–7.

Gardner, H. (2006). *Multiple intelligences.* Basic Books: New York.

Garfinkle, A. N., & Schwartz, I. S. (1998). Observational learning in an integrated pre-school: Effects on peer imitation and social interaction. Unpublished manuscript.

Geist, E., & Baum, A. (2005). "Yeah, but's" that keep teachers from embracing an active curriculum. Overcoming the resistance. *Beyond the Journal. Young Children on the Web.* Retrieved from http://journal.naeyc.org/btj/200507/03Geist.pdf

Gesell, A., Halverson, H. M., Thompson, H., Ilg, F. L., Castner, B. M., Ames, L. B., & Amatruda, C. S. (1993). *The first five years of life: A guide to the study of the preschool child.* Harper and Row: New York.

Getahun, D., Jacobsen, S, J., Fassett, M. J., Chen, W., Demissie, K., Rhoads, G. (2013). Recent trends in childhood attention-deficit/hyperactivity disorder. *JAMA Pediatrics:* 1–7. doi:10.1001/2013.jamapediatrics.401. Published online January 21, 2013.

Gibbs, J. (2001). *Tribes: A new way of learning and being together.* Center Source Publications: Santa Rosa, CA.

Goldman, B. (2009). Promising practices to support friendships in inclusive classrooms *Impact: Feature Issue on Early Childhood Education and Children with Disabilities, 22*(1). Retrieved from http://ici.umn.edu/products/impact/221/221.pdf

Goldstein, H. (1993). Structuring environmental input to facilitate generalized language learning by children with mental retardation. In A. P. Kaiser & D. B. Gray (Eds.), *Enhancing children's communication: Research foundations for intervention.* Brookes: Baltimore, MD.

Gonzalez-Mena, J. (1992). Taking a culturally sensitive approach in infant-toddler programs. *Young Children, 47*(2), 4–11.

Gonzalez-Mena, J., & Eyer, D. W. (2012). *Infants, toddlers, and caregivers.* McGraw Hill: New York.

Good, W. V., & Hoyt, C. S. (1989). Behavioral correlates of poor vision in children. *International Ophthalmology Clinics, 29,* 57–60.

Goode, T. D. (2004). *Cultural competence continuum.* National Center for Cultural Competence, Georgetown University Center for Child and Human Development, University Center for Excellence in Developmental Disabilities: Washington, DC.

Gordon, A. M., & Williams Browne, K. (2010). *Beginnings and beyond: Foundations in early childhood education.* Wadsworth, Cengage Learning: Belmont, CA.

Graue, M. E. (1998). What's wrong with Edward the unready? Our responsibility for readiness. *Young Children, 33*(2), 12–16.

Grayson, J. (1992). Child abuse and developmental disabilities. *Virginia Child Protection Newsletter, 37*(1), 3–7.

Greenberg, M. T., & Kusche, C. A. (1993). *Promoting social and emotional development in deaf children: The PATHS project.* University of Washington Press: Seattle, WA.

Greenberg, P. (1990). Why not academic preschools? *Young Children, 45*(2), 70–80.

Greenberg, P. (1994). How and why to teach all aspects of preschool and kindergarten math. Part 2. *Young Children, 49*(2), 12–18.

Greenberg, P. (1998). Thinking about goals for grownups and young children while we teach writing, reading, and spelling (and a few thoughts about the "J" word). *Young Children, 53*(6), 31–42.

Greenspan, S. I. (1992). *Infancy and early childhood: The practice of clinical assessment and intervention with emotional and developmental challenges.* International Universities Press: Madison, CT.

Greenspan, S. I., & Wider, S. (1997). *Facilitating intellectual and emotional growth in children with special needs.* Addison-Wesley: Reading, MA.

Griffin, C., & Rinn, B. (1998). Enhancing outdoor play with an obstacle course. *Young Children, 53*(3), 18–23.

Grosjean, F. (2001). The right of the deaf child to grow up bilingual. *Sign Language Studies, 1*(2),110–114.

Gross, M. U. (1999). Small poppies: Highly gifted children in the early years. *Roeper Review, 2,* 207–214.

Guralnick, M. J. (1990). Early childhood mainstreaming. *Topics in Early Childhood Special Education, 10*(2), 1–17.

Guralnick, M. J. (1994). Mothers' perceptions of the benefits and drawbacks of early childhood mainstreaming. *Journal of Early Intervention, 12,* 168–183.

Guralnick, M. J., & Neville, B. (1997). Designing early intervention programs to promote children's social competence. In M. J. Guralnick (Ed.), *The effectiveness of early intervention* (pp. 579–620). Brookes: Baltimore, MD.

Gutierrez, A., Hale, M. N., Gossens-Archuleta, K., & Sobrino-Sanchez, V. (2007). Evaluating the social behavior of preschool children with autism in an inclusive playground setting. *International Journal of Special Education, 22,* 25–29.

Hadden, D. S., Fowler, S. A., Fink, D. B., & Wischnowski, M. W. (1995). *Writing an interagency agreement on transition: A practical guide.* University of Illinois: Champaign.

Hadden, S. (1998). The impact of local interagency agreements written to facilitate the transition from early intervention to preschool. Unpublished doctoral dissertation, University of Illinois: Urbana-Champaign.

Haensly, P. (2000). A new lens for detecting giftedness "Becoming." *Gifted Child Today, 23,* 22–23, 52–53.

Hains, A. H., Rosenkoetter, S. E., & Fowler, S. A. (1991). Transition planning with families in early intervention programs. *Infants and Young Children, 3*(4), 38–47.

Hakuta, K., & Diaz, R. M. (1985). The relationship between degree of bilingualism and cognitive ability. In K. E. Nelson (Ed.), *Children's language.* Erlbaum: Hillsdale, NJ.

Halgunseth, L. C., Peterson, A., Stark, D. R., & Moodie, S. (2009). Family engagement, diverse families, and early childhood education programs, An integrated review of the literature. Retrieved from http://www.naeyc.org/files/naeyc/file/ecprofessional/EDF_Literature%20Review.pdf

Hanline, M. F. (1992). Facilitating integrated preschool service delivery transitions for children, families, and professionals. In C. A. Peck, S. L. Odom, & D. B. Bricker (Eds.), *Integrating young children with disabilities into community programs: Ecological perspectives on research and implementation* (pp. 133–146). Brookes: Baltimore, MD.

Hanline, M. F., Nunes, D., & Worthy, M. B. (2007). Augmentative and alternative communication in the early childhood years. *Beyond the Journal. Young Children on the Web.* July.

Hanson, M. J., & Brennan, E. L. (1997). Language, culture, and disability: Interacting influences on preschool inclusion. *Topics in Early Childhood Special Education, 17*(3), 307–334.

Hanson, M. J., & Carta, J. J. (1996). Addressing the challenges of families with multiple risks. *Exceptional Children, 62,* 201–212.

Hanson, M. J., & Lynch, E. W. (1995). *Early intervention*. Pro-Ed: Austin, TX.

Haring, N. G., & McCormick, L. (1994). *Exceptional children and youth*. Merrill: Columbus, OH.

Harms, T., Clifford, R. M., & Cryer, D. (2004). *Early childhood environment rating scale*. Teachers College Press: New York.

Harms, T., Jacobs, E. V., & White, D. R. (1995). *School age care environment rating scale*. Teachers College Press: New York.

Harris, F. R., & Allen, K. E. (1966). Under six: Children in preschool. *KCTS Television Series and Viewers Guide*. University of Washington: Seattle, WA.

Harris, F. R., Wolf, M. M., & Baer, D. M. (1964). Effects of adult social reinforcement on child behavior. *Young Children, 1*, 8–17.

Harry, B. (1992). *Cultural diversity, families, and the special education system*. Teachers College Press: New York.

Harry, B. (1998). Parental visions of "a normal life." In L. Meyer, H. Park, M. Grenot-Scheyer, I. Schwartz, & B. Harry (Eds.), *Making friends: The influences of culture and development* (pp. 47–62). Brookes: Baltimore, MD.

Harry, B., Torguson, C., Katkavich, A., & Guerrero, M. (1993). Crossing social class and cultural barriers in working with families. *Teaching Exceptional Children, 26*, 48–51.

Hart, B. M., & Risley, T. R. (1982). *How to use incidental teaching*. Pro-Ed: Austin, TX.

Hart, B., & Risley, T. (1995). *Meaningful differences in everyday experiences in young American children*. Brookes: Baltimore, MD.

Hart, B., & Risley, T. R. (1999). *The social world of children learning to talk*. Brookes: Baltimore, MD.

Harter, S. (1990). Processes underlying adolescent self-concept formation. In R. Montemeyer, G. R. Adams, & T. P. Gullotta (Eds.), *From childhood to adolescence: A transition period?* (pp. 205–239). Sage: Newbury Park, CA.

Hartup, W. W., & Moore, S. G. (1990). Early peer relations: Developmental significance and prognostic implication. *Early Childhood Research Quarterly, 5*(1), 1–17.

Hatton, Deborah D., McWilliam, R. A, and Winton, P. J. (2002). *Infants and toddlers with visual impairments: Suggestions for early interventionists*. Council for Exceptional Children: Arlington, VA.

Haymes, L. K., Fowler, S. A., & Cooper, A. Y. (1994). Assessing the transition and adjustment of preschoolers with special needs to an integrated program. *Journal of Early Intervention, 18*, 184–198.

Heber, R., & Garber, H. (1975). The Milwaukee Project: A study of the use of family intervention to prevent cultural-familial mental retardation. In B. Friedlander, G. Sterritt, & G. Kirk (Eds.), *Exceptional infant* (3rd ed.). Brunner/Mazel: New York.

Henderson, A. T., & Mapp, K. L. (2002). *New wave of evidence: The impact of school, family, and community connections on student achievement*. National Center for Family and Community Connections with Schools: Austin, TX.

Hepting, N. H., & Goldstein, H. (1996). What's natural about naturalistic language interventions? *Journal of Early Intervention, 20*, 249–265.

Herschkowitz, N., & Herschkowitz, E. C. (2004). *A good start in life: Understanding your child's brain and behavior form birth to age 6*. Dana Press: New York.

Hestenes, L., Laparo, K., Scott-Little, C., Chakravarthi, S., Lower, J. K., Cranor, A., Cassidy, D. J., & Niemeyer, J. (2009). Team teaching in an early childhood interdisciplinary program: A decade of lessons learned. *Journal of Early Childhood Teacher Education, 30*, 172–183.

Hills, T. W. (1993). Assessment in context—Teachers and children at work. *Young Children, 48*(5), 20–28.

Hittleman, J., Parekh, A., & Glass, L. (1987, April). *Developmental outcome of extremely low birth weight infants*. Paper presented at the biennial meeting of the Society for Research in Child Development, Baltimore, MD.

Hitz, R., & Driscoll, A. (1989). Praise or encouragement? New insights into praise: Implications for early childhood teachers. *Young Children, 43*, 6–13.

Hodge, K. A., & Kemp, C. R. (2000). Exploring the nature of giftedness in preschool children. *Journal for the Education of the Gifted, 24*, 46–73.

Hoff, E. (2008). *Language development*. Wadsworth, Cengage Learning: Belmont, CA.

Horowitz, F. D. (1987). *Exploring developmental theories: Toward a structural/behavioral model of development*. Erlbaum: Hillsdale, NJ.

Horowitz, F. D. (1990). Developmental models of individual differences. In J. Columbo & J. Fagan (Eds.), *Individual differences in infancy: Reliability, stability, prediction* (pp. 3–18). Erlbaum: Hillsdale, NJ.

Howard, V. F., Williams, B. F., & Lepper, C. (2009). *Very young children with special needs*. Pearson Prentice Hall: Indianapolis, Indiana.

Hunt, J. M. (1961). *Intelligence and experience*. Ronald Press: New York.

Hyson, M. (2002). "Huh?" "Eek!" "Help": Three perspectives on early childhood assessment. *Young Children, 57*(1), 62–64.

Hyun, J., & Fowler, S. A. (1995). Respect, cultural sensitivity, and communication. *Teaching Exceptional Children, 28*, 25–28.

Institute for Children and Poverty. (2008). *National data on family homelessness*.

IRA & NAEYC. (1998). Learning to read and write: Developmentally appropriate practices for young children. A joint position of the International Reading Association (IRA) and the National Association for the Education of Young Children (NAEYC). Retrieved from http://www.naeyc.org/files/naeyc/file/positions/PSREAD98.PDF

Iwata, B. A., Dorsey, M. F., Slifer, K. J., Bauman, K. E., & Richman, G. S. (1982). Toward a functional analysis of self-injury. *Analysis and Intervention in Developmental Disabilities, 2*, 3–20.

Jacobs, J. C. (1971). Effectiveness of teacher and parent identification of gifted children as a function of school level. *Psychology of the Schools, 8*(2), 140–142.

Janko, S. (1994). *Vulnerable children, vulnerable families.* Teachers College Press: New York.

Jensen, E. (2008). *Brain-based learning and teaching. The new paradigm of teaching.* Corwin Press: New York.

Jeste, S. S., Sahin, M., Bolton, P., Ploubidis, G. B., & Humphrey, A. (2008). Characterization of autism in young children with tuberous sclerosis complex. *Journal of Child Neurology, 23*(5), 520–5. Epub 2007 December 26.

Johnson, C. (2001). *Supporting families in transition between early intervention services and school age programs.* Colorado Families for Hands and Voices: Boulder, CO. Available from www.handsandvoices.org

Johnson, S. C., Mayer, L., & Taylor, B. A. (1996). Supported inclusion. In C. Maurice, G. Green, & S. Luce (Eds.), *Behavioral interventions for young children with Autism: A manual for parents and professionals* (pp. 331–342). Pro-Ed: Austin, TX.

Johnson, T. E., Chandler, L. K., Kerns, G. M., & Fowler, S. A. (1986). What are parents saying about family involvement in school transitions: A retrospective interview. *Journal of the Division for Early Childhood, 11,* 10–17.

Jones, E., & Carr, E. G. (2004). Joint attention in children with autism: Theory and intervention. *Focus on autism and other developmental disabilities, 19,* 13–26.

Jorde, L. G., Carey, J. C., Bamshad, M. J., & White, R. L. (2009). *Medical genetics.* C. V. Mosby: St. Louis, MO.

Kaczmarek, L. A. (1982). Motor activities: A context for language/communication intervention. *Journal of the Division for Early Childhood, 6,* 21–36.

Kaiser, A. (2000). Teaching functional communication skills. In M. E. Snell & F. Brown (Eds.), *Instruction of students with severe disabilities* (5th ed.), pp 453–491). Merrill: Columbus, OH.

Kaiser, A. P., Yoder, P., & Keetz, A. (1992). Evaluating milieu teaching. In S. F. Warren & J. Reichle (Eds.), *Causes and effects in communication and language intervention* (pp. 9–47). Brookes: Baltimore, MD.

Kaiser, B., & Rasminsky, J. S. (1999). *Meeting the challenge: Effective strategies for challenging behavior in early childhood environments.* NAEYC: Washington, DC.

Karnes, M. B., & Taylor, A. R. (1978). *Preschool talent assessment guide.* Illinois University for Child Behavior and Development: Urbana, IL.

Karnes, M., & Johnson, L. (1989). An imperative: Programming for the young gifted/talented. *Journal for the Education of the Gifted, 10*(3), 195–214.

Katz, H. P. (2004). Important endocrine disorders of childhood. In R. Haslam & P. Valletutti (Eds.), *Medical problems in the classroom.* Pro-Ed: Austin, TX.

Katz, L. G., & Chard, S. (2000). *Engaging children's minds: The project approach.* Ablex: Norwood, NJ.

Kaufman, J. M., & Landrum, T. J. (2008). *Characteristics of emotional and behavioral disorders of children and youths.* Prentice Hall: New York.

Keefe, C. H. (1995). Portfolios: Mirrors of learning. *Teaching Exceptional Children, 27*(2), 66–67.

Keith, L. G., MacGregor, S., Freidell, S., Rosner, M., Chasnoff, I. J., & Sciarra, J. J. (1989). Substance abuse in pregnant women: Recent experience at the perinatal center for chemical dependence of Northwestern Memorial Hospital. *Obstetrics and Gynecology, 13,* 715–720.

Kilgallon, P. (2003). Early childhood teachers' knowledge of teaching children with disabilities. *Australian Journal of Early Childhood, 28*(4). Available online at http://www.earlychildhoodaustralia.org.au/australian_journal_of_early_childhood/ ajec_index_abstracts/early_childhood_teachers_ knowledge_of_teaching_children_with_disabilities .html

King, A. M., & Fahsl, A. J. (2012). Supporting social competence in children who use augmentative and alternative communication. *Teaching Exceptional Children, 45*(1), 42–49.

Kinglsey, E. P. (1987). *Welcome to Holland..* Available at http://www.our-kids.org/Archives/Holland.html

Kirk, S. A. & Gallagher, J. J. (2008). *Educating exceptional children.* Houghton-Mifflin: Boston, MA.

Kirk, S. A. (1972). *Early education of the mentally retarded: An experimental study (3rd ed.).* University of Illinois Press: Urbana, IL.

Kishi, G., & Meyer, L. (1994). What children report and remember: A six-year follow-up of the effects of social contact between peers with and without severe disabilities. *Journal of the Association for Persons with Severe Handicaps, 19,* 277–289.

Klein, M. D., Cook, R. E., & Richardson-Gibbs, A. M. (2001). *Strategies for including children with special needs in early childhood settings.* Delmar Thompson: New York.

Klein, T., Bittel, C., & Molnar, J. (1993). No place to call home: Supporting the needs of homeless children in the early childhood classroom. *Young Children, 48*(6), 22–31.

Koball, H., & Principe, D. (2002). *Do nonresident fathers who pay child support visit their children more? Assessing the new federalism.* The Urban Institute: Washington, DC.

Koegel, R., Koegel, L., & Dunlap, G. (1996). *Positive behavioral support: Including people with difficult behaviors in the community.* Brookes: Baltimore, MD.

Koenig, A. J., Holbrook, M. C., Corn, A. L., DePriest, L. B., Erin, J. N., & Priestly, I. (2000). Specialized assessments for students with visual impairments. In A. J. Koenig & M. C. Holbrook (Eds.), *Foundations of education: Instructional strategies for teaching children and youths with visual impairments* (Vol. 2, pp. 103–172). American Foundation for the Blind: New York.

Kohn, A. (2001). Five reasons to stop saying "Good Job!" *Young Children, 56*(5), 24–28.

Kong A, Frigge M.L., Masson, G., et al. (2012). Rate of de novo mutations and the importance of father's age to disease risk. *Nature, 488*(7412), 471–5.

Kontos, S., & Wilcox-Herzog, A. (1997). Teacher's interactions with children: Why are they so important? *Young Children, 52*(2), 4–12.

Kopelwicz, H. S. (1997). *It's nobody's fault: New hope and help for difficult children and their parents.* Three Rivers Press: New York.

Kostelnik, M. J., Whiren, A. P., Soderman, A. K., Stein, L. C., & Gregory, K. (2008). *Guiding children's social development: Theory to practice.* Thomson Delmar Learning: Clifton Park, NY.

Ladd, G. W. (2005). *Children's peer relations and social competence: A century of progress.* Yale University Press: New Haven, CT.

Lally, J. R. (2000). *Infants have their own curriculum: A responsive approach to curriculum planning for infants and toddlers.* Curriculum in Head Start. Head Start Bulletin #67. HHS/ACF/ACYF/HSB.

Lally, J. R., Torres, Y. L., & Phelps, P. C. (1993). Caring for infants and toddlers in groups: Necessary considerations for emotional, social and cognitive development. Presentation at Zero to Three's Eighth Biennial National Training Institute: Washington, DC.

Lally, J. R., & Stewart, J. (1990). *A guide to setting up environments: Infant/toddler care giving.* California Department of Education, Child Development Division: Sacramento, CA.

Lally, J. R., Provence, S., Szanton, E., & Weissbourd, B. (1986). Developmentally appropriate care for children from birth to age 3. In S. Bredekamp (Ed.) [revised in 2009], *Developmentally appropriate practice in early childhood programs serving children from birth through age 8.* National Association for the Education of Young Children: Washington, DC.

Lally, J. R., Torres, Y. L, & Phelps, P. C. (n.d.). *Caring for infants and toddlers in groups.* Zero-to-Three. Retrieved April 11, 2013 from http://www.zerotothree.org/early-care-education/child-care/caring-for-infants-and-toddlers-in-groups.html

Lamorey, S., & Bricker, D. (1993). Integrated programs: Effects on young children and their programs. In C. A. Peck, S. L. Odom, & D. D. Bricker (Eds.), *Integrating young children with disabilities into community programs* (pp. 249–270). Brookes: Baltimore, MD.

Landau, S., & McAninch, C. (1993). Young children with attention deficits. *Young Children, 48*(4), 49–58.

Learning Points Associates. (2007). *Quick Key 1: Understanding the No Child Left Behind Act: Reading.*

Learn NC. (n.d.). *Communicating with Parents.* Retrieved January 4, 2013 from http://www.learnnc.org/lp/pages/2774

Lieber, J., Schwartz, I. S., Sandall, S., Horn, E., & Wolery, R. A. (1999). Curricular considerations for young children in inclusive settings. In C. Seefeldt (Ed.), *Early childhood curriculum: A review of research* (pp. 243–264). Teachers College Press: New York.

Lieber, J., Schwartz, I., Sandall, S., Horn, E., & Wolery, R. A. (2003). Curricular considerations for young children in inclusive settings. *A Research-to-Practice Journal for the Early Intervention Field, 4,* 432–452.

Lim, C. I., & Able-Boone, H. (2005). Diversity competencies within early childhood teacher preparation: Innovative practices and future directions. *Journal of Early Childhood Teacher Education, 26,* 225–238.

Liptak, G. S. (2012). Neural tube defects. In M. L. Batshaw, N. J. Roizen, & G. R. Lotrecchian (Eds.), *Children with disabilities.* Brookes: Baltimore, MD.

Lord, C., & McGee, J. P. (2001). *Educating children with autism.* National Academy Press: Washington, DC.

Lowenbraun, S., & Thompson, M. D. (1994). Hearing impairments. In N. G. Haring, L. McCormick, & T. G. Haring (Eds.), *Exceptional children and youth* (6th ed.). Merrill: New York.

Lozes, M. H. (1988). Bladder and bowel management for children with myelomeningocele. *Infants and Young Children, 1*(1), 42–62.

Luera, M. (1993). Honoring family uniqueness. In S. M. Rehberg (Ed.), *Starting point: A series of definition papers* (pp. 1–9). Office of the Superintendent of Public Instruction: Olympia, WA.

Luetke-Stahlman, B., & Luckner, J. (1991). *Effectively educating students with hearing impairments.* Longman: White Plains, NY.

Lynch, E. M., & Struewing, N. A. (2001). Children in context: Portfolio assessment in the inclusive early childhood classroom. *Young Exceptional Children, 5*(1), 2–20.

Lynch, E. W., & Hanson, M. J. (2011). *Developing cross-cultural competence: A guide for working with young children and their families.* Brookes: Baltimore, MD.

Malatchi, A. (1995). *Together we can: The Virginia project for the integration of children with deaf blindness.* Final report. Virginia Institute for Developmental Disabilities, Virginia Commonwealth University: Richmond, VA.

Malloy, T. V. (2003). *Sign language use for deaf, hard of hearing, and hearing babies. The evidence supports it.* American Society for the Deaf: Washington, DC.

Markussen Linnet, K., Wisborg, K., Obel, C., Secher, N. J., Thomsen, P. H., Agerbo, E., & Brink Henriksen, T. (2005). Smoking during pregnancy and the risk of hyperkinetic disorder in offspring. *Pediatrics 116*(2), 462–467.

Marotz, L. R. (2012). *Health, safety, and nutrition for the young child.* Wadsworth, Cengage Learning: Belmont, CA.

Marotz, L. R., & Allen, K. E. (2012). *Developmental profiles: Pre-birth through adolescence.* Wadsworth, Cengage Learning: Belmont, CA.

Marshal, H. H. (2001). Cultural influences on the development of self-concept: Updating our thinking. *Young Children, 56*(6), 19–25.

Martin, F., & Clark, J. (1996). *Hearing care for children.* Allyn & Bacon: Needham Heights, MA.

Mason, J. A., & Herrmann, K. R. (1998). Universal infant hearing screening by automated auditory brainstem response measurement. *Pediatrics, 101,* 221–228.

Mastergeorge, A. M., Rogers, S. J., Corbett B. A., & Solomon, M. (2003) Nonmedical interventions for autism spectrum disorder. In S. Ozonoff, S. J. Rogers, & D. O. Hendren (Eds.), *Autism Spectrum Disorders: A research review for practitioners.* (pp 133–160). American Psychiatric Publishing, Inc: Washington, DC.

Mather, J., & Weinstein, E. (1988). Teachers and therapists: Evolution of a partnership in early intervention. *Topics in Early Childhood Special Education, 7*(4), 1–9.

Maurice, C. (1994). *Let me hear your voice: A family's triumph over autism.* Balantine Books: New York.

Maxwell, L. E. (2004). Designing preschool classrooms for inclusive programs. Retrieved from http://www.canr.uconn.edu/ces/child/newsarticles/CCC632.html

May, D., Kundert, D. L., Nikoloff, O., Welch, E., Garrett, M., & Brent, D. (1994). School readiness: An obstacle to intervention and inclusion. *Journal of Early Intervention, 18*(1), 290–301.

Mayes, L. C., Bornstein, M. H., Chawarska, K., & Granger, R. H. (1995). Information processing and developmental assessments in 3-month-old infants exposed prenatally to drugs. *Pediatrics, 95,* 539–545.

Mayesky, M. (2011). *Creative activities for young children.* Wadsworth, Cengage Learning: Belmont, CA.

Mayo, L. (1962). *A proposed program for national action to combat mental retardation.* U.S. Government Printing Office: Washington, DC.

McClean, M., Bailey, D. B., & Wolery, M. (2004). *Assessing infants and preschoolers with special needs (3rd ed.).* Prentice Hall: Upper Saddle River, NJ.

McClelland, M. M., Morrison, F. J., & Holmes, D. L. (2000). Children at risk for early academic problems: The role of learning-related social skills. *Early Childhood Research Quarterly, 15,* 307–329.

McEachin, J. J., Smith, T., & Lovaas, O. I. (1993). Long-term outcome for children with autism who received early intensive behavioral treatment. *American Journal on Mental Retardation, 97,* 359–372.

McGregor, G., & Vogelsberg, R. (1998). *Inclusive schooling practices: pedagogical and research foundations a synthesis of the literature that informs best practices about inclusive schooling.* Paul H. Brookes: Baltimore, MD.

McLean, M., Bailey, D. B., & Wolery, M. (2004). *Assessing infants and preschoolers with special needs.* Pearson Education: Columbus, OH.

McWilliam, R. A., & Dunst, C. J. (1985). *Preschool assessment of the classroom environment. Unpublished rating scale.* Family, Infant, and Preschool Program, Western Carolina Center: Morganton, NC.

McWilliam, R., Wolery, M., & Odom, S. (2001). Inclusive preschool programs. In M. Guralnick (Ed.), *Early childhood inclusion: Focus on change.* Brookes: Baltimore, MD.

MedlinePlus (2012). *Hemophilia. Retrieved* October 1, 2012 from http://vsearch.nlm.nih.gov/vivisimo/cgi-bin/query-meta?v%3Aproject=medlineplus&query=hemophilia

Meisels, S. J. (1993). Remaking classroom assessment with the work sampling system. *Young Children, 48*(5), 34–40.

Meltzoff, A. N., & Moore, M. K. (1983). Newborn infants imitate adult facial gestures. *Child Development, 54,* 702–709.

Meltzoff, A. N., & Moore, M. K. (1997). Explaining facial imitation. A theoretical model. *Early Development and Parenting, 6,* 179–192.

Meyer, D. J., & Vadasy, P. F. (2007). *Sibshops: Workshops for siblings of children with special needs.* Brookes: Baltimore, MD.

Mills, P. E., & Cole K. N. (1999). *Mediated learning: Developmentally appropriate early childhood methods designed to facilitate inclusion.* Paper presented at the Early Childhood Special Education Summer Institute: Wenatchee, WA.

Minow, M. L. (2001). *Limited English proficient students and special education.* National Center on Accessing the General Curriculum: Wakefield, MA. Retrieved from http://aim.cast.org/learn/historyarchive/backgroundpapers/lep_sp_ed

Minor, L. (2002). Effective practices in early intervention planning transitions to preschool. *See/Hear Newsletter.* Retrieved from http://www.tsbvi.edu/seehear/summer02/planning.htm

Mitchell, S., Foulger, T. S., & Wetzel, K. (2009). Ten tips for involving families through internet-based communication. *Young Children.* Retrieved from http://www.naeyc.org/files/yc/file/200909/Ten%20Tips%20for%20Involving%20Families.pdf

Montgomery, D. (2005). Communication without harm. Strategies to enhance parent-teacher communication. *Teaching Exceptional Children, 37*(5), 50–55.

Moore, Brian C. J. (Ed.). (2005). *Handbook of perception and cognition (2nd ed.).* Elsevier: Burlington, MA.

Morbidity and Mortality Weekly Report. December 18, 2009; 58 (SS-10). Retrieved February 24, 2010 from http://www.cdc.gov/mmwr/preview/mmwrhtml/ss5810a1.htm

Morris, R. (1993). *What is PDD? Pervasive development disorders in school age children.* Village Press: Carmel, CA.

Moule, J. (2012*). Cultural competence: A primer for educators.* Wadsworth, Cengage Learning: Belmont, CA.

MTA Cooperative Group. (2004). National Institute of Mental Health multimodal treatment study of ADHD follow-up: 24-month outcomes of treatment strategies for attention-deficit/hyperactivity disorder, *Pediatrics, 113,* 754–761.

Mulligan, S. A., Green, K. M., Morris, S. L., Maloney, T. J., McMurray, D., & Kittleson-Aldred, T. (1992). *Integrated childcare: Meeting the challenge.* Communication Skills Builders: Tucson, AZ.

Murphy, K. R., & Barkley, R. A. (1996). The prevalence of DSM-IV symptoms of AD/HD in adult licensed drivers: Implications for clinical diagnosis. *Comprehensive Psychiatry, 37,* 393–401.

National Association for the Education of Young Children. (2009). *Quality benchmark for cultural competence.* Retrieved from http://www.naeyc.org/files/naeyc/file/policy/state/QBCC_Tool.pdf

National Association for the Education of Young Children. (2009). *Where we stand on curriculum, assessment and program evaluation.* Retrieved from http://www.naeyc.org/files/naeyc/file/positions/StandCurrAss.pdf

National Association for the Education of Young Children. (2009). *Developmentally appropriate practice in early childhood programs serving children from birth though 8. A position paper. Retrieved from* http://www.naeyc.org/files/naeyc/file/positions/PSDAP.pdf

National Association for the Education of Young Children. (2003). *Position statement on early childhood curriculum, assessment and program evaluation.* National Association for the Education of Young Children: Washington, DC.

National Association for the Education of Young Children. (1998*). Accreditation criteria & procedures.* Author: Washington, DC.

National Association for the Education of Young Children. *Responding to linguistic and cultural diversity recommendation for effective early childhood education: A position statement* (pp. 1–8). Author: Washington, DC.

National Association for the Education of Young Children. (2009). *Developmentally appropriate practice in early childhood programs serving children from birth through age 8.* Retrieved from *http://www.naeyc.org/positionstatements/dap.*

National Association for the Education of Young Children and the Fred Rogers Center for Early Learning and Children's Media. (2012). *Technology and interactive media as tools in early childhood programs serving children from birth through age 8.* Retrieved from http://www.naeyc.org/files/naeyc/PS_technology_WEB.pdf

National Association of Early Childhood Specialists. (2003). *Still unacceptable trends in kindergarten entry and placement. A position statement.* Retrieved from http://www.naeyc.org/files/naeyc/file/positions/Psunacc.pdf

National Association of State Boards of Education. (1992). *Winners all: A call for inclusive schools.* Author: Alexandria, VA.

National Coalition for the Homeless (2009). *Education of homeless children and youth.* Retrieved January 4, 2013 from http://www.nationalhomeless.org/factsheets/education.html

National Center for Children and Youth with Disabilities. (1994). *A parent's guide: Accessing parent groups.* Available from http://www.NICHCY.org

National Clearinghouse for English Language Acquisition. (2011). *The growing numbers of English learner students, 1998/99–2008/09.*

National Institute of Health, National Institute of Child Health and Human Development. (2001). *Rett syndrome* (NIH Publication No. 01-4960). Author: Rockville, MD. Retrieved October 13, 2007 from http://www.nichd.nih.gov/publications/ pubskey.cfm?from=autism

National Institute of Mental Health. (2009). *Autism Spectrum Disorders (Pervasive Developmental Disorders).* Retrieved February 24, 2010 from http:/ /www.nimh.nih.gov/health/publications/autism/

National Institute of Mental Health. (2006). *New NIMH Research Program Launches Autism Trials.* Press release September 7, 2006. Retrieved April 18, 2010 from http://www.nimh.nih.gov/science-news/2006/new-nimh-research-program-launches-autism-trials.shtml

National Joint Committee on Learning Disabilities. (2006). *Learning disabilities and young children: identification and intervention.* Retrieved October 13, 2007 from http://www.ldonline.org/article/11511

National School Lunch Program (2012) Retrieved from http://www.fns.usda.gov/cnd/lunch/AboutLunch/NSLP-FactSheet.pdf

Nave, G., Nishioka, V., & Burke, A. (2009). *Analysis of the developmental functioning of early intervention and early childhood special education populations in Oregon* (Issues & Answers Report, REL 2009-No. 078). U.S. Department of Education, Institute of Education Sciences, National Center for Education Evaluation and Regional Assistance, Regional Educational Laboratory Northwest: Washington, DC. Retrieved from www.ies.ed.gov/ncee/edlabs

Nielsen, B. A. (2010). *Week by week. Plans for documenting children's development.* Wadsworth Cengage Learning: Belmont, CA.

Neilsen, S. L., Olive, M. L., Donovan, A., & McEvoy, M. (1998). Challenging behaviors in your classroom? Don't react— teach instead. *Young Exceptional Children, 2*(1), 2–10.

Neisworth, J. T., & Bagnato, S. J. (1992). The case against intelligence testing in early intervention. *Topics in Early Childhood Special Education, 12,* 1–20.

Neuman, S. B., Copple, C., & Bredekamp, S. (2003). *Taking stock of what you do to promote literacy. Young Children.* Retrieved from http://www.naeyc.org/files/yc/file/200303/PromotingLiteracy.pdf

Neville, H. F. (2007). *Is this a phase: Child development & parent strategies birth to 6 years.* Parenting Press: Seattle, WA.

NIMH. (2006). *New NIMH research program launches autism trials.* Press release September 7, 2006. Retrieved April 18, 2010 from http://www.nimh.nih.gov/

science-news/2006/new-nimh-research-program-launches-autism-trials.shtml

Nixon, H. L. (1991). *Mainstreaming and the American dream: Sociological perspectives on parental coping with blind and visually impaired children.* American Foundation for the Blind: New York.

Noonan, M.J., & McCormick, L. (1993). *Early intervention in natural environments: Methods and procedures.* Brooks/Cole: Pacific Grove, CA.

Noonan, M. J., & McCormick, L. (2006). *Young children with disabilities in natural environments: Methods & procedures.* Brookes: Baltimore, MD.

Notari-Syverson, A., & Shuster, S. L. (1995). Putting real-life skills into IEP/IFSPs for infants and young children. *Teaching Exceptional Children, 27*(2), 29–32.

Notari-Syverson, A., O'Connor, R., & Vadasy, D. *(2007). Ladders to literacy.* Brookes: Baltimore, MD.

n.p. (2012, October 27). Autism early intervention can help regulate brain activity in kids. *Medical News Today.* Retrieved from http://www.medicalnewstoday.com/articles/252079.php

n.p. (2011). No Child Left Behind. *Education Week.* Retrieved January 26, 2013 from http://www.edweek.org/ew/issues/no-child-left-behind/

O'Roak, B.J., Vives, L., Girirajan, S., et al. (2012). Sporadic autism exomes reveal a highly inter-connected protein network of de novo mutations. *Nature, 485*(7397), 246–50.

Oberti v. Borough of Clementon School District. WL 178480 (3rd Cir. NJ 1993).

O'Brien, C. (2009) *Injuries and investigated deaths associated with playground equipment, 2001–2008.* U.S. Consumer Product Safety Commission: Washington DC.

Odom, S. L. (2000). Preschool inclusion: What we know and where we go from here. *Topics in Early Childhood Special Education, 20*(1), 20–27.

Odom, S. L., & McEvoy, M. A. (1988). Integration of young children with handicaps and normally developing children. In S. L. Odom & M. B. Karnes (Eds.), *Early intervention for infants and children with handicaps.* Brookes: Baltimore, MD.

Odom, S. L., & McEvoy, M. A. (1990). Mainstreaming at the preschool level. *Topics in Early Childhood Special Education, 10*(2), 48–61.

Odom, S. L., & McLean, M. (1996). *Early intervention/early childhood special education recommended practices.* Pro-Ed: Austin, TX.

Odom, S. L., Parrish T. B., & Hikido, C. (2001). The cost of inclusive and traditional special education preschool services. *Journal of Special Education Leadership, 14*(1), 33–41. Retrieved from http://csef.air.org/publications/related/jsel/odom_hik.pdf

Odom, S. L., Peck, C. A., Hanson, M., Beckman, P., Kaiser, A., Lieber, J., et al. (1996). *Inclusion at the preschool level: An ecological systems analysis. SRCD Social Policy Report, 10,* 18–30.

Odom, S., & Bailey, D. (2001). Inclusive preschool programs. In M. Guralnick (Ed.), *Early childhood inclusion: Focus on change.* Brookes: Baltimore, MD.

Office of Head Start (2008). *Head Start program fact sheet.* Head Start Bureau: Washington, DC.

Olswang, L. B., & Bain, B. A. (1991). Intervention issues for toddlers with specific language impairments. *Topics in Language Disorders, 11*(4), 69–86.

Ostrosky, M. M., Donegan, M. M., & Fowler, S. A. (1997). Facilitating transitions across home, community, and school: Developing effective service delivery models. In A. M. Wetherby, S. F. Warren, & J. Reichle (Eds.), *Transitions in prelinguistic communication: Preintentional to intentional and presymbolic to symbolic* (pp. 437–460). Brookes: Baltimore, MD.

Ostrosky, M. M., & Jung, E. Y. (2006). Building positive teacher child relationships. In K. M. Paciorek & J. H. Munro (Eds.), *Early childhood education 05/06,* 131–133.

Ozonoff, S., Iosif, A., Baguio, F., Cook, I. C., Moore Hill, M., Hutman, T., Rogers, S. J., Rozga, A., Sangha, S., Sigman, M., Steinfeld, M. B., Young, G. S. (2010). A prospective study of the emergence of early behavioral signs of autism. *Journal of the American Academy of Child and Adolescent Psychiatry. 49,* 256–266.

PACER Center. (2000). PACER is the Minnesota Parent Training and Information Center, funded by the U.S. Department of Education's Office of Special Education Programs. http://www.pacer.org

PACER Center. (2000). *What is the difference between an IFSP and an IEP?* PACER Center: Minneapolis, MN.

Palmer, D., Borthwick-Duffy, S., Widaman, K., & Best, S. (1998). Influences on parent perceptions of inclusive practices for their children with mental retardation. *American Journal on Mental Retardation, 3,* 272–287.

Palmer, D., Fuller, K., Arora, T., & Nelson, M. (2001). Taking sides: Parent views on inclusion for their children, *Exceptional Children, 67,* 467–484.

Parlakian, (2010). Early literacy and very young children. In K. Menke Paciorek (Ed.), *Annual Editions: Early Childhood Education.* McGraw Hill: New York.

Parten, M. (1932). Social participation among preschool children. *Journal of Abnormal and Social Psychology, 27,* 243–269.

Patterson, G. R. (1975). *Families: Applications of social learning to family life.* Research Press: Champaign, IL.

Peck, C. A. (1993). Ecological perspectives on the implementation of integrated early childhood programs. In C. A. Peck, S. L. Odom, & D. D. Bricker (Eds.), *Integrating young children with disabilities into community programs* (pp. 3–15). Brookes: Baltimore, MD.

Peck, C. A., Carlson, P., & Helmstetter, E. (1992). Parent and teacher perceptions of outcomes for typically developing children enrolled in integrated early childhood programs. A statewide survey. *Journal of Early Intervention, 16,* 53–63.

Peck, C. A., Odom, S. L., & Bricker, D. B. (Eds.). (1993). *Integrating young children with disabilities into community programs: Ecological perspectives on research and implementation.* Brookes: Baltimore, MD.

Perrone, V. (1990). How did we get here? In C. Kamii (Ed.), *Achievement testing in the early grades: The games grown-ups play.* National Association for the Education of Young Children: Washington, DC.

Peters, S. (2004). *Inclusive education an EFA strategy for all children.* World Bank: Washington, DC.

Petitto, L. A., & Maramette, P. F. (1991). Babbling in the manual mode. *Science, 251,* 1493–1496.

Piaget, J. (1992). *The origins of intelligence in children.* International Universities Press: New York.

Pickard, R. E., Thompson, D. C., Helfand, M., Davis, R.L., McPhillips, H., Lieu, T. A., et al. (2002). *Does early identification of deaf newborns lead to later improvements in language skills? JAMA, 287,* 587–588.

Pinker, S. (2007). *The language instinct: How the mind creates language.* Harper Perennial Modern Classics: New York.

Pogrund, R. L., Fazzi, D. L., & Hess, C. L. (Eds.). (2002). *Early focus: Working with young children who are blind or visually impaired and their families.* American Foundation for the Blind: New York.

Powers, L., Singer, G., & Sowers, J. (1996). *On the road to autonomy: Promoting self-competence among children and youth with disabilities.* Brookes: Baltimore, MD.

Powers, M. D. (2000). What is autism? In M. D. Powers (Ed.), *Children with autism: A parent's guide* (2nd ed.), pp. 1–44. Woodbine House: Bethesda, MD.

Prescott, E. (1994). The physical environment—a powerful regulator of experience. *Exchange Magazine, 100,* 9–15.

President's Commission on Mental Retardation. (1972). A proposed program for national action to combat mental retardation. U.S. Government Printing House: Washington, DC.

Pretti-Frontczak, K. L., & Bricker, D. D. (2004). *An activity based approach to early intervention.* Brookes: Baltimore, MD.

Rafferty, Y., Boettcher, C., & Griffin, K. W. (2001). Benefits and risks of reverse inclusion for preschoolers with and without disabilities: Parents' perspectives. *Journal of Early Intervention, 24,* 266–286.

Rafferty, Y., Piscitelli, V., & Boettcher, C. (2003). The impact of inclusion on language development and social competence among preschoolers with disabilities. *Exceptional Children, 69,* 467–479.

Rapin, L., & Katzman, R. (1998). Neurobiology of autism. *Annals of Neurology, 43,* 7–14.

Rathus, S. A. (1988). *Understanding child development.* Holt, Rinehart, & Winston: New York.

Rao, P.A., Landa, R.J. (2013) "Association between severity of behavioral phenotype and comorbid attention deficit hyperactivity disorder symptoms in children with autism spectrum disorders" Autism June 5th 2013. doi: 10.1177/1362361312470494

Ray, A., & Bowman, B. (2003). *Learning multicultural competence: Developing early childhood practitioners' effectiveness in working with children from culturally diverse communities.* Final report to the A.L. Mailman Family Foundation. Initiative on Race, Class, and Culture in Early Childhood. Erikson Institute: Chicago.

Ray J. A., Pewit-Kinder, J., & George, S. (2009). *Partnering with families of children with special needs. Young Children.* Retrieved from http://www.naeyc.org/files/yc/file/200909/ FamiliesOfChildrenWithSpecialNeeds0909.pdf

Reeves, R. R. (1990). ADHD: Facts and fallacies. *Intervention in School and Clinic, 26,* 70–78.

Reichle, J., Mirenda, P., Locke, P., Piche, L., & Johnson, S. (1992). Beginning augmentative communication systems. In S. F. Warren & J. Reichle (Eds.), *Causes and effects in communication and language intervention* (pp. 131–156). Brookes: Baltimore, MD.

Renzulli, J. S., & Reis, S. M. (1991). Building advocacy through program design, student productivity, and public relations. *Gifted Child Quarterly, 35,* 182–187.

Renzulli, J. S., Smith, L. H., White, A. J., Callahan, C. M., Hartman, R. K., & Westberg, K. L. (2002). *Scales for rating the behavioral characteristics of superior students.* Creative Learning Press: Mansfield Center, CT.

Rett Syndrome Research Trust (2009). *Prevalence of Rett and related syndromes.* Retrieved February 20, 2010 from http://www.rsrt.org/about-Rett/prevelance-of-Rett-and-related-disorders.html

Rheingold, H. L., Gewirtz, J. L., & Ross, H. W. (1959). Social conditioning of vocalizations in the infant. *Journal of Comparative and Physiological Psychology, 52,* 68–73.

Rice, M. L., & O'Brien, M. (1990). Transitions: Times of change and accommodations. *Topics in Early Childhood, 9*(4), 1–14.

Rieke, J. A., Lynch, L. L., & Soltman, S. L. (1977). *Teaching strategies for language development.* Grune and Stratton: New York.

Rivkin, M. S. (1995). *The great outdoors. Restoring children's right to play outside.* The National Association for the Education of Young Children: Washington, DC.

Robinson, H. B. (1981). The uncommonly bright child. In M. Lewis & L. A. Rosenblum (Eds.), *The uncommon child.* Plenum: New York.

Roedell, W. C. (1980). *Gifted young children.* Teachers College Press: New York.

Roeser, R. J., Valente, M., & Husford-Dunn, F. (2007). *Audiology diagnosis.* Thieme Medical: New York.

Rogers, K. B. (2001). *Re-forming gifted education: Matching the program to the child.* Great Potential Press: Scottsdale, AZ.

Roizen, N. J. (2002). Down syndrome. In M. L. Batshaw (Ed.), *Children with disabilities* (5th ed.), pp. 307–320. Paul H. Brooks: Baltimore, MD.

Rosenkoetter, S. E., Hains, A. H., & Fowler, S. A. (1994). *Bridging early services for children with special needs* and their families: A practical guide for transition planning. Brookes: Baltimore, MD.

Rosenquest, B. B. (2002). Literacy-based planning and pedagogy that supports toddler language development. *Early Childhood Education Journal, 29,* 241–249.

Roskos, K. A., Christie, J. F., & Richgels, D. J. (2003). The essentials of early literacy development. *Young Children,* Retrieved from http://www .naeyc.org/files/yc/file/200303/Essentials.pdf

Ruenzel, D. (2000). *Desire for learning.* Alison Gopnik spoke at the Brain Connection to Education Spring Conference. Available from www.brainconnections.com

Sainato, D. M., & Carta, J. J. (1992). Classroom influences on the development of social competence in young children with disabilities. In S. L. Odom, S. R. McConnell, & M. A. McEvoy (Eds.), *Social competence of young children with disabilities: Issues and strategies for intervention* (pp. 93–109). Brookes: Baltimore, MD.

Salisbury, C. L., & Chambers, A. (1994). Instructional costs of inclusive schooling. *Journal of the Association for Persons with Severe Handicaps, 19,* 215–222.

Salisbury, C. L., Palombaro, M. M., & Hollowood, T. M. (1993). On the nature and change of an inclusive elementary school. *Journal of the Association for Persons with Severe Handicaps, 18,* 75–84.

Sallows, G. O., & Graupner, T. D. (2005). Intensive behavioral treatment for children with autism: Four years outcome and predictors. *American Journal of Mental Retardation, 110,* 417–438.

Sameroff, A. J., & Chandler, M. J. (1975). Reproductive risk and the continuum of caretaking casualty. In F. D. Horowitz (Ed.), *Review of child development research,* (pp. 187–244). University of Chicago Press: Chicago.

Sandall, S., McLean, M., & Smith, B. (2000). *DEC recommended practices for early childhood special education and early intervention.* Sopris West: Longmont, CO.

Sandall, S. R., & Schwartz, I. S. (2008). *Building blocks for teaching preschoolers with special needs.* Brookes: Baltimore, MD.

Sanders, S. J., Murtha, M. T., Gupta, A. R., et al. (2012). De novo mutations revealed by whole exome sequencing are strongly associated with autism. *Nature. 485*(7397), 237–41.

Sankar-DeLeeuw, N. (2002). Gifted preschoolers: Parent and teacher views on identification, early admission and programming. *Roeper Review, 24,* 172–177.

Schattner, R. (1971). *An early childhood curriculum for multiply-handicapped children.* John Day: New York.

Schickedanz, J. A. (1999). *Much more than the ABC's.* National Association for the Education of Young Children: Washington, DC.

Schickedanz, J. A., Schickedanz, D. I., & Forsyth, P. D. (1982). *Toward understanding children.* Little, Brown: Boston.

Schorr, E. A., Fox, N. A., van Washove, V., & Knudsen, E. I. (2005). Auditory-visual fusion in speech perception in children with cochlear implants. *Proceedings of the*

National Academy of Sciences of the United States, 102, 18748–18750.

Schorr, R. (1990). Peter, he comes and goes. *Journal of the Association for Persons with Severe Handicaps, 19,* 215–222.

Schreibman, L., Koegel, R., Charlop, M., & Egel, A. L. (1990). Infantile autism. In A. S. Bellack, M. Hersen, & A. E. Kaxdin (Eds.), *International handbook of behavior modification and therapy* (pp. 783–789). Plenum Press: New York.

Schwartz, I. S., & Baer, D. M. (1991). Social validity assessments: Is current practice state of the art? *Journal of Applied Behavior Analysis, 24,* 189–204.

Schwartz, I. S., Billingsley, F. F., & McBride, B. (1998). Including children with autism in inclusive preschools: Strategies that work. *Young Exceptional Children, 2*(1), 19–26.

Schwartz, I. S., Garfinkle, A. N., Joseph, G., & McBride, B. (1999). Communication and language disorders. In P. Howlin (Ed.), *Behavioral approaches to problems in childhood.* MacKeith Press: London.

Schwartz, I. S., McBride, B., Pepler, L., Grant, S., & Carta, J. J. (1993, December). *A classroom-based curriculum for facilitating communicative independence in young children with special needs.* Paper presented at the Division of Early Childhood Conference, San Diego, CA.

Schwartz, I. S., Sandall, S. R., Garfinkle, A. N., & Bauer, J. (1998). Outcomes for children with autism: Three case studies. *Topics in Early Childhood Special Education, 18,* 132–143.

Seidenberg, M. S. (1997). Language acquisition and use: Learning and applying probabilistic constraints. *Science, 275,* 1599–1603.

Seltzer, J., McLanahan, S., & Hanson, T. (2001). Will child support enforcement increase father–child contact and parental conflict after separation? In I. Garfinkel, S. McLanahan, D. Meyer, & J. Seltzer (Eds.). *Fathers under fire.* Russell Sage: New York.

Sharpe, M. N., York, J. L., & Knight, J. (1994). Effects of inclusion on the academic performance of classmates without disabilities. *Remedial and Special Education, 15,* 281–287.

Shelton, J. F., Hertz-Picciotto, I., & Pessah, I. (2012). Tipping the balance of autism risk: Potential mechanisms linking pesticides and autism. *Environ Health Perspectives, 120*(7), 944–951. Retrieved from http://www.ncbi.nlm.nih.gov/pmc/articles/PMC3404662/

Shonkoff, J. P., & Phillips, D. A. (Eds.). (2000). Communicating and learning. In *From neurons to neighborhoods: The science of early childhood development* (pp. 124–162). National Academy of Sciences: Washington, DC.

Shore, R. (2003). *Rethinking the brain: Insights into early development.* Families and Work Institute: New York.

Siegel, B. (1998). *The world of the autistic child.* Oxford University Press: New York.

Siegel, B. (2008). *Getting the best for your child with autism: An expert's guide to treatment.* Guilford Press: New York.

Simeonsson, R. J., & Bailey, D. B. (2000). Family dimensions in early intervention. In E. Zigler, J. P. Shonkoff, & S. J. Meisels (Eds.), *Handbook of early intervention* (pp. 428–444). Cambridge University Press: New York.

Simpson, R. L., & Sasso, G. M. (1992). Full inclusion of students with autism in general education settings. Values versus science. *Focus on Autistic Behavior, 7*(2), 1–12.

Skellenger, A. C., Hill, M., & Hill, E. (1992). The social functioning of children with visual impairments. In S. Odom, S. McConnell, & M. McEvoy (Eds.). *Social competence of young children with disabilities* (pp. 165–188). Brookes: Baltimore, MD.

Skinner, B. F. (1957). *Verbal behavior.* Prentice Hall: New York.

Skipper, S. (2006). *Conceptual framework for effective inclusive schools.* Retrieved from http://www.google.com/search?client=safari&rls=en&q=Conceptual+Framework+for+Effective+Inclusive+Schools+Susan+Skipper&ie=UTF-8&oe=UTF-8

Slavin, R. E., & Cheung, A. (2005). A synthesis of research on language reading instruction for English language learners. *Review of Educational Research, 75*(2), 247–284.

Smart, B. A. (2004, Fall). *The costs of asthma and allergy.* American Academy of Allergy, Asthma and Immunology, *Allergy and Asthma Advocate.*

Smith, D. (1993). *Passport for change: Transition planning.* Hints and helps for families with infants and toddlers. F.A.C.T.S. Project, United Cerebral Palsy Association: Washington, DC.

Smith, J. (2006). *Cued speech and cochlear implants powerful partners. Presentation at Cued Speech 40th Anniversary Convention.* PowerPoint available at cuedspeech.org.

Smith, R. (2004). *Conscious classroom management.* Conscious Teaching Publications: San Rafael, CA.

Snow, K. (2009). *Person first language.* Position paper. Available from http://disabilityisnatural.com/

Speech-Language-Hearing Division of Kansas University Affiliated Facility. (n.d.). *Speech, language, hearing development in preschoolers.* Author: Lawrence, KS.

Spitz, R. V. & Tallal, P. (1997). Look who's talking. A prospective study of familial transmission of language impairments. *Journal of Speech, Language & Hearing Research, 40*, 990–1002.

Spodek, B., Saracho, O. N., & Lee, R. C. (1984). *Mainstreaming young children.* Wadsworth: Belmont, CA.

Staff Report of the Select Committee on Children, Youth, and Families. (1990). *Opportunities for success: Cost-effective programs for children.* U.S. Government Printing Office: Washington, DC.

Stainback, W., & Stainback, S. (1996). *Support networks for inclusive schooling: Interdependent integrated education.* Brookes: Baltimore, MD.

Steinberg, A. G., & Knightly, C. A. (2007). Hearing: Sounds and silences. In M. L. Batshaw (Ed.), *Children with Disabilities,* Brookes: Baltimore, MD.

Stevenson, J. (1992). Evidence for Genetic Etiology in Hyperactivity in Children. *Behavior Genetics, 22*, 337–344.

Stile, S., & Kitano, M. (1991). Preschool-age gifted children. *DEC Communicator, 17*(3), 4.

Stockall, N. S., Dennis, L., & Miller, M. (2012). Right from the start. Universal design for preschool. *Teaching Exceptional Children, 45*, 10–17.

Strain, P. S., & Cordisco, L. (2008). LEAP preschool. In S. Harris & J. Handleman (Eds.), *Preschool education programs for children with autism* (pp. 224–252). Pro-Ed: Austin, TX.

Strain, P. S., Lambert, D. L., Kerr, M. M., Stagg, V., & Lenker, D. (1983). Naturalistic assessment of children's compliance to teachers' requests and consequences for compliance. *Journal of Applied Behavior Analysis, 16*, 2143–2149.

Strasser, J. & Seplocha, H. (2010). Using picture books to support young children's literacy. In K. Menke Paciorek (Ed.), *Annual Editions: Early Childhood Education,* McGraw Hill: New York.

Streissguth, A. P., Barr, H. M., & Sampson, P. D. (1990). Moderate prenatal alcohol exposure: Effects on child IQ and learning problems at age 7 1/2 years. *Alcoholism: Clinical and Experimental Research, 14*, 662–669.

Strickland, D. S., & Shanahan, T. (2004). Laying the groundwork for literacy. *Educational Leadership, 61*(6), 74–77.

Strock, M. (2004). Autism spectrum disorders (Pervasive developmental disorders, p. 40; NIH Publication No. NIH-04-5511). National Institute of Mental Health, National Institutes of Health, U.S. Department of Health and Human Services: Bethesda, MD. Available from http://www.nimh. nih.gov/publicat/autism.cfm

Strock, M. (2006). *Attention deficit hyperactivity disorder* (NIH Publication No. 3572). Available from http://www.nimh.nih.gov/publicat/adhd

Sugai, G., Horner, R. H., Dunlap, G., Hieneman, M., Lewis, T. J., Nelson, C. M., Scott, T., Liaupsin, C., Sailor, W., Turnbull, A. P., Turnbull III, H. R., Wickham, D., Wilcox, B., & Ruef, M. (2000). Applying positive behavioral support and functional behavioral assessment in schools. *Journal of Positive Behavior Interventions 2*(3), 131–43.

Swanson, J. M., & McBurnett, K. (1993). Effect of stimulant medication on children with attention deficit disorder: "A review of reviews." *Exceptional Children, 60*, 154–163.

Swim, T. J. (2006). Basic premises of classroom design. In K. M. Paciorek & J. H. Munro (Eds.), *Annual Editions: Early childhood education 05/06* (pp. 101–105), McGraw Hill/Dushkin: Dubuque, IA.

Szabos, J. (1989). Bright child, gifted learner. *Challenge, 34.*

Takanishi, R., & Kauerz. (2008). *PK inclusion: Getting serious about a P–16 education system. Phi Delta Kappan, 89*(7), 480–487.

Teller, D. Y., McDonald, M. A., Preston, K., Sebris, S. L., & Dobson, V. (1986). Assessment of visual acuity in infants and children: The acuity card procedure. *Developmental Medicine and Child Neurology, 28*, 779–789.

The MTA Cooperative Group. (1999). A 14-month random-ized clinical trial of treatment strategies for attention-deficit hyperactivity disorder (ADHD). *Archives of General Psychiatry, 56*, 1073–1086.

Thomas, A., & Chess, S. (1977). *Temperament and development.* Bruner/Mazel: New York.

Thomas, A., & Chess, S. (1986). The New York longitudinal study: From infancy to early adult life. In R. Plomin & J. Dunn (Eds.), *The study of the temperament: Changes, continuities, and challenges.* Erlbaum: Hillsdale, NJ.

Thompson, D., Hudson, S. D., & Olsen, H. M. (2006). How safe are child care playgrounds? A progress report. In K. M. Paciorek & J. H. Munro (Eds.), *Annual Editions: Early childhood education 05/06* (pp. 106–111), McGraw Hill/Dushkin: Dubuque, IA.

Thompson, R. A., & Lamb, M. E. (1982). Stranger sociality and its relationship to temperament and social experi-ence during the second year of life. *Infant Behavior and Development, 5*, 227–228.

Thurman, S. K., & Widerstrom, A. A. (1990). *Infants and young children with special needs.* Brookes: Baltimore, MD.

Tomlinson, C. (1999). *The differentiated classroom: Respond-ing to the needs of all learners.* Association for Supervi-sion and Curriculum Development: Baltimore, MD.

Trahan, C. (2002). *Implications of the No Child Left Behind Act of 2001 for Teacher Education.* (ERIC Document Reproduc-tion Service No. ED477723). ERIC Digest: Washington, DC.

Trivette, C. M., & Dunst, C. J. (2005). DEC recommended practices; Family-Based Practices. In *DEC Recommended Practices.* DEC: Missoula, MT.

Turnbull, A. P., & Turnbull, H. R. (1993). Participatory re-search on cognitive coping: From concepts to research planning. In A. P. Turnbull, J. M. Patterson, S. K. Behr, D. L. Murphy, J. G. Marquis, & M. J. Blue-Banning (Eds.), *Cognitive coping, families, and disabilities* (pp. 1–14). Brookes: Baltimore, MD.

Turnbull, A. P., Turnbull, H. R., Erwin, E. J., & Soodak, L. C. (2005). *Families, professionals, and exceptional-ity: A special partnership.* Prentice Hall: Upper Saddle River, NJ.

U.S. Department of Education. (2013). *ESEA flexibility.* Retrieved January 26, 2013 from http://www2.ed.gov/policy/elsec/guid/esea-flexibility/index.html

U.S. Department of Education. (2009). *Office of Civil Rights.* Retrieved from http://www.ed.gov/about/offices/list/ocr/504faq .html

U.S. Department of Education. (2010). *Twenty-Ninth An-nual Report to Congress on the Implementation of the Individuals with Disabilities Education Act, Parts B and C. 2007. Retrieved January 14, 2013 from http://www2. ed.gov/about/reports/annual/osep/2007/parts-b-c/in-dex.html#about*

U.S. Department of Education, National Center for Educa-tion Statistics. (2006). *Digest of Education Statistics, 2005.* (NCES 2006-030).

U.S. Department of Health and Human Services, Admin-istration for Children and Families, Administration on Children, Youth and Families, Children's Bureau. (2010). *Child maltreatment 2009.* Retrieved from http://www .acf.hhs.gov/programs/cb/pubs/cm09

U.S. Department of Health and Human Services. (1980). *Infant care* (DHHS Publication No. OHDS 80-30015). U.S. Government Printing Office: Washington, DC.

U.S. Department of Health and Human Services. (2002). *Child support report.* XXIV, No. 4. Office of Child Sup-port Enforcement. (20020401).

U.S. Food and Drug Administration (FDA) (2010). *Benefits and risks of cochlear implants.* Retrieved from http://www.fda.gov/MedicalDevices/ProductsandMedical-Procedures/ImplantsandProsthetics/CochlearImplants/ucm062843.htm#a

United Cerebral Palsy. (2009). *The difference between an IFSP and an IEP.* Retrieved from www.mychildwithout-limits.org/?page=ifsp-iep-comparison

United States Conference of Mayors. (2012). *Hunger and Homelessness Survey: A status report on hunger and homelessness in America's cities. A 25-city survey.* Author: Washington, DC. Retrieved on January 2, 2013 from http://www.usmayors.org/pressreleases/uploads/2012/1219-report-HH.pdf

United States Conference of Mayors. (2008). *Hunger and Homelessness Survey: A status report on hunger and homelessness in America's cities. A 25-city survey.* Au-thor: Washington, DC. Retrieved on January 15, 2010 from http://usmayors.org/pressreleases/documents/hungerhomelessnessreport_121208.pdf

United States Conference of Mayors. (2002). *A status report on hunger and homelessness in America's cities,* Author: Washington, DC.

University of Michigan Depression Center. (2007). *Facts about depression in children and adolescents.* Retrieved February 22, 2010 from http://www.med.umich.edu/depression/caph.htm

Volk, H. E., Lurmann, F., Penfold, B., Hertz-Picciotto, I., & McConnell, R. (2013). Traffic related air pollution, partic-ulate matter, and autism. *JAMA Psychiatry, 70*(1), 71–77. *http://archpsyc.jamanetwork.com/article.aspx?articleid=1393589#qundefined*

Volkmar, F. R. (2000). Medical problems, treatments, and pro-fessionals. In M. D. Powers (Ed.), *Children with autism: A parent's guide* (2nd ed.), pp. 73–74). Woodbine House: Bethesda, MD.

Vygotsky, L. (2006). *Mind in society: The development of higher psychological processes.* Harvard University Press: Cambridge, MA.

Walker, H. M., Ramsey, E. & Gresham, F. (2003). *Antisocial behavior in school: Evidence based practices.* Wadsworth/Thompson Publishing: Belmont, CA.

Walker, H., Stiller, B., & Golly, A. (1998). First steps to suc-cess. *Young Exceptional Children, 1*(2), 2–7.

Wang, J., Samir Haj-Dahmane, S., & Roh-Yu Shen (2006). Effects of prenatal ethanol exposure on the excitability of ventral tegmental area dopamine neurons in vitro. *JPET Fast Forward*. Published on August 11, 2006 as DOI:10.1124/jpet.106.109041. Retrieved online April 18, 2010 from http://jpet.aspetjournals.org/content/early/2006/08/11/jpet.106.109041.full.pdf

Warren, D. H. (1994). *Blindness and children: An individual differences approach*. Cambridge University Press: New York.

Warren, S. F., & Kaiser, A. P. (1988). Research in early language intervention. In S. L. Odom & M. B. Karnes (Eds.), *Early intervention for infants and children with handicaps* (pp. 89–108). Brookes: Baltimore, MD.

Washington, K., Schwartz, I. S., & Swinth, Y. (1994). Physical and occupational therapists in naturalistic early childhood settings: Challenges and strategies for training. *Topics in Early Childhood Special Education, 14*, 333–349.

Watson, A. & McCathern, R. (2009). Including children with special needs. Are you and your early childhood program ready? *Beyond the Journal. Young Children on the Web*. March. Retrieved from http://www.naeyc.org/files/yc/file/200903/ BTJWatson.pdf

WebMD.com A-Z Health Guide from WebMD. (2010). *Health topics: Fragile X Syndrome*. Retrieved January 15, 2010 from http://children.webmd.com/ fragile-x-syndrome

WebMD.com. (2008). *Chelation Study for Autism Called Off—Controversial Trial Too Risky, Panel Says*. Retrieved from http://www.webmd.com/brain/autism/news/20080918/chelation-study-autism-called-off

Wein, C. A., & Kirby-Smith, S. (1998). Untiming the curriculum: A case study of removing clocks from the program. *Young Children, 53*(50), 8–13.

Whitebrook, M., Phillips, D. A., & Howes, C. (1994). Who cares? Childcare teachers and the quality of care in America. In E. Galinsky, C. Howes, S. Kontos, & M. Shinn (Eds.), *The study of children in center, family, and relative-based child care*. Families and Work Institute: New York.

The White House. (2010). *Remarks by the President at the Signing of the 21st Century Communications and Video Accessibility Act of 2010*. Retrieved from http://www.whitehouse.gov/the-press-office/2010/10/08/remarks-president-signing-21st-century-communications-and-video-accessib

The White House. (2011). *Improving Latino Education to Win the Future*. Retrieved March 4, 2013 from http://www.whitehouse.gov/blog/2011/04/27/improving-latino-education-win-future

Widerstrom, A., Mowder, B., & Sandall, S. (1997). *Infant development and risk* (2nd ed.). Brookes: Baltimore, MD.

WIC (2012). *Fact Sheet*. Retrieved January 3, 2013 from http://www.fns.usda.gov/wic/WIC-Fact-Sheet.pdf

Will, M. (1986). *Educating students with learning problems—a shared responsibility*. U.S. Department of Education, Office of Special Education and Rehabilitative Services: Washington, DC.

Willard-Holt, C. (1999). *Dual Exceptionalities*. The ERIC Clearinghouse on Disabilities and Gifted Education (ERIC EC). (ERIC EC Digest #E574): Reston, VA.

Winton, P., McCollum, J., & Catlett, C. (1997). *Reforming personnel preparation in early intervention*. Brookes: Baltimore, MD.

Wolery, M. (2007). *Conditions necessary for desirable outcomes in inclusive classrooms*. National Early Childhood Technical Assistance Center: Chapel Hill, NC.

Wolery, M. (1994a). Designing inclusive environments for young children with special needs. In M. Wolery & J. S. Wilbers (Eds.), *Including children with special needs in early childhood programs*. National Association for the Education of Young Children: Washington, DC.

Wolery, M. (1994b). Implementing instruction for young children with special needs in early childhood classrooms. In M. Wolery & J. S. Wilbur (Eds.), *Including children with special needs in early childhood programs*. National Association for the Education of Young Children: Washington, DC.

Wolery, M. R., & Brookfield-Norman, J. (1988). (Pre)academic instruction for handicapped preschool children. In S. L. Odom & M. B. Karnes (Eds.), *Early intervention for infants and children with handicaps* (pp. 109–128). Brookes: Baltimore, MD.

Wolery, M., & Bredekamp, S. (1994). Developmentally appropriate practices and young children with disabilities: Contextual issues in the discussion. *Journal of Early Intervention, 18*, 331–347.

Wolery, M., & Wilbers, J. S. (Eds.). (1994). *Including children with special needs in early childhood programs*. National Association for the Education of Young Children: Washington, DC.

Wolery, M., McWilliam, R. A. A., & Bailey, D. B. (2005). *Teaching infants and preschoolers with disabilities*. Prentice Hall: Upper Saddle River, NJ.

Wolery, M., Strain, P. S., & Bailey, D. (1992). Reaching potentials of children with special needs. In S. Bredekamp & T. Rosegrant (Eds.), *Reaching potentials: Appropriate curriculum and assessment for young children*. National Association for the Education of Young Children: Washington, DC.

Wolfensberger, W. (1996). *The principle of normalization in human services*. F. Allan Roeher Institute: Downsview, ON.

Wolfle, J. (1989). The gifted preschooler: Developmentally different but still 3 or 4 year olds. *Young Children, 44*(3), 41–48.

Wolraich, M. L., Hannah, J. N., Pinnock, T. Y., Baumgaertel, A., & Brown, J. (1996). Comparison of diagnostic criteria for attention-deficit hyperactivity disorder in a countywide sample. *Journal of the American Academy of Child and Adolescent Psychiatry, 35,* 319–324.

World Federation for the Deaf. (2012). *Sign language.* Retrieved from http://www.wfdeaf.org/human-rights/crpd/sign-language

Wood, J. J., & McCormick, K. M. (2002). Toward an integration of child- and family-centered practices of assessment in preschool children: Welcoming the family. *Young Exceptional Children, 5*(3), 2–11.

Yeargin-Allsopp, M., Rice, C., Karapurkar, T., Doernberg, N., Boyle, C., & Murphy, C. (2003). Prevalence of autism in a US metropolitan area. *The Journal of the American Medical Association, 289*(1), 49–55.

Zebrowski, P. M. (1995). The topography of beginning stuttering. *Journal of Communication Disorders, 28*(2), 75–91.

Zeece, P. D., & Wolda, M. K. (1995). Let me see what you say; let me see what you feel! *Teaching Exceptional Children, 27*(2), 4–10.

Zero to Three: National Center for Infants, Toddlers, and Families. (2005). *Diagnostic classification of mental health and developmental disorders of infancy and childhood.* Author: Washington, DC.

Zigler, E., & Hodapp, R. M. (1991). Behavioral functioning in individuals with mental retardation. *Annual Review of Psychology, 42,* 29–50.

Zirkel, P. A. (2006). What does the law say? *Teaching Exceptional Children, 38*(5), 67–68.

Index

Classification, 458
Classroom adaptations, for physical disabilities, 155–156
Classroom practices
    adaptive materials, 153
    confidentiality, 168
    emergency considerations, 168
    and health problems, 167–168
    health records, 167
    medication administration, 167–168
Class websites, 236
CMV virus (cytomegalic inclusion disease), 103
Cocaine, maternal use of, 104
Cochlea, 121
Cochlear implant, 122
Cognitive capacities, 406
Cognitive development
    brain research, 444–446
    emerging literacy, 442–444, 460–461, 463
    impact of hearing loss on, 124
    impact of vision impairment on, 134
    interwoven with motor development, 84
Cognitive disorders, 184
Combined loss, 121
Combined type of ADHD, 175
Committee on Pediatric AIDS, 162
Communication, 125, 414. *See also* Parents
Communication development, 68–69. *See also* Speech,
        language, and communication skills
Community, creation of, 67–68, 70–71
Community-based preschool programs, 58–59
Compensatory education, 31
Competition, 324–325
Comprehensive screening, 250
Computer-based information systems, 275
Computers and assistive technology, 449, 451
Concept formation, 457
Conception, prevention of developmental disabilities
        before, 47
Conceptual skills, 112
Conduct disorder (CD), 177
Conductive hearing loss, 121–122
Confidentiality, 168, 231
Conflict, 486
Congenital anomalies, 113
Congenital conditions, 99
Congenital dislocation of the hip, 148
Connecting Developmentally Appropriate Practice to
        Brain Research
    brain-based research, 445
    cognitive, emotional, and social capacities, 406
    early intervention model and autism, 198
    executive function skills and social problem solving, 498
    experiences and brain development, 83
    imitation and mirror neurons, 324
    parent's use of technology and impact on child's
            development, 430
    recess and brain development, 163, 352
    redshirting and readiness, 516
    relationships, importance of, 13
Consequences, 310, 479–480
Consistency, 292–293, 492
Consolidation, 297

Constructivists, 416
Contextually based assessment, 72
Contingent stimulation, 289, 389
Continuity of services, 513
Contractures, 144
Cooing, 418
Cooperation, and toddlers, 85
Cooperative play, 394, 395
Corporate child care, 58
Cortical blindness, 130
Cost issues, and inclusion, 15
Council for Exceptional Children (CEC), 32
CP (Cerebral palsy), 110, 144, 145–146
CPR training, 168
Creative materials, 154
Criterion-referenced assessment, 247
Critical periods, 11–12, 123
Cross body midline, inability to, 183
Cross-disciplinary practices, 61
Cross-lateral movements, uncertain, 183
Cruising, 84
Crying, 417–418
Cubby areas, 335
Cued speech, 125
Cueing, 321–322
Cultural bias, avoidance of in assessment process, 253
Cultural competence, 217, 219, 221
Cultural differences, and assessment, 252–253
Culturally competent programs, 61
Cultural mediators, 219
Cultural self-awareness, 221
Cumulative deficits, 48–49
Cumulative effect, 123
Curriculum
    for ages six to eight, 71
    for ages three to five, 68–69
    integrated, 71
    and self-care skills, 363–367
CVS (Chorionic villus sampling), 47
Cyanosis, 159
Cystic fibrosis, 102, 114, 157
Cytomegalic inclusion disease (CMV virus), 103

D

Daily schedule, sample, 349–352
Daniel, Jerlean, 7
DAPs (Developmentally appropriate practices), 56, 62,
        291, 444
Data collection, and challenging behaviors, 482–485
Dawdling, 86
DDA (Developmental Disabilities Act), 35
DDH (Developmental dislocation of the hip), 148
Deafness. *See also* Hearing loss
    case study, 128
    as cause of developmental differences, 99
    combined with blindness, 115
    definition of, 121
    under IDEIA, 113
DEC. *See* Division for Early Childhood (DEC)
Deficit model, 19
De novo mutations, 194
Denver II screening instrument, 250–251

M

Mainstreaming, 5
Mand-model, 428
Manipulative materials, 153–154, 339, 456
Manual interpreter, 127
Manual prompting, 321
Mapp, Karen, 216
Marcellino, Rosa, 112
Match, problem of the, 307
Materials and equipment for social learning, 402
Maternal diabetes, 103
Maturation, 378
Maturationists, 307
Maurice, Catherine, 194
Mayes, Linda, 104
MBD (Minimally brain damaged), 175. *See also* Autism spectrum
    disorder (ASD)
Mealtimes, 365
Mediated learning, 297
Mediator, teacher as, 297–298
Medicaid, 51
Medication
    for ADHD, 177–178
    administration of, 167–168
    for autism spectrum disorders, 200
Membership, 6
Memory, 459–460
Meningitis, 105
Meningocele, 147
Mental Health: A Report of the Surgeon General, 196
Mercury, 200
Metabolic disorders, 102
Metabolization, 102, 159
Milieu (incidental) teaching, 197, 290–291, 429
MIND Institute, 194
Minimally brain damaged (MBD), 175. *See also* Autism spectrum
    disorder (ASD)
Minimum brain dysfunction, 180
Minority-language children, 91, 111. *See also* English Language
    Learners (ELL)
Mirrow neurons, 324
Mobiles, 351
Mobility devices, 150–151
Modeling, 323–325, 402, 403, 454–455
Mona, Marie, 463
Montessori, Maria, 308
Motherese, 416
Motor development, 84, 134
Motor skills, in preschool years, 85
Multicultural practices, 61
Multidimensional concept, readiness as, 289
Multi-disciplinary assessments, 38
Multidisciplinary team, 270
Multimodal Treatment Study of Children with Attention Deficit
    Hyperactivity Disorder, 177
Multiple disabilities, 113
Multiple intelligences, 90
Muscular dystrophy, 148
Music, rhythms, stories, 352
Mutual gaze, 390
Myelomeningocele, 147
Myopia, 131

N

NAEYC. *See* National Association for the Education of Young
    Children (NAEYC)
National Association for Retarded Children (NARC), 8, 32
National Association for the Education of Young Children (NAEYC)
    on assessment of young children, 246
    Early Childhood Inclusion: A Joint Position Statement, 7
    guidelines for early childhood programs, 56
    joint position paper on Inclusion, 60
    on literacy development, 69
    normalization, 62
    Position Statement on Developmentally Appropriate Practice, 331
    Position Statement on Early Childhood Curriculum, 246
    "Responding to Linguistic and Cultural Diversity," 283
    "Taking stock of what you do to promote literacy," 464
    on technology and interactive media, 449
    on transitions, 355
    on working with families, 224–226
National Association of State Boards of Education, 9
National Center for Cultural Competence, 221
National Center for the Education of the Gifted, 46
National Center on Educational Outcomes (NCEO), 43
National Dissemination Center for Children with Disabilities
    (NICHCY), 239
National Immunization Survey, 50
National Institute of Child Health and Human Development, 196
National Institute of Mental Health (NIMH), 200
National Mental Health and Special Education Coalition, 189
National Professional Developmental Center on Inclusion (NPDCI), 7
National Program for Playground Safety (NPPS), 341
National Scientific Council on the Developing Child, 406
National Society for the Gifted and Talented (NSGT), 46
National Society for the Prevention of Blindness, 114, 132
National Survey of America's Families, 57
National Survey of Children's Health, 193
Natural consequences, 313
Naturalistic language-learning environment, 426–429
NCEO (National Center on Educational Outcomes), 43
NCLB (No Child Left Behind), 41–44, 69–70, 163, 442, 443
Need for attention, 488
Needs identification, 265–266
Negative reinforcement, 311
Neural activity, 82
Neurological processes, 102
Neuroscientists, 82
Newsletters, 236–237
A New Wave of Evidence (Mapp), 216
NICHCY (National Dissemination Center for Children with
    Disabilities), 239
NIMH (National Institute of Mental Health), 200
No Child Left Behind (NCLB), 41–44, 69–70, 163, 442, 443
Nonambulatory, 378
Noncompliance, 489–492
Nondisadvantaged ruling on learning disabilities, 180
Nondiscriminatory evaluation, 36
Non-intrusiveness, 266–267
Nonverbal communications, 414, 423
Normal development. *See* Typical (normal) development
Normal deviations, 474
Normalization, 62
Normalized practices, 62
Norm-referenced assessment, 247